D1161251

HIGHLIGHTS FROM THE REVIEWS OF
THE LETTERS OF SAMUEL BECKETT
VOLUME 1: 1929–1940

"The most bracing read [of 2009] was *The Letters of Samuel Beckett Volume 1: 1929–1940*, a portrait of the Dubliner as a young European with a hard gemlike gift for language, learning and mockery … Constantly Beckett is veering between certainty about his need to write and doubt about the results, all expressed in prose that is undoubting, delighted and demanding." Seamus Heaney, "Books of the year 2009," *The Times Literary Supplement*

"This edition of letters has been annotated with knowledge and care, using vast research. It will, for the most part, please admirers of Beckett's art and satisfy those who respect his wishes that only letters which have bearing on his work should appear." Colm Tóibín, *The London Review of Books*

"The editorial work behind this project has been immense in scale. Every book that Beckett mentions, every painting, every piece of music is tracked down and accounted for. His movements are traced from week to week. Everyone he alludes to is identified; his principal contacts earn potted biographies. When he writes in a foreign language, we are given both the original and an English translation … The standard of the commentary is of the highest … *The Letters of Samuel Beckett* is a model edition." J. M. Coetzee, *The New York Review of Books*

"One of the highlights of the year was the publication of *The Letters of Samuel Beckett Volume 1: 1929–1940* … Every page is a hoot. Beckett comes across as even smarter, and more smarting, than one already knew." Paul Muldoon in "Books of the Year 2009," *The Times Literary Supplement*

"*Imagination Dead Imagine* is the title of one of his late pieces, but the point is that the Beckettian imagination continued lively to the very end. In that letter to Axel Kaun he placed himself on 'the road toward this, for me, very desirable literature of the non-word,' but a few lines later he states his program with a contrary succinctness: 'Word-storming in the name of beauty.' *The Letters of Samuel Beckett Volume 1: 1929–1940* is a preliminary record of that storm." John Banville, *The New Republic*

"Can a writer's letters – occasional and ephemeral as these tend to be – really qualify as great literature? In Beckett's case, yes. For here is the most reticent of twentieth-century writers, one who refused to explain his plays and fictions, wrote almost no formal literary criticism, and refused to attend his own Nobel Prize ceremony – revealing himself in letter after letter as warm, playful, unfailingly polite even at his most vituperative and scatological, irreverent but never cynical, and, above all, a brilliant stylist whose learning is without the slightest pretension or preciosity." Marjorie Perloff, *Bookforum*

"This edition ... is a triumph. The introductory and supplementary material is well judged and helpful, the annotations and identifications are tirelessly thorough. The later Beckett declared that 'every word is like an unnecessary stain on silence and nothingness,' but these letters are packed with wonderfully necessary words." Stefan Collini, "Books of the Year 2009," *The Times Literary Supplement*

"The editorial labor in this first volume is immensely impressive." Denis Donoghue, *The New Criterion*

"The first volume of Beckett's letters, *The Letters of Samuel Beckett Volume 1: 1929–1940* (Cambridge), was the funniest, most intelligent and most poignant book I read this year, and since three more volumes are promised by Cambridge University Press we should be moved and entertained for some years to come." Gabriel Josipovici in "Books of the Year 2009," *The Times Literary Supplement*

"This first of a promised four volumes (to include 2,500 out of a total 15,000 items of correspondence) represents already a heroic achievement by the editors who embarked on the project nearly a quarter of a century ago ... Each letter has demanded a dense undergrowth of notes in minuscule print, providing information on every allusion, every reference, even acknowledging where such information has been sought but not found ... The editorial team deserves all our thanks for their patience, their stamina and their scholarly rigour." Nicholas Grene, *The Irish Times*

"An elating cultural moment is upon us. It is also a slightly surprising moment. Beckett, in his published output and authorial persona, was rigorously spare and self-effacing. Who knew that in his private writing he would be so humanly forthcoming? We always knew he was brilliant – but this brilliant? ... The knowledge of what lay ahead for Beckett – the writing of the plays and the great prose fiction – makes one very impatient for the further volumes of letters, almost as if Beckett were in actual correspondence with oneself." Joseph O'Neill, *The New York Times Sunday Book Review* and *The International Herald Tribune*

"Admirers of Samuel Beckett, arguably the greatest writer in English of the second half of the twentieth century, have grown used to waiting for Godot, who will surely come tomorrow or, just possibly, the day after. In the meantime, these similarly anticipated letters have quite definitely arrived, and in an edition more sumptuous than one ever imagined. Has any modern author been better served by his editors than Beckett?" Michael Dirda, *The Washington Post*

"An extraordinary work of scholarship . . . a revelatory triumph." Tim Rutter, *The Los Angeles Times*

"Since Samuel Beckett was incapable of writing a duff sentence, the first volume of his letters, 25 years in the making, has been awaited with high anticipation." Jonathan Bate, *The Sunday Telegraph*

"Judging by this exemplary inaugural selection, the overall enterprise promises to be an extraordinary commitment, not only to the scholarly virtues of patience, concentration and scrupulousness but to a deep sense of the cultural value of the writer as a twentieth-century avatar . . . As Beckett himself said, in *Proust*: 'We cannot know and we cannot be known.' Even so, we must be grateful for the opportunity this magnificent work of scholarship provides to reflect on what there is to be known, and the conflicts and crises its subject underwent in his fidelity to the strange, demanding and all too human need to speak his mind." George O'Brien, *The Dublin Review of Books*

". . . the editorial team, with their astonishingly detailed annotations, are to be congratulated for making the life work of this heroically perverse illuminist a lot clearer." Hugh Haughton, *The Literary Review*

"If volume one is any indication of the whole, we can expect three more thoroughly researched and professionally documented volumes, arranged yearly with handy chronologies, useful indexes, intelligent translations, clear introductions, large print, and helpful profiles of the main characters." James McNaughton, *Modernism/Modernity*

"Compulsively readable, these letters from Samuel Beckett's most prolific decade show up all the Irish master's literary virtuosity and playfulness." "Books of the Year," *The Economist*

"'I find it more & more difficult to write, even letters to my friends,' Beckett wrote in 1936, midway through this volume. You would never know it from the natural grace and ease of these missives, which more than validate the editors' statement in the introduction to this volume that Beckett 'was one of the great literary correspondents of the twentieth century, perhaps of any century.' His editors have done him justice by providing the fullest context imaginable, backed up by their impressive scholarship." Martin Rubin, *The Washington Times*

"Here is the authentic early Beckettian tang, straight from the source, unmediated by artifice … Beckett's strong language is one of the things that give the letters their pungency and drive; it is a testament also to the suppleness, rigour and strength of his writing that they don't seem in any way dated, unless a wide frame of cultural reference is these days in itself passé … There are treasures upon treasures here." Nicholas Lezard, *The Guardian*

"Anyone who knows a lot about Beckett will be thrilled to discover a great deal more from these pages. Readers who know little or nothing will get an incomparably in-depth introduction to his literary beginnings … The cornucopia of letters to come in the remaining three volumes, reflecting the mind behind the cornucopia of his major works over the subsequent five decades, should prove as well worth having waited for as the non-arrival of that enigmatic Monsieur Godot." Michael Horovitz, *The Times*

"For Beckett enthusiasts, these letters are crammed with unexpected treasures … There will be three more volumes in this admirable series; the next will cover 1945 to 1956 (the year *Waiting for Godot* was first produced in Britain, and the unknown author suddenly became world-famous). Like Vladimir and Estragon, we fans will find it hard to wait." Kevin Jackson, *The Sunday Times*

THE LETTERS OF SAMUEL BECKETT

Volume I *The Letters of Samuel Beckett: 1929–1940*
Volume II *The Letters of Samuel Beckett: 1941–1956*
Volume III *The Letters of Samuel Beckett: 1957–1967*
Volume IV *The Letters of Samuel Beckett: 1968–1989*

Letter from Samuel Beckett to Georges Duthuit,
Wednesday 28 October [1948].
Duthuit collection.

THE LETTERS
OF
SAMUEL BECKETT

Volume II: 1941–1956

George Craig, *Editor and French Translator*

Martha Dow Fehsenfeld, *Founding Editor*

Dan Gunn, *Editor*

Lois More Overbeck, *General Editor*

CAMBRIDGE UNIVERSITY PRESS

Cambridge, New York, Melbourne, Madrid, Cape Town,
Singapore, São Paulo, Delhi, Tokyo, Mexico City

Cambridge University Press
The Edinburgh Building, Cambridge CB2 8RU, UK

Published in the United States of America by Cambridge University Press, New York

www.cambridge.org
Information on this title: www.cambridge.org/9780521867948

First published 2011

Printed in the United States of America

A catalogue record for this publication is available from the British Library

ISBN 978-0-521-86794-8 Hardback

Major support from The National Endowment for the Humanities (1991–1997,
2008–2011) has facilitated the preparation of this Edition. Any views, findings,
or conclusions expressed in this publication do not necessarily reflect those
of the National Endowment for the Humanities.

CONTENTS

ILLUSTRATIONS

GENERAL INTRODUCTION

If Volume I of *The Letters of Samuel Beckett* began to give evidence to substantiate the editors' claim that Samuel Beckett was one of the great literary correspondents of the twentieth century, Volume II, which is concerned with the period 1941–1956, is destined to render the claim irrefutable. For although there are few letters for the period 1941–1944, and not a single letter about the work, owing to Beckett's circumstances during the War, the lack is more than compensated for by what follows. The post-War period is probably the richest in Beckett's literary life, seeing him write, in a remarkably short time, much of the work for which he is most celebrated – *En attendant Godot*, *Molloy*, *Malone meurt*, and *L'Innommable*, as well as *Fin de partie*, and many shorter pieces (all those named being subsequently translated by him – either alone or with others – into English). Yet the intensity of Beckett's literary production is practically matched by his letter-writing. While it might be imagined that the flurry of texts produced by Beckett in these years would leave little time or inclination for writing to friends and acquaintances, the exact opposite proves to be the case; almost as if the very withdrawal required for the writing of fiction and drama called for a supplement in the more immediately relational writing that is correspondence, directed as that is toward a single individual. For, surprising though it may seem in retrospect, it is the case that, through the first decade covered here, Beckett remained a writer largely unknown, unpublished, and un-produced. Indeed, one of the many fascinating insights offered by these letters is into a Beckett who must learn for the first time, in his late forties, to react to a large and increasingly enthusiastic public; into a Beckett for whom letters will therefore no longer be his only immediate way of connecting to others through written words.

The final letter of Volume I of *The Letters of Samuel Beckett* was dated 10 June 1940, and was written from Paris only two days before Beckett chose to leave the city, four days before the German army entered and occupied it.[1] The four and a half years between this letter and the first letter presented in the body of the present volume, dated 17 January 1945, mark a major interruption in Beckett's sixty years of epistolary writing. The reason for the hiatus will be obvious to a reading public aware as it now is that Beckett worked with the French Resistance, and had to go into hiding to save his life. However, the way in which Beckett's wartime years came to bear on his letter-writing is likely to be one of the many things that readers of the current volume will speculate on, if only perhaps to wonder how far the range and urgency of his correspondence after the War was related to its dearth during it.

THE WAR YEARS

The editors, whose primary concern is the letters, clearly cannot ignore this long interruption. But the intricacies of Beckett's movements during these years, and of the changing political scene, are such as to warrant a full historical account.[2] As this is a general introduction to a volume of letters, mention will be made principally of individuals and events which affected Beckett the letter-writer either directly or indirectly through his friends and associates.

This period was one of many, often abrupt, moves for Beckett. He and his partner Suzanne Deschevaux-Dumesnil left Paris on 12 June 1940, heading first to Vichy where they met James Joyce, as Beckett later recalled in a letter to Patricia Hutchins: "In 1940 I was for a few days with the Joyces at their hotel in Vichy and saw them leave for St. Gérand. It was the last time I saw him."[3] Through Joyce, Beckett arranged to borrow money from Valery Larbaud, before making his way with Suzanne Deschevaux-Dumesnil to Toulouse, then on to Arcachon, where Mary Reynolds and Marcel Duchamp helped them settle for the summer. They returned to Paris in early September 1940.

The Occupation caused extensive disruption in public administration: there was no direct postal service between France and Britain or Ireland, and money transfers were restricted.[4] Even postal deliveries within France, between the Occupied and the Unoccupied Zones, were far from reliable or easy, something apparent from Beckett's last letter to James Joyce.

It is a pre-printed postcard which presents prefabricated phrases, allowing the sender to strike out phrases that were inappropriate. Only family news could be transmitted, and even this was subject to censorship. Beckett sent his missive on 12 January 1941, addressing it to Joyce at the Hôtel du Commerce, Saint-Gérand-le-Puy, Allier, unaware that the Joyces had left there for Switzerland on 14 December 1940.[5] Beckett's letter was forwarded to Joyce at the Pension Delphin in Zurich on 17 January, but Joyce never saw it. He had died on 13 January, the day after the letter was written.

(a)

(b)

1. Lettercard from Samuel Beckett to James Joyce, 12 January 1941

On 18 January 1941, Beckett's brother Frank, answering a letter from Tom McGreevy, wrote: "We are not in communication with Sam nor have we been for some time. The last we heard of him was that he was back in Paris & I am able to get him some dough now & again so it might be worse. I suppose you saw that J. Joyce died in Zurich."[6] Communication with Ireland was possible only through diplomatic channels, as is clear from the letter that Beckett wrote to Count Gerald O'Kelly at the Irish Legation on 4 June 1941, requesting that the following message be sent to his family, in reply to their message: "'Monsieur Beckett est en excellente santé et ne manque de rien.'"[7]

Under the Occupation, Jews, Communists, and other "undesirables" were rounded up and sent to internment camps. Among the victims was Joyce's friend and assistant Paul Léon, arrested on 21 August 1941.[8] Of the ten surviving letters from Beckett to Lucie Léon, Paul's wife, only a few have dates or postmarked envelopes (these range from 17 July 1941 to 10 February 1942).[9] Many offer his assistance in her Red Cross work, for example in procuring chocolates for distribution to internees. Others are expressions of anxiety over the fate of her husband Paul, or of Beckett's eagerness for news, since, as he says, "I don't know what's happening anywhere."[10]

During the Occupation, Beckett occasionally helped André Salzman, husband of Ruth Salzman, a friend of Suzanne Deschevaux-Dumesnil, by acting as courier ("agent de liaison"). Salzman's Resistance activities involved securing money for clandestine publications. As an Irish passport holder, Beckett did not need special permission to move about at night in Paris, hence he could safely deliver documents and money with discretion.[11]

On 1 September 1941, Beckett formally joined the French Resistance réseau "Gloria SMH," by that time "part of the British SOE (Special Operations Executive)."[12] Less than one year later, the réseau was broken, and more than fifty of its members were arrested. One of these was Alfred Péron, who had recruited Beckett to the Resistance, and whom Beckett had known since their days at the Ecole Normale Supérieure. His wife Mania sent a telegram to Beckett and Suzanne Deschevaux-Dumesnil with a coded warning: "Alfred arrêté par Gestapo. Prière faire nécessaire pour corriger l'erreur."[13] The two immediately warned others and took flight. In late September, they were helped by a "passeur" into the Unoccupied Zone, reaching Vichy on the 29th.[14]

Unsurprisingly, there are few letters from this period. There is, however, one puzzle in this connection, from an unexpected source. Francis Stuart, an Irish writer resident in Berlin throughout the War, claimed in his published journal, and in an interview later with the editors, that, having written to Beckett, he received on 9 August 1942, "A letter from Sam

Beckett in Paris which I was glad to get." Stuart went on: "He seems to be living there even more cut off from Ireland and isolated than am I. One of the small number of those from days of peace with whom I had something in common."[15] Although Stuart claimed the letter was subsequently lost, he recalled that Beckett had written that he had "'nearly finished a novel,' that is, he had done the first chapter."[16] The novel was *Watt*; the letter from Beckett arrived in Berlin just days after Stuart had given his first radio talk from Germany to Ireland, on 5 August, and days before Beckett was compelled to leave Paris.

Through the Irish Legation in Vichy in October 1942, Beckett renewed his Irish passport.[17] He and Suzanne Deschevaux-Dumesnil "received a provisional safe-conduct pass which allowed them two days to travel to Avignon. There they reported to the central police station"; then, as "a special favour," they were given until 6 October to leave Avignon."[18] On Sunday, 11 October, Beckett writes from "'Les Roches Rouges,' Roussillon, par/ Cavaillon, Vaucluse" to inform Cornelius Cremin, the First Secretary of the Irish Legation then in Vichy, that he has found a place to live:

> The above is my address henceforward. A little bled in the hills about 30 miles from Avignon, landscape all that could be desired, food all that could not. The worst drought for years, historic famine, etc. No one knows where the winter food is coming from, I less than the next.
>
> . . .
>
> Have had prolonged interviews with the local Gendarmes, in their barracks 6 miles from here. My history almost day by day from my first setting foot in France. They can't believe that I can be called Samuel and am not a Jew. Yesterday they took away my identity card I suppose to see if it had not been tampered with. My movements are restricted in the extreme, radius of ten kilometres about.
>
> . . .
>
> Can you suggest what I should do, or what could be done, to have my tether lengthened. I suppose you could support any application I might make in that sense, but I doubt if that is enough. For the moment I do not intend to try and go home.[19]

Informed that a "permis de circuler" for travel within the Department is "almost impossible to obtain and that even a safe-conduct" pass to travel to the nearby town of Apt would require reasons "of the utmost gravity, such as illness," Beckett writes on 27 October to Cremin:

> If this is indeed the extent of my rights, in what exactly do the advantages of Irish nationality consist? Might I not as well be a Pole? This view as put forward by me having met with no success up to the present, I think perhaps it is time for the Legation to put it forward for me, with particular enquiry as to why I cannot move about freely in "free France", as I should have to do if … I decided to take the necessary steps preparatory to going home, and as to what I have done to deserve incarceration in the Commune of Roussillon. May I count on the Legation for a little representation in this sense?[20]

On 24 June of the following year, Beckett was summoned to appear "without delay" before "'prefectorial authorities of Vaucluse, Service des Etrangers'" for yet another "'examination of my situation.'" On 30 June, the day he received the summons, Beckett writes to Seán Murphy, Irish Minister to France (then in Vichy), expressing frustration with the continued restrictions on his movement and repeated interrogations:

> But with regard to this constant prying into my identity, my past movements, my present movements, my means of existence, my mode of existence, why I am called Samuel, etc., etc., when all my papers are perfectly in order, when since arriving in the "free zone" I have neglected none of the formalities of declaration, registration, etc., imposed on foreigners in this country, when my only offence, I mean that of having clandestinely crossed the line of demarcation, has been judged in the police-court of Apt and presumably purged by the payment of a fine of 400 francs, and when all this has been made clear time and again and apparently accepted as satisfactory in the course of repeated interrogations, I feel obliged to appeal to you to intervene. Would a Swiss citizen be baited in this manner, or a Swedish? Or is an Irishman less entitled than they to the common courtesies and privileges extended to non-belligerents?
>
> …
>
> I do not know what you can do, or if you can do anything, to have an end put, once and for all, to this inquisition. If I might, without impertinence, venture a suggestion, it would be that you telephone before Tuesday next to the Préfecture of Vaucluse, Service des Étrangers, to find out if possible for what reason I am thus badgered and to assure them at least that I am known to you. You might even mention, if you could be so kind, that you believe me to be inoffensive.[21]

Finally the results Beckett sought were forthcoming, at least in part because a recently passed law had addressed the broader issue of displaced foreigners in France: on 17 July, Beckett could report to Seán Murphy:

> The "examination of my situation" at the préfecture of Vaucluse differed in no way from those with which I am familiar. My identity card was briefly inspected and the hope expressed that I continued to receive a subsidy from the *Swiss* Legation.
>
> I am happy to be able to inform you that I was successful, on this occasion, in establishing my right, in virtue of the Decree of May 20th last, published in the J.O. of June 3rd last, to travel freely in France, without other papers than my passport and identity card, and without other territorial restrictions than those now in vigour for travellers generally.[22]

From Roussillon in Unoccupied France Beckett's communication with his family continued to be directed through the Irish Legation in Vichy, by telegram to and from Ireland. One such – "ALL WELL LETTER DATED FIFTH APRIL RECEIVED LOVE SAM" – was sent on 31 May 1943.[23] Funds could now be transferred, the transfer confirmed and receipt acknowledged, all by telegram.

The Liberation of Paris took place on 25 August 1944. Beckett and Suzanne Deschevaux-Dumesnil had returned to the flat at 6 Rue des Favorites by 12 October, the date on which Beckett wrote to the Irish Legation in Vichy to indicate his change of address. He asked that his subsidy and its arrears be sent to him there, and noted: "I expected to find the Legation back in Paris, but was informed to-day, Rue de Villejust, that you are not expected before the end of the month."[24] By 20 September, his brother Frank was trying to contact him. Only on 9 November 1944 did Frank report that Beckett had sent the message to his family via the Irish Legation: "Back in Paris. All well. Impossible move at present. Love to you all."[25]

Not until April 1945 could Beckett make his way from France to England, where the manuscript of *Watt* was confiscated and inspected for "code," and on to Ireland for a family visit. Several years later, in a letter to George Reavey, he remarked that *Watt* was "written in dribs and drabs, first on the run, then of an evening after the clodhopping, during the occupation."[26] The *Watt* notebooks confirm that the novel was begun before Beckett left Paris, and that he continued writing even when in hiding.[27] To Gottfried Büttner, Beckett wrote: "It was written as it came, without preestablished plan"; and to George Reavey: "It is an unsatisfactory book [. . .] But it has its place in the series, as will perhaps appear in time."[28] Later still, Beckett claimed that he had written it "to keep himself sane."[29] Two points are worth noticing here. One is that incomparably laconic "clodhopping," catching up Beckett's months of rural drudgery. The other is the fact, so different from what was very soon to come, that *Watt* was written in English.

Given the exceptional fact of the gap in Beckett's letters, it was the editors' original intention to signal it by entitling the present volume *1945–1956*. Yet the War years were decisive and formative, and the editors had no wish to diminish, still less elide, their significance. After much deliberation, it was decided that the helpfulness of identifying the gap in Beckett's correspondence was less important than establishing the continuity of the period and of the edition; hence the title *1941–1956*.

RESEARCH FOR VOLUME II

The nature of the research carried out in preparation of the edition has been fully described in the Introduction to Volume I. There is one important shift which should be noted here. Many of the people addressed or referred to in the post-War period were still alive when, decades later, the edition was being prepared. In the case of those who had died, it was possible to interview their colleagues and members of their families. Some of the major collections from which the letters published here are drawn remain in private hands. One example is the letters written to Georges Duthuit and held by his son Claude Duthuit, who with great generosity not only released the letters but provided abundant background information.

In those rare instances where Beckett himself had kept letters containing requests and drafts of his responses to these, the editors followed the trail to the individuals who had sent them, in order to track down Beckett's reply. Sometimes, luck joined intuition, as in seeking one Desmond Smith, who had written to Beckett from Toronto in 1956 to pose questions about *Waiting for Godot*. Forty-five years later, the editors tried every Desmond Smith in the Toronto telephone directory – and found the man in question, who indeed remembered having written to Beckett. He was engaged in packing up his affairs before a move, but promised to look for his letter from Beckett. Some weeks later, he faxed a copy of this letter; it had been found lying in a box of old newspapers, ready for discarding. Then the letters to Edouard Coester: these were among papers that Beckett had kept, but locating Coester was a challenge of both name and address, for he had composed music under one name and practiced law under another. An inquiry at Coester's last known address in a small village was forwarded to his daughter. She reported that, while her father was unable to reply to the inquiry, he had indeed been a musicologist and composer as well as a magistrate. When sent a copy of the letter, she confirmed that the handwriting in the letter that Beckett had kept was that of her father. For members of Coester's family, the discovery brought forward a story none of them had known; for readers of Volume II, the letters give clear evidence of Beckett's strong views on the relation of words and music.

For Beckett, the gap between completion of a work and its publication gradually narrows as Les Editions de Minuit, Fischer Verlag, Suhrkamp Verlag, Faber and Faber, John Calder, and Grove Press establish themselves as his publishers in France, Germany, England, and the United States. From the archives of publishers and agents it became evident that Beckett grew to depend upon his representatives – in publishing, in licensing productions, and in granting permissions. In some instances Beckett's desire to be amenable led to conflicts of interest: if permissions were not granted in a regularized way, contracts could be compromised. By following requests for permissions, the editors were led to discovery of publications and productions of Beckett's work, and to persons responsible for these, that would not otherwise have come to light.

Beckett's exchanges with his BBC producers document the evolution of the texts for radio drama and readings of his work, as well as the arrangements for recorded performance. The BBC Written Archive as well as its Sound Archive provided valuable contextual information on production, casting, broadcast schedules, and audience response.

The records of theatre productions and scripts, production photos, reviews, and memoirs helped the editors to fill out the account. Issues of contract, licensing, and censorship that arose in producing *Waiting for Godot* in London's West End affected both the Dublin Pike Theatre and New York productions. Newspaper reports, now more readily available thanks to the internet, provide one index of public response, while the records of censorship of the London production by the Lord Chamberlain's Office, now in the public domain, offer a view of what was happening, literally, behind the scenes. Not all publicity was favorable, as was seen when the opening of *Godot* in Miami was unhelpfully billed as "the laugh sensation of two continents," and its socialite audiences walked out in droves.[30]

In the years covered by this volume, Beckett, scrupulous as ever, answered virtually all his own mail. The exceptions were letters to publishers about matters of contract; some of these were dealt with, first, by Jacoba van Velde, then by Suzanne Deschevaux-Dumesnil who represented

Beckett's interests in early negotiations with Editions de Minuit, and later by Beckett's French publisher Jérôme Lindon, Director of Editions de Minuit, who drafted letters concerning legal or business matters for Beckett to sign. Examples of letters drafted for Beckett's signature are included in the notes as cross-reference when they provide context for a letter by Beckett himself.

SELECTION, PRESENTATION, AND ANNOTATION

When Beckett resumed his life in Paris after the War, it was to find a city much changed – and not, in his view, for the better. And of course it was as a man himself much changed that he returned, in ways that he hardly ever evokes directly, but which will be reflected in the tone of the post-War letters, and in his choice of language. One half of the pages of letters presented in the present volume were written by Beckett in French – written in French both for practical reasons and because Beckett wanted it so. As his desire to write in French grew stronger, and his circle of acquaintance widened, so the number of letters he wrote increased. Volume I printed approximately 60 percent of the total corpus for the years 1929–1940, whereas in the present volume closer to 40 percent of the letters consulted are published. Beckett had more correspondents in the post-War period and more of his letters were kept; this is due partly to his increased productivity, partly to the critical success of his fiction in France, partly to the response to productions of *En attendant Godot* in Paris, of *Warten auf Godot* in Germany, and of *Waiting for Godot* in London and New York.

The principles guiding the editors' selection have been set out in full in Volume I. The founding principle has been that laid down by Beckett himself: that the choice should be of letters "having bearing on my work." Given that there was so little published work to go on, the preparation of Volume I was fraught for the editors with difficulties of interpretation. For the present volume, selection has been more straightforward, even though the number of letters has increased. A first reason for this is that there is much more work produced in these years, and that Beckett is concerned in his letters with little else; even by the strictest standards of acceptability, there is an abundance of work-related letters. A second reason is offered by the shift in tone mentioned earlier. Beckett is no longer just a young writer making his way, impatient of others' failure to give him recognition, irritated by the success of authors of whom he is contemptuous.

Beckett's own experience of the War years, and his awareness of the experiences of his friends, had a profound effect on him – something of which we are aware not from things he says, but, paradoxically, from the fact that he will not speak of them; a phenomenon dismally familiar from survivors of the camps. The occasional petulance to be found in the early letters, the occasional harsh word for this person or that: these are hardly ever to be seen. In Volume II, with the exception of unresponsive or unreasonable publishers, Beckett complains of no one but himself and of little but what he sees as his own inadequacies.

The letters presented here are addressed to a much wider range of friends and acquaintances than before, as well as to strangers – an Italian translator, a South American publisher, a Canadian journalist. The proportion of letters included varies widely depending upon the recipient. Thus nearly all of the letters to Georges Duthuit have been included, while those to Thomas MacGreevy, which formed the backbone of Volume I, are far fewer during this period, and from this a smaller proportion is published. Beckett's relationship with MacGreevy was not as close as formerly; as their common Irishness came to matter less, and as they were occupied with professional endeavors, their letters tended more toward the familial or personal than toward exchanges about their writing.

The other shift is of language. There are letters in French in Volume I, but nothing to compare, in number or in length, with what is in the present volume. Editorial policy is unchanged: letters are presented in their original language, with a translation immediately following, and notes (which refer to both original and translation) following that. The higher proportion of letters in French has inevitably led to a reduction in the number of letters that can be included since the translations take space; but that has been judged by the editors to be a price worth paying, since it makes Beckett's originals available to the reader, as well as conveying their sense and something of their tone to the reader without French. The implications of Beckett's move to French are discussed in the "French translator's preface" and in the "Introduction to Volume II." Editorial policy has been to publish certain letters that have been previously published, including many to Barney Rosset, to Alan Schneider, and to Maurice Nadeau, since they are too important to be ignored, and since here the context, being that of the œuvre rather than that of an individual correspondent, opens up something of the singularity of Beckett's response to each.

Of the principles guiding the presentation of the letters (explained in full in Volume I), it need only be said that the letters are presented as they were written, preserving Beckett's habits, idiosyncrasies, and lapses. They appear as *clear copy*, reflecting the changes that Beckett made as or after he wrote – that is, the letter as it was received by the addressee. Where a correction made by Beckett is deemed of particular significance, it is referred to in a note. Wherever possible the editors have tried to avoid interrupting the flow of the letters. Where that is not possible, editorial emendations are presented within square brackets (preceded by a question mark if a reading is doubtful) to signal that these are not Beckett's words. Exception to this principle is made in the case of letters by writers other than Beckett, where trivial errors (typos, accidental omissions, etc.) have been silently corrected.

Each letter is prefaced by the name of the recipient and the place to which the letter was sent, when that is known, since Beckett rarely included the recipient's name and address in the body of his letters. The date and place of writing are given as written, as is Beckett's signature. Postscripts are placed following the signature, and their placement in the original is noted if it differs. The bibliographical note following each letter presents a description of the document and of its location. This information is followed by an indication of previous publication and a discussion of dating where these are relevant. The letters of this volume have offered some difficult challenges of dating, often because the letters in question contain no references to people, places, or events in the outside world. Beckett's letters are often undated owing to the possibility of rapid exchange permitted by multiple mail deliveries in a single day, and in Paris by the existence of the pneumatique. Dating supplied by the editors is given within square brackets, with doubtful dating noted. Occasionally it is impossible to propose anything more precise than a date range.

A full account of the principles chosen for annotating the letters is given in Volume I. What requires mention here is a shift in emphasis from the earlier volume. In the years – more than the editors like to remember – since research was first carried out on background to the letters, the research climate has changed in unforeseeable ways. Volume I of the edition bore something of the traces of its own research history, for there, while the editors tried to restrict the notes to what was essential to an understanding of the letter, the assumption was that readers would have access to only basic research tools. Here, with Volume II, the situation has changed. First, the period covered by the present volume is less distant from present-day readers, hence more ground may be common. Second, and crucially, the editors can now assume that most readers will have access to the vast resources of the internet, offering research tools of a sophistication and range literally unimaginable only twenty years ago. Hence, for example, where policy was to give some indication of the reasons for individuals' notoriety ("Florentine painter," "German composer") and their life dates, policy now is to give brief identifications and dates only to less well-known individuals. Where persons, often themselves recipients of letters, had a particular and enduring connection to Beckett, their brief biographies are given in the "Profiles" appendix in the volume where they first substantively appear. The same applies to significant publications, institutions, and organizations. Fuller detail concerning editorial practice, including abbreviations, notations, and idiosyncrasies in Beckett's usage, as well as a discussion of the approach to translation, are presented later in the introductory materials to this volume; a chronology precedes each year of letters and provides an overview of events.

In Volume I, numerous passages were elided from the letters at the request of the Samuel Beckett Estate. In Volume II there have been far fewer such elisions. There has been close, easy, and fruitful collaboration between the editors and the Estate, and there remain only a very few letters which the editors would have included but which were not approved.

The editors have decided that certain letters by Suzanne Deschevaux-Dumesnil should be presented within the body of the text of Beckett's letters. For several months during the years 1949–1951 she acted at Beckett's request and on his behalf in negotiations with publishers. Without these letters, it is not possible to trace the steps by which Beckett came to be published by Editions de Minuit. This exceptional case is signaled by the typographical particularity of these letters being presented in italics.

LACUNAE

There were times, during the War especially, when Beckett and his correspondents were moving frequently between cities or countries, carrying little more than what a suitcase could hold: non-essential papers were often jettisoned. Places changed, of course, over time: certain buildings no longer exist; streets, even whole countries, were redrawn. Paris itself underwent huge changes. The editors have tried to signal such changes where relevant.

Letters from this period that are known to exist but which have not been consulted are relatively few. One major collection relevant to the corpus of this volume has eluded the editors: the letters sent by Beckett to friends he made while in hiding in Roussillon, Josette and Henri Hayden. The person who purchased the collection when it was sold by auction at Sotheby's in 2008 has not permitted access, despite the repeated requests of the editors, supported as these were by the Estate of Samuel Beckett. When Beckett mentions writing letters which the editors have not been able to trace, this has been signaled in the notes. Letters which are discovered after publication of the relevant volume will be published, following the principles of selection adopted hitherto, as supplementary material in Volume IV.

Many readers have speculated as to why, in Volume I, certain crucial figures in Beckett's life were not represented by letters addressed to them: his mother, his father, his brother, Peggy Sinclair, Lucia Joyce, Peggy Guggenheim, to name but a few. The reason for this is simple and prosaic: to the best of the editors' knowledge, no letters from Beckett to these individuals have survived. Readers of the present volume may wonder why none of Beckett's letters to his brother or to his companion Suzanne Deschevaux-Dumesnil is included. The explanation is equally simple: despite the full cooperation and the best endeavors of the Beckett family and heirs, the editors have found no evidence that any such letters survive.

The editors readily recognize that there are gaps in their knowledge, and have not hesitated to report the limits of what they have been able to discover: indicating, for example, when handwriting is illegible, when a reference is unclear, when evidence is insufficient, or when the relevant information or document has simply not been found.

NOTES

1 SB to Marthe Arnaud, 10 June 1940.
2 An account of Samuel Beckett's Resistance activities and his escape to Roussillon can be found in James Knowlson's authorized biography of Beckett, *Damned to Fame: The Life of Samuel Beckett* (New York: Grove Press, 2004) 273–308.
3 SB to Patricia Hutchins, TCD, MS 4098/8.
4 A report, "Irish Legation in France, 1941," issued in February 1942, indicated that communication "between Ireland and the occupied zone" was impossible, and that facilitating inquiries "from relatives in Ireland and from residents in the occupied zone" imposed new burdens on the Legation, as did facilitating "payments to nationals and other persons and bodies entitled to money from Irish sources" (NAI, Irish Legation Vichy, Schedules including situation reports and transmitted messages to individuals).
5 Zurich James Joyce Foundation, Hans E. Jahnke Bequest.
   Richard Ellmann, *James Joyce: New and Revised Edition* (Oxford: Oxford University Press, [paperback with corrections] 1983) 738–739.
6 Frank Beckett to Thomas McGreevy, 18 January 1941, TCD, MS 10402/170.
7 (Mr Beckett is in excellent health and wants for nothing.) SB to Count Gerald O'Kelly, Ministre Plénipotentiaire Conseiller Spécial, 4 June 1941. A telegram relaying this information was sent by the Irish Legation through Swiss radio to Dublin on 13 June 1941 (NAI, DFA Paris 29/40).
8 Knowlson, *Damned to Fame*, 279.
9 SB to Lucie Léon (pen name, Lucie Noel, 1900–1972), NLI, MS 36,907/8.
10 SB to Lucie Léon, NLI, MS 36,907/8.
11 Interviews with Claude Salzman (16 March 1996; 9 October 2009).

12 For a fuller discussion of Beckett's involvement in the Resistance, see Knowlson, *Damned to Fame*, 278–298.

13 (Alfred arrested by Gestapo. Pray take all steps to have error corrected.) Knowlson, *Damned to Fame*, 287–288.

14 Knowlson, *Damned to Fame*, 292–293.

15 Stuart said he had obtained Beckett's Paris address from the Irish Consul in Berlin, William Warnock (1911–1986), who had contacted the Paris Legation (then in Vichy). Cornelius Cremin, First Secretary of the Irish Legation there (1939–1943), knew Beckett. In the typed manuscript of the journal, the date for the entry is given as "AUGUST Sunday," and it is preceded by an entry dated 6 August and followed by one dated 10 August; 8 August was on Sunday in 1942 (ICSo, Collection 167, Geoffrey Elborn Collection of Francis Stuart Box 1/ F. 15). When published as "Selections from a Berlin Diary 1942," the date "August 9" is supplied (Francis Stuart, *The Journal of Irish Literature*, 5.1 [January 1976] 88); when published in *The Irish Times*, the date for the entry is given as 5 August 1942 [Francis Stuart, "Extracts from a Berlin Diary Kept Intermittently between 1940 and 1944," *The Irish Times*, 29 January 1976: 10]).

16 Interview with Francis Stuart, 8 September 1993.

17 NAI, DFA Paris 202/166A; DFA France 49/34.

18 Knowlson, *Damned to Fame*, 293.
    SB to Cornelius Cremin, 27 October 1942, NAI DFA Paris Embassy 49/17 (Catriona Crowe, Ronan Fanning, Michael Kennedy, Dermot Keogh, and Eunan O'Halpin, eds., *Documents on Irish Foreign Policy*, VII [Dublin: Royal Irish Academy, 2010] 254).

19 SB to Cornelius Cremin, 11 October [1942], NAI DFA Paris Embassy 49/17 (Crowe et al., eds., *Documents on Irish Foreign Policy*, 251–252). The words "tether lengthened" are supplied from transcription of the original.

20 SB to Cornelius Cremin, 27 October 1942, NAI DFA Paris Embassy 49/17 (Crowe et al., eds., *Documents on Irish Foreign Policy*, 253–254). The words "of the utmost gravity" and "this" in "if this is indeed" are supplied from transcription of the original.
    Cornelius Cremin's letter to Beckett of 6 November 1942 indicates that an inquiry into the restrictions on Beckett's movement had been undertaken (Crowe et al., eds., *Documents on Irish Foreign Policy*, 254).

21 SB to Seán Murphy, 30 June 1943, NAI DFA Paris Embassy 49/17 (Crowe et al., eds., *Documents on Irish Foreign Policy*, 314–315). This publication corrects SB's mispelling ("non-belligerants"). Writing on 8 July, Seán Murphy assured Beckett that his case had been brought to the attention of the Ministry of Foreign Affirs (Crowe et al., eds., *Documents on Irish Foreign Policy*, 317–318).

22 SB to Seán Murphy, 17 July 1943, NAI DFA Paris Embassy 49/17. In the original, Beckett writes "identity-card", "20th," and "3rd," and underscores "Swiss"; SB's Gallicism is noted in this publication: "Beckett appears to have been translating directly from the French 'en vig[u]eur', meaning 'in force'" (Crowe et al., eds., *Documents on Irish Foreign Policy*, 319).
    A draft of this letter is in notebook 3 of *Watt* (TxU, Samuel Beckett collection, Works I, folder 3). SB refers to "Décret n° 1505 du 20 mai 1943 réglementant le séjour et la circulation des étrangers en France" (governing the duration of stay and movements of foreigners within France), *Journal Officiel de la République Française* 75.132 (3 June 1943) 1514–1515.

23 NAI, DFA Paris 207/316/43.

24 NAI, DFA Paris 106, Samuel Beckett.

25 NAI, DFA 106, Samuel Beckett; on 9 November 1944, Frank Beckett replied to this message via the Irish Legation.

26 SB to George Reavey, 14 May 1947.

27 The *Watt* notebooks (TxU, Samuel Beckett collection, Works, Box 6, folders 5–7, Box 7, folders 1–4). The first notebook was begun on 11 February 1941; the second notebook is dated 3 December 1941, and on page 39 includes the reference "Vanves 4 Sept. 42"; the third notebook is dated 5 May 1942; the fourth bears the date of 4 October 1943; the fifth contains various texts as well as a continuation of *Watt* (to page 99, with a note to see "the end" in notebook 6) and includes a date of 18 February 1945; in notebook 6 Beckett wrote: "Dec 28th 1944/ End." (Carlton Lake *et al.*, *No Symbols Where None Intended: A Catalogue of Books, Manuscripts, and Other Material Relating to Samuel Beckett in the Collections of the Humanities Research Center* [Austin: Humanities Research Center, The University of Texas at Austin, 1984] 75–76; Samuel Beckett, *Watt*, ed. Chris Ackerley [London: Faber and Faber, 2009] viii.)

28 SB to Gottfried Büttner, 12 April 1978, published in Gottfried Büttner, *Samuel Becketts Roman "Watt": Eine Untersuchung des gnoseologischen Grundzuges* (Heidelberg: Winter, 1981) 14–16; Büttner, *Samuel Beckett's Novel* Watt, tr. Joseph P. Dolan (Philadelphia: University of Pennsylvania Press, 1984) 5; SB to George Reavey, 14 May 1947.

29 Knowlson, *Damned to Fame*, 323.

30 Alan Schneider, *Entrances: An American Director's Journey* (New York: Viking, 1986) 229.

FRENCH TRANSLATOR'S PREFACE

Translation is inseparable from all but the earliest of Beckett's writing: as idea (necessity, challenge, burden), and as activity (practice, result). It is not the only way in which we are made aware of Beckett the linguist: the letters show continual recourse to Latin, French, Italian, and German. Both his translating and his letter-writing raise, directly or indirectly, the question of *competence*: how *good* are Beckett's French, Italian, etc.? His decision to write for publication in French – and later to conceive and compose a particular work in that language, in the awareness that he will at some later point translate it into English – makes the question inescapable. Can the letters help us to answer it?

In the imposed silence of the War years we have only a very few letters, messages of reassurance for his family sent to the Irish Legation. Beckett goes on living. More than that: he goes on living *in France*, and a very different France from the one that he has known, which could be summed up crudely as Paris and a few trips outside. But the difference is not only one of location. In these years he is no longer surrounded exclusively by writers, painters, publishers, art historians, professionals of all kinds: he is living in the country, in Roussillon-sur-Apt in the Vaucluse – part of what Nationalists used to call "la France réelle." This brings in a crucial new factor. The French that he, gifted linguist that he is, has absorbed over thirty-odd years – in school, at university, in the circle of his acquaintance – is not the French of rural and southern France, of what dismissive Parisians refer to generically as "Trou-en-Brie." These years – and the farm-work he shares in to ensure his own survival – more than make up for that, while the fact that throughout this time he is living with Suzanne Deschevaux-Dumesnil (who spoke almost no English) ensures regular contact with standard French.[1]

This is far from being a simple matter, a mere adding on of new sounds, new words, new constructions. Still less is it an index of some slide into regionalism. What matters is a (wholly justified) strengthening of his confidence: a sense of being in touch with the full range of "French."

This is not something that can be documented: Beckett does not keep that kind of diary. It is, precisely, the letters that he goes on to write after the War which allow us to glimpse the change. For it is one thing to send a typescript in French to a publisher (a person with whom dealings are seldom intimate), quite another to send an important and deeply felt letter in French to someone whom one knows and respects. From the end of the War, Beckett is writing in French. It is at this point that he meets the art critic Georges Duthuit. At the heart of this second volume of his letters is the extraordinary sequence that he writes to Duthuit between 1948 and 1952: letters in which he finds himself reaching for the finest possible delineation of his views on art and artists. But if these offer the most detailed evidence of his range and characteristic style, they are not the only letters illustrating the new confidence. It is in these years that dealings with publishers move from the minimal–businesslike to the personal, as he begins his long association with Jérôme Lindon and the Editions de Minuit. Then there is his correspondence with Jacoba van Velde, sister of the painters Bram and Geer, for a time his agent for France and later his translator into Dutch. This too starts out as a matter of arrangements and gradually shifts to the ground of friendship and, on Beckett's side, concern. And there are the letters to Mania Péron, whose husband Alfred, a friend whom he had known in Trinity College Dublin and later at the Ecole Normale Supérieure in Paris, had died during his return from Mauthausen Concentration Camp. Beckett can help her as teacher of English and writer; she can help him with everything from everyday matters to questions of grammar and style. In short, there is nothing now that cannot be expressed in a letter. That is not to say that his French is indistinguishable from that of a native speaker. There will be occasional oddities of tone: writing to Mania Péron he can say "J'entreprends après-demain une randonnée de 60 kilomètres à bicyclette" (Tomorrow I am undertaking a 60-kilometre bicycle ride). The solemn "j'entreprends" contrasts almost comically with what Beckett is planning.[2] And there are occasional lapses, as when, writing to Helmut Castagne at Fischer Verlag, he uses the phrase "lui accorder les facilités dont il a besoin." The French "facilités" will not do where what is meant is "equipment" or "available services," or simply "helpfulness."[3] Such instances are few. At the same time, it is important not to dismiss them out of hand, for Beckett himself is a severe critic of lapses, and will take great pains, particularly in his exchanges with Mania Péron, to avoid or correct textual imperfections. His general ease of movement, however, is never in doubt. And these immediate post-War years lead into the time when Beckett will need to be able to represent in the words of a letter exactly what he has in mind for directors and actors, as requests for guidance flow in from theatres all over Europe and the Americas.

But more is at issue than an increased confidence – more even than the freedom that that brings. The letters to Duthuit in particular reveal a Beckett not only ready but eager to pass on *all* his promptings and feelings: to write to another as he might talk to himself. They abound in violent contrasts, laudings (few), and dismissals (many); they assert, in terms at once insistent and fiercely idiosyncratic, a possible way of seeing, thinking, feeling, in which he wants to include Duthuit. The "I" is predicated throughout on a "we." To read these letters is to be given a glimpse into the imaginative and affective space where Beckett's words are forged.

The translator must hope to stretch English to a point where it will allow a glimpse of the sheer strangeness of Beckett's French. A glimpse of this strangeness seen from the inside comes in a letter to Barney Rosset where, on the subject of Erich Franzen's translation of *Molloy*, Beckett talks of Franzen's "irritating way of turning the unusual into the usual so that it won't read like a translation."[4] For the most part, the task is formal–tonal: to represent, for example, the special function Beckett attaches to this or that word, in ways that differ from ordinary usage. The word "empêchement," for instance, normally signals prevention: being stopped from doing this or that. From whatever angle we look at it, its function would be negative. Beckett can follow this pattern, as here: "Je voulais passer te voir hier soir. Encore ce soir. Empêchement chaque fois." (I wanted to go round to see you last night. This evening again. Each time something cropped up.)[5] But he can also write: "Non, la seule chose à maintenir dans ce morceau de bravoure verdâtre [. . .] c'est le motif peinture empêchement" (No, the only thing in that ugly green purple patch worth keeping [. . .] is the *painting / preventedness* motif).[6] For what Beckett argues is that only when "preventedness" is accepted can a true painting, no longer driven by desire or memory, emerge. In an earlier letter he chooses a different word to similar effect: "coincement."[7] This signals the state of being stuck, cornered, trapped – again an essentially negative notion. It is Bram van Velde's ability to accept this state that is, for Beckett, his great gift – and the gift that he himself aspires to. Meanwhile, he decides to make sure that these words carry that extra – and unlikely – weight.

But there is a major structural problem here. The more Beckett pursues and develops this view of Van Velde, the more he risks creating a *coherence*: a settled, finite, recognizable, and therefore acceptable perspective. That is, his own words may set up the familiar triangle of critic/painter/painting, to be inserted in the larger space of general culture: the unwarranted process of recuperation, realignment, and consolation that he so much wants to repudiate. The sentences grow wilder and wilder as he casts about for a line that will evade that trap (Jérôme Lindon, Beckett's publisher and, later, literary executor, commenting on the Beckett of these letters, said with a publisher's rueful indulgence, "Mais il était exalté" [But he was over-excited]).[8] Consider this sentence about Bram van Velde:

> Mais il s'y essaie, ou y tient si tu préfères, en se créant au fur et à mesure une [*for* un] espace paradis qui l'y autorise, espace nouveau où traînent forcément quelques réminiscences de ceux si généreusement mis à notre disposition et dont tant d'artistes se sont si bellement gargarisés et dont d'autres encore ont simplement pris leur parti, fait leur affaire, comme il semble naturel en effet qu'on fasse bonne face contre mauvaise fortune, à supposer qu'elle soit mauvaise, et tous finissent bien par s'assoupir dans l'unanimité faite à ce sujet. (But he does try his hand at it, or has a mind to it if you prefer, by creating for himself a paradise-space which allows him to do so, a new space in which there are still, inevitably, a few lingering reminiscences of those so generously put at our disposal and which so many artists have gone on about so eloquently, and which others have simply resigned themselves to, settled to, since it seems natural that one should put on a show of making the best of a bad job, if bad it be, and all concerned end up settling comfortably into the unanimity that surrounds the whole business.)[9]

Beckett adds immediately: "Pardonne ce ton doctoral, mais sous le bonnet quel chahut" (Forgive this doctoral tone, but what a din there is going on under the Tudor bonnet). For no one is more aware of the trap than Beckett himself, and he will quite suddenly stop the torrent of argument and move to something deflatingly different, as for instance when he breaks off an intricate exploration of necessary lessness to say "Mais je commence à écrire" (But I'm starting to write) – and quickly ends the letter.[10]

Why does he *allow* himself to be drawn on to the ground of argument? There can be no certain answer, but there is one unresolved tension that cannot be ignored: that between his deep-seated distaste for the role of critic and the forcefulness of his actual views. Duthuit drops in front of him this or that assertion or question, his own or someone else's, about art; Beckett pounces on it at once, deploying, if necessary inventing as he goes, a language that will reveal precisely how and where the assertion is wrong – until he suddenly becomes aware of what he is doing, and, embarrassedly or comically, backs away. The shift is always rapid, as when, in a letter to Mania Péron, he writes of Geer van Velde: "Je l'ai toujours beaucoup estimé. Mais pas assez je crois. Ne le dis pas à Bram. Entre les oeuvres, pas d'hésitation. Mais ce n'est pas un jugement." (I have always had a high opinion of him. But not high enough, I think. Don't say that to Bram. Between the one's work and the other's, no hesitation. But that is not a judgement.)[11] Or again, when, writing to Georges Belmont about a play that Belmont has sent him:

> La pièce est étrange, très littéraire et en même temps, il me semble, faite pour être jouée, comme une démonstration du tort qu'on a de considérer ces deux aspects comme ennemis, c'est le cas probablement de tout ton théâtre, mais je ne le connais pas assez bien. Une vraie trouvaille, les deux masques et leurs jeux de scène, et indispensable, je me suis même demandé s'il n'y aurait pas intérêt à leur donner plus d'impor-tance. J'espère pouvoir te sortir tout ça, et autre chose, mieux en bavardant. Par le papier je ne suis plus bon qu'à aller dans la bêtise, l'ignorance, l'impuissance et le silence. (The play is strange, very literary and at the same time, it seems to me, made to be performed, as a demonstration of the wrongness of considering these two aspects as opposed to each other. Probably the case for all your plays, but I don't know them well enough. A real find, the two masks and the byplay with them, and indispensable. I even wondered if it might not be worth making more of them. I hope to be able to get all this out to you, along with other things, better when we can chat. On paper all I'm good for now is going on into silliness, ignorance, impotence, and silence.)[12]

Beckett will always be the first to see inadequacy or inappropriateness in his own words. For the translator, the problem is to recognize that, but to make sure that the movement is seen as closer to a conditioned reflex than to a considered judgment.

The new confidence is at work too, although to very different effect, in what he writes to Jacoba van Velde. It is not just that he moves from the businesslike to the friendly. The more important point is that he can see in her letters (although she too is writing in a language that is not native to her) features which warrant a progressively less detached approach: to the point, for example, where he feels able to offer suggestions on how to deal with the alarming slide into alcoholism and depression of the man she lives with, or how to overcome her own writer's block. This terrain is differently dangerous: a slip or an awkwardness here may cause untold distress. Beckett faces it with effortless honesty: in one letter passing from an opening paragraph on the death of her mother through some pleasantly shareable business to a final paragraph that runs "Et Paolo et Francesca? Et Tristan et Yseult? Merde alors, les grands mamoureux, il n'y a que ça." (What about Paolo and Francesca? And Tristan and Isolde? Hell's bells, they're all over the place, these Great Looovers.)[13] For even in these letters Beckett is wary of any slippage into solemnity: what the French call so neatly "le sérieux." Venturing a hope about improvement in her husband's condition, he immediately changes the tone:

> J'espère qu'il va bientôt rappliquer et que son père finira par cracher de quoi vous installer tous les deux solidement à Paris, si c'est ça que vous voulez. Vivement 57, et 67, et 77, après ça ira, sinon avant. Voilà à quoi vous vous exposez, en me demandant de vous écrire (ce que j'aurais fait de toute façon). Laissez-moi vous souhaiter – en homme bien élevé – beaucoup de bonheur dans cette putain d'année qui vient. (I hope he's going to get back soon and that his father will eventually cough up the wherewithal to get the two of you properly housed in Paris, if that's what you want. Let 57 come soon, and 67, and 77. It'll be all right after that, if not before. See what you bring on yourself by asking me to write [I'd have done so anyway]. Allow me to wish you – well brought up as I am – much happiness in this bloody awful coming year.)[14]

With Mania Péron he is right in the business of translation: she looks over, and offers suggestions for, his French-language writings; he responds to these, and gives her advice for her work as teacher of English. Here is a sample (the text under translation is "Le Saltimbanque," one of Baudelaire's "Petits Poèmes en Prose"):

> "Sa destinée était faite" – difficile à traduire. On ne peut pas dire "drawn out for him" à mon avis. "Drawn out" ne peut signifier, au figuratif, que "protracted" – traîné en longueur. Le sens en est en effet "it was all over". "His destiny was at an end,

accomplished, achieved". J'aimerais assez, quoique ça fasse un peu étrange, "his destiny was done". "His course was run", pas mal non plus. Non, non, ne me remerciez pas. ("Sa destinée était faite" – difficult to translate. One cannot say "drawn out for him" in my view. "Drawn out" can only mean, figuratively, "protracted" – traîné en longueur. The meaning is "it was all over". "His destiny was at an end, accomplished, achieved". I would quite like, although it sounds a bit odd, "his destiny was done". "His course was run", not bad either. No, no, don't thank me.)[15]

It is worth keeping in mind this level of care when we read, in a letter to an English correspondent: "I am by no means a good translator, and my English is rusty, but I simply happen to be able still to write the queer kind of English that my queer French deserves."[16] Here, of course, we must allow for Beckett's characteristic self-depreciation. That itself takes innumerable forms. In another letter to Mania Péron we find this reference to his Ussy cottage:

> Depuis que je suis ici la valeur de ces 2000 mètres a baissé de 20% au bas mot. Pommiers et poiriers lâchent leurs fruits à peine formés et les groseill[i]ers, comme surpris pour me faire plaisir, redeviennent sauvages. (Since I've been here, the value of these 2,000 metres has gone down by 20%, to put it no higher. Apple trees and pear trees shed their fruit barely formed and the currant bushes, as if taken by surprise in order to please me, are going back to the wild.)[17]

But such wry claims of general incompetence never stop him from making a point when he wants to, as when he says, in another letter to Mania Péron: "Lisez laid à la place de lay. Lie actif n'existe pas, sinon comme archaisme [sic] ou par erreur: the cloth was lain." (Read "laid" instead of "lay." "Lie" does not exist in the active, except as an archaism or an error: "the cloth was lain.")[18] The to-and-fro about word-values is accompanied throughout by a warm and easy concern for Mania and her family. For what we are looking at here – the concurrent generous warmth toward those close to him and uncompromising severity in anything to do with written expression – is a constant of Beckett's world.

This is apparent, for example, in his dealings with Patrick Bowles, to whom he entrusts the translation into English of *Molloy*. He likes Bowles, and gets on well with him, but is increasingly uneasy over some features of the proposed translation. To his unfailing distaste for translating his own work is added now irritation at having to struggle with Bowles's version. This we know of only from letters to friends, but the implication is clear: willingly or not, he decides that translation is a burden he must in future shoulder himself.

But translation is not the only kind of boundary-crossing in which we can see Beckett's resourcefulness. Here is the opening of a letter to Duthuit: "Assez de ce vous garou, veux-tu?"[19] A literal rendering is impossible: this invented piece of French takes off from a familiar word, "loup-garou" (werewolf; the "bugbear" of stories told to children). As Beckett senses an increasing closeness to Duthuit, he makes a verbal move toward marking it: a change from the earlier, formal "vous" to the intimate "tu." The importance of this shift will be familiar to all French-speakers aged over fifty; current practice makes much less of it. However, rather than simply making the change, Beckett proposes it by way of this extraordinary formula, banishing as it were for ever the "big bad 'vous,'" and hoping for Duthuit's favorable reaction. English has no obvious linguistic or cultural parallel. The translator can do no more than suggest the range implied. My suggestion (borrowed from the early Quakers) is "Shall we stop the scraping and bowing, and go for thee-ing and thou-ing? What say you?" As with all explained jokes, the instantaneous has become the laborious.

Cultural difference brings another kind of difficulty, related this time not to "foreignness" but to Irishness: the habit, common among speakers of Irish English, of shaping the sentence along oral lines, the vocal stress-pattern indicating the meaning. I should say here that my own Irishness makes it impossible for me not to recognize the effects of this oral shaping, which may appear anywhere in Beckett's work – the apparently unbroken succession of words on a typical double page of *The Unnamable* is in reality shaped and ordered by speech patterns and rhythms. Here is Beckett writing to a woman whom he has known since childhood about the fatuities of critics of *En attendant Godot*: "Like a lot of seaside brats digging for worms people are."[20] The pitch rises steadily to "worms," then falls sharply for the last two words, spoken on the same level. These two words drive the sentence. The importance of this oral dimension is fascinatingly illustrated by Beckett's frequent omission of commas and semi-colons where they might be expected. How deliberate this is can be seen when he writes to H. O. White: "Trinity News made a great hames of my text with their unspeakable paragraphs and varsity punctuation. I asked them either not to print it at all or to print it as it stood and above all to send me proofs. Well I suppose I should be used to being improved behind my back and to the horrible semi-colons of well brought-up young blue pencils."[21] The natural punctuation for Beckett is that of the breath group. I have tried to follow that preference except where, for those unaccustomed to the dominance of the oral, it could lead to confusion or incomprehensibility. Nothing with Beckett is entirely straightforward, but there can be few more surprising claims than the one we find in a letter to Georges Duthuit (whose strong bias is toward the eye): "nous qui ne sommes tout de même pas des auditifs" (we who are all the same not ear-people).[22] There cannot have been many finer-tuned ears than Beckett's.

I shall finish with two further examples of the sheer range of Beckett's epistolary styles: examples as different from each other as they very well could be. We can only guess at what the first cost Beckett. He has learned that the review *Les Temps Modernes* (founded just after the War by Jean-Paul Sartre), which, he believed, had undertaken to publish his story "Suite," has published only the first part of it. When, over one month later, the second part of his story was submitted to the journal, it was rejected. This least litigious of writers finds himself forced to protest – at a time when, it must have seemed, his long-frustrated career was about to take off. If ever there was a test of Beckett the writer and Beckett the linguist, this is it. The letter he writes to Simone de Beauvoir, then one of the editors of *Les Temps Modernes* and a writer whose work he respects, is a triumph. Here is a crucial passage:

> J'ai suffisa[m]ment confiance en vous, finalement, pour vous dire tout simplement mon sentiment. Le voici. Vous m'accordez la parole pour me la retirer avant qu'elle n'ait eu le temps de rien signifier. Vous immobilisez une existence au seuil de sa solution. Cela a quelque chose de cauchemar-[d]esque. J'ai du mal à croire que des soucis de présentation puissent justifier, aux yeux de l'auteur de L'Invitée, une mutilation pareille. (I have sufficient trust in you, in the end, simply to tell you what my feelings are. They are as follows: You are giving me the chance to speak only to retract it before the words have had time to mean anything. You are immobilising an existence at the very moment at which it is about to take its definitive form. There is something nightmarish about that. I find it hard to believe that matters of presentation can justify, in the eyes of the author of *L'Invitée*, such a mutilation.)[23]

Not hurt pride, not the revelation of some narcissistic wound, not mere fury at being crossed. On the contrary it is as if Beckett were defending one of his own friends against grossly unfair attack: it is the friend that matters. But this moral stance, with its notable self-abnegation, is itself a powerful piece of writing. He is facing Simone de Beauvoir the writer with her professional failure of imagination, her betrayal of the literary. In the severely intellectualist context of *Les Temps Modernes*, Beckett's unembarrassed but firm deployment of words informed rather by feeling ("J'ai suffisa[m]ment confiance en vous, finalement, pour vous dire tout simplement mon sentiment" [I have sufficient trust in you, in the end, simply to tell you what my feelings are]) is breathtaking. Faced with the very different verbal signals of the arbiters of current intellectual fashion, Beckett will not break faith either with his "creature," or, more important, with his own characteristic utterance.

And finally, a reaching out in which neither defense nor attack matters. One of Beckett's most admirable characteristics is his willingness to help younger writers. One in particular needs encouragement, so low is his self-esteem – Robert Pinget – and Beckett is unfailingly supportive, but not always in the same way. Rather than offer (from a position of strength) this or that piece of practical advice, or just sympathy, he tells Pinget that he is unable to

> vous conseiller en connaissance de cause. Du reste cela ne servirait à rien, ces causes-là on ne les connaît jamais. Il faut que vous vous décidiez tout seul, en vous disant autant que possible que quoi qu'on fasse on est sûr de le regretter. Je ne connais que trop bien ce que vous éprouvez devant un dilemme pareil. J'ai toujours été intransigeant et je l'ai quelquefois regretté. Dites oui ou non et débarrassez-vous de cette histoire. (give you advice based on an informed inside view. In any case it would get us nowhere: those sorts of insides we can never view. You must make up your own mind, telling yourself as much as possible that whatever one does, one is bound to regret it. I am only too familiar with what you are going through, faced with a dilemma of this kind. I have always been uncompromising, and I have sometimes regretted it. Say yes or no and be shot of the whole business.)[24]

George Craig

NOTES

1 "Trou" (hole).
  For further information on these years, see Knowlson, *Damned to Fame*, 291–308.

2 SB to Mania Péron, 28 August 1951.
3 SB to Helmut Castagne, 14 July 1956.
4 SB to Barney Rosset, 11 February 1954.
5 SB to Georges Duthuit, [? end December 1950].
6 SB to Georges Duthuit, 26 May [1949].
7 SB to Georges Duthuit, 2 March 1949.
8 Interview with Jérôme Lindon, 19 November 1996.
9 SB to Georges Duthuit, 2 March 1949.
10 SB to Georges Duthuit, 11 August 1948.
11 SB to Mania Péron, 28 August [1951].
12 SB to Georges Belmont, 8 August 1951.
13 SB to Jacoba van Velde, 25 November 1952.
14 SB to Jacoba van Velde, 27 December 1956.
15 SB to Mania Péron, 28 March 1952, second letter of this date.
16 SB to Cyril Lucas, 4 January 1956.
17 SB to Mania Péron, 6 September 1951.
18 SB to Mania Péron, 17 August [1951].
19 SB to Georges Duthuit, 2 March 1949.
20 SB to Mary Manning Howe, 18 August 1955 (see SB to Pamela Mitchell, 18 August 1955, n. 5).
21 SB to H. O. White, 2 July [1956].
22 SB to Georges Duthuit, Saturday [on or after 30 April, before 26 May, 1949].
23 SB to Simone de Beauvoir, 25 September 1946.
24 SB to Robert Pinget, 14 December 1955.

EDITORIAL PROCEDURES

Letters are transcribed as written and presented as a clear text, that is, the final text as sent to the recipient. While some letters were repeatedly revised before being sent, letters to friends were not always checked. Inevitably, eccentricities appear: slips of the pen, typos, accidental substitutions, oddities of spelling (particularly of proper names that Beckett had misheard or misremembered), and persistent confusions (sent/send). To signal each one with "sic" or "for" would interfere with reading, hence only when Beckett's eccentricities might prevent or distort understanding are they noted.

Sequence Letters are presented chronologically. When more than one letter was written on the same day, the letters are ordered alphabetically by recipient's name, unless internal evidence suggests another sequence. When the editors supply dating, the letter appears in sequence according to the date deduced. When Beckett sends a letter enclosing another letter, both letters are presented, with the enclosure following the letter itself.

Recipient The full name of the recipient, with a corporate identification if relevant, and the city to which the letter was sent, are indicated in small capitals as a header; these are editorial additions. Beckett himself seldom included a recipient's name and address in a letter; however, when he does, this is shown as written.

Date Dates are presented as written by Beckett, who most often follows European format (day, month, year), but placement is regularized. If the date, or any portion of it, is incomplete or incorrect, editorial emendation is given in square brackets; if a date, or any portion of it, is uncertain, this emendation is preceded by a question mark. The rationale for the dating is given, if needed, in the bibliographical note following the letter.

Place Place is presented as written, but placement is regularized. Where place is incomplete or missing, editorial emendation is given in square brackets, preceded by a question mark if uncertain. Occasionally, the place of writing is not congruent with the place of mailing; for example, Beckett may write in Paris, but post the letter in La Ferté-sous-Jouarre. This is not corrected. Imprinted letterheads are given in small capital letters.

Orthography Beckett's idiosyncratic spelling, capitalization, and abbreviation are preserved: this includes abbreviations without punctuation (wd, cd, yrs), varying presentation of superscripts (M^r, Y^r, $14^{\underline{me}}$), use of ampersands, contractions written without an apostrophe ("wont" *for* "won't"), and use of diacriticals and hyphens ("Ca" *for* "Ça," "c'est à dire" *for* "c'est-à-dire"). Beckett's practice of indicating the titles of works is inconsistent: sometimes he underscores titles, sometimes he does not, sometimes he underscores partially.

Beckett often uses words or phrases from other languages when writing in English or French, but he seldom underscores such words or phrases. If Beckett's moves from one language to another produce what appears to be a variant spelling in the dominant language of the letter, this is marked or explained in a note.

Beckett frequently spells a name incorrectly. When a person's name, a title, or another reference is misspelled in the text of a letter, this is signaled in the notes. On occasions when the misspelled name is likely to confuse, its first use is corrected within square brackets in the text: e.g. "Marcel [*for* Maurice] Nadeau" and "Roland [*for* Ronald] Searle." When, as in a joke or pun made with a name, a misspelling is judged to be deliberate, it stands as written; standard spelling is given in the notes and the index. As in Volume I, Beckett always spells the name of Gwynedd Reavey as "Gwynned"; this is noted at the first occurrence and then silently emended.

Beckett presents ellipses with spaced dots; however, these are variously two dots or three dots. Beckett occasionally punctuates with a dash instead of a period at the end of a sentence.

Authorial emendation The results of Beckett's cancelations, insertions, and inversions are presented as a clear text. When a reading of an emendation by Beckett is uncertain, it is given within square brackets in the text, preceded by a question mark.

Beckett often overwrites or overtypes to self-correct; when typing, he sometimes cancels a word or phrase if it does not fit the space on the page, and sometimes leaves it in partial form before writing it fully on the next line or page. Beckett changes his mind as he writes: sometimes omitting or inserting a word, phrase, or sentence; inverting word order; extending a thought in the margins. Typed letters contain both typed and handwritten corrections. Drafts of letters show many more changes. Where Beckett's changes are substantive – that is, not merely corrections of spelling or typos or false starts – these are presented in the notes. Scholars interested in the patterns of Beckett's changes will wish to consult the original manuscripts. When grammatical or spelling variants interfere with sense, these are editorially expanded or corrected within square brackets in the text, or are signaled in the notes.

Editorial emendation Editorial emendations to the text are supplied only when necessary to understanding and are shown within square brackets. Other than obvious typographical errors (overtypes, space slips, extra spacing, false starts), and what is stated above, there are no silent emendations. For the sake of readability, in the case of letters by writers other than Beckett, the editors have made silent corrections where there appeared to be trivial errors (typos, accidental omissions, etc.).

Placement and indentation of date, address, closing and signature lines have been regularized. Paragraph indentations are standardized. Line ends are marked only in poetry. Postscripts are presented following the signature; if their original placement differs, this is described in a note.

Editorial ellipses in letters and other unpublished manuscripts are shown by three unspaced dots within square brackets; editorial ellipses in published materials are shown with three spaced dots.

Illegibility Illegibility is noted in square brackets [illeg]. If a reading is uncertain, it is given within square brackets and preceded by a question mark. Damage to the original manuscript that obscures or obliterates the text is described in the bibliographical note and is marked in the text as illegible. When the illegible words can be surmised, these are presented within square brackets within the text.

Signature The closing and signature lines are regularized. An autograph signature or initial can be assumed for an autograph letter; in a typed letter, the notation "s/" indicates a handwritten signature or initial. A typed letter may have both an autograph and a typed signature. When these are not identical, both are shown. When these are identical, the existence of an autograph signature is indicated only by "s/" and the typed signature is presented in the line that follows:

With best wishes
s/
Samuel Beckett

An unsigned carbon copy presents only a typed signature, but spacing allows for an autograph signature in the original:

With best wishes

Samuel Beckett

Bibliographical note Following each letter is a bibliographical note which gives a description of the letter. Description of the physical document may include its letterhead, the image on a postcard, and enclosures. This description also includes the address on a postcard or envelope, the postmark, and any additional notation on the envelope, whether written by Beckett or in another hand (e.g. forwarding address, postal directives). Postmarks are indicated by city (not by post office) and date. Editorial markers are given in italics: e.g. *env to* George Reavey; *pm* 1–3–54, Paris. The ownership of the physical property is given with the designated library abbreviation, collection name and accession information, or dealer's name; private ownership is indicated according to the owner's preference, by name or simply as "private collection." Previous publication is noted when the letter has been published in full or in a substantial portion (more than half); facsimile reproductions are indicated in this note.

Notations used in the bibliographical description indicate whether the letter is handwritten or typed; whether a letter, postcard, lettercard, telegram, or pneumatique; the bibliographical description indicates the number of leaves and sides, and whether the letter is signed, initialed, or unsigned. A leaf is a physical piece of paper; a side is a page written on, whether recto or verso. A postcard may bear an address on the recto (1 leaf, 1 side) or on the verso (1 leaf, 2 sides). Beckett sometimes folded a single piece of paper so that it had four sides (1 leaf, 4 sides). All editorial notations are detailed under "Abbreviations."

Discussion of dating When the date of a letter is corrected or derived from internal or external evidence, the rationale for the assigned date or date-range is given following the bibliographical note. Undated or partially dated letters are not unusual. Beckett may neglect to date a letter when it is part of a frequent exchange or when it follows or anticipates a personal meeting; he often misdates letters at the beginning of a new year. If envelopes are clearly affiliated with the letter in question, the postmark may be helpful in dating. Some correspondence received by publishers and other businesses was routinely date-stamped; this is signaled in the bibliographical note and may help with dating. While Beckett occasionally delivers a note personally, it is also the case that some stamped letters are sent without cancellation. Telegrams may bear only the date of receipt.

Translation Letters written entirely in a language other than English are translated immediately following the transcription of the original and its bibliographical note.

Translations of words or phrases are provided in the notes to the letter. Translations are given as in the following example: "Bon travail & bon sommeil" (work well & sleep well). The language of the original is not indicated in the translation unless there may be ambiguity; if required, the following abbreviations are used: colloq., colloquial; Fr., French; Ger., German; Gk., Greek; Ir., Irish; It., Italian; Lat., Latin; Sp., Spanish. Published translations are used for literary quotations, if available and deemed appropriate by the editors, and are so noted (see below).

Beckett may write the name of a German city with German, French, or English spelling; however, translations and editorial material present the English spelling of city and place names. Translations do not repeat Beckett's mistakes (slips of the pen, misremembering or misspelling of proper names, and the occasional incoherence inevitable in unrevised writings). In the rare cases where spelling norms have changed (well into the 1950s Beckett wrote "to-day" and "to-morrow"), current practice is followed. Although Beckett practiced English-style capitalization when writing the titles of books in other languages, translations and notes use the capitalization practice of the language in which the book was written. In the translation of letters, all titles of books are indicated by italics.

Translators' initials are given when the translator is other than George Craig for French, Viola Westbrook for German, and Dan Gunn for Italian. In this volume, the German in Samuel Beckett's letters is limited to his discussion with Erich Franzen, the German translator of *Molloy*. Translation is provided in the annotations for passages from corollary correspondences or printed sources when these are not in English.

In the chronologies, notes, and profiles, Samuel Beckett is referred to as "SB." Translations follow British spelling and punctuation practice; all other editorial materials follow American English spelling and punctuation. Although all letters are presented as written, in line with standard French practice the edition does not put accents on initial capitals in editorial matter. All other accents are displayed, even where, as in editorial headers, the material is represented in small capitals. This affects only editorial matter in French; other languages have other conventions.

Identifications of persons The first reference gives a person's name (including birth name, and/or acquired appellations including pseudonyms and nicknames, where relevant). Identifications and life dates are not given for well-known figures such as William Shakespeare, René Descartes, or Dante Alighieri. Dates are given for less well known public figures. Dates and a brief statement of identification are given for figures who, in the editors' judgment, may not be known to readers or about whom information is not readily available. Additional statements of identification may be given over the course of a volume, or over the four volumes, when a person's primary occupation, affiliation, or relationship to Samuel Beckett changes.

Names Names are not necessarily constant over time. Thomas McGreevy chose to change the spelling of his family name to "MacGreevy" in 1941; Beckett follows the new spelling, with occasional hesitations, and so editorially from Volume II onwards his name is spelled "MacGreevy." Members of MacGreevy's family retained the original spelling of the family name. As a result, the two spellings may appear in close succession. After World War II, Georges Pelorson changed his name to Georges Belmont. Some women assume their husband's surname when they marry: Mary Manning became Mary Manning Howe and then Mary Manning Howe Adams, but she used her maiden name professionally. Jacoba van Velde is also known in the letters as Tonny and Tony Clerx (a married name). Editorial practice is to follow Beckett's spelling of the name at the time of writing (but not his misspellings), but also to refer to writers by the name given on the title page of their books.

Some persons become known by their initials, some by their nicknames, and some by both. Abraham Jacob Leventhal generally gives his name in publications as A. J. Leventhal, but he is most often referred to in Beckett's letters by his nickname, "Con." Beckett's cousin Morris Sinclair may also be addressed as "Maurice," or by his family nickname "Sunny," which in German becomes "Sonny" (indeed he was the only son in the Sinclair family).

When a name changes, a note signals this change. Both/all names are entered as one heading in the Index.

Dates Approximate dates are preceded by c. (circa), fl. (floruit), or a question mark; when dates are approximated as a range, the earliest birth year and the latest death year are given, preceded by c. to indicate approximation. If only the birth year or death year is known, it is given as, for example, (b. 1935) or (1852–?) or (d. 1956). Rarely, the only date known is a marriage date; this will be given as (m. 1933). When a date is unknown, it is indicated as (n.d.).

Titles In editorial material (introductions, translations, annotations, appendices), titles are presented with the capitalization and spelling conventions of the original language. The title of a work of art is italicized and commonly presented in English since the language of the artist may not be the same as the language of the museum or collections that have owned it. Generally, a catalogue raisonné gives titles in several languages. Titles of musical works are sometimes in the language of the composer and remain untranslated; however, lines from songs, recitatives, and arias are always translated. Titles of books that are referred to in the text appear in the notes in their original language, followed by date of first publication and title in English if there is a published translation, e.g. *Léviathan* (1929; *The Dark Journey*); if the English title is given in roman font, e.g. *Die notwendige Reise* (1932; The Necessary Journey), this indicates that no English translation has been found and that the translated title has been supplied by the editors.

For titles, dates, and names, including variant spellings of names, editorial practice has been to rely upon *The Grove Dictionary of Music*; *The Grove Dictionary of Art*; *The Cambridge Biographical Encyclopedia*, second edition; *The Dictionary of Irish Biography*; the catalogues of the Bibliothèque Nationale de France, the British Library, the National Library of Ireland, the Library of Congress, as well as other national libraries; and *The Oxford Dictionary for Writers and Editors*.

Glosses Unusual or archaic English words or foreign-language terms that have entered common English usage are not glossed if they can be found in the second electronic edition of *The Oxford English Dictionary* (OED Online, 2009).

References References to unpublished materials give the archive and manuscript identification of the documents. References to published materials give a full bibliographical citation at the first mention, and a short-title reference thereafter. The Bibliography includes all published materials that are cited, with the exception of newspapers. Titles that are identified in the text but not cited do not appear in the Bibliography.

Cross-reference Cross-reference that refers back to specific material within the edition is given by indicating the date of the letter and the number of the pertinent note, e.g. 9 January 1936, n. 5. This holds for all volumes of the edition: cross-references do not include volume number. Cross-references are rarely given forward. It is presumed that most readers will read sequentially; those who wish to pursue a single figure or work will be able to do so by use of the Index.

Choice of editions Although it is necessary to select standard editions for editorial reference, these choices are not governed by a single rule. For example, most often the Bibliothèque de la Pléiade edition of French texts is used, or the more recent of these where two editions exist, because these editions take into account earlier editions. Exceptions have been made when a reference requires a first edition or an edition that Beckett refers to in a letter, or one he is known to have read, or the only one he could have read. The choice of edition may change over the course of subsequent volumes. Where there is no standard edition, editions are selected for their accessibility, for example the Riverside edition of Shakespeare's works. Biblical references are to the King James Version. Publication information is given for all first and subsequent editions of Beckett's texts, when this information is germane to the context of a letter; English-language quotations are generally taken from the first Grove Press editions.

Choice of translations Published English translations are provided for Beckett's foreign-language citations where these are available, unless the editors have determined that none of these is suitable. Beckett nearly always read in the original language, and so the choice of a translation is seldom directed by his reading.

Chronologies Chronologies precede each year of the letters in order to present an overview of the events mentioned in Beckett's correspondence; these include certain significant world events.

Profiles Biographical profiles of persons who have a continuing role in the narrative of *The Letters of Samuel Beckett* appear in the Appendix. Those who have a profile are indicated by an asterisk following their name in the first reference to them; this asterisk appears with their name in the Index. A profile presents a narrative of a person's life and work, with regard particularly to his or her association with Beckett. Profiles appear in the first volume of the letters in which the person becomes a figure of significance for Beckett. As profiles will not be reprinted in subsequent volumes of the edition, they cover the historical range of a person's association with Beckett. Profiles given in other volumes are indicated, at the point of first reference in each volume, with the notation, e.g., "Profile, I." Profiles are also given for certain institutions, publications, and organizations.

ACKNOWLEDGMENTS

The family of Samuel Beckett has been welcoming as well as generous in sharing memories and documents. The editors warmly thank Edward and Felicity Beckett, Caroline and Patrick Murphy, and remember with gratitude the late Ann Beckett, John Beckett, Deirdre Hamilton, Sheila Page, and Morris Sinclair.

FUNDING AND CONTRIBUTIONS

The James T. Laney School of Graduate Studies of Emory University has supported the research for *The Letters of Samuel Beckett* since 1990. The editing project at Emory, known as The Correspondence of Samuel Beckett, also serves as a laboratory for humanities research in which graduate students in several disciplines of the humanities are engaged. Emory faculty and staff colleagues have been willing partners in what has become a world-wide endeavor.

The extensive process of gathering, organizing, and preparing documents and oral histories, fundamental to a project such as *The Letters of Samuel Beckett*, was facilitated by major support from The National Endowment for the Humanities from 1991 to 1997, and 2009 to 2011. The research for this edition is international and cross-cultural. The Florence Gould Foundation supported the French and American partnership of this research from 1995 through 2003. The James T. Laney School of Graduate Studies, Emory University, Emory College, and The American University of Paris contributed to cost-sharing for these grants. The support of the Gould Foundation helped to establish a Paris center for the research at The American University of Paris, directed by editor Dan Gunn; students there served as interns, conducting research in French collections.

The Mellon Foundation supported research at the Harry Ransom Center, University of Texas at Austin (1993–1994); the Huntington Library / British Academy Exchange Fellowship (1994–1995) supported research at the Huntington Library; the Everett Helm Visiting

Fellowship supported research at the Lilly Library, Indiana University (1997–1998, 2002–2003). The Rockefeller Foundation enabled the entire editorial team to meet at its Bellagio Study Center, Italy (2005), to work together on the first two of the edition's four volumes. The Friends of the University of California San Diego Libraries supported research in the collections of the Mandeville Special Collections Library (2008).

The Cultural Division of the Department of European Affairs of Ireland has undertaken to distribute copies of each of the four volumes of *The Letters of Samuel Beckett* to universities and public libraries overseas, and those operated through the various Irish Diplomatic Missions abroad.

The contributions of Emory Professors Alice N. Benston and the late George J. Benston to *The Letters of Samuel Beckett*, along with their intellectual mentorship and personal encouragement, are an immeasurable gift.

We are grateful for the efforts of Joseph Beck of Kilpatrick Stockton LLP, who has provided pro bono assistance to the edition in the area of copyright law.

The editors greatly appreciate the generous in-kind contributions of the following persons: Nori Howard-Butôt, Brenda Bynum, R. Cary Bynum, David Hesla, Linda Matthews, Alexandra Mettler, James Overbeck, Eduardo Paguaga, Donald Saliers, Lynn Todd-Crawford, and Eugene Winograd.

The edition has also been the beneficiary of gifts from individual donors, each of whom has additionally enriched this endeavor with his or her continuing interest: H. Porter Abbott, Laura Barlament, Alice N. Benston and George Benston (d.), Jean B. Bergmark, Matthew Bernstein and Natalie Bernstein, Brenda Bynum and Carey B. Bynum, Claydean Cameron, Hilary Pyle Carey, Brian Cliff, Mary Evans Comstock, Barnaby Conrad III, Judith Schmidt Douw and John Douw, Robert D. Graff, Christopher Herbert, David Hesla in memory of Thor Hesla, William Hutchings, Jennifer Jeffers, Kimball King, Park Krausen, Ann Madden Le Brocquy and Louis Le Brocquy, Eleanor Lee and Timothy Smucker in honor of David Hesla, Jay Levy and Sandra Levy, Terence McQueeny, Linda Matthews, Mary Lynn Morgan, Martin Muller, Victoria R. Orlowski, Frances L. Padgett in honor of Brenda Bynum, Lucia Pulgram, Ranny Riley, Robert Sandarg, David Schenck, Lawrence Shainberg, and Arvid Sponberg.

EMORY UNIVERSITY

The vision and support of the Deans of the James T. Laney School of Graduate Studies and Emory College have been instrumental in the

l

research and preparation of the edition and the involvement of students in this work. The editors especially thank Lisa Tedesco, Dean and Vice Provost of Academic Affairs of Graduate Studies, and Robert A. Paul, Dean of Emory College.

The Advisory Board at Emory University, chaired by Alice N. Benston, includes Maximilian Aue, Geoffrey Bennington, and Ronald Schuchard. The editors wish to recognize them and the contributions of other Emory faculty colleagues: Brenda Bynum, Michael Evenden, David Hesla, Geraldine Higgins, Peter Hoeyng, Viola Westbrook.

Emory University Libraries have been at the heart of the research for the edition: at The Woodruff Library – Director Richard Luce; librarians Rachel Borchardt, Lloyd Busch, Joyce Clinkscales, Margaret Ellingson, Erika Farr, Marie Hanson, Lisa Asling Macklin, Elizabeth Patterson, Chuck Spornick, Alain St. Pierre, James Steffens, Sandra Still, Ann Vidor, David Vidor, Erik Wendt; in the Manuscript, Archives, and Rare Book Library (MARBL) – Ginger Cain, David Faulds, Naomi Nelson, Elizabeth Russey, Kathy Shoemaker; in the Woodruff Health Sciences Center Library – Barbara Abu-Leid, Carolyn M. Brown.

The dedicated support team in the Beckett Project office over the years has managed the demands of the edition with effectiveness and good humor: in addition to those named in Volume I, Daphne Demetry and Melissa Holm. The editors appreciate the assistance of Katie Busch, Rosemary Hynes, Ulf Nilsson, José Rodriguez, and Geri Thomas in the James T. Laney School of Graduate Studies, as well as the technical assistance of Darwin Diocares.

Emory University Graduate Fellows have served the research of the project with thorough scholarship and ingenuity: in addition to those named in Volume I, Levin Arnsperger, Jenny Davis Barnett, Jacob Hovind, Eduardo Paguaga, John Peck, and Jan Steyn. Emory University Undergraduate Assistants have facilitated the research and record-keeping of the edition: in addition to those named in Volume I, Jes Gearing, Mario Kolev, Cameron LeBlanc, Hannah Shin, and Lisa Sutton.

THE AMERICAN UNIVERSITY OF PARIS

Initiated with the award of a grant from the Florence Gould Foundation, the edition's partnership with The American University of Paris has included faculty, staff, and students. The editors appreciate the assistance and support of President Celeste Schenck, and faculty: Geoffrey Gilbert, Daniel Medin, Richard Pevear, Roy Rosenstein, Jula Wildberger, and librarian Jorge Sosa, as well as the assistance of Béatrice Laplante and Brenda Torney. AUP Student Interns have conducted effective research in libraries and interviews in Paris: in addition to those named in Volume I, Christiane Craig, Antal Neville, Jan Steyn, Marion Tricoire, Lilyana Yankova.

ADVISORY TEAM

A number of colleagues have served the edition in an informal but important advisory capacity. The editors convey warm appreciation for their scholarship, counsel, and wisdom: Walter Asmus, Alice N. Benston, Brenda Bynum, Ruby Cohn, David Hesla, James Knowlson, Gerard Lawless, Breon Mitchell, Mark Nixon, Catherine Putman (d.), Hilary Pyle, Ann Saddlemyer, Susan Schreibman, Ronald Schuchard, Caroline Swift (d.), Dirk Van Hulle, Katharine Worth, and Barbara Wright.

For their insight and assistance with the research for Volume II of *The Letters of Samuel Beckett*, the editors wish to thank:

Viviane Abrouk-de Seynes, Chris Ackerley, Jacob Adams, Mary Manning Howe Adams (d.), Avigdor Arikha (d.), Anne Atik. Mark J. Batty, Jean-François Bauret, Georges Belmont (d.), Christophe Bident, Georges Borchardt, Barbara Bray (d.), Desmond Briscoe, Terence Brown. John Calder, James Campbell, Eléonore Chatin, Brian Coffey (d.) and Bridget Coffey (d.), John Coffey, Stefan Collini, Anne-Marie Colombard, Thomas Cousinau, Robert Craft, Brian Croxall, Melanie Cuming.

Mary Warner Darley, Emile Delavenay (d.), Michel Delon, Gerry Dukes, Claude Duthuit (d.). Richard Ellmann (d.), Stephen Enniss, Linwood M. Erskine, Jr., Roni Eshel. Margaret Farrington, Raymond Federman (d.), John Fletcher, M.R.D. Foot, Samuel Foster, M. Pierre Fourcaud, Hans Freitag. Stanley E. Gontarski, Nicholas Grene, Margaret Grimm.

Nagib Hague, Anthony Harding, Lawrence Harvey (d.), Sheila Harvey, David Hayman, Jocelyn Herbert (d.), Phillip Herring, Joseph Hone, Fanny Howe, Susan Howe, Tina Howe. Hans Jahnke (d.), Robert Joesting, Harry Johnson, Ann Johnston and Jeremy Johnston, Tina Johnston, Bettina Jonič, Stephen Joyce. Gérard Kahn, Damien Keane, Marek Kedzierski, Elizabeth Knowlson, Erika Kralik. Rémi Labrusse, Geneviève Latour, Alex Léon, Roger Little, Christopher Logue, Herbert Lottman, Cyril Lucas, John Luce.

William R. McAlpine (d.), Joe McCann, Ian Macdonald, Caroline McGee, Mark McGee, Barry McGovern, James McGuire, Simone McKee, Dougald McMillan (d.), Franz Michael Maier, John Manning (d.), Gwenythe Martelock, Georges Matisse, Alexandra Mettler, James Mays, Deryk Mendel, Charles Mott. Maurice Nadeau, R. Northridge. Marjorie Perloff, Alexis Péron, Yves-Marie Péron, Giulio Pertile, Lino Pertile, Isabelle Poncet, Eric Price. Jean-Michel Rabaté, Claude Rawson, Evelyn Rhodes, Philip Roberts, Astrid Rosset, Barney Rosset, Anthony Rota (d.), Elizabeth Ryan (d.). Claude Salzman and Zoubeida Salzman, Luca Scarlini, Peter Schippel (d.), Pierre Schneider, Dominic Shellard, Carolyn Somers, Claire Stoullig, Francis Stuart (d.). Marco Tomaschette, Erika Tophoven. Christiana Vila. Victor Waddington (d.), David Wheatley. Anne Yeats (d.), Michael Yeats (d.), Duncan Youngerman.

Contributions that pertain primarily to later volumes of the edition will be accordingly acknowledged there.

LIBRARIES AND ARCHIVES

Research for *The Letters of Samuel Beckett* began in libraries and archives. Behind the electronic catalogues, on-line finding aids, databases, and textbases that have broadened access to collections are the scholars, librarians, and archivists who have developed valuable collections. In particular, the editors appreciate the efforts of the Beckett International Foundation at the University of Reading; by gathering and organizing a central archive of the papers of Samuel Beckett, it has provided access for generations of international scholars. We wish to thank James Knowlson for his vision in building this collection and fostering the collaboration of Beckett scholars. We also thank Mary Bryden, Sean Lawlor, Mark Nixon, and John Pilling for their collegial assistance.

The editors acknowledge with gratitude colleagues in libraries, archives, museums, and other offices of record, who have assisted them with queries.

Agnes Scott College Library: Elizabeth Bagley. *Archives of American Art*: Susan Marcott, Judy Throm. *BBC Sound Archive*: Gösta Johansson, Guinevere Jones. *BBC Written Archives*, Caversham: Trish Hayes, John Jordan, Jacqueline Kavanagh, Erin O'Neill, Julie Snelling, Jeff Walden, Tracy Weston. *Bibliothèque Nationale de France*: Département Littérature et Art – Bernard Krespine; Département des Arts du Spectacle – Joëlle

Garcia. *Bibliothèque Polonaise*, Paris. *Bibliothèque Publique d'Information Centre Georges Pompidou*, Paris. *Bibliothèque de la SACD*, Paris: Florence Roth. *Bibliothèque Sainte-Geneviève*, Paris. *La Biennale di Venezia Archive*: Daniela Ducceschi. *Boston College*, John J. Burns Library of Rare Books and Special Collections Library: John Atteberry, Shelley Barber, Amy Braitsch, David E. Horn, Robert O'Neill, Susan Rainville. *Boston University*, Howard Gotlieb Archival Research Center: Margaret Goostray, Howard Gotlieb (d.), Ryan Henrickson, Christopher Noble, Sean Noel, Alexander Rankin, Kim Sulik. *British Library*: Jamie Andrews, Christopher Fletcher, Kathryn Johnson, Andrew Levett, Kate O'Brien, Rupert Ridgewell.

Centro Nacional de las Artes (CENART), Biblioteca de las Artes, Mexico City: Arturo Diaz. *Cornell University*, Fiske Collections, Division of Rare Books and Manuscript Collections – Patrick J. Stevens; Carl Kroch Library – Ana Quimaraes; Olin Library Department of Rare Books – David R. Block. *Dartmouth College*, Rauner Special Collections Library: Joshua Berger, Philip Cronenwett, Stephanie Gibbs, Sarah I. Hartwell, Jay Satterfield, Joshua Shaw. *Department of Foreign Affairs*, Dublin: Bernadette Chambers. *Deutsches Literaturarchiv*, Marbach: Ute Doster, Gunther Nickel. *The Dictionary of Irish Biography*: James McGuire. *Dublin Zoo*: Kathleen Molloy. *Editions Julliard*: Vanessa Springora.

Faber and Faber, Archive: Robert Brown. *Fédération Française de Ski*: Marie-Jo Paillard. *Féis Ceóil, Dublin*: Ita Beausang, Maeve Madden. *Fondation Maeght*, Saint-Paul-de-Vence: Annette Pond. *Fondazione del Teatro Stabile di Torino*: Anna Peyron. *The Frick Collection*, Frick Art Reference Library: Lydia Dufore, Sue Massen. *Global Village*, New York: John Reilly. *Grolier Club Library*, New York: J. Fernando Peña.

Harvard University: Houghton Library – Michael Dumas, Elizabeth Falsey, Susan Halpert; The Pusey Theatre Collection – Annette Fern, Pamela Madsen, Hope Mayo, Fredric Woodbridge Wilson. *Illustrated London News*: Richard Pitkin. *Indiana University*, Lilly Library: Erica Dowell, David Frasier, Breon Mitchell, Joel Silver, Saundra Taylor. *Institut Mémoires de l'édition contemporaine (IMEC)*: Olivier Corpet, André Derval, Albert Dichy, Nathalie Léger, Martine Ollion, Claire Paulhan. *Institute of Contemporary Arts*, London. *Instituto Nacional de Bellas Artes* (CITRU/INBA), Centro de Investigación Teatral "Rodolfo Usigli," Mexico City: Rodolfo Obregón. *Iowa Center for the Book*: Sidney Huttner.

Jamestown Historical Society, Rhode Island: Rosemary Enright. *Kungliga Biblioteket*, Stockholm: Anders Burius. *Library of Congress*, Department of Manuscripts: Alice Love Birney, Jeffrey M. Flannery, Thomas Mann.

McMaster University, William Ready Division of Archives and Research Collections: Jane Boyko, Eden Jenkins, Carl Spadoni, Charlotte A. Stewart-Murphy. *The Joan Mitchell Foundation*: Jen Dohne, Kira Osti, Carolyn Somers. *The Pierpont Morgan Library*, New York: Clara Drummond, Maria-Isabel Moestina. *Musée de Grenoble*: Hélène Vincent. *Musée de la Monnaie*, Paris: Sylvie Juvénal. *Museum of Modern Art*, New York: Kate Adler, Michelle Harvey.

National Archives, Washington, DC: John Taylor (d.). *National Archives of Ireland*: David V. Craig, Aideen Ireland, Catriona Crowe, Tom Quinlan. *National College of Art and Design*, Dublin: Alice Clarke. *National Gallery*, London, Libraries and Archive Department: Flavia Dietrich-England, Jacqueline McComish. *National Gallery of Ireland*: Leah Benson, Marie Bourke, Niamh MacNally, Ann M. Stewart. *National Library of Ireland*: Patricia Donlon, Catherine Fahy, Patrick Hawe, Elizabeth M. Kirwan, Noel Kissane, Gerard Lyne, Colette O'Daly. *New York Public Library*: Berg Collection – Stephen Crook, Isaac Gewirtz; Billy Rose Theatre Collection – Mary Ellen Rogan, Nina Schneider, Robert Taylor; Theatre on Film and Tape Archive – Betty Corwin. *New York University*, Fales Library and Special Collections: Ann E. Butler, William J. Levay. *Northwestern University*, McCormick Library of Special Collections: Scott Krafft, Susan R. Lewis, R. Russell Maylone, Sigrid P. Perry, Allen Streicker.

Ohio State University Libraries, Department of Rare Books and Manuscripts: Rebecca Jewett, Geoffrey D. Smith. *Princeton University Libraries*, Rare Books and Special Collections: Tad Bennicoff, Anna Lee Pauls, Jean F. Preston, Margaret M. Sherry Rich, Don C. Skemmer. *Radio Telefis Éireann (RTE)*, Dublin: Brian Lynch. *Random House*: Jean Rose, Jo Watt. *Royal National Theatre*, London: Gavin Clarke, Nicola Scadding.

Paul Sacher Stiftung, Basel: Robert Piencikowski. *Società Italiana degli Autori ed Editori (SIAE)*: Valentino Ballarin, Tony Ciancaglioni. *Sotheby's*, London: Peter Beal, Sarah Cooper, Barbara Heeton-Smith, Anthony W. Laywood, Tessa Milne, Peter Selley, Bruce W. Swan. *Southern Illinois University at Carbondale*: Randy Bixby, David V. Koch, Judy Simpson. *Staatsbibliothek zu Berlin*: Roland Klein, Jutta Weber. *Stanford University Libraries*: Pamela Dunn, Sara Timby. *State University of New York at Buffalo*, The Poetry Collection: Michael Basinski, Robert J. Bertholf, Heike Jones, Sue Michael, Sam Slote. *Syracuse University Libraries*, The George Arents Research Center: Carolyn Davis, Nicolette A. Dobrowolski, Kathleen Manwaring.

The Tate Modern, Archives: Jennifer Booth. *Théâtre National de l'Odéon*: Laure Benisti. *Trinity College Dublin*, Alumni Office: Jean O'Hara, Dolores Pocock. *Trinity College Dublin*, Library, Department of Manuscripts: Jane Maxwell, Bernard Meehan, Linda Montgomery. *Ulster Museum*: S. B. Kennedy. *UNESCO Library*, Paris: Jens Boel. *Universal Edition*: Elisabeth Knessl. *University of California San Diego*, Mandeville Library: Linda Corey Claassen. *University of California Los Angeles*, University Research Library: David Zeidberg. *University of Chicago Libraries*, Regenstein Library, Special Collections Research Center: Betsy Bishop, Stephen Duffy, Robert Kovitz, Daniel Meyer, Alice Schreyer, Suzy Taraba. *University College Dublin*, Special Collections: Seamus Helferty, Norma Jessop. *University College London*, Archives. *University of Delaware Libraries*, Special Collections: L. Rebecca Johnson Melvin, Timothy D. Murray. *University of Manchester*, John Rylands Research Institute: Stella Halkyard, Peter McNiven. *University of Maryland*, College Park: Beth Alvarez, Naomi Van Loo. *University of Reading*: Archives – Verity Andrews, Guy Baxter, Michael Bott, Brian Ryder; Location Register of English Literary Manuscripts – David Sutton. *University of Texas at Austin*, Harry Ransom Center: Patrice Fox, Elizabeth L. Garver, John Kirkpatrick, Carlton Lake (d.), Richard Oram, Thomas Staley, Maria X. Wells, Richard Workman. *University of Tulsa*, The McFarlin Library, Special Collections: Melissa Burkart, Lori N. Curtis.

Vassar College, Special Collections Library: Dean M. Rogers. *Victoria and Albert Museum*: The National Art Library – Nina Appleby, Alison Baber, Mark Evans, Francis Keen; Theatre and Performance Collections – Janet Birkett, Kate Dorney. *Ville de Menton*, Département des Affaires Culturelles: Catherine Gourdet. *Washington University*, Olin Library, Special Collections: Chatham Ewing, Holly Hall (d.), Anne Posega, Kevin Ray. *Wildenstein and Co.*, New York: Ay-Whang Hsia. *Yale University*: Beinecke Library – Vincent Giroud, Nancy Kuhl, Patricia Willis, Tim Young; Gilbert Music Library – Suzanne Eggleston Lovejoy. *Zurich James Joyce Foundation*: Fritz Senn, Ursula Zeller.

The following manuscript dealers have been helpful to the research for the edition, especially for informing us of offerings and forwarding our inquiries. We thank the following: Alan Clodd (d.); Seamus De Búrca; R. A. Gekoski; Thomas A. Goldwasser; Glenn Horowitz; George J. Houle; Index Books; Joseph the Provider; Kennys; Kotte-Autographs; Maggs Bros. Ltd.; Bertram Rota Ltd.; Sotheby's; Swann Gallery; Steven Temple Books; Ulysses Books; Waiting for Godot Books; Wildenstein and Co.

PUBLISHERS

Barney Rosset was Samuel Beckett's trusted American publisher at Grove Press. The editors especially appreciate his efforts on behalf of the edition as its original General Editor. The editors also thank all those at Grove Press who assisted with the research for the edition, with special mention of Judith Schmidt Douw, Fred Jordan, and Astrid Rosset.

John Calder and his former associate Marion Boyars (d.), Beckett's London publisher of the poetry and prose, have generously responded to research questions and provided assistance in contacting individuals.

Faber and Faber, especially archivist Robert Brown, have made research in the firm's archives productive; Helene Ritzerfeld (d.) at Suhrkamp Verlag and Barbara Neu at Fischer Verlag have made the archives of these firms available for research.

The editors gratefully acknowledge the assistance of the many associates who read the manuscript of this volume and who made helpful suggestions; any errors that remain are the editors' responsibility.

PERMISSIONS

The editors and publishers acknowledge the following sources of copyrighted material. While every effort has been made, it has not always been possible to trace all copyright holders. If any omissions are brought to our notice, we will be pleased to include the appropriate acknowledgments in subsequent editions.

Letters, manuscripts, and other documents written by Samuel Beckett are reproduced in this volume by permission of The Estate of Samuel Beckett.

Other letters and documents are reproduced with the kind permission of the following copyright holders: Viviane Abrouk-de Seynes; Lady Albery; Anne Atik-Arikha; The Baeza Estate; The BBC Written Archives Centre; The Estate of Frank Beckett; Jacques Blin; André-Thierry Bordas; The Curtis Brown Group Limited; Susan Bullowa and Jane Bullowa; John Calder Publisher Ltd.; Joanna Marston, Rosica Colin Ltd.; Melanie Daiken; The Estate of Suzanne Deschevaux-Dumesnil; Harriet Devine; François Dutertre; Claude Duthuit; Faber and Faber Ltd.; Margaret Farrington and Robert Ryan; S. Fischer-Verlag GmbH, Frankfurt am Main; the Boris Ford family; Marianne Fouchet; Hans Freitag; Arethusa Greacen; David H. Greene; F. A. Herbig Verlagsbuchandlung GmbH; Frances Hickey, widow of Vincent Hickey, for Tim Hickey; Aidan Higgins; Indiana University Press; Betsy Jolas; Louise L. Lambrichs; Peter Lieberson and The Estate of Goddard Lieberson; Cyril Lucas; Les Editions de Minuit; James P. Montgomery, Rose Mary O'Brien, and Ruth Bourke; Paul and Tony Myerberg; Archives Jean Paulhan / IMEC; Barney Rosset; Routledge, an imprint of Taylor and Francis Publishing Group, Abingdon, Oxon; The Estate of Alan Schneider; Eileen Simpson, widow of Alan Simpson; Stanford University Libraries; Eva Stroux; Suhrkamp-Verlag, Berlin; Erika Tophoven; The Trustees of the Estate of Feliks Topolski; The Trocchi Estate.

Permission to publish has also been granted by the following owners of letters, manuscripts, and other documents: The Archive of the Akademie der Künste; The BBC Written Archives Centre; The Beckett International Foundation, The University of Reading;

The Bibliothèque Jacques Doucet; The Bibliothèque Nationale de France: Département des Arts du Spectacle, and Département des Manuscrits; Terence Brown; The John J. Burns Library, Boston College (Alan Schneider – Samuel Beckett Collection, Barney Rosset – Samuel Beckett Collection, Robert Pinget – Samuel Beckett Letters); The Estate of Cyril Cusack; The Deutsches Literaturarchiv, Handschriftenabteilung, Marbach; Claude Duthuit; Martha Fehsenfeld; Indiana University Press; The Lilly Library, Indiana University; Institut mémoires de l'édition contemporaine (IMEC); Herbert Lottman; Christian Ludvigsen's Beckett Collection, Denmark; The William Ready Division of Archives and Research Collection, McMaster University Library; Joe McCann for Maggs Brothers, Ltd. (Alan Clodd collection); Ernst Mannheimer; Joanna Marston for Rosica Colin, Ltd.; Les Editions de Minuit; The Pierpont Morgan Library, New York; The National Archives of Ireland; The Board of the National Library of Ireland; The Kungliga Biblioteket, National Library of Sweden; The Estate of Ernest O'Malley; The Special Collections Library, The Pennsyvlania State University Libraries; Françoise Porte; The Estate of Jacques Putman; The Royal Archives and the British Library, Department of Manuscripts (The Lord Chamberlain's Office papers); The Paul Sacher Foundation, Basel (Igor Stravinsky Collection); The Sinclair Family; Edith Smolens; Bibliothèque de la Société des Auteurs et Compositeurs Dramatiques, Fonds d'archives Georges Neveux; Special Collections Research Center, Morris Library, Southern Illinois University Carbondale; Eva Stroux; Grove Press Records, Special Collections Research Center, Syracuse University; Erika Tophoven; The Board of Trinity College Dublin; UNESCO; Mandeville Special Collections Library, University of California San Diego; University of Reading, Special Collections; The Harry Ransom Center, University of Texas at Austin; Wisconsin Historical Society; The Beinecke Rare Book and Manuscript Library, Yale University; The Gilmore Music Library, Yale University; Gráinne Yeats; Duncan Youngerman; The Zurich James Joyce Foundation, Hans E. Janke Bequest.

ABBREVIATIONS

LIBRARY, MUSEUM, AND INSTITUTIONAL ABBREVIATIONS

BIF	Beckett International Foundation, The University of Reading
BL	British Library
BNF	Bibliothèque Nationale de France
Burns Library	John J. Burns Library, Boston College
CLU	University of California Los Angeles
CtY, Beinecke	Beinecke Rare Book and Manuscript Library, Yale University
CtY, Gilmore	Gilmore Music Library, Yale University
Doucet	Bibliothèque Jacques Doucet
ICso	Southern Illinois University Carbondale
IMEC, Beckett	Institut Mémoires de l'édition contemporaine, Collection Samuel Beckett
IMEC, Blin	Institut Mémoires de l'édition contemporaine, Collection Roger Blin
IMEC, Bordas	Institut Mémoires de l'édition contemporaine, Collection Editions Bordas
InU	Lilly Library, Indiana University
IUP	Indiana University Press
McM	The William Ready Division of Archives and Research Collections, McMaster University
Minuit	Editions de Minuit
MOMA	Museum of Modern Art, New York
Morgan	The Pierpont Morgan Library, New York
NAI	National Archives of Ireland
NGI	National Gallery of Ireland
NGL	National Gallery, London
NhD	Rauner Special Collections Library, Dartmouth College

NjP	Manuscripts Division, Department of Rare Books and Special Collections, Princeton University Library
NLI	Manuscripts Department, National Library of Ireland
NLS	The Kungliga Biblioteket, National Library of Sweden
NSyU	Grove Press Records, Special Collections Research Center, Syracuse University
OSU	Rare Books and Manuscripts Library, Ohio State University, Columbus
PSt	Special Collections Library, Pennsylvania State University, College Park
SACD	Bibliothèque de la Société des Auteurs et Compositeurs Dramatiques
TCD	Manuscript Department, Library, Trinity College Dublin, when used with reference to manuscript identifications; in other instances, a short form for Trinity College Dublin
TxU	Harry Ransom Center, University of Texas at Austin
UCSD	Mandeville Special Collections Library, University of California San Diego
UNESCO	Archives, UNESCO, Paris
UoR	Department of Special Collections, University of Reading
WHS	Wisconsin Historical Society

PRIVATE COLLECTIONS

Rosica Colin collection	Private collection of Rosica Colin, Ltd.
Cusack collection	Private collection of the Estate of Cyril Cusack
Duthuit collection	Private collection of Claude Duthuit
Fehsenfeld collection	Private collection of Martha Fehsenfeld
Lefèvre collection	Private collection of Yvonne Lefèvre
Lottman collection	Private collection of Herbert Lottman
Ludvigsen collection	Private collection of Christian Ludvigsen

Mannheimer collection	Private collection of Ernst Mannheimer
Porte collection	Private collection of Françoise Porte
Reid collection	Private collection of Alec Reid
Sinclair collection	Private collection of Morris Sinclair
Smolens collection	Private collection of Edith Smolens
Yeats collection	Private collection of Gráinne Yeats

ABBREVIATIONS FOR PUBLICATIONS

NNRF	*Nouvelle Nouvelle Revue Française*
OED	*Oxford English Dictionary* (OED Online, 2009)
Pyle	refers to numbers assigned to paintings by Jack B. Yeats in Hilary Pyle, *Jack B. Yeats: A Catalogue Raisonné of the Oil Paintings* (London: Andre Deutsch, 1992), and Hilary Pyle, *Jack B. Yeats: His Watercolours, Drawings and Pastels* (Dublin: Irish Academic Press, 1993)
SBT/A	*Samuel Beckett Today/Aujourd'hui*

EDITORIAL ABBREVIATIONS

b.	born
c.	circa
d.	died
f.	folio
fl.	floruit (flourished)
[illeg]	illegible word or words
ins	inserted
m.	before date of marriage or to indicate married name
n.d.	no date
np	no page
pseud.	pseudonym
s/	signed
?	uncertain

ABBREVIATIONS IN BIBLIOGRAPHICAL NOTES

A	autograph
ACI	autograph card initialed
ACS	autograph card signed

AH	in another hand
AL draft	autograph letter draft
ALI	autograph letter initialed
ALS	autograph letter signed
AMS	autograph manuscript
AN	autograph note
ANI	autograph note initialed
ANS	autograph note signed
APCI	autograph postcard initialed
APCS	autograph postcard signed
APS	autograph postscript
corr	corrected
env	envelope
illeg	illegible
imprinted	imprinted with SB's name
Lettercard	folding lettercard
letterhead	imprinted letterhead (shown in small caps)
pm	postmark
Pneu	pneumatique
T	typed
PS	postscript
TLC	typed letter copy
TLcc	typed letter carbon copy
TLdraft	typed letter draft
TLI	typed letter initialed
TLS	typed letter signed
TMS	typed manuscript
TPc	typed postcard
TPCI	typed postcard initialed
TPCS	typed postcard signed

INTRODUCTION TO VOLUME II

"Bien Cher Tom – I should have written long ago. You know how it is. I am overwhelmed with silly requests and letters most of which I feel I have to answer. Till I hate the sight of pen and paper."[1] Nothing – but *nothing* – from the early letters selected for the present volume, that is to say from 1945 or 1946, could lead a reader to imagine that, ten years later, Samuel Beckett would be writing to his old friend Tom MacGreevy in such terms: with so much concern at incursions made upon his time and privacy by an often unknown public, and so pervasive a despondency at the rebuffs he feels obliged to send to the numerous inquiries and requests he receives. As becomes clear from his letters, nobody is more surprised than Beckett himself at the critical – even more at the popular – success his work achieves during the period represented here, 1941–1956. This period is not only the most productive in Beckett's writing life but is also the one which brings about the most defining transformations: from the writer familiar to and respected by a narrow group of readers to the writer known to and admired by a growing international audience; from the English-language writer to the author known best for works written first in French; from the writer in one, and then in two languages, to one of the major translators of the twentieth century; from the writer of prose fictions and verse to arguably the most important dramatist of his era.

The transformations have their corollaries in Beckett's letter-writing activity: no longer do his letters go out (as was frequently the case with the letters included in Volume I of the present edition) into an epistolary space where the interest of the other was far from certain, hoping to arouse curiosity and cultivate an audience; now the audience is assured, and is avid for information. By the end of the present volume, letters will frequently be serving a purpose which, while standard

1 SB to Thomas MacGreevy, 30 July 1956.

enough, was relatively rare in the years during the period up to achievement of literary notoriety, a period that includes the time when the great works are being written (*Molloy, Malone meurt, L'Innommable; En attendant Godot, Fin de partie*) – that purpose being one of conveying information, often to correspondents whom Beckett has not met or with whom he has scant acquaintance. From the watershed of *Godot*'s success, the letter that will be increasingly common is one which is informative and direct rather than exploratory and complex, and this will hold through the remainder of Beckett's life until his death in 1989. Nobody who has read the letters of the period up to Beckett's being "damned to fame," which is to say the letters of Volume I and of most of the present volume, can doubt that this fame was sought, at least as regards his work.[2] For the letters attest not just to the dogged endeavor to write, against odds which often seem insurmountable, but also to the author's determination to enable his "creatures" (as he occasionally calls them) to live and make their way in the world: letters to publishers, to translators, to academics, to journalists, to theatre directors, to theatrical agents, to radio producers. Yet nobody reading the letters from the later years represented in the present volume could doubt the strength of Beckett's ambivalence about his literary career; the depth of his wish to remove himself from the public sphere and its bold affirmations, posturings, and assertions; his sense of himself as one (as he humorously understates it in 1952 to the aspiring novelist Aidan Higgins) "deficient in the professional outlook."[3]

In the rhythm of approach and withdrawal, release and withholding, confident prediction and radical uncertainty, commitment to the work and indifference (feigned or real) to its fate, the need to express and the commitment to a non-expressive art – in such a rhythm and play, occurring on nearly every level, the letters presented here find their tortuous paths. If this was to some extent the case for the letters which preceded the War, something crucial, if hard to describe, has changed when in 1944 Beckett returns from his years of hiding in Roussillon in the Free France Zone: less in the strength of the ambivalence felt toward his own activities than in a new absence of hostility and recrimination, a lack of grievance toward the world and its inhabitants. A subtle shift has occurred in the prevailing *tone* of the letters: just when one might expect umbrage or infuriation – at the years spent in hiding, at the loss

2 The title of James Knowlson's authorized biography is *Damned to Fame: The Life of Samuel Beckett.*
3 SB to Aidan Higgins, 8 February 1952.

of numerous friends deported and dead, at the disastrous conditions in the ruins of the bombed Normandy town of Saint-Lô where he works for the Irish Red Cross – what one in fact finds is resignation and reticence; gone, or almost, are the fizzling tirades of the early years, the self-pity, the rancour, and the occasional self-indulgent displays of cleverness, almost as if so much suffering witnessed had put the cap for ever on a merely personal expression of disadvantage or misprision; as if, perhaps, the sight of so much brutal activity had confirmed him for ever in his inclination to a – however paradoxically rigorous and positively charged – *passivity*. Not once does Beckett, who being Irish and therefore neutral in the War, rue his engagement with the cause of the French Resistance or regret what it has cost him; not once, indeed, does he even mention it. Very rarely does he voice resentment, as if bitterness had been transmuted into something more deeply reflective: not an acceptance of horror or injustice, but an awareness of the communality of loss and the reversibility of roles of victim and persecutor. Less narcissistic and self-consciously literary, his letters are more thoroughly literary too – if literary in a way that can be recognized as such only because their author is at the same time writing works that will change our very conception of *the literary*. When he writes from the "Capital of the Ruins," Saint-Lô, of how he and his companions have reacted to the lack of lodging, water, and sanitary arrangements, he remarks that "The apparent apathy doesn't irritate me as it does the other two, whose reaction to the people is more or less the classical anglo-saxon exasperation." Of his companions' attitude he adds: "It is a tune of which I am tired."[4] When he replies to his cousin Morris Sinclair, who has written to inquire about possible topics for a Doctoral thesis, he mentions not a word of the conditions at the Saint-Lô Hospital, but dispenses advice on Jean-Paul Sartre, Husserl, and Kierkegaard, restricting his comment on himself to a terse "I shall be leaving here at the end of the year, no matter what happens, or whether I can get money from Ireland or not, and returning to Paris."[5]

When Beckett does return to Paris in early 1946, the city that will remain his home for the remainder of his life, he does not much like what he finds: "It is hard sometimes to feel the France that one clung to, that I still cling to," as he later sums it up.[6] Yet complaints are far fewer than before the War, and the tenor of the letters is curiously measured,

---

4 SB to Thomas MacGreevy, 19 August 1945.
5 SB to Maurice Sinclair, 21 October 1945.
6 SB to Thomas MacGreevy, 4 January 1948.

almost hushed, between January 1946 and May 1948, the date of the first in the great sequence of letters to the art critic Georges Duthuit (which sequence forms the backbone of the present volume rather as the letters to MacGreevy did for Volume I). This is the crucial period of innovation in French, during which are written the four novellas ("La Fin," "L'Expulsé," "Premier amour," and "Le Calmant") as well as *Mercier et Camier*, *Molloy*, *Malone meurt*, and the first of the plays, *Eleutheria* – the correspondence with Duthuit gathering pace at the very time when *En attendant Godot* and *L'Innommable* are being conceived. As with mentions of the War, what is remarkable is how rarely or cursorily these incomparably important works are in fact referred to, so that in November 1947 he can write to George Reavey of *Molloy*, not even mentioning its title: "I have finished a longish book in French. Murphy is out in French. Shall send you a copy some day." Which bald statement is instantly dismissed by: "No news of any account."[7]

The letters convey a sense, during these years, of Beckett's hardly daring to presume on his correspondents' patience, when many of them have suffered greater privation than he has: correspondents such as Mania Péron with whom he enters into regular exchange now, whose husband Alfred died in 1945 shortly after being liberated from the Mauthausen Concentration Camp. Gone, or severely curtailed, are complaints about the body and its ailments, the insistent listing of the pains and humiliations imposed by physical being – though any reading of the works being written contemporaneously with the letters reveals that ailments, if no longer deemed appropriate for communication to correspondents, are anything but forgotten. Corresponding with this, attenuated too is Beckett's paradoxical confidence in the body as the source of the most compelling metaphors of genuine artistic process, his conviction – for which he was only ever partly indebted to André Breton – that "Beauty will be convulsive or will not be."[8] The correlation between the necessity of art and involuntary physical processes, especially the spasm of defecation or ejaculation, still occasionally appears here, as when he writes to Georges Duthuit, "Now I must buckle down to doing the wearisome tidying up of my play, which will

---

7 SB to George Reavey, 18 November 1947.
8 "La beauté sera CONVULSIVE ou ne sera pas." André Breton's novel *Nadja* concludes, famously, upon this dictum (*Œuvres complètes*, I, ed. Marguerite Bonnet, Philippe Bernier, Etienne-Alain Hubert, José Pierre, Bibliothèque de la Pléiade [Paris: Gallimard, 1988] 753).

probably be called *En attendant Godot*. Above all I must make sure the anus is clear."[9] Of his work to date, which the job of translating is obliging him to review, he can still write: "Sick of all this old vomit and despair more and more of ever being able to puke again."[10] But where formerly the body was the site of a bedevilled authenticity, now there is a growing awareness that the body's very excitability may be a problem as well as a solution. Where once "mental aspermatism" was a threat or a curse, now, after a long discussion of the possibilities of "the pure manstuprations of Orphic and abstract art," it can appear more like a promise or reward, to the point that he can write hopefully to Georges Duthuit: "What if we simply stopped altogether having erections? As in life. Enough sperm floating about the place."[11]

The impotence here courted finds echoes in several other shifts that are perceptible in the letters of the pre-War period. The scorn at those from amongst Beckett's acquaintance who have chosen the good life, particularly in its bourgeois manifestations, is here palliated into a wry acceptance. And this can on occasion extend even to himself, if only in an inverted form: where earlier he felt impelled to write of his various schemes for alternative lives – careers more profitable, more conventional, more explicable to his family – now he barely even thinks of applying himself to anything except the next act of writing. When visiting Ireland in 1946, he is briefly tempted, as he explains to George Reavey: "I see advertised in to-day's *Irish Times* an editorial vacancy on the staff of the RGDATA (Retail Grocery Dairy and Allied Trades-Association) Review at £300 per an. I think seriously of applying." Though even this temptation is seen in terms of a possible – if implausible – literary apprenticeship, as he makes clear when he continues: "Any experience of trade journalism would be so useful."[12] Material conditions for Beckett and his companion Suzanne Deschevaux-Dumesnil are no less constraining after the War than they were before it – on the contrary. Yet guilt at a failure of duty to any task other than the literary, guilt that once led Beckett to imagine himself a university lecturer, a museum curator, a surveyor, even a commercial airplane pilot, has winnowed here into something almost

---

9 SB to Georges Duthuit, Tuesday [? March 1949]. For the purpose of this Introduction Beckett's letters will be cited in English; Beckett's original is of course to be found in the body of the text.
10 SB to Barney Rosset, 22 January 1954.
11 SB to Thomas McGreevy, 28 November 1937 [*for* 1936]. SB to Georges Duthuit, 2 March 1949.
12 SB to George Reavey, 25 April 1946.

wistful, what can be conveyed in a perfect conditional tense, as when he writes to Pamela Mitchell in 1954, again from Ireland, whither he has returned to be with his dying brother Frank: "And most evenings the walk along the beach, or over the hill to the mountain view, but not this evening. Should have made quite a good butler, no, too much responsibility, but a superior kind of house-boy, a head house-boy, no, just an ordinary house-boy."[13]

Further shifts are striking, that have implications for Beckett's letters, though what may be the most important of these is more like the opposite of a shift, a settling rather, an acceptance of France as once-and-for-ever home. While this was announced in 1937, only after the enforced residency in the South during the War years do the implications ramify. Where, during the 1930s, Beckett was on the move – one would be tempted to say *tirelessly*, were he not for ever lamenting how tired he is while traveling – between Dublin, London, Paris, the major cities of Germany, now he travels less and often reluctantly, from 1953 occasionally accepting an invitation to participate in a production of his theatre abroad. Beckett recovers the flat he occupied from 1938 to August 1942, and his address at 6 Rue des Favorites in Paris's 15th arrondissement becomes the point of departure for most of his letters. A second shift is of both tone and object, and represents a further diminishment of dispersal: a reduction in the number and intensity of mental or literary journeys taken, when these are not of the author's own initiation. So many of Beckett's letters in the pre-War period were concerned with his reading, with his often humorous disillusionment with authors minor and major, ancient and modern. Here, when books are read, they are judged less severely. (When asked about his reading and literary influences in 1954 in the wake of the *Godot* success, he turns the critique upon himself: "I am not trying to seem resistant to influences. I merely note that I have always been a poor reader, incurably inattentive, on the look-out for an elsewhere."[14]) And an enthusiasm for literary works is magnified when it is conveyed, as it increasingly is, to those whom he wishes to encourage in their reading: enthusiasm, for example, for Albert Camus's *L'Etranger*; for Jules Verne's *Le Tour du monde en 80 jours*; for Maurice Blanchot on the Marquis de Sade; for J. D. Salinger's *The Catcher in the Rye*; for Theodor Fontane's *Effi Briest*; for Racine's *Andromaque*; for E. M. Cioran's *La Tentation d'exister*; for

13 SB to Pamela Mitchell, 6 August 1954, in SB to Pamela Mitchell, 19 August 1954, n. 1.
14 SB to Hans Naumann, 17 February 1954.

W. B. Yeats, about whom he has earlier been disparaging, for *At The Hawk's Well* in particular.

The Beckett of these post-War years is, then, more settled and more concentrated, "a sadder and a wiser man" perhaps, even when no more satisfied with his own literary endeavors. Since, in this period before the telephone became ubiquitous (the telephone to which Beckett was never reconciled), letters tended to be written when distances were too great for direct daily contact to be feasible, this change in him, particularly when coupled with the intensity of his literary writing, might have made his letter-writing the poorer. If this is not the case, if this is in fact one of the very richest of periods for his letters, this must be attributable principally to the urgency of his need to express himself (even on the undesirability of expressiveness), as well as to his acute perception of the requirements of his epistolary interlocutors, who turn to him for his words – of support, of encouragement, of consolation – more needily than ever before. Yet there are, I believe, two further factors contributing to making this so very fertile a period for his letters; it is as easy to be confident and precise about the first of these as it is hard to be more than intuitive and tentative about the second.

The first and most obvious reason for the profusion of letters during this period is that, while Beckett does indeed choose to curtail his international peregrinations, he none the less continues to write to those living far from the French capital; he is obliged repeatedly if reluctantly to visit Ireland; and, more crucially, he chooses to engage in a reduced-scale motion ideally suited to the dialogue of letter-writing. From early in 1949, Beckett is exploring the countryside between the towns of Meaux and La Ferté-sous-Jouarre, taking first a room in a farmhouse. By 1953, the room has turned into a small and basic house near the village of Ussy-sur-Marne which Beckett gives orders to be built on a patch of land he has acquired, and to which he retreats with increasing regularity when life in Paris becomes too hectic. The solitude of the countryside satisfies something of the "need [for] a thousand years of silence, my own above all," and from within that silence an apprehension of the unrehearsed and unaccountable in nature that enchants and also irritates.[15] "Yesterday in the Bois de Meudon we startled a huge woodpecker, green and yellow (of course)," he writes to Duthuit in 1949 (the "we" referring to himself and Suzanne

15 SB to Jérôme Lindon, 19 August 1952.

Deschevaux-Dumesnil); "It dug its claws into the trunk, briskly put that between us and it, then ran up, to the top branches, I suppose"; following this with an expression of delight which is barely dimmed by its symptomatic qualifying adjective: "An absurd joy welled up in me."[16] The surprises offered by nature seem to offer relief from the burden of selfhood, from the humanly predictable realms of endeavor and achievement; yet perhaps for this very reason accounts of them in the letters tend to make Beckett uneasy, as in a 1955 letter to Pamela Mitchell where the unfathomable in his environment leads to instant self-disparagement, as if between self and nature there were no comfortable middle-ground: "Visited by partridges now daily, about midday. Queer birds. They hop, listen, hop, listen, never seem to eat. Wretched letter, forgive me. Hope you can read it all the same."[17] Out of the delight and the exasperation produced by nature – two sides, as they may be, of the same coin – what frequently emerges is narrative, as in a marvellous passage in a letter of 1949 to Duthuit, which begins: "In the fields, on the roads, I give myself over to deductions on nature, based on observation! No wonder I am irritable. It produces grim results." There follows an expression of incomprehension as to why the larks would choose to nest in clover and sainfoin when in the corn fields they could nest undisturbed. Which leads in turn to another initially mystified observation: "One evening as we were on our way back to Ussy, at sunset, we suddenly found ourselves being escorted by ephemerids of a strange kind, 'may-flies', I think. They were all heading in the same direction, literally following the road, at about the same speed as us." The explanation that emerges, uniting *eros* and *thanatos*, turns the flies into veritable Beckett actors: "In the end I worked out that they were all going towards the Marne to be eaten by the fish, after making love on the water."[18] Infancy and old age, nourishment and loss, join in a further observation of birds that is entirely typical of the way in which nature – it is especially true of his observations of nature in Ireland – is linked to mourning: "Never seen so many butterflies in such worm-state, this little central cylinder, the only flesh, is the worm. First flights of the young swallows, the parents who feed them on the wing. Yesterday, about 2 o'clock, a year ago, my mother was dying, not even capable of forgetting that, or of thinking of it too late."[19]

16 SB to Georges Duthuit, 1 March 1949.
17 SB to Pamela Mitchell, 13 March 1955.
18 SB to Georges Duthuit, 1 June 1949.
19 SB to Georges Duthuit, 26 July [1951].

Of all observations made at Ussy, perhaps none fills Beckett with greater incredulity and awe than those of the trees which he plants, as they take root and grow: "I have looked at my trees, the negundo, prunus and limes are actually budding, the chestnut too, and the cedar hangs on to its needles," he writes to Pamela Mitchell in 1955; in which statement by far the most surprising word, coming from someone so resistant to the urge to possess, from this least house-proud of individuals, is *my*.[20] Possessive adjective notwithstanding, what Ussy seems to permit Beckett is not just avoidance of the madding crowd, but a space where the sort of dispossession or impossibility – not strictly nameable as such – which fascinates him at the time is the more readily perceived and achieved. The form this dispossession takes is, we hinted above, perhaps closest to the psychic mechanisms and peculiar temporality of mourning. But if Ussy lets Beckett mourn, then it is not just for the numerous loved ones lost during the War or the years which follow (including his mother and his brother), but in some curious sense for himself as well, for what has to be shed when the path chosen – path human but above all path literary – is as straitening as his own.

To Beckett's instinct for mourning and quietism corresponds most nearly the act not of writing, but rather of *gardening*, as he intimates in a letter to Duthuit in 1951: "I feel that my unceremonial retreat, from what, I wonder, is nigh, and that I am starting on my apprenticeship. Fifteen or twenty years of silence and solitude, brightened up by gardening and walks, shorter and shorter, I feel this evening that that would suit me, and suit me the least badly possible."[21] To George Reavey in 1953, he expresses something similar: "I possess two rooms on a remote elevated field beyond Meaux about 30 miles from Paris and hope to live there mostly in the future, watching the grass try to grow among the stones and pulverizing the pretty charlock with Weedone."[22] And within the fantasy of a life spent silently gardening-to-death there is one activity which catches, more than any mere observation can do, the way in which the countryside offers solace and requires it as well: the activity of *digging*. "Orgy of digging, ground-clearing rather," Beckett writes to Duthuit, having just returned to Ussy.[23] Again in the winter months and again to Duthuit, just before remarking on his meeting a grave-digger, Beckett writes: "Impossible to do anything with the earth,

20 SB to Pamela Mitchell, 17 February 1955.
21 SB to Georges Duthuit, [c. 9–14 April 1951].
22 SB to George Reavey, 12 May 1953.
23 SB to Georges Duthuit, Wednesday evening [? 10 January 1951].

half frozen, half muddy. I long to be digging, digging over as they say here."[24] To Pamela Mitchell in 1953, he tells of the holes he has dug for trees he intends to plant, turning the holes into graves as he adds, of the trees, "They'll probably all die long before the Spring to judge by the look of the holes." It is with a brief account of a parallel near-demise, experienced while translating *Molloy*, that he continues: "I was kilt entirely co-translating in Paris, 8 stupid hours daily, and the result not very satisfactory." And he returns to digging later in the letter: immediately after noting his enthusiasm for Salinger's *The Catcher in the Rye*, he remarks: "Going out suddenly now for no reason to do some digging." Only to follow this, presumably after interruption for a dig, with a statement that catches something of the very swing of promise and disappointment, of emptying and filling, that digging permits and engenders: "That was a mistake, what is not?"[25] From Paris, as he writes to his American publisher Barney Rosset, when unable to face work on the new play that will become *Endgame* or the task of translating *L'Innommable*, he can think back on other holes he has dug: "I have not looked at the new play for some weeks now nor, I confess, pursued struggle with L'Inno. But have dug fifty-six large holes in my 'garden' for reception of various plantations, including 39 arbores vitae and a blue cypress."[26] And when digging holes literal is not an option, the activity does not necessarily disappear, metaphor as it also is for so much of what Beckett attempts in these years of most intense creativity. To his American stage director Alan Schneider, who has encouraged him to visit the US for the New York premiere of *Godot*, he writes: "If I don't get away by myself now and try to work I'll explode, or implode. So I have retreated to my hole in the Marne mud and am struggling with a play."[27] In one of the last letters of the present volume, to Barney Rosset, feeling drained by the surge of work that has produced *Molloy*, *Malone meurt*, *L'Innommable*, *Godot*, and *Fin de Partie* (to name just the most important), Beckett writes: "I am tired and depressed with all this fuss of rehearsal and the feeling of barking up the wrong monkey-bread and look forward to the moment when I can dig in again here and see are there any bits left of the solitary worth trying to stick together."[28]

24 SB to Georges Duthuit, Wednesday [3 January 1951].
25 SB to Pamela Mitchell, 25 November 1953.
26 SB to Barney Rosset, 15 March 1956.
27 SB to Alan Schneider, 27 December 1955.
28 SB to Barney Rosset, 1 December 1956.

It is not that Ussy offers, in its occasions for digging of all sorts, a simple palliative. One moment Beckett is able to write "I am thinking seriously of settling myself, of settling us both, in the country, just keeping the flat as a pied à terre"; while at another moment he can "Feel an urge to go to the cinema, to sit at a café terrasse," and write to Tom MacGreevy (in 1953): "There is the country to go to, but I often wish there was not, it's a burden, a house and garden, if Suzanne wasn't there I'd get rid of it."[29] But the come and go between Ussy and Paris seems to suit Beckett well, and will indeed structure much of the remainder of his life: as well as being – we have suggested – a vital contributor to the richness of his correspondence, given that from Ussy the chief way to be in touch is by letter. *Come and go*: nowhere does he state the ambivalence implied more starkly than he does here, in that same letter to Pamela Mitchell in which he talks of Salinger and digging: "When I'm here never want to leave the place and when in Paris wish I was rid of it, I must have told you that before."[30]

It may be no coincidence that in that same letter in which Beckett writes of "digging in," he permits himself, for one of the first times, to admit that he is not only "tired" – which term has done service throughout his correspondence for a gamut of states running from the mildly disconsolate to the downright desperate – but "tired and depressed" (even if he qualifies this by "tired and depressed with all this fuss of rehearsal and the feeling of barking up the wrong monkey-bread"). As his physical symptomatology eases, Beckett is left during this period with a need to find new ways to express his own dejection, for which "tiredness" is scarcely adequate, and "depression" little better. The letters do not encourage us to psychologize the aesthetic which Beckett is developing, but they do allow an insight into the intimate correlation between what he is living and what he is thinking through in the literary and aesthetic fields. And more than that, they offer an intimation of how, even whilst conveying their dark vision, letters also are doing something quite other, as they reach out to their addressee through a shared experience of loss and discomfiture. To Robert Pinget, who in 1956 is still a little-known writer and who is struggling to make a life for himself in London, Beckett concludes his letter of

---

29 SB to Georges Duthuit, 10 September [1951]; SB to Georges Duthuit, 26 July 1951; SB to Thomas MacGreevy, 27 September 1953.
30 SB to Pamela Mitchell, 25 November 1953.
31 SB to Barney Rosset, 1 December 1956.

encouragement with: "Don't lose heart: plug yourself into despair and sing it for us."[32] To his old friend from the pre-War years Georges Pelorson (who has renamed himself Georges Belmont after his collaboration in the Vichy Government and his subsequent disgrace), Beckett writes from Ussy with none of the rancour that might be expected from someone who has risked his life in the Resistance Movement, but rather with a sort of companionable abjection – holes again: "Cannot manage to interest myself in work, past, present and to come. I ask for nothing more than to be able to bury myself in this beetroot-growing hole, scratch the earth and howl at the clouds."[33] From Ireland where he has traveled to tend his dying brother, to Jacoba van Velde, sister of the artists Geer and Bram van Velde, he depicts his life as little more than a stay of execution, assured of how well this tone, with its distant echo of Edgar from *King Lear*, will chime with her own difficulties: "Here things are as bad as they could be. We say that, even though we know that we've seen nothing yet [. . .] My life here – nothing; better not mentioned. It will end like everything else, and the way will again be free that goes towards the only end that counts."[34]

By the end of the period represented here, Beckett will be fifty years old. Letters increasingly serve as a means of facing, together with another, the implacable advance of age and endings of all sorts. Perhaps surprisingly, the death of his mother May Beckett in 1950 prompts no major letter of mourning, nothing comparable to the astonishing letter to MacGreevy on the death of his father.[35] However, as Beckett learns early, from his reading of Proust if not from his own experience, the process of grieving is never predictable or linear; a flight of birds, as in the passage cited above from 1951, can be enough to afflict the bereft. And if there is no salient letter mourning the mother, there is none the less an astonishing passage of *pre-mourning* (which anticipation may be implicit in all mourning), from when Beckett travels to Ireland in 1948 to visit his family. To Georges Duthuit he poses a question which indicates that, though elsewhere he claims not to have read Dante for

32 SB to Robert Pinget, 8 March 1956.
33 SB to Georges Belmont, Friday [c. 28 September 1951].
34 SB to Jacoba van Velde, 20 August 1954. Edgar: "And worse I may be yet: the worst is not / So long as we can say, 'This is the worst.'" (Shakespeare, *King Lear*, in *The Riverside Shakespeare: The Complete Works*, General and Textual Editor G. Blakemore Evans, assisted by J.J.M. Tobin, 2nd edn. [Boston: Houghton Mifflin, 1997] IV.i.27–28.) Anne Atik notes SB's particular fondness for these lines in her book *How It Was: A Memoir of Samuel Beckett* (Emeryville, CA: Shoemaker and Hoard, 2005) 25.
35 SB to Thomas McGreevy, 2 July 1933.

years, the *Commedia* is still present to him: "Do you know the cry common to those in purgatory?" The answer he offers is one which perfectly matches his own sense of the burden of existence: "Io fui" (I was). He continues with an account of a family visit to church in which, even as one tries not to read retrospectively, it is almost impossible not to hear harbingers of the short dramas of later years: "I went with my mother to church last Sunday, a distant church, so that she could find the pillar behind which my father would hide his noddings off, in the evening, his physical restlessness, his portly man's refusal to kneel. The parson announced: 'Mr Frost, loved and respected by us all, entered life yesterday morning, funeral tomorrow'." Apologizing to Duthuit for taking him into such intimate spaces, Beckett continues: "Poor old Georges, no luck for you this evening. The weather is fine, I walk along my old paths, I keep watching my mother's eyes, never so blue, so stupefied, so heartrending, eyes of an endless childhood, that of old age." And in the extraordinary statement that follows, it is almost as if – the eyes, the mourning, the loss, the gain, infancy and great old age – Beckett were mapping out the literary space that he is going to make his own (even if it will take him another decade fully to inhabit it): "Let us get there rather earlier, while there are still refusals we can make. I think these are the first eyes that I have seen. I have no wish to see any others, I have all I need for loving and weeping, I know now what is going to close, and open inside me, but without seeing anything, there is no more seeing."[36] The call to a sort of collective immolation – "Let us get there," "Allons-y" – contains, of course, its contrary: an assertion of life and companionship almost as powerful as those of the moribunds of whom he writes in his fictions, the Molloys, Malones, and Unnamables, whose claim to be dying is ever undercut by the urgency of their utterance.

It is in 1954, when he returns to Ireland again in order to be with his ailing brother, that Beckett writes letters which, taken as a sequence, are almost like stations of a mourner's cross. "I am afraid my brother is not going to recover," he writes to Barney Rosset; "I must stand by here as long as I am need[ed]. Probably for some months longer."[37] During these months that he will spend at his brother's bedside, his letters attempt to share what he believes cannot be shared, with Duthuit and above all with Pamela Mitchell. The fact that Mitchell has been his lover, and that he is resigned to terminating their affair, seems to allow him, through a double loss, to grieve the more freely: for his

36 SB to Georges Duthuit, 2 August [1948].
37 SB to Barney Rosset, 12 July 1954.

brother, for himself, for the love he judges irredeemable; almost as if, were he successfully to convince Mitchell how abject he is, she might feel inclined to move on and spare him the pain of causing her pain. "Never felt less like writing and I haven't felt like for years," he none the less *writes*, continuing, "and never so revolted at the thought of the work done. Sometimes feel like letting myself be sucked in by this exquisite morass, just lie down and give up and do nothing more." Again he almost imagines anticipating his brother, as he concludes: "The old Irish slogan 'Die in Ireland'. It's a dangerous place to come back to for any other purpose."[38] Rarely does Beckett permit himself the lyricism, however world-weary, that pervades this series of letters. Here, to Mitchell – to "Mouki" as he has rechristened her – living and dying, loving and losing, are purged of the bitterness which marked their pre-War fusings. As he takes himself wearily off to bed after a day of watching over his brother, the remembrance of her bed mixes with the memory of his parents' deaths, with the echo of the sea on the shore, reminding him of the need to continue once the dead are long gone. "Fortunately there is plenty to do," he writes to her, "more than ever, and fortunately the nights are still long and fairly good with the old sea still telling the old story at the end of the garden. My room has a French window out to the garden and I can slip out of an evening and prowl without disturbing anyone."[39] A tone emerges, new, of almost paternal care and affection, however tinged it may be with frustrated erotic longing.

The suspicion that he really does have something to *offer* in a letter, something other than loyalty or interest, is one which, to this most and least self-confident of men, gradually turns into an unavoidable conviction. It is not merely to his young cousin Morris Sinclair or to Robert Pinget that he offers advice. For Pamela Mitchell, from Ireland, he can take time off from caring for his brother to pen a list of "a few books you could read, if you have not already."[40] And with public recognition, however uneasy Beckett feels about it, goes gratitude, not least for those who have supported him when that recognition seemed unimaginable. To Max-Pol Fouchet, who has written favorably of the recently published *Molloy* in the journal *Carrefour*, Beckett responds: "Allow me to thank you for this latest generous expression of your regard and to

38 SB to Pamela Mitchell, 23 June 1954, in SB to Barney Rosset, 12 July 1954, n. 3.
39 SB to Pamela Mitchell, 19 August 1954.
40 SB to Pamela Mitchell, 19 August 1954.

tell you how happy I am to feel that you belong to the small number of those to whom so poor and distant a voice really speaks."[41] To the writer and publisher Maurice Nadeau, who has reviewed *L'Innommable* favorably in *Les Lettres Nouvelles*, Beckett comes as close to being effusive as he ever will – a sign no doubt of how much this novel means to him, as well as of the improbability of its ever being appreciated: "But do understand what that means for me, and the scale of what you are giving. The 'he was' becomes 'he will be', with me to the end. I can no longer even thank you. I can only send you my affectionate friendship."[42] To the nascent interest among academics, Beckett responds in kind, as to David Hayman in 1955, who has given him his thesis on Mallarmé and Joyce, in a letter which serves as a reminder of the formidable scholar of literature Beckett remains, even in a period when he spends more time disguising this than foregrounding it.[43] As Beckett's work passes into languages he does not master, a special gratitude goes out to his translators, a gratitude founded on his own experience of the arduousness of the task. To C. G. Bjurström, who is translating "L'Expulsé" into Swedish, after a wonderfully pedantic explanation of "pompier et mimi" (oral sex), he writes: "Thank you again for all the pains you have taken."[44] To Mania Péron, who supervises his usage of French, he writes: "I shall never be able to thank you enough for all the trouble you have taken. You must be very tired, almost as much as I am."[45] And as he tentatively makes his way in the world of theatre, Beckett finds plenty of reason, amidst frustrations at the difficulties of getting his plays produced, to express a debt toward those who take his work from page to stage. No individual will be as crucial in this process as Roger Blin. When he first meets him, Beckett likes the man – "Nice fellow, very Montparnasse" – but is skeptical of his abilities: "Not very good either as actor or as director, if I am to judge by the Sonata that we saw."[46] The letters chart the transformation of this opinion, as Blin succeeds in having *Godot* produced at the Théâtre de Babylone, playing the role of Pozzo himself; to the point where, learning that Blin is suffering from a hernia, Beckett first urges him to rest, then joins him in the club of the afflicted: "I'm too tired and too sad to be able to write a proper letter." Yet he closes this missive with

41 SB to Max-Pol Fouchet, 4 May 1951.
42 SB to Maurice Nadeau, 5 September 1953.
43 SB to David Hayman, 22 July 1955.
44 SB to C. G. Bjurström, 4 November 1953.
45 SB to Mania Péron, Tuesday [? after 18 October 1955].
46 SB to Georges Duthuit, Monday 27 [February 1950].

recognition not only of the debt but also of the role of letters, permitting as they do what cannot otherwise be shared: "The latest work has ground to a halt, but I'm not giving up. There's a play there somewhere, but how weak one is! And then one uses up the moments of strength on silly things. If I ever get there, it will be thanks to you. I've never been able to put into words how fond I am of you, or show it."[47]

While the debt Beckett feels toward those in the theatre is great, it is scarcely greater than what is felt toward those who publish him, as certain negative examples may begin to illustrate. If, as has been suggested, the occasional bitterness of the letters from the pre-War period is almost invisible here, righteous anger has not vanished. On at least three occasions Beckett's indignation reaches outrage, and each time toward individuals responsible for publishing his work. When in 1946, whether by design or oversight, Simone de Beauvoir decides not to publish the second part of his story "Suite," having published the first part in *Les Temps Modernes*, Beckett's rejoinder, while remaining polite, barely conceals his sense of having been very shoddily treated – or rather of his *work* having been subjected to what he calls a "mutilation."[48] When Alexander Trocchi publishes Beckett's story as "The End" in his journal *Merlin*, without first letting him correct the page-proofs, he reacts with what he describes (to Pamela Mitchell) as "a stinker," expanding to Barney Rosset: "Most extraordinary thing for one writer to do to another. So for the moment we are not on speaking terms."[49] Yet the animus toward Beauvoir and Trocchi is short-lived compared to what is felt toward Jean Paulhan, who in 1953 publishes, in the *Nouvelle Revue Française*, a censored version of an extract from *L'Innommable*. Beckett is so infuriated by the mere report of this that he pens a letter of complaint so abrasive that he sends it first to his publisher Jérôme Lindon for approval. Perhaps unsurprisingly, Beckett's letter of complaint to Paulhan has not been found, but its tenor and content can be reconstituted from what he says of it elsewhere: "I would like it to be as nasty as possible."[50] When he does then read his censored story, he writes again to Lindon, stating: "It makes me literally ill. A letter, even a stinger, no longer seems to me enough."[51] Beckett is determined, despite his own temperament, to pursue a court

---

47 Letter to Roger Blin, 29 January 1955.
48 SB to Simone de Beauvoir, 25 September 1946.
49 SB to Pamela Mitchell, 27 August 1954; SB to Barney Rosset, 18 October 1954.
50 SB to Jérôme Lindon, 9 February 1953.
51 SB to Jérôme Lindon, 11 February 1953.

case against Paulhan, whose letter of excuse does nothing to appease him, describing it to Lindon as a "supplementary infamy," before inquiring again if he might have a case in law against Paulhan.[52]

It is in the context of such affronts, of his pre-War failure to find a publisher to represent his work consistently on either side of the English Channel, as well as of his short-lived satisfaction with the publisher Bordas (who takes on the French version of *Murphy*), that can be understood the depth of gratitude to one who was to become so much more than a mere publisher, Jérôme Lindon. These are the years during which Beckett discovers two of the publishers who will work with him most closely for the rest of his life: Lindon and Barney Rosset. When Lindon and his young house Les Editions de Minuit commit to Beckett, the nightmare of dealing with publishers is transformed into something bearable – even at times into a pleasure. The letters to Lindon, written first by Beckett's companion Suzanne Deschevaux-Dumesnil, chart the growth of a remarkable literary friendship between an author and his publisher (as well as testifying indirectly to the extent to which publishers have changed in the past sixty years). For Lindon swiftly becomes more like a business manager, an agent, and an advisor. In 1951, in the very first letter he himself writes to Lindon, Beckett can already state: "Allow me to tell you how touched I am by the interest you are taking in my work, and the trouble you are taking to defend it."[53] By 1955 this will have become, in response to Lindon's own gratitude expressed at being Beckett's publisher: "You are the only French publisher who, five years ago, wanted anything to do with me. Whose is the debt of gratitude?"[54] With his American publisher Barney Rosset, the sense of debt may not be so great, yet the relief is considerable, especially as in time relations with Rosset become even less formal than with Lindon. "And I do appreciate," Beckett writes to him in 1954, "that in taking on me you are taking on a pretty pickle."[55] When in 1956 a London publisher new to Beckett, John Calder, proposes an English edition collecting all three novels of the trilogy into a single volume, he describes the offer as "A dream, for my rheumatics"; a dream which was for more than thirty years to become a working reality, as Calder became the principal British publisher of Beckett's fiction.[56]

52 SB to Jérôme Lindon, 17 February 1953.
53 SB to Jérôme Lindon, 10 April 1951.
54 SB to Jérôme Lindon, 18 October 1955.
55 SB to Barney Rosset, 18 October 1954.
56 SB to Jérôme Lindon, 11 November 1956.

It might be tempting, with hindsight, to see Beckett as a sure bet, a publisher's dream. However, Beckett never failed to remind his loyal supporters of how poor a bet he judged himself. "It's hard to go on with everything loathed and repudiated as soon as formulated, and in the act of formulation, and before formulation," he writes to Rosset, ending his letter, "I'm horribly tired and stupefied, but not yet tired and stupefied enough. To write is impossible but not yet impossible enough."[57] One of the most disconcerting, and at the same time compelling, aspects of the letters collected here is the combination of Beckett's utter commitment to his work, so great that it leads him almost to challenge Jean Paulhan to pistols at dawn, and at the same time his indifference toward it, when not his utter contempt for it. That both the attachment and the revulsion are real, letter after letter certifies. Recounting to Pamela Mitchell the mess made of his story in Trocchi's *Merlin*, Beckett follows his account by saying, "None of this has the slightest importance."[58] Partly this may be attributable to Beckett's aversion to any self–importance, heightened here by the dire context of his brother's illness. But that this is not the whole story, that such matters could be both important and unimportant, is confirmed repeatedly. To Jérôme Lindon who is asking for unpublished texts, he responds, quite typically: "'Le Calmant' is available, but I would rather nobody ever read that."[59] His critical writings are even more virulently reviled than his fictions, as when he writes to Tom MacGreevy who has praised the second of his published articles on Bram van Velde: "Thanks for your friendly reference to the van Velde preface, abominable 'machine' that I shall always regret, no less than its Cahiers d'Art predecessor."[60] Every time a set-back occurs to the staging of *Godot*, Beckett is ready – despite his attempts to find a director, a theatre, subventions, actors – with assurances that no set-back is critical; even that no set-back is set-back enough. And when eventually the play is successfully staged? "I went to Godot last night for the first time in a long time," he tells Pamela Mitchell; "Well played, but how I dislike that play now. Full house every night, it's a disease."[61] And later, of *Malone Dies* (again to Pamela Mitchell): "Don't buy a copy for God's sake and don't even read the one I'll have sent to

57 SB to Barney Rosset, 11 February 1954.
58 SB to Pamela Mitchell, 19 August 1954.
59 SB to Jérôme Lindon, 19 August 1952.
60 SB to Thomas MacGreevy, 26 September [1948].
61 SB to Pamela Mitchell, 1 November 1953 [*for* 31 October 1953].

you"; before generalizing the case – "My God how I hate my own work."[62]

Stalking the revulsion every step of the way is the infinite care taken in the detail of each stage of the work, from the layout to the proofs, to the stage designs, and so on. Beckett's resistance to explication of his own work, which became legendary, is in these letters still in its infancy: it can be viewed either as an aspect of the revulsion or as an aspect of the care and defense – or even perhaps of both. Emblematic in this regard is the letter he writes in 1952 to journalist Michel Polac, who is one of the first to ask him to expatiate upon *Godot* and its absent eponym. To Polac's very first question, Beckett replies: "I have no ideas about theatre. I know nothing about it. I do not go to it. That is allowable." Taking a new paragraph for each statement, in a move so contrary to his usual epistolary style that it seems almost as if he were responding to a criminal indictment, Beckett continues: "What is less so, no doubt, is first of all, in these conditions, writing a play, and then, having done so, having no ideas about it either." Paragraph break. "This is unfortunately my case." The four next paragraphs begin with protestations of ignorance ("Je ne sais pas"), as Beckett disavows any acquaintance with the meaning of his work or the intentions or thoughts of his characters, beyond what he has indicated.[63] In time, the response becomes virtually a refrain, sounding ever more frequently over the next thirty-seven years of his life – already confirmed here by a refusal to give interviews to newspapers or radio, or to make himself available for literary prizes. Ralph Richardson, to take one more example, has a mind to play the role of Vladimir in the British premiere of *Godot*, and Beckett has met him in London. "I [. . .] had a highly unsatisfactory interview with SIR Ralph Richardson," Beckett writes to Rosset, "who wanted the low-down on Pozzo, his home address and curriculum vitae, and seemed to make the forthcoming of this and similar information the condition of his condescending to illustrate the part of Vladimir." The bigger the name of the inquirer ("SIR Ralph"), the smaller the inclination to oblige: "Too tired to give satisfaction I told him that all I knew about Pozzo was in the text, that if I had known more I would have put it in the text, and that this was true also of the other characters. Which I trust puts an end to that star."[64]

---

62 SB to Pamela Mitchell, 12 March 1956.
63 SB to Michel Polac, [after 23 January 1952].
64 SB to Barney Rosset, 18 October 1954.

Fortunately for the present edition, such resistance to comment is itself as frequently resisted as it is asserted. At almost the very time Beckett is disclaiming to Polac all knowledge of theatre, he is writing the following to Duthuit:

> Yes, of course, theatre is a spectacle; but not of a place. What goes on in it could go on as well, or as badly, anywhere else – not to mention what is said in it. Even when I was a youngster I went through passion and death listening to my French tutor spend whole lectures on contemporary settings of the *Comédie du Palais*, and I used to say to myself, if that is what theatre is . .[65]

Two years later he writes to MacGreevy – with so much implied for his own work in his use of the word "too": "Last night a marvellous Bérénice on the air, with Barrault Antiochus. There too nothing happens, they just talk, but what talk, and how spoken."[66] And commentary of a somewhat different order is offered, at times hesitantly but at other times almost peremptorily, as Beckett becomes increasingly involved in theatre and the directorial process, as in a letter to Blin, in which he bemoans the fact that Estragon's trousers are not being allowed to drop fully to his ankles – "It must seem silly to you, but to me it's vital."[67] To Carlheinz Caspari who is staging *Godot*'s premiere in Germany, Beckett yields an explicit account of why the play is not, and never could be, expressionist, dragging his title figure firmly back into the realm of the human: "Godot himself is not of a different species from those he cannot or will not help." What follows may contain the familiar disavowal, but in the sentence's final clause is contained a key to Godot as powerfully explicative as any he will ever offer: "I myself know him less well than anyone, having never known even vaguely what I needed."[68] To Alan Schneider, who during this period will become Beckett's leading American director, indications almost become instructions; when they bear on character they are nosologically precise, as when he writes of the same Pozzo whose CV he has declined to hand over to Ralph Richardson: "He is a hypomaniac and the only way to play him is to play him mad."[69]

---

65 SB to Georges Duthuit, Wednesday [3 January 1951].
66 SB to Thomas MacGreevy, 27 September 1953.
67 SB to Roger Blin, 9 January 1953.
68 SB to Carlheinz Caspari, 25 July 1953.
69 SB to Alan Schneider, 27 December 1955.

One of the things of which his move into theatre serves to remind Beckett is that no play reaches its audience unmediated, that interpretation begins the moment the author lays down his pen, if not before; like a composer, a writer for the theatre *requires* interpretation as much as fears it, and this when the gap between interpretation and adaptation – and appropriation – will for ever be perilously fine. "We have to be careful with this adaptation business," Beckett writes to Lindon in 1953.[70] When one Edouard Coester inquires a year later about the possibility of producing a musical accompaniment to *Godot*, Beckett replies, "I have already publicly expressed my opposition to any stage music."[71] And when Coester repeats his request, the response is unequivocal: "You speak as a musician, I as a writer, I fear that our two positions are irreconcilable."[72] Yet even as he is issuing the "No" for which he will become famous, Beckett is also saying "Yes" to Coester, his text to be viewed now as generative starting-point rather than end-in-itself: "But this drama which you seem to have felt so keenly, if you thought fit to translate it, however freely, into pure music, that would interest me a great deal and give me great pleasure."[73] The term "translate" ("traduire") is the crucial one, and it will occupy Beckett more and more, in its several forms – as all translators know, purity goes out the window from the moment tough choices need to be made. To Goddard Lieberson, who has produced a gramophone recording of *Godot*, Beckett writes, little more than two years after turning down Coester: "You may also quote me as saying that I appreciate your reasons for introducing a musical element into your Godot recording and consider you have done it with success and discretion."[74]

There is a popular view of Beckett as inflexibly opposed to adaptation of his work; the letters reveal how far this is from the truth, as his ideas on theatre and the newer media of radio and television develop.[75] "I would not consent to a film being made of Godot," he writes to

70 SB to Jérôme Lindon, Saturday [before 18 May 1953].
71 SB to Edouard Coester, 11 March 1954.
72 SB to Edouard Coester, 23 March 1954.
73 SB to Edouard Coester, 11 March 1954.
74 SB to Goddard Lieberson, 23 September 1956.
75 See, for example, Milan Kundera: "It is as if Stravinsky and Beckett wanted to protect their work not only against the current practice of distortion but also against a future less and less likely to respect a text or a score; it is as if they hoped to provide an example, the ultimate example of the supreme concept of author" (*Testaments Betrayed*, tr. Linda Asher [London: Faber and Faber, 1995] 274).

Rosset – while leaving open the possibility of a version for television.[76] He briefly considers making a recording of his own voice reading his work in French, even while expressing his doubts – "It was all very well for Joyce with his fine trained voice, but when you have a gasp-croak like mine you hesitate."[77] When he hears that the BBC would like a play for radio, he avers to Nancy Cunard: "Never thought about Radio play technique but in the dead of t'other night got a gruesome idea full of cartwheels and dragging feet and puffing and panting which may or may not lead to something."[78] Two days later, to Aidan Higgins, this becomes: "feet dragging and breath short and cart wheels and imprecations from the Brighton Road to Foxrock Station and back, insentient old mares in foal being welted by the cottagers and the devil tattered in the ditch – boyhood memories."[79] Within a short time, Beckett has completed his first play for radio, *All That Fall* – only the experience with *Godot* has taught him that, as he later puts it of what will become *Fin de partie*, "I shall only have the final text of the play – title still unknown – after a certain number of rehearsals."[80] And of course, even when the text is finished, the choice of cast and theatre can alter everything. The enthusiasm Beckett shows for a *Godot* that would star Buster Keaton and Marlon Brando gets the better of his usual reticence and even elicits a rare exclamation mark: "Imagine Keaton as Vladimir and Brando as Estragon!"[81] And when he hears of the possibility of an "all negro" production of *Godot*, "the thought of which pleases me immensely," he reverts to the topic repeatedly and hopefully.[82]

One further form of "adaptation" that Beckett is obliged to confront during this period – not for the first time, but now more pointedly than before – is that imposed by the custodians of public propriety. His acceptance of the proposal by Merlin Press to publish *Molloy* with Olympia Press, known for its production of erotica and illicit texts, already signals his sympathies. In his very first letter to Rosset he sees fit to warn his new publisher of the dangers: "With regard to my work in general I hope you realize what you are letting yourself in for. I do not mean the heart of the matter, which is unlikely to disturb anybody, but

76 SB to Barney Rosset, 23 September 1956.
77 SB to Barney Rosset, 1 August 1956.
78 SB to Nancy Cunard, 4 July 1956.
79 SB to Aidan Higgins, 6 July 1956.
80 SB to Helmut Castagne, 14 July 1956.
81 SB to Pamela Mitchell, 17 February 1955.
82 SB to Goddard Lieberson, 23 September 1956.

certain obscenities of form which may not have struck you in French as they will in English, and which frankly (it is better you should know this before we get going) I am not at all disposed to mitigate."[83] It is with a tone of anything but surprise that he remarks to Rosset, later, "I suppose you have heard that all editions of <u>Molloy</u> have been banned in Ireland."[84] Yet it is neither in the United States nor in Ireland that Beckett encounters the stiffest opposition, but in England, where the Lord Chamberlain demands a series of modifications and cuts, first to *Godot* and then to *Endgame*, that will result in the latter being premiered in London not in English but in French (and under club conditions). "We were all set for a London West End performance until the Lord Chamberlain got going," Beckett writes, of *Godot*, to Rosset in 1954.[85] The changes and excisions demanded can from today's perspective look laughably prim: Beckett finally accepts, amongst other changes, to "Replace <u>fly</u> by <u>coat</u> [...] <u>arse</u> by <u>backside</u> [...] <u>privates</u> by <u>guts</u>."[86] But the letters reveal that such alterations were no laughing matter to Beckett, reminding him as they do of why he left Ireland and of all he finds obnoxious in bourgeois conventionality.

It is, however, in the passage of texts from one language to another that the question of adaptation, of what is fidelity and what betrayal, obtrudes most insistently. If the crossings of the water between Ireland and England, and between England and France, have linguistic implications Beckett is prepared for, the implications of crossing the Atlantic have not been foreseen. To Rosset, who is about to publish *Molloy* in the United States, he writes, "I understand your point about the Anglicisms and shall be glad to consider whatever suggestions you have to make in this connexion." Yet even as he signals a willingness to change the odd word, he warns Rosset that "the mere substitution here and there of the American for the English term is hardly likely to improve matters, on the contrary."[87] And the translation within versions of English is of course child's-play compared to what must occur across languages. Beckett's sympathy for translators is mitigated only by his even greater sympathy for his own texts. The letters present the beginnings of several key collaborations between Beckett and his translators, most

---

83 SB to Barney Rosset, 25 June 1953.
84 SB to Barney Rosset, 2 February 1956.
85 SB to Barney Rosset, 21 April 1954.
86 SB to Donald Albery, 23 June 1954.
87 SB to Barney Rosset, 1 September 1953.

significantly with Jacoba van Velde who works on the Dutch versions and with Elmar Tophoven who becomes his chief German translator. "I'm glad that you're taking on the translating of *Godot*, I'm sure you'll do it very well," he writes to Jacoba van Velde, extending his willingness to help her – "Ask me anything you like about it": a statement that might seem unthinkable to anyone familiar only with the Beckett of such letters as those to Michel Polac.[88]

That transposition into a second language is liable to be a complex and arduous process is only to be expected. Far less predictable is the extreme difficulty that Beckett experiences in moving *his own* texts into *his own* language. That English does remain *his own* language he informs Hans Naumann in 1954, in response to Naumann's question about why he has shifted to writing in French: "I do not consider English a foreign language, it is my language."[89] As early as 1946, Beckett predicts to George Reavey – as it turns out, accurately for the short term if mistakenly for the long: "I do not think I shall write very much in English in the future."[90] And translating himself does constitute *writing in English*, about this the letters leave no doubt. To Alexander Trocchi, who hopes for a translation of *Molloy* – "It won't go into English," he states; adding a conclusion which he later wishes he had stuck to, since he finds working with Patrick Bowles, the translator with whom he collaborates on *Molloy*, fails to yield the hoped-for results: "It would have to be entirely rethought and rewritten which is I fear a job only myself can undertake and which I simply can't face at present."[91] When it comes to *Malone meurt*, which he does translate alone, he describes the process as "child's play after the Bowles revision."[92] Occasionally, the letters do echo what Beckett describes (in 1951 to Duthuit) as "my fading English," though the Gallicisms may at times be tongue-in-cheek: "if the edition is exhausted as they say" – though say it more readily in the expression's French equivalent; "hope to hear soon you have hung the pot-hanger with all due solemnity and jollity," which phrase transposes directly the French expression for "having a housewarming": "pendre la crémaillère"; "I am having copies made of ALL THAT FALL (BBC script), emission probably January," where the standard French "émission" does service for "transmission" (or the more familiar

88 SB to Jacoba van Velde, 24 June 1953.
89 SB to Hans Naumann, 17 February 1954.
90 SB to George Reavey, 15 December 1946.
91 SB to Alexander Trocchi, [on or before 5 February 1953].
92 SB to Barney Rosset, 18 October 1954.

"broadcast").[93] Indeed, on the evidence of the letters presented here, few would be inclined to contradict the remark made to Trocchi, "My English is queer"; though one might wish to add, no queerer than his French.[94] Asked by Duthuit to translate the Marquis de Sade for the journal *Transition*, Beckett hesitates, claiming that "my English is going off noticeably," before finding a silver lining: "I am only comfortable now with a sort of pastiche of 18th-century style – which does not come amiss as it happens."[95] While to George Reavey, remarking on a publisher's interest in his novel *Watt*, Beckett writes, with a turn of phrase and word order that might seem at first to bear out the probable accuracy of the prediction they contain – before prompting the thought that as English itself is becoming a foreigner it may one day again become acceptable: "Perhaps, to encourage him with Watt, I should say I expect soon to resume writing in English, than which, entre nous, few things are less likely."[96]

I suggested, near the start of this Introduction, that there exist *two* shifts of crucial importance to the letters in this volume, the first of which – the relative settledness of Beckett during the period – has implications relatively easy to describe, the second of which has implications much harder to account for (but which George Craig addresses in his Translator's Preface to the present volume). We have in fact been following this second shift for some time now, as it consists of Beckett's wholesale adoption of the French language. Of the reasons behind that shift he writes, to Hans Naumann, "I prefer to let them stay in the half-light"; though no sooner does he state this than he adds an incomparably rich suggestion: "I will all the same give you one clue: the need to be ill equipped" ("le besoin d'être mal armé").[97] To Duthuit, who is trying to coax out of him some publishable views on the painting of Bram van Velde, Beckett excuses himself, saying, "It is perhaps the fact of writing directly in English which is knotting me up. Horrible language, which I still know too well."[98] Without some sense of the release that writing in French represents to Beckett – a sense which often has to be inferred, as he would be unlikely to talk in terms of

93 SB to Georges Duthuit, 26 July 1951; SB to George Reavey, 15 December 1946; SB to Mr and Mrs A. J. Leventhal, 18 October 1956; SB to Barney Rosset, 1 December 1956.
94 SB to Alexander Trocchi, [on or before 5 February 1953].
95 SB to Georges Duthuit, Wednesday [3 January 1951].
96 SB to George Reavey, 15 August 1947.
97 SB to Hans Naumann, 17 February 1954.
98 SB to Georges Duthuit, Tuesday [? 28 June 1949].

release – it may be hard to understand the further major change which his letters undergo, from 1948 when they cease to be the rather measured acts of reporting that they largely are from 1945 and turn into the most ardent outpourings in his letter-writing life.

Without a sense of what it means to avoid an excessive "knowledge" of a language, to shed the arms implied by "ill equipped" or "mal armé" – with perhaps an echo of the poet who made impotence so central to his œuvre, Mallarmé – it may also be hard fully to gather why one man, Georges Duthuit, becomes the recipient for so much of this outpouring, for the single most intense – if relatively short-lived – surge of letters Beckett ever offers. For, unlike in the case of his great correspondent of the pre-War years, Thomas MacGreevy, whose experience was much closer to Beckett's own, there is little in Duthuit, his background or station, that makes him the obvious privileged Beckett interlocutor. What the two men do share, indubitably, is a rich and long-nurtured fascination with and love for visual art, for painting in particular, and a wish to fathom what the possibilities are for contemporary painting. As Beckett says of Duthuit, to Bram van Velde, the artist who means more to him than any in this period: "He sees things as they are."[99] To Duthuit, in tone even more than in content, Beckett can write as to none other: "I am spilling my guts out."[100] Duthuit's replies also matter incomparably. At the end of an opening sentence which has already lunged for over ten lines, Beckett writes with relief: "I find your long letter which makes up for everything, or many things, including not being drunk enough to go straight to sleep."[101] Another letter closes: "Write to me, dear old friend. That is the only post I have any wish for."[102] And again: "feeling that affection which needs no words and is stronger than those I do spew out in all directions."[103] To Duthuit,

---

99 SB to Bram van Velde, 14 January 1949.

  Two articles throw some further light onto Beckett's friendship with Duthuit, both by Rémi Labrusse: "Beckett et la peinture: le témoignage d'une correspondance inédite," *Critique*, 46.519–520 (August–September 1990) 670–680, and "Samuel Beckett and Georges Duthuit," in *Samuel Beckett: A Passion for Paintings*, Fionnuala Croke, ed. (Dublin: National Gallery of Ireland, 2006) 88–91.

  Georges Duthuit's son Claude Duthuit has suggested to the author of the present Introduction that a further link between the two men was established by their being outsiders to the French cultural mainstream, Duthuit having spent the War years in the United States and having been viewed with some suspicion upon his return to France after the War.

100 SB to Georges Duthuit, Wednesday [3 January 1951].
101 SB to Georges Duthuit, 11 August 1948.
102 SB to Georges Duthuit, [c. 9–14 April 1951].
103 SB to Georges Duthuit, 10 September [1951].

Beckett writes with unheralded energy and abandon, with an utter confidence that, despite any differences in temperament and understanding (differences which are caricatured in the publication which eventuates from the letters, the "Three Dialogues"), he will be understood, even when what he is trying to express is on the far edge of the expressible – up to the point where he begins to take his distance, as evinced when he writes to Duthuit in 1954, "In the end, I think that our preoccupations are of two very different orders as if separated by a zone of shadow where, exiled from each other, we vainly seek a meeting point."[104]

It is to Duthuit that Beckett writes letters that bring all the elements of his genius as a letter-writer together, as in that missive from which I have already quoted, from early in 1951. This letter begins with an assertion of the importance of the epistolary relation and the satisfaction (cited immediately above) of receiving Duthuit's letter; a confirmation of connection, and its importance, when Beckett is freezing in the wintry Marne Valley at Ussy. There follows the characteristic word on Beckett's health – rarely glorious. And then the familiar wish, thwarted by the frost, to be digging. Next comes a narrative of encounters, first with a gravedigger, then with a peasant whose wife has broken her hip – if it were not that Beckett recounts it as real, one might be forgiven for thinking he had invented the whole episode, so thoroughly *Beckettian* does it sound. There follows a reminder of an earlier question as to the suitability of the name "Godot" – a salutary reminder of the hesitation behind a title that has since become canonical. And all this, all the anecdotes and *trouvailles*, by way of warm-up – a warm-up almost literal in the prevailing winter cold – to the main matter, which consists of an exposition of why Beckett rejects the offer by Nicolas de Staël of a stage set for the as-yet-unproduced *En attendant Godot* (of as-yet-uncertain title). Rejecting what he dismisses as "aestheticism" and "Wagnerism," Beckett sets down his theatrical credo in terms as clear as are to be found anywhere in his œuvre: "I do not believe in collaboration between the arts, I want a theatre reduced to its own means, speech and acting, without painting, without music, without embellishments." With only a hint of an apology for what he suspects Duthuit will take to be extremism, and with one more gesture toward the possibilities of digging, he appeals to an inexpressiveness which has been, and will remain, the very heart of

---

104 SB to Georges Duthuit, 2 March 1954. Of the numerous articles on the "Three Dialogues," particularly noteworthy is the section on Beckett, "Inhibited Reading," in Leo Bersani and Ulysse Dutoit, *Arts of Impoverishment: Beckett, Rothko, Resnais* (Cambridge, MA, and London: Harvard University Press, 1993) 11–91.

his debate with Duthuit (focused as this usually is on the work of Bram van Velde): "I should like to see it set up any old how, sordidly abstract as nature is, for the Estragons and Vladimirs, a play of suffering, sweaty and fishy, where sometimes a turnip grows, or a ditch opens up. Nothing, it expresses nothing, it is an opaque no one bothers to question anymore." Asking to be excused for "my unloading all this," Beckett closes by moving his letter away from "spilling my guts out," to the life-giving zone of the heart: "Write to me again here, if your heart is in it. Mine would like it."[105] Only, even after having signed his name, he cannot quite let go of his argument about drama, and without even pausing for a "PS" returns to it with the passage cited above, about his off-putting childhood experience of theatre.

If we are right in inferring that it is partly the possibility of letting go in a foreign tongue that fuels the letters to Duthuit, then in the central idea that Beckett presents in this signal letter, form and idea coincide. For if French offers a chance to shed the co-ordinates of a knowledge inherited from earliest experience, a chance to be "mal armé," then this loss is encapsulated in the artistic "indigence" which Beckett here – and elsewhere, insistently – extols. "Indigence," Beckett remarks, thinking of de Staël's suggestion for a stage set, "we can never say it often enough, and, decidedly, painting is incapable of that."[106] He here denies the capacity of painting to be sufficiently "mal armé," in the teeth of his own attempt to prove otherwise throughout the correspondence with Duthuit: his attempt over years of letters to sustain that art *is* capable of meeting the conditions of an aesthetic of indigence, the art of Bram van Velde in particular – even if it is an attempt Beckett makes in spite of himself, committed as he is to the belief that he has nothing whatsoever of interest or worth to say about art.

Having arranged in 1954 for a group of *hommages* to be published on one of the artists – and men – he most admires, Jack B. Yeats, Beckett then faces the fact that he too must say something: "I have dreadful difficulty with this form of writing, it is real torture, and spent days before the blank sheet before I could do anything, and the result is no more than the most clumsy of obeisances."[107] And when it comes to Bram van Velde, who is most important of all: "I am no longer capable of writing in any sustained way about Bram or about anything" – a

---

105 SB to Georges Duthuit, Wednesday [3 January 1951].
106 SB to Georges Duthuit, Wednesday [3 January 1951].
107 SB to Thomas MacGreevy, 1 March 1954.

statement which turns into the potentially crippling "I am no longer capable of writing *about.*"[108] This statement is belied not only by the pages of the letter which precede it, but also by practically every letter Beckett sends to Duthuit, as, for example, two years later when he writes of Van Velde, in a phrase of extraordinary beauty that recalls his fondness for Rimbaud, and where self-deprecation does nothing to dim the éclat: "I think continually of those last paintings, miracles of frenzied impotence, streaming with beauties and splendours like a shipwreck of phosphorescences, decidedly one is literary all one's life, with great wide ways along which everything rushes away and comes back again, and the crushed calm of the true deep."[109] And alongside the vision, always, undercutting it, Beckett's sense that what matters most in Van Velde's work is its very inexpressiveness: "It is new," he writes to Duthuit, "because it is the first to repudiate relation in all its forms."[110] What Van Velde has achieved is precisely what makes it impossible for Beckett to comment upon it – comment though he does. Van Velde has dared what Beckett calls, in this same letter, the "gran rifiuto." The reference is to Dante, where the one who has "made the great refusal" is – significantly for Van Velde, for Beckett, and for the work Beckett has written and is yet to write – to be found amongst the "neutrals" of *Inferno* Canto Three, those who suffer horribly because, having refused to commit in life, they have been rejected even by Hell. The fact that, as Beckett would certainly have known, scholars have disagreed for centuries over who it was that Dante had in mind is all to the purpose, since it makes the unnamed figure the more requiring of attention. What Dante describes as having occurred "per viltade" (from cowardice) is turned by Beckett into an act of utmost courage: "We have waited a long time for an artist who is brave enough, is at ease enough with the great tornadoes of intuition, to grasp that the break with the outside world entails the break with the inside world, that there are no replacement relations for naive relations, that what are called outside and inside are one and the same."[111]

Refusal, indigence, impotence, passivity, absence of relation, inexpressiveness: the terms which Beckett uses to attempt to wring some sense from what he knows cannot make sense in any direct or rational fashion. "One must shout, murmur, exult, madly, until one can find the

108 SB to Georges Duthuit, 9 March 1949.
109 SB to Georges Duthuit, 10 September [1951].
110 SB to Georges Duthuit, 9 March 1949.
111 SB to Georges Duthuit, 9 March 1949.

no doubt calm language of the no, unqualified, or as little qualified as possible."[112] Beckett's terms are, in fact, as he reminds Duthuit, an extension of the domain he has been trying to map out ever since *Murphy*, his novel written in 1936, which contains the phrase borrowed from the philosopher Geulincx: "Ubi nihil vales, ibi nihil velis" (Where you are worth nothing, may you also wish for nothing).[113] What the letters collected here attest to is the fact that no position Beckett might ever adopt with respect to any writer or artist, especially with respect to himself, is ever as important as the position in which he already finds himself, a position that is – almost invariably – an awkward one, if not worse. From that position too these extraordinary letters emerge, struggling to articulate what is the case while painfully aware that in articulation the case is forever being altered: normalized, palliated, returned to the realm of the expressive. Within Beckett's "No," a "Yes" forever seems to be inscribed, be it only the "yes" represented by the name at the head of the page, the fact that this is never – even when as to Duthuit he turns his most disquisitional – anything other than a letter, addressed to a particular individual who, he hopes, will comprehend even his most abstract and paradoxical or self-effacing epistles. For, as he writes to Duthuit, closing a letter from June 1949, in a statement which makes it clear – as the letters do throughout – that for him, as for a certain Dante to whom the statement may again allude, the aesthetic position is also, always, first and foremost an existential necessity: "Never again can I admit anything but the act without hope, calm in its damnedness."[114]

Dan Gunn

112 SB to Georges Duthuit, 11 August 1948.
113 Translation by George Craig. SB to Georges Duthuit, Saturday [on or after 30 April, before 26 May 1949]. See SB to Thomas MacGreevy, 16 January 1936, n. 5.
114 SB to Georges Duthuit, Thursday 9 June [1949].

LETTERS
1941–1956

CHRONOLOGY 1940–1945

1940	12 June	SB and Suzanne Deschevaux-Dumesnil leave Paris for Vichy; they stay at the Hôtel Beaujolais, where the Joyces were living. Valery Larbaud lends money to SB.
	mid-June	SB and Suzanne Deschevaux-Dumesnil travel to Toulouse; lacking adequate papers, they go to Cahors, and from there to Arcachon, where Mary Reynolds and Marcel Duchamp help them settle.
	14 June	Germans occupy Paris.
	18 June	General de Gaulle broadcasts from London urging the French to resist the Germans.
	22 June	Armistice between France and Germany signed at Compiègne; France divided into Occupied and Unoccupied Zones.
	23 June	Hitler in Paris for one day.
	1 July	French Government set up in Vichy in what is now to be called the Etat Français (French State).
	10 July	Philippe Pétain named Chef de l'Etat Français by vote of the Assemblée Nationale in Vichy.
	9 August	Irish Legation receives message on behalf of SB's family: "Please wire position Samuel Beckett."
	19 August	P. J. O'Byrne, Irish Legation in Spain, writes to George Reavey in Madrid, in response to Reavey's (misplaced) concern that SB has sought a way to leave France for Ireland by way of Spain.
	mid-September	SB and Suzanne Deschevaux-Dumesnil return to Paris.
	21 September	The first Verordnung requiring Jews in the Occupied Zone to register as Jews with local police offices.
	28 September	Otto Abetz, then Diplomatic Botschafter (Head Diplomat) with the German Embassy in Paris, asks

		French publishers to purge their lists of Jewish authors.
	3 October	The Vichy Government excludes Jews from the administration, armed forces, entertainment, arts, media, and liberal professions (including teachers, lawyers, doctors).
	28 November	The Irish Legation in Vichy confirms SB's profession as a writer, which allows him to receive food allowances in Paris.
	14 December	James, Nora, Giorgio, and Stephen Joyce leave Saint-Gérand-le-Puy for Switzerland.
1941	12 January	SB sends pre-printed lettercard to James Joyce.
	13 January	Death of James Joyce in Zurich.
	February	Georges Pelorson named by the Vichy government Chef de la propagande des jeunes in the Secrétariat général à la jeunesse.
	11 February	SB begins first notebook of *Watt*.
	14 May	First of three mass round-ups of Jews, carried out by the French police in Paris.
	4 June	SB asks Count O'Kelly, Special Counsellor to the Irish Mission in France, to arrange for a message to be sent to his family.
	22 June	Hitler invades Russia.
	21 August	Paul Léon arrested by French police, as part of a second mass round-up of Jews in Paris.
	1 September	SB joins the Resistance réseau "Gloria SMH," part of the British Special Operations Executive (SOE).
	3 December	SB begins second notebook of *Watt*.
	7 December	Japanese attack Pearl Harbor.
	8 December	The United States and Britain declare war on Japan.
	11 December	Germany and Italy declare war on the United States. The United States declares war on Germany and Italy.
	12 December	Third mass round-up of Jews in Paris.
1942	27 March	Paul Léon deported to Auschwitz.
	4 April	Death of Paul Léon.
	5 May	SB begins third *Watt* notebook.

29 May	Paris Jews over the age of six required to wear a Star of David, a law enforced from June.
5 August	Francis Stuart gives first radio broadcast in Berlin.
9 August	Francis Stuart records in his journal receiving a letter from SB.
16 August	Alfred Péron arrested by the Gestapo; Mania Péron alerts SB and Suzanne Deschevaux-Dumesnil by telegram; they warn others in their réseau and quit their Paris apartment.
4 September	SB and Suzanne Deschevaux-Dumesnil arrive at Vanves. Date in second notebook of *Watt*: "Vanves 4 Sept. 42."
early to mid-September	SB and Suzanne Deschevaux-Dumesnil move from Vanves to Janvry, where they stay for ten days with Nathalie Sarraute.
29 September	SB and Suzanne Deschevaux-Dumesnil arrive on foot in Vichy; they receive a safe-conduct pass and continue their travel to Avignon.
1 October	SB requests renewal of his Irish passport (which had expired on 22 September 1942).
6 October	SB and Suzanne Deschevaux-Dumesnil arrive at Roussillon, where friends of hers live.
9 October	SB rents half of a small house, "Les Roches Rouges," in Roussillon.
18 October	SB's passport is renewed.
27 October	SB writes to Cornelius Cremin, Irish Legation in Vichy, to protest against limitations on his travel beyond the Commune of Roussillon.
11 November	Germans and Italians move into the Occupied Zone; Germans take command of Vichy.
18 November	First mention of Roussillon in third notebook of *Watt*.
1943 January	SB works on a farm owned by the Aude family.
27 May	SB acknowledges receipt of funds and a letter from his family sent 5 April; requests cable be sent to family through Irish Legation in Vichy (sent 31 May).
6 July	Appears before the Service des Etrangers, Préfecture du Vaucluse; he is now allowed to travel within "Free France."

	September	Henri and Josette Hayden arrive in Roussillon.
	23 September	Alfred Péron deported to the Mauthausen Concentration Camp.
	4 October	SB begins fourth *Watt* notebook.
1944	May	SB offers his services to the Forces Françaises de l'Intérieur.
	June	De Gaulle proclaims the Gouvernement Provisoire de la République Française (GPRF).
	6 June	D-Day: Allied landings in Normandy.
	11 July	Allies begin siege of Saint-Lô.
	25–26 July	Allies capture Saint-Lô.
	August	Intensive Resistance action in the Vaucluse; Americans reach Roussillon.
	17 August	German troops begin to leave Paris.
	20 August	Vichy officials and supporters move to Sigmaringen, Germany, and establish a government in exile there, until April 1945.
	25 August	Liberation of Paris.
	31 August	The GPRF is installed in Paris.
	12 October	SB returns to his apartment at Rue des Favorites, although he stays, temporarily, in the Hôtel Lutétia.
	23 October	The GPRF is recognized as the legitimate government of France by the Allies.
	28 December	SB completes first "end" of *Watt*, sixth notebook.
1945	January	Writes "La Peinture des van Velde ou le monde et le pantalon."
	17 January	SB sends message to his brother through the Irish Legation; none of his previous letters sent from Paris has been received.
	18 February	Writes this date in the fifth notebook of *Watt*, having made revisions to the novel.
	30 March	SB awarded the Croix de Guerre. (At an unknown later date he receives the Médaille de la Reconnaissance Française.)
	from 8 April	Leaves Paris for Dublin. The typescript of *Watt* is confiscated on entry into England. SB stays for several

	days in London. He is interrogated and retrieves his passport as well as the typescript of *Watt*. Comes across Jeannine Picabia there.
from 16 April	In Dublin.
19 April	Purchases *Regatta Evening* from Jack B. Yeats.
28 April	Death of Mussolini.
30 April	Death of Hitler.
30 April / 1 May	Death of Alfred Péron in Samedan, Switzerland, in transit from Mauthausen to France.
2 May	Berlin falls to Soviet troops.
8 May	VE Day.
25 May	SB sends *Watt* to Routledge and Kegan Paul, London.
4 June	France issues new franc notes; requires that all old notes be exchanged by 23 June.
6 June	Routledge rejects *Watt*.
8 June	Robert Desnos dies after liberation from Buchenwald. SB appointed to the Irish Red Cross Hospital in Saint-Lô.
9 June	SB's poem "Dieppe 193?" [sic] published in *The Irish Times*.
11 June	Opening of the Jack B. Yeats National Loan Exhibition at the National College of Art, Dublin. Thomas MacGreevy publishes *Jack B. Yeats: An Appreciation and an Interpretation*.
9 July	The Louvre reopens.
16 July	The French Government orders that foreign currency must be exchanged for new French bank notes.
4 August	SB's review "MacGreevy on Yeats" published in *The Irish Times*.
7 August	SB leaves Dublin for Saint-Lô with the Irish Red Cross Hospital team, traveling via London and Paris.
9–12 August	In Paris.
13 August	Arrives in Saint-Lô.
29 August	Supplies for the Irish Red Cross Hospital reach Saint-Lô.

14 October	SB in Paris, briefly.
1 November	The Louvre closes for the winter because of lack of fuel.
13 November	Charles de Gaulle elected Head of the GPRF.
16 November	UNESCO charter signed in London.
21 November	Coalition French Government formed.
14 December	SB drives Colonel Thomas J. McKinney from Saint-Lô to Paris; stays at his Rue des Favorites apartment.
21 December	SB in Dieppe, awaiting arrival of Mary Crowley, Matron of the Irish Red Cross Hospital.
25 December	Returns to Paris. Devaluation of French currency.

January 17th 1945   6 Rue des Favorites
                                     Paris 15me

Dear Mr MacDonald[1]

I am surprised to hear that my family is without news of me. I write them regular cards.

Perhaps you would be good enough to have the following message sent to my brother (Frank Beckett, 6 Clare Street, Dublin):[2]

> "Sorry to hear you are without news. Write you regularly. All well here. Love. Sam."[3]

I am trying at present to get the necessary permissions for a return journey to Dublin.[4] If I succeed in obtaining the French and British return visas I shall ask you for yours.

> Yours sincerely
> s/ Samuel Beckett

TLS; 1 leaf, 1 side; *AN pencil AH* L.T. 33; NAI, DFA 106 "Samuel Beckett."

1   Denis Ronald McDonald (1910–1983) was posted to the Irish Legation in Vichy in November 1943 and was Second Secretary of the Irish Legation in Paris from 1945 to 1946 (Michael Kennedy, "Denis Ronald McDonald," in *Dictionary of Irish Biography*, V, ed. James McGuire and James Quinn [Cambridge: Cambridge University Press, 2009] 929). SB types MacDonald.

2   On 9 January 1945, SB's brother Frank Beckett (1902–1954; Profile, I) wrote to the Department of External Affairs to cover costs of wiring the Irish Legation in Paris to inquire about SB; the telegram received at the Irish Legation on 15 January: "BROTHER ANXIOUS BECKETTS WELFARE PLEASE WIRE REPLY AND ASK BECKETT TO WRITE" [NAI, DFA/PARIS 207/316/43; NAI, DFA 49/12(17)].

3   Having received their telegram of 17 January, SB wired his family through the Irish Legation in Paris on 19 January: "SORRY HEAR YOU ARE WITHOUT NEWS WRITE YOU REGULARLY ALL WELL LOVE SAM" [NAI, DFA 49/12(17)]. Apparently Frank Beckett did not receive SB's message, because it is repeated in a letter from the Department of External Affairs in Dublin to Frank Beckett on 2 February (NAI, 207/316/43).

4   Documentation of SB's efforts to obtain permission from France and England to return to Dublin has not been found; however, on 19 January, the Chargé d'Affaires at

the Irish Legation in Paris asked SB if he wished to be placed on a list "of Irish citizens who propose to return home" that was "to be put before the Anglo-French Priorities Board which controls the grant of passages on the sea/rail service to England." He added that SB would not require an Irish visa (NAI, DFA 49/12/(17)).

On 4 April, the Ministre d'Irlande wired Dublin: "BECKETT LEAVING PARIS NEXT SUNDAY NIGHT" (NAI, DFA 29/12(17)); the following Sunday was 8 April. An internal memo from the Department of External Affairs to the Irish Legation in Paris on 26 April indicated that SB arrived in Dublin "a couple of days" after 14 April and that he had called at the Department in Dublin on 25 April (NAI, 310/3).

GWYNEDD REAVEY

LONDON

May 10th 1945   6 Clare Street
                                                  Dublin

dear Gwynned[1]

Many thanks for your letter. Delighted to have the good news of George, & look forward to making a night of it soon.[2]

Already sent a couple of shirts to Geer & Bram, which I hope arrived safely, by a friend going over. So far have bought no clothes proprement dits – question of coupons.[3] Don't bother to send any money for the time being. Shall let you know.

Have seen a little of Tom. Not much. He is very busy helping to organise a big Yeats loan exhibition to take place next month. Apotheosis (of Yeats). I bought a new Yeats, by the way. <u>Night</u>. I have <u>Morning</u> in Paris. Tom seems happy & busy. He works a great deal with the Capuchins (art criticism) & is generally very active. Last time he was looking for a nice lavatory to change into his dinner jacket in, so that he would be wearing the right clothes for his discourse on Swift at University College. I think he is doing the kind of work he likes, for the kind of people he likes.[4] He sends you affectionate messages.

I have been busy cleaning up my book, which I hope to see off to Routledge this week or next.[5]

I had a glimpse of Brian over to bury his father looking very married & tired. I think its 4 children he has and an awful life in some school in England, teaching everything. He talks now of going to Palestine.[6]

However towards the end he placed some pseudo philosophical or rather logical absurdity almost like the old days. Caught a glimpse of Denis, on the same occasion, on leave from Washington. He seems to have been writing a lot of poetry, & publishing it, in America. Tom says he has made records saying his own poems. I thought he was married too, & congratulated him. But this was a mistake, as he is not married, & through no fault of his own apparently. Haven't seen him since.[7]

I am having a nice sleep here & I suppose putting on what is called weight. I believe whiskey can be obtained, at moderate prices. But all prices seem moderate to me, to whom all prices used to seem immoderate. And yet my pension has not increased.

Love & à bientôt.

Sam

ALS; 1 leaf, 2 sides; TxU, Reavey collection.

1   Gwynedd Reavey (1901–?; Profile, I). Because SB always misspells her given name as "Gwynned," hereafter it is silently corrected.

2   On 20 April 1945, Gwynedd Reavey reported that she had seen SB in London in a letter to her husband George: "He spent 24 hours, on his way to Dublin. He looked thin & rather older, but is not otherwise changed. I can't tell you his adventures in a letter." SB's stay in London was longer than this. Gwynedd Reavey also writes of his plans: "Sam will be in London again in June on his way back to Paris" (TxU, Reavey collection).
SB deleted "delightful letter" and inserted "your letter. Delighted to have the good news."
George Reavey (1907–1976; Profile, I) had been in Moscow from 1 April 1942 where he was attached to the Ministry of Information of the British Embassy in Kuibyshev; he returned to London in June 1945 (George Reavey, *Soviet Literature To-day* [London: Lindsay Drummond, 1946] viii; TxU, Reavey collection, Draft, Proof of Evidence [Divorce], 25 May 1950).

3   Dutch painters Abraham Gerardus van Velde* (known as Bram, 1895–1981), and Gerardus van Velde* (known as Geer, 1898–1977). In her letter of 20 April to her husband, Gwynedd Reavey reports that SB brought "direct news" from Geer and Bram, "safe, well, and in Paris" (TxU, Reavey collection). The Dublin friend who took shirts to Bram and Geer van Velde in Paris has not been identified.
"Proprement dits" (worth the name).

4   Thomas MacGreevy (né McGreevy, 1893–1967; Profile, I). The Jack B. Yeats National Loan Exhibition was held at the National College of Art, Dublin, in June–July 1945. MacGreevy, a close friend of Jack B. Yeats (1871–1957; Profile, I), was on the selection committee for the exhibition of Yeats's paintings from the period 1907–1945 (TCD, MS 8153/2).
The painting that SB calls "Night" is entitled *Regatta Evening*; SB bought it at Yeats's home on 19 April 1945 (Pyle 652; Hilary Pyle, *Jack B. Yeats: A Catalogue*

Raisonné of the Oil Paintings, II [London: Andre Deutsch, 1992] 596; private collection). The painting called "Morning" by SB is now in the National Gallery of Ireland (*A Morning*, NGI 4628, Pyle 482; Pyle, *Jack B. Yeats: A Catalogue Raisonné of the Oil Paintings*, I, 436).

The Capuchin Annual (1930-1977) was published by the Capuchin Franciscan Fathers (Susan Schreibman, "Introduction to *The Capuchin Annual*," The Thomas MacGreevy Archive, 1999: www.macgreevy.org, accessed 4 June 2009). MacGreevy contributed to *The Capuchin Annual* from 1941 and joined its editorial staff in 1943. No record of MacGreevy's talk on Swift at University College, Dublin, has been found.

5   SB refers to *Watt*. Routledge had published SB's novel *Murphy* (1938).

6   Brian Coffey (1905-1989; Profile, I). His father Dr. Denis Joseph Coffey (1865-1945) was President of University College, Dublin, until 1940; he died on 3 April ("Denis Joseph Coffey," *The Irish Times*, 4 April 1945: 4).
Coffey was teaching at St. Cecilia's School, Spinkhill, Derbyshire; he and his wife Bridget (née Baynes, 1914-1996) had four children at this time. Brian Coffey did not go to Palestine. SB writes "its" for "it's."

7   Denis Devlin (1905-1959; Profile, I) was First Secretary of the Irish Legation in Washington, DC (1940-1947). Between 1939 and 1945, Devlin had published poems in *Accent, Briarcliff Quarterly, Calendar, Maryland Quarterly, The New Republic, Poetry, The Sewanee Review, The Southern Review*, and *University of Kansas City Review* (Denis Devlin, *Collected Poems of Denis Devlin*, ed. J. C. C. Mays [Dublin: The Dedalus Press, 1989] 20). Devlin's reading of poems with comment to the Writer's Club of the Library of Congress (3 January 1945) was recorded by the Library of Congress (LWO 6117, reel 18, side a). Devlin married Marie Caren Radon (n.d.) in 1946.

T. M. RAGG, ROUTLEDGE AND CO.
LONDON

25th May, 1945   6, Clare Street,
                                                    Dublin

Dear Mr. Ragg,[1]

I am sending you by registered post the manuscript that I mentioned to you while in London last month.[2]

I gave your message to Mr. and Mrs. Yeats who were very glad to hear news of you and who send you their best wishes.[3]

I look forward to seeing you again in London next month or the month after.

Yours sincerely,

s/ <u>Samuel Beckett</u>
(Samuel Beckett)

Mr. Ragg
c/o Messrs. Routledge & Co.,
68/72 Carter Lane
London E.C. 4

TLS; 1 leaf, 1 side; UoR, Routledge and Kegan Paul, MS 1489, Box 1858.

1   T. M. Ragg (1897–1953), Editor at Routledge and Kegan Paul.

2   Receipt of *Watt* was acknowledged by Ragg on 29 May: "I am looking forward with the greatest of pleasure to reading this, and to discussing it with you when you are next in London, in June or July, if I have not already written to you about it before then" (UoR, Routledge Kegan Paul, MS 1489, Box 1858).

2. Samuel Beckett, Dublin, August 1948

3   Jack Yeats had recommended SB's novel *Murphy* to Routledge, which had published his own novel *The Amaranthers* (Samuel Beckett, *The Letters of Samuel Beckett: 1929–1940*, I, ed. Martha Dow Fehsenfeld, Lois More Overbeck, George Craig, Dan Gunn [Cambridge: Cambridge University Press, 2009] 566, 568).

Mrs. Mary Cottenham Yeats (Cottie, Cotty, née White, 1867–1947).

T. M. RAGG, ROUTLEDGE AND CO.,
LONDON

11.6.45   6, Clare Street,
                                                                      Dublin

Dear Mr. Ragg,

   Thank you for your letter and prompt return of M.S.

   Will you give my kind regards to Mr. Read.[1]

      Yours sincerely,

      s/

      (Samuel Beckett.)

Mr. Ragg

c/o Messrs. Routledge & Co.,

68/72 Carter Lane

London E.C. 4

TLS; 1 leaf, 1 side; UoR, Routledge and Kegan Paul, MS 1489, Box 1858.

1   T. M. Ragg had given the manuscript of *Watt* to Herbert Read (1893–1968) to consider. On 6 June 1945, Ragg wrote to SB:

> My dear Beckett,
>   Both Herbert Read and myself have read WATT, and both of us I am afraid have very mixed feelings about it and considerable bewilderment. To be quite frank, I am afraid it is too wild and unintelligible for the most part to stand any chance of successful publication over here at the present time, and that being so, we cannot see our way to allocating any of our very limited supply of paper to its production. I am sorry about this, and sorry indeed that we cannot feel the same whole-hearted enthusiasm for WATT as we did for MURPHY, but there it is! Perhaps some other publisher will feel more sympathetic, and at the same time have more paper at his disposal.
>   In the circumstances I think I had better return the typescript to you at once so that you can take action in other directions. (UoR, Routledge and Kegan Paul, MS 1489, Box 1858.)

GWYNEDD REAVEY
GEORGE REAVEY
LONDON

June 21ˢᵗ 1945   6 Clare Street
                                                Dublin

dear Gwynedd

Many thanks for letter & cheque.[1]

I am returning to France as (tenez-vous bien) interpreter-storekeeper to the Irish Red Cross Hospital Unit in Normandy.[2]

They are setting up a hospital at St. Lo. This is the only way in which I can return to France with the certainty of being able to keep on my flat.[3] It is impossible to get sterling out of here to France for any other than strictly commercial purposes.[4]

The date of my return is not yet certain. It may be early next month. I hope so. I have no idea how much time I shall have in London. Being now a slave again I can make no plans. And as you are much in the country it may be difficult to arrange a meeting. I should be disappointed not to see you again, & George, after so long, before reintegrating the decurtations.[5]

All as usual here. Tom sends his love,[6]

　　　Yours ever
　　　　　Sam

June 21ˢᵗ 1945

dear George

Delighted to know you home again, safe. I hope indeed that we may meet in July. I want very much to hear you on Russia.[7]

I caught one glimpse of Brian, more diaphanous than ever. He has a terrible job, teaching 9 subjects in a Yorkshire Jesuit school. He has 4 children now – I understand looks forward to having ten. He was over to bury his father in April.[8] His address is:

S$^{\underline{t}}$ Cecilia's
  Spinkhill
  Near Sheffield
    Derbyshire

I saw a little of Denis Devlin also, home on leave. He continued to Washington last week. He has a book or books coming out in New York.[9] He looks very well and is not married, contrary to rumours.

Tom McGreevy is flourishing & very busy with Capuchin periodicals & the Yeats Exhibition. His long essay on Yeats is appearing here next week in book form.[10]

My book <u>Watt</u> has been turned down by Routledge. M$^{\underline{r}}$ Ragg and M$^{\underline{r}}$ Read agreed that it was "wild & unintelligible" and felt very sorry for the author of <u>Murphy</u>.[11] I have forgotten the name of the agents who took over from you and don't know if they exist still.[12] If you know of any agent, preferably young, with even half the tenacity you displayed in handling <u>Murphy</u>, I should be glad to know his name. One copy of the book went with Denis to America.

Alfred Péron is dead. Arrested by Gestapo 1942, deported 1943, died in Switzerland, on his way home May 1$^{\underline{st}}$ 1945.[13]

Shall let you know as soon as I have any definite news about my departure.

    Yours ever
      Sam

ALS; 1 leaf, 2 sides; ALS, 3 leaves, 3 sides; both in *env to* M$^{\underline{r}}$ & M$^{\underline{rs}}$ George Reavey, 43 Vicarage Court, Kensington Church St., LONDON W. 8, *verso*: Beckett, 6 Clare Street, Dublin, EIRE.; *pm* 21-6-45, Dublin; TxU, Reavey collection.

1   Gwynedd Reavey had repaid SB for the shirts he had sent on her behalf to Geer and Bram van Velde (see 10 May 1945).

2   "Tenez-vous bien" (hold on to your chair).

3   The Irish Red Cross had announced on 14 September 1944 that it would set up a hospital in France; its location in Saint-Lô was announced in April 1945. The Ministère Français de la Reconstruction was responsible for the building, and the Irish Red Cross Society provided equipment and staff. As a foreign national, SB was finding it hard to return to France. His friend and one of the Irish doctors helping to establish the hospital, Dr. Alan Thompson (1906–1974), suggested that he "apply for the post of

quartermaster-storekeeper"; SB's fluent French would allow him also to "act as inter-preter" (Phyllis Gaffney, *Healing Amid the Ruins: The Irish Hospital at Saint-Lô (1945–46)* [Dublin: A. and A. Farmar, 1999] 9, 14, 24–26).

4   In order to restore internal monetary control and international monetary rela-tions, France issued new bank notes that went into circulation on 4 June 1945. From 4 to 15 June, French residents were required to exchange all French currency over 50 francs for new currency; short-term bonds, and other bank notes were also affected. "Holders of any such notes in the United Kingdom" were given until 23 June to make the exchange ("Banknote Exchange in France," *The Times*, 4 June 1945: 2; "French Franc Notes," *The Times*, 5 June 1945: 9). Persons in Ireland who held the old currency were advised to contact the French Legation in Dublin ("French Currency Alteration," *The Irish Times*, 5 June 1945: 2).

5   The French verb "réintégrer" is a facetious heavyweight substitute for "rentrer à" (return to). SB's Gallicism is of course deliberate. He follows it with the archaic "decurtations" (abridgments, reductions, shortages).

6   Thomas MacGreevy. SB writes "McGreevy."

7   George Reavey's work in Russia: 10 May 1945, n. 2, and Reavey, *Soviet Literature To-day*, viii–ix. Reavey returned to London by mid-June, having traveled via the Middle East and Cairo (TxU, Reavey collection, Draft of Autobiography, IV, 2).

8   Brian and Bridget Coffey had five more children from 1948 to 1953 (John Coffey, 21 April 2008). The death of Coffey's father: 10 May 1945, n. 6.

9   Devlin published *Lough Derg and Other Poems* (New York: Reynal and Hitchcock, 1946). Devlin's marriage: 10 May 1945, n. 7.

10   MacGreevy's involvement with *The Capuchin Annual* and the Jack B. Yeats National Loan Exhibition: 10 May 1945, n. 4. SB refers to MacGreevy's study, *Jack B. Yeats: An Appreciation and an Interpretation* (Dublin: Victor Waddington Publications, 1945).

11   SB quotes from T. M. Ragg's letter of 6 June 1945 (see 11 June 1945, n. 1).

12   Richard Reginald March (n.d.) took over the European Literary Bureau before 18 September 1939 (Richard March to George Routledge & Sons Ltd., 18 September 1939 [UoR, Routledge and Kegan Paul, RKF 119/9]).

13   Rémy Alfred Péron (1904–1945; Profile, I) was arrested by the Gestapo on 16 August 1942 at Clefs (Maine-et-Loire). He was held for six months at Fresnes, trans-ferred in February or March 1943 to Romainville, and deported to the Concentration Camp at Mauthausen, Austria, on 23 September 1943. On 28 April 1945, Péron was among French and Belgian prisoners released to the Red Cross; he arrived in Schuls on 29 April 1945; he died at Samedan, Switzerland, during the night of 30 April – 1 May (Daniel Palmieri, Historical Research Officer, International Committee of the Red Cross, 30 October 2009, with reference to ACICR, B SEC DAS/Z-168, Rapatriement par colonnes; Mania Péron for the Samuel Beckett Exhibition, University of Reading, 1971; UoR, BIF, 1227/8/1; Georges Loustaunau-Lacau, *"Chiens maudits": Souvenirs d'un rescapé des bagnes hitlériens* [Paris: Edition du Réseau Alliance, 1965] 95). A tribute to Péron appeared in the "Irishman's Diary," *The Irish Times*, 28 July 1943: 3; a rough French translation of the final paragraphs of this, attributed by SB to Alex Newman, is in the "Premier Amour" notebook (TxU, Samuel Beckett collection).

THOMAS MACGREEVY

TARBERT, IRELAND

19 août 1945

Hôpital de la X Rouge
irlandaise
St. Lô,
Manche
France

My dear Tom

We only had 4 days in Paris, and drove down here last Monday.[1] The hospital buildings are far from ready, and there is no question of getting the place running properly before middle of November, if we ever get it running at all. We have been quite misinformed by the French Red X and the whole thing is disappointing. It is complicated further by all kinds of obscure tensions between the local medical crowd and the Red X people in Paris. We have the impression that the locals would like the stuff, but don't want us (very reasonable attitude) and that the French Red X, for reasons not clear, insist on an Irish staff. We hope soon to improvise a dispensary, laboratory & V. D. clinic, and have sent for a couple of doctors & technicians. No sign of the stores yet. They may be arriving in Cherbourg (not Granville after all) to-day. We drive to Cherbourg to-morrow-morning & shall probably remain there until all the stuff is safely on the train for St. Lô. We have to do every thing ourselves, the French Red X nous a laissé tomber.[2]

St. Lô is just a heap of rubble, la Capitale des Ruines as they call it in France.[3] Of 2600 buildings 2000 completely wiped out, 400 badly damaged and 200 "only" slightly. It all happened in the night of the 5th to 6th June. It has been raining hard the last few days, and the place is a sea of mud. What it will be like in winter is hard to imagine. No lodging of course of any kind. We stayed first with the chatelain of *Canisy*, about 4 miles out, in a huge castle with a 12th century half wing still standing.[4] But since last Wednesday we have been with a local doctor in the town, quite near the hospital site, all 3 in one small room and Alan and I sharing a bed! We are chivvying the architect to get at least one hut ready, even without water or sanitary arrangements, so that we can occupy it. The apparent apathy doesn't irritate me as it does the other two, whose reaction to the people is more or less the classical anglo-saxon exasperation. It is a tune of which I am tired.[5]

Apart from the castle crowd, full of the poor old misled man and hero of Verdun, the verdict seems to be universally oppressed. Laval, we read, has a bullet 2 mm. from his heart, cancer of the stomach and a boil on the neck. I thought they had got Déat but it seems not.[6] I didn't have time in Paris to see anyone. There were rooms for us at the Ritz. I stayed at home of course and even permitted myself to decline dinner & lunch invitations from Murphy, McDonald, & Co. And I had to pilot round Alan & the Colonel a certain amount.[7] Suzanne is very well and I would have given a great deal to stay quietly in no. 6. Not much chance of my seeing it again now until my contract is up, i.e. about Xmas. I shall get out then I think, with or without money. As soon as it is possible I shall look up Emile and try and get your things across to my place. Robert Desnos (Corps et Biens) died like Péron on his way home from deportation.[8] I saw an article by Paul Léon advertised in the "Nef", a new literary review. I suppose it is the same, but dare not conclude from that that he is living. Haven't been able to see a copy of the paper so far.[9]

Thanks again for your wire. Your pleasure more than repays me for any trouble it gave me. I am enclosing a payment docket on the I.T.[10] It is signed in the received space and you can cash it at the office. Split a bottle with my shadow.

By the way the Minister assured me in Paris that any Irish citizen here could get money out of Eire into France, up to the equivalent of £50 per month for a single person. The Bank of Ireland told me the absolute contrary. He told me further that they wanted sterling, whereas Ferguson asserted they couldn't touch it, any more than any country outside the sterling area. Qui croire?[11]

Good luck now my dear Tom. Don't let them get you down. The Louvre is open again.[12] I don't [? know] with what pictures. The same crowd, writing & painting, tops the bill that has topped it since the liberation. I had a glimpse of Geer van Velde, full of affectionate enquiries for you, but saw nothing of Bram.[13]

Affectueuses amitiés

Sam

Keep the Hospital information under your hat perhaps. Don't think McKinney has told them much.[14]

ALS; 3 leaves, 6 sides; TCD, MS 10402/172.

1   SB left Dublin on 7 August for France to take up duties with the Irish Red Cross Hospital in Saint-Lô. He arrived in Saint-Lô on Monday 13 August (SB to Thomas MacGreevy, 6 August [1945], TCD, MS 10402/171).

2   Equipment and supplies (250 tons) were shipped from Dublin to Cherbourg on 14 August, loaded onto trains, and arrived in Saint-Lô on 29 August (Eoin O'Brien, "Samuel Beckett at Saint-Lô - 'Humanity in Ruins,'" *Journal of the Irish Colleges of Physicians and Surgeons* 19.2 [April 1990] 138; "Irish Red Cross Ship for Cherbourg," *The Irish Times*, 14 August 1945: 1). On 27 August, Col. Thomas J. McKinney (1887–1973), Director of the Hospital, and Dr. Alan Thompson were joined by additional staff: Dr. Frederick Frank McKee (1916–1960), Assistant Surgeon; Dr. Arthur Warren Darley (1908–1948), Assistant Physician; Dr. James Cyril Gaffney (1913–1952), Pathologist; Mr. Michael Brendan Killick (n.d.), Technician; and Mr. Tommy Dunne (n.d.), Assistant Storekeeper. By November 1946, the hospital barracks were in service; the hospital was formally inaugurated on 7 April 1946 (O'Brien, "Samuel Beckett at Saint-Lô - 'Humanity in ruins,'" 138–140).
"Nous a laissé tomber" (has simply dropped us).

3   For photographs of Saint-Lô before and after the attacks, see Robert Patry, *Saint-Lô, la ville, la bataille: la capitale des ruines / The Capital of Ruins*, tr. Eugène Turboult (Saint-Lô: Editions du Syndicat d'initiative de Saint-Lô, 1948). Beckett's radio talk on Saint-Lô, "The Capital of the Ruins," is dated 10 June 1946; although Dougald McMillan has suggested that the piece was broadcast on Radio Eireann, this has not been confirmed (published in Eoin O'Brien, *The Beckett Country: Samuel Beckett's Ireland*, Photography David H. Davison, Foreword James Knowlson, Illustrations Robert Ballah [Dublin, London: The Black Cat Press in association with Faber and Faber, 1986] 333–337; in John Calder, ed., *As No Other Dare Fail: For Samuel Beckett on his 80th Birthday by his Friends and Admirers* [New York: Riverrun Press, 1986] 73–76, introduced by Dougald McMillan, 71; in Samuel Beckett, *The Complete Short Prose: 1929–1989*, ed. S. E. Gontarski [New York: Grove Press, 1995] 275–278, with discussion of variants, 285–286).

4   The Château de Lassay was located on Mont Canisy and was known locally as Canisy. It was "owned by the Countess de Kergolary who was an active member of the French Red Cross" (Gaffney, *Healing Amid the Ruins*, 28). SB omits the circumflex in "châtelain," and uses the masculine form.
SB canceled "I went" and replaced it by "We stayed."

5   Dr. Jean Bourdon, Dr. Albert Phillippe, Dr. Lecouillard, and Dr. Verrières were local doctors, but it is not known with whom SB stayed; André Hilt (1906–1946) was "the architect responsible for rebuilding the town"; "a French architect, M. Lafont," prepared plans for the hospital which were approved by Dublin architect Michael Scott (1905–

1989) (Gaffney, *Healing Amid the Ruins*, 11, 13, 24; "Irish Red Cross Hospital at St. Lo Opened," *The Irish Times*, 8 August 1946: 2). A report by Alan Thompson (September 1945) indicated that a lack of pipes held up installation of running water and sanitation facilities (O'Brien, "Samuel Beckett at Saint-Lô – 'Humanity in ruins,'" 139).

6   Le Bon Sauveur, the psychiatric hospital in Saint-Lô, had been badly damaged, and displaced inmates had been taken to the Château de Lassay (Canisy) (Simone McKee). SB says of the inmates that all their talk is of "the poor old misled man" and hero of Verdun (1916), Marshal Philippe Pétain."

Under Pétain, Pierre Laval (1883–1945) served as Head of Government in Vichy between April 1942 and August 1944. In August 1941, Laval had survived an assassination attempt, even though a bullet was lodged near his heart (René de Chambrun, *Pierre Laval: Traitor or Patriot?*, tr. Elly Stein [New York: Scribner's Sons, 1989] 68–69). Laval fled France at the end of the War, was arrested by American troops, stood trial for treason in Paris, and was executed on 15 October 1945; preliminary hearings were held during August 1945.

Marcel Déat (1894–1955), Editor of *L'Œuvre*, founded the Rassemblement National Populaire (RNP), a collaborationist party, in 1941. On 16 March 1944, he was named Ministre du Travail et de la Solidarité Nationale in the Vichy Government. In April 1945, Déat left for Italy (Jean-Paul Cointent, *Marcel Déat: du socialisme au national-socialisme* [Paris: Perrin, 1998] 400–401).

7   Seán Anthony Murphy (1896–1964), Irish Minister to France from 1938 to 1950; Denis R. McDonald, Chargé d'Affaires, Irish Legation in France.

8   Suzanne Deschevaux-Dumesnil (1900–1989; Profile, I) lived with SB at 6 Rue des Favorites in Paris. Emile Delavenay (1905–2003), whom MacGreevy knew from their connection with the Ecole Normale Supérieure (Profile, I).

The author of *Corps et biens* (1930), Robert Desnos (1900–1945) was a member of the Resistance group Agir from 1942. He was arrested on 22 February 1944, sent first to Compiègne, next to Auschwitz on 30 April, and then to Buchenwald on 14 May. Following liberation in May 1945, Desnos was taken in weakened condition to Terezin, Czechoslovakia, where he died of typhus on 8 June (Anne Egger, *Robert Desnos* [Paris: Fayard, 2007] 993–994, passim).

Alfred Péron's death: 21 June 1945, n. 13.

9   Paul Léopoldovitch Léon (1893–1942) had been James Joyce's assistant; he was registered as a Jew, arrested in Paris on 21 August 1941, detained first at the Drancy and Compiègne transit camps, and then deported on 27 March to Silesia where he died on 4 April 1942 (Lucie Noel [pseud. of Lucie Léon], *James Joyce and Paul L. Léon: The Story of a Friendship* [New York: Gotham Book Mart, 1950] 48–49, 57, 60).

The article that SB had seen announced was written by a different Paul Léon (1874–1962), who was Directeur Général de l'Art Monumental au Collège de France and a member of the Institut de France: "Du Palais-Royal au Palais-Bourbon (souvenirs)," *La Nef* (*Nouvelle Equipe Française*) 2.9 (August 1945) 19–38.

10   SB refers to his review of MacGreevy's *Jack B. Yeats: An Appreciation and an Interpretation*, and *The Irish Times*'s payment for it (Samuel Beckett, "MacGreevy on Yeats," *The Irish Times*, 4 August 1945: 82).

SB deleted "all" and inserted "any."

11   On 15 January 1945, Ordonnance no. 45–35 restricted the financial operations in France of persons resident in neutral countries.

On 16 July, France ordered that foreign currency in all its forms (cash, checks, letters of credit, trade letters, commerce effects, etc.) be exchanged for French currency ("Ordonnance no. 45–1554, 16 Juil. 1945," *Journal Officiel de la République Française* [17 July 1945] 4358). This followed on the issue of new currency in France (see 21 June 1945, n. 4).

Mr. Ferguson, Bank of Ireland, has not been further identified.

"Qui croire?" (Whom to believe?).

12   The Louvre reopened on 9 July, with "an exhibition of its most famous sculptures and some of its best known paintings," many of which had been restored during their Wartime storage at Montauban in the Midi-Pyrénées. With the eighty-three paintings, a special exhibition showed how the pictures had been kept and hidden during the War, as well as correspondence that documented negotiations between curators and the German and Vichy Governments concerning the collection as a whole (*The Times*, 10 July 1945: 3). The Louvre closed for the winter because of lack of fuel (*The New York Times*, 27 September 1945: 4).

13   Geer van Velde; Bram van Velde.

14   PS written in top left margin, side 1, set off from the text by a horizontal line and from the date by a curving line.

MORRIS SINCLAIR

DUBLIN

21ˢᵗ October 1945   HOPITAL DE LA CROIX ROUGE IRLANDAISE

                                        A SAINT LO

Dear Sunny

Glad to have such good news of you. I agree that a French PH.D. would be more interesting. But not any of the subjects you mention. You might perhaps do a short one on Sartre, if the philosophy wasn't too much for you. You neednt do much more than mention that side of him. His German adhesions would be into your barrow.[1] Husserl – ? (Das Schloss, Der Prozess). Kierkegaarde comes in also. I should be very glad to help you and could introduce you to Sartre & his world.[2]

Afraid I can't put you up in my garret. You will find it difficult to live on 4,500 frs. per month. But as your scholarship is in sterling, that amount will be doubled probably in a short time, and then you could manage all right. I think I could get you grinds also, at from 80 to 100 francs an hour.[3]

Was in Paris a week or so ago and heard Moussorgsky's 'Tableaux d'une Exposition' for the first time. It killed the rest of the programme, including Prokovief's 3rd piano concerto.[4]

I shall be leaving here at the end of the year, no matter what happens, or whether I can get money from Ireland or not, and returning to Paris.

Give my love to Cissie, Nancy, Deirdre, George.[5] As you say its a great chance for you. If you don't know any Sartre and can't get him in Dublin, let me know & I'll have you sent from Paris anything I have.[6]

Yours ever

Sam

Will you thank Con for his note and tell him I am writing.[7]

ALS; 3 leaves, 3 sides; letterhead; Sinclair collection.

1   SB's cousin Morris Sinclair (Sunny, Sonny, 1908–2008; Profile, I) pursued the German influences on Jean-Paul Sartre, but the study was never written, nor did he meet Sartre (Sinclair to editors, 30 April 2006; 5 September 1996).

2   Edmund Husserl. SB refers to Franz Kafka's novels *Das Schloss* (1927; *The Castle*), *Der Prozess* (1925; *The Trial*). SB adds a final "e" to the name of Søren Kierkegaard.

3   Suzanne Deschevaux-Dumesnil continued to occupy the apartment at 6 Rue des Favorites.
SB refers to the increasing value of the British pound against the deflated value of the French franc.

4   SB's spelling of Prokofiev is not standard in either English or French; he uses the French spelling of Mussorgsky.
SB heard the concert at the Salle Gaveau on 14 October, directed by Gustave Cloëz (1890–1970, then Conductor with the Opéra Comique); Samson François (1924–1970) was the soloist in the Piano Concerto no. 3 in C, op. 26, by Sergei Prokofiev and in "Pictures from an Exhibition" by Modest Mussorgsky. Also on the program was Symphony no. 8 in B minor ("Unfinished") by Franz Schubert.

5   Morris Sinclair's mother, Frances Sinclair (Cissie, née Beckett, 1880–1951; Profile, I), his sisters Annabel Lilian Sinclair (known as Nancy, 1916–1969) and Deirdre Morrow (née Sinclair, 1920–2010; later m. Hamilton); Deirdre's husband at this time was George Morrow (1915–1998).

6   SB deleted "let me know" and replaced it with "can't get him in Dublin, let me know."

7   Abraham Jacob Leventhal (known as Con, 1896–1979; Profile, I). His note to SB has not been found.

GEORGE REAVEY
LONDON

31 Oct [1945]   Hopital [sic] Irlandais
                                           Saint-Lô
                                           Manche
                                           France

dear George

No idea you were still in London. I am here since last August,
working with the Irish Red Cross, but expect to be free by end of year,
when I shall return to Paris.[1]

I get up to Paris now & then, & saw Geer & Lisl once. There [*for*
They] are living out somewhere on the Ligne de Sceaux, I forget
where, on the fringe, having of course lost their Paris apartment
and failed like thousands to find another. Bram's exhibition with
Zervos has not yet come off (it should have been held last Spring)
nor the 2nd post-liberation number of the Cahiers with my article on
the 2 v. Velde.[2]

I have nothing at all in London. I dumped <u>Watt</u> with a fellow on
the way through last August and understand that Nicholson &
Watson are nibbling.[3]

Saw a fair amount of Tom in Dublin. He is very active in art circles
and writing in the Capuchins. The same old Tom. Saw a little of Devlin
also, before he returned to Washington, & caught a glimpse of Coffey,
married to extinction.[4]

Life in Paris is pretty well impossible, except for millionaires. Still
I hope we may meet there soon. Or shall I be bottled in a warring
Europe for another 5 or 10 years? Can't say I care much where I'm
bottled, du moment que je suis en bouteille.[5]

best wishes to Gwynedd
    yours ever
        Sam

ALS; 2 leaves, 2 sides; TxU, Reavey collection.

1   SB's "resignation was effective from January 1946, but he continued to give whatever help he could to the hospital from Paris" (O'Brien, *The Beckett Country*, 339).

2   Elizabeth van Velde (née Jokl, known as Lisl, m. Geer van Velde 1933, b. 1908). When they returned to Paris from the South of France in 1944, Geer and Lisl van Velde lived in Cachan, on the rail line from the Luxembourg Station to Sceaux, south of Paris (Germain Viatte, *Geer van Velde* [Paris: Editions "Cahiers d'Art," 1989] 210).

Bram van Velde's exhibition was held from 21 March to 4 April 1946 at the Galerie Mai, Paris. Marcel Michaud (1898-1958), whose Galerie Folklore in Lyon held Van Velde's first exhibition, had become director of the Galerie Mai and wished to inaugurate his directorship with a show of Van Velde's work. The Galerie Mai was owned by Christian Zervos (1889-1970), Editor of *Cahiers d'Art*. Michaud wrote to Marthe Arnaud (née Kuntz, 1887-1959): "C'est toujours par Van Velde que nous débutons à l'ouverture, mais je ne puis encore préciser la date, celle-ci dépendant surtout des Zervos et de leurs démarches" (It is still with Van Velde that we start at our opening, but I cannot yet give a precise date, since this depends above all on the Zervoses and their arrangements) (Claire Stoullig and Nathalie Schoeller, eds., *Bram van Velde* [Paris: Editions du Centre Georges Pompidou, 1989] 160, 164). Geer van Velde's first Paris exhibition took place in March–April 1946 at the Galerie Maeght (Viatte, *Geer van Velde*, 210).

SB wrote "La Peinture des van Velde ou le monde et le pantalon" at the beginning of 1945 (*Cahiers d'Art* 20-21 [1945-1946] 349-356; rpt. in Samuel Beckett, *Disjecta: Miscellaneous Writings and A Dramatic Fragment*, ed. Ruby Cohn [New York: Grove Press, 1984] 118-132).

3   SB left *Watt* with Leslie Herbert Daiken* (né Yodaiken, 1912-1964) when he passed through London on 7 August, asking him to try to place the novel with a publisher. Daiken wrote to A. J. Leventhal, 24 August: "Sam Beckett called on his way to France [...] He left WATT, which we have all enjoyed, and which I am mailing tomorrow to my publishers who have already been primed against the honour they are to be accorded in receiving it" (TxU, Leventhal collection). Nicholson & Watson published Daiken's *They Go, the Irish: a Miscellany of War-Time Writing* (1944).

Covering the return of SB's novel on 17 November, Daiken received a note from Mr. Crindle of Nicholson & Watson indicating that the firm had turned down *Watt* (TxU, Daiken collection).

4   Thomas MacGreevy, Denis Devlin, and Brian Coffey: 10 May 1945, n. 4, n. 7, and n. 6.

5   "Du moment que je suis en bouteille" (Since bottled I am).

CHRONOLOGY 1946

1946

1 January	SB resigns from Irish Red Cross Hospital at Saint-Lô.
17 February	Begins the novella that will become "Suite" and later "La Fin," writing first in English.
22 February	London literary agent A. P. Watt confirms receipt of *Watt*, sent to him by Leslie Daiken.
March–April	Geer van Velde exhibition at the Galerie Maeght.
13 March	SB continues to write "Suite/La Fin," but in French.
21 March	Bram van Velde exhibition opens at the Galerie Mai, Paris.
8 April	Chatto and Windus turn down *Watt*.
before 21 April	SB in London, where he stays briefly with George Reavey, before traveling on to Dublin.
before 15 May	SB's first part of "Suite" accepted by *Les Temps Modernes*.
19 June	Writes that Methuen is considering *Watt*, and that Maurice Fridberg in Dublin is interested in reading it.
24 June	His poem "Saint-Lô" published in *The Irish Times*.
29 June	Returns to Paris.
30 June	Writes to Jacoba van Velde that the second part of "Suite" has been finished.
July	First part of "Suite" published in *Les Temps Modernes*.
2 July	SB sends second part of "Suite" to *Les Temps Modernes*.
5 July	Begins writing *Mercier et Camier*.
28 August	Writes to Routledge requesting copies of *Murphy*.
before 1 September	Learns from Routledge that *Murphy* went out of print in 1942.
3 September	Methuen rejects *Watt*.

25 September	SB writes to Simone de Beauvoir to protest at her unwillingness to publish the second part of "Suite" in *Les Temps Modernes*.
26 September	Final date in second notebook of manuscript of *Mercier et Camier*.
October	SB and Suzanne Deschevaux-Dumesnil in Abondant, occupying the cottage of André and Ruth Salzman.
	"La peinture des van Velde ou le monde et le pantalon" published in *Cahiers d'Art*.
before 13 October	SB revises *Mercier et Camier*.
by 13 October	Has received proofs of "Poèmes 38-39" from *Les Temps Modernes*.
6–14 October	Writes "L'Expulsé."
16 October	Returns to Paris from Abondant.
28 October	Begins writing "Premier amour."
29 October	Pierre Bordas sends SB contract for *Murphy* and future work.
November	*Les Temps Modernes* publishes the twelve "Poèmes 38-39."
4 November	UNESCO charter in force (ratified by twenty countries).
12 November	SB completes "Premier amour."
19 November	Goes to Abondant.
December	"L'Expulsé" published in *Fontaine*.
before 3 December	Sends "Premier amour" to Jacoba van Velde.
15 December	Sends *Mercier et Camier* to Editions Bordas.
c. 16–17 December	Returns to Paris from Abondant.
23 December	Begins writing "Le Calmant."

GEORGE REAVEY
LONDON

April 25th 1946   Dublin

dear George

I want to thank you again for your kindness to me while I was in London. I got a taxi and the train all right, but was nearly left behind at Holyhead, with a number of unfortunates. There were 1500 on board, the limit being 1000.[1]

I am taking things very easy here, writing a little and walking a lot. The place is lousy with guzzling tourists. I haven't seen Tom or anyone else so far.[2]

I had a note from Watt (which?) regretting that he had not seen me and acknowledging my remarks on the Chatto-Cape-Routledge etc. caucus.[3]

I see advertised in to-day's Irish Times an editorial vacancy on the staff of the RGDATA (Retail Grocery Dairy and Allied Trades-Association) Review at £300 per an. I think seriously of applying. Any experience of trade journalism would be so useful.[4]

Yours ever

Sam.

ALS; 1 leaf, 2 sides; TxU, Reavey collection.

1 Shortly before Easter (21 April), SB stayed one or two nights with Reavey in London as he traveled from Paris to Dublin. Reavey recalls that they discussed "what to do with Beckett's new novel Watt" (TxU, Reavey collection, Draft of Autobiography, iv, 3). Holyhead, Wales, was the departure point of ferries to Dublin; travel from England to Ireland was noticeably heavier than usual this Easter holiday ("Heavy Advance Booking for Holiday Season," The Irish Times, 18 April 1946: 1).

2 Thomas MacGreevy.

3 Leslie Daiken had placed SB's novel Watt with the London agents A. P. Watt & Son. As Daiken explained to A. J. Leventhal, 26 February: Sam "asked me to put Watt in the hands of an agent, and, – in re the Joyce joke about Cork framed in cork, I trust he will appreciate the delicacy of my choice in agents!" (TxU, Leventhal collection; for the

Joyce reference, see Ellmann, *James Joyce*, 551). When R. P. Watt wrote to Daiken on 22 February to confirm receipt of the typescript of *Watt*, he returned the letter from Nicholson and Watson to Daiken of 17 November 1945 (see 31 October 1945, n. 3) that had been inadvertently left within the typescript (TxU, Daiken collection).

The letter from A. P. Watt to SB has not been found; SB's report of it implies that he had either visited the firm while in London or written to them. Chatto and Windus had published SB's *Proust* and *More Pricks Than Kicks*, but had rejected *Murphy*; Jonathan Cape had rejected *Murphy*; Routledge published *Murphy*.

4 The Retail Grocery, Dairy and Allied Trades' Association advertised for a "full-time officer . . . to assist in the editing and management of 'The RGDATA Review'"; the post offered "attractive prospects to candidates capable of building further the high reputation which the paper enjoys in the trade" (*The Irish Times*, 25 April 1946: 8).

JACOBA VAN VELDE

PARIS

15 mai 1946   NEW PLACE

                                               FOXROCK

                                               C° DUBLIN, EIRE

Ma chère Tony[1]

J'apprends de Suzanne que vous avez placé "<u>Suite</u>" aux <u>Temps Modernes</u>.[2] Félicitations. Il n'y a qu'une chose qui me chiffonne, s'il est possible qu'un chiffon soit chiffonné, c'est que j'ai l'impression, d'après ce que Tzara m'a dit, que <u>Fontaine</u> (rédacteur Fouché) l'a déjà pris. Il est naturellement possible que Tzara ait dit ça pour se débarrasser de moi.[3] En tout cas il faudra s'assurer que cela ne passe pas dans les 2 revues à la fois, ou d'avance dans l'une alors que l'autre comptait dessus pour un numéro futur. Vous avez probablement déjà fait le nécessaire, mais sinon vous seriez tout à fait gentille de vous en occuper. Suzanne me dit que vous n'auriez pas à joindre Tzara. Vous savez qu'il devait soumettre <u>Murphy</u> à Calmann-Lévy.[4]

Je peux rentrer au courant du mois prochain. J'en ai marre de cette vie de buffet-sanctuaire.

J'espère que vous avez de bonnes nouvelles de votre mari et qu'il commence à avoir assez de la vie paramilitaire.[5]

Merci de tout le mal que vous vous êtes donné. Je crains que vous n'ayez entrepris là un travail bien ingrat.

Bien amicalement
Sam Beckett

ALS; 2 leaves, 2 sides; BNF, 19794/1.

15 May 1946

NEW PLACE

FOXROCK

C° DUBLIN, EIRE

Dear Tony[1]

I hear from Suzanne that you have placed "Suite" at the *Temps Modernes*.[2] Congratulations. There is only one thing that makes me jumpy, if an invertebrate can jump, it is that I have the impression, from something Tzara told me, that *Fontaine* (edited by Fouchet) has already taken it. Naturally it is possible that Tzara said that to get rid of me.[3] Whatever happens we shall have to make sure that it does not appear in the two reviews at the same time, or in one of them early, when the other is planning on putting it in a later number. You have probably already done all that is needed, but if not, it would be really nice if you could deal with it. Suzanne tells me that you would not have to get in touch with Tzara. You know that he was to show *Murphy* to Calmann-Lévy.[4]

I may come back this month some time. I am sick of this open-house/bolthole life.

I hope that you have good news of your husband, and that he's beginning to tire of paramilitary life.[5]

Thank you for all the trouble you've taken. I fear that you may have taken on a pretty unrewarding task.

Yours ever

Sam Beckett

1   Catharina Jacoba van Velde* (Jacoba, Tonny, Tony; m. Polak, m. Clerx; 1903–1985), sister of Geer and Bram van Velde, was SB's French agent at this time.

2   Suzanne Deschevaux-Dumesnil.

3   SB incorrectly spells Fouchet as "Fouché."
It is not known if "Suite" was simultaneously offered to Max-Pol Fouchet (1913–1980), founding Editor of *Fontaine: Revue Mensuelle de la Poésie et des Lettres Françaises*.

Fontaine was founded, in 1939, in Algeria; it published French poets and writers opposed to the German Occupation.

Tristan Tzara (1896–1963).

4   Calmann-Lévy did not publish *Murphy*.

5   Jacoba van Velde was married to Dutch journalist, actor, and writer Arnold Clerx (Bob, 1897–1968); he was on military service in Germany in 1945 (G. J. van Bork, *Schrijvers en dicters*, www.dbnl.org/auteurs, accessed 21 May 2009).

GEORGE REAVEY

LONDON

May 27th 1946   New Place

                                                          Foxrock

dear George

Many thanks for the poems. I think your translations remarkable, if I can judge without knowing the originals. Perhaps a little over-rimed and over-accented, but extraordinarily resourceful. I should think you would have little difficulty in getting them published. Let me know if you want them back. I should like to keep them.[1]

I expect to go home next month, towards the end probably, but shall fly direct if I possibly can. There is to be a direct Dublin-Paris service starting some time next month. I am restless to be gone.

I am glad you did not take the German job. The cultural thing you mentioned would be more in your line.[2] In any case I look forward to seeing you in Paris in the near future.

I have seen something of Tom. Rather under the Capuchin weather and longing to get away and not able to. He has published a useful little book on the Irish Nation Gall., with plates.[3]

Keidrych Rhys is here, fat and serious and full of autonomous balls about Wales. He is to be received by Dev! I think you knew him.[4]

Remember me to Bill and Helen.[5]

I have finished my French Story, about 45:000 words I think. The first half is appearing in the July <u>Temps modernes</u> (Sartre's canard). I hope to have the complete story published as a separate work.[6] In France they dont bother counting words. Camus's <u>Etranger</u> is not any longer. Try and read it, I think it is important.[7]

Our little Europa group was evoked at a debate at the National University Literary Society. Con Leventhal said nice things about us. I wasn't there but Tom was, of course.[8]

Alan Duncan's widow, Belinda, has married Brian Lunn.[9]

Sur quoi . .[10]

>Amitiés

>Sam

I heard from the Watts. <u>Watt</u> is now with Methuen, who wrote asking to see it. Another stamp gone bang.[11]

ALS; 2 leaves, 4 sides; AN AH, incorrectly dated as "1956?"; TxU, Reavey collection. *Dating*: from publication of the first part of "Suite" in *Les Temps Modernes* (1.10 [1 July 1946] 107–110).

1 The specific poems translated by Reavey and sent to SB are not known. Reavey's translations of poems presented in his critical study *Soviet Literature To-Day* (130–153) are new, with the exception of an excerpt from Nikolai Tikhonov's "The Horses" which was published in *Soviet Literature: An Anthology* (ed. and tr. George Reavey and Marc Slonim [London: Wishart and Co., 1933; rpt. Westport, CT: Greenwood Press, 1972] 368–369).

2 Gwynedd Reavey had taken a position with the Control Commission in Germany in October 1945 and remained there until December 1947 (George Reavey to Mr. Churchill, Clapham and Co., London [after 25 May 1950], TxU, Reavey collection). Neither the position in Germany that Reavey had considered, nor the position related to culture has been identified; Reavey remained in London.

3 Thomas MacGreevy as Editor of *The Capuchin Annual*: 10 May 1945, n. 4. MacGreevy's *Pictures in the Irish National Gallery* was a reprint of photographic reproductions and texts that appeared in the 1943 *Capuchin Annual* (London: B. T. Batsford, 1945). It was intended "to help our own people [become] more familiar with the treasures of the National Gallery [. . .] I wrote the introductions to the different schools of painting and notes on thirty-four pictures under journalistic conditions and mostly from memory" (MacGreevy to James White, 26 January 1965, TCD, MS 8132/223).

4 Welsh poet and anthologist Keidrych Rhys (1915–1987) edited the literary journal *Wales* (1937–1940, 1943–1949). Rhys met the Prime Minister of Ireland Éamon de Valera to present his views on recognition of Wales "as a Dominion." In "An Irishman's Diary," Quidnunc described Rhys as a "large and literary young Welshman," and hoped his success in the Welsh language would inspire De Valera to promote Gaelic language and literature (*The Irish Times*, 27 May 1946: 5).

5 George Reavey had introduced SB to William McAlpine (1913–1994) in London. Born in Belfast, with a degree in Engineering from Queen's University, McAlpine had literary interests and friends (Dylan Thomas, Stephen Spender). Helen McAlpine (1906–1989, m. 1947).

6 SB refers to the first part of "Suite" (see 15 May 1946, n. 3).

7 *L'Etranger* (1942; *The Stranger* [US], *The Outsider* [UK]) by Albert Camus.

8 Europa Press published SB's *Echo's Bones and Other Precipitates* (1935), Denis Devlin's *Intercessions* (1937), Brian Coffey's *Third Person* (1938), and two books by George Reavey, *Signes d'Adieu (Frailty of Love)* (1935) and *Quixotic Perquisitions* (1939). The meeting of the National University (UCD) Literary Society was held on 18 May 1946; the minutes of this debate do not indicate its subject beyond the proposition: "That Romantic England is dead and gone" (Seamus Helferty, Archives, University College, Dublin, 27 July 2005).

9 Belinda Duncan (née Atkinson, 1893-1964; Profile, I), widow of Alan Duncan (1894-1943; Profile, I), married Brian Lunn (1893-1974) in 1946; Lunn's first wife Betty Duncan (1893-1977) was Alan's sister.

10 "Sur quoi" (On which).

11 The letter from A. P. Watt to SB has not been found.

JACOBA VAN VELDE
PARIS

June 11th 1946   New Place Foxrock
                                             Dublin Eire

Dear Tony

Thanks for your letter. I am writing to Madame Allard. I don't think I can let her have <u>Suite 2</u> before first week in July. If this is too late for August number I suppose they can put it in the September number.[1]

Very sorry to hear you are deprived of some of the things that make life bearable. Doctors are all Puritans. Have a good rest at Gresse.[2] I leave here end of this month. Shall see you in Paris in July.

Love to Bram & Geer if you see them, or write to them.[3]

    Yours ever

    Sam Beckett

ALS; 1 leaf, 2 sides; BNF, 19794/2.

1 There was no August issue of *Les Temps Modernes*, but rather a combined August/ September number (1.11/12) released in September to mark the first anniversary of the journal; it was devoted to American writers.

SB's letter to Paule Allard (n.d.) has not been found; SB identifies her as a "sub-editrix" with *Les Temps Modernes* when, on 11 December 1946, he writes to Arland Ussher (1899-1980; Profile, I; TxU, Beckett collection).

2 Gresse-en-Vercors, south of Grenoble.

3 Bram and Geer van Velde.

GEORGE REAVEY

19th June [1946]   Dublin

dear George

Many thanks for letter and poems. I liked them well.[1]

I am leaving for Paris, direct by air next Saturday week. I shall be very glad to be back.[2]

By all means suggest my doing something for <u>Documents</u>.[3] I should be glad of the money. They might write to me at my Paris address.

Thanks for your suggestions re <u>Watt</u>. I have heard nothing from the agents since they informed me that they had sent the ms to Methuens, at Methuens' request.[4] Fridberg, now in business here, wants to see it also, and is writing for it to <u>Watt</u>.[5] I wish I could get it to you. I wish I'd never given it to Watts. That blasted fellow Devlin has the only other copy in Washington and I suppose is doing nothing about it.[6] I shall write to Watts again and tell them to let you have a quick look at it.

No I didn't see the <u>Horizon</u> you mention.[7]

First half of my French récit is appearing in July <u>Temps Modernes</u>. They want the 2nd half for the following number, but I fear it wont be cleaned up in time, though the writing is finished.

Daiken is over. I have given him nothing so far.[8]

No telephone in Paris.

I shall be sorry not to see you on the way and to profit by your hospitable suggestion. I hope we may get together again this year some time in Paris.

Shall give your message to Geer & Lisl. I think they have gone to the south, to prepare Geer's number of <u>Pierre à Feu</u>.[9]

I have seen a little of Tom. More than ever tied up with the men of God.

Love to Gwynedd when you write.[10]

> Yours ever
> Sam

ALS; 2 leaves, 4 sides; TxU, Reavey collection. *Dating*: from publication of SB's "Suite" in *Les Temps Modernes* (July 1946).

1   Reavey's poems have not been identified.

2   Aer Lingus inaugurated a direct Dublin–Paris route on 17 June; commercial service began on Saturday 22 June.

3   *Documents: A European Review of Politics, Literature and Art* was advertised in the July 1946 issue of *Horizon* as a new monthly published "in Paris in two editions: English and French"; the announcement indicated that there would be contributions by George Reavey, Dylan Thomas, and André Gide in the first issue. The "specimen copy of 1st issue for sale in England 1/8/46" (dated June 1946) is in the British Library; the Bibliothèque Nationale de France possesses three issues (June–December 1946), directed by Stéphane Cordier (1905–1986), edited by J.-A. Capuano (n.d.); it appears that no further issues were published.

4   A. P. Watt as agent for *Watt*, and Methuens' request: 27 May 1946.

5   London publisher Maurice Fridberg (n.d.) opened an office at 27/28 Clare Street, Dublin, in 1945 (Patrick Gordon Campbell, *An Irishman's Diary* [London: Cassell and Company, 1950] 132). His firm published the Hour Glass Library series and works by Rhys Davis, Norah Hoult, Gertrude Stein, Donagh McDonagh, John Brophy, Roy Campbell, Elizabeth Bowen, and Frank O'Connor. Fridberg's letter to A. P. Watt has not been found. SB does underscore "Watt."

6   Denis Devlin in Washington: 10 May 1945, n. 7.

7   Vivian Mercier's essay on Irish censorship, "Letter from Ireland II," included a mention of *Murphy* (*Horizon* 13.76 [April 1946] 276–285).

8   Leslie Daiken's project is not known, but it appears that he was expecting to hear from Reavey. Daiken wrote to Reavey on 22 May: "I've been patiently – and then impatiently – waiting to hear from you ever since before Easter when Sam told me that you would certainly be getting in touch" (TxU, Reavey collection).

9   Geer and Lisl van Velde. Following Geer van Velde's first Paris exhibition at the Galerie Maeght (March 1946), five lithographs and two reproductions of paintings were published with Jacques Kober's catalogue "Le Noir est une couleur," *Derrière le Miroir* 1 (December 1946–January 1947).

10   Gwynedd Reavey's work in Germany: 27 May 1946, n. 2.

JACOBA VAN VELDE

30 juin 1946   Paris
chère Tony

Merci de vos lettres. Je regrette que les miennes vous aient donné tant de mal. J'écris comme je pense, voilà.

Je suis rentré hier.[1] J'ai terminé aujourd'hui la deuxième partie de Suite. Il ne reste plus qu'à la taper. Je l'enverrai aux T.M. après-demain au plus tard. Si c'est trop tard pour août tant pis.[2]

Faites-moi signe dès votre retour.[3] Suzanne va bien et vous remercie de votre carte.

Retapez-vous bien. Sans tabac ni alcool la vie n'est pas possible.

Amitiés

Sam

Merci beaucoup ma chère Tony de votre gentille carte. J'espère que le temps ne vous semble pas trop long et que vous allez rentrer en pleine forme – Toutes mes amitiés.

Suzanne

ALS; 1 leaf, 1 side; ANS Suzanne Deschevaux-Dumesnil; BNF, 19794/5.

30 June 1946   Paris

Dear Tony

Thank you for your letters. I am sorry that mine have given you so much trouble. I write as I think, that is how it is.

I came back yesterday.[1] Today I finished the second part of "Suite". Only remains to type it out. I shall send it to the T. M. the day after tomorrow at the latest. If it is too late for August, too bad.[2]

Let me know as soon as you are back.[3] Suzanne is well and thanks you for your card.

Get well soon. Without tobacco or drink no life is possible.

Yours ever

Sam

Thank you very much, Tony dear, for your nice card. I hope that the time doesn't seem to be going by too slowly, and that you're going to come back in top form. – Much love.

Suzanne

1   SB had been in Dublin since shortly before 21 April.

2   Submission of "Suite" to *Les Temps Modernes*: 15 May, 27 May, and 11 June 1946.

3   Jacoba van Velde's vacation: 11 June 1946, n. 2.

3. Geer van Velde in his studio, Cachan, 1949

GEORGE REAVEY
LONDON

Sept 1st 1946   6 Rue des Favorites
              Paris 15me

Dear George

  Thanks for your letter. Hope I shall have the pleasure of seeing you here soon.

  I wrote the other day to Routledge asking them to send me copies of <u>Murphy</u> and have received the following reply:

"We are in receipt of your letter dated the 28th August but would point out that our edition of your book MURPHY went out of print in 1942 and a royalty statement was rendered to your agent, giving particulars, in 1943. For this reason we are unable to send a copy to the address you gave, or six copies to yourself." Signed J. G. Carter.[1]

I have no recollection of any statement of royalties and you probably never received it either.[2] I am quite helpless about these things and do not even know what exactly is the significance of "went out of print". Or what are my rights if any in the matter of a new edition. Should I ask Watt etc to deal with the matter, or should I apply to the Authors' Society? Before I write an imbecile reply to Routledge I should like to know from you if you have any record of the statement of royalties that they say they sent you. I am sorry my dear George to pester you with this, but I should like the thing cleared up. The more so as Harper wrote me asking about AMerican [sic] rights of Murphy. Quelle misère tout ça.[3]

I saw Geer and Lisl lately back from the Midi and living at Cachan. Very prosperous.[4]

I am working on a new book in French.[5] The first part of my story Suite has appeared in the July number of the Temps Modernes and the second and last part will appear in October. I hope all is well with you and Gallimard.[6]

Love to Gwynedd.

Yours ever

s/ Sam

TLS; 1 leaf, 1 side; TxU, Reavey collection.

1 Routledge published *Murphy* (1938). J[ohn] G[rant] Carter (1902–1966) was Sales Manager of Routledge from 1933, and later Chairman (1961–1966). Neither SB's letter to Routledge, nor the letter that he cites has been found.

2 No record of royalty payments on *Murphy* has been found, nor has any indication that the book was formally declared out of print (Routledge Archives, UoR [1943]; Routledge Archives at The University of London).

3 A. P. Watt, London, was SB's agent for *Watt*. SB refers to the Society of Authors, which represents authors in rights issues, especially with regard to negotiations with

publishers. Harper's interest in *Murphy* has not been documented; the novel was eventually published in the United States by Grove Press (1957).

"Quelle misère tout ça" (What wretched stuff, all this).

4   Geer and Lisl van Velde: 31 October 1945, n. 2.

5   SB began *Mercier et Camier* on 5 July 1946 (Lake, ed., *No Symbols Where None Intended*, 151–152).

6   Reavey had just published his study *Soviet Literature To-day*, for SB wrote to him on 15 July: "Congratulations on your book. I am very glad indeed, and the more so as it brings yourself to Paris" (TxU, Reavey collection).

SIMONE DE BEAUVOIR
PARIS

le 25 Septembre 1946   6 Rue des Favorites
                                                    Paris 15me

Chère Madame

Hier Madame Clerx m'a appris votre décision au sujet de la deuxième partie de <u>Suite</u>.[1]

Je regrette le malentendu qui vous met dans l'obligation d'arrêter ma nouvelle à mi-chemin.[2]

Vous pensez à la bonne tenue de votre revue.[3] Cela est naturel. Moi je pense au personnage de <u>Suite</u>, frustré de son repos. Cela aussi est naturel, je pense. Je me mets difficilement à votre place, puisque je ne comprends rien aux questions de rédaction. Mais j'ai lu vos livres et je sais que vous pouvez vous mettre à la mienne.

Je ne voudrais pas que vous vous mépreniez sur le sens de cette lettre, que je n'écris qu'après de longues hésitations. Je n'ai pas envie de discuter. Je ne vous demande pas de revenir sur ce que vous avez décidé. Mais il m'est décidément impossible de me dérober au devoir que je me sens vis-à-vis d'une créature. Pardonnez–moi ces grands mots. Si j'avais peur du ridicule je me tairais.

J'ai suffisa[m]ment confiance en vous, finalement, pour vous dire tout simplement mon sentiment. Le voici. Vous m'accordez la parole pour me la retirer avant qu'elle n'ait eu le temps de rien signifier. Vous immobilisez une existence au seuil de sa solution. Cela a quelque chose de cauchemar-[d]esque. J'ai du mal à croire que des soucis de présentation puissent justifier, aux yeux de l'auteur de L'Invitée, une mutilation pareille.[4]

Vous estimez que le fragment paru dans votre dernier numéro est une chose achevée. Ce n'est pas mon avis. Je n'y vois qu'une prémisse majeure.

Ne m'en voulez pas de cette franchise. Elle est sans rancune. Il existe simplement une misère qu'il s'agit de défendre jusqu'au bout, dans le travail et en dehors du travail.

Croyez à mon estime la plus sincère.

(Samuel Beckett)

TLcc; 1 leaf, 1 side; Fehsenfeld collection. The AL draft in AMS notebook "Voyage de Mercier & Camier autour du pot dans les bosquets de Bondy" differs from the final version (TxU, Beckett collection). Previous publication, AL draft, Lake, ed., *No Symbols Where None Intended*, 81–82.

25 September 1946   6 Rue des Favorites
                                          Paris 15

Dear Madam

Yesterday Madame Clerx told me of your decision on the second part of Suite.[1]

I regret the misunderstanding which compels you to cut off my story half way.[2]

You have in mind the reputation of your review.[3] That is natural. I am thinking of the character in "Suite", denied his rest. That too is natural, I think. I find it hard to put myself in your position, since I know nothing whatever about editorial matters. But I have read your books and I know that you can put yourself in mine.

I would not want you to misunderstand the point of this letter, which I am writing only after long hesitations. I have no wish to engage in argument. I am not asking you to go back on your decision. But it is quite impossible for me to evade the duty I feel towards a creature of mine. Forgive these grand words. If I were afraid of ridicule I would keep quiet.

I have sufficient trust in you, in the end, simply to tell you what my feelings are. They are as follows: You are giving me the chance to speak only to retract it before the words have had time to mean anything. You are immobilising an existence at the very moment at which it is about to take its definitive form. There is something nightmarish about that. I find it hard to believe that matters of presentation can justify, in the eyes of the author of *L'Invitée*, such a mutilation.[4]

Your view is that the fragment which appeared in your last number is a finished piece. That is not my view. I see it as no more than a major premise.

Do not be offended by this plain speaking. It is without rancour. It is simply that there exists a wretchedness which must be defended to the very end, in one's work and outside it.

With my sincere regard

Samuel Beckett

---

1   SB surmised that *Les Temps Modernes* would publish "Suite" in two parts, the first in July. SB did not finish the story until the end of June and submitted the second part of the story after the first had been published (see 30 June 1946, 11 June 1946).

2   In her biographies of both Samuel Beckett and Simone de Beauvoir, Deirdre Bair claims that Beauvoir thought the text was complete as published in the July issue of *Les Temps Modernes*, "'because it had no beginning or end and none of it made any real sense.'" Bair adds that when SB submitted the second half of "Suite," Beauvoir, "thinking it 'a second submission,' rejected it without reading it" (*Simone de Beauvoir: A Biography* [New York: Simon and Schuster, 1990] 346; Raymond Federman and John Fletcher, *Samuel Beckett: His Works and His Critics* [Berkeley: University of California Press, 1970] 49–50).

3   The August/September issue of *Les Temps Modernes*: 11 June 1946, n. 1. Because this number featured American authors, October was the earliest that the second part of "Suite" could have appeared, had the story been announced in the July issue as having two parts. In an interview with Deirdre Bair, Beauvoir said that the second part of the story "'was simply not in keeping with what we wanted to print in the magazine,' which was her standard rejection" (Bair, *Simone de Beauvoir*, 346).

4   *L'Invitée* (1943; *She Came to Stay*) was Beauvoir's first published novel.

JACOBA VAN VELDE
PARIS

mercredi [25 September 1946]   [Paris]
Ma chère brave Tony

Réflexion faite, j'envoie à Madame de Beauvoir la lettre ci-jointe. Cela ne changera rien à l'affaire, mais j'aurai fait ce que j'avais à faire.[1]

Encore merci du mal abominable que vous vous donnez, pour me dépoubeller.

Affectueusement de nous deux
s/ Sam

TLS; 1 leaf, 1 side; letterhead HÔPITAL DE LA CROIX ROUGE IRLANDAISE À SAINT LÔ *canceled with diagonal line; enclosure*: the copy of SB to Simone de Beauvoir, 25 September 1946, is not extant in Jacoba van Velde collection; BNF, 19794/3.

Wednesday [25 September 1946]   [Paris]
Dear good-hearted Tony

On second thoughts, I am sending the enclosed letter to Madame de Beauvoir. It will make no difference, but I shall have done what I had to do.[1]

Thank you again for the appalling trouble you've been taking to get me out of the rubbish bin.

Love from us both
Sam

1   SB to Simone de Beauvoir, 25 September 1946.

JACOBA VAN VELDE
PARIS

dimanche [13 October 1946]   Abondant[1]
Chère Tony – Nous rentrons mercredi. Voulez-vous venir dîner à la maison jeudi. Nous vous attendrons sauf contre-avis.

J'ai écrit une nouvelle ici et revu <u>Mercier</u>, qui me dégoûte déjà.[2]
J'ai reçu les épreuves des poèmes, et la fade lettre de P. A. Rien de la B.[3]
Affectueusement de nous deux. Sam

APCS; 1 leaf, 1 side; "Château d'Abondant (E.-et-L.), côté Ouest. – Le Miroir"; *to* Madame Tony Clerx, 4 ^{bis} Rue Antoine Bourdelle, Paris 15me; *pm* 15-10-46, Abondant; BNF 19794/6. *Dating*: 13 October was the Sunday before the postmark of 15 October 1946.

Sunday [13 October 1946]   <u>Abondant</u>[1]

Dear Tony – We're coming back on Wednesday. Can you come and have dinner with us on Thursday? We'll expect you unless we hear from you.

I've written a short story here, and gone back over *Mercier*, which already sickens me.[2] I've received the proofs of the poems, and the insipid letter from P. A. Nothing from the B.[3]

Love from us both. Sam

1   Abondant is a village 4 miles northeast of Dreux, Eure-et-Loir; SB and Suzanne Deschevaux-Dumesnil were staying in a house lent to them by André (1908–1964) and Ruth Salzman (née Stern, 1908–1995). Suzanne and Ruth had been friends for several years; Suzanne had been the girlfriend of Ruth's brother Paul Stern (1902–1944). (Interviews with Claude Salzman, 16 March 1996, October 2009.)

2   SB dates the manuscript of "L'Expulsé" as "begun 6 October 1946, completed 14 October 1946" (TxU, Beckett collection; *Fontaine* 10 [December 1946 – January 1947] 685–708; revised, in *Nouvelles et Textes pour rien* [Paris: Editions de Minuit, 1955] 11–40).
     The AMS of *Mercier et Camier* is in three notebooks. The first is headed "La Forêt de Bondy / Camier et Mercier / I / Autour du pot / Les Bosquets de Bondy," and is annotated by SB as "one of first writings in French circa 1945 unpublished jettisoned." The notebook is dated by SB as "begun 5 July 1946"; the date of the beginning of Chapter X, in notebook 2, is given as "Sept. 26." Two pages at the beginning of the notebook containing "L'Expulsé" constitute the final pages of the AMS of *Mercier et Camier*, which is dated "3 October 1946" (TxU, Samuel Beckett Collection 6/1; Lake, ed., *No Symbols Where None Intended*, 151–152).

3   "Poèmes 38–39," *Les Temps Modernes* 2.14 (November 1946) 288–293.
     Paule Allard: 11 June 1946, n. 1. Apparently Simone de Beauvoir had not replied to SB's letter of 25 September 1946.

PIERRE BORDAS
PARIS

<u>30 Oct 1946</u>   <u>Paris</u>

cher Monsieur Bordas

    Ci-joint les deux contrats dûment signés.[1]

    Amicalement à vous

        Sam Beckett

ALS; 1 leaf, 1 side; IMEC, Beckett, Boîte 1, S. Beckett, Dossier Murphy 1946–1957.

30 Oct 1946   Paris

Dear Mr. Bordas

    Enclosed are the two contracts duly signed.[1]

    Sincerely yours

        Sam Beckett

1 Pierre Bordas (1913–2000), who founded Editions Bordas in 1946, sent SB a contract for *Murphy* on 29 October, as well as a "contrat général prévoyant les conditions financières pour vos autres oeuvres" (general contract setting out the financial conditions for your other works). With this letter, payment was made to SB for the translation and the author's rights of *Murphy* (IMEC, Beckett, Boîte 1, S. Beckett, Dossier Murphy 1946–1957).

    Pierre Bordas describes his initial meeting with SB and Jacoba van Velde:

> Son auteur, Samuel Beckett, était tout à fait surprenant: grand et maigre, le visage profondément marqué de rides profondes, front élevé, regard semblant fixer le vague. Totalement muet, il était accompagné par une jeune femme qui parlait à sa place. (*L'Edition est une aventure* [Paris: Editions de Fallois, 1997] 186.) (Its author, Samuel Beckett, was quite astonishing: tall and thin, his face deeply marked by deep lines, high forehead, his gaze fixed on the middle distance. Wholly silent, he was accompanied by a young woman who spoke for him.)

45

JACOBA VAN VELDE
PARIS

<u>vendredi</u> [before November 1946]
Chère Tony

J'ai laissé passer une toute petite faute dans l'un des poèmes, le quatrième, intitulé <u>Ascension</u>, avant-dernier vers. Il faut <u>rôde</u>, avec circonflexe, à la place de <u>rode</u>, sans circonflexe. Vous seriez gentille de circonflexer avant de les apporter aux T.M.[1] Merci.

A lundi

Votre

Sam

ALS; 1 leaf, 1 side; BNF 19794/13. *Dating*: "Ascension" was published in November 1946.

Friday [before November 1946]
Dear Tony

I overlooked a tiny mistake in one of the poems, the fourth, entitled "Ascension," in the last line but one. It should be *rôde*, with a circumflex, instead of *rode*, with no circumflex. Please circumflex it before you take them to the *T. M.*[1] Thanks.

Till Monday

Yours

Sam

1 "Ascension" was fourth in the poem cycle "Poèmes 38-39," 288–293; the published text does not include this correction.

ARLAND USSHER
DUBLIN

11 December 1946   Abondant – E. et L. [Eure-et-Loir]

Dear Arland

Thank you for the 19th Century. You do them proud, I must say. Flourishing, particularly the military representatives, they are happily engaged in reorganising the salvation of the country. They are prepared to forget and forgive – the so rude interruption.[1]

Forgive my not having replied before now to your letter of Oct. 26th. I spoke to Paule Allard, sub-editrix of the Temps Modernes, about your book, and she did not seem aware of its existence, which is extraordinary, since everything goes through her hands.[2] Did you leave a copy with the T.M. for review, or merely submit to Gallimard? It is difficult for me, having had a resounding difference of opinion with Simone de Beauvoir, to intervene. But PAULE ALLARD is well disposed, and you might write to her yourself, using my name if you wish.

I have been in the country for the past month, ill nearly all the time, not serious but tiresome. We expect to return to Paris next week. Suzanne desires to be remembered to you.

I shall not be home before March or April, and I look forward to seeing you again then.

Best wishes to all three for Xmas, Sylvester et sqq.[3]

yours ever

Sam

ALS; 1 leaf, 1 side; TxU, Beckett collection.

1 SB refers to Arland Ussher's essay "The Meaning of Collaboration," *The Nineteenth Century and After* 140.1333 (July 1946) 330–331.

2 Ussher was pursuing French publication of his book *Postscript on Existentialism* (1946). In his letter of 28 August, SB responded to Ussher's concern about identifying a French translator for the book: "If Gallimard accepts the work they will find the translator [. . .] But if Gallimard turns down the book, I could have my agent here handle it, if you wish [. . .] I could also speak of the book to Sartre (whom I met the other day) if you wish" (TxU, Beckett collection). Ussher submitted the book for consideration by Gallimard in November; it was rejected (Dionys Mascolo, Librairie NRF, Gallimard, to Arland Ussher, 6 January 1947 [TCD, MS 9042/233]).

In his letter of 28 August, SB had congratulated Ussher on a favorable review of *Postscript on Existentialism*, "Seen from Dublin," in the *Times Literary Supplement* (by E. C. Blunden, *TLS* (2322 [3 August 1946] 367). In his letter of 26 October (which has not been found), Ussher may have asked SB to see about the possibility of a review in *Les Temps Modernes*.

3   SB sends seasonal greetings to Ussher's wife Emily (née Whitehead, 1898–1974) and daughter Henrietta Owen (Hetty, m. Staples, b. 1926).

GEORGE REAVEY

LONDON

Dec. 15$^{\underline{th}}$ 1946   Abondant – Eure-et-Loir

dear George

Abjectest apologies for delay in replying to your letters of 8$^{\underline{th}}$ & 13$^{\underline{th}}$ October. Thank you indeed for all the trouble you have taken to furnish me with advice, addresses, etc. Since my last letter to you my position has been considerably simplified. I have signed a contract with the Editions Nouvelles Françaises (Bordas) for all future work in French & English (including translations) and my affairs are now entirely in their hands. They do editions in English here & in America and it is they too who will look after any future London editions of work in English. They are publishing in the first place my French translation of Murphy and have already paid me handsomely enough (to one used to British generosity) both for my translation and an advance on royalties.[1] They are also reading a shortish novel in French (Mercier et Camier) written since my return to France last July.[2] They have withdrawn Watt (not What, Watt) from the ineffable Watt quartet.[3] It is a great relief for me to have my literary affairs centralized in this way, by a firm prepared to act in a sense as my agents as well as my publishers. I don't know much about them, except that they do a lot of luxury editions. They wanted me to do a translation for an American luxury edition of new poems by Eluard, illustrated by Chagall, also a translation of the Symphonie Pastorale, but I turned both down.[4] Thirteen poems in French written 1938–39 are appearing soon in the Temps Modernes and a longish short story (L'Expulsé) dealing with the same deadbeats as in Suite has been taken by Fontaine.[5] I hope to have a book of short stories ready for the Spring (in French).[6] I do not think I shall write very much in English in the future. A long article on the Van Velde brothers, written a year ago, is appearing, or perhaps has appeared, in the Cahiers d'Art.[7] As to Murphy in English, I shall get Bordas to deal with the bastards. I received in all £20 (– income tax) for Murphy, and imagine I am due a little more if the edition is exhausted as they say. And if they have remaindered it, why don't they say so? I get letters from inconnus in England complaining that they can't get a copy.[8]

Forgive all this autobiography.

I hope you have clinched things with Gallimard.[9] I wonder is it quite the right firm for a book of that kind? I hope you will soon be able to get over to Paris in person.

I have been here in the country, on the edge of the Dreux forest, for the past month, in poorish health. I am returning to Paris to-morrow or the day after. I was to go to Dublin for Xmas but can't face it and shall not go before March or April, and then I fear not via London, but by air direct.

I had a note from Jack Lindsay of the Bookhouse, naming you & asking for work. I have not had the common politeness up till now to reply, but shall do so.[10] I have been horribly busy, & then poorly.

I also had a friendly letter from Daiken offering to send me Murphy.[11] I managed to find a few copies here, given to friends, donkeys years ago.

I haven't seen Peggy. She was in Italy and is now I understand in New York. The latest companion is of Italian nationality, I am told, and of royal birth, I seem to remember. A palace on the Grand Canal is on the mat, for purchase.[12]

I saw a long anti-Franco article in French in Action by Nancy Cunard.[13]

The boys are very cross with Koestler.[14]

The van Veldes are all well. I see a good deal of the Clerxes. He was in UNRAN, but has left it. I thing the 2 brothers & sister are at present in Holland, to see the mother, very poorly.[15]

Have you dropped the UNESCO idea? They haven't got going here at all yet and don't seem to know what they intend to do.[16] Are you not tempted by the chance of spending some time in Paris? The franc will doubtless be cheaper soon.

What news of Gwynedd? Give her my love. Best wishes to you both for Xmas etc.

Don't be talionic, drop me a line soon.

Yours ever

Sam

ALS; 1 leaf, 4 sides; TxU, Reavey collection. *Dating*: although SB refers to the November 1946 issue of *Les Temps Modernes* as a future publication, he may simply not yet have seen it, as he was away from Paris from about 11 November (according to his letter to Arland Ussher, 11 December 1946).

1 SB's previous letter to Reavey was dated 1 September.

The contract with Editions Bordas for *Murphy* and future works: 30 October 1946. Although Bordas published such works as Léonie Villard's *La Poésie américaine: trois siècles de poésie lyrique et de poèmes narratifs* (1945) under the imprint Editions Françaises Nouvelles, there exists no indication of English-language publication in France or the United States.

Bordas paid SB 35,000 francs (Bordas to SB, 29 October 1946, IMEC, Beckett, Boîte 1, S. Beckett, Dossier Murphy 1946–1957).

2 The dates of composition of *Mercier et Camier*: see [13 October 1946], n. 2. A note of an advance of 10,000 francs for *Mercier et Camier* dated "Janvier 1947" was appended by Beckett to the contract of 30 October; however, Bordas did not publish the novel (IMEC, Beckett, Boîte 1, S. Beckett, Dossier Murphy 1946–1957).

3 On 29 October, Pierre Bordas wrote to the British publisher of *Murphy* for confirmation that the rights were available; on 31 October, Routledge confirmed: "The rights of MURPHY are the property of Mr. Samuel Beckett and he is, therefore, entitled to deal with you direct as far as we are concerned" (IMEC, Beckett, Boîte 1, S. Beckett, Dossier Murphy 1946–1957).

No documentation has been found to indicate that Bordas withdrew *Watt* from A. P. Watt in London. SB refers to the familial partners of A. P. Watt as "the quartet."

4 Arnold-Bordas published a limited edition of *Le dur désir de durer* (1946) by Paul Eluard with twenty-five original etchings and a colored frontispiece by Marc Chagall; it was published in both French and English with translations by Stephen Spender and Frances Cornford (*Le dur désir de durer* [Philadelphia: Grey Falcon Press, 1950]). Although SB was asked to translate it, Bordas did not publish an English translation of André Gide's *La Symphonie pastorale* (1925); it had already appeared in English as *Two Symphonies* [Isabelle and The Pastoral Symphony], tr. Dorothy Bussy (New York: Cassell, 1931).

5 "Poèmes 38–39" presented twelve, not thirteen, poems. These are misnumbered: poem IV, "Ascension," is followed by the titled but unnumbered poem [V] "La Mouche"; there is no poem XI (288–293) (Federman and Fletcher, *Samuel Beckett*, 50). Neither correspondence with *Les Temps Modernes* nor the corrected proofs has been found to indicate whether or not a poem was indeed omitted. That SB continues to refer to thirteen poems suggests that he had not seen the twelve poems as published (SB to George Reavey, 14 May 1947). Ruby Cohn speculates that the unpublished "Les joues rouges" may have been grouped with these poems (Ruby

Cohn, *A Beckett Canon* [Ann Arbor: The University of Michigan Press, 2001] 99; UoR, BIF, MS 2912).
Publication of "L'Expulsé": [13 October 1946], n. 2.

6   SB describes the collection of stories to George Reavey on 14 May 1947 as *Quatre Nouvelles*, suggesting that originally he considered "Premier amour" as one of the four, with "L'Expulsé," "Suite" (published later as "La Fin"), and "Le Calmant" (they were later published together as *Four Novellas* [London: John Calder, 1977]). The manuscript of "Premier amour" is dated "28 October to 12 November 1946"; SB sent it to Jacoba van Velde before 3 December, saying <u>Premier Amour</u> semble m'avoir achevé. L'avez-vous au moins bien reçu?" ("Premier Amour" seems to have finished me off. Have you at least received it?) (BNF, 19794/8).
SB dates the beginning of the manuscript of "Le Calmant" as "23 December 1946" (Lake, ed., *No Symbols Where None Intended*, 83, 147; Cohn, *A Beckett Canon*, 144, 147).

7   Beckett, "La Peinture des van Velde ou le monde et le pantalon," 349–356; the issue of *Cahiers d'Art* in which it appeared is dated as 1945–1946; as the imprint date is the fourth trimester of 1946, SB may not have seen the issue.

8   *Murphy* was out of print from Routledge in 1942 (see 1 September 1946). "Inconnus" (unknowns).

9   Reavey may have approached Gallimard about publishing his study *Soviet Literature To-day*; Gallimard had published the French edition of his anthology edited with Marc Slonim, *Anthologie de la littérature soviétique, 1918–1934* (1935), but it did not publish anything further by Reavey.

10   Jack Lindsay (né Robert Leeson Lindsay, 1900–1990) may have contacted SB with regard to his edited collection, *Anvil: Life and the Arts: A Miscellany* (London: Meridian Books, 1947); work by Reavey was published in the 1947 edition (dated spring 1947, although publication was delayed to autumn 1947). SB's letter to Lindsay has not been found; Bookhouse has not been identified.

11   Leslie Daiken's letter to SB has not been found.

12   Marguerite Guggenheim (Peggy, 1898–1979; Profile, I) had been in Venice in the summer of 1946, and in the autumn went to New York, where her gallery Art of This Century closed at the end of May 1947; Guggenheim purchased the Palazzo Venier dei Leoni on the Grand Canal in Venice in December 1948 (Jacqueline Bograd Weld, *Peggy: The Wayward Guggenheim* [New York, E. P. Dutton, 1998] 351–354, 359, 363, 369–370). The friend of Peggy Guggenheim referred to here has not been identified.

13   Nancy Cunard, "Manuel Alvarez sera exécuté au garrot," *Action, Hebdomadaire de l'Indépendance Française* 111 (18 October 1946): 6.

14   Arthur Koestler (1905–1983) was in Paris in October and November for rehearsals of his play *Bar du Soleil* (*Twilight Bar*), produced by Jean Vilar (1912–1971) at the Théâtre de Clichy. Presumably, SB refers to Albert Camus and Jean-Paul Sartre as "the boys." Koestler's friendship with them dates from this period; however, his political positions put him at odds with them on several occasions (David Cesarani, *Arthur Koestler: The Homeless Mind* [New York: The Free Press, Simon and Schuster, 1999] 272–278; Arthur Koestler and Cynthia Koestler, *Stranger on the Square*, ed. Harold Harris, [London: Hutchinson, 1984] 66–70, 72; Ronald Hayman, *Sartre: A Life* [New York: Simon and Schuster, 1987] 246–247).

15   Geer and Lisl van Velde, Bram van Velde and Marthe Arnaud, Jacoba van Velde Clerx and her husband Bob.

It is probable that SB meant the United National Relief and Rehabilitation Administration (UNRRA), operated by the United Nations to resettle displaced persons in the liberated countries of Europe.

The mother of Jacoba, Geer, and Bram van Velde was Hendrika Catharina van Velde (née Van de Voorst, 1867–1952).

SB wrote "thing" for think.

16   The UNESCO charter had been signed on 16 November 1945, and by 4 November 1946 it had been ratified by twenty countries; from 19 November to 10 December 1946, the first general conference of UNESCO developed a draft program for the new organization headquartered in Paris ("UNESCO's Task: Conference Opened in Paris," *The Times* 20 November 1946: 3; "The Task of UNESCO," *The Times* 8 November 1946: 5; "UNESCO Conference Ended: Agreement on First Task," *The Times* 11 December 1946: 3).

CHRONOLOGY 1947

1947 January   Editions Bordas pay SB an advance for *Mercier et Camier*.

18 January   SB begins writing his play *Eleutheria*.

24 February   Finishes *Eleutheria*.

before 14 April   Travels to London, where he stays with George Reavey for a few days, before going on to Dublin.

14 April   In Dublin.

15 April   Imprint date of French translation of *Murphy*.

May   Exhibition of French pictures, Victor Waddington Gallery, Dublin, including three paintings by Geer van Velde.

2 May   SB begins writing *Molloy*.

5 July   Flies from Dublin to Paris.

23 July   SB and Suzanne Deschevaux-Dumesnil go to Menton. SB works on *Molloy* there.

15 August   Jean Vilar reading *Eleutheria*.

27 August   London publisher Hamish Hamilton considering *Watt*.

end of September   SB returns to Paris from Menton.

1 November   Finishes *Molloy*.

18 November   First day of National Strikes in France that will last through the winter of 1947–1948.

by 24 November   Hamish Hamilton has rejected *Watt*. Maria Jolas has asked SB to translate for the new *Transition*.

27 November   Begins *Malone meurt*. Grenier-Hussenot theatre company shows an interest in *Eleutheria*.

14/5/47

New Place
Foxrock
Co Dublin

Dear George

Thanks for your letter. Forgive my not having written to you long ago. Thank you again for your kindness to me while I was in London.[1]

You write "I saw Denis and got Murphy" but I think you must mean Watt. I am glad to see you confusing them. I am glad you were able to read it and should be delighted for you to handle it, but on condition that you accept the usual wretched commission, as well on extracts as on the whole work if ever taken. It is an unsatisfactory book, written in dribs and drabs, first on the run, then of an evening after the clodhopping, during the occupation. But it has its place in the series, as will perhaps appear in time.[2] Anyhow do with it as you please. Some firm, I forget which (Daiken could tell you) would have taken it long ago if I had consented to make certain changes. They wanted notably the work to open in the railway-station! You might as well know that I can't make any changes, in case the suggestion is made to you that I should.[3]

As to works in French, Murphy is [for in] French is due this month from Bordas, my own translation, and not a very good one. A novel Mercier et Camier, short, has also been accepted by Bordas and should be out this autumn.[4] A book of long short stories (Quatre Nouvelles) is ready but has not yet found a publisher. Two have appeared separately, in the Temps Modernes (Suite) and Fontaine (L'Expulsé).[5] Thirteen poems, old, have appeared in the Temps Modernes.[6] And shortly before leaving Paris I finished a play in three acts called Eleuthéria or Eleuthéromane, I'm not quite sure, and which Madame

Clerx is handling as she handles all my work in French, with more or less success. Ecco.[7]

I expect to be here until the end of June. My mother is very shaky and I fear I can't invite you to stay with us here, as I should so much have liked to do. I thought perhaps you might like to stay in a nice country pub in Enniskerry, not so far from here, with frequent buses to town at your door. Plenty of goodfood and drink and lovely country.[8] Brian Lunn and his wife ex-Mrs Alan Duncan were staying there recently.[9] I dispose of a car and could help you get around. I think you would be happier there than in Dublin where it is almost impossible to get a hotel room. Joe Hone would be a neighbour.[10] If you think well of this let me know in good time so that I may book your room.

An exhibition here now of modern French painting, very pleasant. Three pictures from Geer of which one sold already for £150.[11]

Almost certain that I shall fly straight back thus by-passing the wen, so do try and get over here for a bit.[12]

Many thanks again for everything.

> Yours ever
>
> s/ Sam

TLS; 1 leaf, 2 sides; TxU, Reavey collection.

1   It is likely that SB stayed with George Reavey in London on his way to Ireland, although in his letter to Arland Ussher of 17 February, SB had mentioned a plan to fly directly to Dublin in April (TxU, Reavey collection).

2   SB canceled "a" and inserted "the" before "series."
Denis Devlin had a copy of the typescript of *Watt* (see 19 June 1946). At this time, what SB calls "the series" was *Murphy*, *Mercier et Camier*, and *Molloy*, which he had just begun to write in French in Foxrock on 2 May (Richard L. Admussen, *The Samuel Beckett Manuscripts: A Study*, ed. Jackson Bryer, A Reference Study in Literature [Boston: G. K. Hall, 1979] 68–69; Lake, ed., *No Symbols Where None Intended*, 53).

3   Before giving *Watt* to A. P. Watt, Leslie Daiken had sent the manuscript to Nicholson and Watson, who returned it; it is not known whether changes had been requested (see 31 October 1945, n. 3). In the published text, the scene in the railway station takes place near the end of the novel (*Watt* [New York: Grove Press, 1959] 223).

4   The imprint date of the French translation of *Murphy* published by Bordas is 15 April 1947. Although the advance paid by Bordas in January 1947 for *Mercier et Camier* was noted by SB on their contract dated 30 October 1946, the novel was never published by Bordas (see 15 December 1946, n. 2).

5 *Quatre Nouvelles*: 15 December 1946, n. 6. *Premier amour* was omitted when "L'Expulsé," "Le Calmant," and "La Fin" were eventually published in *Nouvelles et Textes pour rien*.

Publication of the first portion of "Suite" (later entitled "La Fin") in *Les Temps Modernes*: 15 May 1946, n. 2, and 25 September 1946 to Simone de Beauvoir. Publication of "L'Expulsé" in *Fontaine*: 13 October 1946, n. 2.

6 SB's poems in *Les Temps Modernes*: 15 December 1946, n. 5.

7 The manuscript of SB's first play *Eleutheria* notes that it was begun on "18 January 1947" and completed on "24 February 1947" (Admussen, *The Samuel Beckett Manuscripts*, 106; Lake, ed., *No Symbols Where None Intended*, 51).

Jacoba van Velde Clerx.

"Ecco" (It., That's it).

8 Maria Jones Beckett (née Roe, known as May, 1871–1950; Profile, I).

Enniskerry, Co. Wicklow.

9 Brian Lunn and his wife Belinda, the widow of Alan Duncan: 27 May 1946, n. 9.

10 Joseph Maunsell Hone (1882–1959; Profile, I) lived at Ballyorney House, Enniskerry, from 1946 to 1951 (David Hone, 14 August 2009).

11 None of the three paintings by Geer van Velde included in the exhibition of French pictures at the Victor Waddington Gallery in May 1947 has been identified (Leah Benson, National Gallery of Ireland, 28 November 2008).

12 "The wen" (London).

ERNEST O'MALLEY

DUBLIN

4-7-47   Foxrock

My dear Ernie[1]

I am leaving to-morrow & am sorry not to have seen you before my departure.

I am sending back the Aragon. Forgive me. I can't read it let alone review it. And if I had been able to read it I wouldn't have been able to review it. This is a reflexion on me, not on Aragon.[2]

Kindest regards again to Helen.[3]

Good luck to you.

Yrs ever

Sam Beckett

ALS; 1 leaf, 1 side; Cormac O'Malley collection.

1   Ernest O'Malley (1897–1957) was Book Editor for *The Bell* (1947–1948), and contributed to that and other Irish and international journals, as well as to broadcasts for Radio Éireann and the BBC.

2   SB was asked to review the English translation of Louis Aragon's *Les Voyageurs de l'impériale* (1942; *Passengers of Destiny*, tr. Hannah Geffen Josephson [1947]). It was reviewed by Christine Longford: "Novels of High Society," *The Bell* 15.2 (November 1947) 76–80.

3   Helen Hooker O'Malley (née Reolofs, 1905–1993), American sculptor.

MARIA JOLAS
PARIS

2.8.47   56 av. Aristide-Briand
                                                     Menton-Garavan
                                                     A[lpes]-M[aritimes]

My dear Maria

I'm afraid I can't undertake the translation you propose. I'm not doing any translations now.[1]

I should be glad eventually to contribute to the Workshop if you are interested in my work in French.[2]

How did you find Lucia? I feel guilty that I never go to see her. I imagine I upset her.[3]

I expect to return to Paris at the end of this month & shall probably be there all of September & October. I would like very much to see you, & Gene, to whom my kindest remembrance.

Good luck to the new Transition.

        Yrs. ever
        Sam Beckett

ALS; 1 leaf, 1 side; CtY, Beinecke, Gen MSS 108, Series VII, Box 28, Folder 535.

1   Maria Jolas (née MacDonald, 1893–1987; Profile, I). Her inquiry about translations referred to preparation of the post-War *Transition**, edited by Georges Duthuit* (1891–1973). Maria Jolas described the new project to Continental Publishers and Distributors in London in her letter of 24 July 1947:

> In the framework of "Transition Press", Eugene Jolas, American poet and founder and editor of "Transition" (1927–1938), and Georges Duthuit, French

poet and critical writer, are planning the following activities for the fall of 1947: "Transition Cahiers", a bi-monthly review in English of contemporary French writing, and "Transition Workshop", an intercontinental collection of new writing and hitherto untranslated documents.

"Transition Cahiers" will appear six times a year in small book-size format and contain some 160 to 190 pages of text. Its aim will be to present in English translation the most important writing, either as to form or content, as it appears in contemporary French publications: essays, articles, enquêtes, stories, poems etc. as well as a general view of French activities in the fields of philosophical, sociological, religious or esthetic research, historical, scientific or economic thought.

"Transition Workshop" plans include: an occasional volume entitled "Transition Word," devoted to the works of writers who are conscious of the problems of language; Romantic and post-Romantic documents, with which the English-speaking public is unfamiliar; contemporary pamphlets, in both French and English, to include the work of writers throughout the Atlantic community which, for commercial reasons, frequently remains unpublished; a "Verticalist" series, to include poems and other texts of a metaphysical-mystic nature; a "James Joyce Year-Book", to contain critical and other material devoted to the personality and works of the Irish writer.

Eugene Jolas will edit and direct the "Workshop" and the "Cahiers" will be edited and directed by Georges Duthuit. (CtY, Beinecke, Gen MSS 108, Series XII, Transition, Box 59, Folder 1381.)

Eugene Jolas (1894–1952; Profile, I).

2   SB canceled "my" and inserted "you."

3   Lucia Joyce (1907–1982; Profile, I) remained institutionalized in the Maison de Santé in the Paris suburb of Ivry, run by her doctor, François Achille-Delmas (1879–1947).

GEORGE REAVEY

LONDON

15-8-47   56 Av. Aristide-Briand

                                             MENTON-GARAVAN

                                             A.-M.

My dear George –

Many thanks for your letter and good news. I knew if anyone could get the book out of the drawer it was you. I myself forget what it's all about, but suppose it will come back to me, with the proofs. Domicile me wherever you think best, all I want is money.[1]

We have been here for past three weeks and hope to stay 3 weeks more, which would get me back to Paris just in time to see your man from Hamiltons.[2] I have been in bad health with an abscess in the jaw and tooth trouble, but am better now. I am getting on with another book in French, entitled probably Molloy.[3] I don't know what I can say to Hodge about future work. All I would have to offer in English being translations from my own French. Perhaps, to encourage him with Watt, I should say I expect soon to resume writing in English, than which, entre nous, few things are less likely.

It has been raining here for the past two days which strikes me as being against the rules. We are camping in a fenestrated villa & cooking our food in the open-air, on charcoal and the debris of period furniture.[4]

Hope you feel restored after your whiff of Europe. Imagine you'll need plenty of vital reserves to face the coming winter in London. We expect to return here this winter, if all goes not too badly.

My play in French was almost taken by Hussenot - Grenier (playing at Théâtre Agnès Capri), but only almost. They were very nice about it. And recommended it to Jean Vilar, who has it at present.[5]

All the best and many thanks for all you've done.

Yrs ever   Sam

ALS; 3 leaves, 3 sides; TxU, Reavey collection.

1   SB refers to his novel *Watt*.

2   In his letter to George Reavey of 20 July, SB writes "We leave for Menton next Wednesday and hope to stay there 3 weeks at least" (TxU, Reavey collection); the Wednesday after 20 July 1947 was 23 July.
   Alan Hodge (1915–1979) edited Hamish Hamilton's series The Novel Library from 1946 to 1952. The American novelist Raymond Chandler wrote of him to Jamie Hamilton: "Your man Hodge is a superb editor, the rarest kind of mind … Hodge is concerned with the book and damn all else" (*Selected Letters of Raymond Chandler*, ed. Frank McShane [New York: Columbia University Press, 1981] 202–203).

3   SB began writing *Molloy* on 2 May in Foxrock (Lake, ed., *No Symbols Where None Intended*, 53). The AMS notebooks of *Molloy* are dated throughout: notebook II is dated as "22.7.47 Paris" on the flyleaf; it continued from "Menton 27.7.47" on page 9; the section dated "15.8" extends from page 73 to page 78 (TxU, Beckett collection).

4   SB and Suzanne Deschevaux-Dumesnil were staying at the Villa Irlanda in Menton-Garavan that belonged to Ralph Cusack (1912–1965) and SB's cousin Nancy Sinclair (Knowlson, *Damned to Fame*, 332). SB mentions open windows and cooking

out-of-doors; in an interview, Morris Sinclair, who knew the house, said that this suggested that there was no electricity.

5   SB deleted "It is now" and inserted "And recommended."

SB's play *Eleutheria* was written in January and February 1947, and Jacoba van Velde had it circulated on his behalf (Knowlson, *Damned to Fame*, 328–333). The theatre company of Jean-Pierre Grenier (1914–2000) and Olivier Hussenot (1913–1978) was formed in 1946; they produced works of popular entertainment and light comedy.

The cabaret singer and actress Agnès Capri (née Sophie-Rose Friedmann, 1915–1976) studied at the Schola Cantorum and with actor Charles Dullin (1885–1949); a friend of Paul Nizan, Louis Aragon, and Max Ernst, she performed in Jean Cocteau's *Le Bœuf sur le toit*, before opening her own theatre, Le Capricorne, in Paris in 1938. At the outbreak of the War, she left Paris for Algeria; in 1944, she returned and re-established her company in Paris.

Theatre director Jean Vilar established the Avignon Theatre Festival in 1947, and from 1951 to 1963 was the head of the Théâtre National Populaire (TNP).

JACOBA VAN VELDE
PARIS

27.8.47   56 A$^{\underline{v}}$ Aristide-Briand
                                                Menton-Garavan
                                                Alpes-Maritimes

Ma chère Tony

J'aurais dû vous écrire plus tôt. J'ai eu un mauvais abscès [*for* abcès] à la mâchoire, c'est ma seule excuse.

Je ne pense pas d'ailleurs que vous ayez grand'chose à me communiquer, en fait de nouvelles littéraires.

Il est possible que nous restions ici jusque vers la fin septembre. Ce n'est pas un empêchement à la parution de Murphy, vous le savez. Si vous arrivez à tirer quelque chose de ce salaud, vous seriez gentille de me l'envoyer, mais moins votre part et le coût du mandat.[1]

Je suis toujours en rapports avec Leyris, qui demande maintenant des textes pour la Licorne. Connais pas. Si ça vous tombe sous la main, je serais content d'en voir un exemplaire.[2]

J'ai pensé que vous pourriez peut-être présenter les nouvelles aux Editions Pierre à Feu (Maeght) mais c'est sans doute là une très mauvaise idée.[3]

61

Reavey m'écrit de Londres qu'il y a des chances que la maison d'édition Hamish Hamilton prenne Watt.

Toujours rien de Vilar au sujet de ma pièce.

Bien amicalement de nous deux à vous deux.

Sam

Nous espérons que vous avez pu vous échapper de Paris pendant la grosse chaleur, que vous vous portez bien tous les deux et que vous n'êtes bien [*for* pas] trop emmerdés.

ALS; 2 leaves, 2 sides; BNF 19794/10-11.

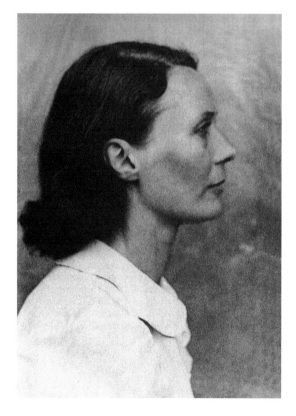

4. Jacoba van Velde

27.8.47 56 Aᵛ Aristide-Briand
Menton-Garavan
Alpes Maritimes

Dear Tony

I ought to have written to you sooner. I've had a bad abscess on my jaw, my only excuse.

In any case I don't think you can have much to tell me in the way of literary news.

We may stay on here till late September. That doesn't interfere with the publication of *Murphy*, as you know. If you manage to wring anything out of that bastard, do please send it on, minus your cut and the cost of the money-order.[1]

I'm still having exchanges with Leyris, who is now asking for texts for *La Licorne*. Means nothing to me. If you should come across it, I'd be glad to see a copy.[2]

It occurred to me that you might offer the stories to the Editions Pierre à Feu (Maeght), but I dare say this is a very bad idea.[3]

Reavey writes from London that there's a chance that Hamish Hamilton will take Watt.

Still nothing from Vilar about the play.

Warmest regards from us both to you both.

Sam

We hope that you managed to get out of Paris during the great heat, that you're both well, and that things aren't too awful.

---

1 The dépôt légal of *Murphy* is the second trimester of 1947, and on 14 May 1947, SB writes to George Reavey that *Murphy* is "due this month from Bordas"; SB's words suggest that the book has not yet appeared. The first press announcements of the novel are in *Paru: L'Actualité Littéraire, Intellectuelle et Artistique* 37 (December 1947) 134 and in *Bibliographie de la France* (15 [January 1948]) 94 (IMEC, Bordas, Service de communication, Beckett, S., *Murphy*, BDS 03.14).

2   Pierre Leyris (1907–2001) translated into French works by Shakespeare, Milton, Blake, Dickens, Hopkins, T. S. Eliot, Melville, Henry James, and D. H. Lawrence. At this time, he was working with Uruguayan poet Susana Soca (1906–1959), Editor of *La Licorne*; the journal appeared in three issues: Spring 1947, Autumn 1948, and Winter 1948. SB's letters to and from Leyris have not been found.

3   SB refers to the stories "Premier amour," "L'Expulsé," "Le Calmant," and "La Fin." Aimé Maeght (1906–1981) founded the Galerie Maeght in 1945 in Paris. Jacques Kober (b. 1925) was its first Director; he also founded and directed its publication, *Pierre à Feu*. He attracted poets and writers to its pages ("Valéry, Beckett, Bataille, Paulhan, Breton, Bachelard, Char, Queneau, Eluard, Prévert"), and also contributed his own poetry. "For Aimé Maeght, the union of text and image – through publications linked to the Maeght Gallery – was therefore of pivotal importance" (Jan K. Birksted, *Modernism and the Mediterranean: The Maeght Foundation* [Aldershot: Ashgate, 2004] 106–108).

GEORGE REAVEY

LONDON

<u>18.11.47</u>   <u>Paris</u>

My dear George

Thanks for your letter. I knew H.H. was hatching a dead egg, or rather that <u>Watt</u> was under a dead hen. Thanks for all the trouble you have taken.[1]

I have nothing at all in English. I have finished a longish book in French. <u>Murphy</u> is out in French. Shall send you a copy some day.[2]

No news of any account. We are back from Menton some time. The annual struggle against cold & restrictions has well begun. Things here get daily worse. I expect there will be some trouble before the end of the winter, pitchforks versus [? gilda].[3]

Hope all is well with you & that your work goes satisfactorily.

Yours ever

Sam

ALS; 1 leaf, 1 side; TxU, Reavey collection.

1   Hamish Hamilton had rejected *Watt*.

2   SB finished *Molloy* on 1 November 1947 (Lake, ed., *No Symbols Where None Intended*, 53). Publication of *Murphy* in French by Bordas: 27 August 1947, n. 1.

3   On 5 November 1947, the French Cabinet announced new financial policies which included elimination of the subsidy for coal. On 10 November, news came that French currency, along with other European currencies, would be devalued in the near future. On 13 November, Charles de Gaulle was elected head of the French government. On 14 November, there was an increase in the "prices of gas and electricity by 45 per cent, of railway and subway fares by 25 per cent, and of freight rates by 28.5 per cent," which was described as "an application of 'the price policy ordered by Wall Street'" (Harold Callender, "French Communists Adopt Political Isolationist Policy," *The New York Times* 15 November 1947: 1, 3). The United States European Recovery Program provided long-term aid, but it also imposed policies intended to stabilize the economy of post-War Europe; this exceptional exercise of power incited strong response in France (Anne O'Hare McCormic, "Street Scenes in a Show Staged for Congress," *The New York Times* 17 November 1947: 20).

Beginning on 10 November, there was a wave of strikes in France. Following a general strike in Marseille on 15 November, conflicts escalated until 10 December, when they were halted by mobilization of 80,000 reservists and the enactment of laws for the "défense de la République" (Anne Simonin, Hélène Clastres, *Les Idées en France 1945–1988: Une chronologie*, Le Débat [Paris: Gallimard, 1989] 58).

THOMAS MACGREEVY
DUBLIN

24.11.47   6 rue des Favorites
                                                Paris 15

My dear Tom

Forgive my long silence.

We had a couple of months in Menton, difficult months, but with good sun & sea. The winter is setting in now in Paris. No heating in this house for the 6th year in succession. Things are very bad, with a badness that won't lead anywhere I fear, perhaps only, after an ineffectual skirmish, to French Yankeeism and then war. Life even for margin people like me is increasingly difficult. Only the low rent makes it possible.[1]

I have been working very hard and have just finished another book, a longish one for me, called *Molloy*, in French. *Murphy* is out in French, badly translated by me, and is not worth reading. "The Edition" is in a bad way here and there are bankruptcies all over the place. Hamish Hamilton sat on "Watt" for 6 months, then turned yellow in the end. *Mercier et Camier* is due from Bordas next year sometime.[2]

I had a letter from Charles, from London, on his way to S. Africa.[3]

I had hoped mother would come to France this winter, at least as far as Paris, and perhaps to the south, but she is worse and can't face it. I am sending her a new Swiss medicine that I hope may do her good. She is very lonely and desolate and can't write to me any more. There seems to be some conspiracy (nothing to do with Frank) to have her put away in a nursing home. I hope she will never consent to this.[4]

I had a letter from Maria Jolas asking me to do translations for the "new" Transition. I declined, in spite of poverty. No news of Norah & Giorgio. I haven't been to see Lucia.[5]

I hope things with you are as well as they can me [*for* be] and that all the family is well. I see nobody, just work and struggle to keep going. Sauf imprévu I won't be in Dublin before summer. Write to me. My love to Jack Yeats. And my greetings to all your household.[6]

> Ever affectionately
>
> Sam

ALS; l leaf, 2 sides; TCD, MS 10402/174.

1   Menton: 15 August 1947, and n. 4.
SB refers to the economic unrest and waves of strikes, devaluation, and shortages (see 18 November 1947, n. 3). By 22 November, "coal production was brought nearly to a standstill and other industries were halted by strikes, which Communist leaders proclaimed were designed to defeat the European Recovery Program" (Harold Callender, "French Crisis, at Bottom, is an Economic One," *The New York Times* 23 November 1947: 119).

2   *Molloy*: 15 August 1947, n. 3.
Murphy: 27 August 1947, n. 1. The financial difficulties of Bordas may have delayed the release of *Murphy*, for SB's first mention of having it in hand is in November 1947.
The first reference to Hamish Hamilton's interest in *Watt* comes in SB's letter to George Reavey of 15 August; news of the publisher's rejection is mentioned in SB's letter to Reavey of 18 November. By saying that the novel has been with Hamish Hamilton for six months, SB implies that *Watt* had been sent to them as early as 14 May, when SB wrote to Reavey: "Anyhow do with it as you please." That Reavey had acted on behalf of the novel is confirmed by SB's letter to Reavey of 25 June: "Thanks for your letter, & for the trouble you are going to about Watt. If anyone can place the book you can" (TxU, Reavey collection).
Although *Mercier et Camier* was contracted by Bordas, it was not published by them.

3   Charles Prentice (c. 1892–1949; Profile, I).

4   SB's mother suffered from Parkinson's disease. Parpanit, produced by Geigy in Switzerland, is mentioned by SB in his letter of 23 June [after 1944, before 1950] to Yvonne Lefèvre (b. 1921), a pharmacist in Isigny-sur-Mer, Calvados. SB had known her family in Saint-Lô (James Knowlson and Elizabeth Knowlson, eds., *Beckett Remembering, Remembering Beckett: A Centenary Celebration* [New York: Arcade, 2006] 91–92).

Frank Beckett.

5   SB's refusal, at this time, to undertake translations for *Transition*: 2 August 1947.

James Joyce's widow Nora Joyce (née Barnacle, 1884–1951; Profile, I) and their son Giorgio (1905–1976; Profile, I) were living in Zurich. Lucia Joyce was in a sanatorium in the Paris suburb of Ivry. SB incorrectly writes Nora with a final "h."

6   "Sauf imprévu" (barring accidents).

MacGreevy had warmly reviewed Jack B. Yeats's exhibition at the Victor Waddington Galleries in October 1947; he urged that Yeats's painting *Above the Fair* (NGI, 1147; Pyle 774) be acquired by the National Gallery of Ireland, an effort that resulted in the presentation of the painting to the National Gallery by "Reverend Senen on behalf of a group of private citizens" ("Brilliant Yeats Exhibition," *The Sunday Independent* 5 October 1947: 2; *National Gallery of Ireland: Illustrated Summary Catalogue of Paintings*, intro. Homan Potterton [Dublin: Gill and Macmillan, 1981] 205; Pyle, *Jack B. Yeats: A Catalogue Raisonné of the Oil Paintings*, II, 697–698).

MacGreevy's widowed sister, Honora Phelan (née McGreevy, known as Nora, 1891–1974), and her daughters Elizabeth, Margaret, and Patricia lived with MacGreevy (www.macgreevy.org/about.jsp, accessed on 17 August 2009).

CHRONOLOGY 1948

1948	before 4 January	SB unable to receive money from Irish Bank; applies to UNESCO for employment.
	13 January	Pierre Bordas informs Jacoba van Velde that he cannot publish *Molloy* immediately.
	15 February	Publication of *Transition Forty-Eight* no. 1.
	8–27 March	Bram and Geer van Velde exhibition, Kootz Gallery, New York; SB writes text for the invitation card.
	May	"Peintres de l'empêchement" published in *Derrière le Miroir*.
	14 May	Declaration of the State of Israel.
	21 May	SB takes Georges Duthuit to see Bram van Velde's work.
	30 May	Finishes *Malone meurt*.
	4 June	Opening of Geer and Bram van Velde exhibition, Galerie Maeght.
	15 June	SB's "Three Poems" published in *Transition Forty-Eight*, no. 2.
	21–28 June	MacGreevy in Paris. SB attends *Andromaque* with him at the Comédie-Française.
	24 June	Blockade of Berlin by the Soviet Union.
	8 July	SB retyping *Malone meurt*.
	14 July	Travels to Dublin.
	19 July	MacGreevy is made Chevalier de l'Ordre de la Légion d'Honneur for his services to the arts.
	11 August	SB attends the private viewing of the Irish Exhibition of Living Art at the National College of Art.
	c. 1 September	Travels from Dublin to Paris.
	29 September	Finishes retyping *Malone meurt*.

October	Publication of *Transition Forty-Eight*, no. 3.
9 October	SB begins writing *En attendant Godot*.
November	Patrick Waldberg reviews *Murphy* in *Paru*.
30 December	Death of Arthur Darley. Shortly after, SB writes the poem "Mort de A.D."

4.1.48   Paris

My dear Tom

Very glad to have your letter from Dunquin and to know you were enjoying your time there. It would do you good to get away more often, from family and drudgery. I wish you could go to Lugano or Vevey, with plenty of money and no obligations.[1] I should like to get out of Paris myself, not to the south, to flat green country, not too green but as flat as possible, with only woods interrupting the horizons. However there is no prospect of our going anywhere. Fortunately the weather is wonderful. To-day I had a long walk along by the Seine in flood, the water spilling over the banks at the Pont de l'Alma, in the warm sunshine, without a coat.[2] I am tired, from overwriting probably. A book of short stories, two "novels" and a play in under two years.[3] They go out into the usual void and I hear little more about them. Jean Vilar is taken with the play and nibbling. The French Murphy fell stillborn from the press as I think Dr J. said.[4] Molloy is a long book, the second last of the series begun with Murphy, if it can be said to be a series. The last is begun and then I hope I'll hear no more of him.[5] Watt was "nearly" taken in London, I forget by whom. Reavey is looking after it. Perhaps in another couple of years a mug will be forthcoming. Forgive all these details about my work. My life seems to be little else. I am glad the little poem lasts for you. I shall send you the Bones this week. I had quite forgotten you had asked me for them. Also the Confessions for Margaret. I am very glad to hear she has had the courage to break away from her teaching. Don't hesitate to ask me for any texts she can't get in Dublin or that you would like to have yourself.[6]

It was good of you to remember mother at Xmas. She really can't write at all any more. I seldom have news from her. I have hopes that the new medicine I sent over will do her good. Alan has been to great trouble in administering it and writes me encouraging news of the effects. I wish she was back in New Place with her old maid Mary back again.[7]

I saw Maria Jolas. She wrote asking me to help her revise her husband's translations of René Char! Je suis une bonne poire.[8] She had seen Nora and Giorgio in Switzerland. They seem to be knocking it out better. Lucia is still at Ivry. All debts paid off. Delmas, the director, is dead. I don't go out any more. Maria has been out and is kind to her. She told me that Delmas said to her one day that he had hopes for Lucia as long as I continued to visit her, but none any more when I ceased going. Full of news and chat the Jolas woman always was.[9] Gilbert is back on the eastern island. I haven't seen him.[10]

While I was in Ireland Nora McGuinness gave me a pound to buy an art publication for her here. I haven't been able to find it and wrote asking her for more details or to name an alternative purchase. No reply. You might bring the matter up if you see her. If I don't hear from her this month on the subject I'll send her back her pound.[11]

The news of France is very depressing, depresses me anyhow. All the wrong things, all the wrong way. It is hard sometimes to feel the France that one clung to, that I still cling to. I don't mean material conditions, which are appalling. It is quite impossible for me to live now with my pittance. I had hoped that my books would make up the difference. But there is little chance of their pleasing here more than elsewhere. The ten or fifteen thousand francs advance, when they are taken, last about a fortnight.[12] I have been reduced to applying for employment to UNESCO.[13] Suzanne earns a little money with her dressmaking. That is what we are living on at present. To crown everything my bank is having trouble with the department of finance over my account, I mean the bank in Dublin. I don't understand what it's all about. So it's a quiet and meagre life. With no friends, with only work to give it meaning.

I hope Eire will be given the Savonarola and Boccaccio she merits, by the Pearl and Killiney Golf Club. I haven't read Dante for years. Have you read Malebranche?[14] I have been too restless and nervous to read anything this long time, but feel the old lust for study stirring in me. I hear great accounts of Jouvet's Dom Juan. But I havent been to a theatre or a concert or a gallery since returning from the south.[15]

Remember me very affectionately to Jack Yeats. I have his Morning and Evening and long thoughts of him and his work.[16] I feel he doesn't mind my not writing.

Remember me very kindly to your sister and nieces. And for yourself, my dear Tom, all you know.

Ever

s/ Sam

TLS; 1 leaf, 2 sides; TCD, MS 10402/175.

1 Dunquin, Co. Kerry, is a cliff-top village overlooking the Blasket Islands, near the Dingle Peninsula.

Lugano, Switzerland, is on the northern shore of Lake Lugano; Vevey, Switzerland, is on the northeastern shore of Lake Geneva.

2 The Pont de l'Alma crosses the Seine between the Place de l'Alma, Paris 8, and the Place de la Résistance, Paris 7.

3 SB refers to the stories "Premier amour," "L'Expulsé," "Le Calmant," and "La Fin," the novels *Mercier et Camier* and *Molloy*, and the play *Eleutheria*.

4 Pierre Bordas wrote of the French edition of *Murphy*: "J'envoyai plus de deux cents exemplaires de services de presse, sans qu'un seul article sortît" (I sent more than 200 review copies, not a single article came of it) (Bordas, *L'Edition est une aventure*, 186). The first review appeared in *L'Age Nouveau* 24 ([? January] 1948) 92–93 (IMEC, Bordas, 03.14, Dossier de presse, *Murphy*).

"All, all but truth, drops dead-born from the press" is from Alexander Pope's *Epilogue to the Satires*, "Dialogue II" (*Imitations of Horace, with An Epistle to Dr. Arbuthnot, and The Epilogue to the Satires*, ed. John Butt, 2nd edn. [London: Methuen and Co., 1953] 325). Samuel Johnson adapts the original when writing of Sir Richard Blackmore's *Eliza* (1705): "She 'dropped,' as it seems, 'dead-born from the press'" (*Lives of the English Poets*, II, ed. George Birkbeck Hill [Oxford: Clarendon Press, 1905] 242).

5 SB had begun to write *Malone meurt*; the AMS is dated as "begun 27 November 1947, completed 30 May 1948" (Lake, ed., *No Symbols Where None Intended*, 57).

6 The poem that MacGreevy admires has not been identified: it may have been published in SB's *Echo's Bones and Other Precipitates* (1935). MacGreevy's niece Margaret Phelan had been a primary school teacher for two years, and then in 1947 went to University College, Dublin, to read French and Irish; she does not recall the book referred to here only as *Confessions* (Margaret Farrington, 30 April 2010).

7 Alan Thompson, with whom SB had worked at the Irish Red Cross Hospital in Saint-Lô, was administering the medication, Parpanit, to May Beckett; it was most effective as one of a combination of drugs, and dosages had to be closely monitored.

New Place was May Beckett's home in Foxrock, built after she sold Cooldrinagh. Her maid was Mary Blane (b. 1885), who had been with the Beckett family for many years (Census of Ireland, 1911).

8 The first issue of *Transition* published "The Pulverized Poem," a translation by Eugene Jolas of *Le Poème pulvérisé*, by René Char (1907–1988) (*Transition Forty-Eight* no. 1 [February 1948] 33–55).
"Je suis une bonne poire" (I am a soft touch).

9 By 1948, Nora and Giorgio Joyce were getting on better (Brenda Maddox, *Nora: The Real Life of Molly Bloom* [Boston: Houghton Mifflin, 1988] 358).
   Dr. François Achille-Delmas died on 8 October 1947 (Michèle Rault, Archives, Ivry, 2 September 2009; "Le Carnet du Monde," *Le Monde* 12–13 October 1947: 4).

10 Stuart Gilbert (1883–1969) lived on the Ile Saint-Louis, Paris.

11 Irish artist Norah McGuinness (1883–1969). SB was last in Ireland in April and May 1947.

12 In December 1945, the French franc had been devalued from 200 to 480 francs to the British pound; in the face of low wages, rising prices, and the need to be competitive in world markets, the French franc was devalued again on 26 January 1948, from 480 to 864 francs to the British pound.

13 Jean Thomas (1900–1983; Profile, I), Jean-Jacques Mayoux (1901–1987), and Emile Delavenay, all of whom Beckett had known while at the Ecole Normale Supérieure, were with UNESCO when SB applied for work as a translator there. Thomas was Director of Cultural Activities with UNESCO from 1947 to 1954; Mayoux, who had been Director of the International Institute of Intellectual Cooperation when it became part of UNESCO, worked as Director of Translation of Great Works within the Department of Culture from 1947 to 1952; Delavenay was Head of the Documents and Publications Service from 1949. Mayoux proposed SB as a translator (Emile Delavenay, 11 October 1992; Unesco/Biographies/Secretariat).

14 The Pearl was a Dublin pub frequented by the literati; Killiney is a suburb of Dublin. MacGreevy's essay "Dante – and Modern Ireland" was published in *The Father Matthew Record* (41.1 [January 1948] 3–4). SB refers MacGreevy to the French Cartesian Nicolas Malebranche (1638–1715).

15 Louis Jouvet (1887–1951) was performing in the production of Molière's *Dom Juan* then at the Théâtre de l'Athénée in Paris; Robert Kemp wrote: "Non, ce n'est pas Molière. Mais c'est très beau ... Jouvet est admirable" (No, this is not Molière. But it is very fine ... Jouvet is admirable); "Don Juan à l'Athénée," *Le Monde* 15 December 1947: 3).

16 *A Morning* and *Regatta Evening* by Jack B. Yeats: 10 May 1945, n. 4.

THOMAS MACGREEVY
DUBLIN

18.3.48   Paris
My dear Tom

   Many thanks for your goodness in the matter of the flowers. You went I fear to a great deal of trouble and it looks as if you paid the carriage out of your own pocket. Mother was delighted.[1]

I feel from her letters she is very much worse and very depressed in spirits. Frank seldom writes, so I have no means of checking this impression.

I continue to receive no money from Ireland, so have been stupidly busy with lessons & translations.[2] I have a great desire to get on with my own work, but can't get near it at the moment. I see a little clearly at last what my writing is about and feel I have perhaps 10 years courage and energy to get the job done. The feeling of getting oneself in perspective is a strange one, after so many years of expression in blindness.[3] Perhaps it is an illusion. Eleutheria is hithering, thithering and beginning to be spoken of a little. I think it will see the boards in time, even if only for a few nights. But never those of the Gate.[4] The French Murphy so far has sold 6 copies! There is one very friendly review. Bordas (the editor) blames it on me who refuse, mulishly perhaps, to do the "service de presse", i.e. send enhommaged copies to the critics.[5]

I have not seen Thomas since. He suggested, when we meet, my looking him up at UNESCO and our spending an evening together. But I haven't done so. It appears he is all-powerful in the place.[6] There is an atmosphere of futility & incredulity there that is overwhelming. I don't think it will last very long, or in a very modified form.

I am glad to have news of Jack Yeats. I shall write to him soon. In the meantime give him my affectionate salutations.

Artaud died the other day in Lucia's home at Ivry.[7]

I shall be in Ireland in June or July at the earliest. If one dare speak of the future. If it must be as bad as is feared here, it will be bad for me in France & not in Ireland.[8]

Yes I received your Dante article and reading it was reminded of our old talks 20 years ago in Paris. Not because the article owed anything to me, but because it was you. I felt you constrained, as in all your work for The Record, and found myself wishing again you were writing more for yourself and less for Ireland. I know you are doing what you want to do, in a sense. But it must leave you often with a starved feeling.[9]

Bon courage, my dear Tom, & kindest regards to sister and nieces.
Ever yours affectionately
Sam.

ALS; 2 leaves, 2 sides; *env to* Thomas MacGreevy Esq, 74 Fitzwilliam Place, Dublin. IRLANDE., *pm* 20-3-48, Paris; TCD, MS 10402/176.

1   May Beckett's birthday was 1 March.

2   SB's difficulty in receiving money from Ireland: 4 January 1948.

3   SB replaced "days" by "years" in this sentence.

4   *Eleutheria* had been read by Agnès Capri and Jean Vilar; SB refers to Dublin's Gate Theatre.

5   The dossier de presse for the French edition of *Murphy* includes many announcements of the book, but only one review, by René Dam, who said of the novel: "Un chef-d'œuvre du genre" ("Le Disciple," *L'Age Nouveau* [? January 1948] 92–93; see IMEC, Bordas, Service de communication, Beckett, S., *Murphy*, Bordas 03.14). The only other review that has been found is by American poet and art historian Patrick Waldberg (1913–1985) ("Murphy, par Samuel Beckett," *Paru* 48 [November 1948] 22–23).

6   Jean Thomas.

7   Antonin Artaud died on 4 March 1948 at the age of fifty-two at the Maison de Santé, Ivry.

8   SB replaced "may" by "dare."
SB refers to the instability in France following devaluation (see 4 January 1948).

9   MacGreevy's essay on Dante in *The Father Matthew Record*: 4 January 1948, n. 14.

BRAM VAN VELDE

mardi 18 mai [1948]   6 Rue des Favorites
                                                       Paris 15me

Cher ami

Georges Duthuit, que j'aime bien et qui sait ce que c'est que la peinture, est passé chez moi hier et a été très impressionné par vos deux tableaux.[1] Puis-je l'amener chez vous vendredi prochain le 21 entre quatre et cinq heures? Il part le mois prochain à New York où il va représenter la France dans un débat sur l'art moderne, et il serait souhaitable qu'il puisse parler de votre travail en connaissance de cause.[2] Il a été visiblement très touché hier, surtout par la gouache.

Pas la peine de parler de ceci à Maeght, je vous expliquerai pourquoi.[3]
Donc sauf contre-avis à vendredi.

Affectueusement à vous deux

s/ <u>Sam</u>

TLS; 1 leaf, 1 side; Putman collection. *Dating*: Friday was 21 May 1948. Previous publication, Stoullig and Schoeller, eds., *Bram van Velde*, 165.

Tuesday 18 May [1948]   6 Rue des Favorites

                                         Paris 15me

Dear Bram

Georges Duthuit, of whom I'm very fond, and who really knows what painting is, called round here yesterday and was much impressed by your two pictures.[1] May I bring him along to your place next Friday 21st between four and five o'clock? He is leaving next month for New York where he will be representing France in a debate on modern art, and it would be desirable if he could talk about your work from first-hand knowledge.[2] He was clearly much touched yesterday, especially by the gouache. No point in mentioning this to Maeght; I'll explain why.[3] See you on Friday, then, unless I hear from you to the contrary.

Love to you both

s/ Sam

1   The untitled oil and untitled gouache by Bram van Velde then in SB's possession are now in the Musée National d'Art Moderne, Centre Georges Pompidou (*Sans titre*, 1937, Inv. AM 1982–244; *Sans titre*, 1939–40, Inv. AM 1982–243).

2   Georges Duthuit was invited to participate in a panel of fifteen experts in *Life* magazine's "Roundtable on Modern Art" held in the Penthouse of the Museum of Modern Art in New York from 11 to 13 June. The question posed: "Is modern art, considered as a whole, a good or bad development? … Is it something that responsible people can support, or may they neglect it as a minor and impermanent phase of culture?" (Russell W. Davenport, with Winthrop Sargeant, "A Life Round Table on Modern Art," *Life* [11 October 1948] 56; the James Thrall Soby Papers in the MOMA Archives contain a transcript of the symposium and Soby's notes on the discussion: I.21.16.)

In an interview with *The New York Times*, Duthuit mentioned Bram van Velde's work. Duthuit was described as a "well-known writer on art, literature and philosophy and editor of the now-revived magazine, 'Transition.'" The article went on to say, "As he is a leader in the advance-guard circles which set the patterns of taste the public ultimately follows, his sentiment has significance." Duthuit said, "Most of the younger painters whom I admire are trying to keep as close as possible to the initial sensation, to keep in touch with the object at the same time that they indulge in the greatest possible freedom of interpretation." He named Edouard Pignon (1905–1993), Pierre Tal-Coat (né Pierre Jacob, 1905–1985), Francis Tailleux (1913–1981), and Van Velde (presumably Bram): "all concerned with capturing the first sensation" (Aline B. Louchheim, "A French Viewpoint: Visiting Writer Sums Up the Post-War Scene," *The New York Times* 27 June 1948: II, 6).

3   Aimé Maeght, at whose Galerie Maeght Bram and Geer van Velde's exhibition was to open on 4 June 1948.

GEORGES DUTHUIT
PARIS

27.5.48   Paris
Cher ami

Je suis obligé de vous demander de l'argent. 6000 francs. En voici le détail.

Appréciation	
texte Gracq	500
Pichette Lettre	
Ponge	3000
3 séances avec	
Maria (12 heures)	2500
	6000[1]

Je ne sais pas quelle impression vous ont laissée les peintures de van Velde. J'ai senti à un moment donné que vous faisiez beaucoup de réserves. Moi avec mon coupe-fil je perds facilement la tête.[2] C'est la misérable envie de ne pas être toujours seul. Ou d'être seul impunément, d'errer sous les palmiers sans que les vautours vous chient dessus.[3] Aussi cet infini de l'empêchement tire-t-il sur   [Fragment]

AL; 1 leaf, 1 side, fragment; Duthuit collection.

27.5.48   Paris

Dear Georges

I am forced to ask you for money. 6000 francs. Here are the details.

Appreciation	
Gracq text	500
Pichette Letter	
Ponge	3000
3 sessions with	
Maria (12 hours)	<u>2500</u>
	6000[1]

I do not know what impression the Van Velde paintings made on you. I felt at one moment that you had quite a few reservations. I, with my special free pass, lose my head easily.[2] It is the wretched longing not to be always alone. Or to be alone with impunity, to wander beneath the palm-trees without being shat upon by the vultures.[3] And so this infinity of preventedness reaches over into   [Fragment]

1   SB completed many translations, and revised translations by others, at Duthuit's request; opinions differ as to what exactly his contribution consists in, not least because he did not sign his own translations. It is not known what "Appréciation" refers to; "texte Gracq" may refer to "Literature Hits below the Belt" by Julien Gracq (1910–2007), though this was not published until more than two years later, in *Transition Fifty* no. 6 ([October 1950] 7–26), where translation is credited to J. G. Weightman; translation of "Letter – Red" by Henri Pichette (1924–2000; *Transition Forty-Eight* no. 2 [June 1948] 5–15) is credited to Jack T. Nile and Bernard Frechtmann, while translation of Pichette's "APoème 4" which appears in the same issue (24–43) and receives no translator's credit is probably by SB. "Ponge" probably refers to an article by Francis Ponge (1899–1988), "Braque, or Modern Art as Event and Pleasure" (*Transition Forty-Nine* no. 5 [December 1949] 43–47), which receives no translator's credit.

SB had been working with Maria Jolas on translations for *Transition*.

2   SB omits the "e" required on "file" in "coupe-file."

Duthuit's visit to Bram van Velde's studio: SB to Bram van Velde, 18 May [1948]. An exhibition of Geer and Bram van Velde's work was forthcoming at the Galerie Maeght, Paris.

3 SB adapts a phrase from Goethe's *Die Wahlverwandtschaften*: "Es wandelt niemand ungestraft unter Palmen" (No one wanders beneath palm trees with impunity) (in *Die Leiden des jungen Werthers, Die Wahlverwandtschaften, Kleine Prosa, Epen*, ed. Waltraud Wiethölter and Christoph Brecht [Frankfurt: Deutscher Klassiker Verlag, 1994], VIII of *Sämtliche Werke: Briefe, Tagebücher und Gespräche*, ed. Friedmar Apel, Hendrik Birus, and Dieter Borchmeyer [1985–] 452).

GEORGE REAVEY
LONDON

July 8th [1948]   Paris
My dear George

Glad you improved the obscure hour on leaving us. Now you are back in the vicarage.[1]

I fear there is little chance of my having 30000 words for Horizon by the date you mention. If French was not a bar I could let them have the first half of Molloy, about that length. As you know, I can't work in Ireland, where I shall be from next Wednesday till probably the end of August. But if anything starts, continues and ends I shall let you know.[2] I am now retyping, for rejection by the publishers, Malone Meurt, the last I hope of the series Murphy, Watt, Mercier & Camier, Molloy, not to mention the 4 Nouvelles & Eleuthéria. A young publisher here is interested, I forget his name, Editions K I think, and I am preparing him for burial. All that will see in time the sorry light of the domaine public. Until when smile boys smile.[3] Write to me in Ireland to my mother's address, New Place, Foxrock, Co Dublin. I am sending you Transition 2 and have not forgotten, for Bill, the Paru or Critique, I forget which, with the panegyric of the poet whose name sincerely I can't recall at the moment.[4] We had a card this morning from Bram & Marthe, happy in the rain and shine of the Vosges. Tom MacGreevy left a week ago, exhausted with arting around. He stood us Andromaque at the Français. Je ne sais de tout temps quelle injuste puissance Laisse le crime en paix et poursuit l'innocence. De quelque part sur moi que je tourne les yeux, Je ne vois que malheurs qui condamnent les Dieux. Voire.[5] Remember me to Bill and Helen and believe me yours, my dear George, ever.[6]

s/ Sam

TLS; 1 leaf, 1 side; *AN, figures, in AH*; TxU, Reavey collection. *Dating*: confirmed by MacGreevy's visit to Paris to attend the International Congress of Art Critics, 21-28 June 1948.

1 Reavey, who had recently spent an evening with SB in Paris, lived at 43 Vicarage Court, Kensington Church St., London 8. SB plays with words from the Victorian hymn by Isaac Watts: "How doth the little busy bee / improve each shining hour."

2 Cyril Connolly (1903-1974) edited *Horizon: A Review of Literature and Art*, from 1940 to 1950; the journal included French writing in translation. The first part of *Molloy* is over 100 pages (7-124).

3 SB had completed the manuscript of *Malone meurt* by the end of May 1948 (see 4 January 1948, n. 5).

In the left margin, on the line with *Malone meurt*, SB types L'Absent, which was the initial title of *Malone meurt* (Admussen, *The Samuel Beckett Manuscripts*, 66).

Alain Gheerbrant (b. 1920), French poet and explorer, headed the Paris publishing house K éditeur from 1945 to 1949 (Alain Gheerbrant and Léon Aichelbaum [interview], *K éditeur*, bibliography by Léon Aichelbaum and Raymond-Josué Seckel, [Cognac: Le Temps qu'il fait, 1991]). The bibliography of *K éditeur* lists the books published by this firm, as well as projects that remained unpublished; there is no mention of SB.

SB invokes the First World War song "Pack Up Your Troubles in Your Old Kit Bag".

4 *Transition Forty-Eight* no. 2 had been published on 15 June 1948.

SB refers to George Reavey's friend William McAlpine.

Critique: Revue Générale des Publications Françaises et Etrangères was founded in 1946 by Georges Bataille (1897-1962) and published by Editions de Minuit. *Paru: l'Actualité Littéraire, Intellectuelle et Artistique* was published in Monaco from January 1944 to August/September 1950 when it merged with *Cahiers du Monde Nouveau* to form *Monde Nouveau Paru*.

The "panegyric" to which SB refers has not been found.

5 Thomas MacGreevy attended the first International Congress of Art Critics from 21 to 28 June, organized by the review *Arts* and held at UNESCO; he describes the experience in his essay "Art Criticism, and a Visit to Paris," *The Father Matthew Record* 41.9 (September 1948) 4-8.

MacGreevy also describes seeing Jean Racine's *Andromaque* with Annie Ducaux (1908-1996) in the title role, saying that he saw it "with friends" at the Comédie-Française "the night before I came away"; it was performed on 24 and 29 June ("Les Spectacles," *Le Monde* 25 June 1948: 6; 30 June 1948: 6).

Oreste: "Je ne sais de tout temps quelle injuste Puissance / Laisse le crime en paix et poursuit l'innocence. / De quelque part sur moi que je tourne les yeux, / Je ne vois que malheurs qui condamnent les Dieux." (I do not know what immemorial power / Leaves crime in peace, harasses innocence. / Wherever in my life I turn my eyes, / I see misfortunes that condemn the gods.) (Jean Racine, *Andromaque*, in *Théâtre complet de Racine*, ed. Maurice Rat [Paris: Librairie Garnier Frères, 1947], III.i.65-68; *Andromache*, in

Andromache, Britannicus, Berenice, tr. John Cairncross [London: Penguin Books, 1967] III.i.773–776).

"Voire" (Indeed so).

   6   William and Helen McAlpine.

G E O R G E S D U T H U I T
P A R I S

27/7/48

                                          N E W P L A C E
                                          F O X R O C K
                                          C$^{\underline{O}}$ D U B L I N

Mon cher vieux

    Ce soir je ne dirai rien qui vaille mais en avant quand-même. Merci de votre voix d'un autre monde, de votre amitié, du mal que vous vous donnez pour <u>Murphy</u>. Murphy. Il ne savait pas que ce serait si long, qu'il serait si vil. Il est bien usé, il a très peur, mais il a encore des sourires en réserve, plus jaunes qu'hideux. Aspire-t-on là? Peu him-porte. Fouchet sera gentil peut-être. Queneau – pas la peine, il est contre, et *Murphy* est par trop vulnérable.[1] Vos nouvelles de notre note sont intéressantes. Heureusement que vous êtes là pour nous freiner, dans les premiers temps. Il y en aura d'autres. Ce que nous tenons (!) là est, pour moi, d'une telle évidence, qu'il me semble impossible que d'autres n'y aient pas songé. Mais l'acceptation de l'ignorance, de la pure faiblesse, il faut sans doute la chercher ailleurs que chez les porte-plumes et -pinceaux. Ici je me tais. Mais l'autre soir, aveuglé par le whiskey, je me suis mis à crier et à faire des gestes frénétiques. Mes spectateurs, genre fortement cultivé, ont vite fait de me rappeler à la décence, à renfort de citations des intouchables habituels. J'ai entendu, de loin, des voix graves, douces et raisonnables, profitant du criard pour se faire encore plus merdeuses que d'habitude. Il me semble me rappeler que l'on a cité St. François d'Assise pour me montrer l'antiquité de ce que j'appelais de mes hurlements. Vous parlez d'une pauvreté. Il existe, dans notre Galerie Nationale, un por-trait de lui soi-disant par Rubens et que l'on pourrait à la rigueur accorder au palefrenier de Teniers. Il apparaît dans l'embrasure d'une porte, l'oeil vif et savamment hagard, les stigmates immanquables bien en vue, incapable par amour de Jésus de payer une tournée, le poveretto! Amie mouche! Encore un Chazal au fond.[2] On m'a fait lire du Rimbaud. "Pavillon de viande saignante sur la soie des mers et des fleurs arctiques". J'aimais beaucoup ça il y a 20 ans. "Douceurs".[3] Voire. Ici on a du mal à croire qu'il existe de la poésie et une pensée autophage et maigrissante. De votre équation Sartre-Breton, on peut émerger en effet, il me semble, dans un air pur de grandeur, de conation distinguée et de splendeurs utilitaires, où cesse la duperie où ils se rejoignent, où tous depuis toujours (je vous entends grogner) se sont rejoints, la duperie de l'humain et de l'achevé.[4] Je sens si bien ce que vous dites sur l'espace des Italiens.[5] Je me rappelle un tableau au ZWINGER, un Saint Sébastien d'Antonello da Messina, formidable, formidable. C'était dans la première salle, j'en étais bloqué chaque fois. Espace pur à force de mathématique, carrelage, dalles plutôt, noir et blanc, en longs raccourcis genre Mantegna à vous tirer des gémissements, et le lapidé exposé, s'exposant, à l'admiration des courtisans prenant l'air dominical au balcon, tout ça envahi, mangé par l'humain.[6] Devant une telle oeuvre, une telle victoire sur la réalité du désordre, sur la petitesse du coeur et de l'esprit, on manque se pendre. Demandez-moi de vous en montrer la reproduction, vous la connaissez sans doute. Dire qu'on veut remettre ça, yeux irrémédiablement baissés pour ne pas faire de la peine, en laissant voir tout l'ahurissement de l'ignorance retrouvée, en partie tout au moins. Je voudrais que vous soyez là pour entre autres choses voir les dernières peintures de Yeats.[7] Je pense qu'un jour vous viendrez peut-être. Le poème d'Arp m'a rappelé la manière de Gene. Qu'attend ce dernier pour Sophiser Maria?[8] De qui à propos j'ai reçu une longue lettre sur les démarches à faire pour faire rapatrier, aux frais des amis sinon de la République, les restes que vous devinez. Au fond, c'est Norah et Giorgio qu'il s'agit de ramener en Irlande. Jusqu'au delà des vers il les aura possédés. Ils doivent avoir de belles conversations, les vers, les cadavres cuvés, sur Joyce et Klee, sur Witz aussi peut-être, tel que la tradition l'a conservé.[9] Merci à vous deux d'être gentils pour Suzanne, triste, seule, ne sachant où donner de l'âme, lasse du silence, vite dégoûtée des mots. D'elle ce matin 4 Francs-Tireurs, avec des gauloises dedans.[10] J'ai rêvé de Matisse, il disait, dans un argot de Dublin, qu'il n'en pouvait plus (<u>I'm bet</u>). Mon père disait, dans son dernier coma, Fight, fight, fight.[11] Oui, j'ai de beaux souvenirs. Et qui ne pourront que s'épaissir. Je vais déjeuner, puis aller me promener sur les longues pentes vertes, d'où enfant je voyais par temps clair les montagnes du Pays de Galles. A la nuit tombante mon père, pour m'amuser, mettait feu au genêt. Je boirai quelques pintes dans les auberges de la montagne, ce ne sont pas des auberges, des comptoirs, aux beaux noms de propriétaires défunts, Fox, Lamb, Silke, et le soir viendra enfin, et la mer qui s'allume, le port, la ville, les promontoires.[12] Paysage romantique mais promeneur bien sec. Votre ami

Sam

ALS; 3 leaves, 6 sides; Duthuit collection.

NEW PLACE

FOXROCK

C$^{\underline{o}}$ DUBLIN

<u>27/7/48</u>

My dear Georges,

This evening I shall have nothing sensible to say, but on we go all the same. Thank you for your voice from another world, for your friendship, for the trouble you are taking over *Murphy*. Murphy. He did not know it would take so long, that he would be so base. He is worn out, he is very much afraid, but he still has smiles in reserve, grim rather than hideous. Is that what we aspire to? Hoo cares. Maybe Fouchet will be nice. Queneau – not worth bothering: he is anti, and *Murphy* is far too vulnerable.[1] Your news about our note is interesting. It is fortunate that you are there to put the brakes on for us, in the early stages. There will be others. What we have got hold of (!) there is, for me, so obvious that it seems impossible that other people have not thought of it. But acceptance of ignorance, of pure weakness: for that one must look beyond the pen- or brush-holders. Here I hold my tongue. But the other evening, blinded by whiskey, I started to shout and make frantic gestures. My audience, the highly cultivated kind,

5. Georges Duthuit in his studio at 96 Rue de l'Université in 1962. Behind him, paintings by Jean-Paul Riopelle, Nicolas de Staël, and Henri Matisse

brought me back in no time to decent behaviour, with shoals of quotations from the usual untouchables. From far off I could hear voices grave, sweet and reasonable, taking advantage of the loud-mouth to become even more stinkingly poisonous than usual. I seem to remember that St Francis of Assisi was quoted in order to show me the ancient nature of what I was calling for with my bellowings. Now there is poverty! There exists, in our National Gallery, a portrait of him, supposedly by Rubens, that one might just about allow to be by Teniers' groom. He appears in a doorway, eyes bright with a studied wildness, the inevitable stigmata well on display, unable for love of

Jesus to buy a round, poveretto! Brother fly! Another Chazal, really.[2] I was handed some Rimbaud to read. "The flag of red meat over the silk of the seas and the Arctic flowers". I was very fond of that twenty years ago. "Happiness".[3] Well ... Here it is hard to believe that poetry and a self-devouring, ever-reducing thought can even exist. From your Sartre-Breton equation one may indeed emerge, I think, into a pure air of grandeur, distinguished conation and utilitarian splendour, in which an end is made of the pernicious illusion in which they are at one, in which people everywhere have always been at one (I can hear you groaning), the illusion of the human and the fully realised.[4] I feel so clearly what you say about space and the Italians.[5] I remember a picture in the Zwinger, a St Sebastian by Antonello da Messina – tremendous, tremendous. It was in the first room, and it stopped me in my tracks every time. Pure space by dint of mathematics, tiling, flagstones rather, black and white, with long, Mantegna-style fore-shortenings, that would draw moans from you, and the victim of the stoning, displayed, displaying himself, to the admiration of the courtiers taking the Sunday air on their balconies, the whole thing invaded, eaten into by the human.[6] In front of such a work, such a victory over the reality of disorder, over the pettiness of the heart and mind, it is hard not to go and hang yourself. Get me to show you the reproduction, no doubt you know it. And to think that they intend to go through the whole thing again, eyes irremediably lowered so as not to cause offence by revealing the full bewilderment of ignorance regained, in part at least. I wish you could be here to see, among other things, Yeats's latest paintings.[7] I think maybe one day you will come. The Arp poem reminded me of Gene's manner. What is that gentleman waiting for to do a Sophie gesture on Maria?[8] From whom while I am on the subject I have had a long letter about getting the remains of you-know-who repatriated, at the expense of the friends, if not the Republic. The real point is to get Norah and Giorgio brought back to Ireland. Even from beyond the worms he will have put one over on them. They must have great conversations, the worms, with the bodies fermenting, on Joyce and Klee, on Witz too maybe, as tradition has preserved him.[9] Thanks to both of you for being so kind to Suzanne, sad, lonely, not knowing what way to turn her spirit, weary of silence, soon sickened by words. From her this morning four Francs-Tireurs, with Gauloises inside.[10] I had a dream about Matisse – he was saying, in Dublin slang, that he was exhausted ("I'm bet"). My father, in his final coma, kept saying Fight, fight, fight.[11] Yes, I have wonderful memories. Which can only grow in volume. I am going to have lunch, then go for a walk on the long green slopes from where, on a clear day, when I was a child, I used to see the mountains of Wales. As night fell my father, to amuse me, used to set fire to the broom. I shall drink a few pints in the mountain inns – they're not inns, just bars, with the lovely names of dead proprietors, Fox, Lamb, Silke, and finally evening will come, and the sea light up – the harbour, the town, the headlands.[12] Romantic landscape, but dry old stick of a traveller. Your friend

    Sam

---

1 Georges Duthuit was attempting to raise interest in SB's *Murphy*, published one year previously in French. Max-Pol Fouchet was, amongst other things, a reviewer and Advisory Editor on *Transition*; Raymond Queneau (1903–1976) held at this time, among other influential roles, that of Secrétaire Général of the Editions Gallimard.

2 *St. Francis of Assisi* (NGI 51) by Peter Paul Rubens. SB probably refers to David Teniers the Elder (1582–1649) rather than to his son David Teniers the Younger (1610–1690). Mauritian writer (and later painter) Malcolm de Chazal (1902–1981) was becoming known in Paris at this time; he will be the subject of an article by Aimé Patri, "Discovery of Malcolm de Chazal," in *Transition Forty-Eight* no. 3 (October 1948) 5–13.

    "Poveretto" (poor little man).

3 SB cites from Arthur Rimbaud's "Barbare," misquoting "Le pavillon en viande" (Rimbaud, *Œuvres complètes*, ed. André Guyaux and Aurélia Cervoni, Bibliothèque de la Pléiade [Paris: Gallimard, 2009] 309; *Rimbaud: Complete Works, Selected Letters*, tr. Wallace Fowlie [Chicago: University of Chicago Press, 1966] 244–245).

4 SB refers to Georges Duthuit's article "Sartre's Last Class II" (tr. Colin Summerford, *Transition Forty-Eight* no. 2, 98–116), in which much scornful play is made with a rumor that André Breton, the high priest of Surrealism, and the fiercely rational Jean-Paul Sartre are making common cause.

5 It is not possible to say with certainty which text SB was reading, but hostility to the Western mimetic tradition was cardinal to Duthuit's aesthetic, hostility to Italian art in particular. Probably, SB was reading a draft of the early pages of Duthuit's work which incorporated and modified articles Duthuit had written between 1929 and 1931 for *Cahiers d'Art*, which was published as *Les Fauves* (Geneva: Editions des Trois Collines, 1949; re-edited in a critical edition by Rémi Labrusse [Paris: Michalon, 2006]; all future references are to the latter). *Les Fauves* was translated, with SB's help, as *The Fauvist Painters* (tr. Ralph Manheim [New York: Wittenborn, Schultz, 1950]; for a history of the publishing of this work, see Rémi

Labrusse, "Note sur l'histoire du texte et sur la présente édition," in Duthuit, *Les Fauves*, xxvii-xxxvi). Duthuit writes:

> Classical paintings remain flat, and this everyone knows, but people prefer not to say so, because that's how our masterpieces are, and any attempt to discuss them meets with a stern reprimand. We live in material extension, it has depth and the masterpiece has not, but represents an ideal world: therefore silence and respect. And it is into the midst of the ideal that we are thrust by these captivating and redoubtable geniuses, shackled by space and bowed beneath the axe of time, once and for all, without reprieve. And that is why their works had become unbearable, why it became necessary to impeach the lofty tenors and noble basses of the Italians. No point in seeking to prolong one's suffering. None of these prodigious personalities of the art galleries, churches and palaces which they transform instantly into museums, catacombs in which no glimmer of things to come is tolerated, none of these personalities overthrew the barriers which space and time interpose between the minds of men. On the contrary, it was rather to be feared that, after them, the bolts were drawn forever. (*The Fauvist Painters*, 7.)

Duthuit's hostility to Italian art was so radical and pervasive that Yves Bonnefoy opens his essay on Duthuit's early writings: "Georges Duthuit n'aura jamais eu de mots assez durs pour discréditer l'art italien" (For Georges Duthuit, there will never have been words harsh enough with which to discredit Italian art) ("Georges Duthuit" [Introduction] in Georges Duthuit, *Représentation et présence: premiers écrits et travaux (1923-1952)* [Paris: Flammarion, 1974] 5).

6 *The Martyrdom of Saint Sebastian* (c. 1475, RPG 52) by Antonello da Messina is housed in the Gemäldegalerie Alte Meister, Dresden. SB had admired the painting during a visit to the Zwinger Museum in 1937 (see 16 February 1937 to McGreevy). SB's choice of the word "lapidé" (victim of a stoning) to describe Saint Sebastian is odd, given the painting presents him in the traditional manner as transfixed with arrows.

In his article "Beckett et la peinture: le témoignage d'une correspondance inédite," Rémi Labrusse cites this passage as illustrative of SB's understanding of Duthuit's view of the adverse consequences of the Italian Renaissance, which for Duthuit committed painting to a mimetic mastering of appearances rather than what was to be found in Byzantine art and in the work of Fauvist painters: a new illumination of space, and thereby a reanimation of the viewer's relation to reality, what Labrusse calls "des représentations qui fussent un début plutôt qu'une fin, une impulsion plutôt qu'une expression, et qui, dénouant les chaînes de l'espace, ne constitueraient pas du sens comme tel" (representations that would be a beginning rather than an end, an impulsion rather than an expression, and which, loosening the chains of space, would not make sense as such) (*Critique*, 46.519-520 [August-September 1990] 670-671).

7 From 1947 to 1948, Jack B. Yeats produced 113 paintings; it is not known which of these SB particularly admired (Pyle, *Jack B. Yeats: A Catalogue Raisonnné of the Oil Paintings*, II, 738-875).

8 The poem by Jean Arp (1886-1966) that SB has read is likely to have been "Sophie" (Jean Arp, *On My Way: Poetry and Essays 1912-1947* [New York: Wittenborn, Schultz, 1948] 28-31; rpt. in Jean Arp, *Jours effeuillés: poèmes, essais, souvenirs 1920-1965* [Paris: Gallimard, 1966] 301-302). Its style reminds SB of that of Eugene Jolas. Arp's wife Sophie Taeuber-Arp had died as a consequence of an accident in 1943, and in the following years Arp wrote many tributes to her, including "Sophie"; this leading, presumably, to SB's suggestion that Eugene Jolas might "Sophiser" his wife Maria.

9   Reburial in Ireland was discussed for James Joyce, who had died in Zurich in 1941. "Nora, backed by Giorgio, felt that the Irish government should do no less for its greatest writer of prose than for its greatest writer of poetry [Yeats]"; she enlisted the help of Maria Jolas and Joyce's patron Harriet Shaw Weaver (1876–1961), and she later approached Constantine Curran (1880–1975) and Count Gerald Edward O'Kelly de Gallach (1890–1968, first Irish Minister to France in 1929 and Special Counsellor to the Irish Mission in France during the Second World War), to see if "the Irish government or the Royal Irish Academy would consider requesting the return of Joyce's body to Ireland" (Maddox, *Nora*, 362–363).

Paul Klee died in 1940 and was also buried in Switzerland. Konrad Witz (c. 1410–c. 1445) also died in Switzerland, in either Geneva or Basel.

SB incorrectly adds an "h" to the end of "Nora."

10   *Franc-Tireur* was a newspaper, published clandestinely in France between December 1941 and August 1944, and as a daily from 21 August 1944 to 17 November 1957.

Gauloises: at the time, the most popular brand of French cigarette, manufactured and sold by the State-owned SEITA.

11   The painter Henri-Emile-Benoît Matisse, who was Duthuit's father-in-law. "I'm bet" (Irish colloquialism for "I'm beaten").

Beckett's father's dying words (see 2 July 1933 to McGreevy).

12   Johnnie Fox's Pub had been in business since 1798 in Glencullen, near Dublin. Lamb Doyle's pub and restaurant is in Sandyford, Co. Dublin; its owner was named "The Lamb" to distinguish him from the other Doyles in the area. *Thom's Directory of Ireland for the Year 1934* indicates a J. T. Silke, Wine and Spirit Merchant, on the Kill Rd., Monkstown ([Dublin: Alex. Thom and Co., 1934] 2019).

GEORGES DUTHUIT

2/8/[48]   NEW PLACE

Mon cher vieux

Ce matin votre grande enveloppe. Puisque vous me demandez mon avis, m'est avis que vous pouvez publier tout ça, puisqu'il faut bien publier quelque chose.[1] Le Breton surtout est moche, quelle prose quand même, et le Frédérique. Le Genêt mieux traduit pourrait aller. Le Tardieu me semble assez bien traduit, surtout le 2ème poème. A la fin du troisième il y a quelque chose qui cloche, et à vrai dire, en les relisant, le premier est assez plat.[2] Je n'ai pas compris si vous voulez que je traduise quelque chose (je le ferais volontiers pour vous) ou que je révise, même à l'aveuglette, les traductions déjà faites. Si dans les textes à moi que vous avez vous trouvez des passages qui vous tentent pour Transition, ils sont bien entendu à vous. Vous me connaissez trop bien pour y voir une prière d'insérer.[3]

Ici j'ai du mal à croire qu'il m'est jamais arrivé, qu'il m'arrivera peut-être encore, d'écrire. Je m'en dédommageais autrefois, m'en réjouissais si vous voulez, en parlant d'abondance, dans cette ville d'abondants parleurs. Pas aujourd'hui. Mais il faut bien voir les 2 ou 3 qui vous aiment, qu'on aime aussi c'est probable, fidèlement. "Ange plein de beauté connaissez-vous les rides, Et la peur de vieillir et ce hideux tourment, De lire …?"[4] Les vers qui importent sont ceux qu'on oublie, les autres on les cite incorrectement avec facilité. Donc l'autre soir encore grand tir de connaissances, académie néoplatonicienne, Masaccio, Foppé, Michel Ange mort et Galilée né même année et ce vieux cheval du Giorgionisme de nos jours, de leurs jours. Et sous entendu, surentendu, ce Christ Pickwick mort pour les durs et les bourreaux.[5] Connaissez-vous le cri commun aux purgatoriaux? Io fui.[6] J'ai accompagné ma mère au temple dimanche dernier, temple lointain, pour qu'elle y retrouve le pilier derrière lequel mon père abritait ses somnolences, le soir, ses agitations, son refus de corpulent de s'agenouiller. Le pasteur a annoncé: "Monsieur Frost, aimé et estimé de nous tous, entré dans la vie hier matin, obsèques demain."[7] Mon pauvre Georges, ce soir, vous êtes mal tombé. Il fait beau, je marche dans mes vieux chemins, je guette les yeux de ma mère, jamais si bleus, si stupéfaits, si déchirants d'enfance sans issue, celle de la vieillesse. Allons-y plutôt un peu plus tôt, pendant qu'il est encore des refus à faire. Je crois que ce sont les premiers yeux que je voie. Je ne tiens pas à en voir d'autres, j'ai là de quoi aimer et pleurer suffisamment, je sais maintenant ce qui va se fermer, et s'ouvrir en moi, mais sans rien voir, ça ne voit plus rien. Envoyez–moi des textes à traduire, de vous autant que possible. Je ne sais pas si nous pourrons faire quelque chose. Moi, je sais mal combattre. On fera peut-être quelque chose en ne pouvant combattre. Après tout c'est un talent répandu, celui-là. Dans la mêlée, bien sûr, pas au-dessus, poilu peu poilu indifférent aux causes, dans une autre guerre depuis toujours, sans espoir de

permission ni d'armistice, banni des gains et des pertes sans tomber toutefois dans le nouveau testament. Bien des choses à Marguerite.[8]
Affectueusement

Votre Sam

ALS; 2 leaves, 4 sides; Duthuit collection. *Dating*: dated 1948 by reference to Mr. Frost's obituary.

2/8/[48]   NEW PLACE
My dear Georges,

This morning your big envelope. Since you want my opinion, my opinion is that you can publish it all, since something has to be published.[1] The Breton above all is poor stuff, what prose all the same, and the Frédérique. The Genet better translated would be all right. The Tardieu seems to me quite well translated, especially the second poem. At the end of the third there is something wrong, and, to tell the truth, re-reading them, the first is rather flat.[2] I have not understood whether you want me to translate something (that I would gladly do for you) or revise, even cursorily, the translations already done. If in the texts by me that you have you find passages that tempt you for *Transition*, they are of course yours. You know me too well to see that as a hint.[3]

Here I have difficulty in believing that it has ever happened to me, that it may happen to me again, to write. In the old days, I used to make up for that, used to rejoice in it if you like, by talking in abundance, in this city of abundant talkers. Not these days. But you do have to see the two or three who are fond of you, and that you are probably fond of too, faithfully. "Ange plein de beauté connaissez-vous les rides, Et la peur de vieillir et ce hideux tourment, De lire . . .?"[4] The lines that matter are those one forgets. The others one quotes easily and incorrectly. And so again the other evening great firing-off of knowledge, Neoplatonic academy, Masaccio, Foppa, Michelangelo dead and Galileo born the same year, and that old warhorse the

91

Giorgionism of our times, of their times. And understood, overstood, this Pickwick of a Christ who died for the hard men and the executioners.[5] Do you know the cry common to those in purgatory? <u>Io fui</u>.[6] I went with my mother to church last Sunday, a distant church, so that she could find the pillar behind which my father would hide his noddings-off, in the evening, his physical restlessness, his portly man's refusal to kneel. The parson announced: "Mr Frost, loved and respected by us all, entered life yesterday morning, funeral tomorrow."[7] Poor old Georges, no luck for you this evening. The weather is fine, I walk along my old paths, I keep watching my mother's eyes, never so blue, so stupefied, so heartrending, eyes of an endless childhood, that of old age. Let us get there rather earlier, while there are still refusals we can make. I think these are the first eyes that I have seen. I have no wish to see any others, I have all I need for loving and weeping, I know now what is going to close, and open inside me, but without seeing anything, there is no more seeing. Send me texts for translation, of yours as far as possible. I don't know whether we'll be able to do anything. I am not good at fighting. Perhaps we can do something by not fighting. After all, that is a widely shared talent. In the free-for-all, of course, rankest of rankers, not above it, indifferent to causes, caught up since the beginning in another war, without hope of leave or armistice, banished from the gains and the losses yet without falling into the New Testament. Warmest greetings to Marguerite.[8] Fondly

    Your Sam

---

1   The purpose and policy of *Transition*: see Profile and 2 August 1947, n. 1.

2   The only work by André Breton appears in *Transition Forty-Eight* no. 2, which is already published by this time. No work by André Frédérique (1915–1957) appeared in *Transition*; it is not known to which text SB is referring.

SB incorrectly adds a circumflex accent to the name "Genet"; no work by Jean Genet or by Jean Tardieu (1903–1995) appeared in *Transition*. Four poems by Tardieu ("Les portes de l'inanimé," "Les femmes de ménage," "Contre-point-du-jour," and "Passant qui rentre ravi") did appear in "Poèmes," *Empédocle* (1.4 [August–September 1949] 53–56), and it may be to these that SB is referring.

3   SB publishes "Trois Poèmes," with his translations of them, "Three Poems": "je suis ce cours de sable qui glisse" / "my way is in the sand flowing," "que ferais-je sans ce monde sans visages sans questions" / "what would I do without this world faceless

incurious," and "je voudrais que mon amour meure" / "I would like my love to die" (*Transition Forty-Eight* no. 2, 96–97). In the "Notes about Contributors" (146–147, unsigned, but probably written by Duthuit and possibly translated by SB himself) he is described as follows:

> Samuel Beckett is a Dublin poet and novelist who, after long years of residence in France has adopted the French language as his working medium. Invited to give some account of his reasons for now writing in French, rather than in this [sic] native language, he replied that he would be happy to do so and seemed then to have some views on the subject. But some months later he wrote saying that he did not know why he wrote in French, nor indeed why he wrote at all. Some considerable time later however, as we chanced to encounter him emerging in unusual good humour apparently from the *Multicolor* in the *Avenue de Wagram*, we begged him to make a further effort, in his own interest and in that of literature as a whole. Drawing us then aside into the little frequented semi-circular *Rue de Tilsitt*, and having first looked round in every conceivable direction to make sure no doubt that we were not observed, he confessed at last in a strong or rather weak Dublin accent: "*Pour faire remarquer moi.*"
>
> Despite this undoubtedly original syntactical usage of his adopted tongue, Beckett has nevertheless contributed to such French reviews as *Les Temps Modernes*, *Fontaine*, etc. Any mention here of his English-language writings would, we feel, be out of place, despite their indisputably excellent quality.

4   Charles Baudelaire, "Réversibilité" ("Reversibility"):

> Ange plein de beauté, connaissez-vous les rides,
> Et la peur de vieillir, et ce hideux tourment
> De lire la secrète horreur du dévouement
> Dans des yeux où longtemps burent nos yeux avides?
> Ange plein de beauté, connaissez-vous les rides?
> (Fair as you are, what could you know of fear -
> the fear of ageing and the unspeakable pain
> of finding only half-concealed disgust
> in eyes from which we once drank greedily!
> Being so fair, what do you know of fear?)

(Charles Baudelaire, *Œuvres complètes*, I, ed. Claude Pichois, Bibliothèque de la Pléiade [Paris: Gallimard, 1975] 44; Charles Baudelaire, *Les Fleurs du mal: The Complete Text of The Flowers of Evil*, tr. Richard Howard [Boston: David R. Godine, 1982] 49–50.)

5   SB mocks the participants "in this 'great firing off of knowledge'" by appearing to ascribe to them the virtues of those neo-Platonists who, in the Italian Renaissance, took up the torch lit by Plato in his Academy.

Vincenzo Foppa (c. 1427–c. 1515) whom SB misspells "Foppé"; Michelangelo died in 1564, the year of the birth of Galileo Galilei; "Giorgionisme" refers to the style of Giorgione or to that of his imitators and disciples.

SB evokes Charles Dickens's benignly ineffectual Mr. Pickwick from *The Posthumous Papers of the Pickwick Club* (better known as *The Pickwick Papers*, published serially 1836–1837).

6   In Dante's *Purgatory* the phrases "Io fui" and "I' fui" (I was) are used repeatedly, though no more frequently than in *Inferno*.

7   The funeral of Sydney William Frost took place at All Saints' Church, Blackrock, on 26 July (*The Irish Times* 26 July 1948: 8; 29 July 1948: 3).

8   SB's play on "poilu" is not translatable directly. It depends on the coincidence of the standard meaning ("hairy") with slang ("private or other low-ranking soldier"). "Peu poilu" (not very hairy) is depreciative in one way; a different depreciation is suggested in the translation.

Marguerite Duthuit-Matisse (1894–1982), daughter of Henri Matisse and his model Camille Joblaud (1873–1954), wife of Georges Duthuit, was administrator of *Transition*.

GEORGES DUTHUIT

11/8/48   [Dublin]

Mon cher vieux Georges

Retour (je vais essayer d'écrire lisiblement) à la maison (ça ne durera pas) après quelle journée, retour de bonne heure, 9 heures, après passage en revue des sociétés possibles, des pubs possibles, retour à la maison après exposition "art vivant" avec des peintures "françaises", Manet navet, Derain inconcevable, Renoir dégob (n'y a pas que Pichette, pardon), Matisse beau bon coça colà, peintre qui me parlait de Macakio le sperme à la queue, un Clavé (?) qui faisait baver tout le monde, peintre (même) qui m'entretenait de l'art abstrait (unique espoir), critique d'art qui n'avait pas (quand) été sans se laisser impressionner par les "abstractionnistes" chez Denise je ne sais plus qui, et j'en passe, de retour dis-je après panne par absence d'essence sur route nationale à l'heure des premiers ivrognes, dans le crépuscule gris, je trouve votre longue lettre qui me dédommage de tout, ou de beaucoup de choses, dont ne pas être ivre à dormir.[1] Avant d'y répondre, là où j'en suis capable, et les endroits ne sont pas nombreux, de par ma faute (coule français de faible des Halles) je dirai que je suis tombé sur un type ici qui vaut la peine, mon cousin, un cousin, musicien, 22 ans, ours obsédé, il m'a joué ses chansons (Shelley, Blake (le pauvre)) en sifflant la voix, son quatuor, son concerto pour flûte et cordes, en hurlant, c'est pas de la blague, c'est un ?, il nous a quittés sans un mot, volte-face vers je sais bien quelles ruelles dépeuplées, j'ai fait ça, qu'il le fasse mieux que moi, et le reste, il viendra en France, me faire chier, ce sera volontiers, enfin – si je suis là, mais il va falloir que nous disparaissions, c'est évident, dans Paris ou en dehors.[2] Le mot illisible n'est sans doute pas autre chose que <u>moche</u>, sans garantie, tel que je ne me connais que trop bien.[3] Je verrai demain pour les textes, dont le Michaux, et je reverrai le Genet.[4] Je me rappelle bien la phrase à vous que vous me citez et l'avoir mal traduite en effet. Je vous proposerai autre chose mais pas ce soir. Vous savez vraiment je ne tiens pas à être libéré, ni à être secouru, que ce soit par l'art ou que ce soit par autre chose. Des jeunes, après lecture d'Eleuthéria, m'ont dit, mais vous nous renvoyez découragés. Qu'ils prennent de l'aspirine ou qu'ils fassent du footing, avant le petit déjeuner. Rien ne me sera jamais assez contre, pas même la douleur, et je ne crois pas en avoir spécialement besoin. I say confusedly what comes uppermost, comme Browning.[5] Je tombe, tombe, dans une sorte d'idiotie vraiment, où je m'entends parler de Berlin et d'André Marie, comme je viens d'entendre passer le train, au fond du jardin, avec sa charge de passagers se disant, nous ne l'avons pas raté.[6] Victor (nom d'ailleurs à changer, j'ai besoin à la place de Nick quelque chose) est on ne peut plus sans défense, il s'entend de loin aussi, ce qu'il doit dire, pour avoir le droit de se taire, c'est les vieilles blagues au fond, il a peur, il dit Monsieur l'Inspecteur, il a l'air de les engueuler, en réalité il leur lèche les bottes, leur parler c'est leur sucer le cul.[7] Mon cher Georges, ne vous donnez pas de mal avec ça, je veux dire pour faire jouer, nous rigolerons mieux autrement, nous puiserons ailleurs, loin de là, un meilleur sérieux. Je ne saurai jamais assez à quel point espace et temps sont indicibles, et moi alors pris là-dedans. D'accord, tout le monde les escamote, avec leur prétention de savoir où ils sont, parmi quoi, depuis quand, et pour combien, suivant les gigotements. On peut également oser être simple et dire que ne pas savoir c'est non seulement ne pas savoir ce que l'on est, mais aussi où l'on est, et quel changement attendre, et comment sortir de là, où que ce soit, et comment savoir, quand il semble que quelque chose bouge, qui apparemment ne bougeait pas jusqu'alors, ce que c'est qui bouge, qui ne bougeait pas, et ainsi de suite. Hier il faisait si clair que j'ai cru, des hauteurs où j'étais, loin au-dessus de la mer, voir les montagnes du Pays de Galles. Ça se fait – à plus de 100 kilomètres. Suzanne m'écrit des lettres de plus en plus lamentables. Elle est inconsolable, au fond, de vivre. J'ai retenu ma place sur l'avion pour la fin du mois. L'erreur, la faiblesse tout au moins, c'est peut-être de vouloir savoir de quoi on parle. A définir la littérature, à sa satisfaction, même brève, où est le gain, même bref? De l'armure que tout ça, pour un combat exécrable. Je crois savoir ce que vous ressentez, acculé à des jugements, même suggérés seulement, chaque mois, enfin régulièrement, arrachés de plus en plus difficilement à des critères haïs. C'est impossible. Il faut crier, murmurer, exulter, insensément, en attendant de trouver le langage calme sans doute du non sans plus, ou avec si peu en plus. Il faut, non, il n'y à [*for* a] que ça apparemment, pour certains d'entre nous, que ce petit bruit de halali insensé, et puis peut-être le débarras d'au moins une bonne partie de ce que nous avons cru avoir de meilleur, ou de plus réel, au prix de quels efforts, et peut-être l'immense simplicité d'une partie au moins du peu redouté que nous sommes et avons. Mais je commence à écrire. Minuit vient de sonner. A demain.

    Votre Sam

ALS; 4 leaves, 8 sides; Duthuit.

11/8/48   [Dublin]

Georges my old friend,

    Back (I am going to try to write legibly) home (but it will not last) after what a day, back early, nine o'clock, after survey of all the possible clubs, all the possible pubs, back home after "living art" exhibition, with "French" paintings, dud Manet, unthinkable Derain, pukeworthy Renoir (there is not just Pichette, you know), fine good sew-sew Matisse, painter who talked to me of Macakio with sperm in his cock, a Clavé (?) that had everybody oh-ing and ah-ing, painter (same) who talked at length of abstract art (only hope), art critic who had been (when) not unimpressed by the "abstractionists" at Denise somebody's place, and more, and more, back I say after breakdown for lack of petrol on main road at the hour of the earliest drunks, I find your long letter which makes up for everything, or many things, including not being drunk enough to go straight to sleep.[1] Before answering, at those points where I am able, and there are not many of those, on account of my own fault (flow freely, weedy French), I shall tell you that I have come across someone really worth knowing here, my cousin, a cousin, musician, 22, obsessive bear of a man, he played me his songs (Shelley, Blake [poor man]), whistling the voice, his quartet, his concerto for flute and strings, bellowing, no joke, he's a ?, he left us without a word, about turn towards I well know what deserted side streets, I have done that, let him do it better than I could, and the rest, he will come over to France, get on my nerves, well, willingly enough – if I am there, but we will have to disappear somewhere, in Paris or outside it.[2] The illegible word is doubtless nothing other than "moche", no guarantees, knowing myself as I do all too well.[3] I shall see to the texts tomorrow, including the Michaux, and I shall go back over the Genet.[4] I remember clearly the sentence of yours that you quote, and that I did indeed translate it badly. I shall come up with something but not this evening. You know I really have no wish to be set free, nor to be helped, by art or by anything else. Young people, after reading *Eleutheria*, have said to me, but you are sending us away discouraged. Let them take aspirin, or go for long walks, before breakfast. Nothing will ever be sufficiently against for me, not even pain, and I do not think I have any special need for it. I say confusedly what comes uppermost, like Browning.[5] I fall, fall, into a sort of idiocy really, in which I hear myself talking about Berlin or André Marie, as I have just heard the train go by, at the bottom of the garden, with its cargo of passengers thinking, we have not missed it.[6] Victor (name to be changed, incidentally, I need Nick something instead) is utterly defenceless, he too can be heard from afar, what he has to say, in order to have the right to be silent, is in the end the old nonsense, he is afraid, he says Mr Inspector sir, he seems to be telling them off, in reality he is licking their boots, talking to them is sucking their arses.[7] Georges my old friend, don't go to any trouble over it, I mean trying to get it put on, we will have a better laugh another way, we will dig out, somewhere else, well away from there, a better kind of seriousness. I shall never know clearly enough how far space and time are unutterable, and me caught up somewhere in there. Yes, all right, everyone makes free with them, with their claim to know where they are, amid what, since when, and for how long, according to the twitchings. One may just as well dare to be plain and say that not knowing is not only not knowing what one is, but also where one is, and what change to wait for, and how to get out of wherever one is, and how to know, when it seems as if something is moving, which apparently was not moving before, what it is that is moving, that was not moving before, and so on. Yesterday it was so clear that I thought I could see, from the high ground where I was, well above the sea, the mountains of Wales. It can be done from more than 100 kilometres. Suzanne writes, letters that are more and more dismal. At bottom, she is inconsolable at living. I have booked my seat on the plane for the end of the month. The mistake, the weakness at any rate, is perhaps to want to know what one is talking about. In defining literature, to one's satisfaction, even brief, where is the gain, even brief? Armour, all that stuff, for a loathsome combat. I think I know what you are going through, forced back into judgements, even if merely suggested, every month, at any rate regularly, pulled out with greater and greater difficulty according to hateful criteria. It is impossible. One must shout, murmur, exult, madly, until one can find the no doubt calm language of the no, unqualified, or as little qualified as possible. One must, no that is all there is, apparently, for some of us, this mad little tally-ho sound, and then perhaps the shedding of at least a good part of what we thought we had that was best, or most real, at the cost of what efforts. And perhaps the immense simplicity of part at least of the little feared that we are and have. But I'm starting to write. It has just struck midnight. Until tomorrow.

Your Sam

1 On 11 August, the private view of the annual Irish Exhibition of Living Art took place at the National College of Art, Kildare Street, Dublin, which opened to the public on the following day and ran until 11 September. Exceptionally, included in the show were French paintings from the private collection of H. J. P. Bomford (d. 1978). Two

paintings by Edouard Manet (1832–1883) appeared: *Madame Manet dans la Serre* (1878) and *Tama, the Japanese Dog* (National Gallery of Art [Washington], 1995.47.12); and one painting "Attributed to Edouard Manet" in the exhibition catalogue, *Ile de St. Ouen*. Two works by André Derain (1880–1954) were exhibited: *Portrait of a Lady* and *Still Life* (1921–1922, Australian Art Gallery of New South Wales, 355.1987). By Auguste Renoir (1841–1919) appeared *Cagnes, Still Life with Melon and Peaches* (Musée des Beaux-Arts de Montréal, 2001.220), *Printemps* (private collection), *Girl in Blue*, and *Girl in Red*. By Matisse appeared a single painting, *Still Life*.

SB runs together "comme ci, comme ça" or its more colloquial version "couci-couça" (so-so) with "'Coca Cola" to suggest something carefully prepared but undistinguished.

SB is presumably reporting a mangling of Masaccio's name by some anglophone.

One painting by Antoni Clavé (1913–2005) was on show: *Girl with Cockerel* (Dublin City Gallery The Hugh Lane, 1568).

The painter and the art critic have not been identified.

Denise René (née Bleibtreu, b. 1913) co-founded the enterprise "Société Denise René" in 1939 in her Paris apartment-studio at 124 Rue La Boétie; after the War, this became the Galerie Denise René which held its first exhibition in July 1944, Dessins et compositions graphiques, by Victor Vasarely. The gallery promoted abstract art (Denise René, *Denise René, l'intrépide: une galerie dans l'aventure de l'art abstrait, 1944–1978* [Paris: Centre Georges Pompidou, 2001] 11–17).

2   "Un fort des Halles" is the sort of strapping, loud-mouthed lad who might be a porter in Les Halles de Paris, the food market in the 1st arrondissement which was operational until the early 1970s. SB, characteristically, invents himself as a "faible [weak fellow] des Halles," with speech to match.

John Stewart Beckett* (1929–2007), SB's cousin, son of SB's paternal uncle Dr. Gerald Paul Gordon Beckett (1888–1950). None of the musician's songs based on work by Percy Bysshe Shelley and William Blake, nor his quartet or his flute and string concerto, has "survived his determined destruction" of his own compositions (Edward Beckett, 14 April 2009).

3   SB elucidates what he has written in his previous letter, of 2 August: "Le Breton est moche."

4   In *Transition Forty-Eight* no. 4 [January 1949] appears "To right nor left" by Henri Michaux (1899–1984), translated by SB (14–18); and "Thief's Journal (Extracts)" by Jean Genet, in a translation by Bernard Frechtman which SB revises (66–75).

5   This line is spoken by Paracelsus in the poem "Paracelsus" by Robert Browning (*Robert Browning: The Poems*, I, ed. John Pettigrew and Thomas J. Collins [New Haven: Yale University Press, 1981] 83, line 372).

6   Former Resistance worker, prisoner of Buchenwald Concentration Camp, and Garde des Sceaux André Marie (1897–1974) had been appointed Head of Government on 27 July.

7   Victor Krap is *Eleutheria*'s principal figure. The words "Monsieur l'inspecteur" do not appear in the play; rather, they suggest here a displeasing tendency to compliance in Victor Krap.

GEORGES DUTHUIT

Jeudi [12 August 1948]   [Dublin]
Cher vieux

Hier soir je vous ai écrit une lettre on ne peut plus con, que j'ai envoyée quand même étant on ne peut plus con et m'en doutant. Je n'ai rien à cacher, au contraire. Hier ce fut la fatigue, plus que le "déprimant" de je ne sais quel psychiâtre écossais, McDougall peut-être, et puis le plaisir de votre lettre, que j'attendais, espérais.[1] Ce soir, n'ayant bu que 3 double whiskeys avec mon vieux prof. de golf, je serai d'une dignité à peine titubante.[2] J'ai travaillé pour vous, nous, cet après-midi de malheur, ci-joint une partie du pauvre résultat. J'ai commencé le Michaux, dont je me charge. Je ferai l'ARP aussi. Peu à peu, si ça ne presse pas. J'ai commencé également la révision du Genêt.[3] Ça ne donnera jamais grand'chose, je le crains, je n'aime pas ce travail de sauvetage qui ne sauve même pas la face, qui vise une chose horripilante. Où trouver les termes, les rythmes, les halètements, sans quitter le trésor de nos conneries, qui nous révèle un peu. Ce soir, parmi les fougères ruisselantes, dans cette lumière de soleil couchant éclairant l'orage d'en dessous, il m'a semblé qu'il nous manque un motif fait pour faire exploser tout ce triste mélange. Il est à chercher sûrement là où tout est à chercher désormais, dans l'éternel larvaire, non, c'est autre chose, dans le courage de l'imperfection du non-être aussi, où vient nous assaillir la tentation d'être encore, un peu, et la gloire d'avoir été un peu, sous un ciel inoubliable. Oui, à chercher dans l'impossibilité d'avoir jamais assez tort, d'être jamais assez ridicule et sans armes. Vous parlez de tous ces mondes fermés, achevés, qui font un grincement de solitudes, d'orgueils. Et du même coup d'une tota-lité de l'être possible. Pour moi tous les Titans sont d'accord, les Hercule, quel que soit le genre de labeur, entre Pichette et Buonarotti l'addition se fait aisément.[4] Ne pas avoir à s'exprimer ni à se mêler d'un maximum quelconque, dans son monde sans nombre ni valeur ni accomplissement, c'est quand même un jeu à tenter, une nécessité à tenter, et qui ne réussira jamais, si ça réussit. Coller à la nécessité, comment faire autrement, en s'en sachant loin, en souffrant de dire savoir, et en le disant, de loin en loin. On n'a même pas besoin de prêter l'oreille, pour être étourdi par l'avalanche de son impossibilité à chaque fragment d'instant, par son étalage, diluement, inconcevable, à travers autant d'enfers que, dans sa vie à soi pour commencer, ou pour finir, et puis dans celle des autres, morts et mourants pour ne parler que de l'humain, des bonheurs et des malheurs soi-disant, de fausses réussites et des échecs à pisser des ronds de chapeau. Une grande fatigue, soudain, et besoin du noir et du lit étroit et du lent abandon des choses, des arbres, du vent, des veuleries et volontés passées et proches. A demain.

Vendredi [? 13 August 1948]   [Dublin]

Aujourd'hui je n'ai rien fait, pour Transition. J'ai écumé les campagnes, les auberges, il est tard, je ne suis bon qu'à aller me coucher, tout en comptant peu sur un sommeil amical. Je pense pouvoir finir Genêt, Michaux, Arp, la semaine prochaine. J'espère que ça ne presse pas trop. Ici je réponds mal de moi. Demain je m'en vais loin de Dublin, je ne ferai rien demain, je passerai la journée à me pénétrer de la nécessité de rentrer ici. Les lettres de Suzanne se font de plus en plus désespérées, faites-lui signe, même si ce n'est pas votre tour. Ce soir j'ai vu trois éperviers qui chassaient, la mère, ou le père, et 2 petits. Ça me fascine, les oiseaux de proie, plus que les tigres ou lions. Pardonne-moi maintenant et toujours toutes mes stupidités et blancheurs, je ne suis d'un être qu'une toute petite partie, des vestiges se haïssant, des restes d'une vieille envie, quand j'étais petit, d'arrondissement, même à petit rayon. Ça vous enferme toute la vie. Et on pousse en vain vers l'absence de figure. Mais vous ne me mépriserez pas, je vous choquerai souvent mais vous serez

avec moi, j'ai d'autres amis mais un seul Georges Duthuit. Je le sens.
Je le sais.

     Sam

ALS; 3 leaves, 6 sides; Duthuit collection.

Thursday [12 August 1948]   [Dublin]

Dear Georges

    Yesterday I wrote you an unbelievably silly letter, which I never-theless sent, being myself unbelievably silly and suspecting as much. I have nothing to hide, quite the opposite. Yesterday it was tiredness, more than the "depressant" of some Scottish psychiatrist, McDougall maybe, and then the pleasure of your letter, which I was waiting for, hoping for.[1] This evening, having drunk no more than three double whiskeys with my old golf teacher, I shall be dignified, with hardly a hint of a stagger.[2] I have been working for you, for us, this wretched afternoon, herewith part of the unimpressive result. I have started the Michaux, which I am taking on. I shall do the ARP as well. A little at a time, if there's no hurry. I have also started revising the Genet.[3] It will never amount to much, I'm afraid; I do not like this rescue work which does not even save face, and which is directed at something exasperating. Where can one find the terms, the rhythms, the pant-ings, without leaving the treasure-house of our vulgar nonsense, which does rather show us up. This evening, among the dripping bracken, in this light from the setting sun, illuminating the storm from below, I had the feeling that we need a motive to blow up all this dismal mixture. It is surely to be sought where everything must be sought now, in the eternally larval, no, something else, in the courage of the imperfection of non-being too, in which we are intermittently assailed by the temptation still to be, a little, and the glory of having been a little, beneath an unforgettable sky. Yes, to be sought in the impossibility of ever being wrong enough, ever being ridiculous and defenceless enough. You speak of all those closed, achieved worlds that give off a grinding of solitudes, prides. And at the same time of a possible totality of being. For me all the Titans are in agreement, the Herculeses, whatever the kind of labour: between Pichette and Buonarroti the adding-up is easily done.[4] Not to have to express oneself, nor get involved with whatever kind of maximum, in one's numberless, valueless, achievementless world; that is a game worth trying, all the same, a necessity worth trying, and one which will never work, if that works. To stick close to necessity, how can one do otherwise, knowing one is far away from it, suffering at saying "knowing," and very occasionally saying it. No need even to listen out in order to be dazed by the avalanche of one's impossibility at every fragment of a moment, by one's long spreading out, diluting, unthinkable, through as many hells as, in one's own life to start with, or to finish with, and then in other people's, dead and dying, to speak only of the human, so-called happinesses and unhappinesses, false successes and failures that would just make you gawp open-mouthed. A great weariness suddenly, and need for darkness and the narrow bed, and the slow letting go of things, the trees, the wind, failures of nerve and efforts of will past and to come. More tomorrow.

Friday [? 13 August 1948]   [Dublin]

Today I have done nothing for *Transition*. I have been scouring the countryside, the inns, it's late, all I'm good for is bed, though I have no great confidence of finding friendly sleep. I think I can finish Genet, Michaux, Arp next week. I hope there is no great hurry for them. Here I cannot answer for myself. Tomorrow I am going to get right away from Dublin. I shall do nothing tomorrow, I shall spend the day convincing myself of the necessity of coming back here. Suzanne's letters are becoming more and more desperate: do get in touch with her, even if it is not your turn. This evening I saw three sparrowhawks hunting: the mother, or the father, and two little ones. Birds of prey fascinate me, more than tigers or lions. Forgive me now and always for all my stupidities and blanknesses, I am only a tiny little part of a creature, self-hating vestiges, remains of an old longing, when I was little, for rounding out, even on a small radius. That shuts you in your whole life long. And one drives in vain towards figurelessness. But you will not despise me, I shall shock you often but you will be with me. I have other friends, but only one Georges Duthuit. I feel it. I know it.

Sam

1   SB adds an inappropriate circumflex to the French word "psychiatre"; he also writes below "diluement" for "dilution," "Buonarotti" for "Buonarroti," and twice adds an unwarranted circumflex to the name "Genet."

William McDougall (1871–1938) was an English-born psychologist who worked from 1920 in the United States. Knowlson reports that SB came across McDougall in 1934–1935 while he was in London following his psychoanalysis with W. R. Bion (Profile, I) (*Damned to Fame*, 171).

2   SB's golf coach was James Barrett (1882–1950), the professional at Carrickmines Golf Club from 1906 until 1950 (Cedric R. Bailey, Hon. Secretary, The Carrickmines Golf Club, 16 May 2009).

3   Translations of Michaux and Genet: 11 August 1948, n. 4; translation of Arp: 27 July 1948, n. 8.

4   The Titans were those gods considered in Greek mythology to precede, and to have been conquered by, the Olympian gods. Hercules (or Herakles), son of Zeus and Alcmena, was known throughout the Greek world as the paragon of strength and courage, as the universal helper, and for his accomplishing of his twelve labors.

In "Notes about Contributors" in *Transition Forty-Eight* no. 2, Henri Pichette is described as "author of the poetic drama, *Les Epiphanies*, which attracted wide if controversial attention when it played last winter to crowded houses." The "Notes" continue: "By certain critics he was hailed as 'the genius, the poet we have been waiting for' and his play was termed 'an astonishing renewal of the dramatic art, a remarkable event'. Even his opponents were willing to concede that he possessed an 'abundant, surging gift for verbal creation'" (150–151).

Michelangelo Buonarroti.

THOMAS MACGREEVY
DUBLIN

26th September [1948]   Paris

My dear Tom

Many thanks for Record with your Paris notes which I read with much pleasure and interest, though not always with you in the nice things you say of the critic and his relation to the artist, this perhaps because of my own feeling of helplessness, finally, and of speechlessness, and of restlessness also I think, before works of art.[1] Thanks for your friendly reference to the van Velde preface, abominable "machine" that I shall always regret, no less than its Cahiers d'Art predecessor.[2]

Mother sent me Irish Times with account of Yeats reburial. I suppose the intention was to do him proud. And to think there are people who want that kind of thing for Joyce! Nichols wrote to me that exhumation before 25 years after burial was forbidden by the sanitary authorities of the Canton of Zurich except in exceptional circumstances. They suggest that the Joyce "committee" should write them a letter justifying "ideologically" the return to Ireland of the celebrated remains. This ends my part in the proceedings.[3]

Mother seems in good form. The new maid is incompetent but very kindly. Usually mother dictates her letters to a girl who comes in, but the last was in her own hand, four whole pages.

It is a relief, physically and the other way, to be back here. I have finished typing out Malone meurt (may he never come back) and am now happily doing nothing, working at Chopin's 3rd Sonata and the Etudes symphoniques.[4] Arthur Darley turned up with bicycle and rucksacks and Gerald's son John, the musician, is arriving soon with a scholarship from the London College of Music.[5]

We are having a real St Martin's summer. There is some chance of our being lent a little chalet on the edge of the Forest of Fontainebleau. Suzanne could do with a rest in the country.[6] She asks to be very kindly remembered to you.

My regards to your sister and nieces. And an affectionate message to dear Jack Yeats.[7]

> Yours ever
> Sam

ALS; 2 leaves, 2 sides; TCD, MS 10402/177. *Dating*: 1948 is established by references to Yeats's reburial and discussion of reinterment of James Joyce in Ireland.

1   SB refers to MacGreevy's "Art Criticism, and A Visit to Paris" in *The Father Matthew Record*, in which MacGreevy writes: "I suggested . . . that the rôles of the reason and the imagination, of the thinker – which is to say the critic – and the artist, are most properly regarded as twin servants of something that is greater than either of them, which is truth" (6).

2   MacGreevy wrote: "At one exhibition of abstract paintings by the Dutch artists, Bram and Geer Van Velde, the catalogue had a closely reasoned preface in admirable French by the Irish writer, Samuel Beckett" (6). SB's essay "Peintres de l'empêchement" introduced the paintings of Geer and Bram van Velde at the Galerie Maeght, Paris (*Derrière le Miroir*, 11–12 [June 1948] 3, 4, 7). SB's earlier essay on their work was "La Peinture des van Velde ou le monde et le pantalon," commissioned by *Cahiers d'Art*, 349–356.

3   When W. B. Yeats died on 28 January 1939, he was buried in Roquebrune, France; the "concession temporaire" with the cemetery there was for ten years, and so the family made plans for reinterment in Drumcliff, Co. Sligo, Ireland (Ann Saddlemyer, *Becoming George: The Life of Mrs W. B. Yeats* [Oxford: Oxford University Press, 2002] 604–611). The reburial took place on 17 September 1948 ("Yeats Rests under Ben Bulben," *The Irish Times* 18 September 1948: 1, 3).
   Reburial of James Joyce in Ireland: 27 July 1948, n. 9. The Dublin undertakers J. and C. Nichols had been consulted by SB at the request of Maria Jolas. (Eventually, on 16 June 1966, the remains of Nora and James Joyce would be reinterred together, not in Ireland, but in the Fluntern Cemetery in Zurich.)

4   SB's typing of the MS of *Malone meurt*: 8 July [1948], n. 3.
   Frédéric Chopin, Piano Sonato no. 3 in B minor, op. 58; Robert Schumann, *Etudes symphoniques*, op. 13, a set of twelve studies for piano.

5   Arthur Darley, with whom SB had served at the Irish Red Cross Hospital at Saint-Lô in 1945 where Darley was in charge of the tuberculosis ward, was a gifted musician. SB wrote the poem "Mort de A.D." after his friend's death from tuberculosis on 30 December 1948 in Dublin.
   John Beckett.

6   "St. Martin's Summer" is SB's term for an Indian summer.

7   MacGreevy's family who lived with him: 24 November 1947, n. 6.
MacGreevy had accompanied Jack Yeats to the reinterment of his brother in Sligo.

GEORGES DUTHUIT

mercredi 28 oct [*for* jeudi 28 octobre 1948]
Mon cher vieux Georges,
   Merci de votre gentille lettre avec l'article de Blanchot.[1]
   Oui, à l'abri des mots, mais venant s'y mêler par moments, la chose entre nous est en lieu sûr. Le reste compte peu.

Il ne faut pas vous tracasser au sujet de la maison de Beauzelle.[2] Il y a peu de chances qu'on puisse profiter de votre générosité. C'est trop loin. D'ailleurs nous finirons sans doute par comprendre que la place des boeufs est devant la charrue et que la campagne est dans la tête.

Ni au sujet de Gabrielle, à qui j'ai écrit et dont j'attends le consentement pour me mettre au travail. Je lui ai dit que cela lui serait payé dans les 7 à 8 mille francs. Je ferai ça rapidement et avec ce qui, chez moi, tient lieu de joie.[3]

Cela m'a fait du bien de vous parler de ma pièce, en bafouillant.[4] J'ai fort bien compris ce que vous avez dit au sujet des accessoires. Cela m'aidera, m'a déjà aidé. Je les vois d'une iniquité plus grande que nature. A l'ombre dérisoire d'un arbre pas même foutu de vous pendre.

Quand nous verrons-nous? Vendredi? Chez vous autant que possible. Le bougnat a une clientèle qui ne me revient pas.

      Affectueusement

        Sam

ALS; 1 leaf, 1 side; Duthuit collection. *Dating*: 28 October fell on a Wednesday in 1942 and 1953, but these years are not contextually possible. The letter should be dated as prior to March 1949 as SB addresses Duthuit as "vous" rather than "tu." The first page of the manuscript of *En attendant Godot* is dated "9 octobre 1948." This suggests that the letter was written in October 1948, and if the date is correct as the 28th, then it should be Thursday 28 October; if, however, it is the date that is mistaken, it should be Wednesday 27 October; the editors have chosen the former.

Wednesday 28 Oct. [*for* Thursday 28 October 1948]

My dear Georges

Thank you for your kind letter with the Blanchot article.[1]

Yes, protected against words, but working its way in among them at moments, what goes on between us is safe from attack. The rest hardly matters.

Do not worry yourself about the Beauzelle house.[2] There is not much chance of our being able to take advantage of your generosity. It is too far. In any case we shall no doubt finally realize that the place of oxen is before the plough and that countryside is in the head.

Nor about Gabrielle, to whom I have written, and whose consent I am waiting for before starting work. I told her that she would be paid seven or eight thousand francs for it. I shall do it quickly and with what, for me, does duty for gladness.[3]

It did me good to talk to you about my play, in my stammering way.[4] I have really taken in what you said about stage props. It will help me, it has already helped me. I see them as having a larger-than-life-size iniquity, in the derisory shade of a tree you could not even hang yourself on.

When shall we meet? Friday? At your house if at all possible. The bar has the kind of customers I really do not like.

Fond regards

Sam

1   It is not known which article by Maurice Blanchot Duthuit has sent to SB; Blanchot published some five articles in 1948 alone.

2   Beauzelle, a village in the Haute-Garonne, was the site of the family home of Henri Matisse's wife Amélie Noélie Matisse (née Parayre, c. 1871-1958). When Matisse and his wife separated, she rented a manor there (until 1949), to which Marguerite and Georges Duthuit would go on holiday; it is to this house that Duthuit has invited SB (Claude Duthuit).

3   The article to which SB refers, and which he translates, is "Apollinaire" by Gabrielle Picabia, published in *Transition Fifty* no. 6 (110-125). Gabrielle Picabia (née Buffet, 1881-1985) trained at the Schola Cantorum in Paris, was a friend of Apollinaire, and in 1909 married the painter Francis Martinez Picabia (1879-1963); she was the mother of Gabrielle Cécile Martinez Picabia (known as Jeannine, 1913-1977), founder of the Resistance réseau Gloria SMH of which SB had been a part. *Transition*'s "Notes about Contributors" has: "GABRIELLE PICABIA. A woman of steady, quiet, invincible courage, who ranks with the foremost heroines of the Resistance. She was early married to Francis Picabia, that anti-painting painter who continues to paint; hence her precocious acquaintance with Dada and kindred circles" (151).

4   SB had begun the writing of *En attendant Godot* nearly three weeks before, on 9 October.

CHRONOLOGY 1949

1949 January — Publication of *Transition Forty-Eight* no. 4.

29 January — SB finishes writing *En attendant Godot*.

February — Bram and Geer van Velde exhibition at the Galerie Folklore, Lyon.

before 27 March — SB submits *Eleutheria* for the Prix Rivarol; the play is being read by director Raymond Rouleau. Begins retyping *En attendant Godot*. Translates Apollinaire's poem "Zone."

by 27 March — SB and Suzanne Deschevaux-Dumesnil take a room in a farmhouse in Ussy-sur-Marne.

29 March — SB begins writing *L'Innommable*.

April — "Three Poems" published in *Poetry Ireland*.

12 May — Berlin blockade lifted.

before 1 June — SB begins translations for *Sélection*, the French edition of the *Reader's Digest*.

June — Begins working on "Three Dialogues."

30 June — Charles Prentice dies in Nairobi.

July — SB in Dublin.

1 August — Flies from Dublin to Paris.

20 October — Sends an extract from *Watt* to John Ryan, Editor of *Envoy*.

10 December — "Three Dialogues" published in *Transition Forty-Nine* no. 5.

mardi [? 1949]

Cher vieux Georges

La glace est tout au fond, au 9me cercle, réservé aux traîtres, répartis entre 4 zones: Caina (traîtres des parents), Antenora (traîtres de la patrie), Giudecca (traîtres des hôtes) et Giudecca (traîtres des bienfaiteurs).

Tu pourrais peut-être te servir des vers suivants:

O sovra tutte mal creata plebe,
che stai nel luogo onde parlare è duro,
me' foste state qui pecore o zebe! (32. 13–15)[1]

En fait de vers descriptifs glacés je n'ai rien trouvé qui puisse faire l'affaire.

Encore si de temps en temps les Innuit mangeaient leurs petits, comme Ugolin . . .

Poscia, più che il dolore, potè il digiuno.

Interprétation d'ailleurs fort douteuse, mais à laquelle je tiens.[2]

A bientôt, cher vieux.

s/ Sam

TLS; 1 leaf, 1 side; *A corr in red ink*; Duthuit. *Dating*: Duthuit's completion of *Une fête en Cimmérie* (see n. 2 below).

Tuesday [? 1949]

My dear Georges,

The ice is right at the bottom, in the 9th circle, reserved for the traitors, divided across four zones: Caina (traitors to parents), Antenora (traitors to country), Giudecca (traitors to hosts), and Giudecca (traitors to benefactors).

You could perhaps use the following lines:

O sovra tutte mal creata plebe
che stai nel luogo onde parlare è duro
me' foste state qui pecore o zebe! (32. 13–15)[1]

In the way of descriptive frozen verses I have not found anything that would do.

It would not be so bad if from time to time the Innuit ate their young, like Ugolino . . .

Poscia, più che il dolore, potè il digiuno.

A very dubious interpretation, incidentally, but one to which I am attached.[2]

Enough for now, my old friend.

Sam

---

1 Accurately transcribing his 1926 Salani edition of the *Commedia*, SB cites this passage from the nethermost, frozen floor of Dante's Hell, Cocytus, where (in *Inferno* Cantos XXXII–XXXIV) four degrees of treachery are punished; he inadvertently calls the third level "Giudecca" instead of "Ptolomea" (Dante, *La Divina Commedia*, comment by Enrico Bianchi [Florence: Adriano Salani, 1927]; on editions of Dante's work read by SB and used here, see SB to Thomas McGreevy, Friday [? summer 1929], n. 6).
Dante addresses the inhabitants of Cocytus as he prepares to enter this icy realm: "O beyond all others misbegotten crowd who are in the place it is hard to speak of, better had you here been sheep or goats!" (Dante Alighieri, *The Divine Comedy of Dante Alighieri*, I, *Inferno*, tr. and comment John D. Sinclair [London: John Lane The Bodley Head, 1939; revised 1948] 395).

2 Duthuit had published an article entitled "Le Don indien: sur la côte nord-ouest de l'Amérique" (*Labyrinthe* 2.18 [April 1946] 9). He returns to the theme of ice, cold, and the Poles, in his *Une fête en Cimmérie* (completed in 1949) which contains illustrations by Henri Matisse (several of which represent Inuits); it is almost certainly in this connection that Duthuit has sought SB's guidance (though in the event he does not cite Dante); this text was published only years later ([Paris: Fernand Mourlot, 1964] 21–32).
SB cites one of the most famous lines in the *Commedia*, and one of the most disputed: "Then fasting had more power than grief" (*Inferno*, Canto XXXIII, line 75, 408–409). This is the final utterance of Count Ugolino della Gherardesca (c. 1220–1289), who, locked in a tower in Pisa, has watched his children die. Interpretation has hinged on whether or not Dante's line implies that Ugolino, before himself dying of starvation, first eats his own children; SB chooses to believe that he does.

BRAM VAN VELDE

14/1/49   Paris
Mon cher Bram

Nous sommes furieusement enrhumés tous les deux et il est même possible que Suzanne fasse un commencement de grippe. Il vaut donc mieux que nous renvoyions notre soirée à dimanche en huit le 23. Nous sommes très déçus, mais pas moyen de faire autrement.

J'ai beaucoup pensé à votre travail ces derniers jours et compris l'inutilité de tout ce que je vous ai dit. Vous résistez en artiste, à tout ce qui vous empêche d'oeuvrer, fût-ce l'évidence même. C'est admirable. Moi, je cherche le moyen de capituler sans me taire – tout à fait. Mais quand je vais chez vous regarder ce que vous avez fait, il ne devrait pas être question de moi. J'entends encore votre dernier "j'ai compris". Je l'avais mérité. J'espère que vous aurez fait venir Duthuit chez vous. Il voit les choses telles qu'elles sont.

Si vous passez dans la semaine nous apporterons les tableaux Rue de l'Université.[1]

Bien des choses à Marthe.[2] Et de toute manière à dimanche en 8.

Affectueusement de nous deux

s/ <u>Sam</u>

Ci-joint le dernier silence raté.[3]

TLS; 1 leaf, 1 side; enclosure not extant; Putman collection. Previous publication, Marianne Alphant, Nathalie Léger, and Amarante Szidon, eds., *Objet Beckett* (Paris: Centre Pompidou, IMEC-Editeur, 2007) [plate 80]; Stoullig and Schoeller, eds., *Bram van Velde*, 165.

14/1/49   Paris
My dear Bram

We both have dreadful colds and it may even be that Suzanne is coming down with flu. So we'd better postpone our evening till a week next Sunday, the 23rd. We're very disappointed, but there's no way round it.

I've thought a lot about your work these last few days. And understood the uselessness of all I've said to you. As an artist, you hold out against everything and anything that might prevent you from making your works, even the plain facts. That is admirable. I am searching for a way of capitulating without giving up utterance – entirely. But when I go round to your studio to look at what you've been doing, the subject of me ought not to come up. I can still hear your final "now I see". I had deserved it. I hope that you've had Duthuit round. He sees things as they are.

If you can come round some time during the week, we can take the pictures to the Rue de l'Université.[1]

Very best wishes to Marthe.[2] And in any case, see you a week on Sunday.

> Love from us both
> Sam

Enclosed is the last failed silence.[3]

1 Duthuit's studio-office was located at 96 Rue de l'Université, Paris 7.

2 Marthe Arnaud.

3 The enclosure has not been found or identified.

GEORGES DUTHUIT

Lundi 17 janvier [1949]   Paris
Mon cher vieux,

Je comptais passer aujourd'hui, mais suis trop mal fichu. Suzanne ne vaut guère mieux.

Je n'ai pas fait grand'chose pour vous. La Promenade de Picasso de cet ignoble Prévert et la suite Picasso d'Eluard que je trouve belle. Je ne sais plus si vous m'avez demandé de traduire le 2ème poème Picasso de Prévert. Vous me le direz. Maintenant je vais faire le Jarry.[1]

Je suis allé mardi dernier voir le dernier travail de Bram.[2] Il m'a un peu déconcerté. Je m'attendais à autre chose. J'ai proféré mon chapelet de conneries habituel n'ayant rien à voir avec l'affaire. J'aurais naturellement voulu l'encourager. Je crois que je l'ai seulement enfoncé un peu plus. J'ai pensé à ce que nous allons faire sur lui. Je crois que ça serait mieux sous forme de dialogue, mais pas parlé, écrit. Vous m'enverriez – ou je vous enverrais – une première perche, et ainsi de suite. C'est peut-être une mauvaise idée. Tout ce que je sais, c'est que j'ai sérieusement besoin qu'on m'attise, j'espère que ce n'est pas une obscénité, à ce sujet comme aux autres.

Passez nous voir n'importe quel après-midi. Si je ne suis pas accroché à ma planche, je n'en serais pas bien loin, ni pour bien longtemps.

Affectueusement de nous deux

Sam

ALS; 1 leaf, 1 side; Duthuit collection. *Dating*: 17 January fell on a Monday in 1949.

Monday 17 January [1949]   Paris

My dear Georges

I was planning to drop in today, but am not feeling at all well. Suzanne is not much better.

I have not done much for you. The "Promenade de Picasso" by the ignoble Prévert and the Picasso sequence by Eluard which I think is lovely. I do not know if you asked me to translate Prévert's second Picasso poem. Let me know. Now I am going to do the Jarry.[1]

I went last Tuesday to see Bram's latest work.[2] It rather took me aback. I was expecting something different. I let out my usual string of embarrassing rubbish with no bearing on the matter in hand. Naturally I would have wanted to encourage him. I think I only pressed him back down a little. I have been thinking of what we are going to do on him. I think it would be better in the form of a dialogue, but written, not spoken. You would give me a first nudge, or I you, and so on. Maybe that is a bad idea. All I know is that I really need someone to get me going. I hope that this is not an obscenity, on this subject as on others.

Monday 17 January [1949], Duthuit

Come round and see us any afternoon. If I am not hunched over my desk, I could not be very far, or for very long.

Fond regards from us both.

Sam

---

1 SB refers to translations he is doing for *Transition Forty-Nine* no. 5, all of which go unsigned: "Promenade de Picasso" by Jacques Prévert (1900–1977) was translated as "Picasso goes for a Walk" (50–53) (only one Picasso poem by Prévert is printed); "Le travail du peintre – A Picasso" by Paul Eluard (*Poésie ininterrompue* [Paris: Gallimard, 1946] 65–72), was translated as "The Work of the Painter – To Picasso" (6–13); an extract from *Gestes et opinions du Docteur Faustroll, Pataphysicien* by Alfred Jarry (1873–1907; rpt. in *Le Surmâle* [Paris: Les Humanoïdes Associés L. F. Editions, 1979] 165–170) was translated as "The Painting Machine" (38–42).

2 It is not known which particular paintings SB saw on his visit.

GEORGES DUTHUIT

Mardi [? March 1949]   [Paris]

Mon cher vieux

Merci de votre mot. Je me sens morne et plat. Un soir chez Hayden, je suis sorti de mes pauvres gonds, en poussant des hurlements d'enragé.[1] Nous ne nous reverrons pas de sitôt. Je l'ai traité de plombier. Il avait une fluxion et ressemblait au white monkey de Galsworthy.[2] Je n'en ai pas de remords, c'est étrange. Je me trompe peut-être du tout au tout sur la peinture de Bram, quoiqu'il m'assure que non, mais au fond nous ne parlons pas de la même chose, Bram et moi, il me semble. Il veut vaincre, il y revient tout le temps. Et ces splendeurs où j'entends l'hymne de l'être fonçant à rebours et libre enfin dans les quartiers interdits, ce sont peut-être des splendeurs comme tant d'autres, rapport à l'espèce bien sûr, celle de la corde tendue où l'on se vautre. Mais ça m'arrange mieux de ne pas le croire – pour le moment, excusable faiblesse. Il a été beaucoup question chez Hayden d'une bouteille (elle était vide), son galbe bien entendu, et puis d'autres uniques particularités. Je lui ai dit qu'il n'avait jamais vu une bouteille de sa vie. Mais il paraît qu'il n'y a que les poètes qui ne voient pas les bouteilles. Mon pauvre George[s], je me demande de quel recours je vais pouvoir vous être, pour votre numéro sur la peinture.³ Je crains d'aucun. Nous sommes très contents qu'Amarre vous ait plu. Ce n'est pas ce titre qu'il faudrait. La dernière phrase se prête en effet difficilement à l'articulation.⁴ Gabirol, c'est finalement nul autre qu'Avicebron.⁵ Je m'en suis débarrassé et j'ai fait les ajustements Reverdy dans le sens indiqué. Le résultat est pareil. Que les étoiles l'aient déjà abattu ou qu'elles n'y aient pas encore tout à fait arrivé, c'est sans importance.⁶ D'accord, Rimbaud ne tient pas très bien, mais par moments c'est incomparable. A nous aussi on nous vole nos papillons. Resteront toujours quelques chenilles.⁷

J'irai vous serrer la main et vous souhaiter bon voyage et bon repos demain en fin d'après-midi, sauf contre-avis.⁸ Je dois maintenant m'atteler à la fastidieuse toilette de ma pièce qui s'appellerait probablement En attendant Godot. Il faut surtout bien dégager l'anus.

    Affectueusement

      Sam

ALS; 1 leaf, 2 sides; Duthuit collection. *Dating*: SB is typing up *Waiting for Godot* in March 1949; see 27 March 1949.

Tuesday [? March 1949]   [Paris]

My dear Georges

Thank you for your note. I feel gloomy and flat. One evening at Hayden's, I lost my wretched temper, and let out the roars of a madman.¹ It will be a while before we see each other again. I called him a plumber. He had some kind of inflammation and looked like Galsworthy's white monkey.² It is strange, I do not feel remorseful. Perhaps I am entirely wrong about Bram's painting, although he assures me that I am not, but basically we are not talking about the same thing, Bram and I, it seems to me. He wants to conquer, he keeps coming back to that. And these splendours, in which I can hear the hymn of Being blasting out back to front, and free at last in the forbidden quarters, are perhaps splendours like so many others, thinking of the species, of course, that of the tightrope over which we sprawl. But it suits me better not to believe it – for the moment: a pardonable weakness. There was much talk at Hayden's of a bottle (it was empty), its curve of course, and then other unique peculiarities. I told him that he had never seen a bottle in his life. But it seems it is only poets that do not see bottles. Poor old Georges, I do not know what help I can be to you, for your issue on painting.[3] None, I fear. We are very pleased that you liked "Amarre". That is not the right title for it; sure enough, the last sentence is not easily speakable.[4] Gabirol, it turns out, is none other than Avicebron.[5] I got rid of it and made the Reverdy adjustments along the lines indicated. The result is the same. Whether the stars have already floored him, or whether they have not quite got there yet is unimportant.[6] Agreed, Rimbaud does not hold up very well, but at moments it is incomparable. Our butterflies get stolen too. There will always be some caterpillars left over.[7]

I shall come round to say goodbye and wish you bon voyage and a good rest tomorrow late afternoon, unless there is a change of plan.[8] Now I must buckle down to doing the wearisome tidying up of my play, which will probably be called *En attendant Godot*. Above all I must make sure the anus is clear.

Fond regards

Sam

1 Henri Hayden* (1883–1970) lived at this time at 205 bis Boulevard Raspail, Paris 14.

2 In his novel *The White Monkey* (1924), John Galsworthy writes of the eponymous creature:

> Stripping the coverings off the picture, Fleur brought it in, and setting it up on the jade-green settee, stood away and looked at it. The large white monkey with its brown haunting eyes, as if she had suddenly wrested its interest from the orange-like fruit in its crisped paw, the grey background, the empty rinds all round – bright splashes in a general ghostliness of colour, impressed her at once.

The character Aubrey Greene expands: "When they're still, a monkey's eyes are the human tragedy incarnate. Look at them! He thinks there's something beyond, and he's sad or angry because he can't get at it" ([New York: Charles Scribner's Sons, 1924] 156, 159).

3 SB refers to *Transition Forty-Nine* no. 5, which was in preparation.

4 "L'Amarre" is a two-page story by Suzanne Deschevaux-Dumesnil which exists (typewritten) in the Duthuit collection. Its final line, as typed, is: "Dites-le, qu'avez-vous? Et moi, qu'ai-je?" This line has been canceled, and in handwriting, probably her own, has been added: "Dites-le ah qu'avez-vous ah qu'ai-je qu'ai-je ah."

5   Avicebron is the standardized Latin-derived form of the name of the Spanish-born Jewish poet and Neoplatonic philosopher Solomon ben Yehuda Ibn Gabirol (c. 1022–c. 1058).

6   SB writes "qu'elles n'y aient pas encore tout à fait arrivé" where, strictly, grammar requires "qu'elles n'y soient pas … arrivées."

Two parts of *Transition Fifty* no. 6 (October 1950) are given over to Pierre Reverdy (1889–1960). The first, "Where Poetry Comes into Being," is translated by Lothian Small (27–32); the second, "Poèmes – Poems," contains sixteen poems translated by SB (unsigned, 34–65). SB is probably referring to lines from the poem "Etape" ("Halt"): "Le cavalier mourant levait pourtant sa tête / Les étoiles le fusillaient" ("Shot by the stars the dying rider / Raised his head withal") (46, 47).

7   SB may be invoking the last lines of the penultimate verse of Rimbaud's *Le Bateau ivre*, a poem he translated in 1932: "Un enfant accroupi plein de tristesses, lâche / Un bateau frêle comme un papillon de mai" ("a child, full of sadness, / Squatting, looses a boat as frail / As a moth into the fragrant evening") (Rimbaud, *Œuvres complètes*, 164; Arthur Rimbaud, *Drunken Boat*, tr. Samuel Beckett [Reading: Whiteknights Press, 1976] 33).

8   Duthuit's destination is unknown.

6. From left to right: Georges Duthuit, Bram van Velde, Marguerite Duthuit-Matisse, Jacques Putman, Andrée Putman. Chez Fernand, Rue Saint-Nicolas, Paris 11

GEORGES DUTHUIT

1.3.49   Paris

Cher vieux

J'ai envie de vous écrire. C'est ma seule excuse.

Côté travaux :

Vitrac Traduction souvent mauvaise et incorrecte. J'ai revu seule-ment le 1er acte. Puis éprouvé le besoin de changer d'air.[1]

Leibnitz C'était évidemment à dire.[2]

Préface pour Ponge Il paraît que ça plaît à Ponge, qui cependant à mon avis en émerge drôlement vulnérable. Fénéon, Chazal, Ponge, ne serait-ce pas finalement au fond la même boulimie? Mais chut. Et zut.[3]

Textes Ponge Ne peux rien faire sans l'original.[4]

Ponge sur Braque C'est dégoûtant. "Braque a maintenant plus de 60 ans et le monde commence à rentrer dans sa rainure"!![5] Qu'en termes galants. Pour un élève des réalistes en politique, c'est un élève qui titube drôlement.[6] Il a du mal à s'en tirer, de sa rainure, à la faveur de verbes "amortis" et de parenthèses. Quel soulagement de nous savoir revenus à tout jamais de la fête galante et jetés à nouveau nus devant le poisson mort (et le morceau de charbon).[7] Jolie image de Braque sur le "ber". Que veut dire exactement "porte à faux" entre les gencives de l'esthète?[8] Bram a rencontré notre grand chosier à son exposition chez Michaud. Il a tout regardé (enfin presque tout) avec autant d'attention que s'il s'était trouvé bloqué devant un oursin puis a posé une question à laquelle Bram, n'y ayant rien compris, n'a pu répondre. Fin des rapports.[9]

Queneau. Est-ce absolument nécessaire? "La servante, qui s'était [illeg 1 word] dans la cuisine . .": Traduction: "Who had wanted . . ."[10]

Mallarmé Je me suis permis de substituer à la divagation De même, rapport avec mes compétences, celle ayant pour immolé Edouard Manet, à cause de quelques pittoresques balbutiements sur l'oeil et la main.[11]

Introduction à Fénéon. Je l'ai entamée. Coup de sang à huitaine.[12]

Jolie phrase de Suzanne:
  "Ici est tombée face au temps la jeunesse de . . . . . Halte."[13]

Nous avons passé quelques bonnes soirées avec Marguerite. Nous lui souhaitons de trouver vite ce qu'elle cherche et puis de prendre un peu de bon repos.

Hier nous avons surpris dans le bois de Meudon un énorme pivert vert et jaune (naturellement). Il s'est agrippé au tronc, l'a mis vivement entre lui et nous, puis est monté en courant, je le suppose, jusqu'aux branches supérieures. Une absurde joie m'a rempli.[14]

Bram s'est remis au travail. Marthe est revenue. J'ai raconté à Bram l'histoire Martin – Tal-Coat, que je tenais d'André. Il a ri, mais vraiment comme un fou, en rosissant, comme disait l'autre.[15] Marguerite nous a parlé d'une dame anglaise qui s'intéresse aux tableaux et n'a rien pu voir chez Maeght.[16]

J'ai lu aussi sur la peinture, avec vos notes, mais n'ai rien pu y ajouter. Je crois que c'est le côté descriptif qui m'a paralysé, ou plutôt qui ne m'a pas déparalysé. Je suis arrivé à faire les 3 premières strophes des Phares, c'est tout. Je ne crois pas pouvoir aller plus loin. André m'a dit que ça pourrait servir, si je pouvais y ajouter l'envoi (c'est à dire rien moins que les 3 dernières strophes!). Mais il me semble que c'est tout ou rien. Nous en reparlerons.[17]

Vous pouvez être content, à mon avis, du 4ème numéro. Puis il y a un côté scoop qui impressionnera les Améros avertis.[18]

On a dévalisé l'appartement de Picabia, volé fourrures (tiens!), bijoux (tiens! tiens!), etc., mais épargné les toiles. Trop orphiques peut-être.[19] Ça me rappelle que j'ai terminé enfin le texte de Gabrielle sur Apollinaire. Vous pensiez peut-être que vous alliez y couper![20]

Revenez vite tous les deux pleins d'oxygène et de courage. Vous nous en passerez un peu.

Affectueusement à tous 2 de nous deux.

Sam

ALS; 2 leaves, 3 sides; Duthuit collection.

1.3.49   Paris

Dear old friend

I feel like writing to you. That is my only excuse.

On the work front:

<u>Vitrac</u> Translation often bad and incorrect. I have only gone back over the 1st act. Then felt the need for a change of air.[1]

<u>Leibniz</u> Obviously had to be said.[2]

<u>Preface for Ponge</u> I gather that Ponge likes it, though in my view he comes out of it as pretty damned vulnerable. Fénéon, Chazal, Ponge, maybe in the end it is all the same bulimia? But hush. And pish.[3]

<u>Ponge texts</u> Can do nothing without the original.[4]

<u>Ponge on Braque</u> It is revolting. "Braque is now over 60 and the world is beginning to fit into his groove"!![5] What oft was thought. For someone who is a pupil of the realists in politics, he is pretty unsteady on his feet.[6] He has a struggle to get out of that groove of his, making great play with "muffled" verbs and parentheses. What a relief to know that we are back for good and all from the fête galante, and pitched, naked once more, in front of the dead fish (and the lump of coal).[7] Nice image of Braque's on the "cradle". What exactly does "awkward position" mean, coming from between the gums of our aesthete?[8] Bram met our great thinger at his exhibition at the Michaud gallery. He looked at everything (well, almost everything) as attentively as if he had found himself stuck in front of a sea-urchin, then asked a question to which Bram, who had no idea what he meant, had no reply. End of dealings.[9]

<u>Queneau.</u> Is it absolutely necessary? "The servant girl, who had [illegible, 1 word] into the kitchen . .": Translation: "Who had wanted ..."[10]

<u>Mallarmé</u> I have taken the liberty of substituting for the "divagation" <u>De même</u>, thinking about my competence, the one that has Edouard Manet as sacrificial victim, on account of a few picturesque stammerings about the eye and the hand.[11]

<u>Introduction to Fénéon.</u> I have made a start on it. Aneurism in a week's time.[12]

A nice phrase by Suzanne:

"Here fell, facing time, the youth of . . . . . Halt."[13]

We have spent a few enjoyable evenings with Marguerite. We do hope she will soon find what she is looking for, and then have a good rest.

Yesterday in the Bois de Meudon we startled a huge woodpecker, green and yellow (of course). It dug its claws into the trunk, briskly put that between us and it, then ran up, to the top branches, I suppose. An absurd joy welled up in me.[14]

Bram has taken up his work again. Marthe has come back. I told Bram the Martin – Tal-Coat story, which I had from André. He laughed like a man demented, really, going all pink, as the man said.[15] Marguerite told us about an English lady who is interested in the paintings and did not manage to see any chez Maeght.[16]

I have been reading too about painting, with your notes, but I have not been able to add anything. I think it is the descriptive side that paralysed me, or rather that did not unparalyse me. I managed to do the first three stanzas of the "Phares" ("The Lighthouses"), that is all. I do not think I can go any further. André told me that would do, if I could just add on the Envoi (that is, the last three stanzas, no less!). But I think that it is all or nothing. We shall talk about this another time.[17]

You can feel pleased, I think, with the fourth issue. And then there is a "scoop" side to it that will impress the better-informed Yanks.[18]

Someone broke into Picabia's flat, stole furs (well, well!), jewellery (well, well, well!), etc., but spared the paintings. Too Orphic, maybe.[19] That reminds me that I have at last finished Gabrielle's piece on Apollinaire. Perhaps you thought you were going to get away without it![20]

Come back, both of you, full of oxygen and courage. You can pass some on to us.

   Love to you 2 from us both.

   Sam

1   It is not known which work by Roger Vitrac (1899–1952) Duthuit has asked SB to look over; nothing by Vitrac appears in *Transition*.

2   It is not known to what SB is referring by "Leibnitz"; nothing by or about Gottfried Leibniz appears in *Transition*.

3   "Préface pour Ponge" by Duthuit's assistant and collaborator Pierre Schneider (b. 1925) appears translated by SB as "Introduction to the Works of Francis Ponge," in *Transition Fifty* no. 6 (October 1950) 68–74. In *Transition Forty-Nine* no. 5, there appears an article by André du Bouchet (1924–2001), in a translation by SB, lauding the art criticism of Félix Fénéon (1861–1944): "Félix Fénéon or The Mute Critic" (76–79); this is directly followed by "La Grande Jatte: Extracts from the Collected Works of Félix Fénéon," in an unsigned translation almost certainly by SB (80–85).

4   SB is probably referring to Francis Ponge's "Poems," which appear in a translation by Pierre Schneider and Richard Wilbur (*Transition Fifty* no. 6, 75–86).

5   Francis Ponge's article "Braque, or Modern Art as Event and Pleasure" is published in SB's translation. The present sentence is translated as "Braque has passed his sixtieth year and the world has begun to enter his groove" (*Transition Forty-Nine* no. 5, 45).

6   Molière, *Le Misanthrope*, I.ii.325: "Ah! qu'en termes galants ces choses-là sont mises" (Oh how gracefully these things are put) (*Le Misanthrope*, ed. Jacques Arnavon, L'Interprétation de la Comédie Classique [Paris: Plon, 1914] 167).
  Ponge writes: "Well, to the political realists whose disciple and friend I flatter myself I am" ("Braque, or Modern Art as Event and Pleasure," 43). Context is furnished by Bernard Beugnot, editor of Ponge's collected works:

> Le public auquel Ponge s'adresse l'amène à adopter un ton à la fois pédagogique et tendu, un peu insistant, côtoyant par moments la polémique, anticipant les objections … Ponge, qui n'a pas rompu avec le Parti et qui s'affiche encore comme "l'élève et l'ami" des "réalistes en politique" (les communistes) ne renouvelle toutefois pas sa carte de membre en 1947. (Francis Ponge, *Œuvres complètes*, I, ed. Bernard Beugnot, Bibliothèque de la Pléiade [Paris: Gallimard, 1999] 950.) (The readership that Ponge is addressing leads him to adopt a tone at once pedagogical and stiff, somewhat insistent, edging at moments towards polemic, dealing in advance with objections … Ponge, who has not broken with the Party, and still makes bold to present himself as "the disciple and friend" of the "political realists" [the Communists], nonetheless does not renew his membership in 1947.)

7   Ponge writes of Braque's work: "We are again flung naked, like primitive man, face to face with nature. The canons of Greek beauty, the charms of perspective, historiography, *fêtes galantes*, concern us no further. Not even decoration. What is there to decorate? Our dwelling is destroyed, and our palaces and temples; at least in our mind; they revolt us" ("Braque, or Modern Art as Event and Pleasure," 46).

8   Ponge's original runs: "L'idée, dit Braque, est le *ber* du tableau. C'est-à-dire l'échafaudage d'où le bateau se libère, pour glisser à la mer. Point de porte-à-faux. Surtout point de recherche du porte-à-faux" ("Braque ou l'art moderne comme événement et plaisir," *Œuvres complètes*, I, 139); SB translates this: "The idea, says Braque, is the *cradle* of the picture. That is to say the scaffolding from which the ship frees itself, and slips to the sea. Above all no gratuity, no search after gratuity" ("Braque, or Modern Art as Event and Pleasure," 46). SB's Gallicism – "gratuity" for

"gratuité" – masks a further difficulty, as neither is part of the normal connotations of "porte-à-faux," used in the present letter to mean "awkwardness."

9   Francis Ponge's best-known work was *Le Parti pris des choses* (1942; *The Nature of Things*).
SB probably refers to Bram van Velde's exhibition of 1946 at the Galerie Mai in Paris, of which Marcel Michaud was director (see 31 October 1945, n. 2).

10   It is not known which Queneau text SB is translating; no text by Queneau appears in *Transition*.

11   "De Même" appears in "Variations sur un sujet" by Stéphane Mallarmé (*Œuvres complètes*, II, ed. Bertrand Marchal, Bibliothèque de la Pléiade [Paris: Gallimard, 2003] 242–244). Mallarmé's "Edouard Manet" finishes, in SB's translation:

> Memory: he said, then, so well: 'The eye, a hand', that I muse again. This eye – Manet – this child eye of old urban stock, new, set on things, on persons, virgin and abstract, preserved, only yesterday, the immediate freshness of meeting, in the claws of glancing smile, in mockery then, before the pose, of the fatigues of a twentieth sitting. His hand – the pressure felt clear and prompt affirming in what mystery the limpid vision coursed within it, to establish, vivid, pale, profound, keen, haunted with dark, the new and French masterpiece. ("Edouard Manet," *Transition Forty-Nine* no. 5, 88; *Œuvres complètes*, II, 146–147.)

12   SB refers to his translating of André du Bouchet's article, "Félix Fénéon or The Mute Critic."

13   No written source has been found for this quotation.

14   The Forest of Meudon is situated close to Paris, southwest of the city.

15   Bram van Velde, Marthe Arnaud, André du Bouchet.
Paul Martin (1895–1984) had founded the Galerie de France in Paris in 1942, which highly influential gallery he ran until late 1950. André du Bouchet suggested that Martin returned Tal-Coat's recent work to him, asking for "more color" (interview with André du Bouchet, 1 December 1994). The year 1949 saw Martin preparing an exhibition of Tal-Coat's work which opened on 6 December: Tal-Coat, peintures (1927–1939). Being unpersuaded of the value of Tal-Coat's recent work, Martin chose to exhibit only early works by the artist (Claire Stoullig ed., *Tal-Coat devant l'image* [Geneva: Musées d'Art et d'Histoire, Genève; Musée d'Unterlinden, Colmar; Musée Picasso, Antibes; Kunstmuseum, Winterthur, 1997] 206).

16   The English inquirer has not been identified.

17   The first three stanzas of Baudelaire's poem "Les Phares" start with the names of artists: "Rubens," "Léonard de Vinci," and "Rembrandt" (*Œuvres complètes*, I, 13). SB's translation did not appear in *Transition* or elsewhere.

18   The fourth issue of *Transition*, though entitled *"Forty-Eight,"* was printed only on 15 January 1949. By "scoop," SB may be referring to the lengthy "Documents" section with which the journal ends, dealing as it does with two controversial issues: "The Church and French Writers (II)," and "The 'German Question' in France" (113–150).

19   The journal *Qui Détective? Le Magazine de l'énigme et de l'aventure* devoted a long article to the burglary on 26 February of Francis Picabia's studio at 82 Rue des Petits Champs, Paris 2, reporting that a fur coat and several pieces of jewelry were stolen,

and that the hunt for the burglars had been successful (Robert Buffet, "Course au Trésor," *Qui Détective? Le Magazine de l'énigme et de l'aventure* 142 [21 March 1949] 3–5).

20 "Apollinaire" by Gabrielle Picabia was translated by SB (*Transition Fifty*, no. 6, 110–125).

GEORGES DUTHUIT

2.3.49   Paris

Mon cher vieux Georges

Assez de ce vous garou, veux-tu?[1]

Ta très belle lettre ce matin. Elle me plonge dans trop de courants pour que je puisse me soucier de ma nage. Donc seulement quelques signaux, après lecture répétée. Je tâcherai qu'ils soient simples.

Bram et moi, nous sommes loin l'un de l'autre, si je nous ai bien devinés, quoique réunis à un moment, c'est à dire à tout moment, dans un même coincement, car il y en a qui ne lâchent pas. Je veux dire – non, pas de ça. C'est un endroit (drôle que je voie toujours tout en termes de boîte) d'où l'on ne peut sortir vers aucun des espaces que tu énumères, et certes Bram n'y parvient pas plus que moi. Mais il s'y essaie, ou y tient si tu préfères, en se créant au fur et à mesure une [*for* un] espace paradis qui l'y autorise, espace nouveau où traînent forcément quelques réminiscences de ceux si généreusement mis à notre disposition et dont tant d'artistes se sont si bellement gargarisés et dont d'autres encore ont simplement pris leur parti, fait leur affaire, comme il semble naturel en effet qu'on fasse bonne face contre mauvaise fortune, à supposer qu'elle soit mauvaise, et tous finissent bien par s'assoupir dans l'unanimité faite à ce sujet. Pardonne ce ton doctoral, mais sous le bonnet quel chahut. Pour Bram aussi c'est un mauvais pas, d'où chaque fois ces montagnes et ce foudroiement – et ces longs silences où il récupère. Ce n'est pas pour rien qu'il parle si souvent de dominer et de vaincre, c'est à dire de sortir, et on voit de lui émerger en effet, 5 ou 6 fois par l'an dont il ne veut pas, une main, une épaule, un oeil, implorant vers la prise qu'il n'a pas su s'assurer. J'ai cru à un moment donné qu'il finirait par y renoncer, par peindre le coincement, ne serait-ce que par épuisement. Il m'a semblé voir s'amorcer cette grande aventure dans certaines toiles, par exemple dans la peinture qui est chez toi, et d'une façon beaucoup plus nette et dramatique encore dans quelques-unes des grandes gouaches sombres exposées chez Michaud et qu'il faut absolument que tu ailles voir chez Boré.[2] Mais je commence à croire depuis quelque temps qu'il est trop tard et que ce sera jusqu'à la fin ces formidables tentatives de rétablissement vers une cime furieusement rêvée, et qu'à vrai dire il porte dans ses bras, et que ce sera chez lui jusqu'à la fin la seule beauté de l'effort et de l'échec, au lieu de celle, tellement calme et même gaie, dont j'ai la prétention de me laisser hanter. N'empêche que pour moi ça reste une peinture sans précédent et où je trouve mon compte comme dans nulle autre, à cause justement de cette fidélité à l'oubliette et de ce refus d'une liberté à surveiller. De cette nécessité de génie où il se trouve de reconnaître à son trou, tout en s'obstinant à vouloir s'y arracher, la liberté, les hauteurs, la lumière et les seuls dieux qui le regardent et qu'il n'y a d'évasion que partielle et vers une mutilation. Et cependant le tableau c'est la trappe qui s'ouvre. Tou[t] ça est littéraire, simpliste, mais à chacun son poumon. Je ne parlerai pas de moi, je t'en ai assez parlé pour qu'il ne me reste plus à répondre à la question que tu me poses et que tu saches combien je suis de compagnie avec B et combien peu. Je t'entends dire que ce sont des échecs fort réussis et en effet, en tant que peinture, cela doit être le cas, quoique je n'en sache absolument rien. J'ai cru y voir force "désagréments et défauts", comme dit Ponge, sans vouloir un seul instant les convertir en qualités.[3] Mais je suis fermé aux questions de facture (en peinture, où elle se taille de si jolis succès à la Hayden) et il est certain que je verrai toujours à celle de Bram l'arrière-faix de l'infaisable. Je me rappelle m'être fendu autrefois, il y a les 20 ans règlementaires, étant moins peu que maintenant, d'un article furibond sur les poètes nodernes irlandais, où je posais en critère de la poésie valable moderne la conscience prise de l'objet disparu. Déjà! Et de parler, comme du seul terrain accessible au poète, du no man's land qu'il projette autour de lui, un peu comme la flamme sa zone d'évaporation.[4] Triste escamotage en effet, où la chasse continue. J'y pense en te lisant sur l'école d'Aix.[5] On trouve le même respect frisson[n]ant du dehors dans un van Goyen, et Dieu sait si je l'aime.[6] Quelles affreuses noces depuis toujours que celles de l'artiste se frottant, de plus en plus câlin comme tu le dis, contre ses meubles, dans la terreur d'en être délaissé.[7] A quoi on nous oppose, comme la seule alternative, les pures manstuprations de l'art orphique et abstrait. Et si l'on ne bandait tout simplement plus? Comme dans la vie. Assez de sperme répandu.

> Dans un bordel d'Athènes,
> Un jour que Démosthènes
> Enculait Cicéron
> (Enculait Cicéron),
> Le jus philosophique
> De sa bitte héroique
> Coulait à gros bouillon
> (Coulait à gros bouillon).

Voilà les canons qui nous foutent le tabès encore.[8]

Ce que Vigny dit du mépris, je le dirais volontiers de ce monde, ou si tu veux cet état, que je ne fais encore qu'entrevoir, car il n'est pas trop d'une vie pour s'habituer à cette obscurité-là, et dont par conséquent je n'ai jamais pu te parler qu'en bavant des ronds de cagoule.[9] Le fait est que d'y être vous décourage de parler et de ne pas y être vous en disqualifie. Mais je sais que tu as senti quand même ce que je voulais dire. Et moi qui croyais ne pas avoir à parler de moi. Je ne sais pas ce que c'est (d'y être vous décourage de savoir), mais je sais que c'est une grande consolation, à tout, partout, devant la feuille surtout, et moi j'ai grandement besoin d'être consolé, je suis fier, mais pas de cette fierté-là. Mes forces diminuent? Parfait, elles se foutront un peu moins dans mes jambes. Tout ce qui me diminue, à commencer par ces chers souvenirs, m'en facilitent l'accès. Je ne risquerai rien à y vivre, j'aurai à peine le temps d'y naître. Et c'est sans doute à cette naissance, enfin, que le travail devra s'arrêter. Comme ça on voit un peu mieux ce qu'il y a à faire, et par quels

moyens. Ce sera un travail de frontière, de passage, où par conséquent le vieux charabia peut encore servir, en mourant. Une longue estompe. On cesse. Mais à la faveur quand même d'un autre être qui, s'il ne doit jamais s'exprimer (et qui sait?), n'en est pas moins pour beaucoup dans . . . l'affaire. Si c'est ça la mort, allons-y.
[Fragment]

TL; 1 leaf, 2 sides, fragment; Duthuit collection.

2.3.49   Paris

My dear Georges,

Shall we stop the scraping and bowing, and go for thee-ing and thou-ing? What say you?[1]

Your lovely letter this morning. It pushes me out into too many currents for me to worry about how I swim. So just a few signals, after much re-reading. I shall try to keep them simple.

Bram and I are a long way apart from each other, if I have sensed us right, although at one moment, that is at any moment, close together in one and the same stuckness, for that can come in forms that do not easily let go. I mean – no, none of that. It is a place (odd how I always see things in terms of boxes) from which there is no way out towards any of the spaces that you list, and certainly Bram makes no more headway than I do. But he does try his hand at it, or has a mind to it if you prefer, by creating for himself a paradise-space which allows him to do so, a new space in which there are still, inevitably, a few lingering reminiscences of those so generously put at our disposal and which so many artists have gone on about so eloquently, and which others have simply resigned themselves to, settled to, since it seems natural that one should put on a show of making the best of a bad job, if bad it be, and all concerned end up settling comfortably into the unanimity that surrounds the whole business. Forgive this doctoral tone, but what a din there is going on under the Tudor bonnet. For Bram too it is a bad place to be stuck, hence each time those mountains, and that thunderbolt action – and those long silences in which he recovers. It is not for nothing that he so often talks of dominating and conquering, that is, getting out, and sure enough you can see emerging, five or six times in a year, unwanted, a hand, a shoulder, an eye, reaching imploringly towards the grasp that he has not been able to secure. I thought at one point that he would end up giving that up, and painting the stuckness, if only from exhaustion. I felt I was seeing the beginnings of that great adventure in certain paintings, for instance in the painting you have, and much more sharply and dramatically in some of the great dark gouaches that were exhibited at the Michaud, and which you must go and see chez Bauret.[2] But for some time now I have been beginning to think that it is too late and that right up to the end there will be those tremendous attempts at getting back up towards a peak furiously dreamed of, and which in actual fact he holds in his own arms, and that in his case, right to the end, there will only be the beauty of attempt and failure, instead of the kind, so calm and even gay, that I claim haunts me. For all that, it is still, for me, a painting without precedent, in which as in no other I find what I am seeking, precisely because of this fidelity to the prison-house, this refusal of any probationary freedom. Because of that necessity of genius where he finds himself, to recognise, in his hole, even as he obstinately seeks to pull himself out of it, the freedom, the high places, the light and the only gods that concern him, and that there is no escape other than partial, and even then only towards mutilation. And yet the painting is the trapdoor opening. All this is literary, over-simplified, but we breathe as best we can. I will not talk about myself – I have done that often enough for me not to have to give any further answers to the question you ask me, and for you to know how much and how little I stand together with B. I can hear you saying that these are highly successful failures, and indeed, as painting, that must be true, although I have absolutely no idea. I thought I could see in it a great many "blemishes and defects", as Ponge says, without wanting for a moment to convert them into qualities.[3] But I am closed to questions of craftsmanship (in painting, where it can produce such nice successes à la Hayden) and it is certain that I shall always see in Bram's the afterbirth of the unfeasible. I remember coming out once, the regulation 20 years ago, being at that time less little than now, with an angry article on modern Irish poets, in which I set up, as criterion of worthwhile modern poetry, awareness of the vanished object. Already! And talking, as the only terrain accessible to the poet, of the no man's land that he projects round himself, rather as the flame projects its zone of evaporation.[4] A dismal kind of dodging, right enough, where the hunt goes on. I am thinking about it as I read you on the Aix school.[5] One finds the same quivering respect for what lies outside in a van Goyen, and God knows I am fond enough of him.[6] What ghastly ceremonies over the years: the artist rubbing himself, more and more wheedlingly as you say, against his furniture, out of terror of being abandoned by it.[7] To which, as only alternative, we find ourselves being faced with the pure manstuprations of Orphic and abstract art. What if we simply stopped altogether having erections? As in life. Enough sperm floating about the place.

> One day in Athens
> Old man Demosthenes
> Was buggering Cicero
> (Buggering Cicero)
> The intellectual stock
> From his most heroic cock
> Flowed soupily out
> (Flowed soupily out).

There: sung in the round it would give us the clap again.[8]

What Vigny says about contempt, I would gladly say it about this world, or this state, if you like, of which I can still only catch a glimpse, for a lifetime is not too long for us to get used to that darkness, and which as a result I have never been able to talk to you about except by mouthing extravagant nonsense.[9] The fact is that being in it discourages you from talking about it and not being in it disqualifies you from talking about it. But I know that you have all the same felt what I meant. And there I was, thinking I did not have to talk about me. I do not know what it is (being in it discourages you from knowing), but I know that it is a great consolation, for everything, everywhere, above all in front of the blank page, and I badly need to be consoled; I am proud, but not proud in that way. Is my strength ebbing away? Fine, it will make its miserable way into my legs a bit less. Anything that lessens me, starting with my precious memories, makes access to it easier. I shall be running no risks by living in it – I shall hardly have time to be born in it. And no doubt it will be at that birth that, at last, the work will have to stop. That way one can see a little better what has to be done, and by what means. It will be boundary work, passage work, in which as a result the old rubbish can still be some use, while the dying is going on. A long slow fading. One ceases. But with the help, all the same, of another being who, if he is never to find expression (and who knows?), is nonetheless heavily involved ... the business. If that is what death is, let's have it.

1 For discussion of this opening and its translation, see George Craig's "Translator's Preface," p. xxxvi.

2 Georges Duthuit owned Bram van Velde's *Nature morte* (Putman 51) (Rainer Michael Mason, ed., *Bram van Velde: 1895–1981, Rétrospective du centenaire* [Geneva: Musée Rath, Musées d'Art et d'Histoire, 1996] 95, plate 35).

The Michaud exhibition: 1 March 1949, n. 9.

Jean Bauret (1907–1990), whose surname SB mistakenly spells "Boré," then resident at Fontenay-Mauvoisin, was a friend and collector of Bram van Velde.

Bauret owned *Peinture I* (c. 1937–1938, Putman 112; Mason, ed., *Bram van Velde*, 105, plate 44); this is mentioned by SB in "La Peinture des van Velde ou le monde et le pantalon," 351. Bauret also owned an untitled gouache (now referred to as *Grande gouache brune*, Putman 105, Stuttgart Staatsgalerie inv. 2708; Mason, ed., *Bram van Velde*, 116, plate 55); this is the subject of a work by Bauret's son, Jean-François Bauret, *L'Analyse photographique d'un tableau de Bram van Velde* (Fontenay-Mauvoisin: chez l'auteur, 1960).

3 Ponge elaborates, in SB's translation:

> In what then shall taste consist, in the matter of modern art? Doubtless in being able to discern, among the causes of surprise or irritation that the works afford me, those that are, in virtue of some call *deep down* within me, efficient and motivated. In being able to discern, beneath the *blemishes* or *defects* of such-and-such a work, so solid a foundation of qualities (better still, in those very defects such quality) that the defects will be deemed qualities, eventually. ("Braque, or Modern Art as Event and Pleasure," 44.)

4   SB refers to his article "Recent Irish Poetry," published under the pseudonym Andrew Belis in *The Bookman* (86.515 [August 1934] 235–236; rpt. in Beckett, *Disjecta*, 70–76). The article opens:

> I propose, as rough principle of individuation in this essay, the degree in which the younger Irish poets evince awareness of the new thing that has happened, or the old thing that has happened again, namely the breakdown of the object, whether current, historical, mythical or spook . . .
>
> The artist who is aware of this may state the space that intervenes between him and the world of objects; he may state it as no-man's-land, Hellespont or vacuum, according as he happens to be feeling resentful, nostalgic or merely depressed. (235.)

SB puts a grave rather than an acute accent on "réglementaires," and mistypes "nodernes" for "modernes." His expression "étant moins peu que maintenant" is enigmatic; the translation suggests one possible reading.

5   Georges Duthuit is visiting the home of André Masson (1896–1987) at Le Tholonet near Aix-en-Provence. By "l'école d'Aix" SB is presumably referring to artists working in and around Aix-en-Provence, often under the influence of Cézanne, particularly André Masson and Tal-Coat, the latter of whom was also resident at this time at Le Tholonet; as well perhaps as to other artists and collectors of their circle, such as Cecil Michaelis (1913–1997) and Fernand Pouillon (1912–1986) (Florian Rodari, "Biographie commentée par les textes," in Stoullig, ed., *Tal-Coat devant l'image*, 189–225). From Masson's home, on 28 February, Duthuit has written to SB:

> André était en train d'expliquer ses préoccupations actuelles avec lesquelles je suis depuis pas mal de temps familier, et qui sont également celles de Tal-Coat [...] d'un accord tacite, ils prétendent, plutôt qu'à affirmer des formes, à délivrer l'une de l'autre, à créer des zones de silence entre elles, des champs de repos. Le mot de "vide" revient souvent dans les conversations. Au bord de ce vide, se trouve un signe, une valeur juste indiquée et qui en donne la clé, qui l'anime et qui l'ouvre. On essaye, en travaillant, de ne pas se laisser paralyser par l'idée du tableau à faire, à terminer. On s'arrête quand il n'y a plus rien à dire, quand on ne peut pas alléger, aérer les masses plus qu'elles ne le sont. On essaie de dénouer les nœuds de vipères de l'espace, et permettre à notre esprit de se mouvoir plus aisément dans cette blancheur, mise en œuvre, en mouvement par des notes infiniment discrètes de gris, d'ocre presque éteints. Rester intense pourtant, mais avec légèreté. Mais dans ces deux cas, on part toujours d'une perception normale, d'une sensation éprouvée, d'un ordre latent, peut-être, de la nature, et qu'il s'agit de dégager, de perpétuer. (Undated letter [28 February 1949], Duthuit collection; also published in Rémi Labrusse, "Extraits de la correspondance entre Georges Duthuit et Samuel Beckett," in Stoullig, ed., *Tal-Coat devant l'image*, 106.) (André was busy explaining his current concerns, with which I've been familiar for a fair while now, and which are also Tal-Coat's [...] by some tacit agreement they claim that, rather than putting down forms, they are setting them free from one another, creating between them zones of silence, fields of non-movement. The word "void" often crops up in their conversations. On the edge of this void stands a sign, a value just set there that offers a key to it, opens it up, breathes life into it. One tries, while working, not to be paralysed by the idea of the picture that has to be made, to be finished. One stops when there's no more to say, when one can no longer lighten, aerate the masses more than has already been done. One tries to untangle the vipers' nests of space and allow

the mind to move more easily in this blankness set out, set moving by infinitely discreet, almost faded tones of grey, of ochre. Remain intense though, but with a light touch. But in both their cases one starts out from a normal perception, a lived sensing of a latent order, of nature perhaps, which it is their task to bring out, to perpetuate.)

6   Jan van Goyen (1596–1656).

7   In his letter of 28 February, Duthuit has written:

> Mes amis peintres, ici, dans un paysage de toute splendeur, cherchent comme nous leur vie dans le travail et sans doute ne rejettent-ils pas l'idée qu'il y a, qui nous guettent, parmi les vapeurs qui nous empoisonnent et les villes qui nous usent, des monstres de stupeur ou de brutalité, et que par ailleurs, nous aussi, chacun à notre manière, nous sommes des monstres. C'est pourquoi sans doute ils ne se lancent plus sur l'univers avec la fougue d'autrefois, pourquoi ils n'essayent plus de le violenter, ne l'abordent qu'avec des mains comme tremblantes, et murmurent quand ils auraient crié. Ils parviennent à faire un accommodement avec la vie, avec la matière, et tâchent de tourner en vie des poisons qu'ils n'absorbent plus qu'à très faible dose. (Duthuit collection; also published in Labrusse, "Extraits de la correspondance entre Georges Duthuit et Samuel Beckett," 106–107.) (My painter friends, here, in a countryside of surpassing splendour, are, like us, seeking their life in their work, and no doubt not denying the idea that there are, lying in wait for us, among the vapours that are poisoning us, the towns that are wearing us down, monsters of stupidity or brutality – and that, from another angle, we too, in our way, are monsters. That no doubt is why they no longer set about the universe with the passionate enthusiasm of earlier times; why they no longer try to force it, and only come at it with hands that are almost trembling, and murmur where once they shouted. They are contriving to reach some accommodation with life, with matter, and trying to turn into life poisons which now they absorb only in tiny doses.)

8   SB cites a "chanson de carabins" (medical student song); he adds an "s" to the standard French spelling "Démosthène."

9   SB may be thinking of lines from Part III of "La Flûte" by Alfred de Vigny: "Si, plus haut parvenus, de glorieux esprits / Vous dédaignent jamais, méprisez leur mépris" (If, reaching higher, glorious minds / Ever disdain you, meet their contempt with contempt) (*Œuvres complètes*, I, Bibliothèque de la Pléiade, ed. François Germain and André Jarry [Paris: Gallimard, 1986] 148).

GEORGES DUTHUIT

9.3.49

Cher Vieux

Partons cette fois-ci du rapport. C'est là où nous semblons nous rejoindre le mieux.[1]

Par rapport nous entendons, naturellement, non seulement celui, primaire, entre l'artiste et ce que le dehors lui propose, mais aussi et surtout ceux qui, en-dedans de lui, lui assurent des lignes de fuite et de recul et des changements de tensions et lui dispensent, entre autres bienfaits, celui de se sentir plusieurs (au bas mot), tout en restant (bien entendu) unique. Il peut donc se détourner du visible immédiat sans que cela tire à conséquence, sans cesser pour autant d'être un terme de relation. Inutile de nommer la peinture, hystérique ou raisonnée, sortie de ces miradors de repli qui, sommés d'avoir à nourrir l'expression, se prennent à ressembler d'étrange façon à celui du chevalet secoué par le mistral, devant le tohu-bohu des instants irremplaçables.

Est-ce à dire qu'un Bram, se refusant (à supposer qu'il y soit pour quelque chose) au rapport primaire, tire forcément son expression du jeu des autres? Si c'est oui, pourquoi diffère-t-elle tellement, d'une différence qui vraiment ne se laisse pas exprimer en degrés, de ce qu'on en a tiré déjà? Est-ce que parce que, chez lui, ces rapports intimes gardent le caractère propre du milieu où ils se nouent, alors que chez d'autres ils sont dénaturés par l'habitude de l'observation extravertie? Ou parce que, en raison de son peu d'aptitude pour ce genre de prospection, ils se nouent peu et mal? Et si c'est non, peut-on concevoir une expression en l'absence de rapports quels qu'ils soient, aussi bien entre le moi et le non-moi qu'à l'intérieur de celui-là?

Faut-il préciser la nature de ces rapports de soi en soi? Je suis mal placé pour le faire, n'en bénéficiant plus guère. Et je tendrai irrésistiblement à ramener au mien le cas de Bram, puisque c'est là la condition de pouvoir y être et en parler, et puis pour d'autres raisons moins avouables. Mettons qu'il s'agisse de l'agréable faculté d'exister sous diverses espèces, dont en quelque sorte les unes constatent les autres, ou qui se font constater à tour de rôle par celle préposée à cet office et qui, gorgée des visions ainsi obtenues, se livre de temps en temps à une petite séance d'autologie, avec un bruit goulu de succion.

Ainsi térébré, pour parler comme Fénéon, l'artiste peut se rouler dans la peinture dite non-figurative en toute tranquillité, avec l'assurance de n'être jamais à court de thèmes, d'être toujours devant lui-même et avec autant de variété que s'il n'avait jamais renoncé à flâner aux bords de la Seine.[2] Et ici encore triomphe la définition de l'artiste comme celui qui ne cesse d'être devant. Au lieu d'être devant les précipitants il est devant les précipités. Tu parles d'une villégiature.

Pour moi la peinture de Bram ne doit rien à ces piètres consolations. Elle est nouvelle parce que la première à répudier le rapport sous toutes ces formes. Ce n'est pas le rapport avec tel ou tel ordre de vis-à-vis qu'il refuse, mais l'état d'être en rapport tout court et sans plus, l'état d'être devant. Il y a longtemps qu'on attend l'artiste assez courageux, assez à son aise dans les grandes tornades de l'intuition, pour saisir que la rupture avec le dehors entraîne la rupture avec le dedans, qu'aux rapports naïfs il n'existe pas de rapports de remplacement, que ce qu'on appelle le dehors et le dedans ne font qu'un. Je ne dis pas qu'il ne cherche pas à renouer. Ce qui importe, c'est qu'il n'y arrive pas. Sa peinture est, si tu veux, l'impossibilité de renouer. Il y a, si tu veux, refus et refus d'accepter son refus. C'est peut-être ce qui rend cette peinture possible. Pour ma part, c'est le gran rifiuto qui m'intéresse, non pas les héroïques tortillements auxquels nous devons une chose si belle.[3] J'en suis navré. Ce qui m'intéresse c'est l'au-delà du dehors-dedans où il fait son effort, non pas la portée de l'effort même. L'exilé béat n'habite pas Montrouge.[4]

Que peint-il donc, avec tant de mal, s'il n'est plus devant rien? Dois-je vraiment essayer de le redire, en rafraîchissant les images? Quoi que je dise, j'aurai l'air de l'enfermer à nouveau dans une relation. Si je dis qu'il peint l'impossibilité de peindre, la privation de rapport, d'objet, de sujet, j'ai l'air de le mettre en rapport avec cette impossibilité, avec cette privation, devant elles. Il est dedans, est-ce la même chose? Il les est, plutôt, et elles sont lui, d'une façon pleine, et peut-il y avoir des rapports dans l'indivisible? Pleine? Indivisible? Evidemment pas. Ca vit quand même. Mais dans une telle densité, c'est à dire simplicité, d'être, que seule l'éruption peut en avoir raison, y apporter le mouvement, en soulevant tout d'un bloc. S'il faut néanmoins y voir l'aboutissement d'un sourd travail de rapports secrets, mon Dieu, je me résignerai à ne pas être ridicule. Je ne veux rien prouver et les théories étanches ne me sont pas plus chères que celles qui laissent passer cette chère Vérité. J'essaie seulement d'indiquer la possibilité d'une expression en dehors du système de rapports tenu jusqu'à présent pour indispensable à qui ne sait pas se contenter de son seul nombril. Si tu me demandes pourquoi la toile ne reste pas blanche, je peux seulement invoquer cet inintelligible besoin, à tout jamais hors de cause, d'y foutre de la couleur, fût-ce en y vomissant son être.

Finalement, pour reprendre un motif où je n'ai jamais su bien te suivre, je ne vois pas du tout comment un travail pareil peut accrocher des considérations sur le temps et l'espace, ni pourquoi, dans ces toiles qui nous font grâce de ces catégories, on serait tenu de les remettre, sous des espèces plus riantes que celles familières de la division, extensibilité, compressibilité, mesurabilité, etc., à l'infini. On connaît déjà de ces honorables tentatives de bonification.[5] Et dire que le peintre, en enduisant une toile de couleurs, s'engage nécessairement dans la voie des relations spatiales et temporelles, me semble vrai uniquement pour celui qui n'a pas cessé de les faire intervenir sous la forme de rapports, ce qui n'est pas le cas de Bram, si j'ai bien bafouillé. Et dans ces servitudes de métier qui obligent à s'acoquiner à une surface matérielle imparfaitement plane et à mettre à s'y soulager une durée plus ou moins hoquetante, je ne peux voir un aveu que là où il y a en même temps propos d'en tirer parti. Que Bram fasse état de son passé, d'avenir meilleur et de Pietà à double vierge-mère, me laisse bien sûr froid comme Malone, c'est à dire à peine tiède, exception faite des extrémités, dont la tête. J'ai toujours pensé qu'il n'avait pas la moindre idée de ce qu'il faisait et que moi non plus. Mais c'est de préférence à cette dernière appréciation que j'essaierai de m'agripper, jusqu'au jour où je n'aurai plus besoin d'une main dans la mienne dans mon tort.

Voilà, mon cher Georges, j'ai fait un gros effort et nous ne sommes pas plus avancés. Je n'ai fait que dire la même chose que par deux fois déjà. Je ne peux plus écrire de façon suivie sur Bram ni sur n'importe quoi. Je ne peux pas écrire sur. Alors il va falloir, si tu n'es pas complètement dégoûté de moi, que tu me poses des ques-tions.[6] J'essaierai d'y répondre. Mais sache que moi qui ne parle guère de moi ne parle guère que de ça.

A samedi. Affectueusement

s/ Sam

10.3.49

Ta si gentille lettre ce matin. Il n'y a que toi pour saisir combien je suis peu à mon affaire dans ces histoires d'éclairage.[7] C'est pour Bram, c'est une affaire entendue. Mais à quel point est-ce un service? Qu'on en parle, qu'on en parle, mais autant que possible pas comme moi, il me semble. Et même si c'en est un, il y a des moments où l'impatience me gagne. Enfin, le plus clair de l'histoire, c'est mon envie de t'aider dans une besogne pas commode. Samedi nous verrons comment ça peut se goupiller à la satisfaction générale.

TLcc photocopy; 3 leaves, 3 sides with PS 10.3.49 side 3; UoR, BIF, MS 2907. TLS, 2 leaves, 2 sides (leaf 2 missing, but photocopied from UoR, BIF, MS 2907); Duthuit collection. Previous publication, Samuel Beckett, "Lettre à Georges Duthuit à propos de Bram," in Mason, ed., *Bram van Velde*, 45–48; Samuel Beckett, "Sam over Bram," tr. Matthijs Engelberts, Ruth Hemmes, and Erik Slagter, *Het Beckett Blad* 11 (Autumn 1996), 19–22; Samuel Beckett, "Lettre à Georges Duthuit 9 mars 1949–10 mars 1949," in S. E. Gontarski and Anthony Ulhmann, eds., *Beckett after Beckett* (Gainesville: Florida University Press, 2006) 15–21.

9.3.49

Dear Georges,

Let us start out this time from relation. That is where we seem to be closest.[1]

By relation we understand, naturally, not only the primary form, that between the artist and the outside world, but also and above all those which, within him, ensure that he has lines of flight and retreat, and changes of tension, and make available to him, among other benefits, that of feeling plural (to put it no higher), while remaining (of course) unique. He can therefore turn away from the immediate visible without that's having particular importance, yet still not ceasing to be a term of relation. No point in naming the painting, hysterical or reasoned, that comes out of those fall-back miradors which, called upon to have to give substance to the expression, begin to resemble strangely that of the easel shaken by the mistral, before the hurly-burly of irreplaceable moments.

Does that mean that a Bram, refusing (if, that is, he has any part in it) the primary relation, must necessarily draw his expression from the play of the others? If the answer is "yes", why does that expression differ so much – a difference which can really not be measured in degrees – from what others have already drawn from it? Is it because, in his work, these intimate relations retain the specific character of the frame within which they are formed, whereas in others they are distorted by the habit of outward-turned observation? Or because, by reason of his scant aptitude for this sort of prospecting, they form so seldom and so badly? And if not, can one conceive of expression in the absence of relations of whatever kind, whether those between 'I' and 'non-I' or those within the former?

Do we have to have exact definition of the nature of these self-to-self relations? I am ill equipped to provide it, having as I now do the benefit of so few. And I shall tend irresistibly to pull Bram's case over towards my own, since that is the condition of being in it and talking about it, and then for other reasons less easy to admit. Let us say that what is at issue is the enjoyable possibility of existing in diverse forms, all of them, as it were, confirming the existence of the others, or each in turn confirmed by the one designated for that purpose and which, bursting with the visions thus obtained, indulges from time to time in a little session of autology, amid greedy sounds of suction.

Thus terebrated, to speak like Fénéon, the artist can wallow untroubled in what is called non-figurative painting, assured of never being short of themes, of always being in front of himself and with as much variety as if he had never left off wandering idly along the banks of the Seine.[2] And here again we see triumphing the definition of the artist as he-who-is-always-*in-front-of*. Instead of being in front of the precipitants he is in front of the precipitates. Talk about a rest cure.

For me Bram's painting owes nothing to these feeble consolations. It is new because it is the first to repudiate relation in all these
forms. It is not the relation with this or that order of opposite that it
refuses, but the state of being in relation as such, the state of being in
front of. We have waited a long time for an artist who is brave enough,
is at ease enough with the great tornadoes of intuition, to grasp that
the break with the outside world entails the break with the inside
world, that there are no replacement relations for naive relations,
that what are called outside and inside are one and the same. I am not
saying that he makes no attempt to reconnect. What matters is that
he does not succeed. His painting is, if you will, the impossibility of
reconnecting. There is, if you like, refusal and refusal to accept
refusal. That perhaps is what makes this painting possible. For my
part, it is the *gran rifiuto* that interests me, not the heroic wrigglings to
which we owe this splendid thing.[3] It is awful to have to say so. What
interests me is what lies beyond the outside-inside where he does his
striving, not the scale of the striving itself. The visionary exile does
not live in Montrouge.[4]

What then does he paint, with such difficulty, if he is no longer in
front of anything? Must I really try to say it again, livening up the
images? Whatever I say, I shall seem to be locking him back into a
relation. If I say that he paints the impossibility of painting, the lack
of all relation, object, subject, it will look as if I am putting him into
relation with this impossibility, this lack; in front of them. He is
inside: is that the same thing? Rather he is them, and they are him,
fully. And can there be relations within the indivisible? Full?
Indivisible? Obviously not. But still, life goes on. But with such den-
sity, that is, simplicity, of being, that only eruption can get the better
of it, give it movement, by forcing everything upwards in one single
mass. If nevertheless we do have to see in it the outcome of the
unobservable working out of secret relations, well, I shall resign
myself to not being ridiculous. I have no wish to prove anything,
and watertight theories are no dearer to me than those that allow
dear Truth to slip through. I am only trying to point to the possibility
of an expression lying outside the system of relations hitherto held to

be indispensable to anyone who cannot be content with his own navel. If you ask me why the canvas does not stay blank, I can only invoke this unintelligible, unchallengeable need to splash colour on it, even if that means vomiting one's whole being.

Finally, to take up a theme in which I have never been much good at following you, I really do not see how work of this kind can bring in considerations of time and space, nor why, in paintings which let us off those categories, we should be obliged to put them back, in forms jollier than the familiar division, extensibility, compressibility, measurability, etc., ad infinitum. We know about these honourable attempts at improving.[5] And to say that the painter, by spreading colour on a canvas, is necessarily setting out along the road of spatial and temporal references, seems to me true only for someone who has never stopped bringing them in in the form of relations, which is not the case for Bram, if I have misexpressed myself aright. And in those servitudes of the craft that oblige painters to have dealings with an uneven material surface, and to put into relieving themselves on it a more or less jerky length of time, I see no kind of admission, except where there is at the same time intention to make something of it. That Bram should bring up his past, his better prospects, and a Pietà with a double virgin mother, naturally leaves me as cold as Malone, that is just about lukewarm, apart from my extremities, which include the head. I have always thought he had not the faintest idea about what he was doing, and neither had I. But my preference will still be to hold on to this last appreciation, until the day comes when I shall not need another hand to hold in my wrongness.

There, my old friend, I have made a great effort and we are no further forward. All I have done is say the same thing I have already said twice. I am no longer capable of writing in any sustained way about Bram or about anything. I am no longer capable of writing *about*. So, if you are not altogether sick of me, you are going to have to ask me questions.[6] I shall try to answer. But bear in mind that I who hardly ever talk about myself talk about little else.

Till Saturday. Love

Sam

10.3.49

Such a lovely, kind letter from you this morning. Who else would grasp how ill at ease I am in all this clarification business.[7] Agreed, it is all for Bram. But how much of a service is it? By all means let us have him talked about, but as far as possible not the way I do it, that is how I see it. And if service it is, there are moments when I feel impatience coming on. Anyhow, the one thing clear in the whole business is my wish to help you out in an awkward task. On Saturday we shall see how we might knock up something that will do for all concerned.

1   SB is probably responding to Duthuit's letter of 5 March, written from Masson's house at Le Tholonet. While composing this long letter (three single-spaced typed pages), Duthuit receives SB's of 2 March, and comments on SB's invitation to "tutoiement": "C'était un bien beau présent que la première phrase de ta lettre" (That was a lovely present, that first sentence of your letter) (Duthuit collection).

2   Félix Fénéon uses the word "térébrer" (meaning "bore," "pierce," or "perforate") in one of the extracts from his collected works translated by SB for publication in *Transition Forty-Nine* no. 5: "Etretat in particular solicits this painter of seascapes; he delights in these uprearing blocks, these terebrated masses, these abrupt ramparts whence, like trunks, flying buttresses of granite spring" ("La Grande Jatte: Extracts from the Collected Works of Félix Fénéon," 80).

3   Before he crosses the River Styx and enters Hell proper, Dante the pilgrim encounters the "neutrals": those who have in life made no commitment to a cause, and who must now desperately follow a standard-bearer while being stung by flies and wasps; among these he identifies "l'ombra di colui / che fece per viltà il gran rifiuto" (the shade of him who from cowardice made the great refusal; *Inferno*, Canto III, lines 59–60); traditionally, this was thought to be Pope Celestine V, who abdicated the papacy in 1294, though more recent commentators have suggested alternatives.
SB drops the dieresis in his spelling of "héroïques."

4   Bram van Velde's studio was in the Paris suburb of Montrouge, at 3 Rue Aristide-Briand (Jacques Kober, *Bram van Velde et ses loups* [Gap: Bartavelle, 1989] 11).

5   In his letter of 5 March to SB, Duthuit writes:

Aujourd'hui en effet André [Masson] cherche, de compagnie avec Tal Coat, à s'éloigner de la conception européenne (gréco-) scénique et policée du monde pour s'en remettre à une vision diffuse et découvrir, aux antipodes de "l'espace-limite", un espace mouvant, changeant, actif, qui s'évanouirait, fleurirait, mûrirait, disons un espace humain … Je pourrais tenter d'expliquer le fait d'un commencement de libération de ces lieux inimaginables qu'on appelle le Temps et l'Espace, où ma dépouille mortelle est priée de sauter dérisoirement, là d'un moment semblable à un autre, ici d'une partie superposable et identique à un autre, et où je suis condamné à faire le singe jusqu'à extinction complète de ma petite réserve de forces, pendant que les savants s'y dilatent et s'y congratulent du succès de leurs opérations, pendant que les peintres, depuis les Grecs surtout, depuis la préhistoire, depuis je ne sais quand, y logent des abstractions, des concepts, dans lesquels on s'obstine à me présenter le fin fond de la réalité. Ils n'arrêtent pas le temps, puisqu'ils se placent dans un temps qui n'est qu'une succession d'arrêts, qui n'est qu'immobilité. Ils n'approfondissent pas l'espace pour s'en dégager et nous aider à en sortir, puisque leur espace ne compte ni pour le corps, ni pour le cœur ni pour une pensée qui a ses racines dans le corps et le cœur. (Duthuit collection; also published in Labrusse, "Extraits de la correspondance entre Georges Duthuit et Samuel Beckett," 107, 109.) (Nowadays André [Masson], along with Tal Coat, is seeking to get away from the Graeco-scenic, European, institutionally ordered conception of the world, and move to a diffuse vision, there to discover, at the opposite pole from "space as limit", a space that is moving, changing, active, capable of vanishing, blossoming, ripening – shall we say a human space? ... I might try to explain the fact of a beginning of liberation of those unimaginable places called Time and Space, in which my mortal coil is requested to perform its derisory jiggling – there, from one similar moment to another, here from one superposable, identical part to another – and where I am condemned to carry on the grotesque pantomime till the last drop of my feeble reserves of strength, while the scientists grow great within it, congratulate each other on the success of their operations, while the painters, above all since the Greeks, since prehistoric times, since who knows when, embed in it abstractions, concepts which they go on and on presenting to me as being the very core of reality. They do not stop time, because they place themselves in a time which is no more than a succession of stops, which is nothing other than immobility. They do not reach a deeper understanding of space in order to step outside it and help us to emerge from it, since their space counts neither for the body, nor for the heart, nor for a thought whose roots are in the body and the heart.)

SB omits the circumflex on "connaît."

6   Duthuit's letter to SB of 5 March opened by stating: "Il ne s'agit pour moi que de vous inciter, aussi maladroitement que les circonstances l'exigent, à écrire un peu sur Bram – ne serait-ce que par la fureur d'avoir à me répondre. La fureur, ce serait magnifique." (For me the only issue is to incite you, as awkwardly as the circumstances require, to write something about Bram – if only out of fury at having to give me an answer. That fury would be magnificent.) (Duthuit collection; Rémi Labrusse, "Hiver 1949: Tal-Coat entre Georges Duthuit et Samuel Beckett," in Stoullig, ed., *Tal-Coat devant l'image*, 102).

7   Duthuit's letter referred to here has not been found.

It is not certain whether SB is using "éclairage" in the sense given in the translation, or whether he has in mind that other sense of the word which is "way of lighting," as in references to the way in which a painter deploys effects of light.

7. Bram van Velde, in his studio, Montrouge, c. 1950–1952

THOMAS MACGREEVY
DUBLIN

27.3.49   Paris
My dear Tom
    Very glad to have news of you. I had heard from Cauvet-
Duhamel of your Légion d'Honneur and should have written long
ago to congratulate you. I do so now, with all my affection.[1] I am

sorry to hear you have been in such poor health since your return. I think it is impossible to have health in Dublin. Of any kind. And the depressing feeling of always working for others and never for yourself does not make things easier for you. I wish you could get away for long months, without any obligations or anyone to look after, to your Vevey or wherever it is you fancy.[2] Cauvet very kindly sent me from Liverpool a newspaper cutting about a new discovery for treatment of Parkinsonism. I sent it to Frank rather than to mother directly, as I am not sure that she accepts the idea of Parkinsonism and in any case so as not to raise her hopes lightly. I hope he has got Alan to look into it. He writes with difficulty. It is probably only another form of palliative, but perhaps more satisfactory than the Parpanit.[3] I was very touched by Cauvet's kind thought. Mother writes, dictates rather, in fairly good form apparently. Frank says she is getting slowly more bowed and stiff and would like to have a nurse with her permanently. It will certainly come to that sooner or later, the later the better. There was some talk of Frank coming for a week or so to Paris, and I urged him to do so. But office and family tie him by the leg and there is little chance of him making the break. All more or less well with us. We are both tired, especially Suzanne. We have found and taken a room in a farmhouse at Ussy-sur-Marne, between Meaux and La Ferté-sous-Jouarre. Only 6 pounds a year, unfurnished. We are trying to get together a few scraps and hope to go there for a first short stay about Easter. Marvellous country, peace. The woman of the house, with a husband out of work and a small boy, seems a decent sort and won't bother us, will be even probably glad to help Suzanne for the honest penny. It is big dilapidated room on the ground looking out on old fruit trees and lilacs. The Marne 100 yards away, i.e. bathes of a sort. The little village was mentioned in dispatches 1914–18.[4] It is a relief to have a refuge for when the strain of noise, neighbours, visits and art cackle becomes unbearable. I expect to visit mother some time in July, shall probably stay not longer than a month. Morris Sinclair's Dutch wife has calved at Baudelocque, a daughter. Now their fun begins.[5] I have no news of anyone you know. We heard Rue Jacob, in the premises of some musical society, Schoenberg's Quintet for intestines presented by the indefatigable dodecaphonist Leibowitz. Suzanne loathed it. I was very interested, having only heard Pierrot Lunaire I think once, without pleasure, and now want to hear some Berg and Webern and more Schoenberg, never or hardly ever played in Paris. We heard Bartok's 3rd piano concerto (last work, unfinished) on the wireless, with great pleasure both of us.[6] Bram van Velde is in poor health and can't get on with his work. I have a kind of joint study on him with Duthuit in a coming Transition, dragged out of me, as the articles for Zervos and Maeght were dragged out of me. Each time I say never again and each time I am told it is for the sake of Bram. But what I write on him will do him more harm than good, as I have told him. However this time Duthuit is there to mollify my generalisations.[7] I have finished a second play in two acts: <u>En Attendant Godot</u>, and am now typing it out. The first is being read by Rouleau! Three novels in French are dragging around somewhere.[8] I don't see the possibility of anything else for a long time. I submitted the first play for the Prix Rivarol (not yet awarded as far as I know) and was told unofficially a little later that all plays and verse would be eliminated ipso facto and only novels considered! This between ourselves. Also that Gide, named among the committee, had lent his name on condition that he would not have to read anything![9] I translated Apollinaire's <u>Zone</u> (first poem of Alcools) for Duthuit.[10] There are some admirable passages. My kindest remembrances to Jack Yeats. I am writing to him very soon. Remember me also to your sister and nieces. Suzanne sends you her greetings. And from me, my dear Tom, affectionately as always.

s/ <u>Sam</u>

TLS; 1 leaf, 2 sides; TCD, MS 10402/178.

1   Benjamin Frédéric Cauvet-Duhamel (1903–1991) was a career diplomat who served as Secretary of the French Legation in Dublin (1937–1944), Chef du Service du Chiffre au Ministère des Affaires Etrangères (1945–1947), and Consul Général in Liverpool (1947–1955); among his translations into French were Yevgeny Zamiatin's novel *Nous Autres* (1929) and Alexis Tolstoy's *Aventures de Nevzorov* (1926). Thomas MacGreevy was named Chevalier de l'Ordre de la Légion d'Honneur for services to

the arts on 19 July 1948 (José Tomas, Grande Chancellerie de la Légion d'Honneur, 7 December 2009).

2   Vevey: see 4 January 1948, n. 1.

3   Alan Thompson.
Use of the drug Parpanit in the treatment of Parkinson's disease: 24 November 1947, n. 4. It is not known what article Cauvet sent to SB. Several synthetic drugs to treat Parkinson's disease were developed at this time. Myanesin was marketed in England from 1949, but it was only effective when taken in very large doses; however, Artane had proven effective without toxic side effects (Lewis J. Doshay and Kate Constable, "Newer Drugs in the Treatment of Parkinsonism," *Neurology* 1 [1951] 68–74).

4   SB and Suzanne Deschevaux-Dumesnil rented a room at 4 Rue de Changis (Paule Savane, *Samuel Beckett à Ussy sur Marne* [Ussy-sur-Marne: Association pour la Sauvegarde d'Ussy, 2001] 11). The family name of the woman of the house is not known.

5   Morris Sinclair's wife Hermina (née de Zwart, known as Mimi, 1919–1997) gave birth to their daughter Anne at the Clinique Universitaire Baudelocque, 123 Boulevard de Port-Royal, Paris 14.

6   SB refers to the Quintet for Winds, op. 26, by Arnold Schoenberg, played by René Leibowitz (1913–1972) who had studied with Schoenberg and Anton von Webern in Berlin before settling in Paris as a conductor, teacher, and composer in 1945; Leibowitz founded the International Festival of Chamber Music in 1947. SB refers to Schoenberg's song cycle "Pierrot Lunaire," op. 21. The location and date of this concert have not been found.
Béla Bartók's Piano Concerto no. 3 in E major was unfinished at his death in 1945. It was completed from his notes by Tibor Serly (1901–1978), a student and friend of Bartók. The broadcast that SB heard has not been documented.

7   SB refers to "Three Dialogues: Samuel Beckett and Georges Duthuit" (*Transition Forty-Nine* no. 5, 97–103), to "La Peinture des van Velde ou le monde et le pantalon" published in *Cahiers d'Art*, and to "Peintres de l'empêchement" published in *Derrière le Miroir* by the Galerie Maeght.

8   *En attendant Godot* was written between 9 October 1948 and January 1949 (Knowlson, *Damned to Fame*, 342). Belgian actor and director Raymond Rouleau (né Roland Edgard Marie Rouleau, 1904–1981), who worked with Antonin Artaud and Charles Dullin in the 1930s, and directed Sartre's *Huis clos* at the Théâtre du Vieux-Colombier (1944), was considering SB's *Eleutheria*. SB's novels in French, *Mercier et Camier*, *Molloy*, and *Malone meurt*, were as yet unpublished.

9   The Prix Littéraire Antoine de Rivarol was created in 1949 by the Librairie Bonaparte in memory of the author of the *Discours sur l'universalité de la langue française*; the first award was made to Russian writer Wladimir Weidlé (1895–1979) for *En marge de l'Occident* and to Lebanese writer Farjallah Haik (1907–1994) for *Abou Nassif*. The jury consisted of André Gide, Jules Romains, Georges Duhamel (1884–1966), and Jules Supervielle (1884–1960) (Charles C. Zippermann, "Literary Landmarks of 1949," *Books Abroad* 24.2 [Spring 1950] 140).
SB types "unofficially" into the left margin.

10   Guillaume Apollinaire published *Alcools* in 1913. SB's unsigned translation of "Zone" was published in *Transition Fifty* no. 6, 126–131; rpt. as *Zone* (Dublin: Dolmen Press, 1972).

GEORGES DUTHUIT

Samedi [on or after 30 April,
   before 26 May 1949]   Ussy sur Marne
Cher vieux

    Ta lettre ce matin.[1] Tu me sembles triste. J'espère que tu ne l'es pas trop. Tu as raison, vouloir que le cerveau fonctionne, c'est le comble de la connerie, ou sinistre, comme les amours du vieillard. Il a mieux à faire, le cerveau, s'arrêter et s'écouter par exemple. Curieux combien on est acculé au mot écouter, nous qui ne sommes tout de même pas des auditifs. Mais tu ne vas pas pouvoir me lire.

    Ci-joint les feuilles. La sympathie que j'ai pour André me déconseille tout commentaire. Je ne me suis permis de rien couper. J'ai essayé d'arranger par-ci par-là, mais il faut bien le dire – non, je ne le dirai pas. Du reste, il y a sans doute un nombreux public pour des orgies pareilles.[2]

    A Masson on pourrait dire peut-être qu'il est temps d'arrêter ces inutiles hostilités, de faire sien le bois d'où il ne sortira jamais. Mais il y verrait peut-être la honte d'un abandon, ou mourrait, comme le sexagénaire retiré des affaires.[3] C'est vraiment très simple, mon cher Georges, et pas métaphysique ni mystique pour un liard, ce que nous avons pigé. C'est même le sens commun, bon et rond comme le dos de d'Alembert.[4] Dans la vieille phrase de Geulincx citée dans Murphy, un peu à l'aveuglette il est vrai, tout est dit: Ubi nihil vales, ibi nihil velis.[5] Il s'agit seulement de s'entendre sur le domaine où l'on ne vaut rien. On ne risque guère d'en exagérer l'étendue.

    Je fais du vélo avec frénésie, je veux dire celui qui est censé de me représenter.[6] Le même pauvre con cloue, visse, scie et lime pestant et content. C'est de loin ce qu'il a de mieux à faire. Et devant la feuille, il voudrait s'affairer encore, se précipiter pour mesurer, prévoir et faire tenir debout. Mais un peu honteux quand même, sachant que ce n'est pas sa place.

Nous resterons encore 10 jours probablement, question de sous. Envoie donc ta lettre ici, avant qu'elle arrive à l'océan. Je vais m'attaquer aux Documents. Pour que de tels textes mordent, il faudrait un long travail dessus, et pas mal de renoncements, il me semble. Mais je suis maniaque.[7]

Bien affectueusement, mon cher vieux, et à Marguerite, de nous deux.

Sam

ALS; 1 leaf, 2 sides; Duthuit collection. *Dating*: SB writes to Thomas MacGreevy on 27 March 1949 that he plans to go to Ussy for Easter (17 April 1949), but SB writes to Yvonne Lefèvre on 26 April from Paris. The following Saturday is 30 April, the earliest date for this letter. SB indicates that he is about to work on "Documents," which he returns to Duthuit on 26 May, hence the latest date for this letter is before 26 May 1949.

Saturday [on or after 30 April,
   before 26 May 1949]   Ussy sur Marne
My dear Georges,

Your letter this morning.[1] You seem sad. I hope not too sad. You are right, to want the brain to function is the height of crassness, or is sinister, like the loves of an old man. The brain has better things to do, stopping and listening to itself, for instance. Odd how we are driven back on the word listening, we who are all the same not ear-people. But you are not going to be able to read me.

Herewith the sheets. My fondness for André warns me off any comment. I have not allowed myself to cut anything. I have tried to do some tidying-up here and there, but I have to say – no, I will not say. Besides, there is no doubt a sizeable public for this kind of orgy.[2]

Masson could perhaps be told that it is time to stop these pointless hostilities, to make his peace with the wood from which he will never emerge. But he might see in that the shame of giving up, or he might die, like the sixty-year-old who retires from business.[3] What you and I have managed to get hold of, Georges my old friend, is very simple and not the least little bit metaphysical or mystical; indeed it is common sense, good and round, like d'Alembert's back.[4] It is all in

149

the old sentence from Geulincx quoted in *Murphy*, admittedly a little hastily: *Ubi nihil vales ibi nihil velis.*[5] The only point is to be clear about the domain in which one is worth nothing. There is little risk of anyone's exaggerating its extent.

I cycle frantically, I, that is the person who is supposed to represent me.[6] The same poor fool nails, screws, saws and files, cursing and swearing, and happy. By far the best thing for him to do. And in front of the blank page, he would like to be busy too, rush in to measure, foresee, prop up. But a bit shamefaced all the same, knowing that it is not his place.

We shall probably stay on for another ten days: a matter of money. So send your letter here, before it gets to the ocean. I am going to make a start on the *Documents*. For texts like this to bite, a long working over would be needed, and a fair few abandonings, I feel. But I am by nature obsessive.[7]

Love to you and Marguerite, my old friend, from us both.

<u>Sam</u>

1 Duthuit's letter has not been found.

2 Almost certainly, SB has been revising Dorothy Bussy's translation of the articles by André du Bouchet on André Masson, Tal-Coat, and Joan Miró that become "Three Exhibitions: Masson – Tal-Coat – Miró" (*Transition Forty-Nine* no. 5, 89–96), which piece immediately precedes "Three Dialogues: Samuel Beckett and Georges Duthuit."

3 André du Bouchet's review of Masson's recent work begins:

> Through the dim and transparent canvases of Masson's youth, a streak of blood pierces like a germ of disorder. Today it winds back into landscape – a landscape enriched by the alluvial deposits that it has torn away in its adventurous course. It is exciting to surprise Masson at the turn of a new metamorphosis, at the very moment he emerges from his night, still dazed, dazzled by the light, but firmly resolved not to turn back. ("Three Exhibitions," 89.)

4 SB picks up on the famously hump-backed Jean le Rond d'Alembert (1717–1783), whose mathematical abilities made him one of the most important contributors to that monument of "sense," the *Encyclopédie Générale* (1751–1780).

5 SB cites the phrase by Arnold Geulincx in *Murphy* ([New York: Grove Press, 1957] 178) (Where you are worth nothing, may you also wish for nothing). For further details, see SB to George Reavey, 9 January 1935 [*for* 1936], and n. 5 of that letter.

6 SB writes "censé de me représenter," where one would expect "censé me représenter."

7   Each issue of *Transition* ends with a "Documents" section. That of no. 5, which SB is revising, is headed "A pre-war and a post-war questionnaire: 'Art and the Public,' Braque, Henri Laurens, Masson, Matisse, Miró, *etc.*" (110–126).

GEORGES DUTHUIT

26 May [1949]   Ussy-sur-Marne
Mon cher vieux Georges
      Merci de ta lettre avec 1ere partie du travail annoncé.[1] J'ai commencé à te répondre hier soir. Je recommence aujourd'hui. Sans beaucoup d'espoir de finir.

      Ce sera en tout cas
      1.   Une suggestion
      2.   l'article des Cahiers
      3.   les Italiens

      Entrevoir à l'avance ce que je vais essayer de dire, avoue que ça ne m'arrive pas souvent.

      Je vais également m'efforcer d'écrire lisiblement.

      Quel programme.

1.   Je suggère que je traduise ton travail tel quel, dès que tu l'auras mis au point, et que j'y ajoute un court texte de moi, rien qu'un petit hurlement, où je ferai mes adieux (positivement les derniers) à l'esthétique. Ça n'empêchera point que je commente ton travail, puisque tu y tiens, au fur et à mesure, mais j'aimerais souligner les conditions dans lesquelles m'ont été extorqués l'article Zervos et la préface Maeght (il y a longtemps que ça me pèse sur l'estomac) et dire tout le mal que je pense du rôle que j'ai joué dans l'histoire van Velde.[2]

2.   L'article des Cahiers est chose faite et il n'y a pas à y revenir. Il ne m'appartient pas de regretter qu'on en fasse le point de départ d'une étude sur Bram. Je dirai seulement qu'en le faisant on ajoute, à mon avis, à des difficultés suffisamment grandes sans cela, sans parler du risque d'affaiblir, dès le début, les humbles suggestions que nous serons peut-être d'accord, finalement, pour émettre à ce sujet. Cette

malheureuse composition, qu'on m'a arrachée à coups de lèche, à une époque où déjà je me foutais de Geer comme de mon dernier suspensoir, je ne l'ai ni sous la main ni dans la tête. Je crois seulement me rappeler que je me suis laissé aller, afin d'en finir plus vite, à une antithèse dont je suis le premier à goûter toute l'absurdité, tout en lui reconnaissant une certaine valeur explicative, ce qui est loin de me consoler.[3] Tu dis qu'il y a là de belles images. C'est possible. Elles ne nous mèneront pas loin, les belles images. Elles me semblent même furieusement déplacées, accolées à ce malheureux Bram. Non, la seule chose à maintenir dans ce morceau de bravoure verdâtre, et qui s'y est glissée par je ne sais quel hasard (un moment d'inattention sans doute), c'est le motif peinture empêchement, escamoté aussitôt, bien fringué, les cheveux partagés aussi précisément qu'un jeune cul.[4] Les contradictions réelles et apparentes que tu y relèves si gentiment, avec une retenue dont je me flatte de connaître les raisons, se laisseraient sans doute sans trop de mal résoudre, à grand renfort de distinguos. Ne me serait imputable alors que le péché mignon, pardonné d'avance aux critiques d'art, de m'être exprimé comme un cochon. En disant tout cela, c'est surtout à Bram que je pense. Je sais bien que tu n'en es pas encore là (dans ce que tu m'as envoyé) et qu'à partir de mes propos des Cahiers tu engages un travail de déblayage pur et simple. Je sais également que tu as ta propre position à établir et qu'elle sera assez différente de la mienne (dans la mesure où j'en ai une), tout au moins quant à la formulation. Il serait inadmissible, dans ces conditions, que je te demande de ne retenir de ce premier essai forcé que ce qui vaut d'être retenu. Mais j'y songe, c'est sans doute ce que tu es en train de faire. Et ainsi de suite, sur le même ton geignant.

3.   Toute la partie sur les Italiens est admirable de clarté et de vigueur. Un entrain formidable. La seule remarque que j'aie à faire, c'est que ça a l'air de cotoyer [*for* côtoyer] par moments la vieille opposition formalisme–réalisme (supérieur bien sûr). Entre se complaire dans une convention qui peut sembler issue de la nature et des conditions de la peinture même, au défi de l'expérience de tous les instants, et s'attacher à traduire celle-ci dans une forme d'expression

qui s'y oppose, la différence semble en effet énorme, et l'est sans doute, mais vu par mon trou de serrure à moi, voilé de solitude, ça revient à la même chose, dans le sens qu'il s'agit de 2 maxima, un maximum dans le possible et un maximum dans la vérité. Entre un Gozzoli tel quel et un Gozzoli de nos catégories éclatées, je mourrais d'inanition.[5] Pour moi la question devient intéressante vraiment seulement à partir du moment où l'on s'occupe de ce qui est derrière les 2 attitudes, à savoir d'une part la passion du faisable, où les plus nobles recherches sont viciées par le besoin d'en faire reculer les limites, et d'autre part, peut-être, enfin, bientôt, le respect de l'impossible que nous sommes, impossibles vivants, impossiblement vivant, dont ni le temps du corps, ni l'investissement par l'espace, ne sont pas davantage à retenir que l'ombre le soir ou le visage aimé, et peignant tout simplement un sort, qui est de peindre, là où il n'y a rien à peindre, rien avec quoi peindre, et sans savoir peindre, et sans vouloir peindre, et cela de manière à ce qu'il en transpire quelque chose, tant qu'à faire. Voilà, je vais trop loin, j'irai toujours trop loin, et jamais assez loin. Singulièrement peu habilité, mon pauvre Georges, à participer à un débat pareil, dont je m'écarte à chaque instant, le mors entre les dentiers. Le fait est que la question ne m'intéresse pas. Quelle idiotie! Mais elle me rend enragé et je dis n'importe quoi. D'ailleurs je suis moins agacé que toi par les Italiens, sans doute parce que je ne sens pas assez fort la rupture dont tu parles. Que m'importe que la tyrannie du ton local soit révolue, du moment qu'on a mis quelque chose à sa place? Et détroner les objets en faveur de ce qui les sépare, ou de ce qui les lie, car j'ignore l'effet de l'interspace, pour moi c'est préférer Bonnard blanc à blanc Bonnard. Assez.[6]

Les Documents, que ci-joint, c'est du bon boulot. J'ai corrigé un peu l'anglais. Quelques passages que je n'ai pas compris, mais qu'il ne peut pas laisser tels quels. Je les ai marqués d'un point d'interrogation. Nous verrons ça ensemble.[7] Je ne suis pas très bien, ne suis pas sorti de la journée. Je n'aime pas t'envoyer une lettre pareille, mais tant pis, je ne ferais pas mieux la prochaine fois. De qui sont les jolis vers, cités dans ta lettre? Connaissais pas la définition de Dante.[8] Il appelait la poésie "una bella menzogna".[9] La Renaissance devait être d'accord.

Affectueusement Sam

ALS; 4 leaves, 4 sides; Duthuit collection.

26 May [1949]   Ussy-sur-Marne

Georges my old friend

Thank you for your letter with 1st part of the promised work.[1] I started to reply last night. Am starting again today. With no great hope of finishing.

In any case there will be

1. A suggestion

2. the article from the *Cahiers*

3. the Italians

Having some idea beforehand of what I am going to say, you must admit that does not happen to me every day.

I am also going to make an effort to write legibly.

What a programme.

1.   I suggest that I translate your work as it stands, as soon as you have put the finishing touches to it, and that I add to it a short text of my own, just a little howl, in which I take my (positively final) farewell of aesthetics. That will not stop me from commenting on your work as I go, since you want me to, but I would want to emphasise the conditions in which the Zervos article and the Maeght preface were wrung out of me (that has been weighing on my mind for a long time), and to say how bad I feel about the part I played in the Van Velde business.[2]

2.   The article in the *Cahiers* is over and done with, and there is no going back over it. It is not my place to regret that it should be made the starting-point of a study of Bram. I shall say only that doing so adds, in my view, to difficulties that are great enough already without

that, not to mention the risk of weakening, from the start, the humble suggestions which we may yet finally agree to put out on this subject. This wretched piece, winkled out of me by base flattery, at a time when I already cared for Geer about as much as for my last truss, I can neither put my hand on nor see in my mind's eye. All I think I can remember is that I indulged, in order to have done with the thing, in an antithesis, the total absurdity of which I am the first to savour, even though I see it has some explanatory value, which is far from a consolation.[3] You tell me that there are fine images in it. That may be. Fine images will not get us anywhere. Indeed they seem to me wildly out of place, when linked to the unfortunate Bram. No, the only thing in that ugly green purple patch worth keeping, and which slipped into it by some chance that escapes me (a momentary oversight, no doubt), is the *painting/preventedness* motif immediately retracted, smartened up, its hair parted as neatly as a young arse.[4] The real and apparent contradictions which you pick out so uncensoriously, showing a discretion the reasons for which I flatter myself I recognise, could no doubt without undue difficulty be resolved in a flurry of 'on-the-one-hand's'. I could then be charged with nothing more than that most trivial of offences, for which art critics are forgiven in advance, of having expressed myself like a pig. In saying all this, I am thinking above all of Bram. I know you are not as far on as that yet (in what you have sent me), and that, starting out from my words in the *Cahiers* you are setting about an exercise in ground-clearing pure and simple. I know too that you have your own position to establish, and that it will be rather different from mine (in so far as I have one), at least in terms of formulation. In these conditions, it would be quite improper for me to ask you to keep only what is worth keeping in that first, forced essay. But I am thinking of doing so, and no doubt that is what you are now doing. And so on and so on, in the same whining tone.

3.   The whole section on the Italians is marvellously clear and vigorous. Tremendous energy. The only point I would make is that it occasionally seems to come uncomfortably close to the old formalism–realism distinction (much superior of course). Between delighting mindlessly in a convention which can seem to have come direct from

nature and from the very conditions of painting, against the evidence of every moment, and attempting to translate that convention into a form of expression opposed to it, there does indeed seem to be, indeed no doubt is, a huge difference, but seen through my keyhole, and veiled as I am in solitude, it amounts to the same thing, in the sense that what we have are two maxima: one maximum in the possible, and one maximum in the truth. Between a Gozzoli as such and a Gozzoli from our exploded categories, I would die of starvation.[5] For me the question only becomes interesting from the moment when one concerns oneself with what lies behind the two attitudes, that is on the one hand the passion of the achievable, in which the noblest researches are vitiated by the need to extend its limits, and, on the other, perhaps, well, soon, respect for the impossible that we are, impossible living creatures, impossibly alive, of whom neither the time of the body, nor the investment by space are any more to be retained than the shades of evening or the beloved face, and painting quite simply a destiny, which is to paint, where there is nothing to paint, nothing to paint with, and without knowing how to paint, and without wanting to paint, and all this in such a way that something comes of it, while they are at it. There, I am going too far, I shall always go too far, and never far enough. Singularly ill equipped, my poor Georges, to join in a debate like this, which I pull away from every moment, with the bit between my false teeth. The fact is that the question does not interest me. What nonsense! But it maddens me and I say any old thing. Besides, I am less irritated by the Italians than you are, no doubt because I do not feel so keenly the break that you speak of. What matter that the tyranny of local colour has gone for ever, once something else has been put in its place? And unseating objects from their thrones in favour of what separates them, or what connects them, for I do not know what the effect of interspace is, for me means preferring Bonnard white to white Bonnard. Enough.[6]

The *Documents*, enclosed, are very well done. I have corrected the English a little. A few passages which I have not understood, but which cannot be left as they stand. I have put a question mark against them. We can look at them together.[7] I am not very well, have not been out all day. I do not like sending you a letter like this, but too bad: I would not do any better the next time. Whose are those lovely lines quoted in your letter? Did not know Dante's definition.[8] He called poetry "una bella menzogna".[9] The Renaissance must have agreed.

    Love Sam

1   Duthuit's letter has not been found. SB omits the grave accent in "1ᵉʳᵉ."

2   Duthuit is apparently proposing a collaborative article on one or both of the Van Veldes. The two articles to which SB refers, both on Geer and Bram van Velde, are "La Peinture des van Velde ou le monde et le pantalon" and "Peintres de l'empêchement."
   Notwithstanding SB's reservations, in the opening pages of *The Fauvist Painters* (as in *Les Fauves*) Duthuit himself cites SB's article "La Peinture des van Velde ou le monde et le pantalon":

> Writing of one of the painters who turned Matisse's fauvist researches to their own use, the poet Samuel Beckett declared this artist to be turned entirely outward, towards the turmoil of things in light, towards time. For, says Beckett: "We take cognizance of time only through the things that it agitates, that it prevents us from seeing. It is by giving himself entirely to the outward world, by revealing the macrocosm shaken by the tremors of time, that he realizes himself, that he realizes man if you prefer, in his most immovable being, in his certainty that there is neither present nor repose. His work is a representation of that river into which, according to the modest estimate of Heraclitus, no man ever steps twice." (Duthuit, *The Fauvist Painters*, 5–6.)

3   SB repeatedly contrasts the work of A. (Abraham/Bram) and G. (Gerardus/Geer) van Velde, perhaps most schematically when he writes:

> Il serait préférable de ne pas s'exposer à ces deux façons de voir et de peindre, le même jour. Du moins dans les premiers temps.
>   Mettons la chose plus grossièrement. Achevons d'être ridicule[s].
>   A. van Velde peint l'étendue.
>   G. van Velde peint la succession.
> (Beckett, "La Peinture des van Velde ou le monde et le pantalon," 353; Beckett, *Disjecta*, 128.)
> (It would be preferable not to expose oneself to these two ways of seeing and painting on the same day. At least in the early stages.
>   Let's put it more crudely. Let's get through to being ridiculous.
>   B. van Velde paints extent.
>   G. van Velde paints succession.)

4   SB does not in fact use the term "empêchement" in his article, though this forms the theme, and the title, of his second article on the Van Veldes, which he claims to be in substance a repetition of his first. The closest he comes to "empêchement" may be when he writes:

> Pour le peintre, la chose est impossible. C'est d'ailleurs de la représentation de cette impossibilité que la peinture moderne a tiré une bonne partie de ses meilleurs effets.
>
> Mais ils n'ont ni l'un ni l'autre ce qu'il faut pour tirer parti plastiquement d'une situation plastique sans issue. (Beckett, "La Peinture des van Velde ou le monde et le pantalon," 354; Beckett, *Disjecta*, 129.)
>
> (For the painter, the thing is impossible. In any case, it is from the representation of this impossibility that modern painting has drawn a fair proportion of its best effects.
>
> But neither the one nor the other has what is needed to take advantage, in plastic terms, of an insoluble plastic situation.)

5   SB was revising Ralph Manheim's translation of Duthuit's *Les Fauves*, in which "the Italians" are mentioned repeatedly, and always critically. SB may well be alluding to the following passage, which makes reference to Matthew Stewart Prichard (1865–1936), an English curator and philosopher of art whose thinking had had a decisive influence on Duthuit as a young man:

> The audience play along, because they know that they are at the theatre, that the Italian painters are born dramatists and actors, and that they have always confused, as Prichard said, action with acting. To describe and to mimic does not mean to animate and to live . . . The painter contents himself with giving us the result of whole series of perceptions corrected and amplified by the memory and arbitrarily interrelated – and this he does with an inconceivable dexterity. Hence these narratives have a certain power of enchantment, but they are none the less palpable tissues of concepts. To be sure, it is no banal concept that Leonardo and his fellows exploit to the top of their bent. They perceive the vague, hovering, half-hidden tints of phenomena with extraordinary clarity and are capable of translating them with a decision, a subtlety, a firmness which leave them no equal in the category of interpretative genius. No one can aspire to decompose the obsessive smile of Leonardo or the bowed neck of Michelangelo and reconstruct them, that goes without saying. It is none the less true that both artists draw the constant features of their characters, or prepare the mould on which the individual features are impressed, according to the dictates of opinion. The structure of their personages, so original in appearance, the coordinating principle which they obey, are determined merely by the habits of conventional vision. Even the ground on which so many inimitable accents are superimposed is common property, a product of the impersonal eye. All this partakes of the language of foreseen action and systematized behavior. All is subordinate, once again, to the traditional conception of an absolute time, independent of its content of events, of an absolute space independent of its content of objects and which I cannot even call rigid and immutable, since it does not exist for me and for the true artist, or exists merely as an instrument conceived and utilized by another, by the scientific artist, to take me by the scruff of the neck and thrust me against a gigantic barrier, the barrier of the art of representation. (Duthuit, *The Fauvist Painters*, 50–51.)

Benozzo Gozzoli (c. 1420–1497).

6   SB may be alluding to another passage in *Les Fauves*, where Duthuit writes: "The Italians saw an immediate and complete perception of movement and change in a

crystallization of that perception, a pragmatic solidification later disguised as movement by a series of artifices" (Duthuit, *The Fauvist Painters*, 64).

SB omits the circumflex in "détrôner."

The colloquial phrase is "bonnet blanc, blanc bonnet" and indicates an alleged difference where none exists; the form of the painter's name allows SB to play with this.

7   The "Documents" of *Transition Forty-Nine* no. 5: Saturday [on or after 30 April, before 26 May 1949], n. 7.

8   It is not known which lines, or which definition by Dante, Duthuit cited in his letter.

9   Dante uses this expression in the context of his explanation of the four ways in which a text can be interpreted: "L'altro si chiama allegorico, e questo è quello che si nasconde sotto 'l manto di queste favole, ed è una veritade ascosa sotto bella menzogna" ("The second is called allegorical: this is the sense concealed under the cloak of these fables, and consists of a truth hidden under a beautiful lie") (Dante Alighieri, *Convivio*, ed. Piero Cudini [Milan: Garzanti, 1980] 65–66; *The Banquet*, tr. Christopher Ryan [Saratoga, CA: ANMA Libri, 1989] 42.

GEORGES DUTHUIT

1.6.49   Ussy

Mon cher vieux Georges

Ta si gentille lettre ce matin.[1] Navré de te savoir mal fichu. Froid, le vin est meilleur. Remets-toi vite. Moi, je crois que je suis simplement prodigieusement fatigué, des nerfs surtout, le moindre pépin me met dans tous mes états. Le temps est affreux. Nous pensons rentrer samedi ou dimanche. Je passerai certainement te voir mardi, vers 6 heures comme d'habitude, sauf contre-ordre.

C'est curieux, la façon du temps (mais oui) de procéder par petits paquets de choses associées. Je retrouve ici, au grenier, un vieux numéro de Transition (1938), avec un poème de moi, jeunettement déchaîné, que j'avais tout à fait oublié, et un article (de moi aussi) sur un jeune poète irlandais (jeune alors) qui venait de publier un recueil de poèmes dans la même série que Echo's Bones. Le lendemain je reçois une carte du type en question, de Paris. Il y a 4 ans que je ne l'ai vu ni eu de ses nouvelles.[2]

On m'envoie la publicité du poète Dupret, avec extraits d'une lettre de Breton et invitation à souscrire. J'espère que l'enthousiasme de ce parfait lettré n'aura pas sur les autres pressentis le même effet que sur moi. "Eclairage formidable." J'aurais voulu savoir quel genre.[3] Sur le prospectus d'une entreprise de peinture, ramassé sur la route, à cause des ronds de couleur avec le nom écrit dessous, je trouve le "gris irlandais", pour la 1ère fois. Renversant de désolation hideuse.

Dans les champs, sur les routes, je me livre à des déductions d'ordre naturel, basées sur l'observation! Pas étonnant que je sois irritable. Ça donne des résultats sinistres. Pourquoi se trouve-t-il des alouettes pour nicher dans les champs de trèfle et de sainfoin, qu'on fauche déjà, alors que dans les blés elles seraient tranquilles pendant des mois encore? Un soir que nous rentrions à Ussy, au coucher du soleil, nous nous sommes vus tout d'un coup escortés par des ephémères d'une espèce étrange, des "mouches de mai" je crois. Ils allaient tous dans le même sens, suivaient littéralement la route, à peu près à la même vitesse que nous. Ce n'était pas un tropisme solaire puisqu'on allait vers le Sud. J'ai cru comprendre finalement qu'ils allaient tous vers la Marne, pour se faire manger des poissons, après avoir fait l'amour sur l'eau.

Continue à m'envoyer tes examens de conscience esthétiques, spirituels plutôt. J'aime bien les lire. Je suis parti l'autre soir sur ta phrase "si l'existence à une valeur etc", mais ai dû désister faute de sang au cerveau. Ta "fenêtre sur l'avenir" a failli prendre un bon coup … de bile mélangée de leucocytes.[4] Je ne sais pas parler, seulement crier ou bouder. J'ai travaillé un peu. Chaque fois que je m'y mets, ça vient assez facilement, mais je répugne à m'y mettre, plus que jamais. J'ai fait une chose qu'il ne m'était jamais arrivé de faire, j'ai écrit la dernière page du livre en cours, alors que je n'en suis encore qu'à la 30me. Je n'en suis pas fier. Mais l'issue déjà fait si peu de doute, quels que soient les tortillements, ce dont je n'ai qu'une idée des plus vagues, qui m'en séparent.[5]

J'ai reçu un travail de "Sélection" – texte très noble et statistique sur les méfaits des appareils à sous. A ma grande surprise, car le type qui m'a présenté s'est fait foutre à la porte, et mon "bout d'essai" n'était guère brillant. Tant mieux. C'est de l'argent assez vite gagné. J'achèterai une chambre à air (pas pour y vivre) et un pneu arrière.[6]

Je lis "Le Tour du monde en 80 jours". C'est alerte. Te rappelles-tu le déjeuner de Fogg au Reform club, se composant "d'un hors-d'oeuvre, d'un poisson bouilli relevé d'une 'Reading Sauce' de premier choix, d'un roast-beef écarlate farci de tiges de rhubarbe et de groseilles vertes, d'un morceau de chester, le tout arrosé de quelques tasses d'excellent thé."[7]

Bella menzogna = beau mensonge, tout bonnement. Je crois que c'est dans le Convivio. La poésie était autre chose bien sûr, mais il fallait que la fausseté y fût, aussi bien fondée que possible.[8]

Je suis inquiet du côté de Paris, je ne sais pourquoi. J'ai envie d'y être. Est-il vrai que Masson et Giacometti se sont mis à faire des médailles – de Malraux et Sartre respectivement?[9]

Bien affectueusement à vous deux, et à mardi.

    Sam

ALS; 2 leaves, 4 sides; Duthuit collection.

1.6.49   Ussy

Georges my old friend

Such a lovely letter from you this morning.[1] Really sorry to learn that you are in a bad way. Wine is better cold. Get well soon. As for me, I think I am just prodigiously tired, nervous fatigue most of all. The smallest thing that goes wrong puts me in a state. The weather is awful. We are thinking of coming back on Saturday or Sunday. I shall certainly come round to see you on Tuesday, about 6 as usual, unless I hear from you.

It is odd, the way time (yes, yes) works in little tight groups of associated things. Here in the loft I find an old copy of *transition* (1938), with a poem of mine, the wild youthful kind, which I had quite forgotten, and an article (also by me) on a young Irish poet (young then) who had just published a volume of poems in the same series as *Echo's Bones*. The next day I get a card from the bloke in question, from Paris. Have not seen or heard of him for four years.[2]

Have been sent the publicity for the poet Duprey, with extracts from a letter by Breton and invitation to subscribe. I hope that the enthusiasm of this accomplished literary gent will not have the same effect on the other people approached as it had on me. "Tremendous power of illumination." I wondered what kind.[3] On the brochure of a paint firm, picked up along the road because of the coloured rings with the name written underneath, I find "Irish grey" for the first time. Side-splitting in its hideous desolation.

In the fields, on the roads, I give myself over to deductions on nature, based on observation! No wonder I am irritable. It produces grim results. Why are there larks to nest in the fields of clover and sainfoin, which are already being cut, when they could be undisturbed in the corn for months yet? One evening as we were on our way back to Ussy, at sunset, we suddenly found ourselves being escorted by ephemerids of a strange kind, "may-flies", I think. They were all heading in the same direction, literally following the road, at about the same speed as us. It was not a solar tropism, for we were going south. In the end I worked out that they were all going towards the Marne to be eaten by the fish, after making love on the water.

Keep on sending me your aesthetic, or rather spiritual exercises. I really enjoy reading them. I was set off the other night by your sentence "if existence has any value . . .", but I had to give up for want of blood in the brain. Your "window on the future" nearly got hit with . . . bile mixed with leucocytes.[4] I do not know how to talk, only to shout or sulk. I have done a little work. Each time I get down to it, it comes fairly easily, but I am reluctant to get down to it, more than ever. I have done one thing that I had never happened to do before: I wrote the last page of the book I am working on, whereas I am only on my 30th. I am not proud of myself. But the outcome is already so little in doubt, whatever the writhings that lie between me and it, of which I have only the vaguest of ideas.[5]

I have been given some work by *Sélection* – a very noble and statistical piece about the awfulness of gambling machines, to my great surprise – the bloke who introduced me has been sacked, and my "sample" was not particularly good. All the better. It is money easily made. I shall buy an inner tube and a back tyre.[6]

I am reading *Around the World in 80 Days*. It is lively stuff. Do you remember Fogg's lunch at the Reform Club, made up of "an hors d'oeuvre, boiled fish with a first-rate 'Reading Sauce', scarlet roast beef stuffed with stalks of rhubarb and gooseberries, a piece of chester, the whole thing washed down with a few cups of excellent tea."[7]

Bella menzogna = beautiful lie, quite simply. I think it is in the *Convivio*. Poetry was something else, of course, but there had to be some falsehood in it, as well founded as possible.[8]

I am worried in some way to do with Paris, I do not know why. I feel like being there. Is it true that Masson and Giacometti have started making medals – of Malraux and Sartre respectively?[9]

Love to both of you, and see you on Tuesday.

Sam

1 Duthuit's letter to SB has not been found.

2 SB's poem "Ooftish" and his review of Denis Devlin's *Intercessions*, "Denis Devlin," appeared in *transition*, 27 (April–May 1938) 33; 289–294. *Echo's Bones and Other Precipitates* and Devlin's *Intercessions* were both published in George Reavey's Europa Poets series (Paris: Europa Press, 1935; Paris: Europa Press, 1937). The card from Devlin has not been found.

3 André Breton's laudatory letter is printed in full as preface to *Derrière son double* by Jean-Pierre Duprey (1930–1959), whose name SB misspells ([Paris: Le Soleil Noir, 1950] 15–16). It ends: "Vous êtes certainement un grand poète, doublé de quelqu'un d'autre qui m'intrigue. Votre éclairage est extraordinaire." (You are certainly a great poet, twinned with, to me, someone intriguingly other. The play of light in your work is extraordinary.)

4 The context of Duthuit's comments is not known. SB adds an unwarranted grave accent to "a" in "a une valeur."

5 The manuscript of *L'Innommable* indicates that SB began writing it on "29 March" (Lake, ed., *No Symbols Where None Intended*, 58).

6 The article SB has received from the American edition of the *Reader's Digest* is by Norman and Madelyn Carlisle, "The Big Slot-Machine Swindle" 54 (June 1949) 46–49. This article was not published in the French edition of the journal, but at least one article was indeed translated by SB: T. E. Murphy, "Open Every Door" (*Reader's Digest* 1955 [August 1949] 109–111), was published as "Ouvrons toutes les portes," in SB's unsigned translation (*Sélection du Reader's Digest* 3 [October 1949] 1–4). It is not known who introduced SB to the staff at the *Reader's Digest* (Eleanor Swink, Senior Editorial Director, *International Reader's Digest*, 17 November 1995).

SB's joke is untranslatable. It depends on the normal meaning of "chambre" ("a place where one can live" ["vivre"]), whereas the specialized meaning of "chambre à air" can only be "inner tube."

7 *Le Tour du monde en quatre-vingts jours* (1873; *Around the World in Eighty Days*) by Jules Verne. In recalling the passage, SB somewhat telescopes his citation. The original runs:

"d'un hors-d'œuvre, d'un poisson bouilli relevé d'une 'reading sauce' de premier choix, d'un roastbeef écarlate agrémenté de condiments 'mushroom', d'un gâteau farci de tiges de rhubarbe et de groseilles vertes, d'un morceau de chester, – le tout arrosé de quelques tasses de cet excellent thé" ([Paris: Flammarion, 1978] 50–51).

8   "Bella menzogna": 26 May 1949, n. 9.

9   The medals SB mentions were indeed discussed with the artists and commissioned by the Monnaie de Paris (ref. Archives Monnaie de Paris RP-8, fonds monétaires et contemporains – Série RP). That of André Malraux by André Masson was minted in 1949 (Med 071781, *Catalogue général des éditions* [Musée de la Monnaie de Paris] IV, 1267A); that of Jean-Paul Sartre by Alberto Giacometti was never produced.

GEORGES DUTHUIT

jeudi 9 juin [1949]

Cher ami

Je profite d'un instant (passager) de lucidité pour te dire que je crois voir ce qui nous sépare, ce sur quoi nous finissons toujours par buter, après bien des locutions inutiles. C'est l'opposition possible-impossible, richesse-pauvreté, possession-privation, etc. etc. A ce point de vue les Italiens, Matisse, Tal Coat et tutti quanti sont dans le même sac, en chanvre supérieur, du côté de ceux qui, ayant, veulent encore, et, pouvant, davantage. Davantage de quoi? Ni de beauté, ni de vérité, d'accord, si tu veux, ce n'est pas sûr, ce sont des concepts fourre-tout, mais d'un rapport soi-le reste qui autrefois s'exprimait en termes de beauté et de vérité et qui maintenant cherche d'autres répondants, et ne les trouve pas, malgré des airs voulus de capharnaüm, vide et périclitation. L'affolement que je crois volontiers authentique du Matisse de 1905 et du Masson d'aujourd'hui, des crises, à surmonter, mauvais moments à passer, même pas, substance de lutte héroïque.[1] Tal Coat, tel qu'entrevu aujourd'hui, ça a une belle allure de renoncement. Je t'en fous. Une bien belle chose, une chose bien vraie. Disons-le une fois pour toutes, car moi je ne pourrai que m'enfoncer: on reste en plein championnat. Ce que tu reproches aux Italiens, au fond c'est un manque à gagner. Ils ont perdu leur temps, gaspillé leurs talents, à mettre une absurdité sur pied, une absurdité pernicieuse, qui empêche de vivre, de respirer. Pour moi ils ont seulement eu le tort de croire bien faire, peu importe par quels moyens. Tu opposes un temps quotidien, utilitaire, à un temps vital, de tripes, d'effort privilégié, le vrai. Tout ça revient à vouloir sauver une forme d'expression qui n'est pas viable. Vouloir qu'elle le soit, travailler pour qu'elle le soit, lui en donner l'air, c'est donner dans la même pléthore que depuis toujours, dans la même comédie. Apoplectique, petant [*for* pétant] des artères, comme Cézanne, comme van Gogh, voilà où il en est, le pâle Tal Coat, et où en serait Masson, s'il le pouvait. Pas la peine de parler de détails. Existe-t-il, peut-il exister, ou non, une peinture pauvre, inutile sans camouflage, incapable de l'image quelle qu'elle soit, dont l'obligation ne cherche pas à se justifier? Que je l'aie vue là où il n'y aurait qu'un renouvellement sans précédent du rapport, du banquet, ça n'a pas d'importance. Je ne pourrai jamais plus admettre que l'acte sans espoir, calme de sa damnation.

    Affectueusement et à samedi.

      s/ <u>Sam</u>

TLS; 1 leaf, 1 side; *A notes in left margin in AH*; Duthuit collection. *Dating*: 9 June fell on Thursday in 1949. Previous publication, Labrusse, "Extraits de la correspondance entre Georges Duthuit et Samuel Beckett," 110–111.

Thursday 9 June [1949]

Dear Georges,

    I am taking advantage of a (passing) moment of lucidity to tell you that I think I see what separates us, what we always end up banging our heads against, after a great many useless phrases. It is the opposition possible-impossible, wealth-poverty, possession-deprivation, etc., etc. From that point of view the Italians, Matisse, Tal-Coat and *tutti quanti* in the same bag, made of high-grade hemp, alongside those who, having, want more, and having the ability, want more still. More what? Not beauty, nor truth, all right, if you like, and that's not sure, these are general-purpose concepts, but more of a relation: self – the rest, which once expressed itself in terms of beauty and truth, and which is now seeking other guarantors and not finding them, in spite of posturings like junk-heap, vacuum, and ruination. Matisse's wild panic of 1905, which I am ready to see as genuine, the wild panic of the Masson of today, crises, to be overcome, bad times to be lived through, not even, substance of heroic struggle.[1] Tal-Coat, as glimpsed today, has all the trappings of renunciation. My eye. Something really beautiful, something really true. Let us say it out clearly once and for all, for I can only get more deeply entrenched: we are still in the world of competition, of winning and losing. What you complain about in the Italians, in the end, is failure to take their chances. They have wasted their time, frittered away their talents, setting up an absurdity, a pernicious absurdity that is inimical to living, to breathing. For me their only mistake was believing that they were doing the right thing, no matter by what means. You oppose a quotidian, utilitarian time to a vital time, a time of guts, privileged effort, the true one. What all that amounts to is the wish to save a form of expression which is not viable. To want it to be, to work at making it be, to give it the appearance of being, is to fall back into the same old plethora, the same play-acting. Apoplectic, bursting at the arteries, like Cézanne, like van Gogh, that is what he is about, the pale Tal-Coat, and what Masson would be about, if he could. No point in talking about details. Does there exist, can there exist, or not, a painting that is poor, undisguisedly useless, incapable of any image whatever, a painting whose necessity does not seek to justify itself? The fact that I should have seen it where there is really no more than an unprecedented renewal of the relationship, of the banquet, is of no importance. Never again can I admit anything but the act without hope, calm in its damnedness.

> Regards, and till Saturday.
> Sam

---

1 In *Les Fauves*, Duthuit stresses 1905 as the cardinal fauvist date in the career of Henri Matisse, as when he writes, "... je me décide, tout compte fait, à réserver le nom de fauvisme à la période qui trouve son axe et sa pointe dans le cours des années 1905–1906" (363) (I am deciding, all things considered, to reserve the name of fauvism for the period that finds its axis and apex in the years 1905 and 1906) (*The Fauvist Painters*, 96).

SB omits the dieresis in his spelling of "héroïque."

8. *Sketch of Georges Duthuit* by André Masson, 1945

GEORGES DUTHUIT

Mardi [? 28 June 1949]   Ussy

Mon cher vieux,

Merci de ta lettre, avec page Marguerite.[1]

Je ne sais plus du tout où j'en suis. Je me débats avec le dialogue
Bram. Ça donne une chose abominable. Je ne sais pas si je pourrai

m'en sortir. Je n'en peux plus. Ça devient de la folie furieuse où personne n'a le droit d'entraîner un autre. Pas un seul instant un tableau de lui ne surgit, pour me freiner. Je suis incapable de repenser notre débat; incapable de reprendre des choses plus ou moins acceptables dites déjà. Je ne peux remplacer ta voix; celle qui me rappelle qu'il ne s'agit pas que de moi. Je me demande s'il ne va pas falloir que nous fassions ça ensemble vendredi soir. J'aurais le temps de le traduire le lendemain. J'espère que ce ne sera pas nécessaire, car je voudrais être libre la veille de mon départ. Je vais encore faire quelques efforts, mais ce seront les tout derniers. J'ai fait tout ce qu'il est en mon pouvoir de faire pour Bram, c'est fini. Le mal que je lui ai fait est fini également. J'aurais voulu profité [*for* profiter] de ta gentillesse pour m'expliquer une bonne fois là-dessus. Mais je vois que je ne peux pas. Dès que je m'y mets, sans personne pour me retenir, au lieu de mettre de l'eau dans ma piquette, je trouve qu'il y en [a] déjà trop et qu'un peu de vitriol ferait mieux l'affaire. Comme tu vois, j'ai complètement perdu la tête.

C'est peut-être le fait d'écrire directement en anglais qui me noue. Horrible langue, que je sais encore trop bien.[2]
Example:
"B: Are you suggesting that the painting of van Velde is inexpressive? A. (A fortnight later) Yes."[3]
Pour <u>moi</u>, c'est la seule réponse possible. Répondre, comme j'ai déjà eu la lâcheté de le faire, qu'elle exprime l'impossibilité de rien exprimer, c'est le ramener tambour battant au bercail.

Parce que j'ai la frénésie d'aménager pour moi-même une situation littéralement impossible, ce que tu appelles l'absolu, voilà que je l'y colle à mes côtés.

Pendant ce temps je suis à la campagne. Mille indices me le prouvent.

La semaine prochaine je serai auprès de ma mère mourante.

Et au mois d'août je pourrai me consacrer à nouveau aux joies de la composition littéraire.

En ayant bien soin de ne pas trop boire ni fumer, afin de me conserver le plus longtemps possible.

Et en me disant vaillamment, sans pouvoir y croire, que je ne suis pas le seul.[4]

Ton ami

Sam

ALS; 2 leaves, 4 sides; Duthuit collection. *Dating:* SB planned to be in Dublin for a month in July 1949 (SB to Thomas MacGreevy, 27 March 1949, and SB to Yvonne Lefèvre, 26 April 1949 [Lefèvre collection]). SB here talks of completing the "Three Dialogues" with Duthuit on Friday evening, and doing the translation on Saturday if necessary, although he would like to have the evening before he left free: this suggests that his departure was Saturday 1 July or Sunday 2 July 1949; the previous Tuesday was 28 June 1949.

Tuesday [? 28 June 1949]   Ussy.

My dear old friend,

Thank you for your letter, with Marguerite page.[1]

Now I have no idea where I am. I am wrestling with the Bram dialogue. What is coming out is appalling. I do not know if I shall be able to make anything of it. It is wearing me out. It is turning into a kind of madness into which no one has the right to drag anyone else. Not one moment where one of his paintings springs up in front of me, to check me. I am incapable of rethinking our debate; incapable of taking up again more or less acceptable things already said. I cannot replace your voice; the voice that reminds me that it's not all about me. I am wondering if we will not have to do it together on Friday evening. I would have time to translate it the next day. I hope it will not be necessary, for I should like to be free the evening before I leave. I shall make a few more efforts at it, but they will be the very last. I have done everything it is in my power to do for Bram, but it is all over. The harm I have done him is over too. I would have wanted to take advantage of your niceness to speak my mind fully and finally about it all. But I see that I cannot. As soon as I start, with no one to hold me back, instead of watering down my wine, I find that there is already too much water in it and that a little vitriol would do better. As you see, I have completely lost my head.

It is perhaps the fact of writing directly in English which is knotting me up. Horrible language, which I still know too well.[2]
Example:

"B: Are you suggesting that the painting of van Velde is inexpressive? A. (A fortnight later) Yes."[3]

For *me*, that is the only possible answer. To answer, as I have already been cowardly enough to do, that it expresses the impossibility of expressing anything is just to march him back into line with the others.

Because I have this frantic urge to fix up for myself a situation that is literally impossible, what you call the absolute, there I am dragging him along beside me.

Meanwhile I am in the country. A thousand signs prove it to me.

Next week I shall be with my dying mother.

And in August I shall once again be able to devote myself to the joys of literary composition.

Taking great care not to smoke or drink too much, in order to preserve myself as long as possible.

And telling myself valiantly, without being able to believe it, that I am not the only one.[4]

Your friend

Sam

1   Neither Duthuit's letter to SB nor its enclosure has been found.

2   This paragraph was inserted in the left margin.

3   These lines appear in the "Three Dialogues: Samuel Beckett and Georges Duthuit" (101); only there the words "One moment." appear before "Are you suggesting . . ."; "B" becomes "D" (for Duthuit), and "A" becomes "B" (for Beckett).

4   Georges Duthuit was known to drink only wine (and that in moderation), but he was an inveterate smoker of cigarettes, cigars, and pipe (Claude Duthuit).

GEORGES DUTHUIT
AIX-EN-PROVENCE

<u>30 juillet [1949]</u>   Dublin

Mon cher vieux Georges,

Ta lettre d'Aix ce matin.[1] Je ne tiens pas à grand'chose, tu le sais, mais je tiens à ton amitié. Si je ne t'ai pas écrit plus souvent, c'est qu'ici il est dangereux de sortir même brièvement du rôle, rôle qui cette fois-ci n'a pas été trop mal reçu et qui semble avoir servi à quelque chose.

Je pars après-demain, de très bonne heure, serai à Paris vers midi. A vrai dire ça m'étonnerait beaucoup, que j'y sois à l'heure susdite, qu'il ne se produise rien, d'ici là, qui m'en empêche. Mais je connais trop bien ce sentiment.

Je me demande si tu as reçu ma lettre écrite il y a 3 semaines à peu près.

Suzannne m'a écrit que tu étais bien fatigué. J'espère pour toi que ç'en sera bientôt fini de <u>Transition</u> et de ces corvées. Encore si ça rapportait.

Moi? Dégringolade lente comme chaque fois, un peu plus de whiskey tous les jours, travail néant. Je fais le chauffeur, en me disant, fais attention, tiens-t'en au stout. J'ai vu quelques vieux copains, ne sais plus de quoi ils parlent, ni de qui. Ils doivent penser que je joue à l'idiot. Suzanne s'est donné du mal avec les 2 pièces, Vitaly a l'air de s'y intéresser.[2] Merci pour le Gall.[3] Dans l'état d'ahurissement où je suis, je n'ai pas d'envies d'ordre littéraire. J'ai envie de somnoler, un peu détendu, dans le demi-jour de la chambre d'Ussy, conscient vaguement des branches du dehors. Et en croyant que c'est fini, comme cela m'arrive chaque jour, je sais que je me flatte, que c'est parce que je suis ici, où je serais sans doute resté, sans une histoire de clefs que je ne crois pas t'avoir racontée. Morne d'ailleurs, l'histoire.[4]

Ce que tu vois de la fenêtre me tente beaucoup, j'aimerais beaucoup y aller un hiver, si la place est libre.[5]

Rendez-vous à Paris, bientôt. Je pense que nous irons presque aussitôt à Ussy, Suzanne en aura surement très envie, elle n'a pas bougé de Paris.[6]

Il n'est que 8½$^{\underline{h}}$ du soir, mais je vais aller me coucher. Demain c'est dimanche. Famille au grand complet. Derniers sourires. Le fait est qu'il n'existe qu'un seul moyen de disparaître. Les chambres à la campagne, c'est de la littérature.

Affectueusement à Marguerite et à Madame Matisse.[7]

A toi, mon vieux Georges, toute mon amitié, vieille il me semble déjà de ce que j'ai eu de meilleur.   Sam

ALS; 1 leaf, 2 sides; Duthuit collection. *Dating*: 30 July fell on a Saturday in 1949; internal evidence concerning SB's return from Dublin confirms 1949.

30 July [1949]   Dublin

Georges my old friend,

Your letter from Aix this morning.[1] There are not many things that matter to me, as you know, but your friendship matters. If I have not written more often, it is because it is dangerous here to step, even briefly, out of role, a role which seems to have gone down not too badly this time, and to have done some good.

I leave the day after tomorrow, very early, will be in Paris about noon. But to tell you the truth, I should be amazed if I was there at the aforementioned hour, amazed if nothing turned up between now and then to stop me. But that is a feeling I know only too well.

I wonder if you got my letter, written about 3 weeks ago.

Suzanne said in one of her letters that you were very tired. I hope for you that you will soon be finished with *Transition* and all that drudgery. If it even brought in any money.

Myself? Slow decay, like every other time, a little more whiskey each day, work nil. I do the driving, and tell myself to be careful, to keep to stout. I have seen a few old pals, no idea what they are talking about (nor of whom). They must think I'm playing the fool. Suzanne has been going to a lot of trouble over the two plays. Vitaly seems to be showing an interest.[2] Thank you for the Le Gall.[3] In the state of bewilderment I find myself in, I have no desires of a literary kind. I feel like dozing off, lying back a bit, in the half-light of the bedroom at Ussy, vaguely aware of the branches outside. And thinking it is all over, as happens to me every day, I know I am indulging myself, that it is because I am here, where no doubt I would have stayed, had it not been for a whole business involving keys, which I do not think I ever told you about. A dismal business, I may say.[4]

What you see from your window tempts me greatly. I should love to go there one winter, if the place is free.[5]

See you in Paris, soon. I think we shall go off to Ussy pretty well straight away. Suzanne will surely want that: she has not set foot outside Paris.[6]

It is only 8.30 in the evening, but I am going to go to bed. Tomorrow is Sunday. Whole family coming. Last smiles. The fact is that there is only one way to disappear. Bedrooms in the country, that is story-book stuff.

Love to Marguerite and Madame Matisse.[7]

To you, my dear old Georges, all my friendship, a friendship into which, it seems to me, whatever is best in me has long gone. Sam

1   Duthuit's letter to SB has not been found.

2   *Eleutheria* and *En attendant Godot*. Ukrainian-born Georges Vitaly (1917–2007) was an actor and director who in 1947 founded the Théâtre de la Huchette, Paris 5, which he ran until 1952.

3   It is not known what Duthuit has done for SB with respect to theatre director Yves Le Gall (b. 1925). Le Gall was best known for his 1949 production of *Akara*, by Romain Weingarten (1926–2006), whose third act appeared in *Transition Forty-Eight* no. 4 (42–59), prefaced by a short "Introduction to Akara" by Le Gall (40–41), both of these in unsigned translations by SB. (Michel Vaïs claims that SB was so enthused by Weingarten's play that he translated it all, but advances no evidence in support of the claim [*L'Ecrivain scénique* (Quebec: Presses de l'Université du Québec, 1978) 84].) The entry in "Notes about Contributors" in *Transition Forty-Eight* no. 4, runs: "Yves Le Gall has already found time to spend fifteen years in Africa, in spite of his being only 23 years old. It seems then that it was in the region of Dakar that he first began to give thought to theatrical problems. He has since staged and directed *Akara* and is working on different essays about the technique and the meaning of the theatre" (153).

4   What exactly SB is referring to with respect to keys is not known for sure, but it seems probable that his story relates to his abandoning of his academic post at Trinity College Dublin in 1931 – and of the attendant stability and respectability wished for

him by his family – rather than to his later more definitive break from Ireland in 1937. Probably the story relates to the keys SB was given when he became a member of staff at Trinity College in 1930, one of which permitted entrance to the staff Common Room, another to Front Square, and another to Back Gate, without passing through the main entrance. Return of these keys would have been required when SB quit his post the following year, in circumstances that were deeply embarrassing for himself, his family, and his supporters at the College (James Knowlson, 24 January 2010). As a result of SB's failure to return the keys, all the locks had to be changed. SB's father had been very proud of being able to let himself in by Back Gate with his son's key. All in all, the family was thoroughly embarrassed (Edward Beckett).

5   Duthuit was presumably looking out over the rooftops of Aix-en-Provence, from the attic room he used as a studio in the house his mother-in-law had bought earlier in the year, at 10 Rue Cardinale (Claude Duthuit).

6   SB omits the circumflex accent in "sûrement."

7   Duthuit's wife, and his mother-in-law Amélie Noélie Matisse.

SEAN O'SULLIVAN

DUBLIN

18th October 1949

My dear Sean

I received your letter, and Mr. Ryan's, only yesterday.[1]

I remember the short story you mention. I think it is included in More Pricks than Kicks. But not possessing a copy of that work, I can't say for certain. In any case, even if it is not, I would not consent to its publication now.[2]

I have not written anything in English for a long time. The best I can do for Envoy is an extract from an unpublished work called Watt, written during the occupation. I hope to get this off to them next week.[3]

Yes, I knew Adler was dead. Benno has been in America since 1940 I think.[4]

All the best.

s/ Sam

TLS; 1 leaf, 1 side; AN AH bottom right; ICso, MSS 043 Box 4/5.

1   John Ryan (1925–1992) wrote to SB as Editor of the new Dublin journal *Envoy: A Review of Literature and Art* (December 1949 – July 1951); *Envoy* was intended to serve "abroad as *envoy* of Irish writing and at home as *envoy* of the best in international

writing" (John Ryan, Valentin Iremonger, and J. K. Hillman, "A Foreword to Our First Issue," *Envoy* 1.1 [December 1949] [8]). Ryan was an artist regularly exhibiting from 1946 at the Royal Hibernian Academy, a set designer in Dublin and London, and later Editor of *Dublin Magazine* (1969–1974).

Seán O'Sullivan (1906–1964; Profile, I) had asked SB, on Ryan's behalf, for a contribution.

2 O'Sullivan's letter to SB has not been found; the story he had suggested from *More Pricks Than Kicks* has not been identified.

3 SB responded to John Ryan's letter on 20 October, sending him ten pages of TMS, "an extract from an unpublished work, <u>Watt</u>, finished in 1945. If you decide to use it, please let me have proofs" (ICso, MSS 43/1/3). "An Extract from Watt" was published in *Envoy* 1.2 (January 1950) 11–19.

4 Jankel Adler (1895–1949) died on 25 April; SB had arranged for O'Sullivan to use Adler's studio in Paris in 1939.

The American artist Benjamin G. Benno (né Benjamin Greenstein, 1901–1980) studied in Paris (1926–1930, 1932–1933) and maintained a studio in Paris from 1932 to 1939. His first solo exhibition was sponsored by Picasso at the Galerie Pierre (1934). Benno returned to New York in October 1939, where, in the following year, he exhibited at the Pinacotheca Gallery (Donna Gustafson, "Benjamin Benno," in *Benjamin Benno: A Retrospective Exhibition* [Rutgers, NJ: Jane Voorhees Zimmerli Art Museum, 1988] 1, 5, 9, 11, 18, 19, 23).

ANDRE-CHARLES GERVAIS, BORDAS
PARIS

8 Nov [1949]
Cher Monsieur,

Je ne veux pas attendre davantage pour vous dire que je n'ai pas encore vu Max-Pol Fouchet. Je suis allée plusieurs fois à son hôtel sans résultat. Finalement je lui ai écrit pour lui demander un rendez-vous il y a de cela une huitaine de jours.[1] *Maintenant j'attends sa réponse. Vous voyez, je ne m'y prends pas encore très bien.*

Merci mille fois pour la copie de la lettre que M.-P. Fouchet vous a envoyée. Votre geste une fois de plus me touche énormément et je dois vous dire que vous avez déjà apporté du réconfort à la maison. Quant à la lettre de M.-P. Fouchet elle est, elle aussi, réconfortante à sa façon, c'est déjà beaucoup.[2]

Je vous envoie mes sentiments très amicaux.

> *s/ Suzanne Dumesnil*

6 rue des Favorites 15°

ALS; 1 side, 2 leaves; IMEC, Beckett, Boîte 1, S. Beckett, Correspondance 1946–1953.

8 Nov [1949]

Dear Mr. Gervais

I do not want to wait any longer before telling you that I have not yet seen Max-Pol Fouchet. I have been to his hotel several times, fruitlessly. In the end I wrote to him to ask for an appointment, a week or so ago.[1] Now I am waiting for his reply. You can see, I am not going about this in the right way.

A thousand thanks for the copy of the letter from Max-Pol Fouchet sent to you. Your gesture once more touches me a great deal, and I must tell you that you have already brought much comfort to us here. As for M.-P. Fouchet's letter, it too is comforting in its way, and that itself is quite something.[2]

> *With my very best wishes*
> *Suzanne Dumesnil*

6 rue des Favorites 15°

---

1   On 21 October, in response to a visit from Suzanne Deschevaux-Dumesnil, André-Charles Gervais (1910–1996), Editions Bordas, wrote to Max-Pol Fouchet asking him to receive her "et étudier avec elle les moyens de venir en aide à un écrivain trop humain et trop fier pour notre époque" (and examine with her the ways in which help might be provided to a writer too human and too proud for the time we live in). Gervais added, "J'essaie de mon côté de trouver une solution: mais je suis bien mal placé pour obtenir ce qu'il lui faudrait" (I am trying from my side to come up with a solution, but I am not in a good position to arrange what would be needed).

Fouchet replied to Gervais on 23 October offering to receive Madame Deschevaux-Dumesnil, "Et ferai tout mon possible" (And will do everything I can): "Je m'honore d'être l'un de ceux qui tiennent M. Samuel Beckett pour l'un des plus importants écrivains d'aujourd'hui" (I feel honoured to be one of those who regard Samuel Beckett as one of the most important writers of today) (IMEC, Beckett, Boîte 1, S. Beckett, Correspondance 1947–1953).

2   On 27 October, Gervais sent a copy of Fouchet's letter of 23 October to Suzanne Deschevaux-Dumesnil (IMEC, Beckett, Boîte 1, S. Beckett, Correspondance 1947–1953).

CHRONOLOGY 1950

1950 January   SB commissioned by UNESCO to translate the *Anthology of Mexican Poetry* edited by Octavio Paz.
"An extract from *Watt*" published in *Envoy* (Dublin).
SB finishes a draft of *L'Innommable*.

27 February   Requests extension on deadline to 1 May to complete translations for UNESCO's *Anthology of Mexican Poetry*.

March   Revises translation of Georges Duthuit's *Les Fauves*.

9 May   The "Schumann Declaration," considered to be the beginning of what is now the European Union; later known as Europe Day.

25 June   The Korean War begins.

30 June   May Beckett suffers a broken leg.

c. 2 July   SB travels to Dublin to be with his mother.

25 August   Death of May Beckett.

8 September   SB returns to France.

4 October   Extract from *Malone meurt* accepted by Georges Lambrichs for publication in Editions de Minuit's journal *84: Nouvelle Revue Littéraire*.

6 October   Suzanne Deschevaux-Dumesnil takes *Molloy* to Georges Lambrichs at Editions de Minuit.

before mid-October   Jérôme Lindon reads *Molloy* and writes to Suzanne Deschevaux-Dumesnil that Editions de Minuit will publish the novel.

20 October   Extracts from *Molloy* and *Malone meurt*, translated by SB, published in *Transition Fifty*, no. 6 as "Two Fragments."

15 November	Suzanne Deschevaux-Dumensil returns the signed contracts to Editions de Minuit for publication of the three novels *Molloy*, *Malone meurt*, *L'Innommable*.
December	"Malone s'en conte," an extract from *Malone meurt*, published in *84: Nouvelle Revue Littéraire*.
24 December	SB writes "Texte pour rien, I."

GEORGES DUTHUIT
LONDON

lundi 27 [February 1950]   Paris

Cher vieux Georges,

    Je me demandais où tu étais. Passé chez toi la semaine dernière j'ai seulement appris que tu étais en voyage, avec Marguerite. J'ai griffonné quelques mots sur ta feuille chez la concierge.[1] Je me te disais à Aix ou à Gand et te voilà à portée de cauchemar de la Vale of Health. But in Ken Wood Who shall find me None but the most quarried lovers.[2] Quels souvenirs de ce monticule de malheur. Fléchettes, larmes et hoquets pickwickés mal noyés au Bull et Bush, tentative de thé au Spaniards. En se sachant jeune. Et voué encore cette nuit à la cuvette de World's End.[3] Enfin il y avait, sur le chemin de retour, le Seghers. L'as-tu revu? <u>En existe-t-il une reproduction en couleurs pas trop chère?</u>[4]

    Nous, guère brillantes, les nouvelles. Enorme fatigue. A Ussy ça a été très dur, le sera encore, la prochaine fois, vers la mi-mars. Avec ça les Mexicains. Je verdis dessus. Au tiers du fleuve le Señor Paz s'est ravisé, supprimant une vingtaine de poèmes (dont j'avais déjà traduit une douzaine) et en ajoutant autant.[5] Mon petit normalien, chez qui le sens de l'équité est déjà fort développé, s'est dressé sur ses petits ergots de futur philologue distingué, en proclamant que ce n'était pas dans le <u>bond</u>.[6] Résultat: je dois me débrouiller tout seul avec les nouveaux venus. Et un autre travail venu se greffer là-dessus, de la part de Bordas, 15000 mots sur la sculpture française, de Solutré à nos nuits, co-auteur Gischia, avec je ne sais qui.[7] Plutôt que de refuser j'ai demandé un sursis à l'UNESCO. Accordé. Mais me voilà noyé jusqu'à fin avril. J'ai vu Blin.[8] Il veut, pardon, voudrait monter <u>Godot</u>. Ma nationalité complique les choses, parait-il, les pièces étrangères ne pouvant passer qu'à la cadence d'une pour trois pièces françaises.[9] Gentil type, très Montparnasse, je le connais bien de vue, grand ami d'Artaud, à qui il est en train de faire le coup de Brod, en 3 volumes, mais un peu gêné quand même.[10] Pas très bon ni comme acteur ni comme metteur en scène, à en juger par la Sonate que nous avons vue, avec 17 autres personnes, mais un grand amour du théâtre.[11]

De ce salaud de Paul j'ai dû te citer un fragment du passage suivant (Corinthiens 1, 15):

All flesh is not the same flesh: but there is one kind of flesh of men, another flesh of beasts, and another of birds.

There are also celestial bodies, and bodies terrestrial: but the glory of the celestial is one, and the glory of the terrestrial is another.

There is one glory of the sun, and another glory of the moon, and another glory of the stars: for one star differeth from another star in glory.

So also is the resurrection of the dead. It is sown in corruption; it is raised in incorruption:

It is sown in dishonour; it is raised in glory; it is sown in weakness; it is raised in power:

It is sown a natural body; it is raised a spiritual body. There is a natural body, and there is a spiritual body.[12]

Autre chose quand même qu'Albert Bayet et Pierre Bénard.[13] Un peu bébêtes, peut-être, l'antithèse et chiasme hébraïques, mais comme c'est bien foutu. Ca me rappelle toujours Esaïe 55 (chapitre formidable) dont je t'ai peut-être cité également:

For my thoughts are not your thoughts, neither are your ways my ways, saith the Lord.

For as the heavens are higher than the earth, so are my ways higher than your ways, and my thoughts than your thoughts.[14]

Vu Bram hier, de plus en plus mal fichu. Il part avec Marthe pour deux mois en Haute-Savoie, dans une maison de repos des missionnaires protestants, en pleine brousse.[15] Il a reçu la visite d'un amateur et du directeur du Musée de Grenoble, tous deux désireux d'acheter.[16] Il est grand temps qu'il se libère. Il dit que c'est impossible. Il avait été deux fois voir l'exposition Braque, chez qui il avait cru découvrir des velléités de désordre.[17] Faut que j'aille assister à ça. Une dame enthousiaste, prenant Maeght pour le grand imagier, s'est précipitée sur lui en s'exclamant, Maître, maître, je vous félicite. Public nombreux et rayonnant, pourléchant la marchandise, pur fruit, pur sucre. Article de Reverdy bien en vue.[18]

Fais-moi signe dès ton retour, avant plutôt. Ça fait un bail. Viens dimanche prochain, si tu es rentré.

Affectueusement, mon vieux Georges, à toi.

s/ Sam

TLS; 1 leaf, 2 sides; Duthuit collection. *Dating*: in January 1950, SB received the UNESCO commission to translate the *Anthology of Mexican Poetry* edited by Octavio Paz (SB to Yvonne Lefèvre, 27 April 1950 [Lefèvre collection]). The 27th fell on a Monday in February and March 1950; SB plans to return to Ussy in mid-March.

Monday 27 [February 1950]   Paris

Dear old Georges,

I was wondering where you were. When I called in last week I only found out that you were away travelling, with Marguerite. I scribbled a few words on your note-page at the concierge's.[1] I was imagining you in Aix, or Ghent, and there you are within a nightmare of the Vale of Health. But in Ken Wood Who shall find me None but the most quarried lovers.[2] What memories of that awful hillock. Darts, tears and Pickwicked hiccups not quite drowned at the Bull and Bush, tea attempted at the Spaniards. Knowing one was young. And bound again that night for the basin of World's End.[3] Well, at least there was the Seghers on the way back. Have you seen it again? *Is there a colour reproduction of it, not too expensive?*[4]

From us, nothing marvellous in the way of news. Enormous weariness. It has been very hard at Ussy, will be again, next time, mid-March or so. And then the Mexicans. I am going green over them. A third of the way down the great river, Señor Paz changed his mind, cutting twenty or so poems (a dozen of which I had already translated) and adding on as many.[5] My young Normalien, who already has a highly developed sense of equity, got up on his low horse like the future distinguished philologist that he is, declaring that it was not in his bond.[6] Result: I have to get through the new ones on my own. And another job on top of that, from Bordas, 15,000 words on French sculpture, from Solutré to the present night, co-author Gischia, with I cannot remember who.[7] Rather than refuse I asked for an extension of the deadline at UNESCO. Granted. But now I shall not get my head above water till the end of April. I have seen Blin.[8] He wants, sorry, would like to put on *Godot*. My nationality complicates things, apparently, foreign plays can only be put on at the rate of one for every three French plays.[9] Nice fellow, very Montparnasse. I know him well by sight, great friend of Artaud, on whom he is going to do a Brod, in three volumes. But a bit embarrassed all the same.[10] Not very good either as actor or as director, if I am to judge by the *Sonata* that we saw, along with 17 other people, but great love of theatre.[11]

I must have quoted to you a fragment of the following passage from that bastard Paul (Corinthians 1,15):

All flesh is not the same flesh: but there is one kind of flesh of men, another flesh of beasts, and another of birds.

There are also celestial bodies, and bodies terrestrial: but the glory of the celestial is one, and the glory of the terrestrial is another.

There is one glory of the sun, and another glory of the moon, and another glory of the stars: for one star differeth from another star in glory.

So also is the resurrection of the dead. It is sown in corruption; it is raised in incorruption:

It is sown in dishonour; it is raised in glory; it is sown in weakness; it is raised in power:

It is sown a natural body; it is raised a spiritual body. There is a natural body, and there is a spiritual body.[12]

A bit different from Albert Bayet and Pierre Bénard, all the same.[13] Rather silly, perhaps, the Hebraic antithesis and chiasmus, but how it hangs together. It always reminds me of Isaiah 55 (tremendous chapter) which I have perhaps also quoted to you:

For my thoughts are not your thoughts, neither are your ways my ways, saith the Lord.

For as the heavens are higher than the earth, so are my ways higher than your ways, and my thoughts than your thoughts.[14]

Saw Bram yesterday, looking worse and worse. He is leaving with Marthe for two months in Haute-Savoie, in a rest home for Protestant missionaries, in the middle of nowhere.[15] He had a visit from an art lover and from the Director of the Grenoble Museum, both eager to buy.[16] It is high time he struck out for freedom. He says it is impossible. He had twice been to the Braque exhibition, where he thought he had detected hints of a taste for disorder.[17] I must go. An enthusiastic lady, taking Maeght for the great imager, rushed up to him exclaiming Master, master, I congratulate you. Hordes of people, all beaming, mouths watering over the goods on offer, pure fruit, pure sugar. Reverdy article prominently displayed.[18]

Get in touch as soon as you are back, better still before then. It has been an age. Come next Sunday, if you are back.

Affectionately, my old friend Georges, to you

Sam

1　At this time, the Duthuits were living at 34 Rue de Miromesnil, Paris 8, though SB may have visited Georges Duthuit's studio-office at 96 Rue de l'Université.

2　Duthuit was a regular visitor to Aix-en-Provence, where he often stayed with André Masson and Tal-Coat.
In this period, Duthuit often traveled to Gand (Ghent), Belgium, to lecture at the Institut Français and to visit his friends the Van Nieuwenhuyses (n.d.), who were art collectors.
The Vale of Health is a small and a prosperous neighborhood of North London by Hampstead Heath on which the great Kenwood House is situated. SB cites inexactly from his own poem "Serena I" (written in 1932, first published in *Echo's Bones and Other Precipitates*, [25–27]), which contains the following lines: "hence in Ken Wood who shall find me / my breath held in the midst of thickets / none but the most quarried lovers"; and later in the poem, "but in Ken Wood / who shall find me / my brother the fly" (*Poems: 1930–1989* [London: Calder Publications, 2002] 23–24).

3　SB recollects haunts from his period of residence in London, 1934–1935. The Old Bull and Bush, which has been a pub since 1721 and is commemorated in the popular song "Down at the Old Bull and Bush," is situated on Northend Road, not far from Hampstead Heath. The Spaniards Inn is also on Hampstead Heath (see 8 October 1932, n. 6, to George Reavey). The World's End pub on Kings Road, London SW10 (see 8 September 1934, n. 3, to Thomas McGreevy).

4　SB's "way back" from Hampstead Heath to West Brompton might pass by way of the National Gallery, Trafalgar Square, where (as he comments in his letter to Thomas McGreevy, 8 October 1935) he admired *A Mountainous Landscape* (NGL 4383), then ascribed to Hercules Seghers (c. 1589 – c. 1638).
In the left margin next to the question about a reproduction is written, with double underlining: "ignore."

5   Ricardo Baeza (1890–1956), well-known translator and Spanish Republican in exile, suggested that UNESCO publish an *Anthology of Mexican Poetry* that would be translated from Spanish into both French and English (Octavio Paz with Eliot Weinberger, "Afterword: A Conversation with Octavio Paz," in Samuel Beckett, Octavio Paz, Eliot Weinberger, and Enrique Chagoya, *The Bread of Days: Eleven Mexican Poets / El pan de los días: once poetas mexicanos* [Covelo, CA: Yolla Bolly Press, 1994] 121–122). Octavio Paz selected Guy Lévis Mano (1904–1980) to do the French translation, and, at the suggestion of Jean-Jacques Mayoux, SB to do the English translation (interview with Emile Delavenay, 2 October 1992). As Paz reports:

> Beckett came to see me, and he told me that he didn't speak Spanish, but that he knew Latin very well, and had a friend … who had excellent Spanish. I admired his writing, so I was delighted that he agreed to do the translations.
>
> He began working on the anthology. Sometimes he would call me, and we would go to a café to discuss certain problems – enigmas of the poetry – and I would try to clarify them. He was always very kind, and polite; I liked him as a human being. (Paz and Weinberger, "Afterword," in *The Bread of Days*, 122.)

The Mexican poet Jaime Torres Bodet (1902–1974), who was Director General of UNESCO from late 1948 to 1952, intervened in the textual decisions of the anthology: "Torres Bodet decided that Alfonso Reyes … would be the only living poet admitted in the book … This meant eliminating the work of poets such as Xavier Villaurrutia and José Gorostiza" (Paz and Weinberger, "Afterword," in *The Bread of Days*, x). Comparison of the original list of poems with those published in the English text shows at least forty poems cut or truncated, and nineteen additions, including poems by Reyes (TxU, Beckett collection).

6   SB's helper has not been identified.

7   No such comprehensive work was ever published by Bordas. SB refers to the Paleolithic site of Solutré in Burgundy. Léon Gischia (1903–1991) had co-authored, with Nicole Védrès, a work on recent sculpture, *La Sculpture en France depuis Rodin* (Paris: Seuil, 1945), and later co-authored, with Bernard Champigneulle, *La Sculpture en France, de la préhistoire à la fin du Moyen Age* (Lyon: Audin, 1950), which is probably the book that SB was asked to translate.

8   Roger Blin* (1907–1984). James Knowlson cites SB speaking of Suzanne Deschevaux-Dumesnil during this period: "She hawked everything around … It was the same with Roger Blin. She was the one who saw Blin and got him interested in *Godot* and *Eleutheria*. I kept out of the way" (*Damned to Fame*, 340).

9   SB omits the circumflex on "paraît."

10   In *Roger Blin: souvenirs et propos recueillis*, by Roger Blin and Lynda Bellity Peskine, Blin speaks of his admiration for and friendship with Antonin Artaud, whom he had known since 1928 ([Paris: Gallimard, 1986] 27–34). SB believes that Blin is intending to champion his work, as Max Brod – in his case quite unapologetically – did that of Franz Kafka, perhaps by publishing hitherto unknown works by Artaud, or his papers and letters (of which Blin is reported as possessing an abundance).

11   Roger Blin's production of August Strindberg's *La Sonate des spectres* (*Ghost Sonata*) ran from 23 October 1949 to 13 February 1950 at the Théâtre de la Gaîté-Montparnasse, with Blin in the role of the Student (Odette Aslan, *Roger Blin and Twentieth-Century Playwrights*, tr. Ruby Cohn [Cambridge: Cambridge University Press, 1988] 20).

12   From the King James Bible, SB cites Paul's words in 1 Corinthians 15: 39–44.

13   It is presumably with the styles of these two writers that SB draws his astonishingly odd contrast. Albert Bayet (1880–1961) was Professor of Sociology at the Sorbonne and the Ecole Pratique des Hautes Etudes (Section des Sciences Religieuses), and author of such works as *Les Morales de l'Evangile* (1927). Novelist and journalist Pierre Bénard (1898–1946) wrote for, and from 1936 until his death (with an interruption during the War) was Editor of, the satirical weekly *Le Canard enchaîné*.

14   Isaiah, 55: 8–9.

15   Marthe Arnaud had been a Protestant missionary in Northern Rhodesia (now Zambia). The maison de repos has not been identified.

16   The art lover has not been identified. No work by Bram van Velde entered the collection of the Musée de Grenoble while Jean Leymarie (1919–2006) was its director (1950–1955) (Hélène Vincent, Conservateur en chef, Musée de Grenoble).

17   Braque's exhibition at the Galerie Maeght, Paris, opened on 10 February ("Œuvres récentes," *Combat*, 11–12 February 1950: 4).

18   Georges Braque and Pierre Reverdy, *Une aventure méthodique*, with twenty-six lithographs (Paris: Fernand Mourlot, 1950) 9–61.
The phrase "pur fruit, pur sucre" appears on the jars of many of the best jams.

GEORGES DUTHUIT
PARIS

vendredi [before 1 March 1950]   Ussy
Mon pauvre vieux

Ça ne va pas vite, et cependant je ne fais que ça. Beaucoup traduit cette semaine, et des passages de peu de repos. Ce qui est long, quand la correspondance s'arrête, c'est de repérer où elle reprend.[1]

Nous rentrerons lundi. Le temps de taper mes hiéroglyphes et j'aurai quand même un bon paquet pour Mme Woodward.[2] Veux-tu passer mercredi après-midi, pas trop tôt? J'espère que le compte y sera presque.

1) Veux-tu éclairer ma lanterne sur les implications de l'archange au marché marron, n. 67 des épreuves.[3]

2) Peux-tu m'avoir la Chapelle des Arènes en italien. Je traduis Arena Chapel, ce qui est atroce.[4]

Prière de répondre Rue des Favorites, pour que je puisse disposer de ces atouts dès mon retour.

La maison est vendue. Le 1er mars nous verra sur le pavé.[5]

Il n'a fait que pleuvoir. Aujourd'hui un peu de soleil.

Le grand tableau de Geer me fait enfin des signes. Dommage qu'il ait si mal tourné. Mais ce n'est peut-être pas vrai.[6]

A bientôt, mon cher vieux. Dans mon sommeil je te traduis. D'une façon un peu trop libre.

Fort goûté ton peu de goût pour le désastre à tout faire, à la Bataille.[7]

Comprends toujours pas en quoi l'art peut nous aider à patienter.

Affectueusement

<u>Sam</u>

ALS; 1 leaf, 2 sides; Duthuit collection. *Dating*: prior to sale of the Ussy house where SB had rented a room; reference to SB's work on revision of English translation of Duthuit's *Les Fauves*.

Friday [before 1 March 1950]   Ussy

My poor old Georges,

It is not coming along very fast, and yet it is all I am doing. A lot translated this week, and not the easiest of passages. What takes a long time, when the correspondence breaks off, is spotting where it takes up again.[1]

We shall be coming back on Monday. Just time to type out my hieroglyphs and I shall all the same have a decent bundle for Mrs Woodward.[2] Will you come round on Wednesday afternoon, not too early? I hope it will be almost all there.

1) Will you enlighten me as to the implications of "l'archange au marché marron", no. 67 of the proofs.[3]

2) Can you get for me the "Chapelle des Arènes" in Italian. I am translating it as "Arena Chapel," which is dreadful.[4]

Please reply to the Rue des Favorites, so that I can have all these trump cards at my disposal as soon as I get back.

The house is sold. On the 1st of March we shall be out on the street.[5]

It has done nothing but rain. A little sunshine today.

Geer's big painting is at last beginning to draw my eye. Pity he has turned out the way he has. But maybe it is not true.[6]

I shall see you soon, my old friend. In my sleep I am translating you. Rather too freely.

Greatly enjoyed your lack of enjoyment of the all-purpose-disaster, à la Bataille.[7]

Still do not understand in what way art can help us to wait patiently.

> Love
>
> <u>Sam</u>

1   SB is assisting in the translation of Georges Duthuit's *Les Fauves*.

2   Daphne Woodward (1906–1965), who made her name as a translator of fiction from French, was at this time working as a secretary and translator for Duthuit, translating for example "Nicolas de Staël" by Patrick Waldberg (*Transition Fifty* no. 6, 66–67).

3   The sentence about which SB inquires occurs in the context of Duthuit's argument about the use of light in painting. The French is: "La fulguration de l'éclair, le papillotement de la bougie, l'éclat transcendant de l'archange au marché marron!" (The flash of lightning, the flickering of the candle, the transcendent radiance of the archangel, all very much the worse for wear) (*Les Fauves*, 170; *The Fauvist Painters*, 59).

4   Duthuit discusses Giotto's frescoes for the Chapelle des Arènes (Padua) in *Les Fauves* (262); despite SB's misgivings, the English translation remains "the Arena Chapel" in *The Fauvist Painters* (63), this being indeed one of its standard English names. In Italian, the chapel is usually called the Capella (degli) Scrovegni, after the wealthy merchant, Enrico Scrovegni, who commissioned it.

5   SB had been renting a room in an outbuilding at 4 Rue de Changis, Ussy (Savane, *Samuel Beckett à Ussy sur Marne*, 9).

6   SB owned two paintings by Geer van Velde, *L'Imprévue* and *Composition*, the latter of which was the larger (89 cm × 116 cm); neither of the paintings is dated (Edward Beckett, 12 December 2009). The cause of SB's disappointment with Geer van Velde is not known.

7   "Le désastre" was, along with "le désert," "le désespoir," and "la désagrégation," a key term for Georges Bataille from as early as 1931, when he wrote in *L'Anus solaire*, for example: "Désastres, les révolutions et les volcans ne font pas l'amour avec les astres … A la fécondité céleste s'opposent les désastres terrestres, image de l'amour terrestre sans condition, érection sans issue et sans règle, scandale et terreur." (*Œuvres complètes*, I [Paris: Gallimard, 1992] 86.) (Revolutions and volcanoes, disasters both, do not make love with the stars … Opposing celestial fecundity stand the earthly disasters, image of unconditional earthly love, erection without release or rule, scandal, and terror.)

GEORGES DUTHUIT

Mercredi [? March 1950]

Cher vieux

Merci de tes deux mots et de celui d'Ackerley que voici.[1]

Voici pour le travail. J'y travaille bea[u]coup, pour moi, et cependant n'en ai fait encore qu'une trentaine de pages (du texte américain).[2] C'est très chinois comme boulot, repérer les changements et en même temps contrôler l'anglais à chaque instant. Si je pouvais simplement m'occuper de l'anglais en tant qu'anglais, sans me référer à ce qu'il est censé représenter, ça irait beaucoup plus vite, mais cela est impossible, tant il y a de contresens. Jamais vu un texte aussi difficile à traduire que le tien cette fois. Pour bien faire il faudrait un an, en te consultant tous les deux jours. Voici ce que je te propose. Je t'apporterai samedi ce que j'aurai fait, et si c'est trop peu, et que tu craignes toujours que l'éditeur ne te fasse des histoires, nous aviserons du moyen d'aller plus vite.[3] Je me fais du mauvais sang aussi pour les susceptibilités de ton traducteur américain, je te demanderai de lui présenter tous les changements que j'apporte à son travail, même lorsque ce n'est pas vrai, comme résultant forcément de tes changements à toi, à ne pas lui mettre sous le nez autant que possible.[4]

A samedi, mon cher vieux, sauf contre-ordre. En effet, il est stupide de dire du mal d'une situation dont il est relativement facile de sortir, si on n'est pas content. Quelle veine quand même, on pourrait être des bêtes, où les rats norvégiens sont plutôt rares.[5]

Affectueusement

s/ Sam

Je ne trouve pas page 6 du texte anglais. L'aurais-tu chez toi?

Jamais aussi bien compris qu'en te lisant, même quand je lisais Proust, à quel point le français est la langue de l'infinitésimal.[6]

TLS; 1 leaf, 1 side; APS; Duthuit collection. *Dating*: in March 1950, SB is reworking Ralph Manheim's translation of Georges Duthuit's book, *Les Fauves*; Robert Motherwell's preface to this edition is dated 14 July 1950. By April, most of SB's work on the translation is completed. Duthuit has been in England and has seen Ackerley before 9 March 1950.

Wednesday [? March 1950]

Dear old friend

Thank you for your two notes and for the one from Ackerley which I am returning.[1]

About the work. I am working at it very hard, for me, and yet have done no more than thirty or so pages (of the American text).[2] It is a very Chinese kind of work, spotting the changes and at the same time checking the English at every moment. If I could simply concern myself with the English as English, without referring to what it is supposed to represent, it would go much faster. But that is impossible, so many blunders are there. Never seen a text so difficult to translate as yours this time. To do it properly I should need a year, consulting you every other day. Here is what I propose. On Saturday I shall bring over what I have done, and if it is too little, and you are worried that the publisher will make trouble, we shall work out a way of going faster.[3] Then I cannot stop worrying about hurting the feelings of your American translator. I shall ask you to present all the changes I am making to his work, even when it is not true, as the unavoidable consequence of changes that you have made, to be kept from him as far as possible.[4]

Till Saturday old friend, unless I hear from you. It really is silly to be grumbling about a situation that is relatively easy to get out of if we do not like it. How lucky we are all the same: we might be animals, where Norwegian rats are pretty rare.[5]

Love

Sam

I cannot find page 6 of the English text. Might you have it at home?

Never understood so clearly as when reading you, not even when reading Proust, to what extent French is the language of the infinitesimal.

1   J[oe] R[andolph] Ackerley (1896–1967) was Arts Editor at *The Listener* from 1935, and had been commissioning pieces from Georges Duthuit since before the War. On 10 March, Ackerley wrote to Herbert Read, "It was nice seeing Georges, wasn't it? And you will have seen that he brought me a new article. It was a little out of date, but less inscrutable than the first" (*The Letters of J. R. Ackerley*, ed. Neville Braybrooke [London: Duckworth, 1975] 84). The article was "The French Symbolists," which was published in *The Listener* the day before, 9 March, in a translation probably by SB. In a letter to Ackerley of 9 November 1949, Duthuit had made it clear: "Beckett ne met jamais son nom sur les traductions" (Beckett never puts his name to translations) (Duthuit collection).

2   SB was revising the English translation of Duthuit's *Les Fauves* done by the American translator Ralph Manheim (1907–1992). Manheim would go on to become one of the most celebrated translators into English of the twentieth century, but at this time more of his work had been from German than from French.

3   Reasons for the publisher's haste may be deduced from a publisher's note inserted in the edition of *The Fauvist Painters*:

> The present edition had to wait for its translation, which was checked by the author, and for the color plates, which were made for the Trois Collines edition and reappear here by arrangement. It had been supposed that the American edition would fill a lacuna in regard to fauvism, there having been no book in English on the subject, but the past few months have seen the appearance in America of two volumes of the edition in English of the *History of Modern Painting* edited and published by Albert Skira, Switzerland; the second volume, with extraordinary color plates and conventional texts, is devoted to fauvism and expressionism.

The publisher continues, defensively, "Still, Duthuit's text is conceived on a different level of thought, and the two books can hardly be said to rival one another" (viii).

4   Duthuit had in fact already written to Manheim, on 21 October 1949, to apologize for the changes he was making to his text as he revised it:

> Il me semble que la meilleure manière de nous en sortir maintenant serait, comme il avait été prévu, que je rapporte moi-même ces changements sur votre traduction. Je serai aidé mot à mot, phrase à phrase, pour ce travail, par mon ami Samuel Beckett qui, non content d'être le brillant styliste de langue anglaise que vous connaissez, est un de nos meilleurs écrivains français. Une fois les corrections faites, la traduction vous sera retournée naturellement pour "supervision." (Rémi Labrusse, "Note sur l'histoire du texte et sur la présente edition," in Duthuit, *Les Fauves*, xxxiv.) (It seems to me that the best way out would be, as planned, for me to put these changes into your translation myself. I shall be helped in this work, word by word, phrase by phrase, by my friend Samuel Beckett, who, not content with being the brilliant English-language stylist that you know, is one of our best French writers. Once the corrections have been made, the translation will of course be sent back to you for "supervision.")

Manheim's response of 13 January 1950 sheds light on the extent of SB's contribution:

> The present translation has its curious side but only the connoisseur (and there are very few) will notice it. The curious side is that the idiom reveals pointillistic drops of American and of Franco-British. Curious but perhaps charming.

It is kind of you to say that I need not tell Wittenborn how it was done but unnecessary; I am on very good terms with him and Mrs Wittenborn, who reads copy, will discern at a glance expressions which no American would ever dream of using. Would Samuel Beckett like to sign the translation with me? In the last fifty pages he has done more than I and to me that would be perfectly welcome. He has arrived at brilliant solutions … My only criticism is that here and there he gives evidence of having lived too long in France. (xxxiv–xxxv.)

On 22 January, Duthuit replied to Manheim:

La traduction est bonne. Je n'osais espérer tant. Beckett n'a jamais pensé à signer et ne signera pas: c'est un service qu'il a voulu me rendre et pour lequel je le dédommagerai du mieux que je pourrai, la vente du livre aidant. (xxxv.) (The translation is good. Better than I dared hope. Beckett has never thought of signing, and will not sign: it is a favour that he wanted to do for me, which I shall make up to him as best I can, sales of the book assisting.)

5   This is a literal translation of SB's final sentence, the second clause of which is both ungrammatical and, in the context, incomprehensible. The common or brown rat is also known as the Norway or Norwegian rat, its species being Rattus norvegicus. It is clear that SB intends a joke of sorts, but not what the joke is.

HERBERT LOTTMAN

PARIS

8/3/50   6 Rue des Favorites

                                              Paris 15me

Dear Mr. Lottman[1]

As I am leaving Paris, temporarily, in a few days, it would be difficult to arrange a meeting.

I have written considerably during the past four or five years, but exclusively in French. My last work in English was a novel (Watt), written in France during the occupation.[2] It has not been published.

Of my work in French little has appeared apart from some poems and short stories in Les Temps Modernes and Fontaine, and Murphy (Ed. Bordas), translated by myself.[3]

> Yours sincerely
>
> s/ Sam. Beckett

TLS; 1 leaf, 1 side; Lottman.

1   Herbert R. Lottman (b. 1927) was studying in Paris on a Fulbright Scholarship in 1949–1950, when he was asked by David Herbert Greene (1913–2008), Professor of

English, New York University, if he could contact SB. Greene was editing an anthology in which he then planned to include "a chapter or two" from *Murphy* (*1000 Years of Irish Prose*, ed. David H. Greene and Vivian Mercier [New York: Devin-Adair, 1952]). As Greene wrote to Lottman on 2 February 1950:

> I should like to know
>
> a. what he is doing now, for a living.
>
> b. why has he, or has he, stopped writing.
>
> But none of this is terribly important except that I should like to find that he is a real person, living in the flesh. When I read Murphy I have my doubts sometimes. (Lottman collection.)

Lottman is the author of numerous books on twentieth-century France and French authors. SB here responds to his letter of 7 March 1950 (Lottman collection).

2 SB began writing *Watt* on 11 February 1941 and finished the AMS on 28 December 1944 (Admussen, *The Samuel Beckett Manuscripts*, 90–92).

3 "Suite" and "Poèmes 38–39" were published in *Les Temps Modernes* in 1946, "L'Expulsé" was published in *Fontaine* in 1946, and *Murphy* was published in French by Bordas in 1947.

GEORGES DUTHUIT
PARIS

jeudi [? 30 March or 6 April 1950]   Ussy
Cher vieux Georges,

Bien content d'avoir ta lettre.¹ Oui, je pense très souvent à toi et voudrais te voir plus souvent et t'aider un peu mieux pour Transition. Les sacrés Mexicains m'empêchent de me proposer pour un travail de traduction proprement dite, mais s'il y a des passages qui te turlupinent, envoie-les[-]moi.² Je pense que nous rentrerons autour de Pâques, à contre-canaille, ce ne sera peut-être pas trop tard pour que je puisse t'être utile à quelque chose. J'ai promis l'anthologie pour le 1ᵉʳ mai et ne sais pas si je vais y arriver. Je ne peux faire ici qu'un travail de déblayage, tout devra être repris à Paris. Je ne vais pas non plus très bien, le Belier me fout toujours par terre. Temps sinistre, après quelques belles journées, vent nord-est qui nous tombe en plein dessus d'au-delà de l'horizon. Suzanne étale héroïquement ses glacis demi-satinés sur fond de moiré, moi je pose des contre-poids [de] suspension et plâtre des trous de rat. Les trains passent nombreux, à

100 mètres, jour et nuit. Je vois à peine cette page. Panne ou coupure, depuis ce matin.[3]

Je crois Bram incapable du moindre programme. Pour Stael, l'art doit être très volontaire.[4] Je me sens m'éloigner des idées de pauvreté et de dénuement. Ce sont encore des superlatifs. Non, décidément, je ne vois plus rien, je dois attendre que la lumière revienne. Donc sans doute à demain matin.

---

5 heures plus tard. Après avoir passé toute la soirée dans l'obscurité je viens de me rappeler que j'avais fermé le compteur pour poser mon contre-poids! Nous voyions déjà la grève générale. La lumière revenue, nous avons ri, par acquit de conscience!

Pour revenir à Bram, il y a ne pas avoir et ne pas pouvoir, il y a peut-être trop tendance à les considérer comme solidaires. Les pauvres peuvent plutôt. Pas même pauvres, voilà ce qu'il faut supporter, pas même pauvres et ne pouvant rien. Si encore c'était une chose précise qu'on ne peut, mais on ne sait pas ce qu'il y a à faire. Mais tu connais trop bien ces développements, vieux sans doute comme la tristesse. Et qu'on ne peut pas suivre non plus, à cause de la faiblesse de l'esprit. Faut-il qu'il soit faible, pour ne pouvoir suivre cela! Trésors de la pauvreté, va encore[,] mais ceux de l'impuissance, non, nous nous passerons de trésors. Il ne nous manquera jamais de quoi vivre, dans l'ignorance et la faiblesse, sans fierté vraiment, de quoi vivre, jusque dans les détails les plus saugrenus, au-dessus de ses forces. Elle n'est pas sans joie, cette constatation, que tout effort est l'histoire d'un écroulement, c'est vraiment reposant. Qu'il y ait des esprits supérieurs (sans ironie) qui savent et qui peuvent, je veux bien le croire. Mais lorsqu'on n'est pas doué, vraiment très bête et maladroit, que faut-il faire? Le malin? De l'art? Se taire? Le silence viendra assez tôt, non pas par orgueil, mais de langue lasse.

Paraît qu'Empédocle veut bien d'une nouvelle, ancienne, de moi. Filière Fouchet.[5] Je ne sais plus quoi en penser, de la nouvelle, assez longue, parmi les premiers écrits en français, bourrés de maladresses et de longueurs.[6] Pourrais-tu m'envoyer l'adresse d'Empédocle? Revue inconnue à la Ferté. Faut que Suzanne se mette en rapport avec l'éditeur.[7]

J'ai parcouru l'article de Gracq dans Empédocle. Je n'aime pas ça. Ça me rappelle le peintre en bâtiment qui veut un pinceau qui lisse fin. Véritable cuir de Russie.[8] Il y avait une image – coureur cycliste aspiré par son derny – qui n'en finissait plus, pas une faille, lecteur dans le sillon de l'auteur, raie du cul Braque-Ponge quoi.[9] Lu épatement Breton, Patri, Péret dans Combat. Que de fleurs.[10]

Relevé chez Breton l'image singulièrement percutante du bâtiment de l'humanité jeté par son navigateur, sur les "écueils définitifs". Attendre l'âge atomique pour se faire du mauvais sang, c'est en effet surréaliste. Et la certitude du printemps qui lui réchauffait le coeur pendant les pires moments de l'occupation. Veinard, va.[11]

Pour le mythe, me rappelle pas du tout ce que j'ai bien pu te raconter. A moins – et je ne crois pas – que ce ne soit ce Spoonerism de boite de nuit, du Jockey je crois, raconté par Champi: une mite le soir qui vient se poser parmi un troupeau de cerfs – alors il y avait une grosse bitte dans les miches. Pas possible, n'est-ce pas?[12]

Pour Wittenborn, veux-tu lui demander 10.000 francs pour moi. Comme ça ce sera liquidé.[13]

Pauvre lettre de ma mère ce matin. Où ai-je fourré mes larmes?

Si tu y penses – clefs – reliquaire?

Affectueusement, mon vieux Georges. Moi aussi je m'affole, pour des adjectifs. C'est bête.

Ton Sam

ALS; 4 leaves, 4 sides; [sides 2/3 are numbered]; Duthuit collection. *Dating*: SB reports having read Breton, Péret, and Patri in *Combat*; by 30 March, all three had published there (see n. 10 below). SB speaks of returning to Paris for Easter (9 April 1950); the previous Thursday was 6 April 1950.

Thursday [? 30 March or 6 April 1950]   Ussy

My dear old Georges,

Very glad to get your letter.[1] Yes, I often think of you, and would like to see you more often and be a little more help with *Transition*. These damned Mexicans are preventing me from putting myself forward for a proper translation job, but if there are passages that are bothering you, send them on to me.[2] I think we shall come back at Easter, going the opposite direction of the hordes, perhaps this will not be too late for me to be some use to you. I have promised the anthology for the 1st of May and I do not know if I shall manage it. All I can do here is ground-clearing work, I shall have to go back over it all in Paris. I am not very well either, Aries always gets me down. Weather grim, after several beautiful days, north-east wind that comes straight at us from beyond the horizon. Suzanne is heroically spreading out her dressmaking: glazed demi-satin on a watered (silk) ground, I am putting in counter-weights and plastering up ratholes. Trains continually going by, 100 yards away, day and night. I can hardly see this page. Breakdown or power-cut, since this morning.[3]

I believe Bram to be incapable of any kind of programme. For Staël, art must be a matter of will.[4] I feel myself moving away from ideas of poverty and bareness. They are still superlatives. No, no doubt about it, I cannot see a thing, I shall have to wait for the light to come back. So, till tomorrow morning no doubt.

---

5 hours later. After spending the whole evening in darkness I have just remembered that I had shut off the meter in order to instal my counter-weight! We were already on to general strikes. When the light came back, we laughed, to make up for it!

To go back to Bram: there is not having and there is not being able to, perhaps too much of a tendency to think of them as standing together. The poor are able to, rather. Not even poor, that is what we have to bear, not even poor and yet not able to. If there were even one specific thing that we were not able to do, but we do not know what there is that could be done. But you are only too familiar with these elaborations; old no doubt as sadness. And that we cannot *follow* either, from weakness of mind. How weak it must be, not to be able to follow that! Treasures of poverty, maybe; but of impotence, no, we shall do without treasures. We shall always have enough to keep living, in ignorance and weakness, really without pride, enough to keep living, right down to the most grotesque details, beyond our strength. Not without joy, this observation that every effort is the story of a collapse, it is really restful. That there are superior minds (no irony) which know and are able to, I can readily grant. But when one is not gifted, really stupid and clumsy, what is one to go in for? Cunning? Art? Keeping quiet? Silence will come soon enough, not from pride, but from weariness of speech.

Apparently *Empédocle* wants a story of mine, an old one. The Fouchet connection.[5] I do not know what I think of the story, rather long, one of the first written in French, full of awkwardnesses and longueurs.[6] Could you send me the address of *Empédocle*? Review unknown in La Ferté. Suzanne will have to get in touch with the publisher.[7]

I have skimmed through the article by Gracq in *Empédocle*. I do not like that stuff. It reminds me of the house-painter who wants a brush that *gives a fine finish*. Genuine Russian leather.[8] There was one image – cyclist disappearing up his own derny – which went on and on, without a break, reader in the wake of the writer, Braque-Ponge arse-cleft sort of thing.[9] Read with wonderment Breton, Patri, Péret in *Combat*. What flowery stuff.[10]

Noted in Breton the singularly powerful image of the ship of humanity cast adrift by its navigator on to the "definitive reefs". To wait until the atomic age before feeling really worried, that is indeed surrealist. And that certainty of spring that did his heart good in the worst moments of the Occupation. Lucky thing.[11]

For the myth, no memory at all of what I can possibly have told you. Unless – and I do not think it is that – it is the Spoonerism from some night-club, the *Jockey* I think, told by Champi: a moth one evening which happened to pass among a herd of deer – so there was "une grosse bitte dans les miches". Impossible, don't you think?[12]

For Wittenborn, can you ask him for 10,000 francs for me? That way it will be all settled.[13]

Wretched letter from my mother this morning. Where have I put my tears?

If you think of it – keys – reliquary?

Affectionately, my old friend Georges. I panic about adjectives too. Silly.

Your Sam

1   Duthuit's letter has not been found.

2   The *Anthology of Mexican Poetry*: 27 February 1950, n. 5.

3   SB omits the acute accent in "Bélier."
By this time, SB had moved within Ussy to the "Maison Barbier," a house he rented at 25 bis Rue de la Dehors, at the end of whose garden ran a main train line (Savane, *Samuel Beckett à Ussy sur Marne*, 9).

4   Bram van Velde; Nicolas de Staël, whose name SB spells here without the dieresis.
Duthuit was preparing two publications on Staël at this time: the article "Nicolas de Staël" (*Cahiers d'Art* 25.1 [1950] 383–386), and the pamphlet published on 1 June 1950 by Duthuit's own Transition Press, *Nicolas de Staël*.

5   *Empédocle* was published from April 1949 through June–July 1950. Although not himself on the editorial board of the journal, Max-Pol Fouchet had influence with those who were: Albert Béguin (1901–1957), Albert Camus, René Char, Guido Meister (1892–?), and Jean Vagne (1915–1979) who was also the journal's Director.
On 21 October 1949, in response to a visit from Suzanne Deschevaux-Dumesnil, André-Charles Gervais, Editions Bordas, asked Fouchet to receive her and support SB's work (see Suzanne Deschevaux-Dumesnil to Gervais, 8 November [1949], n. 1).

6   SB is almost certainly referring to one of his stories written in 1946. As "Suite" (later known as "La Fin") and "L'Expulsé" had both already been published, and as SB chose not to publish "Premier amour" in his 1955 collection *Nouvelles et Textes pour rien*, the most likely candidate is "Le Calmant," the fourth of the stories to be written; it was not in the event published by *Empédocle*.

7   *Empédocle* was published from 13 Rue de Buci, Paris 6.
La Ferté-sous-Jouarre is the nearest town to Ussy.
The appeals to Fouchet by Gervais had been made so that he would receive SB's companion Suzanne Deschevaux-Dumesnil, who was more willing than SB to follow up contacts and attempt to place his work.

8   Julien Gracq's essay "La Littérature à l'estomac" (*Empédocle*, 7 [January 1950] 3–33) was also the title of a collection of Gracq's essays (Paris: José Corti, 1950) and was published, in an edited form and in a translation by J. G. Weightman, as "Literature Hits below the Belt" in *Transition Fifty* no. 6, 7–26. In his "Mise au point" in the next number of *Empédocle*, Gracq explains the type of defense of literature he was attempting in his essay (8 [February 1950] 95–96).

9   Gracq writes of the reaction of readers as consisting of "taste" and "opinion." He continues:

> Placé en tête-à-tête avec un texte, le même déclic intérieur qui joue en nous, sans règle et sans raisons, à la rencontre d'un être va se produire en lui: il 'aime' ou il 'n'aime pas', il est, ou il n'est pas, *à son affaire*, il éprouve, ou n'éprouve pas, au fil des pages ce sentiment de légèreté, de liberté délestée et pourtant happée à mesure, qu'on pourrait comparer à la sensation du *stayer* aspiré dans le

remous de son entraîneur; et en effet dans le cas d'une conjonction heureuse on peut dire que le lecteur *colle* à l'œuvre, vient combler de seconde en seconde la capacité exacte du moule d'air creusé par sa rapidité vorace, forme avec elle au vent égal des pages tournées ce bloc de vitesse huilée et sans défaillance dont le souvenir, lorsque la dernière page est venue brutalement 'couper les gaz', nous laisse étourdis, un peu vacillants sur notre lancée, comme en proie à un début de nausée et à cette sensation si particulière des 'jambes de coton.' ("La littérature à l'estomac," 9.) (With only the text for company, the same internal click that happens inside us, without rhyme or reason, on meeting a living creature will take place in him: he 'likes' or 'doesn't like', he is or isn't *in his element*, he is aware or unaware as the pages go by of that feeling of lightness, of freedom untrammelled and yet caught up the while, that might be compared to what is felt by the *stayer* pulled along in the wake of his trainer; and indeed, in the event of a happy conjunction it might be said that the reader is literally at one with the work, that from one second to the next he advances to fill the exact capacity of the mould of air hollowed out by his voracious speed, that he forms with the work, in the steady wind of the pages turned, this solid mass of speed, well oiled, unfailingly smooth which, in memory, when the last page has come along and brutally 'killed the speed', leaves us bewildered, stumbling as we drive forward, as if hit by incipient nausea and that peculiar sensation of legs like jelly.)

This passage is cut from Gracq's article when it is republished in *Transition Fifty* no. 6.

By "Braque-Ponge," SB refers to the article by Ponge on Braque in *Transition Forty-Nine* no. 5 (see 1 March 1949, n. 5).

The derny was (and remains) a bicycle with a small engine attached to it. It was originally manufactured, from 1938, by former racing cyclists Roger Derny et Fils, to serve as a "moto de stayer" or a pacing motorcycle, allowing racing cyclists to pedal in its slipstream.

10 Between March and May, in the *Combat* series "Aux Avant-Postes de 'Combat,'"André Breton published: "Des taches solaires aux taches de soleil" (28 March 1950: 1, 6), and "Ceinturer un monde forcené" (3 April 1950: 1, 6). During the same period and in the same series, Aimé Patri (1904–1983) published "Le Bois dont on fait les masses" (29 March 1950: 1, 6), and "Le grand serpent de mer" (5 April 1950: 1, 6); while Benjamin Péret (1899–1959) published "On ne guérit pas la peste en propageant le choléra" (30 March 1950: 1, 6), "La seule transition concevable" (20 April 1950: 1, 6), "Martyrs préfabriqués" (24 April 1950: 1, 6), "Les trafiquants de la vérité et les faussaires de la paix" (10 April 1950: 1, 4), and "L'obstacle à la révolution sociale" (7 April 1950: 1, 6).

11 SB evokes three moments in Breton's article, "Des taches solaires aux taches de soleil." Breton writes: "Quel contrepoids opposer au fanatisme s'il s'avère que, sourds à tout ce qui n'est pas les voix ensorcelantes qui leur parviennent, les navigateurs qui passent pour les plus hardis s'apprêtent à jeter le bâtiment humain sur un écueil définitif?" (6) (What counterweight can we set up against fanaticism if it is indeed the case that, deaf to all but the Siren voices that reach them, the navigators reckoned to be the boldest are preparing to cast the ship of humanity on to a definitive reef?). Of the "atomic age" Breton writes, "Il est fatal que l'introduction d'un dissolvant – le péril atomique – à l'intérieur du raisonnement logique tel qu'il s'est toujours construit rende ce dernier, pour le moins, aléatoire" (It is inevitable that the introducing of a solvent – the atomic peril – into logical reasoning as it has always been constructed will make this latter uncertain, to say the least). The article opens: "En ces premiers jours de printemps, me revient à l'esprit une des rares idées secourables à quoi je

parvins à m'accrocher aux pires jours de la dernière guerre: tant de dévastations ne pourraient rien contre le retour du printemps, assez grand magicien pour prêter un sourire aux ruines" (In these early Spring days, I am reminded of one of the few helpful ideas that I contrived to hold on to in the worst days of the last war: the many devastations could do nothing to stop the return of Spring, a magician great enough to lend a smile to ruins).

12   SB omits the circumflex on "boîte."

Duthuit has apparently asked SB for information relating to a passage in his article that will appear later in the year as "Sartre's Last Class [conclusion]" (*Transition Fifty* no. 6, 87–90). As published, the relevant passage runs:

> The Kantian myth with Hopi or cognate ditto, as for example the socialo-Fourierist: 'At the sign of the associated leguminists of letters' – plenty and to spare for all the boys and girls in the world. The myth . . .
>
> *La grosse mite dans les biches.*

The Jockey night-club, situated at 146 Boulevard du Montparnasse. Of the club's heyday in the 1930s, Robert McAlmon observed: "Dramas and comedies and fights did occur there, but generally comedy and good will prevailed . . . almost anybody of the writing, painting, musical, gigoloing, whoring, pimping or drinking world was apt to turn up at the Jockey" (Arlen J. Hansen, *Expatriate Paris: A Cultural and Literary Guide to Paris in the 1920s* [New York: Arcade, 1990] 144–145).

SB probably refers to the collections of humorous anecdotes made by Lucien Viéville, *Histoires gauloises de Champi* (1939) and *Nouvelles histoires gauloises de Champi* (1948), though neither volume contains SB's joke, which depends on a spoonerism: "bitte" for "mite" and "miches" for "biches." The innocent version ("une mite dans les biches") means "a moth among the does"; the joke version ("une bitte dans les miches") means "a cock among the tits."

13   Both George Wittenborn (1905–1974) and Heinz Schultz (1904–1954), of the publishing company Wittenborn, Schultz, which was set to publish Duthuit's *The Fauvist Painters* (whose translation SB has been revising), were born in Germany and emigrated to the United States in the 1930s. Together in 1941 they founded their bookshop on East 57th Street, New York, and from 1943 began publishing their highly influential series Documents of Modern Art, directed by Robert Motherwell, which sought to make available English-language versions of important texts by European artists or on European art (www.moma.org/learn/resources/archives/EAD/witten-bornb, accessed on 20 January 2011).

GEORGES DUTHUIT

[before May 1950]   [Ussy]
[Fragment]

Encore rien de décidé ni pour le théâtre ni pour les dates.[1]

Nous sommes ici depuis mardi et rentrerons probablement au début de la semaine prochaine.

J'ai dû me taper une révision de l'Anthologie Mexicaine. J'avais sauté, sans le vouloir, des vers, des strophes et même des poèmes entiers! Et le peu d'Espagnol que j'avais appris à ce moment-là est bien parti. Si leurs plasticiens ressemblent même de loin à leurs poètes, je me dispenserai d'y aller.[2]

Il fait beau, avec un petit vent nord-est bien agaçant et bien desséchant.

Magnifique Symphonie Fantastique de Charles Munch et l'Orchestre de Boston, suivie de la 4me de Brahms mise un peu à nu, elle supporte mal ça. Mal jouée, je l'aimais assez. Je crois que je ne pourrai plus y voir autre chose que du bon boulot.[3]

A bientôt, cher vieux. Tu n'avais pas l'air en train, l'autre jour, avec Bram. J'espère qu'il n'y a rien qui t'embête trop.

    Affectueusement

    Sam

ALS; one leaf, one side, fragment; Duthuit collection. *Dating*: SB to Yvonne Lefèvre, 27 April 1950: "Depuis le mois de janvier je suis très pris par un travail pour l'UNESCO, à peu près terminé" (Since January I have been much taken up with work for UNESCO, nearly done) (Lefèvre collection). Beckett's translation of the *Anthology of Mexican Poetry* was completed in May 1950; he did not further revise this manuscript until 1958.

[before May 1950]   [Ussy]

[Fragment]

Still nothing decided either for the theatre or the dates.[1]

We have been here since Tuesday and will probably go back early next week.

I have had to take on a revision of the *Mexican Anthology*. I had unwittingly missed out lines, stanzas, and even whole poems! And the little Spanish that I had then has well and truly gone. If their practitioners of the plastic arts bear even a remote resemblance to their poets, I shall let myself off going to see them.[2]

The weather is good, with a little north-east wind, very annoying and very desiccating.

Magnificent *Symphonie Fantastique* by Charles Munch and the Boston Orchestra, followed by a rather stripped-down Brahms 4, not made for that. Badly played, it did say something to me. I think that I shall never be able to see in it anything more than good solid work.[3]

Till soon, old friend. You did not look in top form the other day, with Bram. I hope there is nothing too badly wrong.

      Love

        Sam

1 SB is awaiting news of an eventual production of *En attendant Godot*.

2 *Mexican Poetry: An Anthology*: 27 February 1950, n. 5.
SB unconventionally capitalizes "espagnol."

3 The Boston Symphony Orchestra did not visit France in 1950, and so SB must have listened to the concert on the radio. The orchestra's permanent conductor Charles Munch (1891–1968) conducted *Symphonie fantastique* by Hector Berlioz, and Symphony no.4 by Johannes Brahms.

GEORGE REAVEY

ENGLAND

<u>9-5-50</u>   <u>Paris</u>

My dear George

Glad to have news of you after so long and to hear you are safe back from the lanuginous west.[1]

I shall probably be back in Ireland from mid-July to mid-August, sauf imprévu. But we are now more often absent from Paris than formerly, having rented a shack in a little village in Seine-et-Marne.[2] So if you do come to Paris let me know a little in advance.

I saw Geer the other day, in pretty good form. He told me he had something in Leicester Square, but not that Bram had. Bram has been with Marthe in Haute-Savoie for the past month or so. He left very tired. He has not produced very much this past year. Geer had seen Aaronson B^d St Germain, with the usual beautiful wife, setting off on what he calls a walking-tour.[3] Tom McGreevy also went through, lepping hot from Sturm and Drang year, but did not get round to see me.[4]

My adventures, since I last saw you, have all been on paper, now yellowing, or rather turning bare, for I find green paper less expensive. An extract from <u>Watt</u>, massacred by the compositor, appeared in that filthy new Irish rag <u>Envoy</u>.[5]

I received a letter, provoked apparently by my ravings in <u>Transition</u>, from one Elga Lippmann, in which she quotes you. I have not yet had, and fear, shall never, the courtesy to reply. She also quoted Hayter, all new world weariness.[6] I read, but could not follow, not knowing a chisel from a hacksaw, his note on Kandinsky in the American edition of the <u>Spiritual in Art</u>.[7]

Hope you will be happy in the new life, happier than Dante. What has your Faust been doing all this time? In Paris he has fallen foul of René Clair.[8]

Looking forward to seeing you soon.

Ever

Sam

ALS; 2 leaves, 2 sides; TxU, Reavey collection.

1   Reavey's letter to SB has not been found; Reavey left the United States for England on 10 February (Karen A. Bearor, *Irene Rice Pereira: Her Paintings and Philosophy* [Austin: University of Texas Press, 1994] [235]).

2   SB's cottage in Ussy: 27 March 1949, n. 4.
"Sauf imprévu" (barring accidents).

3   Geer van Velde's painting *Composition* (1950) was shown in London as part of the Royal Academy of Arts exhibition, L'Ecole de Paris, 1900–1950 (*L'Ecole de Paris, 1900–1950* [London: Royal Academy of Arts, 1951] 42). There was no work by Bram van Velde in the exhibition. The Royal Academy of Arts is in Burlington House, Piccadilly, not Leicester Square.
Bram van Velde and Marthe Arnaud.
Lazarus Aaronson (1894–1965), poet and Professor of Economics at the City of London College (later the London Polytechnic); his second wife was Dorothy (née Lewin, n.d.).

4   MacGreevy was named Director of the National Gallery of Ireland on 7 June 1950 and took up office in July; having applied in 1936 for the same position, he may have been particularly anxious during the review process in 1950 (*National Gallery of Ireland: Illustrated Summary Catalogue of Paintings*, xxxvi). SB reverts here to the earlier spelling, "McGreevy."

5   "An Extract from Watt," 11–19.

6   Elga N. Lippmann (née Liverman, later m. Duval, 1914 – c. 1984), was an American painter and writer, with whom, according to his petition for divorce, George Reavey had an affair in September 1949 in Massachusetts (TxU, Reavey collection, divorce petition filed 25 May 1950). Her letter to SB has not been found.

SB may refer to "Three Dialogues: Samuel Beckett and Georges Duthuit," published in *Transition*.

The artist Stanley William Hayter (1901–1988) was a friend of George Reavey. It is not certain what Elga Lippmann may have quoted from Hayter's writings. Hayter had published *New Ways of Gravure* (1949). His essay "Techniques of Gravure" appeared in the catalogue for the exhibition Hayter and Studio 17, held at the Museum of Modern Art, New York, from 27 June to 17 September 1944 (6–13). Hayter had also written an introduction for *Jankel Adler* (1946).

7   Stanley William Hayter, "The Language of Kandinsky," in Wassily Kandinsky, *Concerning the Spiritual in Art*, ed. Robert Motherwell (New York: George Wittenborn, 1947) 15–18.

8   Reavey was divorcing Gwynedd Reavey, and planned to marry the American painter Irene Rice Pereira (1902–1971) who joined him in England in June 1950; they married on 9 September 1950; Reavey was working on a thesis on Maxim Gorky and teaching Russian grammar and literature at the University of Manchester (Bearor, *Irene Rice Pereira*, 179, 236).

René Clair (1898–1981) had recently made a film, *La Beauté du Diable* (1950; *Beauty and the Devil*), based on the confrontation of Faust and Mephisto; the text by Jean Marcenac, *La Beauté du Diable*, accompanied by an interview with Clair, "Sur le problème de Faust," had just been published, on 28 April 1950 ([Paris: Les Editeurs Français Réunis, 1950] 45–56).

GEORGES DUTHUIT

[before 30 June 1950]

[Fragment]

Oui, le grand poète tchèque, ayant bien reçu Breton il y a 15 ans, ne peut naturellement avoir fait de mal. On ne parle pas des autres. J'ai lu la lettre ouverte à Eluard. C'est à s'inscrire au Parti.[1]

Je dois partir en Irlande, au début d'août, sinon avant. Ma mère a encore fait une chute. Je n'ai pas de détails.

Tu vois, mon cher Georges, j'avais raison de ne pas t'écrire. Je ne sais pas où je vais, ce n'est pas moi qui bouge. Quelque chose est en train de finir, et je ne vois rien cette fois-ci qui commence à sa place. Je ne m'en plains pas, ne crois pas que je me plaigne. Une chose qui

finit, se plaindre de ça! Ou que rien ne commence! Tout ça sans jugement ni pensée, comme – non, pas d'images non plus.

　　Bonne nuit, mon vieux Georges.

　　　　Affectueusement de nous 2 à vous 2

　　Sam

Ne manque pas de m'écrire à quel moment tu seras à Paris en train de
mettre le dernier numéro debout.

ALS; 1 leaf, 1 side; fragment; Duthuit collection. *Dating*: before 30 June 1950, based on
Frank Beckett's letter of 2 July 1950 to Thomas MacGreevy which reports that May
Beckett has broken her leg, that the doctor has visited on the previous Friday (30 June),
that Frank has asked that SB come to Dublin, and that SB is expected in the coming
week (TCD, MS 10402/179).

[before 30 June 1950]

[Fragment]

Yes, the great Czech poet, having received Breton well 15 years ago, can
naturally have done no wrong. No mention of the others. I have read the
open letter to Eluard. It is enough to make you join the Party.[1]

　　I have to go to Ireland, early in August, if not before. My mother
has had another fall. I have no details.

　　You see, Georges my old friend, I was right not to write to you. I
do not know where I am going, I am not the one who is moving.
Something is coming to an end, and this time I see nothing starting in
its place. I am not complaining, do not think I am complaining.
Complaining of something ending! Or that nothing is beginning! All
that without judgement or thought, like – no, no images either.

　　A good night to you, my old friend.

　　　　Love from us 2 to you 2.

　　Sam

Be sure to tell me when you will be in Paris putting the latest issue
together.

his confession under torture. On 14 June, *Combat* published "Lettre ouverte d'André Breton à Paul Eluard" to ask Eluard to intervene on Kalandra's behalf – Eluard being at this time considered as the quasi-official poet of the French Communist Party (*Combat*, 14 June 1950: 848). Breton begins his "letter" by evoking his visit with Eluard to Prague fifteen years before, and ends, after citing Kalandra's self-condemnation pronounced in court: "Comment en ton for intérieur, peux-tu supporter pareille dégradation de l'homme en la personne de celui qui se montra ton ami?"(3.) (How, in your heart of hearts, can you bear such degradation of man, in the person of him who came forward as your friend?). Eluard's response, was: "'J'ai trop à faire avec les innocents qui clament leur innocence pour m'occuper des coupables qui clament leur culpabilité'" ("I have too much to do with the innocent protesting their innocence to bother with the guilty who profess their guilt") (Henri Béhar, *André Breton: le grand indésirable* [Paris: Calmann-Lévy, 1990] 403).

GEORGES LAMBRICHS, EDITIONS DE MINUIT
PARIS

le 4 octobre 1950

Cher Monsieur Lambrichs[1]

L'unique copie de Molloy *dont je dispose immédiatement n'est vraiment pas sortable. Attendez encore quelques jours et je vous en apporterai une autre, en meilleur état.*[2]

Quant à Mercier et Camier, *je vous en reparlerai à notre prochaine rencontre.*[3]

Pour l'extrait de Malone Meurt *à faire passer dans votre revue, Beckett le croit mal choisi. D'accord quand même.*[4]

> *Cordialement à vous*
> *s/ S. Dumesnil*
> > *6 rue des Favorites 15°*[5]

TLS; 1 leaf, 1 side; Minuit collection; IMEC, Beckett, Boîte 1, S. Beckett, Correspondance – Divers, 1950–1956.

4th October 1950

Dear Monsieur Lambrichs[1]

The only copy of Molloy *that I have to hand is really not presentable. Wait a few days more and I shall bring you another, in better condition.*[2]

As for Mercier et Camier, *I shall talk about that to you again when we next meet.*[3]

For the extract from Malone meurt *that is to go into your review, Beckett* thinks it is not well chosen. Agreed all the same.[4]

 Yours sincerely

 S. Dumesnil

  6 rue des Favorites 15°[5]

---

1   Georges Lambrichs* (1917–1992) joined Editions de Minuit in 1945 as a reader and then became Literary Director.

2   On 5 October, Suzanne Deschevaux-Dumesnil wrote to Lambrichs: "J'ai vu Monsieur Carlier. Il se charge de récupérer Molloy et vous l'apportera demain vendredi, dans l'après-midi je crois." (I have seen Monsieur Carlier. He undertakes to recover *Molloy*, and will bring it to you tomorrow Friday, in the afternoon I think.) (IMEC, Beckett, Boîte 1, S. Beckett, Correspondance – Divers, 1950–1956).

 Robert Carlier (1910–2002) worked with the literary agent Odette Arnaud at this time and directed the Club Français du Livre from 1946 to 1952 (www.gallimard.fr/catalog/html/event/carlier.htm, date accessed 13 November 2009). Carlier had kept typescripts of *Molloy* and *Malone meurt* in order to try to place them with publishers whom he knew (Knowlson, *Damned to Fame*, 341).

3   *Mercier et Camier* had been submitted to Bordas as SB's next work in French; an advance was paid in January 1947, but the novel was not published by them (see 30 October 1946, n. 1, and 15 December 1946, n. 2).

4   Lambrichs was on the editorial board of *84: Nouvelle Revue Littéraire* (1947–1951), edited by Marcel Bisiaux (1922–1990) and published by Editions de Minuit. An excerpt, "Malone s'en conte," appeared in *84: Nouvelle Revue Littéraire* (16 [December 1950] 3–10); it differs from the text as published in *Malone meurt* ([Paris: Editions de Minuit, 1951], 42–52).

5   The address is handwritten.

GEORGE REAVEY

SALFORD, ENGLAND

11/12/50   Paris

My dear George

 Glad to have news of you after so long. Salford 7 sounds diabolic even with fluorescence. Why don't you get a job with UNESCO, that inexhaustible cheese?[1]

Should be very interested to see your wife's painting. The attitude seems quite the antithesis of Bram's, in so far as he has one. I haven't seen much of him lately, or of Geer. The former is struggling to cover enough canvas for an exhibition with Maeght next spring.[2]

I had two dreadful months in Dublin this summer. Hope I shall never have to go back there. My mother died in July. I saw something of Tom, very happy as director of National Gallery, and of Jack Yeats, very frail and stiff, but working away.[3]

I have signed a contract with the Editions of Minuit for all work. They contract specifically for the three "novels" already written. The first, Molloy, should be out in January. Bordas, on the brink of bankruptcy (not entirely my fault), have released me. To my profound astonishment, on my return from Ireland, I found a small cheque from the European Literary Bureau. No explanation. Conscience money perhaps.[4]

Pretty well certain now that the second play, En Attendant Godot, will be put on by Blin at the Noctambules (6 to 8), as soon as Adamov's Grande et Petite Manoeuvre has exhausted its admirers. Non, quelle rigolade. The annus terribilis begins well.[5]

Don't disappear in the fog. Hommages to your wife.

> Yours ever
> s/ Sam

TLS; 1 leaf, 1 side; TxU, Reavey collection.

1   Reavey and his wife lived in Salford in Greater Manchester, near the Manchester Ship Canal; in the 1950s, it was an area of high-density housing mixed with industrial buildings. Salford claimed to have the first buses lit with fluorescent tubes (1949) (web.ukonline.co.uk/m.gratton/Salford%20-%2020th%20Century-Advances%20. htm, accessed on 5 September 2009).

2   Irene Rice Pereira's understanding of the relationship in her painting between perception and spatial systems is discussed by Bearor in *Irene Rice Pereira*.

3   May Beckett died on 25 August 1950 (not July as SB writes here). SB returned to Paris on 8 September; he wrote to Susan Manning on 10 September: "I have been sleeping most of the time since my arrival here the day before yesterday and I feel much better already. To be in the streets of Paris is for me to feel how much I need France and the French way of life and how utterly impossible it would be for me to live in Ireland." (TxU, Beckett collection.)

MacGreevy as Director of the National Gallery of Ireland: 9 May 1950, n. 4.

4   The financial precariousness of Editions Bordas in 1949 and 1950 is suggested by A.-C. Gervais's correspondence with the painter Albert Gleizes (1881–1953), publication of whose book *L'Homme devenu peintre* was twice deferred "owing to the exceptionally difficult circumstances of publishing" (Peter Brooke, *Albert Gleizes: For and Against the Twentieth Century* [New Haven: Yale University Press, 2001] 266).

On 15 November, Suzanne Deschevaux-Dumesnil met Jérôme Lindon* (1925–2001), Director of Editions de Minuit, and learned that he wanted to publish *Molloy*, *Malone meurt*, and *L'Innommable*; she took the contracts to SB to be signed (Jérôme Lindon, "First Meeting with Samuel Beckett," in *Beckett at 60: A Festschrift*, ed. John Calder [London: Calder and Boyars, 1967] 17).

The European Literary Bureau was sold by George Reavey and Gwynedd Reavey to Ronald Duncan (n.d.) on 10 August 1939. SB's *Echo's Bones and Other Precipitates* had been published under the Europa Press imprint of the European Literary Bureau. Although John Pilling suggests that the royalty check was sent from Routledge via the European Literary Bureau which had acted as agent for *Murphy*, this appears unlikely since Routledge had much earlier indicated that this novel was out of print (see 1 September 1946; John Pilling, A *Samuel Beckett Chronology*, Author Chronologies [Houndmills, Basingstoke: Palgrave Macmillan, 2006] 110).

5   Roger Blin's interest in *En attendant Godot* is clear at this point (see 27 [February 1950], n. 8), but no evidence of the plan to produce it at the Théâtre des Noctambules, 7 Rue Champollion, has been found. *La grande et petite manœuvre* (1950; The Large and the Small Maneuver) by Arthur Adamov (1908–1970) opened at the Noctambules on 15 November 1950 and ran "at the 6 o'clock matinée" through 7 January 1951; it was directed by Jean-Marie Serreau (1915–1973), with Roger Blin playing the role of Le Mutilé (Blin and Peskine, *Roger Blin*, 14; Sven Heed, *Roger Blin: Metteur en scène de l'avant-garde, 1949–1959* [Paris: Circé, 1996] 48).

"Non, quelle rigolade" (What a farce).

ROGER BLIN

PARIS

19/12/50   6 Rue des Favorites

Mon cher Blin

J'ai une idée pour le décor. Il faudrait qu'on se voie. Pourriez-vous passez [*for* passer] chez nous un jour de cette semaine? Vous me trouverez toujours au début de l'après-midi, jusqu'à trois heures. Ou bien donnez-moi rendez-vous dehors, si ça vous arrange mieux.

      Amitiés

         s/ <u>Sam Beckett</u>

TLS; 1 leaf, 1 side; IMEC, Blin.

19/12/50   6 Rue des Favorites

Dear Blin,

I have an idea for the set. We ought to meet. Could you call in at our place one day this week? You'll always find me there in the early afternoon, up till 3 o'clock. Or else suggest a time and place for us to meet outside, if that suits you better.

> Regards
> > Sam Beckett

NIALL MONTGOMERY
DUBLIN

29-12-50   Paris

Dear Niall[1]

Many thanks for your card. It was good of you to think of me.

Brain hardening & softening simultaneously makes Joyceology impossible.[2]

Hope to have a book to send you soon, illustrative of this process.[3]

All best wishes to you all for the mauvais quart d'heure[4]

> > Ever yr
> > Sam

ALS; 1 leaf, 1 side; date-stamped 30 DEC 1950; NLI, Accession 6475, Lot 7, Idda (now in Miscellaneous).

1 Dublin architect Niall Montgomery* (1914–1987) wrote poetry, plays, and literary criticism.

2 Montgomery was a friend and early admirer of James Joyce.

3 *Molloy* was published by Editions de Minuit on 10 March 1951.

4 "Mauvais quart d'heure" (the grim moment ahead).

GEORGES DUTHUIT

PARIS

vendredi [? end December 1950]   [Paris]

Cher vieux Georges

Je voulais passer te voir hier soir. Encore ce soir. Empêchement chaque fois. Nous partirons demain, sans acte de Dieu. C'est peut-être une bêtise.

J'ai lu le Sade de Blanchot. Il y a des choses très bien. Quelques citations formidables que je ne connaissais pas, dans le genre de celle que je t'ai bâclée des 120 journées. Difficile d'isoler un passage à traduire, mais j'y suis arrivé et me suis mis à le faire. Je pense que tu seras d'accord.[1]

J'ai été emmerdé en me rappelant tout d'un coup le M. Godeau intime de Jouhandeau. Je cherche à remplacer Godot par un autre nom et ne trouve rien. Crois-tu que ce soit nécessaire?[2]

Je t'écrirai de la campagne.

Bonne année à tous

      Affectueusement

        Sam

On pourrait peut-être corser les choses en donnant quelques extraits de Klossowski (Sade mon Prochain) et de Maurice Heine (avant-propos au Dialogue entre un Prêtre et un Moribond).[3]

Le passage déjà traduit de la Philosophie dans le Boudoir n'est pas mal, mais on pourrait trouver mieux.[4]

ALS; 1 leaf, 2 sides; Duthuit collection. *Dating*: this letter asks the question repeated in that of Mercredi [3 January 1951]: "Tu ne m'as pas répondu pour la question Godeau – Godot."

Friday [? end December 1950]   [Paris]

My dear Georges

I wanted to go round to see you last night. This evening again. Each time something cropped up. We shall leave tomorrow, barring act of God. It may be a silly thing to do.

I have read Blanchot's *Sade*. There are some very good things in it. A few tremendous quotations that I did not know, in the style of the one I knocked up for you from the *120 Days*. Hard to single out one passage to translate, but I managed to and started on it. I think you will agree.[1]

I felt sickened when all of a sudden I remembered Jouhandeau's *M. Godeau intime*. I am trying to replace *Godot* by another name, and cannot find one. Do you think I have to?[2]

I will write to you from the country.

Happy New Year to all

    Affectionately

      Sam

Maybe we could spice things up by putting in a few extracts from Klossowski (*Sade mon prochain*) and Maurice Heine (foreword to the *Dialogue entre un Prêtre et un Moribond*).[3]

The passage already translated from *Philosophie dans le Boudoir* is not too bad, but there are better ones to be found.[4]

1 SB was probably reading Maurice Blanchot's *Lautréamont et Sade* (1949). No record has been found of the quotations SB compiled for Duthuit from Sade's *Les 120 Journées de Sodome, ou l'école de libertinage* (*The 120 Days of Sodom; or, the Romance of the School for Libertinage*), nor of those he compiled from Blanchot's study.

2 *Monsieur Godeau intime* (1926), a novel by Marcel Jouhandeau (1888–1979), was followed by *Monsieur Godeau marié* (1933).

3 *Sade mon prochain* (Paris: Seuil, 1947) by Pierre Klossowski (1905–2001) (*Sade my Neighbor*, tr. Alphonso Lingis [Evanston, IL: Northwestern University Press, 1991]), and *Le Marquis de Sade* by Maurice Heine (1884–1940) (ed. with a preface by Gilbert Lely [Paris: Gallimard, 1950]).

4 It is not known to which passage SB refers.

CHRONOLOGY 1951

1951

22 January	Proofs received for *Molloy*.
4–6 February	SB writes "Texte pour rien, II."
27 February – 5 March	Writes "Texte pour rien, III."
10–12 March	Writes "Texte pour rien, IV."
12 March	*Molloy* published by Editions de Minuit.
19–24 March	SB writes "Texte pour rien, V."
10 April	Publicity photograph taken of SB.
12 April	First review of *Molloy* by Maurice Nadeau in *Combat*, followed by reviews by Jean Blanzat in *Le Figaro Littéraire*, and Max-Pol Fouchet in *Carrefour*.
19 April	Charles Bensoussan expresses interest in SB's plays.
28 April	SB completes "Texte pour rien, VI."
May	Georges Bataille publishes an essay on *Molloy* in *Critique*.
5–21 May	SB writes "Texte pour rien, VII."
25 May	Bensoussan wishes to produce *Eleutheria*, but SB is uneasy about the play.
29 May	*Molloy* had been nominated for the Prix des Critiques.
9 June	SB revising *Malone meurt*.
25 June	Offers an extract from either *Malone meurt* or *En attendant Godot* to *Les Temps Modernes* in response to a request by Simone de Beauvoir.
25 June – 10 July	Writes "Texte pour rien, VIII."
4 July	Delivers *Malone meurt* to Lindon.
8 July	Sends "Texte pour rien, V" ("torn off the placenta of *L'Innommable*") to Jean Wahl for *Deucalion*.

14 July – 6 August	Writes "Texte pour rien, IX."
by 26 July	Has corrected proofs of extract from *Malone meurt* in *Les Temps Modernes*.
8–18 August	Writes "Texte pour rien, X."
20 August – 4 September	Writes "Texte pour rien, XI."
September	"Quel malheur ..." an extract from *Malone meurt*, published in *Les Temps Modernes*.
18 October	Frank and Jean Beckett visit SB for a fortnight.
November	Publication of *Malone meurt*.
7–23 November	SB writes "Texte pour rien, XII" (published as XIII).
December	Extract from *Watt* published in *Irish Writing*.
20 December	SB finishes "Texte pour rien, XIII" (published as XII).

Mercredi [3 January 1951]   Ussy

cher vieux Georges

Ta lettre ce matin. Bien content de l'avoir.[1]

Maison glacée et humide à l'arrivée. Pendant 24 heures ça allait mal. Maintenant on est bien, mais Suzanne ne va pas bien. Toujours un peu de fièvre, toux et grande fatigue. Elle aurait besoin d'un mois au bord de la mer, à l'hôtel, à ne rien faire.

Impossible de toucher à la terre, mi-gelée, mi-boueuse. J'ai envie de bêcher, de labourer comme on dit ici. Fait une longue promenade hier, sans rencontrer personne, si, un fossoyeur, qui sortait d'un cimetière en poussant une brouette. A mi-chemin auberge à la Brouwer, grand [? bouge], paysans intarissables, buvant du vin en attendant l'heure de l'apéritif.[2] Un vieux rentre affolé, sa femme vient de tomber, fracture du col du fémur. "Elle ne tenait déjà pas debout" dit-il, "et maintenant …" Il cherchait une voiture pour la transporter, pour ne pas avoir à payer l'ambulance. On sentait qu'il aurait voulu l'abattre d'un coup de fusil. Le bistrot, peu chaud pour sortir sa voiture, conseillait l'ambulance. Les paysans racontaient, à tour de rôle, par surenchères, les occasions où pareil accident avait failli leur arriver. Je les entendais de bien loin.

Félicitations à Claude. J'avais lu sur le journal que Claude Laroche avait terminé 4me et 1er des Juniors. Est-ce son nom de ski?[3]

Tu ne m'as pas répondu pour la question Godeau–Godot. Je crois que je n'ai qu'à le laisser, mais j'aimerais bien avoir ton avis.[4]

Vu Blin quelques jours avant le départ. Il n'y avait encore rien de fait. Il devait donner le ms à O'Brady le lendemain. Il va également le montrer à Badel du Vieux Colombier, qui pourrait l'aider financièrement si la pièce l'intéresse.[5] Blin extrêmement gentil. Nous avons peu parlé de la pièce.

215

Franchement je suis tout à fait contre les idées de Stael sur le décor, peut-être à tort.[6] Il voit ça en peintre. Pour moi c'est de l'esthétisme. On a fait du décor de ballet et de théâtre, à leur grand dommage je crois, une annexe de la peinture. C'est du Wagnérisme. Moi je ne crois pas à la collaboration des arts, je veux un théâtre réduit à ses propres moyens, parole et jeu, sans peinture et sans musique, sans agréments. C'est là du protestantisme si tu veux, on est ce qu'on est. Il faut que le décor sorte du texte, sans y ajouter. Quant à la commodité visuelle des spectateurs, je la mets là où tu devines. Crois-tu vraiment qu'on puisse écouter devant un décor de Bram, ou voir autre chose que lui?[7] Dans Godot c'est un ciel qui n'a de ciel que le nom, un arbre dont ils se demandent si c'en est un, petit et rabougri. J'aimerais voir ça foutu n'importe comment, sordidement abstrait comme la nature l'est, pour les Estragon et Vladimir, une calvaire à sueurs et à poissons, où quelquefois il pousse un navet, se creuse un fossé.[8] Rien du tout, ça n'exprime rien, c'est de l'opaque qu'on n'interroge même plus. Tout spécifisme formel devient impossible. S'il faut absolument savoir où ils sont, (car à mon avis le texte le dit suffisamment) que la parole s'en charge, de ça aussi, au moyen d'étiquettes, ou mieux encore (mais Blin semble contre) par annonce orale: "Voilà, il paraît que ça c'est le ciel, tout ça, et ce machin-là, c'est un arbre, paraît-il." Indigence, nous ne la dirons jamais assez, et décidément la peinture en est incapable. Ne m'en veuille pas de ce déballage, qui doit t'agacer, je te parle à tripes ouvertes.

J'ai fini le Blanchot. Ca fait 12 pages de texte.[9] Des idées très bien, plutôt des départs d'idées, et quand même pas mal de verbiage, à lire rapidement, pas en traducteur. Il en sort quand même un Sade vraiment gigantesque, jaloux de Satan et de ses supplices éternels, et visant la nature plutôt que les hommes. Ça ne m'ennuie pas du tout, quoique mon anglais baisse sensiblement, je ne me sens plus à l'aise que dans une sorte de pastiche du style 18$^{\underline{me}}$, ce qui ne gêne pas trop en l'occurrence. On pourrait mettre également la fin du texte que je t'ai lu, concernant la disparition de son corps.[10] Je crois qu'il y aurait intérêt à laisser l'avant-propos de Faux Pas, qu'on ne pourrait guère

216

présenter que sous formes d'aphorismes isolés, pour un autre numéro.[11]

Ecris-moi encore ici, si le coeur t'en dit, le mien en serait content. Nous ne rentrons pas tout de suite.

Affectueusement, cher vieux, de nous deux, à vous tous.

Sam

C'est un spectacle bien sûr, le théâtre, mais pas d'un endroit. Ce qui s'y fait se ferait aussi bien, ou aussi mal, n'importe où ailleurs, sans parler de ce qui s'y dit. Déjà gosse j'ai souffert mort et passion en écoutant mon prof. de français parler à longueur de cours des décors d'époque de la Comédie du Palais, et je me disais, si c'est ça le théâtre …[12] Je sais que tu ne veux pas parler de choses pareilles, mais au fond, c'est le même principe, celui de l'épaulage, des effets de manche pétrifiés. Comme on a toujour[s] écrit contre la faiblesse du mot et tonné contre celle du corps. Mais me voilà au bord de mes vieilles rengaines.

ALS; 2 leaves, 4 sides; Duthuit collection. *Dating*: article reporting Claude Laroche's sporting success, 1 January 1951 (see n. 3 below).

Wednesday [3 January 1951]   Ussy

Dear old Georges

Your letter this morning. Very pleased to get it.[1]

House freezing and damp when we arrived. For 24 hours things were bad. Now we are comfortable, but Suzanne is not well. Still a touch of fever, cough, and very tired. She would need a month at the seaside, in a hotel, doing nothing at all.

Impossible to do anything with the earth, half frozen, half muddy. I long to be digging, digging over as they say here. Went for a long walk yesterday, met no one, – yes, I did, a gravedigger coming out of a cemetery pushing a wheelbarrow. Halfway along, large dump, Brouwer-style inn, peasants talking their heads off, drinking wine till it was time for an aperitif.[2] An old man comes in in a terrible state, his wife has just had a fall, broken her hip. "She could hardly stand before", he said, "and now …" He was trying to get a car to transport her, so as not to have to pay for an ambulance. You had the feeling that he would have liked to finish her off with a shotgun. The inn-keeper, not keen to take his car out, was all for the ambulance. The peasants were vying with each other to tell about times when some similar accident had almost happened to them. I could hear them from a long way off.

Congratulations to Claude. I had read in the paper that Claude *Laroche* had come 4th, and 1st of the Juniors. Is that his skiing name?[3]

You did not give me an answer on the Godeau–Godot question. I think I shall just have to leave it, but I should like to have your view.[4]

Saw Blin a few days before we left. Nothing had been done yet. He was to give the ms. to O'Brady the next day. He's also going to show it to Badel at the Vieux Colombier, who could put up some money, if the play interests him.[5] Blin extremely nice. We did not talk much about the play.

Frankly I'm totally opposed to Staël's ideas for the set, maybe wrongly.[6] He sees the whole thing with a painter's eye. For me, that is aestheticism. They have turned ballet and theatre sets into a branch of painting, and done them a great deal of harm, I think. It is Wagnerism. I do not believe in collaboration between the arts, I want a theatre reduced to its own means, speech and acting, without paint-ing, without music, without embellishments. That is Protestantism if you like, we are what we are. The setting has to come out of the text, without adding to it. As for the visual convenience of the audience, you can guess where I put that. Do you really think that one could hear anything, faced with a set by Bram, or see anything other than him?[7] In *Godot* it is a sky that is sky only in name, a tree that makes them wonder whether it is one, tiny and shrivelled. I should like to see it set up any old how, sordidly abstract as nature is, for the Estragons and Vladimirs, a place of suffering, sweaty and fishy, where sometimes a turnip grows, or a ditch opens up.[8] Nothing, it expresses nothing, it is an opaque no one bothers to question anymore. Any formal specificity becomes impossible. If it really is essential to know where they are (and in my view the text makes it clear enough), let the words look after that, that too, by means of labels, or better still (though Blin seems to be against) by announcements: "Well, it seems this is the sky, all this, and that thing over there is a tree, apparently." Indigence, we can never say it often enough, and, decidedly, painting is incapable of that. Please do not mind my unloading all this: it must really irritate you, I am spilling my guts out.

I have finished the Blanchot. It makes 12 pages of text.[9] Some excellent ideas, or rather starting-points for ideas, and a fair bit of verbiage, to be read quickly, not as a translator does. What emerges from it though is a truly gigantic Sade, jealous of Satan and of his eternal torments, and confronting nature more than human-kind. I do not find it any trouble at all, although my English is going off noticeably. I am only comfortable now with a sort of pastiche of 18th-century style – which does not come amiss as it happens. We could put in too the end of the text that I read you, about the disappearance of his body.[10] I think it would be right to leave the foreword to *Faux Pas*, which could really only go out as separate aphorisms, in another issue.[11]

Write to me again here, if your heart is in it. Mine would like it. We are not going back straight away.

Love, old friend, from both of us to all of you.

<u>Sam</u>

Yes, of course, theatre is a spectacle; but not of a place. What goes on in it could go on as well, or as badly, anywhere else – not to mention what is said in it. Even when I was a youngster I went through passion and death listening to my French teacher spend whole lessons on contemporary settings of the *Comédie du Palais*, and I used to say to myself, if that is what theatre is . . .[12] I know you are not trying to talk about things like that, but basically, it is the same principle, that of extras, stilted dramatic gestures. As people have always written against the weakness of the word and inveighed against that of the body. But there I am, starting to harp on about the same old things.

1 Duthuit's letter to SB has not been found.
2 Flemish painter Adriaen Brouwer (c. 1605–1638).

3   Claude Laroche – a skier unconnected to Claude Duthuit – is reported as coming fourth (first of the Juniors) in the downhill in the Paris Ski Championship held at Chamonix ("Yves Moussat enlève la descente du championnat de Paris de ski," *Combat* 1 January 1951: 7).

4   SB's hesitations over the name "Godot": [? end December 1950].

5   Frédéric O'Brady (né Frigyes Ábel, 1903–2003) was a Hungarian-born actor who had played in his first film, Jean Renoir's 1936 *La Vie est à nous*, alongside Blin, and who had been cast with Blin more recently in *Hans le marin*, directed by François Villiers (1949).

In 1943, the Théâtre du Vieux-Colombier, 21 Rue du Vieux Colombier, Paris 6, had been taken over by the businessman Paul Annet (also Anet) Badel (1900–1985), who would run the theatre until 1955. His first production, in 1944, was a premiere of Jean-Paul Sartre's *Huis clos* (Ruby Cohn, *From Desire to Godot: Pocket Theater of Postwar Paris* [Berkeley: University of California Press, 1987] 37–38, 45–46).

6   Duthuit was a close friend of Nicolas de Staël (whom SB here spells "Stael"), and had recently published two articles on his work (see jeudi [? 30 March or 6 April 1950], n. 4). It is not known exactly what Staël's ideas consisted in, but some notion may perhaps be gained from what Staël proposed in another of his rare ventures into the theatrical world. In early 1952, René Char asked Staël to design the set and costumes for a ballet whose libretto he had written, *L'Abominable homme des neiges* (The Abominable Snowman); as a result of which, Staël "multiplie les dessins au crayon, à l'encre de Chine et à la gouache, qu'il soumet à René Char, enthousiaste" (is doing more and more drawings, in pencil, Indian ink, and gouache which he puts up to an enthusiastic René Char) (Eve Duperray, Alexandre Didier, Sandra Chastel, eds., *René Char dans le miroir des eaux* [Paris: Beauchesne, 2008] 155). In a letter of 3 January 1953, Staël wrote to Char: "'Pour ton ballet l'idéal serait une couleur par tableau. Un tableau blanc. blanc. blanc. Un bleu. Un rose. Au point de vue composition, c'est important. Le lieu de l'action ne doit pas changer nécessairement mais alors c'est L'HEURE dans le ciel. Indique-moi cela précisément.'" ("For your ballet. The ideal thing would be one colour per tableau. One tableau white, white, white. One blue. One pink. From the composition point of view this is important. The place of the action doesn't necessarily have to change, but then it's the TIME OF DAY in the sky. Let me know exactly.") Annotating this letter, Germain Viatte suggests that, while the ballet was never produced, traces of the work Staël did for it can be observed in several of his large canvases (Nicolas de Staël, André Chastel, Germain Viatte, Jacques Dubourg, and Françoise de Staël, *Nicolas de Staël* [Paris: Les Editions du Temps, 1968] 244).

7   Bram van Velde.

8   Vladimir and Estragon, the two principal figures in *En attendant Godot*. SB mistakes the gender of "calvaire," writing "une" for "un."

9   SB's attempt to select and translate passages from what was probably Maurice Blanchot's *Lautréamont et Sade*: vendredi [? end December 1950], n. 1. The description SB gives here of Sade matches well the portrait given by Blanchot in this work. However, it is not known to what end SB was compiling – and possibly translating – the extracts from Blanchot's book; no publication eventuated from this labor.

10   In his biography of Sade, Gilbert Lely cites the Marquis's last will and testament in which he gave formal instructions (in the event not respected) on how he wished his corpse to be disposed of. The will ends:

La fosse une fois recouverte, il sera semé dessus des glands, afin que, par la suite, le terrain de ladite fosse se trouvant regarni, et le taillis se retrouvant fourré comme il l'était auparavant, les traces de ma tombe disparaissent de dessus la surface de la terre, comme je me flatte que ma mémoire s'effacera de l'esprit des hommes, excepté néanmoins du petit nombre de ceux qui ont bien voulu m'aimer jusqu'au dernier moment et dont j'emporte un bien doux souvenir au tombeau.

Fait à Charenton-Saint-Maurice en état de raison et de santé ce trente janvier mil-huit-cent-six. (Gilbert Lely, *Vie du Marquis de Sade* [Paris: Jean-Jacques Pauvert, 1965] 690.)

(Once the grave has been filled, acorns are to be sown over it so that, later, the ground of the said grave being once again covered over, and the copse thick with growth as it was before, all trace of my tomb shall disappear from the face of the earth, as I comfort myself my memory shall fade from the minds of men, save however the little company of those who had the goodness to love me until the end, the fond memory of whom I take with me into the grave.

Given at Charenton-Saint-Maurice, in possession of my mind and my health, on this day 30th January eighteen hundred and six.)

11   The foreword to Maurice Blanchot's collection of critical essays *Faux pas*, which heads the opening section entitled "De l'angoisse au langage," consists of nearly nineteen pages of closely argued and tightly set italicized text ([Paris: Gallimard, 1943] 9–26).
SB omits the circumflex on "intérêt."

12   SB may be mistaking the name of Pierre Corneille's comic play *La Galerie du palais* (first published in 1637; *The Palace Corridor*).

GEORGES DUTHUIT

Lundi [? 8 January 1951]   Ussy
Cher vieux

J'ai traduit 4 lettres de Sade (dont une extrêmement belle), en réduisant autant que possible les conneries par lesquelles Lely les relie. Tout le reste du travail qu'il t'a donné me semble sans intérêt et inutilisable. Les notes soi-disant sur la peine de mort n'y font pas allusion. Il faudrait aller chercher ça chez Sade lui-même, dans La Philosophie dans le Boudoir probablement.[1]

Dès que j'aurai tapé ce dernier travail je t'adresserai le tout.

Je suis bien fatigué. Hier je n'ai été bon qu'à lire Un Aller simple, pas mal du tout.[2]

J'espère que ce mot te parviendra et toi à le lire.

Affectueusement et à bientôt

        Sam

ALS; 1 leaf, 1 side; Duthuit collection. *Dating*: ongoing discussion of Sade; the Monday following 3 January was 8 January.

Monday [? 8 January 1950]   Ussy

My dear Georges,

I have translated 4 letters by Sade (one of them extremely beautiful), cutting down as far as possible the rubbish Lely writes as linking material. All the rest of the work he has given you seems pointless and unusable. The so-called notes on the death penalty make no mention of it. For that you would have to go to Sade himself, probably *Philosophy in the Bedroom*.[1]

As soon as I have typed this last piece of work I shall send you off the whole lot.

I am very tired. Yesterday all day I was not up to anything more than reading *Un aller simple*: not bad at all.[2]

I hope that this note will get to you, and that you manage to read it. Fondest regards. Write soon.

Sam

1   It is not known which four letters SB was translating by the Marquis de Sade. At least four volumes edited between 1948 and 1953 by Gilbert Lely (1904–1985) contain both letters by Sade and Lely's commentary: *Morceaux choisis de Donatien-Alphonse-François Marquis de Sade* (1948); Marquis de Sade, *L'Aigle, Mademoiselle ... Lettres*, with preface and commentary by Gilbert Lely (1949); Gilbert Lely, *Vie du Marquis de Sade*, I (1952); and Marquis de Sade, *Le Carillon de Vincennes: lettres inédites*, with notes by Gilbert Lely (1953). SB's translations did not appear in *Transition*.
   The death penalty is indeed discussed – and deplored – in the "Cinquième dialogue" in *La Philosophie dans le boudoir* (Sade, *Œuvres*, III, ed. Michel Delon and Jean Deprun, Bibliothèque de la Pléiade [Paris: Gallimard, 1998] 124–125; "Dialogue the Fifth," *The Complete Justine, Philosophy in the Bedroom and Other Writings*, ed. and tr. Richard Seaver and Austryn Wainhouse [New York: Grove Press, 1965] 310–311).

2   Henry Edward Helseth's 1947 novel *The Chair for Martin Rome* was published as *Un aller simple* (tr. Jean Rosenthal and Minnie Danzas, 1950) in Gallimard's Série Noire.

GEORGES DUTHUIT

Mercredi soir [? 10 January 1951]   [Ussy]

Cher vieux Georges,

Merci pour ces 2 bouquins. Je suis en train de lire le Heine. C'est évidemment très calé, avec je ne sais quoi de déplaisant, il y a de bonnes pages sur l'athéisme au 18me, comment Sade le dépasse, etc. Et sur les 120 journées. Et un essai sur Sade et le Roman Noir bien fait pour vexer les Angliches.[1]

Il fait très beau depuis quelques jours. Orgie de bêchage, de défrichage plutôt. Suzanne va un peu mieux. Nous rentrerons probablement dimanche.

Rien de Blin ni des Editions de M. Offre de travail de l'UNESCO, par pneumatique vu extrême urgence habituelle. Impossible décidément de s'entendre avec ces gens-là.[2]

Peut-être une lettre de toi demain, attendons voir.

Vendredi [? 12 January 1951]
[Fragment]

Ta lettre ce matin. J'ai fini le Heine et commencé à traduire l'avant-propos au Dialogue entre un prêtre et un moribond, texte de Sade publié du reste en Amérique, traduction de ce pauvre Samuel Putnam. Une profession de foi athéiste de Sade très vibrante. Des choses très calées sur l'athéisme des philosophes académiciens, une citation de Sylvain Maréchal.[3] J'ai hésité entre ce texte et celui sur Sade et le Roman Noir, intéressant également. Jeté un coup d'oeil sur le Klossowski. Ça m'a l'air d'un fumisme sans égal, je doute qu'on puisse y trouver un texte potable. Quant à Lely, qui adore Heine, qui adore Sade, n'en attendons pas grand'chose. De tous ces types, c'est Blanchot de loin le plus intelligent.[4]

Nous rentrons dimanche, plutôt vaseux tous les deux. Je vais avoir une première semaine horriblement chargée, je dois passer à l'UNESCO lundi chercher des textes à traduire d'urgence pour leur sacrée revue d'art internationale, en espagnol, allemand et français[.][5]

Je sens que les épreuves de Molloy vont me tomber sur le coin de la nénette en même temps, sans parler de Blin. Enfin, on en a vu d'autres.

Lu le billet contre Paulhan de Saillet. Je crains qu'il ne l'ait raté, dommage, dommage.[6]

Savais–tu que Sade est né au <u>Cochon de Lait</u>, ancien Hôtel Condé?[7]

Je passerai te voir lundi prochain vers 6h, en sortant du passage Kléber.[8]

On s'en jettera un ou deux, des vrais, j'en ai marre du super-11 de l'Union Commerciale.[9]

Bien affectueusement à toi

Sam

ALS; 2 leaves, 3 sides [leaf 2 has two sides]; Duthuit collection. *Dating:* "Nothing from Blin" suggests that this letter precedes that from SB to Roger Blin, 15 January 1951 (IMEC), in which he says that he and Suzanne Deschevaux-Dumesnil have returned to Paris from Ussy on 13 January. The previous Wednesday was 10 January. Proofs for *Molloy* were sent on 22 January 1951 (Philippe Hautefeuille, Editions de Minuit, to Suzanne Deschevaux-Dumesnil, IMEC, Beckett, Boîte 1, S. Beckett, Correspondance 1947–1953).

Wednesday evening [? 10 January 1951]   [Ussy]

My dear Georges,

Thanks for those two books. I am reading the Heine at the moment. It is obviously very bright, but with something disagreeable somehow. Good pages on 18th-century atheism, how Sade goes beyond it, etc. And on the *120 Journées*. And an essay on Sade and the Roman Noir that will really upset ze Engleesh.[1]

Beautiful weather for the past few days. Orgy of digging, ground-clearing rather. Suzanne is a little better. We shall probably come back on Sunday.

Nothing from Blin or the Editions de M. An offer of work from UNESCO, by pneumatique, usual urgent-top-priority. No doubt about it, decidedly impossible to have any sensible dealings with those people.[2]

Perhaps a letter from you tomorrow. We will wait and see.

Friday [? 12 January 1951]

[Fragment]

Your letter this morning. I have finished the Heine and started translating the foreword to the *Dialogue entre un prêtre et un moribond*, a text by Sade, published incidentally in America, translation by poor old Samuel Putnam. A stirring profession of atheistic faith by Sade, brilliant things on the atheism of the Académie philosophers, a quotation from Sylvain Maréchal.[3] I hesitated between this text and the one on Sade and the Roman Noir, equally interesting. Had a quick look at the Klossowski. Reads to me like incomparably woolly rubbish, doubt if we could find a single half-decent text in it. As for Lely, who adores Heine, who adores Sade, we must not expect much from him. Of all of them, Blanchot is by far the most intelligent.[4]

We are coming back on Sunday, both feeling pretty rotten. I shall have a horribly full first week. On Monday I have to go over to UNESCO to pick up texts for urgent translation for their damned international art review, in Spanish, German and French.[5]

I think the proofs of *Molloy* will be dropping on my noggin at the same time, not to mention Blin. Oh well, we have known worse.

Read Saillet's piece against Paulhan. Has not got it quite right, I am afraid. Pity, pity.[6]

Did you know that Sade was born in the Cochon de Lait, formerly Hôtel Condé?[7]

I shall call in to see you next Monday about 6, on my way back from the Passage Kléber.[8]

We shall have a couple of jars – decent ones: I am sick of the Super-11 from the Union Commerciale.[9]

> Much love to you
>
> Sam

---

1   The two books are those which SB goes on to discuss: *Sade mon prochain* by Pierre Klossowski and *Le Marquis de Sade* by Maurice Heine. Heine's collection of essays contains "Avant-propos au *Dialogue entre un prêtre et un moribond*," which focuses on atheism; an "Introduction aux *120 Journées de Sodome*"; and "Le Marquis de Sade et le roman noir" (27–37, 70–72, 211–231). This last essay, originally published in the *Nouvelle Revue Française* in 1933, posits Sade – notwithstanding the fiction of English novelists Horace Walpole and Ann Radcliffe, and notwithstanding Sade's documented admiration for *The Monk* by Matthew Lewis – as practically the founder of the "roman noir" (a genre usually now called "Gothic fiction" in English).

2   SB was awaiting news from Roger Blin about a possible staging of *En attendant Godot*, and from Editions de Minuit about publication of *Molloy*.

UNESCO offer: see n. 5 below.

3 Samuel Putnam (1892–1950; Profile, I), founder of *The New Review* in 1930, translated *Dialogue between a Priest and a Dying Man*, ed. Maurice Heine (Chicago: P. Covici, 1927).

In his "Avant-Propos au *Dialogue entre un prêtre et un moribond*," Heine gives numerous examples of what he judges to be the pusillanimous atheism of the Académiciens. He ends his foreword with a lengthy quotation on how the atheist faces death, taken from the *Dictionnaire des athées* of 1800 by the whole-heartedly atheistic philosopher Sylvain Maréchal (1750–1803):

> Touche-t-il au terme de son existence? Il ramasse toutes ses forces, pour jouir des plaisirs qui lui restent, et ferme les yeux pour toujours, mais avec la certitude de laisser un souvenir honorable et cher dans le cœur de ses proches, dont il recueille les derniers témoignages d'estime et d'attachement. Son rôle fini, il se retire tranquillement de la scène pour faire place à d'autres acteurs, qui le prendront pour modèle. Il éprouve sans doute de vifs regrets à la séparation de tout ce qu'il aimait, mais la raison lui dit que tel est l'ordre immuable des choses. D'ailleurs, il sait qu'il ne meurt pas tout entier, tout à fait. Un père de famille est éternel; il renaît, il revit dans chacun de ses enfants; et jusqu'aux parcelles de son corps, rien de lui ne peut s'anéantir. Anneau indestructible de la grande chaîne des êtres, *l'homme-sans-Dieu* en embrasse toute l'étendue par la pensée, et se console, n'ignorant point que le trépas n'est qu'un déplacement de matière et un changement de forme. Au moment de quitter la vie, il repasse dans sa mémoire, s'il en a le loisir, le bien qu'il a pu faire, ainsi que les fautes. Fier de son existence, il n'a fléchi le genou que devant l'auteur de ses jours. Il a marché sur la terre, la tête haute: et d'un pas ferme, l'égal de tous les autres êtres, et n'ayant de compte à rendre à personne qu'à sa conscience. Sa vie est pleine comme la Nature: *ecce vir.* (Heine, *Le Marquis de Sade*, 37.) (Does he come to the end of his existence? He gathers up all his strength, the better to enjoy the pleasures left to him, and closes his eyes for ever, but in the certain knowledge that he leaves an honourable, a fond memory in the hearts of those close to him, whose final gestures of esteem and love he now receives. His part ended, he withdraws untroubled from the stage, to make way for other actors, who will take him as their model. Doubtless he feels keen regrets over separation from all that he loved, but reason tells him that such is the immutable order of things. Besides, he knows that he does not altogether, not wholly die. A father is eternal: he is reborn, he lives once more in each of his children; not even the smallest particles of him, nothing of him can be utterly brought to naught. An indestructible link in the great chain of being, the *man-without-God* embraces the whole of it in thought, and takes comfort, aware as he is that death is but a displacement of matter and a change of form. As he leaves this life, he goes back in memory, if time allows, over such good as he may have done, over his faults. Proud of his existence, he has bowed the knee to no one save the author of his days. He has walked the earth, with his head held high, his step firm, the equal of every creature, with no account to settle with any save his conscience. His life is full, as nature is: *ecce vir* [behold a man]).

4 Blanchot on Sade: vendredi [? end of December 1950], n. 1.

5 Two of SB's friends from his Ecole Normale Supérieure days were involved in UNESCO's project, initiated in 1949, for a new international art review, to be entitled *World of Art*, whose first issue was to appear in early 1951: Jean Thomas and Emile Delavenay (see 4 January 1948, n. 13). To be published in four languages with

co-publishers from outside UNESCO, "the magazine will be primarily concerned with the plastic arts and architecture and will, through these arts, promote the aims and ideals of Unesco, treating art not as an isolated phenomenon but as an integral part of life. It will be directed not only to the artist, student and educator but also, what is more important, to the general public" (UNESCO, 5 December 1950, D&P/ODG/1236, Annex I, 1). A lengthy official memo of 2 December 1950 from Delavenay to Thomas speaks of his own choice of English translators and of the importance of enforcing a strict and rigorous timetable in completion of the translations (UNESCO, D&P/CUA/1214). A further memo on 5 December 1950, this one confidential, from Delavenay to UNESCO's Director General, while speaking of its author's enthusiasm for the project, concludes that it is "la plus complexe et la plus dangereuse que l'Unesco ait jusqu'ici envisagée" (the most complex and the most dangerous that UNESCO has contemplated up to now) (UNESCO, D&P/ODG/1236, 6). In light of the numerous reservations Delavenay expresses over the project, it is unsurprising that no issues of the review ever appeared.

6   SB has read "Jean Paulhan et la poésie" by Maurice Saillet (1914–1990) (*Mercure de France* 302.1015 [1 March 1948] 505–510; revised and reprinted as "Jean Paulhan et son anthologie," in Maurice Saillet, *Billets doux de Justin Saget* [Paris: Mercure de France, 1952] 229–237). SB's judgment has almost certainly been prompted by the mismatch between Saillet's intention (to attack what he sees as Paulhan's waywardness and self-indulgence) and an approach so prolix and sarcastic as to obscure the very point he wants to make. This is what SB sees as a missed opportunity.

7   SB's joke is probably prompted by his reading of Gilbert Lely's *Vie du Marquis de Sade*, which describes the Hôtel Condé where Sade was born on 2 June 1740: it comprised a vast series of buildings stretching over an area that included what later became the Rue Corneille, Paris 6, where, at no. 7, the Cochon de Lait restaurant was situated (Lely, *Vie du Marquis de Sade*, 34–35).

8   Prior to moving to its current location at Place de Fontenoy, Paris 7, the UNESCO headquarters were situated on Avenue Kléber, Paris 16.

9   The "super-11" was almost certainly a cheap 11° wine on sale at a local shop, the Union Commerciale.

PIERRE BORDAS, EDITIONS BORDAS
PARIS

22/1/51   6 rue des Favorites
                                       Paris 15me

Cher Monsieur Bordas

Madame Dumesnil m'a fait part de votre conversation. Je vous remercie de la confiance et de l'estime que vous avez pour mon oeuvre. Vous l'avez compris, la seule chance pour moi c'est de confier mes livres à un éditeur qui puisse les publier rapidement et leur assurer une publicité convenable. Les Editions de Minuit me font une telle offre.[1]

Tenant compte de votre proposition à Madame Dumesnil et du fait que vous n'avez pu accepter, depuis quatre ans, pour des raisons purement extrinsèques, aucun des livres que j'ai écrits depuis Murphy, je vous fais part de ma décision de considérer, par la présente, comme nul l'additif de la clause 12 du contrat que j'ai signé avec vous et qui engageait mon oeuvre future.[2]

Sans réponse de vous dans les quarante-huit heures à cette lettre que je vous envoie, pour la bonne règle, recommandée, je considérerai votre accord comme acquis.

Il ne me reste qu'à vous remercier encore de votre compréhension, en vous priant de croire à toute mon estime et à mes sentiments les plus sincères.

s/ Samuel Beckett

(Samuel Beckett)

TLS, *AN AH*: contrat; with 2nd TLcc 1946–1957; 1 leaf, 1 side; IMEC, Beckett, Boîte 1, S. Beckett, Dossier Murphy 1946–1957.

22/1/51   6 Rue des Favorites

                 Paris 15

Dear Monsieur Bordas

Madame Dumesnil has told me about your conversation. I thank you for the confidence and the regard that you have for my work. You have understood that for me the only chance is to entrust my books to a publisher who can bring them out quickly and guarantee appropriate publicity. The Editions de Minuit are making me an offer of this kind.[1]

In view of the proposal that you made to Madame Dumesnil, and of the fact that for four years you have been unable, for purely extrinsic reasons, to accept any of the books that I have written since *Murphy*, I hereby notify you of my decision to consider as null and void the addition to clause 12 of the contract that I signed with you covering my future work.[2]

If I do not hear from you within forty-eight hours in response to this letter, which for legal reasons I am sending by registered post, I shall take your agreement for granted.

It only remains for me to thank you once again for your understanding.

> Yours sincerely
> Samuel Beckett
> (Samuel Beckett)

1   It is not known when Suzanne Deschevaux-Dumesnil met Pierre Bordas. The Editions de Minuit contract for Beckett's three latest novels in French was offered on 15 November 1950 (11 December 1950, n. 4).

2   The proposal made by Bordas is not known. SB's contract specified his obligation to permit Bordas to publish future works, and the novel *Mercier et Camier* had been submitted under those terms (30 October 1946, n. 1; 15 December 1946, n. 2).

On 15 February, Suzanne Deschevaux-Dumesnil writes to Lindon that Bordas has not yet replied to the present letter (IMEC, Beckett, Boîte 1, S. Beckett, Dossier Murphy 1946–1957).

MARCEL BISIAUX

PARIS

le 22 mars 1951   6 Rue des Favorites

                                                  Paris 15me

Cher Monsieur Bisiaux

A propos des trois poèmes que vous m'avez dit avoir l'intention de publier dans 84, je me suis rendu compte en les relisant que le troisième est impossible sous sa forme actuelle. Nous allons donc le supprimer, si vous voulez bien, à moins que je n'arrive à le changer, ce qui est fort peu probable.

Pour les deux autres, je ne me rappelle plus s'ils ont des titres dans la version qui vous en a été remise. Si c'est oui, soyez assez gentil de les supprimer (les titres).[1]

> Cordialement à vous

TLcc; 1 leaf, 1 side; Fehsenfeld collection.

22 March 1951   6 Rue des Favorites

                                             Paris 15

Dear Monsieur Bisiaux

In connection with the three poems which you told me you intended to publish in *84*, I have realised on re-reading that the third one is impossible as it stands. We shall therefore leave it out, if you don't mind, unless I can find a way of changing it, which is highly unlikely.

For the two others, I cannot remember if they have titles in the version which you were given. If they have, I should be most grateful if you would take them (the titles) out.[1]

Yours sincerely

---

1 Marcel Bisiaux (1922–1990) was a founder and Editor of *84: Nouvelle Revue Littéraire*, published by Editions de Minuit. The journal began in 1947 and was published irregularly thereafter; its final issue was no. 18 (May/June 1951). It is not known which three poems SB had submitted to *84: Nouvelle Revue Littéraire* as they were not published. Poems dating from 1947–1949 include several without a title: "bon bon il est un pays" (published later as "Accul"); "vive morte ma seule saison"; "que ferais-je sans ce monde sans visage sans questions"; and "je voudrais que mon amour." Those to which SB did make changes when they were published later: "que ferais-je sans ce monde sans visage sans questions" and "je voudrais que mon amour" (Samuel Beckett, *Selected Poems 1930–1989*, ed. David Wheatley [London: Faber and Faber, 2009] 54, 55, 58–59).

Although three poems by SB ("Accul," "Mort de A.D.," and "vive morte ma seule saison") were later published in *Cahiers des Saisons* (2 [October 1955] 115–116), it cannot be assumed that these were the ones previously submitted to *84: Nouvelle Revue Littéraire*.

GEORGES DUTHUIT

[c. 9–14 April 1951]   Ussy sur Marne

                                             (Maison BARBIER)

                                             SEINE & MARNE

cher vieux Georges

Je n'ai pas encore fait le petit boulot que tu m'as demandé. J'ai relu l'article de Heidegger et marqué un passage. A mon avis ce n'est pas la peine d'essayer de sauver l'article de Blanchot. Des extraits de Heidegger, mal traduits par moi d'une traduction française déjà fort embarrassée, ne pouvant y apporter le moindre éclaircissement, au contraire. Ce seraient simplement des passages signés Heidegger, d'aucune vertu relevante en eux-mêmes. Que c'est cotonneux tout ça, et que ce pauvre Hölderlin est mal tombé.[1] Je ne te dis pas ça pour me débiner, je ferai ce petit travail de mon mieux si tu y tiens toujours. De toute façon, il reste à mettre d'accord la version française du poème de Hölderlin avec les allusions que Blanchot y fait. Si tu crois que Mme W. peut le faire, tant mieux. Sinon je le ferai moi. Ecris-moi ce que tu veux que je fasse et si je dois te renvoyer les textes en question.[2]

Ça fait huit jours que nous sommes ici et nous nous fatiguons énormément. A notre arrivée l'herbe commençait à entamer la maison. Je sens que l'heure de ma retraite sans flambeaux, je me demande de quoi, est proche et que j'en fais l'apprentissage. 15 ou vingt ans de silence et de solitude, égayés par le jardinage et des promenades de moins en moins longues, il me semble ce soir que ça ferait mon affaire, me la ferait, aussi peu méchamment que possible. J'ai acheté une brouette, ma première brouette! Elle roule bien, avec sa seule roue. Je surveille les amours des doryphores et m'y oppose, avec succès, quoique humainement, c'est à dire en jetant les parents dans le jardin de mon voisin et en brûlant les oeufs. Que ne m'en a-t-on fait autant! Suzanne a mal aux dents et moi, j'ai la thyroïde qui a l'air de vouloir m'étrangler. Quel triste couple. Je mange déjà, tiens-toi bien, mes propres oignons, c'est bien la première fois que je m'en découvre. J'espère qu'en Suisse, ça a bien marché pour toi.[3] Je n'écris rien, ne lis rien, pas même un policier. Nous pensons pouvoir rester encore 15 jours 3 semaines dans ce triste état, s'il est triste. Ecris-moi, mon vieux Georges, c'est le seul courrier que je me souhaite.

Affectueusement à vous 2 de nous 2

<u>Sam</u>

ALS; 1 leaf, 2 sides; Duthuit collection. *Dating*: Suzanne Deschevaux-Dumesnil in correspondence with Lindon (pm 2 April 1951) wrote that she and SB planned to stay the month in Ussy (IMEC, Beckett, Boîte l, S. Beckett, Correspondance 1946–1953).

[c. 9–14 April 1951]
Ussy sur Marne
(Maison BARBIER)
SEINE & MARNE

My dear Georges,

I still have not done the little job you asked me to do. I have re-read the Heidegger article and marked a passage. In my view it is not worth trying to save Blanchot's article. Extracts from Heidegger, badly translated by me from an already very awkward French translation, and with me unable to throw the faintest light on it, the very reverse. They would only be passages signed Heidegger, of no relevant worth in themselves. How woolly it all is, and what bad luck on Hölderlin.[1] I am not saying that in order to wriggle out of it: I shall do this little job as well as I can if you are still set on it. In any case, I still have to line up the French version of the poem with Blanchot's allusions to it. If you think Mrs W. can do it, so much the better. Otherwise I shall do it. Write saying what you want me to do and whether I am to send you the texts in question.[2]

We have been here a week now and we are wearing ourselves out. When we came the grass was beginning to encroach on the house. I feel that my unceremonial retreat, from what, I wonder, is nigh, and that I am starting on my apprenticeship. Fifteen or twenty years of silence and solitude, brightened up by gardening and walks, shorter and shorter, I feel this evening that that would suit me, and suit me the least badly possible. I have bought a wheelbarrow, my first wheelbarrow! It goes very well, with its one wheel. I keep an eye on the love-life of the Colorado beetle and work against it, successfully but humanely, that is to say by throwing the parents into my neighbour's garden and burning the eggs. If only someone had done that for me! Suzanne has toothache, while I am having trouble with a thyroid that seems to want to strangle me. What a dismal pair. I am already, do not miss this, eating my own onions: the first time I've ever found myself having any. I hope that things went well for you in Switzerland.[3] I am not writing anything, not reading anything, not even a detective story. We think we are going to be able to stay on for a fortnight or three weeks in this sad state, if sad it be. Write to me, dear old friend. That is the only post I have any wish for.

Love from both to both.

Sam

---

1 Friedrich Hölderlin.

Almost certainly, SB is referring to an article by Maurice Blanchot entitled "La parole 'sacrée' de Hölderlin," which reviewed and discussed "A Hölderlin," by Rainer Maria Rilke; "Tel qu'en un jour de fête" and "Dix lettres" by Hölderlin; and "L'hymne 'Tel qu'en un jour de fête' de Hölderlin" by Martin Heidegger (1889–1976) – all of which pieces had been published in *Fontaine* earlier in the year (*Critique* 1.7 [December 1946] 579–596). Heidegger's essay had been translated for *Fontaine* by Joseph Rovan.

SB uses an Anglicism in writing "relevante" in place of, e.g., "pertinente."

2 "Mme. W" is Duthuit's assistant Daphne Woodward.

3 The reason for Duthuit's journey to Switzerland is not known.

JEROME LINDON, EDITIONS DE MINUIT
PARIS

10-4-51   Ussy-sur-Marne
Cher Monsieur Lindon

Bien reçu ce matin votre lettre d'hier. Je vous remercie vivement de votre généreuse avance.[1]

J'ai fait faire la photo cet après-midi. Je l'aurai après-demain et vous l'enverrai aussitôt.[2]

Je sais que Roger Blin veut monter la pièce. Il devait demander une subvention à cet effet. Je doute fort qu'on la lui accorde. Attendons Godot, mais pas pour demain.[3]

La nouvelle dont la première moitié, sous le titre Suite, a paru dans les Temps Modernes, est à votre disposition.[4] Cela peut-il attendre jusqu'à mon retour? C'est mon premier travail en français (en prose). Le Calmant, que Madame Dumesnil a remis à Monsieur Lambrichs, ferait peut-être mieux l'affaire.[5] Ce sera à votre choix.

Je suis très content que vous ayez envie d'arriver rapidement à L'Innommable. Comme je vous l'ai dit, c'est à ce dernier travail que je tiens le plus, quoiqu'il m'ait mis dans de sales draps. J'essaie de m'en sortir. Mais je ne m'en sors pas. Je ne sais pas si ça pourra faire un livre. Ce sera peut-être un temps pour rien.[6]

Laissez-moi vous dire encore combien je suis touché par l'intérêt que vous portez à mon travail et par le mal que vous vous donnez pour le défendre. Et croyez à mes sentiments sincèrement amicaux.[7]

Samuel Beckett

ALS; 1 leaf, 1 side; IMEC, Beckett, Boîte 1, S. Beckett, Correspondance 1947–1953. Previous publication, Lindon, "First Meeting with Samuel Beckett," in Calder, ed., *Beckett at 60*, 18–19 (English), and in Beckett, *Disjecta*, 104–105 (French); both introduce variants from the original.

10-4-51   Ussy-sur-Marne

Dear Monsieur Lindon

Received this morning your letter of yesterday. I am most grateful for your generous advance.[1]

I have had the photograph taken this afternoon. I shall have it the day after tomorrow, and will send it on to you straight away.[2]

I know that Roger Blin wants to put the play on. He was to put in for a grant for this purpose. I very much doubt if they will give him one. Let us wait for *Godot*, but it won't be tomorrow.[3]

The story, of which the first half, under the title "Suite," has appeared in *Les Temps Modernes*, is at your disposal.[4] Can this wait till my return? It is my first work in French (prose). "Le Calmant," which Madame Dumesnil has passed on to Monsieur Lambrichs, would perhaps be more suitable.[5] Your choice.

I am very glad that you want to get on to *L'Innommable* quickly. As I told you, it is this last work that I am most attached to, although it has left me in a sorry state. I'm trying to get over it. But I am not getting over it. I do not know if it will be able to make a book. Perhaps it will all have been for nothing.[6]

Allow me to tell you how touched I am by the interest you are taking in my work, and the trouble you are taking to defend it. And believe me to be[7]

      Yours sincerely

      Samuel Beckett

---

1   The advance was 25,000 old francs (Lindon, "First Meeting with Samuel Beckett," 18).

2   The photo of SB taken at this time is published in Calder, ed., *Beckett at 60*, [facing 25]; the photographer has not been identified.

3   Roger Blin applied for a subvention, "l'aide à la première pièce" (first play grant), for the production of *En attendant Godot*.

4   "Suite" was partially published in *Les Temps Modernes* (see 1 September 1946, and SB to Simone de Beauvoir, 25 September 1946). It was not published by Editions de Minuit until 1955, when the full story appeared as "La Fin" in *Nouvelles et Textes pour rien*. "Suite" was begun on 17 February 1946. It is clear from the notebook draft that SB began this story in English, broke off (28 recto), and then (from 2 March 1946) translated the last paragraph and continued writing in French (Burns Library, Beckett collection, I/5; see also 27 May 1946; Cohn, *A Beckett Canon*, 128–129).

5   "Le Calmant," the fourth of SB's stories: 15 December 1946, n. 6.
The question of who exactly was responsible for the signing of SB at Editions de Minuit, Jérôme Lindon or Georges Lambrichs, has been much disputed. Lindon gave at least three accounts of his role. In a 1989 interview with James Knowlson, he said, "I was going home to lunch. I saw a manuscript on Georges Lambrichs' desk. Doubtless Suzanne had just brought it in to him. I said to him 'What is that?' And he said 'I believe it's very good,' though he hadn't yet read it." (*Damned to Fame*, 341.) This account is very close to what Lindon transmitted to Anne Simonin for her history of the publishing house, *Les Editions de Minuit 1952-1955* ([Paris: IMEC, 1994] 382). Yet in the article published in 1967, "First Meeting with Samuel Beckett," Lindon wrote, "One day in 1950, a friend of mine, Robert Carlier, told me: 'You should read the manuscript of an Irish writer who writes in French. He is called Samuel Beckett. Six publishers have already refused him'" (Lindon, "First Meeting with Samuel Beckett," in Calder, ed., *Beckett at 60*, 17). In this 1967 account, the role of Georges Lambrichs is reduced to a footnote: "George[s] Lambrichs was at this time secretary to the Reading Committee of Les Editions de Minuit" (19).
For his part, Lambrichs was categorical in a 1987 interview:

[SIMONIN]	C'est vous qui avez découvert Beckett?
[LAMBRICHS]	Oui.
[SIMONIN]	Jérôme Lindon prétend que c'est lui.
[LAMBRICHS]	Ça, je sais ... mais enfin aujourd'hui on sait très bien même en Amérique, comment les choses se sont passées. C'est la femme de Beckett qui m'a apporté trois manuscrits: *Molloy, Malone meurt* et *L'Innommable*. J'ai dit à Lindon: "Vous en vendrez cinq cents exemplaires, mais ce sera l'honneur de la maison." Vous connaissez la suite.

                     (Simonin, *Les Editions de Minuit*, 380.)

([SIMONIN] It was you who discovered Beckett?
[LAMBRICHS] Yes.
[SIMONIN] Jérôme Lindon claims he did.
[LAMBRICHS] Yes, I know … but actually nowadays, even in America, people know what went on. It was Beckett's wife who brought me three manuscripts: *Molloy*, *Malone meurt*, and *L'Innommable*. I said to Lindon: "You'll sell five hundred copies, but it will bring lasting honour to the firm." You know the rest.)

6 The new work to which SB refers becomes *Textes pour rien*.

7 Lindon closed his account of his first meeting with Samuel Beckett with the following tribute: "I would like this to be known, and only this: that in all my life I have never met a man in whom co-exist together in such high degree, nobility and modesty, lucidity and goodness. I would never have believed that anyone could exist who is at the same time so real, so truly great, and so good" (Lindon, "First Meeting with Samuel Beckett," 19).

JEROME LINDON, EDITIONS DE MINUIT
PARIS

10 [for 11]-4-51   *Ussy*
Cher Monsieur Lindon

Votre lettre d'hier ce matin. Je ne crois pas que ce soit très grave mais j'estime qu'il faut chercher dès maintenant le moyen de liquider cette situation une bonne fois pour toutes. Il est inadmissible que Bordas continue à faire planer l'équivoque sur les rapports entre les Editions de Minuit et Beckett, qui les veut sans ambiguïté d'aucune sorte. A mon avis il importe simplement de savoir si les démarches déjà effectuées auprès de Bordas suffisent effectivement à annuler les droits de celui-ci sur l'oeuvre future de Beckett et, si elles n'y suffisent pas, quelles sont les démarches qui s'imposent pour que ce résultat soit acquis. Pourriez-vous avoir un avis autorisé à ce sujet?[1] Il faut que vous sachiez que Beckett est entièrement de votre côté et ne se dérobera devant aucune démarche, quelque pénible qu'elle puisse être, qui contribue à dissiper cette atmosphère de double appartenance. Il se peut évidemment qu'on vous dise que l'affaire, telle qu'elle se présente, ne se laisse pas trancher sur le plan strictement juridique. En ce cas il me semble qu'il faudrait dès à présent provoquer l'arbitrage.

Voilà notre première impression à Beckett et à moi. Mais vous êtes certainement plus au courant que nous de ce qu'il convient de faire. Quoi que vous décidiez, soyez sûr que Beckett sera de coeur et activement avec vous.

Vous serez gentil de me tenir au courant, puisque je ne rentre pas avant la fin du mois.

      Sincèrement de nous deux

       Suzanne Dumesnil

P. S. Bordas n'a jamais eu l'Innommable. La question de le lui montrer ne se posait même pas puisqu'il avait renoncé à publier les deux ouvrages dont il dépendait.[2]

J'ai été contente d'apprendre que Molloy a déjà recueilli quelques avis favorables. Pourvu que ça continue.[3]

ALS; 1 leaf, 2 sides; IMEC, Beckett, Boîte 1, S. Beckett, Dossier Murphy 1946–1957.

10 [for 11]-4-51   *Ussy*

Dear Monsieur Lindon

Received this morning your letter of yesterday. I do not think that it is very serious, but my view is that we must start at once to look for a way of resolving this situation once and for all. It is impermissible that Bordas should go on equivocating about the relationship between the Editions de Minuit and Beckett, which he himself wishes to be free of ambiguity of any kind. In my view all that matters is to know whether the measures already taken with Bordas really are sufficient to annul his rights over Beckett's future works, and, if they are not, what steps are needed to ensure that this result is achieved. Might you have an authoritative view on this?[1] *You must know that Beckett is entirely on your side, and will not shrink from any step, however unpleasant, which helps to clear away this atmosphere of double affiliation. It is of course possible that you will be told that the matter as it stands cannot be settled on strictly legal grounds. In that case it seems to me that we would have to go at once to arbitration.*

This is Beckett's and my first impression. But you are certainly better informed than we are about what action is appropriate. Whatever you decide, be sure that Beckett will be in spirit and actively with you.

Please be kind enough to keep me up to date, since I shall not be returning before the end of the month.

Yours sincerely, from both of us

Suzanne Dumesnil

P. S. Bordas has never had L'Innommable. *The question of showing it to him did not even arise since he had abandoned the publication of the two works on which it depended.*[2]

I was pleased to hear that Molloy *has already received a few favourable notices. Long may it continue.*[3]

---

1 Jérôme Lindon's letter of 10 April was directed to Suzanne Descheveaux-Dumesnil, as Lindon said: "Si je vous écris aujourd'hui à vous, c'est qu'il s'agit d'une affaire ennuyeuse pour laquelle il vaudrait peut-être mieux ne pas l'importuner" (If I am writing to you today, it is on account of an awkward matter, about which it would perhaps be better not to bother him) (IMEC, Beckett, Boîte 1, S. Beckett, Dossier Murphy 1946–1957). Lindon reported that Bordas had told him by telephone that their firm held all rights concerning Beckett, and that Beckett's letter to Pierre Bordas of 22 January 1951 did not give grounds for breaking the contract.

2 *Molloy* and *Malone meurt.*

3 There were only brief mentions of *Molloy*, in "Books Received," the *New York Herald Tribune*, *Paris*, 28 March 1951: 5, and in "Vous pouvez lire," *Combat*, 5 April 1951: 4; Lindon may have known about reviews about to be published.

MAURICE NADEAU

PARIS

A Marcel [*for* Maurice] Nadeau

9/b/5 <u>Combat</u>

123 Rue Montmartre

Paris 2<u>me</u>

---

12 avril 1951   Ussy-sur-Marne

Seine-en-Marne

Monsieur

Je suis très touché que vous ayez lu mon travail avec tant d'attention et que vous en ayez rendu compte comme vous l'avez fait dans
<u>Combat</u> d'aujourd'hui et je vous en remercie vivement.[1]

Sincèrement

Sam. Beckett

ALS; 1 leaf, 1 side; *env to* M Maurice Nadeau, 9/b/5 <u>Combat</u>, 123 Rue Montmartre, Paris
2me; Beckett/Nadeau. Previous publication, Maurice Nadeau, *Grâces leur soient rendues*
(Paris: Albin Michel, 1990) 364.

9. Maurice Nadeau

To Marcel [*for* Maurice] Nadeau
9/b/5 *Combat*
123 Rue Montmartre
    Paris 2me

---

12 April 1951   Ussy-sur-Marne
                                   Seine-et-Marne

Dear Monsieur Nadeau

I feel greatly touched that you should have read my work so attentively and reviewed it as you did in today's *Combat*, and I send you my warmest thanks.[1]

Yours sincerely

Sam. Beckett

---

1 Maurice Nadeau* (b. 1911), Director of *Combat* from 1947 to 1951. SB refers to his piece, "Samuel Beckett ou: En avant, vers nulle part!" *Combat* 12 April 1951: 4. Suzanne Deschevaux-Dumesnil wrote to Jérôme Lindon on 13 April about the Nadeau review: "Il n'est pas commode de présenter brièvement un travail aussi glissant et on sent qu'il a fait un véritable effort" (It is no easy task to present briefly a work so elusive, and one feels that he has made a real effort) (IMEC, Beckett, Boîte 1, S. Beckett, Dossier Murphy 1946–1957).

MANIA PERON

PARIS

Lundi [16 April 1951]   <u>Ussy</u>

Chère Mania[1]

Contents d'avoir de vos nouvelles et regrettons qu'elles ne soient pas meilleures.

Tout à fait d'accord avec votre judicieuse critique des critiques. Il fallait vraiment faire inattention pour confondre la victime de Moran avec le père Molloy. Mais ce n'est pas nécessairement Moran lui-même non plus. Que voulez-vous, je ne sais pas tout. Pour moi c'est simplement l'étranger indiqué, j'ai horreur des symboles. L'article de Nadeau avait quelque chose de touchant, il s'est donné du mal. Mais je n'ai pas aimé celui de Blanzat.[2]

Je vous réserve d'autres exemplaires. Malheureusement je ne pourrai pas vous en donner de numérotés n'en ayant reçu que deux.[3]

A Paris j'ai encore quelques petites merdes à vous montrer, genre des deux que vous avez déjà vues. Comment continuer après l'INNommable? Ce sont des petits textes-sondes pour tâter la possibilité d'autre chose.[4]

Dans bientôt 3 semaines 3 belles journées. Nous ne rentrerons guère avant la fin du mois. Entre les giboulées je gratte la boue et observe les vers de terre, d'une observation dépourvue de détachement scientifique. J'essaie de ne pas les blesser, avec la bêche. Tout en sachant que coupés en deux ils élaborent sans tarder une nouvelle tête, ou une nouvelle queue, selon le cas.

     affectueusement de nous 2

     Sam

ALS; 1 leaf, 2 sides; *env to* Madame Péron, 69 Rue de la Tombe-Issoire, PARIS 14me; *pm* 18-4-51, La Ferté-sous-Jouarre; TxU, Lake collection, Beckett.

Monday [16 April 1951]   Ussy

Dear Mania[1]

     We are glad to have your news, and sorry it is no better.

     Agree entirely with your judicious critique of the critics. It really took some serious inattentiveness to confuse Moran's victim with poor old Molloy. But it is not necessarily Moran himself either. What can I say, I do not know everything. For me it is simply the stranger indicated; I cannot bear symbols. The Nadeau article had a touching quality; he took trouble over it. But I did not like the one by Blanzat.[2]

     I am keeping some other copies for you. Unfortunately I shall not be able to give you numbered copies, having received only two.[3]

     In Paris I still have a few little turds to show you, same kind as the two you have already seen. How to go on after *L'Innommable*? These are little text-soundings, trying out something different.[4]

     Out of what will soon be three weeks, three fine days. We are unlikely to go back before the end of the month. Between the April showers I scratch the mud and observe the worms, an observation entirely devoid of scientific detachment. I try not to hurt them, with the spade. All the while knowing that, cut in two, they at once fashion a new head, or a new tail, whichever is the case.

     Love from the two of us

     Sam

1   Maria Péron* (née Lézine-Spiridonof, known as Mania, 1900–1988), widow of Alfred Péron.

2   Nadeau, "Samuel Beckett ou: En avant, vers nulle part!" *Combat* 12 April 1951: 4; Jean Blanzat (1906–1977), "Un livre-événement," *Le Figaro Littéraire* 14 April 1951: 9.

3   Jérôme Lindon sent the two numbered copies to SB on 9 April.

4   SB refers to the stories of what will eventually become *Textes pour rien*.

JEROME LINDON, EDITIONS DE MINUIT
PARIS

19 Avril 51

  Cher Monsieur Lindon. Merci de votre lettre du 17. Nous apprécions toute l'importance, sur le plan pratique, de l'article de Blanzat, mais, comme nous ne lisons pas le Figaro Littéraire, nous ne pouvons comparer le ton de ce dernier feuilleton avec celui qui lui est habituel. Comme critique littéraire, c'est davantage à côté que l'article de Nadeau. Il y a quelques grosses fautes d'interprétation. Il est inconcevable qu'il ait pu confondre la victime de Moran avec le père Molloy.[1] Bien sûr, ça n'a aucune espèce d'importance, et Beckett est très sensible à la chance qu'il a eue d'avoir attiré l'attention de deux critiques aussi écoutés. Vous y êtes pour quelque chose cher Monsieur Lindon, ne vous en défendez pas.

  L'attitude de Beckett envers les prix littéraires est un peu plus difficile à définir. Ce qu'il redoute par-dessus tout, au cas bien peu probable où il aurait un prix, c'est la publicité dont serait alors l'objet, non pas seulement son nom et son travail, mais sa personne. Il estime, à tort ou à raison, qu'il est impossible au lauréat, sans grave discourtoisie, de se refuser aux simagrées de rigueur en de telles occasions: amabilités vis-à-vis de ses supporters, interviews, photos, etc. etc. Et comme il se sent tout à fait incapable d'un tel comportement, il préfère ne pas s'exposer, en briguant un prix, au risque d'y être obligé. Il se fait peut être une idée excessive des devoirs d'un lauréat. Mais si, tout en étant primé, il pouvait sans goujaterie rester dans son coin, il ne verrait aucun inconvénient à l'être. Vous voyez, ce n'est pas une aversion de principe, mais simplement la crainte de la contrepartie. Tout ceci à propos du Prix des Critiques, car il en est d'autres pour lesquels il ne voudrait à aucun prix être présenté. J'espère que je vous aurai fait comprendre sa façon de voir et que vous ne la jugerez pas trop ridicule.[2]

  Avec mon amitié cher Monsieur Lindon, croyez à mon meilleur souvenir.

<u>Suzanne Dumesnil</u>

A l'instant Beckett reçoit une lettre d'un nommé Bensoussan, metteur en scène qui dit s'intéresser à son théâtre et vouloir "bavarder" avec lui. On l'a aiguillé sur les Ed. de Minuit. Faites-en ce que vous voulez, selon la bête, mais préservez-nous-en. Et merci.[3]

ALS; 2 leaves, 3 sides; IMEC, Beckett, Boîte 1, Correspondance 1946–1953.

19 April 51

Dear Monsieur Lindon. Thank you for your letter of the 17th. We do appreciate the full importance on the practical level of the Blanzat article, but, as we do not read the Figaro Littéraire, we cannot compare the tone of this latest piece with his usual one. As literary criticism, it is farther off the mark than Nadeau's. There are a few gross errors of interpretation. It is hard to imagine that he should have confused Moran's victim with old Molloy.[1] Of course, it does not matter in the least, and Beckett is keenly aware of the luck he has had in drawing the attention of two such respected critics. You have some share in that, dear Monsieur Lindon, do not deny it.

Beckett's attitude to literary prizes is a little more difficult to define. What he dreads above all, in the very unlikely event of his receiving a prize, is the publicity which would then be directed, not only at his name and his work, but at the man himself. He judges, rightly or wrongly, that it is impossible for the prizewinner, without serious discourtesy, to refuse to go in for the posturings required by these occasions: warm words for his supporters, interviews, photos, etc., etc. And as he feels wholly incapable of this sort of behaviour, he prefers not to expose himself to the risk of being forced into it by entering the competition. Perhaps he has an exaggerated view of a prizewinner's duties. But if, as prize-winner, he could without unacceptable rudeness stay out of it all, he would see no objection to being one. You see, it is not an aversion of principle, but simply the fear of the other side of the coin. All this in connection with the Prix des Critiques, for there are others for which he would not wish at any cost to be put forward. I hope that I shall have got you to understand his way of thinking, and that you will not judge it too ridiculous.[2]

With friendly greetings and my best wishes, dear Monsieur Lindon

Suzanne Dumesnil

Beckett has just this minute received a letter from one Bensoussan, a theatre director who says he is interested in his plays and wants to "have a chat" with him. We pointed him in the direction of Minuit. Deal with him as you think best, depending on what he's like, but keep him away from us. And thanks.[3]

1 Comparing *Molloy* to *The Odyssey*, Blanzat writes of Jacques Moran: "Par un surcroît de dérision, il tue Molloy sans le reconnaître. En fin de compte, il arrive à la même 'odyssée' nihiliste." (In a final twist of derision, he kills Molloy without recognising him. When all's said, he arrives at the same nihilistic 'Odyssey'.) ("Un livre-événement," 9.)

2 The Prix des Critiques recognizes a literary work published in the previous year. On 17 April, Lindon wrote to Suzanne Deschevaux-Dumesnil: "Il s'agit là du prix littéraire qui, de l'année, est le plus valable, puisqu'il comprend parmi les membres de son jury des critiques comme Nadeau, Blanzat, Paulhan, Marcel Arland, Maurice Blanchot, Armand Hoog, etc." (This is the literary prize which, of all those for the year, is the most influential, since it counts among the members of the panel critics such as Nadeau, Blanzat, Paulhan, Marcel Arland, Maurice Blanchot, Armand Hoog, etc.) (IMEC, Beckett, Boîte 1, S. Beckett, Correspondance 1947–1953).

3 Charles Bensoussan (almost certainly the actor and producer who later took the name Philippe Clair, b. 1930), 26 Rue Racine, Montreuil s/ Bois (Seine).

JEROME LINDON, EDITIONS DE MINUIT
PARIS

le 24 avril 51   Ussy

Cher Monsieur Lindon.

Bien reçu vos deux lettres du 20.[1] *Beckett ne veut pas entendre parler d'interview, que ça se fasse oralement ou par écrit. Je crains qu'il ne soit inébranlable sur ce chapitre. Il donne son travail, son rôle s'arrête là, il ne peut en parler. Telle est son attitude. Quant à "sa vie" ce n'est vraiment pas la peine, d'après lui, qu'un journaliste se dérange pour l'interroger là-dessus. Il a dit à M. Hoffmann, et je vous le confirme, qu'il est prêt à fournir aux Ed. de Minuit, tous les renseignements jugés utiles à ce sujet.*[2] *Il est désolé de ce que cette intransigeance peut avoir de désobligeant et de gênant pour vous en tant qu'éditeur. Je vous l'avais laissé entendre. Il faut le prendre comme il est.*

Si vous jugez possible, sans que les bonnes manières en souffrent trop grandement, de répondre à sa place aux "Nouvelles Littéraires" il serait très content que vous le fassiez. Sinon, envoyez la lettre et il le fera lui-même.[3]

Quant au Prix des Critiques, d'accord pour la candidature de Molloy *si vraiment ça peut se passer comme vous le dites en cas de réussite.*

Je dois ajouter que S. Beckett répugne à invoquer son absence de Paris pour justifier sa carence sur le plan publicitaire. Il veut que ce soit admis – ou inadmis – une fois pour toutes qu'il ne peut pas marcher dans ces histoires-là et qu'il n'est à interroger nulle part ailleurs que dans ses écrits.

Il ne lui reste qu'à vous demander, à vous qui avez fait et faites tant pour lui, de ne pas lui en vouloir.

Nous serons à Paris la première semaine de mai.

Tous mes meilleurs sentiments

    <u>*Suzanne Dumesnil*</u>

ALS; 2 leaves, 3 sides; Minuit collection; IMEC, Beckett, Boîte 1, S. Beckett Correspondance 1946–1953.

24 April 1951

Dear Monsieur Lindon

Your two letters of the 20th safely received.[1] *Beckett will not hear of being interviewed, whether orally or in writing. I fear that on this he is not to be budged. He gives his work, his role stops there. He cannot talk about it. That is his attitude. As for "his life", it is really not, as he sees it, worth a journalist's while to go out of his way to question him about it. He has told M. Hoffmann, and I can confirm this, that he is ready to supply the Editions de Minuit with all the information he judges useful on this.*[2] *He is really sorry for the extent to which this intransigence may be unhelpful and awkward for you as publisher. I had given you to understand as much. One must take him as he is.*

If you think it possible, without too much damage to good manners, to reply on his behalf to the Nouvelles Littéraires, *he would be very glad if you did. If not, send the letter on and he will do it himself.*[3]

As for the Prix des Critiques, go ahead with entering Molloy *if it really can work out the way you say in the event of his winning.*

I must add that S. Beckett would find it very distasteful to invoke his being away from Paris to justify his poor showing in publicity terms. He wants it to be granted – or not granted – once and for all that he will not go along with these performances, and that it is only in his writings that he can be questioned.

It only remains for me to ask you, who have done and go on doing so much for him, not to hold this against him.

We shall be in Paris in the first week of May.

With every good wish

    Suzanne Dumesnil

---

1 One of Lindon's letters of 20 April to Suzanne Deschevaux-Dumesnil mentions that, as she and SB have requested, the Editions de Minuit have intercepted a letter to SB from André Bourin of *Les Nouvelles Littéraires* seeking an interview about *Molloy* (19 April 1951, IMEC, Beckett, S. Beckett, Correspondance 1946–1953).

Lindon's other letter to Suzanne Deschevaux-Dumesnil on 20 April acknowledges the photographic negative sent by SB and responds to her letter of 19 April. In this he indicates the reviews of *Molloy* that have appeared: "outre les articles de Nadeau et de Blanzat, un article de Jacques Brenner dans 'Paris-Normandie', une note de Jean Blanchot dans 'Les Nouvelles Littéraires', et même un article dans 'France-Soir'!" (IMEC, Beckett, Boîte 1, S. Beckett, Correspondance 1946–1953) (besides the articles by Nadeau and Blanzat, an article by Jacques Brenner in *Paris-Normandie*, a note by Jean Blanchot in *Les Nouvelles Littéraires*, and even an article in *France-Soir*!).

2 Michel Hoffmann was Head of Distribution at Editions de Minuit in 1951. Prior to the publication of *Molloy*, he met Alberto Giacometti "to discuss the possibility of a design for the jacket" of the book; "Giacometti submitted three proposals," but the project was canceled "due to financial problems" (*Art impressionniste et moderne: dont un ensemble d'œuvres provenant de l'atelier Degas* [Paris: Christie's, 2006] 120; 24 May 2006, sale 5440, lot 128).

3 Lindon probably wrote to André Bourin, but his letter has not been found.

MANIA PERON
PARIS

29-4-51   Ussy

Chère Mania

Merci de votre lettre.

M'étonne que vous vous étonniez de l'obscurité où je travaille.

Je ne crois pas que Murphy ait pu se suicider, en les circonstances matérielles, mais la possibilité n'est pas à exclure. Il était d'ailleurs déjà mort, à force de suicide mental. Tel est mon humble avis.

Je vous donnerai autant d'exemplaires que vous en voudrez, vous en ferez ce que vous voudrez, mais ne me parlez plus de dédicaces, j'en suis malade (pour Alexis et Michel, bien sûr, très volontiers). Quand j'apprends que je suis un salaud si je ne signe pas un exemplaire pour Tata, l'occasion est vraiment trop belle pour que je la manque, l'occasion d'être un salaud à si bon compte.[1] Et je suis tranquille, vous survivrez, les yeux correcteurs plus perçants que jamais, à cet effroyable affront par omission.

Très touché par la réaction de Michel. Oui, et cher Alfred aurait été content, et vite pénétré, comme moi, du peu de quoi.[2] Car la question n'est pas là, ni dans les environs.

N'ayant pas d'exemplaire ici je ne sais pas ce qui se trouve à la page 59.[3]

J'ai lu la vie de Balzac de Billy, 2 gros volumes remplis de chiffres, et le terrible récit de Mirbeau sur la mort, Balzac crevant comme un chien, abandonné de tous, l'odeur de gangrène remplissant la maison, et Mme Hanska faisant l'amour avec le peintre Gigoux dans une pièce voisine. Et quand, le lendemain, les mouleurs vinrent, ils durent s'en aller, bredouille[s], <u>le nez ayant entièrement coulé sur le drap</u>.[4]

A la semaine prochaine, très probablement.

Affectueusement

Sam

ALS; 1 leaf, 2 sides; *env to* Madame Péron, 69 Rue de la Tombe-Issoire, PARIS 14me; *pm* 30-4-51, La Ferté-sous-Jouarre; TxU, Lake collection, Beckett.

29-4-51   Ussy

Dear Mania

Thank you for your letter.

Amazed that you're amazed at the gloom I work in.

I don't think that Murphy can have committed suicide, in the material circumstances, but the possibility can't be ruled out. In any case he was already dead, as a result of mental suicide. Such is my humble opinion.

I shall give you as many copies as you want, but no more talk, please, about signings – I am ill with doing them (for Alexis and Michel, of course, and very gladly). When I hear that I'm a bastard if I don't sign a copy for Tata, the opportunity is too good to miss: being a bastard at such low cost.[1] And I am not worried – you will survive this affront of frightful omission, with your proofreader's eyes sharper than ever.

Much touched by Michel's reaction. Yes, and dear Alfred would have been pleased, and soon fully aware, like myself, on how little.[2] For the point is not there, nor anywhere near it.

Not having a copy here, I don't know what is on page 59.[3]

I've read Billy's life of Balzac, two fat volumes full of figures, and Mirbeau's terrible account of the death, Balzac dying like a dog, abandoned by all, with the smell of gangrene pervading the house, and Mme Hanska making love with Gigoux the painter in the next room. And the day after, when the moulders came, they had to go away again, empty-handed, *the whole nose having come off on to the sheet.*[4]

Till next week, very probably.

Love

Sam

1 Mania and Alfred Péron's twin sons, Michel Stuart and Alexis Alfred Rémy (b. 1932). "Tata" was the family's name for Mania Péron's maternal aunt Elizabeth Spiridonof (n.d.), who emigrated to France from Russia about ten years later than the rest of the family (interview with Alexis Péron, 11 December 2000).

2 Michel's reaction is not known.

3 It is uncertain whether Mania Péron refers to *Murphy* or to *Molloy*.

4 André Billy, *Vie de Balzac*, 2 vols. (Paris: Flammarion, 1944). "La Mort de Balzac" was originally an incongruous final chapter in Octave Mirbeau's book *La 628-E8* (1907); it was withdrawn, but published in his *Balzac: sa vie prodigieuse, son mariage, ses derniers moments* (1918; *La 628-E8* was later published with the suppressed chapter [Paris: Fasquelle, 1939]).

Eveline Hanska (c. 1806–1882) became Balzac's wife in March 1850; Balzac died on 18 August 1850 (Graham Robb, *Balzac: A Life* [New York: W. W. Norton, 1994] 227, 416).

Jean-François Gigoux (1806–1894), French painter and lithographer.

MAX-POL FOUCHET
PARIS

le 4 mai 1951   6 Rue des Favorites
                                                 Paris 15me

Cher Max-Pol Fouchet

De retour de la campagne je viens seulement de lire votre article sur Molloy dans Carrefour.[1] Il m'a beaucoup touché. Laissez-moi vous remercier de cette dernière si généreuse expression de votre estime et vous dire combien je suis heureux de vous sentir du petit nombre de ceux à qui parle vraiment une voix si pauvre et lointaine.

Madame Dumesnil me charge de vous dire, ainsi qu'à Madame votre mère, bien des choses de sa part.[2]

Croyez, cher Max-Pol Fouchet, à mon amitié.

(Samuel Beckett)

TLcc; 1 leaf, 1 side; Fehsenfeld collection.

4th May 1951   6 Rue des Favorites
                                                 Paris 15me

Dear Max-Pol Fouchet

Back from the country I have just read your article on *Molloy* in *Carrefour*.[1] I was greatly touched by it. Allow me to thank you for this latest generous expression of your regard and to tell you how happy I am to feel that you belong to the small number of those to whom so poor and distant a voice really speaks.

Madame Dumesnil bids me to send, to you, as well as to Madame your mother, every good wish.[2]

I send my own best wishes

(Samuel Beckett)

1   Max-Pol Fouchet, "Molloy," *Carrefour* 24 April 1951: 8.

2   Lucie Fouchet (n.d.).

8 May 1951, Blanzat

JEAN BLANZAT

PARIS

le 8 mai 1951   6 Rue des Favorites

                                                 Paris 15me

Monsieur

    Ce mot bien tardif pour vous dire combien j'ai été touché par votre article sur Molloy dans le Figaro Littéraire.[1] Je crois comprendre tout ce que représente, pour un collaborateur de cet hebdomadaire, une telle prise de position vis-à-vis de ce livre. Et je sais par mon éditeur que l'intérêt que vous portez à mon travail dépasse largement le cadre de la critique écrite. De telles marques de sympathie, venant de vous, effacent bien des amertumes. Croyez à ma reconnaissance émue.[2]

(Samuel Beckett)

TLcc; 1 leaf, 1 side; *AN upper left margin*: Blanchot [sic]; Fehsenfeld collection.

8 May 1951   6 Rue des Favorites

                                                 Paris 15me

Monsieur

    This belated note to say how touched I was by your article on *Molloy* in the *Figaro Littéraire*.[1] I think I know what, for someone working on that weekly, taking such a stand on this book actually means. And I know from my publisher that the interest you have in my work goes well beyond reviewing. Such indications of sympathy, coming from you, offset much past bitterness. In deeply felt gratitude.[2]

(Samuel Beckett)

1   Blanzat, "Un livre-événement," 9.

2   Blanzat, Literary Director of Editions Grasset from 1945 to 1953, wrote for *Le Figaro* from 1946 to 1960. In his review of *Molloy*, Blanzat wrote:

Il est difficile de parler de ce livre. D'un abord déconcertant et rebutant, c'est une de ces oeuvres rigoureusement cohérentes, scrupuleusement honnêtes, pleines d'intentions accumulées, qui ne se laissent approcher que par une fréquentation détendue et confiante … La beauté littéraire, la solidité de la construction, l'originalité des images justifient le mot de l'éditeur: "Il s'agit vraiment d'une des oeuvres capitales de l'après-guerre." (It is difficult to talk about this book. Disconcerting, repellent on first contact, it is one of those works – rigorously coherent, scrupulously honest, full of accumulated intentions – that can only be approached through unhurried, unsuspicious re-reading … The literary beauty, the strength of the construction, the originality of the images justify the publisher's claim: "This truly is one of the outstanding works of the post-War period.")

Jérôme Lindon wrote to Suzanne Deschevaux-Dumesnil on 17 April: "Tout le monde ici a été sensible au ton tout à fait exceptionnel de l'article de Blanzat qui pratiquement ne s'est pas 'engagé' sur beaucoup de livres depuis qu'il tient cette rubrique" (Everyone here has been affected by the wholly exceptional tone of the article by Blanzat, who has almost never taken a committed stand on many books since taking over this column) (IMEC, Beckett, Boîte 1, S. Beckett, Correspondance 1946–1953). And on 20 April, Lindon wrote to Suzanne Deschevaux-Dumesnil: "Il faut que Samuel Beckett sache que Blanzat dit tout simplement: 'Je considère que c'est ça, la critique: pouvoir dire, au moins une fois dans sa vie, qu'un grand écrivain vient d'apparaître'" (Samuel Beckett should know that Blanzat says quite simply: "I consider that this is what criticism is: to be able to say, at least once in one's life, that a great writer has just appeared") (IMEC, Beckett, Boîte 1, S. Beckett, Correspondance 1946–1953).

JEAN WAHL

PARIS

8 mai 1951   6 Rue des Favorites
                                                   Paris 15me

Monsieur

Je me souviens parfaitement de nos quelques rencontres en 1942. Vous étiez à la veille de passer dans l'autre zone et moi, sans le savoir encore, aussi. Je vous ai passé les sonnets de Shakespeare.[1]

Je n'ai pas grand'chose à vous offrir pour Deucalion. J'avais deux poèmes inédits, mais je les ai donnés à 84.[2] Je vous propose un extrait tiré d'un roman à paraître aux Editions de Minuit: Malone Meurt. Si en principe ça vous va, dites-le-moi, et la longueur qu'il vous faut.

Sincèrement

(Samuel Beckett)

TLcc; 1 leaf, 1 side; Fehsenfeld collection.

8 May 1951   6 Rue des Favorites

                                              Paris 15me

Dear Monsieur Wahl

I remember perfectly well our few meetings in 1942. You were just about to cross over to the other zone, and I, without yet knowing it, was too. I gave you Shakespeare's sonnets.[1]

I have nothing much to offer you for *Deucalion*. I did have two unpublished poems, but I gave them to *84*.[2] I suggest an extract from a novel to be published by the Editions de Minuit: *Malone meurt*. If that's all right in principle, let me know, and the length you'd want.

Yours sincerely

Samuel Beckett

1 Jean Wahl* (1888–1974), Professor of Philosophy at the Sorbonne from 1936 to 1967, published influential studies of Hegel and Kierkegaard. In 1942, he was interned at Drancy, escaped, and then took refuge in the United States from 1942 to 1945. He was the founding Editor of *Deucalion*. Wahl's letter to SB has not been found.

2 SB's poems submitted to *84: Nouvelle Revue Littéraire*: 22 March 1951, and n. 1.

JEROME LINDON, EDITIONS DE MINUIT
PARIS

le 12 mai 1951   6 Rue des Favorites

                                              Paris 15me

Cher Monsieur Lindon

Merci de votre lettre du 10 courant.

J'envoie aujourd'hui à Bordas, recommandée, la lettre rédigée par vous, sans rien y changer.[1]

Amicalement

s/ Sam. Beckett

TLS; 1 leaf, 1 side; IMEC, Beckett, Boîte 1, S. Beckett, Dossier Murphy 1946–1957.

12th May 1951   6 Rue des Favorites
                                                 Paris 15th

Dear Monsieur Lindon,

Thank you for your letter of the 10th.

I am sending on to Bordas today, by recorded delivery, the letter composed by you, without making any changes to it.[1]

Best wishes

Sam Beckett

---

1   SB refers to the letter drafted by Lindon ("Projet de Lettre") and enclosed with his letter to SB of 10 May (IMEC, Beckett, Boîte 1, S. Beckett, Dossier Murphy 1946–1957; this draft is incomplete).

JEROME LINDON, EDITIONS DE MINUIT
PARIS

25 Mai 51   *Ussy*

Cher Monsieur,

Bien reçu votre lettre du 22.

Avoir été défendu par un homme comme Blanchot cela aura été le principal pour Beckett quoi qu'il advienne.[1]

A propos d'Eleuthéria, B. est de plus en plus inquiet sur ce travail. Mais il pense qu'il y a peut-être moyen de le remanier. Il aimerait beaucoup que Bensoussan voie Blin (d'autant plus facile que celui-là connaît Adamov). La correction même l'exige, puisque Blin dispose toujours de la pièce (quoi qu'il n'ait pas l'intention de la monter) et annonçait l'autre jour qu'il voulait la montrer à Gélin. Beckett de son côté écrit à Blin pour le mettre au courant et lui demander, s'il n'a plus besoin de son exemplaire, de la passer à Bensoussan.[2]

Nous avons fortement l'impression d'abuser de votre gentillesse en vous laissant servir d'intermédiaire entre metteurs en scène et Beckett. Ne dites pas que ça fait partie de votre travail d'éditeur.

Ne craignez jamais de nous écrire, même s'il s'agit de mauvaises nouvelles, vos lettres nous font plaisir.

25 May 1951, Lindon

> *Croyez à mon amitié et à celle de Beckett*
> *s/ Suzanne Dumesnil*
Toujours rien de Bordas.

ALS; 1 leaf, 2 sides; IMEC, Beckett, Boîte 1, S. Beckett, Correspondance 1946–1953.

25 May 51   Ussy
Dear Monsieur Lindon,

Your letter of the 22nd received.

To have been defended by a man like Blanchot will have been the main thing for Beckett, whatever the outcome.[1]

About **Eleutheria**. B. is more and more worried about this work. But he thinks that there is perhaps a way of reshaping it. He would very much like it if Bensoussan would see Blin (all the easier since the latter knows Adamov). Indeed propriety demands it, since Blin still has charge of the play (although he does not intend to put it on), and was saying the other day that he wanted to show it to Gélin. Beckett for his part is writing to Blin to bring him up to date and to ask him, if he no longer needs his copy, to pass it on to Bensoussan.[2]

We have a strong feeling that we are exploiting your kindness by letting you act as intermediary between directors and Beckett. Do not tell me that this is part of your work as publisher.

Do not ever be afraid to write to us, even if it is with bad news. We enjoy your letters.

Please believe in my own and Beckett's friendship.

Suzanne Dumesnil

Still nothing from Bordas.

1 Blanchot was on the jury for the Prix des Critiques. Lindon wrote in his letter to Suzanne Deschevaux-Dumesnil of 22 May: "Jean Blanzat et Maurice Blanchot défendent le livre sans réserve" (Jean Blanzat and Maurice Blanchot are defending the book unreservedly) (IMEC, Beckett, Boîte 1, S. Beckett, Correspondance 1946–1953).

2 Lindon gave copies of the plays to Charles Bensoussan on 15 May. He reported to Suzanne Deschevaux-Dumesnil on 16 May that Bensoussan had requested permission to put on *Eleutheria* or *En attendant Godot*: "Il m'a donné quelques renseignements sur lui-même et sur son activité; il aurait une salle pour la rentrée" (He gave me some information about himself and his activities. It appears he might have a theatre for the autumn) (IMEC, Beckett, Boîte 1, S. Beckett, Correspondance 1946–1953).

Blin and Adamov had been friends since 1927 (Roger Blin, "Témoignage," in Pierre Mélèse, *Arthur Adamov: textes d'Arthur Adamov, points de vue critiques, témoignages, chronologie*, Théâtre de tous les temps ([Paris: Seghers, 1973] 156–158).

Although he had been given both plays to consider, Roger Blin had already taken steps toward producing *En attendant Godot*. SB's letter to Blin has not been found.

French actor Daniel Gélin (1921–2002).

JEROME LINDON, EDITIONS DE MINUIT

PARIS

30 Mai 51   *Ussy*

Cher Monsieur

   Merci de votre lettre du 30 avec celle adressée à Beckett que vous avez bien fait d'ouvrir.[1]

   Oui, <u>Combat</u> nous a appris le résultat des Prix, c'est dans l'ordre. C'est bien que Nadeau ait tenu bon. Mais la voix de Grenier qu'est-elle devenue? Vous me raconterez tout ça.[2]

   Tant mieux pour <u>Godot</u>. Nous ne savions pas.[3]

   Les comptes Bordas sont arrivés. En voici q.q. aperçus. Ils font état d'une vente de 285 exemplaires et d'un tirage de 3.500, ce qui ne concorde pas avec le minimum 6.000 du contrat. Et finalement Beckett doit à Bordas, et est prié de lui adresser la somme de 20.500 francs, c'est-à-dire supérieure de 5.500 à l'àvaloir qu'il a reçu. Ce document est trop précieux pour que je le confie à la poste. Je vous le donnerai à mon retour.[4]

   Nous rentrons à la fin de cette semaine et j'espère pouvoir passer vous voir lundi prochain dans l'après-midi.

   Croyez à nos très bons sentiments.

   s/ <u>Suzanne Dumesnil</u>

ALS; 1 leaf, 2 sides; IMEC, Beckett, Boîte 1, S. Beckett, Dossier Murphy 1946–1957.

30 May 51   *Ussy*

Dear Monsieur Lindon

   Thank you for your letter of the 30th, together with the one addressed to Beckett, which you did well to open.[1]

Yes, Combat *informed us of the result of the Prix; as expected. It was good that Nadeau held out. But what happened to Grenier's vote? You must tell me about it all.*[2]

So much the better for *Godot. We did not know.*[3]

The Bordas accounts have arrived. Here are a few excerpts. They claim a sale of 285 copies and a print run of 3,500, which does not square with the 6,000 minimum of the contract. And finally Beckett owes Bordas, and is asked to send him, the sum of 20,500 francs, that is, 5,500 more than the advance that he received. This document is too valuable for me to entrust it to the post. I shall give it to you on my return.[4]

We come back at the end of this week, and I hope to be able to come round to see you next Monday afternoon.

With our best wishes
Suzanne Dumesnil

1   On 29 May, Lindon forwarded the letter opened, which he describes only as "une lettre personnelle" (IMEC, Beckett, Boîte 1, S. Beckett, Correspondance 1946-1953). Suzanne Deschevaux-Dumesnil gives the date of this letter incorrectly as 30 May.

2   In his letter of 29 May Lindon writes, "Cependant, Samuel Beckett a bénéficié jusqu'à la fin des voix de Maurice Blanchot, Jean Blanzat et Maurice Nadeau" (However, right to the end Samuel Beckett had the advantage of the votes of Maurice Blanchot, Jean Blanzat, and Maurice Nadeau). The Prix des Critiques was awarded to André Pieyre de Mandiargues for his book *Soleil des loups* "par 8 voix contre 3 à Samuel Beckett et 1 à Ladislas Dormandi" (by 8 votes against 3 to Samuel Beckett and 1 to Ladislas Dormandi) (Geneviève Bonnefoi, "André Pieyre de Mandiargues obtient le Prix des Critiques pour 'Soleil des Loups,'" *Combat*, 29 May 1951: 1, 8).
Jean Grenier (1898-1971) was one of the judges of the Prix des Critiques; he had been one of Camus's teachers at the Lycée Bugeaud in Algiers.

3   Lindon wrote in his letter of 29 May, "Enfin, j'ai su que 'En attendant Godot' est maintenant annoncé officiellement pour la rentrée" (Anyhow, I learned that *En attendant Godot* is now officially announced for the autumn).

4   Pierre Bordas to SB, 26 May 1951 (IMEC, Beckett, Boîte 1, S. Beckett, Correspondance 1946-1953).

JEROME LINDON, EDITIONS DE MINUIT
PARIS

le 7 juin 1951   6 Rue des Favorites
                                Paris 15me

Cher Monsieur Lindon

Après tout je ne vois pas pourquoi je changerais quoi que ce soit à votre lettre aux Ed. Bordas et je n'attends plus que votre accord pour l'envoyer, recommandée, telle quelle.[1]

Amitiés

s/ Sam. Beckett

TLS; 1 leaf, 1 side; IMEC, Beckett, Boîte 1, S. Beckett, Dossier Murphy 1946–1957.

7th June 1951   6 Rue des Favorites
                                Paris 15me

Dear Monsieur Lindon,

After all, I see no reason why I should make any changes at all to your letter to the Editions Bordas, and I am now only waiting for your agreement to send it on, by recorded delivery, as it stands.[1]

Regards

Sam. Beckett

1 The letter drafted for SB's consideration by Jérôme Lindon was signed by SB and sent as written ([6 June 1951], IMEC, Beckett, Boîte 1, S. Beckett, Dossier Murphy 1946–1957).

GEORGES BATAILLE
PARIS

le 9 juin 1951   6 Rue des Favorites
                                Paris 15me

Cher Monsieur

Merci de votre aimable lettre.

Je révise <u>Malone Meurt</u> en ce moment et pense pouvoir en détacher une quarantaine de pages pour <u>Botteghe Oscure</u>. J'aurais préféré quelque chose de moins inchoatif, mais je n'ai rien. J'espère que ça pourra faire l'affaire. Je l'enverrai la semaine prochaine.[1]

J'aimerais vous revoir et pouvoir vous tenir des propos moins incohérents que lors de notre rencontre aux Editions de Minuit. Surtout vous écouter, ça serait beaucoup mieux. Voyager, ou ne plus le pouvoir, dans l'affolement, c'est pardonnable, pour en dire le moins, mais à charge, on dirait, une fois de retour, ou l'affaire abandonnée, de se faire grâce, et aux autres, de ses impressions. Vous l'admettez, je le sens, et qu'on y comprenne, après, aussi peu que pendant, mais avec moins d'à-propos.

J'espère que je serai à Paris lors de votre prochain passage.[2] Je suis souvent à la campagne, mais brièvement. Ne manquez pas, en tout cas, de me prévenir.

    Très cordialement

TLcc; 1 leaf, 1 side; Fehsenfeld collection.

9th June 1951   6 Rue des Favorites

                                       Paris 15me

Dear Monsieur Bataille

    Thank you for your kind letter.

I am revising *Malone meurt* at the moment and think I can take forty pages or so for *Botteghe Oscure*. I would have preferred something less inchoate, but I haven't anything. I hope that this will do. I'll send it next week.[1]

I should like to see you again and be able to talk rather less incoherently than I did at our meeting at the Editions de Minuit. Most of all listen to you, that would be much better. To travel, or no longer be able to travel, within a condition of mad panic is forgivable, to say the least, but on condition, one might say, that once back, or the whole idea dropped, one spares oneself and others one's impressions. You admit as much, I feel, and, let it be clear, afterwards, one understands as little as during, but less pertinently.

I hope I'm in Paris when you next come through.[2] I'm often in the country, though not for long at a time. In any event, do please let me know in advance.

     With my best wishes

1   Bataille's letter to SB has not been found. However, on 6 June 1951, Bataille wrote to Princess Marguerite Caetani (1890–1963, née Chapin), founder of *Botteghe Oscure* (1948–1960), an international literary magazine based in Rome, with Giorgio Bassani as Editor: "J'ai écrit à Samuel Beckett, que j'ai rencontré à Paris il y a trois semaines. Je suis persuadé qu'il vous enverra un manuscrit, d'autant qu'il a aux Ed de Minuit un livre tout prêt dont il devrait être possible de donner un fragment. Je ne l'ai pas encore lu mais on m'a dit que cela était au moins aussi remarquable que *Molloy*." (I have written to Samuel Beckett, whom I met in Paris three weeks ago. I am confident he will send you a manuscript, all the more since he has a book ready at the Editions de Minuit from which it should be possible to extract a fragment. I have not yet read it, but I've been told that it is at least as remarkable as *Molloy*.) (Georges Bataille, *Choix de lettres: 1917–1962*, ed. Michel Surya [Paris: Gallimard, 1977] 434; Bataille published a review, "Le Silence de Molloy," *Critique* 7 [15 May 1951] 387–396.)

2   In June 1951, Bataille was a librarian in Carpentras, Provence; he moved to Orléans in September 1951 to become Conservateur of the Bibliothèque Municipale (Michel Surya, *Georges Bataille: la mort à l'œuvre* [Paris: Librairie Séguier, 1987] 428, 429, 515).

PRINCESS CAETANI, BOTTEGHE OSCURE
ROME

le 14 juin 1951   6 Rue des Favorites
                                      Paris 15me

Madame

    J'apprends par Monsieur Georges Bataille que vous désireriez avoir un texte inédit de moi, soit un long récit soit un extrait de roman, pour votre revue <u>Botteghe Oscure</u>.

    Je vous enverrai donc très prochainement le début d'un roman intitulé <u>Malone Meurt</u> à paraître prochainement (probablement fin octobre) aux Editions de Minuit. J'espère que la longueur de ce texte (10.000 mots à peu près) vous conviendra.

    Je vous prierai de bien vouloir m'envoyer des épreuves.

    Croyez, Madame, à l'assurance de mes sentiments distingués.

               (Samuel Beckett)

TLcc; 1 leaf, 1 side; Fehsenfeld collection.

14th June 1951   6 Rue des Favorites
                                            Paris 15me

Dear Princess Caetani

I learn from Monsieur Georges Bataille that you would like to have an unpublished text by me, either a long story or an extract from a novel, for your review *Botteghe Oscure*.

I shall be sending you very soon the opening sequence of a novel entitled *Malone meurt* that is to be published soon (probably in late October) by the Editions de Minuit. I hope that the length of this text (approximately 10,000 words) seems suitable.

I would ask you to be kind enough to send me proofs.

Yours sincerely

(Samuel Beckett)

SIMONE DE BEAUVOIR
PARIS

le 25 juin 1951   6 Rue des Favorites
                                            Paris 15me

Madame

Merci de votre aimable lettre. Je suis heureux que <u>Molloy</u> vous ait plu, à vous et à Sartre.[1]

Je peux vous donner, pour <u>Les Temps Modernes</u>, soit un extrait de <u>Malone Meurt</u>, roman à paraître aux Editions de Minuit probablement fin octobre, soit <u>En Attendant Godot</u>, pièce en deux actes que doit monter Roger Blin. J'attends votre réponse pour vous envoyer l'un ou l'autre de ces textes.

Croyez, Madame, à mes sentiments les meilleurs.

s/ Sam. Beckett

(Samuel Beckett)

TLccS; 1 leaf, 1 side; Fehsenfeld collection.

25th June 1951   6 Rue des Favorites
                                  Paris 15me

Dear Madame de Beauvoir

Thank you for your kind letter. I am glad that both you and Sartre liked *Molloy*.[1]

I can let you have, for *Les Temps Modernes*, either an extract from *Malone meurt*, a novel to be published by the Editions de Minuit probably in late October, or *En attendant Godot*, a play in two acts which Roger Blin is to put on. I shall wait to hear from you before sending you one or other of these texts.

      Yours sincerely
      s/ Sam Beckett
      (Samuel Beckett)

---

1   Simone de Beauvoir's letter to SB has not been found.

JEROME LINDON, EDITIONS DE MINUIT
PARIS

1/7/51   6 Rue des Favorites
                                  Paris 15me

Cher Monsieur Lindon

Je vous apporterai le texte definitif [*for* définitif] de Malone mercredi prochain le quatre en fin d'après-midi. J'aimerais beaucoup vous voir. Si un autre jour vous convient mieux, soyez assez gentil de me prévenir. Sinon, à mercredi.

      Amitiés
      s/ Sam. Beckett

TLS; 1 leaf, 1 side; IMEC, Beckett, Boîte 1, S. Beckett, Correspondance 1946–1953.

1/7/51   6 Rue des Favorites
                                          Paris 15me

Dear Monsieur Lindon,

I shall bring the final text of *Malone* next Wednesday, the 4th, in the late afternoon. I should very much like to see you. If another day suits you better, please be kind enough to let me know. If not, till Wednesday.

Regards

s/ Sam. Beckett

PRINCESS CAETANI, BOTTEGHE OSCURE
ROME

July 3rd 1951   6 Rue des Favorites
                                          Paris 15me

Dear Princess Caetani

Thank you for your letters of June 25th and 26th, the latter accompanying MS.[1]

Your second letter leaves me in some doubt as to whether I am still invited to contribu[t]e to the November number of <u>Botteghe Oscure</u>.[2]

I hold at your disposal an extract from a third novel, <u>L'Innommable</u>, to be published early next year by the Rditions [*for* Editions] de Minuit, but shall not send it before hearing from you.[3]

Yours sincerely

TLcc; 1 leaf, 1 side; Fehsenfeld collection.

1   The letters from Princess Caetani to SB have not been found, but it is likely that her letter of 26 June returned the selection from *Malone meurt*.

2   Nothing by SB was published in the November issue (7) of *Botteghe Oscure*.

3   It is not known whether SB sent an extract from this novel to *Botteghe Oscure*.

JEAN WAHL, DEUCALION
PARIS

le 8 juillet 1951   6 Rue des Favorites

                                                     Paris 15me

Mon cher Jean Wahl

Voici un petit texte récent qui fera peut-être votre affaire. Lambeau de l'arrière-faix de L'Innommable, il est peu fait pour paraître avant ce dernier. Tel quel, à vous, si vous le voulez.[1]

Amicalement

TLcc; 1 leaf, 1 side; Fehsenfeld collection.

8th July 1951   6 Rue des Favorites

                                                     Paris 15me

My dear Jean Wahl

Here is a recent little text which will perhaps do the trick. A bit torn off the placenta of L'Innommable, not really fit to come out before that does. As it stands, all yours, if you want it.[1]

Best wishes

1   SB sent "Je tiens le Greffe" (*Textes pour rien*, V) to Wahl. This was published, with the second sentence of this letter given as a note ("Je tiens le Greffe," *Deucalion* 36.4 [October 1952] 137–140). On 1 August, SB wrote to Wahl: "Soyez assez gentil de me fixer à ce sujet, afin que je sache si je peux disposer de ce texte ou non" (Do please tell me what's happening, so that I may know whether or not I am free to make other arrangements for this text) (Fehsenfeld collection).

GEORGES BELMONT
PARIS

11/7/51   Paris

Mon cher Georges

Merci de ta lettre avec tes poèmes. Je les emporte, ainsi que la pièce, demain, à la campagne, d'où illisiblement je t'écrirai.[1]

Bien content que Laffont prenne ton livre. En quoi est-ce que ça regarde Julliard, pardonne mon innocence.²

Longue critique sur James dans le dernier numéro de Critique, veux-tu que je te l'envoie, et enthousiasme de Jean Rostand pour la Cosmogonie de Queneau. Ce dernier, je l'ai vu un instant, l'autre jour, avec Duthuit, il haletait littéralement et on voyait sa langue. Très gentil avec moi. Petit article de Jolas, plus révolutionnaire que nature, sur les poèmes de Trakl.³

Je serai certainement à Paris vers la fin du mois et j'espère qu'on pourra se voir. J'ai donné cinquante pages aux Temps Modernes qu'ils ont docilement acceptées et il va falloir que j'aille voir une Madame Sorbets (la connais-tu?) chez Julliard, pour en extirper les épreuves, à la fin du mois.⁴ Fais-moi signe un peu à l'avance, si tu dois être là.

Bon voyage et bonnes vacances à Josée et à Sophie si elles ne sont pas déjà parties.⁵

Ton ami

s/ Sam

Le riz prédigéré est encore meilleur, toujours chez Mono.

TLS; 1 leaf, 1 side; TxU, Lake collection, Beckett.

11/7/51   Paris

My dear Georges

Thank you for your letter with your poems. I am taking them away, along with the play, tomorrow, to the country, from where I shall write to you illegibly.¹

Very pleased that Laffont is taking your book. What business is it of Julliard? Pardon my innocence.²

Long article on James in the last issue of *Critique*, shall I send it, and enthusiasm from Jean Rostand about Queneau's *Cosmogonie*. The latter I saw briefly the other day, with Duthuit, he was literally gasping and you could see his tongue. Very nice to me. Little article by Jolas, ultra-revolutionary, on the poems of Trakl.³

I shall certainly be in Paris towards the end of the month, and I hope we can meet. I have given fifty pages to *Les Temps Modernes* which they docilely accepted, and I shall have to go and see a Madame Sorbets (do you know her?) at Julliard, to dig out the proofs, at the end of the month.[4] Let me know a bit in advance if you are to be there.

Bon voyage and bonnes vacances to Josée and Sophie, if they have not already left.[5]

Your friend

Sam

Predigested rice is even better, again from Monoprix.

---

1 The poems and play sent to SB by Georges Belmont (1909–2008; Profile, I): 8 August 1951, n. 1 and n. 2.

2 From 1946 to 1951, Belmont was a freelance translator of British and American fiction for, among others, Editions Robert Laffont, where from 1951 he was hired as an Advisory Editor. Editions Julliard were allied with Editions Robert Laffont from 1948 to 1962 (Vanessa Springora, Editions Julliard, 27 January 2010).

3 Belmont's translation of *The Ambassadors* by Henry James was reviewed by Monique Nathan: "'Les Ambassadeurs' et les Carnets de James," *Critique* 7.49 (June 1951) 492–498. Jean Rostand (1894–1977) published "Raymond Queneau et la cosmogonie" in the same issue (483–491); Eugene Jolas reviewed Georg Trakl, *Die Dichtungen* (1950), in this number as well (552–554).

4 *Les Temps Modernes* was published by Julliard from January 1949 to September 1965; it had previously been published by Gallimard. Germaine Sorbets was secretary to *Les Temps Modernes* from 1945 to 1974.

5 Joséphine Caliot (n.d.) was Belmont's companion who became his second wife in June 1954; Sophie is their daughter.

GERMAINE SORBETS, JULLIARD, LES TEMPS MODERNES
PARIS

[after 13 July 1951]

Note pour l'imprimeur

Prière de rétablir conformément au ms. la combinais[on] virgule suivie d'une majuscule chaque fois qu'elle se présente:

Ex: Je me disais, Je ne l'aurai jamais
et non pas

Je me disais: Je ne l'aurai jamais[1]

AL draft on verso of G. Sorbets, chez Julliard, to SB, Vendredi 13 juillet [1951]; 1 leaf, 1 side; Fehsenfeld collection. *Dating:* the letter from Sorbets to SB.

[after 13 July 1951]

Note for Printer

Please restore, in line with the ms., the combination comma followed by a capital each time it occurs.

Ex.: Je me disais, Je ne l'aurai jamais

and not:

Je me disais: Je ne l'aurai jamais[1]

1 On 13 July, Mme. Sorbets sent SB proofs for the extract from *Malone meurt* that was to be published as "Quel malheur … ," *Les Temps Modernes*, 71 ([September 1951] 385–416). SB's example: in "Quel Malheur …" (386); in *Malone meurt*, 90.

GEORGES DUTHUIT

20 juillet [1951]   Ussy

Cher Vieux

Bien reçu ta lettre avec ms. Je m'y attaque et espère pouvoir t'envoyer ça, tapé à la machine, dans les premiers jours d'août. Sera-ce assez tôt? Les citations de Mallarmé, sauf celles venant se placer dans ton texte, je les laisse en français, n'est-ce pas? Ce que tu dis m'a l'air très juste. Mais je ne suis pas assez au courant. On pourrait peut-être chicaner sur la pureté de Vuillard.[1]

Il fait beau. Vie shortesque, dehors toute la journée. Résultat: impossible de dormir. Le manque de sommeil, ce n'est pas terrible, mais les images de l'insomnie, non, je préfère le cauchemar.

Dommage que tu n'aies pas pu voir les dernières gouaches de Bram. J'y pense assez, c'est du roman. J'espère que tu feras quelque chose sur lui là-bas à Aix. Je le reverrai probablement à notre retour. J'ai envie de revoir la grande toile restée à Paris.[2]

Merci aussi de l'imprimé que tu as fait suivre, *Irish Writing*, avec une demande de contribution. Je n'ai envie de rien leur donner. Tout ça est proprement écoeurant. Une nouvelle de James Stephens d'un torcheculatif effarant, quel vieux gnome abject.³

Je lis Les Carottes sont cuites. Excellent, le début surmonté.⁴

J'ai corrigé les épreuves pour les Temps modernes. Pas trop affligeantes.⁵

Ton indulgence pour cette pauvre lettre. Je suis abruti, mais mal, comme un gros minou mal coupé.

Affectueusement.

Sam.

ALS; 2 leaves, 2 sides; Duthuit collection. *Dating*: "Quel Malheur ..." published in *Les Temps Modernes* (September 1951).

20 July [1951]   Ussy
Dear old friend

Your letter with ms. duly received. I am setting about it and hope to be able to send it to you, typed, early in August. Will that be soon enough? The quotations from Mallarmé, apart from the ones that have a place in your piece, I should leave in French, should I not? What you say seems very right and proper. But I am not well up in all that. Vuillard's purity is perhaps arguable.¹

The weather is beautiful. Life in shorts, outdoors all day. Result: impossible to sleep. The lack of sleep is no great matter, but the images that insomnia brings – no, I prefer nightmares.

Pity you were not able to see Bram's latest gouaches. I think about them quite often, they are fantastic inventions. I hope you will do something on him while you are down in Aix. I shall probably see him when we get back. I really want to have another look at the big canvas that has stayed in Paris.²

Thank you too for the publication you forwarded, *Irish Writing*, with request for a contribution. I do not feel like giving them anything. The whole thing is genuinely sickening. A short story by James Stephens, that you could not wipe yourself with. Despicable old gnome.³

I am reading *Les Carottes sont cuites*. Excellent, once past the beginning.[4]

I have corrected the *Temps Modernes* proofs. Not too awful.[5]

Your indulgence for this wretched letter. I am in a bad way, really bad, like a big cat that has been poorly neutered.

Love
Sam

1 SB is translating Duthuit's article "Vuillard and the Poets of Decadence," which seeks to combine the painting of Jean-Edouard Vuillard (1868-1940) and Gustave Moreau (1826-1898) with the verse of Stéphane Mallarmé (verse cited on three occasions, in its French original and in translation); the article will wait for three years to appear in *Art News* (53.1 [March 1954] 28-33, 62-63). Here the inside-cover credit runs: "Georges Duthuit, Byzantinologist and advance-guard poet, was hailed by Sir Herbert Read as one of the few critics to bring poetic insights to bear on works of art."

2 It is not known which are the gouaches or the large canvas to which SB refers. Duthuit's intention to write on Bram van Velde: 10 September 1951, n. 3.

3 The quarterly *Irish Writing* was founded in 1946 and edited by David Marcus (1924-2009) and Terence Smith (n.d.), and continued by Seán J. White (1927-1996) from 1954 to 1957. "A Rhinoceros, Some Ladies, and a Horse" by James Stephens (1882-1940) (*Irish Writing* 14 [March 1951] 35-42).

4 SB has been reading *Les Carottes sont cuites*, a translation of *Repeat Performance* (1942) by American crime novelist William O'Farrell (1902-1962) (tr. Maurice Tourneur, Série Noire [Paris: Gallimard, 1951]).

5 *Les Temps Modernes* proofs: see [after 13 July 1951].

GEORGES DUTHUIT

26 juillet [1951]   Ussy-sur-Marne
Cher vieux Georges

Bien content d'avoir ta lettre et de vous savoir bien arrivés à Aix.

Pas question de changer quoi que ce soit à ton texte. A la fin tu dis: "Mallarmé fit de la poésie pure, Vuillard de la peinture pure! Le signe distinctif de Moreau reste, en définitive, l'impureté." Je me suis seulement demandé si "pur" ne changeait pas un peu de sens et de portée, de Mallarmé à Vuillard. Du petit-bêtisme pur et simple.[1]

J'en ai traduit les 3/4. Tu recevras le tout la semaine prochaine, aussi soigné que me le permettent ma lente tête et mon anglais pâlissant.

Je crois que Lindon dépend entièrement de Lambrichs pour le côté littéraire de l'affaire et qu'il ne lit pour ainsi dire jamais rien. Suzanne ira aux nouvelles la semaine prochaine. Elle avait dit à Lindon: "Je crois que c'est très violent." Réponse: "Tant mieux, tant mieux."[2]

J'ai corrigé les épreuves des Temps Modernes. Ca fait une assez grande tartine. C'est pas trop mal quand même, pour avoir été écrit avec des antennes de libellule.[3]

Nom de famille de Marthe: KUNTZ. N'oublie pas le Z.[4]

Nous rentrons à Paris lundi, pour une 15$\underline{\text{aine}}$ de jours, pas plus, puis rappliquerons ici. Envie de cinéma et de terrasse de café. J'ai été très impressionné par Les Carottes sont cuites, tu te rappelles, l'histoire de l'acteur dont la femme boit de l'alcool non purifié, avec un curieux personnage de poète-tapette, William-and-Mary. Formidables passages sur le retour au foyer de la femme aveugle, à sa sortie de la clinique, sur mutisme et le tropisme de la bergère.[5]

Reçu un pneu, un papier des Editions de Minuit, d'un nommé Luc Baquet (?), m'annonçant que Roger Grenier devrait m'interviewer, le surlendemain, dans le cadre de son émission "La Vie des Lettres", et me laissant entendre qu'il y allait de mon salut, sinon de mon devoir.[6] J'entends d'ici mes bêlements de plus en plus nasaux à mesure que les conneries s'accumulent: l'exil: connais pas; la ruse: pour d'autres: silence: volontiers.[7]

J'ai lu, dans Combat, Nadeau sur Glaser, et une interview donnée par ce dernier, pétant de naïf réalisme germanique et de mépris pour ceux à qui suffisent la vie et la mort pas spécialement contemporaines. On commence à bien connaître la rengaine. Envoie le livre quand même, ça doit reposer de la misère sans patère.[8]

Derrière la brouette, peinte par Suzanne en rouge, je ne pense pas à Pascal, depuis l'article de Rostand biologiste sur Queneau dans la Table Ronde.[9] Jamais vu tant de papillons aussi vers, ce petit cylindre central, seule chair, c'est le ver. Premiers vols des jeunes hirondelles, les parents qui les ravitaillent en plein vol. Hier, vers 14 heures, il y a un an, ma mère mourait, même pas capable d'oublier ça, ou d'y penser trop tard.[10]

Bien affectueusement, cher vieux. Passe sur mes conneries, rappelle-toi mon affection.

Sam

ALS; 1 leaf, 2 sides; Duthuit collection. *Dating*: 1951 is confirmed by Maurice Nadeau's piece, "'Secret et Violence' de Georges Glaser" (see n. 8, below).

26 July [1951]   Ussy-sur-Marne

Dear old Georges

Very glad to get your letter and to know that you have all arrived safely in Aix.

No question of changing anything whatsoever in your piece. At the end you say: "Mallarmé produced pure poetry, Vuillard, pure painting! The distinguishing mark of Moreau, finally, remains impurity." I just wondered if "pure" did not change its meaning and its scope a little between Mallarmé and Vuillard. Just silly-little-me-ism.[1]

I have translated 3/4 of it. You will have the whole lot next week, in as finished a state as my slow brain and my fading English allow.

I think that Lindon is entirely dependent on Lambrichs for the literary side of things and that he himself never reads anything, so to speak. Suzanne will make enquiries next week. She had said to Lindon: "I think it is very violent." Response: "So much the better, so much the better."[2]

I have corrected the *Temps Modernes* proofs. It is a sizeable chunk. Not bad, mind you, for something done with a dragonfly's antennae.[3]

Marthe's surname: KUNTZ. Do not forget the Z.[4]

We are coming back to Paris on Monday, for a fortnight, not more, then dashing back here. Feel an urge to go to the cinema, to sit at a café terrasse. I was greatly impressed by *Les Carottes sont cuites*, you remember, the story of the actor whose wife drinks raw alcohol, with a strange character, poet-poof, William and Mary. Tremendous passages on the blind woman's return home from the clinic, on mutism and the tropism of the bergère.[5]

Had a pneumatique, a note from the Editions de Minuit, from someone called Luc Baquet (?), telling me that Roger Grenier was to interview me, the day after tomorrow, as part of his *La Vie des lettres*, and giving out that it was in my best interests, if not indeed my duty.[6] I can hear my bleatings from here, more and more nasal as the nonsense accumulates: exile? don't know; cunning? not my style; silence? gladly.[7]

I read, in *Combat*, Nadeau on Glaser, and an interview given by the latter, bursting with naive Germanic realism and contempt for those for whom life and death, and not just the contemporary kind, are enough. We are beginning to be pretty familiar with the refrain. Send the book all the same; it will make a change from unrelieved wretchedness.[8]

Behind the wheelbarrow, painted by Suzanne in red, I do not think of Pascal, ever since the article by the biologist Rostand in the *Table Ronde*.[9] Never seen so many butterflies in such worm-state, this little central cylinder, the only flesh, is the worm. First flights of the young swallows, the parents who feed them on the wing. Yesterday, about 2 p.m., a year ago my mother was dying, not even capable of forgetting that, or of thinking of it too late.[10]

Warmest feelings, my old friend. Ignore all my nonsense, just remember my love.

    Sam

---

1 SB's translation of Duthuit's article: 20 July [1951], n. 1. As published, SB's version of the sentences runs: "Mallarmé created 'pure' poetry, Vuillard 'pure' painting: the distinctive mark of Gustave Moreau remains, when all is said and done, *impurity*" ("Vuillard and the Poets of Decadence," 63).

2 Whoever first "discovered" SB at Minuit, Lambrichs or Lindon (see 10 April 1951, n. 5), what Anne Simonin posits in her history of Editions de Minuit is that reading and then publishing SB was a turning point for Lindon, transforming him from a rather distant director into a fully engaged literary editor. She cites Lindon:

> En lisant *Molloy*, j'ai eu le sentiment que c'était l'événement de ma vie d'éditeur qui était en train de se produire. Et je continue de penser que c'était vrai. C'est dans les derniers mois de l'année 1950 que s'est produit le seul moment essentiel de ma vie d'éditeur. Par la suite, tous les chocs du même genre étaient,

malgré tout, relativisés par l'antériorité de ma découverte de Beckett. (Simonin, *Les Editions de Minuit*, 383.) (As I was reading *Molloy*, I suddenly had the feeling that what was happening was *the* event of my publishing life. And I go on thinking that this was so. It was in the last months of 1950 that there took place the only essential moment of my life as a publisher. In later times, all shocks of the kind were, in spite of everything, relativized by the precedence of my discovery of Beckett.)

3   "Quel Malheur …" in *Les Temps Modernes*: [after 13 July 1951], n. 1.

4   Marthe Arnaud (née Kuntz), Bram van Velde's companion.

5   In *Les Carottes sont cuites*, a New York actor named Barney Page, deranged by his wife's suicide, strangles his mistress; then, fleeing from the police, he finds himself transported one year back in time with the ability to alter the events leading up to the suicide and murder. Barney's wife Sheila, suffering from manic depression and alcoholism, has drunk a bottle of perfume which has left her blind and choosing to be mute; William and Mary is a cross-dresser who, depending on his attire, is addressed as either "William" or "Mary"; SB also notices admiringly the narrator's device of having the deeply disturbed Sheila turn continually (her "tropisme") to the bergère in the flat as the only safe place to sit or lie.

6   Luc Baquet (n.d.), an employee at Editions de Minuit, had written to SB on 20 July about the importance of the interview, which would give him an opportunity to talk about his work and announce future projects (IMEC, Beckett, Boîte 1, S. Beckett, Correspondance 1947–1953). Roger Grenier (b. 1919), who had worked on *Combat*, from September 1947 ran a literary show, *La Vie des lettres*, which aired on both the "programme national" and the "programme parisien" (Roger Grenier, *Fidèle au poste* [Paris: Gallimard, 2001] 34).

7   SB imagines his interviewer borrowing terms from the conclusion of James Joyce's *A Portrait of the Artist as a Young Man*, where Stephen Dedalus declares: "I will try to express myself in some mode of life or art as freely as I can and as wholly as I can, using for my defence the only arms I allow myself to use - silence, exile, and cunning" (ed. Chester G. Anderson and Richard Ellmann [New York: Viking, 1964] 247).

8   Georg Glaser (1910–1995), a German writer and artisan who had settled in France, was author of *Geheimnis und Gewalt: ein Bericht* (1950) translated by Lucienne Foucrault as *Secret et violence* (1951). Maurice Nadeau published "'Secret et Violence' de Georges Glaser" in *Combat* 28 June 1951: 4. Glaser had been interviewed one week previously by Geneviève Bonnefoi: "Georges Glaser: Allemand fixé à Paris, écrit des livres et cisèle des bijoux" (*Combat* 21 June 1951: 4, 6). Glaser is cited as saying, for example, of novelists of the first half of the century: "Autrefois, ce qui faisait la base de ces romans, c'étaient les rapports sociaux, les relations de l'homme avec sa famille et ses proches, ses amours. Aujourd'hui la question est bien plus vaste: c'est celle de l'homme dans l'univers." (6.) (Time was when what formed the basis of these novels was social connections, man's relationship with family and those close to him, his loves. Nowadays the question is far wider in scope: it is that of man in the universe.)

9   Jean Rostand published "Raymond Queneau et la cosmogonie" not in *La Table Ronde* but in *Critique* (see 11 July 1951, n. 3). His article concludes by correcting Queneau on his acceptance of the popular attribution of the invention of the wheelbarrow to Blaise Pascal.

10   SB's mother May Beckett died on 25 August 1950.

GEORGES DUTHUIT
AIX

mercredi [1 August 1951]   Paris

Cher vieux

Ta lettre ce matin. Voici le boulot. Dire que j'en suis content, non. Mais je suis incapable de faire mieux en ce moment.[1] Je me rappelle fort bien ta lettre Bram, je l'avais encore il n'y a pas longtemps, mais n'arrive pas à mettre la main dessus.[2] Je vais encore chercher. Mais elle a pu être victime du dernier accès du rasoir d'Occam tel que je le promène, quand ça me prend, sur tout ce qui traîne, et souvent à mon dam. Pardonne-moi, cher vieux, si elle n'est plus.

A Paris depuis lundi. Ca n'a pas l'air de trop bien nous réussir. Impossible de dormir. Mais ça déjà à Ussy. Et sans rosé qui m'en console. Nous nous sommes naturellement précipités au cinéma hier soir, Les Chaînes du Destin avec Barbara Stanwyck. Histoire d'une usurpation d'identité conséquemment à un accident de chemin de fer. Je ne l'ai jamais vue aussi bonne, quelques regards d'un pathé-thique [*for* pathétique] extraordinaire.[3]

Personne à l'horizon. Editions de M. désertes, dans l'ex-bordel de la Rue Bernard Palissy.[4] Rien de Blin. Il va falloir essayer de travailler, reprendre les gigotements et les chaînes de fumée. Pour entendre s'exclamer Monsieur Galbriel [*for* Gabriel] Marcel: "Le désordre des idées entraîne celui des choses" (Opera, 1/8/51).[5] Non, c'est bien le vrai meurtrier qu'on arrête à la fin des Carottes. Et il voit venir vers lui les policiers comme des amis enfin et des sauveteurs.[6]

Je sens que nous allons vers une dure année, je voudrais pouvoir bien savourer cet été, à Ussy on y arrive par moments, peut-être qu'on y retournera la semaine prochaine. Suzanne a envie de la mer, possible que nous allions passer quelques jours à Dieppe le mois prochain. J'ai l'impression que le moindre bain de mer m'achèverait, mais j'ai envie d'essayer. Trop de haut vol à l'âge de six ans et de bains glacés tout au long des hivers, trop de choses bonnes et trop de mauvaises. Les galets de la plage se creusent en entonnoirs, je m'y trouvais bien, il y a 13 ans, entre l'Hôtel Select et celui des Arcades, spécialité crustacés. Je ferais mieux de ne plus y jamais foutre les pieds.[7]

Bon courage, cher vieux, pour Bram et le reste. Paraît qu'il s'en va tout seul en Bretagne, chez une amie, au mois de Septembre. Je vais lui faire signe de ce pas, s'il vient à Paris je voudrais le voir, et la grande toile d'avant son départ.[8]

Affectueusement

s/ Sam

TLS; 1 leaf, 1 side; *A corr red ink; AH on verso, red ink*: "a housewife merged in the chores of her house"; Duthuit collection. *Dating*: SB wrote to Duthuit on 26 July [1951] that he was three-quarters finished with the translation he was doing for him, and that he planned to return to Paris on Monday 30 July, for a fortnight. In the present letter he sends the work to Duthuit, and indicates that he has been in Paris since Monday 30 July.

Wednesday [1 August 1951]   Paris

Dear old friend

Your letter this morning. Here is the work. Cannot say I am satisfied with it, no. But I am not capable of doing any better just now.[1] I well remember your Bram letter, I had it not so long ago, but I cannot put my hands on it.[2] I am going to look again. But it may have been a victim of the last fit of Occam's razoring as I practise it, when the humour takes me, on anything that is lying about, often to my own disadvantage. Forgive me, dear friend, if it no longer exists.

Been in Paris since Monday. It does not seem to do either of us any good. Impossible to sleep. But Ussy was no different. And no rosé to console me. Naturally we made straight for the cinema yesterday evening, *Les Chaînes du destin*, with Barbara Stanwyck. An affair of impersonation following a railway accident. I have never seen her so good, a few looks that showed extraordinary pathos.[3]

No one in sight. Editions de Minuit deserted, in the ex-brothel in the Rue Bernard Palissy.[4] Nothing from Blin. I shall have to try to work, go back to the wrigglings and twistings and chains of smoke. In order to hear Monsieur Gabriel Marcel exclaim: "Disorder in the mind brings in its train disorder in things" (*Opéra*, 1/8/51).[5] No, it really is the actual murderer that gets arrested at the end of the *Carottes*. And he sees the two policemen coming towards him as friends and rescuers in the end.[6]

I feel we are in for a hard year, I should really like to be able to enjoy this summer, in Ussy we sometimes manage it, maybe we shall go back next week. Suzanne feels like going to the seaside, perhaps we shall go to Dieppe for a few days next month. I have the impression that the smallest sea bathe would finish me off, but I am keen to try. Too much high diving at age six, too many cold baths all winter long, too many good things, too many bad things. The stones on the beach sink away to form little funnels. I used to enjoy that, 13 years ago, between the Hôtel Select and the Hôtel des Arcades, speciality shellfish. I would be far better off never going near the place again.[7]

Courage, my old friend, for Bram and the rest. Appears he is going off on his own to Brittany, to a woman friend's, in September. I am going to get in touch with him right now. If he comes to Paris I should like to see him, and the great picture still there from the time before he left.[8]

Affectionately

Sam

1 The translation work SB is doing for Duthuit: 26 July 1951.

2 It is not known to which letter SB is referring, of the many letters exchanged between the two men on the subject of Bram van Velde.

3 *Les Chaînes du destin* (*No Man of her Own*) with Barbara Stanwyck (1907–1990) played at the Miramar, 3 Rue du Départ, Paris 14, from 26 July through 1 August.

4 Editions de Minuit had moved from Boulevard St. Michel to its new location in a former brothel at 7 Rue Bernard Palissy in June (Simonin, *Les Editions de Minuit*, 242, 382).

5 Gabriel Marcel (1889–1973) is cited in an article by Paul Morand: "Je repense au mot de Gabriel Marcel, hier au goûter, mot qui m'a tourmenté toute la nuit: 'Le désordre des idées entraîne celui des choses.' N'est-ce pas paraphraser Spinoza, à l'envers?" (I keep thinking about that phrase of Gabriel Marcel's, yesterday at teatime, a phrase that bothered me all night long: "Disorder in ideas brings in its train disorder in things." Is this not a paraphrase of Spinoza, turned round?') ("Charles du Bos chez le dentiste," *Opéra*, 8.316 [1 August 1951] 1.)

6 The reference is to the crime novel *Les Carottes sont cuites* (see 26 July 1951, n. 5). The plot is of such complexity (it includes a rewriting of central events, as well as fantasies induced by drink or drugs) that Duthuit is unsure of the outcome. Here SB reassures him.

7 Dieppe is the port for the Channel crossing to Newhaven, a crossing SB took regularly during the 1930s and after. SB visited Normandy and Brittany during the summer of 1938 in the early days of his relationship with Suzanne

Deschevaux-Dumesnil (Knowlson, *Damned to Fame*, 265) and in 1937 wrote a short poem, "Dieppe," published in 1946 as part of "Poèmes 38–39" (see 15 December 1946, and n. 5). The Hôtel Select was situated at 1 Rue Toustain; the Hôtel des Arcades, still located at the Arcades de la Bourse, had been visited more recently by SB, when he picked up officials from it in 1945, the Irish Red Cross having established headquarters at the hotel (Lawrence E. Harvey, *Samuel Beckett: Poet and Critic* [Princeton: Princeton University Press, 1970] 218).

    8   It is not known to which canvas SB is referring.

MANIA PERON
PARIS

4/8/51   Paris
Chère Mania

    Merci pour vos deux lettres, pour les jolis brins de bruyère si gentiment trois et pour les photos. Si vous voulez que nous envisagions d'orner un jour votre fournil, avant que nous abandonne le goût du pain, faites photographier les chiottes sous tous les angles, avec notamment vue plongeante du siège et de la cuvette, et le chemin qui y mène.[1] Je suis content que Bram se soit decidé, je le verrai peut-être la semaine prochaine, mais n'y compte pas trop.[2] J'ai reçu une demande de contribution d'une mauvaise revue irlandaise Irish Writing (Cork) et leur ai envoyé, dans ma grande bonté, l'extrait de Watt que voici (c'est à dire le commencement et la fin, avec grande coupure et quelques raccords, de la 3me partie), je n'ai rien pu trouver de moins scandalisant, et cependant je ne pense pas qu'il puisse passer là-bas. Par la même occasion j'ai presque entièrement relu ce curieux ouvrage et pu constater, à ma satisfaction, que je n'y comprends plus rien.[3] Ci-joint également le no. 8. Le suivant est en panne. Je commence à en avoir sérieusement marre. Pas la peine de me renvoyer ces textes, mais ne les laissez pas traîner dans vos taillis, vous me les redonnerez à votre retour.[4] Wahl a pris Je tiens le greffe pr. Deucalion.[5] Je n'ai jamais dit que nous ne voulions pas être heureux, vous ne lisez pas mes lettres avec l'attention qu'elles méritent. J'ai dit au sieur Bensoussan de ne pas compter sur Eleuthéria pour la rentrée.[6] Toujours rien de Blin, ce qui veut dire très probablement que l'aide à la première ne sera pas pour moi, ce qui n'a rien de surprenant, vu les octroyeurs, dont les inévitables Marcel et Maulnier.[7]

Affectueusement de nous deux.

s/ Sam

TLS; 1 leaf, 1 side; TxU, Lake collection, Beckett.

4/8/51   Paris

Dear Mania

Thank you for your two letters, for the pretty sprigs of heather, so nicely three, and for the photos. If you want us to think about decorating your bakehouse one day, before we lose our taste for bread, get photographs taken of the shithouse from every angle, with in particular a shot from above of the seat and the pan, and the path leading to it.[1] I am glad that Bram has made up his mind. I shall see him next week perhaps, but am not counting on it.[2] I have had a request to contribute to a bad Irish review, *Irish Writing* (Cork), and have sent them, from my great kindness, the enclosed extract from *Watt* (that is, the beginning, and the end, with much cutting and a few joins, of the third part). I could find nothing less scandalising, and yet I do not think that it will ever get taken on there. While I was about it I re-read almost all of that odd work and was able to establish, to my satisfaction, that I can make no sense of it any more.[3] Herewith also no. 8. The next one is held up. I am beginning to be heartily sick of it. No point in sending these texts back, but don't leave them lying about in your thickets. You can give them back to me when you've returned.[4] Wahl has taken "Je tiens le Greffe" for *Deucalion*.[5] I never said that we did not want to be happy. You are not reading my letters with the attention they deserve. I have told messire Bensoussan not to count on *Eleutheria* for the autumn.[6] Still nothing from Blin, which most probably means that the grant for the first play will not go to me, which is no surprise, granted the granters, among whom the inevitable Marcel and Maulnier.[7]

Love from us both

Sam

1   Mania Péron's letters to SB have not been found; it is not certain what photos she may have sent. Her small cottage in Erquy was formerly a bakehut; it was set on a hill and overlooked the town and the sea (Alexis Péron, 9 October 2009).

2   Bram's decision is not known, but in his letter to Mania Péron of 24 July SB writes "Bram n'ira pas à Erquy, j'ai cette impression, c'est une simple impression" (Bram will not be going to Erquy, I have the impression, it is just an impression) (TxU, Lake collection, Beckett).

3   The letter from David Marcus to SB has not been found. Marcus later wrote: "I had read his startling story collection, *More Pricks Than Kicks*, wrote to him care of his French publishers, told him about *Irish Writing* and asked him if he would contribute" (*Oughtobiography: Leaves from the Diary of a Hyphenated Jew* [Dublin: Gill and Macmillan, 2001] 101–102). The "Extract from Watt" appeared in *Irish Writing* 17 (December 1951) 11–16.

4   SB refers to no. VIII of what will become *Textes pour rien*.

5   "Je tiens le Greffe," *Deucalion* 137–140; no. V of *Textes pour rien*.

6   In his letter of 24 July to Mania Péron, SB wrote: "Soyez heureux, vous en avez l'étoffe, nous pas" (Be happy, you're made for it, we're not) (TxU, Lake collection, Beckett). SB's letter to Charles Bensoussan has not been found. SB's doubts about *Eleutheria*: Suzanne Deschevaux-Dumesnil to Lindon, 25 May 1951.

7   Roger Blin had applied for a government subvention, "l'aide à la première pièce," to produce *En attendant Godot*. The grant was awarded through the Division Arts et Lettres du Ministère de l'Education Nationale (Blin and Peskine, *Roger Blin*, 83–84). SB refers to Gabriel Marcel and Thierry Maulnier (1906–1988).

GEORGES BELMONT

8/8/51   Paris

Mon cher Georges

Merci de ta carte. Dommage qu'on n'ait pu se voir avant ton départ. J'aurais mieux aimé bafouiller sur ton travail de vive voix que noir sur blanc. J'aime les poèmes, surtout Vanité de la Grâce et celui qui commence Ici la vie n'est plus. Par moments je sens un peu la tyrannie de l'image, d'un souffle pourtant jamais forcé, mais c'est là plutôt une critique de moi, de ma faiblesse pour le boîteux et de ma peur du faire. Je retrouve le "bruit de râteaux et de pierres" qui n'est qu'à toi et le vitam continet una dies que tu avais si fort à Dublin, et dont ensuite tu semblais ne plus vouloir, et que voilà ramené, par la vie et les jours.[1] La pièce est étrange, très littéraire et en même temps, il me semble, faite pour être jouée, comme une démonstration du tort qu'on a de considérer ces deux aspects comme ennemis, c'est le cas probablement de

278

tout ton théâtre, mais je ne le connais pas assez bien. Une vraie trou-
vaille, les deux masques et leurs jeux de scène, et indispensable, je me
suis même demandé s'il n'y aurait pas intérêt à leur donner plus
d'importance.[2] J'espère pouvoir te sortir tout ça, et autre chose,
mieux en bavardant. Par le papier je ne suis plus bon qu'à aller dans
la bêtise, l'ignorance, l'impuissance et le silence.

Quelles nouvelles de Laffont-Julliard?[3]

Bonjour à Jose et à Sophie. Reposez-vous bien. Ecris-moi et au
mois prochain.

      Amitiés
         s/ *Sam*

TLS; 1 leaf, 1 side; TxU, Lake collection, Beckett.

8/8/51   Paris

My dear Georges

Thank you for your card. Pity we could not meet before you left. I
would have preferred to stutter about your work directly, rather than in
black and white. I like the poems, especially "Vanité de la Grâce" and
the one that begins "Ici la vie n'est plus". At moments I rather feel the
tyranny of the image, in a surge that is at the same time never forced; but
that is rather a criticism of me, with my weakness for the limping and
my fear of the achieving. I find the "bruit de râteaux et de pierres" which
could only be you, and the *vitam continet una dies* which was so present in
you in Dublin, and which later you seemed not to want any longer, and
which is back there again, by way of life and days.[1] The play is strange,
very literary and at the same time, it seems to me, made to be performed,
as a demonstration of the wrongness of considering these two aspects as
opposed to each other. Probably the case for all your plays, but I don't
know them well enough. A real find, the two masques and the byplay
with them, and indispensable. I even wondered if it might not be worth
making more of them.[2] I hope to be able to get all this out to you, along
with other things, better when we can chat. On paper all I'm good for
now is going on into silliness, ignorance, impotence, and silence.

What news of Laffont-Julliard?[3]

Greetings to Jose and Sophie. Enjoy your rest. Write to me. Till next month.

All best

Sam

1   SB refers to the poems mentioned in his letter of 11 July to Belmont. It is probable that these poems included "Pavana," "Mesure de Dieu," and "Fin de l'élégie" (which begins "Ici la vie n'est plus"), this last of which was dedicated to SB when they were published, along with "Vanité de la Grâce," in "Poèmes," *Nouvelle Nouvelle Revue Française* 2.17 (May 1954) 799–802. (*Nouvelle Nouvelle Revue Française* is henceforth identified in the notes as *NNRF*.)

The "bruit de râteaux et de pierres" comes from a poem written when SB and Belmont (then named Pelorson) were seeing much of each other in Dublin in the early 1930s, and which was published as "Plans" in *transition* 21 (March 1932) 182–183, the same issue that published SB's own "Sedendo et Quiesciendo" [*for* Quiescendo].

"'Vitam continet una dies'" (One day contains the whole of my life) (James Boswell, *Boswell's Life of Johnson, Together with Boswell's Journal of a Tour to the Hebrides and Johnson's Diary of a Journey into North Wales*, ed. George Birkbeck Hill, revised and enlarged L. F. Powell, I, *The Life (1709–1765)* [Oxford: Clarendon Press, 1934] 84).

2   The play by Belmont which SB has read is an early draft of what becomes known as *L'Offense*, which will be performed in November 1956 at the Studio des Champs-Elysées (directed by Maurice Jacquemont). At this time the play, which Belmont originally wrote shortly after the War, was probably still entitled *Jean ou Les dieux du sang*.

3   Laffont-Julliard: 11 July 1951, n. 2.

10. Mania Péron

MANIA PERON
PARIS

vendredi 17 août [1951]   Paris
Chère Mania

Merci de vos précieuses précisions. Et de la belle photo.[1]

Lisez laid à la place de lay. Lie actif n'existe pas, sinon comme archaisme ou par erreur: the cloth was lain.[2]

Ci-joint 9. 10 est en mauvaise voie.[3]

J'ai vu Bram. Il a dormi ici. Sommes allés à l'atelier revoir le travail. Encore plus renversant qu'à la première vision. Il a dit qu'il n'irait pas à Erquy, sans expliquer pourquoi. Je lui ai offert le voyage s'il venait à changer d'avis. C'est tout ce que je sais.[4] Il tourne en rond autour des vieux sphinx. Et moi j'en ai marre depuis vingt ans. C'est sans doute lui qui a raison. Mais ça ne facilite pas la conversation. Egalement revu Geer. Il vient de décrocher, à la 1ère Biennale de Menton, le premier prix pour peintre étranger, 200.000 frs. Bien content pour lui, ça leur paiera des vacances. Je crois que du même coup il est assuré, en sus, de la vente de la toile au Musée de Menton. Concours placé sous la vertigineuse présidence de Matisse et sous le signe de la joie, du soleil, de la santé et autres ignominies. Pas fait pour Bram, également représenté.[5]

Oui, on dit adjurer de.[6]

Sorti un peu avec Blin. Rien de nouveau pour l'aide à la 1ère. Il va falloir s'en passer, probablement.[7]

Je relis Boswell dans la belle édition de Birkbeck Hill. Effet calmant, comme toujours. On a découvert des inédits de Boswell, assez scandaleux paraît-il, à Malahide Castle, près de Dublin. Un 1er volume est sorti chez Heinemann, London Journal. Edulcoré certainement. Traduction française à paraître chez Hachette.[8] Curieux que Boswell ne figure jamais au programme de l'agreg. Ou si? Tout le 18me anglais y passe.

Salut à tous. Affectueusement.
        s/ S.

TLI; 1 leaf, 1 side; TxU, Lake collection, Beckett. *Dating*: although the date "52" is added in AH in the upper margin, 17 August was a Friday, rather, in 1951.

Friday 17 August [1951]   Paris

Dear Mania

Thank you for your invaluable details. And the lovely photo.[1]

Read "laid" instead of "lay". "Lie" does not exist in the active, except as an archaism or an error: "the cloth was lain".[2]

Herewith 9. 10 is ill on the way.[3]

I have seen Bram. He slept here. We went to the studio to have another look at the work. Even more stunning than on first seeing. He said that he would not be going to Erquy, without explaining why. I offered to pay for the trip if he should happen to change his mind. That is all I know.[4] He is going round and round the old sphinxes. And twenty years on I am fed up with it. No doubt he is the one in the right. But it does not make conversation easy. Have seen Geer too. He has just brought off, at the 1st Menton Biennale, the first prize for a foreign painter: 200,000 francs. Very glad for him. That will pay for a holiday for them. I think that, by the same token, he is assured, on top of that, of the sale of his painting to the Musée de Menton. Competition under the dizzying presidency of Matisse and the sign of joy, sun, health and other ignominies. Not made for Bram, also exhibiting.[5]

Yes, one does say "adjurer de".[6]

Been out a bit with Blin. No news of the grant for the first play. We shall have to manage without, probably.[7]

I am re-reading Boswell in the handsome Birkbeck Hill edition. Calming effect, as always. They have found some unpublished manuscripts of Boswell, quite scandalous apparently, in Malahide Castle, near Dublin. A first volume has been published by Heinemann, the *London Journal*. Toned down, for sure. French translation due from Hachette.[8] Odd that Boswell never appears on the Agrégation list. Or perhaps he does? The whole of the English 18th Century is in there.

Greetings to all. Love.

S.

---

1   It is not known what Mania Péron's details concern, or what photo she had sent from Erquy; the photo may have been in response to SB's request (see 4 August 1951).

2   Just as Mania Péron advised SB on French usage, so did he advise her on her English, which she taught at the Lycée Buffon in Paris. SB omits the dieresis in "archaïsme."

3   SB refers to numbers IX and X of what will become *Textes pour rien*.

4   Bram van Velde's movements are recounted because Mania Péron had either invited or expected him to visit her in Brittany.

5   Geer van Velde's oil painting *Composition (intérieur d'atelier)* (Ville de Menton, Musée des Beaux Arts – Palais Carnolès, no. 514) was exhibited in the Première Biennale de peinture de France in Menton from 3 August to 1 October 1951; Van Velde was awarded the Premier Prix réservé à un étranger (Biennale Internationale d'Art de Menton, *Biennale Internationale d'Art de Menton* [Menton, 1951]; Viatte, *Geer van Velde*, 213; Catherine Gourdet, Directrice des Affaires Culturelles, Ville de Menton, 15 September 2009, 8 January 2010). Bram van Velde did not have any work in this exhibition.

6   "Adjurer de" (to entreat to).

7   L'aide à la première pièce: 4 August 1951, Péron.

8   SB refers to Boswell, *Boswell's Life of Johnson*, I.
Over one hundred pages of "the original manuscript of Boswell's 'Life of Samuel Johnson' and the entire original manuscript of his 'Journal of the Tour of the Hebrides'" were found in Malahide Castle in November 1930, and additional manuscript pages were found in 1936 ("Manuscripts of Boswell Reported, Discovery at Malahide Castle," *The Irish Times* 13 November 1930: 4; "Yet More of Boswell," *The Times* 9 March 1936: 15). The purchase of these by Yale University Library was completed in 1951 ("Boswell Papers, More Details of the Yale Purchase," *The Times* 21 September 1950: 3). SB refers to James Boswell, *Boswell's London Journal, 1762–1763: Now Published from the Original Manuscript*, I ed. Frederick A. Pottle, Yale Editions of the Private Papers of James Boswell, (London: W. Heinemann, 1950).

MANIA PERON
PARIS

28 Août [1951]   Ussy-sur-Marne
Chère Mania

Merci de vos 2 lettres et des photographies.[1]

Je n'ai pas de nouvelles de Bram. J'ai passé une agréable soirée avec Geer et Lisl.[2]

Je suis seul à la campagne en ce moment, Suzanne ayant à faire à Paris. J'écris un peu et je jardine un peu. Demain je sèmerai des épinards et repiquerai des poireaux. Je ramasse des Reines-Claude pour faire de l'eau de vie. Moments de calme, moments d'angoisse. Ça fait une endurable moyenne.

Bordas m'attaque en dommages-intérêts.

Irish Writing publie le fragment de Watt.

Je ferai peut-être le 4me avec Alexis, Michel et Tartarin … s'ils veulent de moi.[3]

Merci aussi pr. la bruyère. Elle sentait la bruyère, pas autre chose. Encore. Y a-t-il de la vraie blanche, qui porte bonheur, je l'ai remarqué.

Je fraternise avec un octogénaire veuf et perclus de rhumatismes. Il m'appelle cher ami et mon grand.[4]

J'ai lu, dans Lectures pour Tous de 1904, un poème de Coppée sur les vieux de la vieille, et un reportage sur la Corée, pays du matin calme.[5] Je lis La 628-E8 d'Octave Mirbeau. Fort bien foutu.[6]

J'entreprends après-demain une randonnée de 60 kilomètres à bicyclette. Voilà une nouvelle qui ne pourra manquer de vous intéresser. Ou bien je n'arriverai pas ou bien je n'en reviendrai pas. Mais je partirai, si le temps le permet.

Qu'attendez-vous pour nous donner un roman acerbe sur les hommes et les femmes! Ou enthousiaste, sur la vie? Dite à la dernière extrémité? Je suis au meilleur d'un 11me gigotement.[7] Je vais m'arrêter. Encore une pièce, puis révérence. C'est décidé. C'est comme ça ce soir. Pas la peine d'enfoncer le terminus. Geer dégage un grand courage. Des idées un peu tranchantes, mais peut-être seulement en apparence. Je l'ai toujours beaucoup estimé. Mais pas assez je crois. Ne le dis pas à Bram. Entre les oeuvres, pas d'hésitation. Mais ce n'est pas un jugement.

Allez, au lit. Pour ne pas dormir. Pour écouter la nuit, le silence, la solitude et les morts. Encore un verre. Le courage n'a pas d'odeur.

Affectueusement à tous

Sam

ALS; 1 leaf, 2 sides [*squared notebook page*]; TxU, Lake collection, Péron.

28 August [1951]   Ussy-sur-Marne
Dear Mania

Thank you for your two letters and for the photographs.[1]

I have no news of Bram. I spent a pleasant evening with Geer and Lisl.[2]

I am on my own in the country at the moment, Suzanne having things to do in Paris. I am writing a little and gardening a little. Tomorrow I shall sow some spinach and bed out leeks. I am gathering greengages to make our own eau-de-vie. Moments of calm, moments of near panic. It works out as a bearable average.

Bordas is after me for damages.

Irish Writing is publishing the fragment of *Watt*.

Perhaps I shall make a fourth with Alexis, Michel and Tartarin ... if they will still have me.[3]

Thank you too for the heather. It smelt of heather, nothing else. Still. Is there any of the true white kind, that brings luck? I have seen it happen.

I am making friends with an octogenarian widower, crippled with rheumatism. He calls me "my dear chap" and "big fellow".[4]

I read, in *Lectures pour tous* (1904), a poem by Coppée on "les vieux de la vieille", and a report on Korea, the Land of the Morning Calm.[5] I am reading the *628-E8* by Octave Mirbeau. Damned good piece of work.[6]

The day after tomorrow I am undertaking a 60-kilometre bicycle ride. Now there's a piece of news that cannot fail to interest you. Either I shall not get there or I shall not get back. But I shall set out, weather permitting.

What is holding you back from giving us an acerbic novel about men and women? Or an enthusiastic one, on life? Told in extremis? I am on to the best bit of an 11th twitching.[7] I shall stop. One more play, then my bow. It's decided. That's how it is, this evening. But no need to crash through the buffers. Geer is showing great courage. Ideas a little strident, but maybe only in appearance. I have always had a high opinion of him. But not high enough, I think. Don't say that to Bram. Between the one's work and the other's, no hesitation. But that is not a judgement.

Right, off to bed. So as not to sleep. To listen to the darkness, the silence, the solitude and the dead. Another glass. Courage has no odour.

Love to you all.

Sam

1   Mania Péron's letters and photographs sent to SB have not been found.

2   Bram van Velde; Geer and Lisl van Velde.

3   SB proposes tennis doubles with Mania Péron's two sons and with another – unidentified – nicknamed after the protagonist in Alphonse Daudet's novel *Tartarin de Tarascon* (1872).

4   SB's octogenarian neighbor in Ussy has not been identified.

5   "Un duel au sabre" by François Coppée, which deals with "Les vieux de la vieille," men who had served in Napoleon's Grande Armée (*Lectures pour Tous, Revue Universelle Illustrée* 9 [June 1904] 739–751).
"Au pays du matin calme," a title which uses the sobriquet commonly designating Korea (The Land of the Morning Calm), itself deriving from a loose translation of the country's former name (unsigned, *Lectures pour Tous*, 752–760). The heading summarizes: "rien n'est plus instructif que l'exemple d'un peuple qui, par son apathie et son indifférence à ses propres intérêts, s'est condamné lui-même à subir tour à tour le joug de l'étranger et le caprice des envahisseurs" (nothing is more instructive than the example of a people which, through apathy and indifference as to its own interests, condemned itself to suffering by turns the yoke of a foreign power and the whim of invaders).

6   Octave Mirbeau's unclassifiable book *La 628-E8* (1907) took its title from the license plate of its author's automobile, which vehicle plays a central role in the work.

7   SB was working on *Textes pour rien*.

MANIA PERON
ERQUY, COTES-DU-NORD

6 Septembre [1951]   USSY
Chère Mania

Merci de votre lettre.

Content – encore, je ne sais pas de quoi.

Croyez-moi, je partage vos préoccupations de propriétaire et avisée mère de famille. Un acte de donation semble tout indiqué. Mais il doit y avoir un hic. Enfin c'est un moyen d'arracher à ce cher Reynaud un signe de vie.[1] Le pain qui rend fou n'aurait aucune prise sur Tata, telle est mon opinion.[2]

Assez d'animadversions sur mon écriture. Elle est vigoureuse au moins. Non?

De la bruyère blanche, non pas à 3 branches, obsédée de la Triade.[3]

Ma randonnée de 60 kilomètres s'est fort bien effectuée. Il faut dire qu'une nuit de repos est venue s'intercaler entre l'aller et le retour.

EleuthEria: Le nommé Bensoussan voulait la monter, mais je n'ai pas voulu, je ne sais pas exactement pourquoi. Je n'aimais pas le ton de ses communications. Et c'est un travail qui ne me dit pas grand' chose. Blin est dans la misère, et aucune nouvelle de l'aide à la 1ère.

Je vais probablement avoir les 1res épreuves de Malone cette semaine. Pas la peine de vous emmerder avant les 2mes. Quand pensez-vous rentrer?

Javelage et délavage au chlorate de soude sont les mamelles de ce coin de l'Ile de France. Je connais dans les coins le chiendent et le terrible liseron et la façon d'avoir le pissenlit avec la racine. Qu'est-ce que c'est votre garenne stérile au regard de ces avulsions? Depuis que je suis ici la valeur de ces 2000 mètres a baissé de 20% au bas mot. Pommiers et poiriers lâchent leurs fruits à peine formés et les groseill[i]ers, comme surpris pour me faire plaisir, redeviennent sauvages.

Me demander ce que c'est qui n'existe pas! Voyons! Comme si ça avait de l'importance. Par contre remarque caractéristiquement judicieuse au sujet du lit. J'ai en effet modifié notamment à la correction (vous y êtes d'ailleurs pour quelque chose), et à contre-coeur. Je ne pense pas vous envoyer le 10 pas encore tapé. Il y a un 11me de fait, plus long (contre toute attente) que les autres et encore plus derviche tourneur, et un 12me de parti, autant dire d'arrivé, en pleines Sargasses.[4]

L'eau bout sur l'horrible lampe à alcool, permettez que je prenne mon TUB, avant que la boue sèche.

Suzanne arrive demain ou après-demain, avec des nouvelles des Editions et de Bordas. Je ne sais encore lesquelles.

J'ai fini (c'est pour ne pas gaspiller du papier) le feuilleton de *Lectures pour Tous* de 1904. Du Fond de la Nuit. Du bon travail, vraiment du bon travail, et illustré, je ne vous dis que ça. Traduit de l'anglais. Déjà.[5]

Affectueusement à vous tous.

Sam

ALS; 2 leaves, 4 sides; *env to* Madame Péron, Les Bruyères, La Garenne, ERQUY, Côtes-du-Nord; *pm* 7-9-51, La Ferté-sous-Jouarre; TxU, Lake collection, Péron. *Dating*: follows from 28 August [1951] and in a sequence related to the writing of *Textes pour rien* ("Texte XI" was completed on 4 September 1951).

6 September [1951]   USSY

Dear Mania

Thank you for your letter.

Glad – still. Don't know what about.

Believe me, I can share your preoccupations as house-owner and prudent mother. A gift inter vivos seems to me highly appropriate. But there must be a hitch. Anyhow, it is one way of extracting some sign of life from dear Reynaud.[1] The bread that drives you mad would get nowhere with Tata. That is my view.[2]

Enough animadversions on my handwriting. It is at least vigorous. No?

White heather, not the three-branch kind, you triad-mad woman.[3]

My sixty-kilometre ride went off very well. It has to be said that a night's rest slipped itself in between the outward journey and the return.

Eleutheria: the Bensoussan man wanted to put it on, but I was unwilling, I am not altogether sure why. I did not like the tone of his messages. And it is not work that greatly attracts me. Blin very badly off, and no news of the grant for the first play.

I shall probably get the first proofs of *Malone* this week. Not worth your getting landed with the chore until the page proofs come. When are you thinking of coming back?

Chlorinating and soaking in sodium chlorate are the two breasts of this corner of the Ile de France. I know all about couch grass, and the fearsome bindweed, and the way to get the dandelion with its root. What is your sterile warren in comparison with these uprootings? Since I've been here, the value of these 2,000 sq. metres has gone down by 20%, to put it no higher. Apple trees and pear trees shed their fruit barely formed and the currant bushes, as if taken by surprise in order to please me, are going back to the wild.

Asking me what it is that does not exist! Come on! As if that mattered. Characteristically judicious remark, on the other hand, about the bed. Indeed: I have, in particular, when correcting, made changes (you have some responsibility here), against my better judgement. I am not thinking of sending you the 10, not yet typed. There is an 11th, already done, longer (most unexpectedly) than the others, and even more of a whirling dervish, and a 12th on the way, why not say gone all the way, to the Sargasso weeds.[4]

The water is boiling on the horrible spirit lamp. Please don't mind if I take my TUB, before the mud dries.

Suzanne arrives tomorrow or the day after with news from Minuit and Bordas. I do not yet know what news.

I have finished (so as not to waste paper) the serial in *Lectures pour Tous* from 1904. *Du fond de la nuit*. Good work, really good work, and illustrated. Think of that. Translated from the English. Already.[5]

> Love to you all.
> Sam

---

1   Possibly a reference to French politician Paul Reynaud (1878–1966), who, at this time, advocated fiscal reforms that would increase benefits for families and those without adequate pensions ("'Cette législature n'a pas le droit d'échouer' déclare M. Paul Reynaud," *Le Monde* 5 August 1951: 8).

2   "Tata": 29 April 1951, n. 1. In August 1951, in the village of Pont-Saint-Esprit (Gard), there was an extraordinary and unexplained outbreak of food poisoning (seven dead and forty-six admitted to hospital, many displaying symptoms of serious mental disturbance). The cause, as widely reported in the national press, was thought to be the local bread, which journalists were quick to call "le pain fou" (Steven L. Kaplan, *Le Pain maudit: retour sur la France des années oubliées, 1945–1958* [Paris: Libraire Arthème Fayard, 2008]).

3   SB's writing of the word "blanche" in his previous letter to Mania Péron (28 August) was particularly illegible, leading Péron to read it as "branche."

4   SB refers to *Textes pour rien*.

5   "Du Fond de la Nuit," which consisted of an adaptation of *Called Back* (1884) by Hugh Conway (pseud. of Frederick John Fargus, 1847–1885), was serialized in four parts in *Lectures pour Tous* (March–June 1904).

JEROME LINDON, EDITIONS DE MINUIT
PARIS

le 9 septembre 1951   Ussy-sur-Marne
                                                       Seine-et-Marne

Cher Monsieur Lindon

Tout à fait d'accord avec votre lettre à Bordas.[1]

A remarquer cependant (voir troisième paragraphe de votre lettre) que L'Innommable n'a pas été refusé par Bordas (ne lui ayant jamais été présenté) et que la lettre dont vous faites état ne se rapporte qu'à Molloy. Il est vrai d'autre part qu'en ce qui concerne Malone ma liberté m'a été rendue verbalement et que Gervais peut témoigner en ce sens, que les trois ouvrages doivent être considérés comme n'en faisant qu'un et qu'en tout état de cause il est probable que Bordas ignore lui–même de combien de mes livres il n'a pas voulu.[2] J'ajoute pour mémoire qu'il a commencé par refuser Mercier et Camier.[3]

J'aimerais pouvoir croire que votre lettre mettra le point final à cette histoire. Mais j'ai bien peur que pour cela il n'y ait qu'un seul moyen: porter nous-mêmes l'affaire devant le tribunal compétent. Si vous partagez cette façon de voir, le plus tôt serait le mieux. Enfin vous savez mieux que moi ce qu'il y a à faire. Et quoi que vous décidiez vous pouvez compter sur mon entier accord.

Il ne me reste qu'à vous remercier d'avoir pris encore à votre charge cette fastidieuse affaire.

Amitiés

Sam Beckett

PS. Par l'additif entendez-vous le contrat général visant mon travail futur? Madame Dumesnil ne l'a pas trouvé dans mes papiers à Paris. Mais il doit y être, s'il n'est pas chez vous.[4]

TLS; 1 leaf, 1 side; IMEC, Beckett, Boîte 1, S. Beckett, Dossier Murphy 1946–1957.

9th September 1951

Ussy-sur-Marne
Seine-et-Marne

Dear Monsieur Lindon

Wholly in agreement with your letter to Bordas.[1]

Do note though (see the third paragraph of your letter) that *L'Innommable* was not rejected by Bordas, never having been offered to him, and that the letter to which you refer bears only upon *Molloy*. It is incidentally true that as far as *Malone* is concerned my freedom was given back to me verbally, and that Gervais can bear witness to this; that the three works must be considered as forming one; and that in any case it is probable that Bordas himself has forgotten how many of my books he did not want.[2] I add for the record that he started by turning down *Mercier et Camier*.[3]

I should like to think that your letter will put an end to this business. But I very much fear that for that there is only one way: for us to take the affair to a competent tribunal. If you share this view, the sooner the better. Anyhow, you know better than I what should be done. And whatever you decide, you can count on my full agreement.

It only remains for me to thank you for having again taken on the responsibility of this wearisome affair.

      Best wishes

      Sam Beckett

PS. By 'the additional clause' do you mean the general contract for my future work? Madame Dumesnil has not found it among my papers in Paris. But it must be there, if it is not with you.[4]

---

1 Lindon wrote to Pierre Bordas on 7 September, noting that Bordas had not exercised his contracted option on SB's future works (*Mercier et Camier, Molloy, Malone meurt*). Lindon claimed that the original contract for *Murphy* had not been honored by Bordas, and that SB wished to enter arbitration and proposed to meet Bordas "devant un jury composé pour moitié de membres du Cercle de la Librairie et pour moitié de la Société des Gens de Lettres" (before a jury half of whose members would be drawn from the Cercle de la Librairie, and half from the Société des Gens de Lettres) (IMEC, Beckett, Boîte 1, S. Beckett, Dossier Murphy 1946–1957).

2 The date of the discussion is not known, but evidence of Gervais's goodwill toward Beckett and publication of his work is clear in his letter to Max-Pol Fouchet (see Suzanne Deschevaux-Dumesnil to A. C. Gervais, 8 November [1949]).

SB refers to *Molloy, Malone meurt*, and *L'Innommable*.

3 *Mercier et Camier*: 15 December 1946, n. 2.

4 The additional clause may refer to the addendum to the original contract on which was noted the advance for *Mercier et Camier* (see 15 December 1946, n. 2). The contract of 30 October 1946 is with Editions de Minuit.

GEORGES DUTHUIT

10 Septembre [1951]   Ussy
Cher vieux Georges,

Plus que content de te lire après si longtemps. Je t'ai écrit il y a quelques jours, mais une lettre si triste et si bête que je t'en ai fait grâce. Suis ici depuis trois semaines, seul une bonne partie du temps, Suzanne ayant eu à faire à Paris, où sa mère est venue passer quelques jours. Avant de venir j'ai pas mal vadrouillé à Montparnasse, avec Blin la plupart du temps. Rencontré Hérold, gentil, un peu endormant, et Giacometti, granitiquement subtil et tout en perceptions renversantes, très sage au fond, voulant rendre ce qu'il voit, ce qui n'est peut-être pas si sage que ça, lorsqu'on sait voir comme lui.[1] Mes timides nenni vite balayés, plutôt concassés, moi aidant, comme de bien entendu. Curieuses nuits de Montparnasse, tout compte fait, peu arrosées, grâce à Blin, d'une sobriété de chameau. Très agréable soirée avec Geer et sa femme et un long et maigre et très touchant disciple américain, dont j'ai un peu dérangé les certitudes en lui montrant mes Bram. Vu le tout dernier travail de Geer chez lui, toujours de très loin, mais mieux vu quand même, et accepté comme un but des plus honorables, des trop honorables.[2] C'est le platonicien dans toute sa touchante noblesse (quand on est bien luné), à quatre pattes sur ses millimètres de toile comme un chamois sur une aiguille, pour qui Bram reste "un cas". Pas moyen de sortir de ces antiques querelles. J'avais envie de lui dire qu'il est facile de se dépasser soi lorsqu'on n'y est jamais passé, mais ai bien fait de n'en rien faire, car ç'aurait été plutôt injuste. Enfin un travail pas du tout pour bibi, devrais-je dire pas encore, je me le suis demandé, mais que j'ai certainement sous-estimé. Le congédier, comme le fait Hayden par exemple, comme du post-cubisme pâle, ça non. Et de sa personne grave et incertain, comme je ne l'avais jamais vu. Quelqu'un, sans erreur. Rien de Bram, j'ai du [*for* dû] l'ulcérer, à mon insu et bien malgré moi, tout en lui donnant l'hospitalité de mon mauvais divan. Je pense beaucoup à ses dernières peintures, miracles d'impuissance forcenée, ruisselantes de beautés et de splendeurs comme un naufrage de phosphorescences, on est littéraire décidément pour la vie, avec d'énormes voies par où tout fuit et tout rentre, et le calme écrasé des très grands fonds. Tu vas faire une préface, cher vieux Georges, pour une des grandes expositions de notre temps, je ne te dis pas ça pour te décourager.[3] Vas-y carrément et rentre dedans, dans leurs sagesses d'imagiers, leurs risques calculés et leur capillarisme de modestes universalistes. Côté ton serviteur, histoire de retomber dans le quotidien, menace de ce cher Bordas d'un procès en dommages-intérêts! Et sommation aux Editions de M. d'arrêter tout paiement de droits d'auteur (tu parles d'une privation!). Lindon très gentiment prend l'affaire en mains et m'assure que ce n'est pas sérieux. Moi je m'en fous comme de la dernière des chiffes que je suis. J'attends d'un jour à l'autre les épreuves de <u>Malone</u>, promis pour le 15 Octobre.[4] Vivement <u>L'Innommable</u>, c'est tout ce qui m'intéresse un peu encore. J'écris un tout petit peu, de petits coups de mouche contre la vitre, lor[s]que binage et désherbage m'en laissent le loisir. Je songe sérieusement à m'établir, nous établir, à la campagne, ne gardant l'appartement que comme pied-à-terre, je n'en peux plus, de la ruche et de la Rue de Vaugirard.[5] Et autant que possible ici même. Tu vois, j'ai déjà ma machine à écrire, pour la première fois. Cette fois je crois que c'est sérieux. Il s'agit seulement de trouver une bicoque dans nos cordes. Pour le moment rien. Nous serons certainement à Paris le mois prochain. Première quinzaine, la mère de Suzanne; deuxième, mon frangin et sa femme, à moins qu'il ne décommande, ce qui ne m'étonnerait pas outre mesure. Oui, une chopine avec toi, à l'ombre de n'importe quelle enseigne, ce sont les moments, trops [*for* trop] courts, qui m'importent. Et sentir cette affection qui se passe de paroles et est plus forte que celles que je vomis à tort et à travers.

      Cher vieux, à toi.

      s/ *Sam*

TLS; 1 leaf, 2 sides; side 2: *AN ?AH, blue ballpoint ink and doodle*; Duthuit collection. *Dating*: SB received proofs for *Malone* on 18 September 1951.

10 September [1951]   Ussy

Dear old Georges,

More than glad to read you after such a long time. I wrote a few days ago, but such a dismal, silly letter that I spared you it. Been here three weeks now, alone a good part of the time, Suzanne having things to do in Paris, where her mother has come to spend a few days. Before I came away I spent a fair bit of time wandering round Montparnasse, with Blin most of the time. Met Hérold, nice, bit soporific, and Giacometti, subtle in a granite-like way, all stunning perceptions, very well-behaved underneath it all, wanting to render what he sees, which is perhaps not so well behaved as all that, when one has the ability to see as he does.[1] My timid attempts at disagreement swiftly brushed aside, crushed rather, I of course joining in the crushing. Odd Montparnasse nights, all in all, not much to drink, thanks to Blin, sober as a judge. Very pleasant evening with Geer and his wife and a lanky, thin, very touching American disciple, whose certainties I rather spoiled by showing my Brams. Saw Geer's most recent work in their place, always from a distance, but saw it better all the same, and took it for one of the most honourable goals, the too honourable goals.[2] It is the Platonist in all his touching nobility (if one is in a good mood), on all fours on his millimetres of canvas like a chamois on a needle, for whom Bram is still "a case". No way of getting beyond these ancient quarrels. I felt like telling him that it is easy to get beyond oneself when one has never really been there, and did well to say nothing of the kind, for it would have been rather unfair. Anyhow, a piece of work that is not at all for Muggins, should I say not yet, I wondered, but which I have certainly underestimated. To dismiss it, as Hayden does for instance, as pale post-Cubism, no. And sober and uncertain in his person as I had never seen him. Really someone, no mistake. Nothing from Bram, I must have outraged him, unwittingly and very unwillingly, while all the time offering him the hospitality of my bad divan. I think continually of his last paintings, miracles of frenzied impotence, streaming with beauties and splendours like a shipwreck of phosphorescences, decidedly one is literary all one's life, with great wide ways along which every-thing rushes away and comes back again, and the crushed calm of the true deep. You will be writing a preface, Georges my old friend, for one of the great exhibitions of our time, I am not saying that in order to discourage you.[3] Go at it boldly, drive straight into their image-makers' wisdoms, their calculated risks, their modest universalists' capillarism. As for your humble servant, to fall from the sublime, threat from dear Bordas of a lawsuit! And injunction to the Editions de M. to stop all payment of royalties (what a loss!). Lindon is very nicely taking the matter up, and assures me that it is not worth worrying about. I care about it as much as I would about the wettest of wet rags, which is what I am. I am expecting the proofs of *Malone* any day, they are promised for the 15th of October.[4] Let's get on to *L'Innommable*, that is the only thing that interests me at all now. I am writing a tiny little bit, little fly-splashes against the window, when hoeing and weeding permit. I am thinking seriously of settling myself, of settling us both, in the country, just keeping the flat as a pied-à-terre, I cannot stand la Ruche and the Rue de Vaugirard any more.[5] And settling as far as possible round here. You see, I already have my typewriter, for the first time. Now I think I mean it. Just have to find a hovel we can afford. For the moment, nothing. We shall certainly be in Paris next month. First fortnight, Suzanne's mother; second, my brother and his wife, unless he calls off the trip, which would not surprise me unduly. Yes, a tankard with you, beneath any sign you like, those are the moments, too brief, that matter to me. And feeling that affection which needs no words and is stronger than those I do spew out in all directions.

Dear old friend, your
Sam

---

1   Suzanne's mother was Jeanne Deschevaux-Dumesnil (née Fourniols, 1876–1967). The visit of SB's brother Frank, with his wife Jean (née Wright, 1906–1966): 6 October 1951.

Jacques Hérold (1910–1987), a Romanian-born artist resident in Paris from 1930, was close to many in the Surrealist circle of artists and writers; he illustrated one of the collections of letters by the Marquis de Sade (edited by Gilbert Lely), *L'Aigle, Mademoiselle . . . Lettres.*

2   Geer and Lisl van Velde. The identity of the American disciple, and of the particular works SB was viewing, is not known.

11. Georges Duthuit, Alberto Giacometti, Patrick Waldberg

3   Duthuit was preparing two articles on Bram van Velde's exhibition which ran from 15 February to 10 March 1952 at the Galerie Maeght, Paris: "Bram van Velde ou aux Colonnes d'Hercule" (*Derrière le Miroir* 43 [February 1952] 2–4 and 8; rpt. in Duthuit *Représentation et présence* 357–365; rpt. in Stoullig and Schoeller, eds., *Bram van Velde*, 176–179), and "Maille à partir avec Bram van Velde" (*Cahiers d'Art* 27.1 [July 1952] 79–81; rpt. in Stoullig and Schoeller, eds., *Bram van Velde*, 180). The latter article begins with an echo of SB's estimate: "Un résultat du moins est acquis: nous avons assisté à une des grandes expositions de ce temps" (One outcome at least is certain: we have witnessed one of the great exhibitions of our time).

4   Lindon's letter to Bordas of 7 September: 9 September 1951, n. 1.
SB writes "en mains" for the more standard "en main."

5   The Rue de Vaugirard is the major street round the corner from where SB lived on the seventh floor of 6 Rue des Favorites, Paris 15. La Ruche, an artists' residence in Passage Dantzig, nearby.

MANIA PERON

ERQUY, BRITTANY

Mardi [18 September 1951]   Ussy-sur-Marne

Chère Mania

Bien reçu votre lettre du 13 et, ce matin, votre carte. Très touché que vous preniez tant mes petites affaires à coeur, et par votre offre de raccourcir vos vacances à cause de moi. Rassurons-nous, il n'y a aucune urgence. *Combat* exagère. Les premières épreuves, je les ai reçues seulement ce matin, et je n'aurai certainement pas les autres avant la 1ere semaine d'octobre. Pas grand'chose à signaler jusqu'à présent, sinon que ce travail m'afflige profondément, maintenant [q]u'il est trop tard pour le faire disparaître.[1]

SARGASSES, si j'ai bonne mémoire.

Content que vous ayez des nouvelles des Sarraute, et formulées à votre convenance.[2]

Mes petits textes sont en panne. Le dernier, je n'ai pas le courage de le relire.[3] Décidément je suis dégoûté d'écrire, comme moi j'écris. J'ai envie de m'enterrer, nous enterrer, dans ce trou à betteraves. Qu'il se présente une masure dans mes prix et je m'y engouffre. Trop mou pour chercher ailleurs. Et puis maintenant je connais les têtes d'ici et les dangers, quelle chiffe quand même. Avec le 10me de votre vitalité et de votre courage, non, inutile, je les aurais emprisonnés. Crise de cafard, bien sûr. Mais je ne connais plus que ça.

Oui, j'admire la patte, elle ne ressemble pas aux miennes.[4] Fauchant aujourd'hui, avec ma faux bien battue sur l'enclume à l'anglaise par un Belge trépané et homicide par intermittence, j'ai dévasté un guêpier. Piqué un 50 mètres comme il y a 50 ans, ce qui m'a sauvé la vie. Toutes les quelques minutes un coup de poing sur la terre, c'est un gros fruit qui tombe, à la fois vert et pourri. Ça me dit quelque chose.

Rien de nouveau côté Bordas. Les Editions s'en occupent. J'essaie de lire <u>Notre-D. de Paris</u>. Impossible.[5]

Notre affectueuse amitié à vous tous. Sam

ALS; 1 leaf, 2 sides; *env to* Madame Péron, "Les Bruyères," La Garenne, Erquy, Côtes-du-Nord; *pm* 19-9-51, La Ferté-sous-Jouarre; TxU, Lake collection, Beckett. *Dating:* from pm, 18 September was Tuesday in 1951; date given in AN AH 19.9.51 is that of the pm.

Tuesday [18 September 1951]   Ussy-sur-Marne
Dear Mania

Received your letter of the 13th and, this morning, your card. Much touched that you should show such concern about my little affairs, and by your offering to shorten your holiday because of me. Let us all calm down: there is no urgency. *Combat* is laying it on a bit thick. The first proofs I received only this morning, and I shall certainly not have the others before the first week in October. Nothing worth mentioning so far, except that the work is profoundly distressing, now that it is too late to bury it.[1]

SARGASSO, if I remember correctly.

Glad that you have had news of the Sarrautes, and of the kind that suits you.[2]

My little texts are at a standstill. The latest I had not even the courage to re-read.[3] Decidedly I am sick of writing, the way I write. I feel like burying myself, burying ourselves, in this beetroot-growing hole. Let some hovel turn up that I can afford and I'll disappear into it. Too feeble to go looking anywhere else. And now I know the faces round here, and the dangers – what a spineless creature. With a tenth of your vitality and courage – no, useless, I would have locked them away. Having a bad day, of course. But that's the only kind I know now.

Yes, I admire the paw, it doesn't look like mine.[4] Scything today, with my scythe well hammered out on the English-style anvil by a trepanned and intermittently murderous Belgian, I laid waste a wasps' nest. Did a 50 metres like 50 years ago, which saved my life. Every few minutes there's a thump on the ground, and a big fruit falls, at one and the same time green and rotten. It's telling me something.

Nothing new in the Bordas business. Minuit are dealing with it. I am trying to read *Notre-Dame de Paris*. Impossible.[5]

Our love to you all. Sam

1   Mania Péron was prepared to check SB's proofs, as was her custom. Her concern was sparked by announcement of the publication of *Malone meurt* "dans trois semaines environ" (in about three weeks) ("Offensive d'automne: aux Editions de Minuit," *Combat* 13 September 1951: 4).

2   Ilya Tcherniak, father of Nathalie Sarraute, emigrated from Russia to Paris at the same time as Mania Péron's family, the Lézines, and the families remained close friends; Tcherniak repaid an old debt incurred in Russia by helping to educate Mania and her sister Irène Lézine (Alexis Péron). The news of the Sarrautes is not known.

3   SB refers to the series of *Textes pour rien*. The last that he had sent to Péron was no. IX; in his letter of 17 August 1951, SB is stuck in no. X, which may be the one referred to here.

4   "Patte," translated here as "paw," may refer to handwriting or to some other sense of the word.

5   Victor Hugo's *Notre Dame de Paris* (1831; *The Hunchback of Notre-Dame*).

GEORGES BELMONT
PARIS

Vendredi [c. 28 September 1951]   Ussy-sur-Marne
Mon cher Georges

Merci de ta bonne lettre. Content que ça aille mieux pour toi. Pour ta pièce, penses-tu attendre une huitaine de jours? Sinon n'hésite pas de me prévenir et je ferai un saut à Paris te l'envoyer. Bien content que Marchat s'y intéresse, ça doit donner quelque chose.[1]

J'ai fini de corriger les premières épreuves de Malone. Sale besogne.

Bordas (entre nous) me menace d'un procès en dommages ... intérêts pour rupture de contrat soi-disant. Je n'arrive pas à m'en émouvoir.[2]

Gentil de ta part d'avoir insisté auprès de Queneau pour qu'il lise mon livre. Mais il doit y être aussi peu apte que moi à lire les siens.[3]

Je bricole, maussadement. Aujourd'hui concocté une table avec des chutes de chêne. Elle tient debout. N'arrive pas à m'intéresser au travail, passé, présent et à venir. Je ne demande qu'une chose, pouvoir m'enterrer dans ce trou à betteraves, gratter la terre et bayer aux nuages. Entouré de bons murs.

Je ne crois pas avoir d'autres poèmes, à part les 2 donnés à 84.[4] Il n'y en aura certainement plus et ce ne sera pas un malheur. J'essaierai de récupérer un Godot (la pièce en panne chez Blin) pour te la passer. Et j'ai une dizaine de petits textes écrits ces derniers temps, arrière-faix de l'Innommable et inabordables directement.[5] Mais si le coeur t'en dit ...

Friday [c. 28 September 1951], Belmont

Voilà une bien pauvre lettre et sans doute illisible.

A bientôt mon vieux Georges. Je te ferai signe de Paris, pas la semaine prochaine, l'autre. C'est Suzanne qui arrive avant moi qui t'enverra ta pièce.

Amitiés à tous

Sam

ALS; 1 leaf, 2 sides; Belmont. *Dating*: writing on 18 September 1951 to Mania Péron, SB reports that he has just received proofs of *Malone meurt*; on 4 October 1951, writing to Susan Manning (TxU, Beckett collection), he reports that he has just finished correcting the proofs. The Friday before 4 October 1951 was 28 September.

Friday [c. 28 September 1951]   Ussy-sur-Marne

My dear Georges

Thank you for your kind letter. Glad things are going better for you. As for your play, can you wait a week? If not, don't hesitate to let me know and I will hop up to Paris and send it to you. Very pleased that Marchat is showing interest. That should produce something.[1]

I have finished correcting the first proofs of *Malone*. Rotten job.

Bordas (between ourselves) is threatening to sue me for loss of earnings (he says). I cannot get worked up about it.[2]

Nice of you to have pressed Queneau to read my book. But he must be as little fitted to read it as I am to read his.[3]

I go on doing odd jobs, gloomily. Today knocked together a table with offcuts of oak. It holds up. Cannot manage to interest myself in work, past, present and to come. I ask for nothing more than to be able to bury myself in this beetroot-growing hole, scratch the earth and howl at the clouds. Surrounded by good walls.

I don't think I have any other poems, apart from the two given to 84.[4] There will certainly not be any more, and that will be no misfortune. I shall try to get back a *Godot* (the play that is getting nowhere with Blin) to let you have. And I have ten or so little texts written recently, the afterbirth of *L'Innommable* and not to be approached directly.[5] But if you feel like it ...

This is a poor sort of letter and no doubt illegible.

Till soon, my dear Georges. I shall give you a call from Paris, not next week, the one after. Suzanne, who will get there before me, will send you the play.

> Best wishes to all
>
> Sam

1   SB refers to the play he has read by Belmont (see 8 August 1951). The actor and director Jean-Pierre Marchat (1902–1966), who had trained with Charles Dullin, was a member of the Comédie-Française from 1927 to 1932, and again after 1953; with Marcel Herrand (1897–1953), he founded the company Rideau de Paris (1929–1953) which performed at the Théâtre des Mathurins (Catherine Steinegger, *La Musique à la Comédie-Française de 1921 à 1964: aspects de l'évolution d'un genre* [Sprimont, Belgium: Mardaga, 2003] 48, 149).

2   Bordas contract: 9 September 1951; 10 September [1951], and n. 4.

3   Belmont and Raymond Queneau had founded *Volontés* together. SB had sent *Murphy* to Queneau in 1938 shortly after he was appointed as a reader for Gallimard (3 April 1938). Queneau was on the jury of the Goncourt Prize in 1951, for which SB's *Malone meurt* came runner-up (R. J. Davis, M. J. Friedman, J. R. Bryer, P. C. Hoy, *Samuel Beckett: œuvres et critique franco-anglaise*, Calepins de bibliographie [Paris: Minard, 1972] np).

4   SB had sent Bisiaux three poems for *84: Nouvelle Revue Littéraire*, and later withdrew one of them (see 22 March 1951).

5   SB refers to *Textes pour rien*; by this time he had completed ten of the texts.

MANIA PERON

PARIS

[6 October 1951]   <u>Ussy</u>

Chère Mania

Et voilà!

Pour les épreuves, ce sont les secondes que je compte vous soumettre. Je ne les ai pas encore reçues.[1] Lors des premières j'ai copieusement modifié la fin. Je n'en ai jamais été content et ne le suis toujours pas. Il fallait que ça travaille, mais pas trop, pas au point d'éteindre l'effort pour finir. Très difficile. Et n'y étant plus, je ne suis pas arrivé.[2] Et je crois qu'il y a 2 passages sur la lune que vous ne connaissez pas.[3] Plus rien de Bordas. Peut-être qu'il attend que le livre sorte pour faire opposition.[4]

Content que l'extrait ait plu à Alexis. Il y a quelques accents de terrible[s].[5] Ma faute. Le correcteur les avait corrigés et je les ai remis dans le mauvais sens. Ça m'a rapporté 16.000 fr. De quoi nous payer un gueuleton à tous les cinq quand mon frangin sera là.[6] Nous irons dans une boîte russe et vous commanderez des spécialités caucasiennes.

Affectueusement chère Mania

<u>Sam</u>

	I	II	III	IV	V	VI	VII	VIII	IX
1	G	O	D	I	L	L	O		T	S
2	A	F	O	■	I	■	S	R	A
3	L	F	■	I	L	E	■	E	M
4	L	I	B	E	L	L	E	S	■
5	I	C	O	N	E	■	U	■	D
6	N	I	A	■	■	A	R	M	E
7	A	E	■	B	E	S	O	I	N
8	C	L	E	■	V	■	P	T	T
9	E	■	A	V	A	L	E	E	■

Horizontalement. 1. *Un auteur moderne constate leur lourdeur* – 2. *Anagramme: colonies. Phonétiquement: tâchera* 3. *couronnes* – *La tortue en est une* – *Renversé: pronom* – 4. *Ecrits diffamatoires* – 5: *au[-]dessus du samovar* – 6: *refusa de se mettre à table. Froide quand elle est blanche* – 7: *diphtongue. Naturel, quelquefois* – 8. *Des champs et des songes* – *service* 9: *La couleuvre l'est quelquefois.*

Verticalement. 1. *Polygame* – 2. *Tel un journal* – 3. *note* – *Manque encore à la Garenne* – *voyelles* 4. *attache insuffisante* – 5. *Dans le Nord* – *... qui donc es-tu?* – 6. *Renversé: pronom* – *Peu prisé aux dés* – 7. *Pour Tarzan* – *Ravie* 8. *Adverbe* – *Petite gourmande* 9. *De haut en bas: au noir. De bas en haut: au soleil* – *L'est quelquefois de lait.*

ALS; 1 leaf, 2 sides [verso, a crossword with clues, in Péron's hand, completed in SB's; squared notebook paper, torn from top edge] date added in AH 6-10-51; env to Madame PÉRON, 69 Rue de la Tombe-Issoire, PARIS 14<u>me</u>; pm 6-10-51, La Ferté-sous-Jouarre; TxU, Lake collection, Beckett.

[6 October 1951]   <u>Ussy</u>

Dear Mania

There you are!

For the proofs, it is the second batch that I am expecting to send you. I have not yet received them.[1] At the time of the first ones I made copious changes to the ending. I have never been satisfied with it, and am still not. It had to work actively, but not too much, not to the point of extinguishing the effort to end. Very difficult. And, not being there any more, I didn't manage it.[2] And I think that there are 2 passages on the moon that you do not know.[3] No word from Bordas. Perhaps he is waiting for the book to come out to register his opposition.[4]

Glad that Alexis liked the extract. There are some dreadful accents.[5] My fault. The proof-reader had corrected them, and I put them back wrong way round. It brought in 16,000 fr. for me. Enough to pay for a slap-up meal for the five of us when my brother comes.[6] We'll go to a Russian place and you can order Caucasian specialities.

Affectionately dear Mania

Sam

1 On 15 October, Philippe Hautefeuille at Editions de Minuit wrote to SB that he had just received the second proofs of *Malone meurt*, and asked where he should send them (IMEC, Beckett, Boîte 1, S. Beckett, Correspondance 1947–1953).

2 SB writes "Je ne suis pas arrivé" instead of the expectable "je n'y suis pas arrivé."

3 There are a dozen evocations of the moon in *Malone meurt*; though the AMS is in archive (TxU, Beckett collection), without the corrected proofs it would be difficult to assert what the two new passages might be.

4 *Molloy*, which was published by Editions de Minuit in March, had been offered to Bordas under the original contract, but Pierre Bordas wrote on 13 January 1948 to Jacoba van Velde that as he could not publish it immediately, she could dispose of it elsewhere (IMEC, Beckett, Boîte 1, S. Beckett, Dossier Murphy 1946-1957). *Malone meurt* was published in November 1951. On 3 October, Pierre Bordas wrote to Jérome Lindon that he would pursue "un règlement équitable de cette affaire" (an equitable settlement of this matter) (IMEC, Beckett, Boîte 1, S. Beckett, Dossier Murphy 1946-1957).

5 SB refers to "Quel Malheur ..."

6 Frank and Jean Beckett visited SB during the last two weeks of October (SB to Susan Manning, 4 October 1951, TxU, Beckett collection; SB to Thomas MacGreevy, 10 November 1951, TCD, MS 108402/180).

BRAM VAN VELDE, MARTHE ARNAUD-KUNTZ
PARIS

3-12-51   Paris
Chers amis,

Content d'avoir de vos nouvelles. Je suis en effet mal fichu, et ça depuis pas mal de temps. Je ne sors pour ainsi dire plus depuis 15 jours, un tour de 5 minutes dans le quartier et puis vite retour à la tanière. Et comme ça n'a pas l'air de vouloir s'arranger, ne comptez pas me voir à St. Brice de sitôt.[1] Mais vous, quand vous venez à Paris, pourquoi ne passez-vous pas nous voir?

Je n'ai pas bien compris ce que veut Maeght de moi. Si c'est faisable, et que ça fasse plaisir à Bram, c'est accordé sans autre forme de procès.[2] Mais tant de choses ne sont plus faisables pour la loque que je suis devenu. Il y a longtemps que je n'ai vu Georges, mais j'ai lu sa préface pr. l'exposition et la trouve tout simplement admirable.[3]

Que Bram surtout ne s'imagine pas que je m'éloigne de lui, c'est tout le contraire. Plus je m'enfonce et plus je me sens à ses côtés et combien, malgré les différences, nos aventures se rejoignent, dans l'impensé et le navrant. Et s'il devait y avoir pour moi une âme soeur, je me flatte que ce serait bien la sienne et nulle autre, qu'on se voie ou qu'on ne se voie pas, ça ne change rien à l'affaire. Et que je ne puisse plus, autant qu'autrefois, l'encourager, n'est que l'effet d'une faiblesse et d'une fatigue qui me le rendent encore plus cher, si cela est possible. Bram est mon grand familier. Dans le travail et dans l'impossibilité de travailler, et ce sera toujours ainsi.

Affectueusement de nous deux

Sam

ALS; 1 leaf, 2 sides; Putman collection. Previous publication, facsimile and transcription, with variants, Stoullig and Schoeller, eds., *Bram Van Velde*, 175; Alphant, Léger, and Szidon, eds., *Objet: Beckett*, plates 82–83.

3-12-51   Paris

Dear both,

Glad to hear from you. Yes, I am in a bad way, and have been for quite a while. I haven't been outside to speak of for a fortnight: a five-minute walk somewhere nearby, then quickly back to the den. And since it doesn't seem to be getting any better, don't count on seeing me at Saint-Brice in the next while.[1] But why don't you come and see us when you're in Paris?

I can't quite understand what Maeght wants from me. If it's feasible, and Bram would like it, then it's granted without further ado.[2] But so many things are not feasible any more for the human wreck I've turned into. I haven't seen Georges for ages, but I've read his preface for the exhibition and find it quite simply admirable.[3]

Above all, let Bram not get the idea that I'm moving away from him. The very reverse. The farther I sink down, the more I feel right beside him, feel how much, in spite of the differences, our ventures come together, in the unthought and the harrowing. And if there had to be for me a soul-mate, I make bold to say that it would be his soul and no other. Whether we see each other or not makes no difference. And the fact that I can't encourage him the way I used to is nothing more than the result of a weakness and a weariness which endear him to me still more, if that's possible. Bram is my great familiar. In work and in the impossibility of working. That's how it will always be.

      Love from us both

      Sam

---

1   Bram van Velde and Marthe Arnaud-Kuntz were resident in a damp and dilapidated house at 2 Rue Eugène Chatenay, Saint-Brice-sous-Forêt, just north of Paris (Kober, *Bram van Velde et ses loups*, 27)

2   SB had been asked for a text for Bram van Velde's exhibition at the Galerie Maeght which was to take place from 15 February to 10 March 1952.

3   Georges Duthuit's preface for the exhibition was "Bram van Velde ou aux Colonnes d'Hercule."

CHRONOLOGY 1952

1952	January	Roger Blin seeking a theatre for *En attendant Godot*.
	6 February	An excerpt from *En attendant Godot* recorded on 6 February for broadcast on French radio on 17 February.
	15 February – 10 March	Bram van Velde exhibition, Galerie Maeght. SB writes text for the carte d'invitation.
	26 February	*En attendant Godot* awarded a subvention "pour aider le montage" (in support of the production).
	28 April	Allied occupation of Japan ends; peace treaty signed in San Francisco.
	26 May	Death of Eugene Jolas. SB writes a tribute.
	2 June	*En attendant Godot* in rehearsal: autumn production anticipated.
	23 July	Agreement signed with France Guy, Théâtre de Poche, to qualify for subvention payment for *En attendant Godot*.
	12 August	*Merlin* interested in publishing a work by SB.
	Autumn	SB having a cottage built in Ussy.
	October	"Je tiens le Greffe" ("Texte pour rien, V") published in *Deucalion*.
	17 October	Publication of *En attendant Godot*.
	November	Geer van Velde exhibition, Galerie Maeght.
	1 November	United States tests the first hydrogen bomb in the Marshall Islands.
	2 November	Subsequent to broken agreement with the Théâtre de Poche, SB signs contract with Théâtre de Babylone for production of *En attendant Godot*.
	13 November	Rehearsals of *En attendant Godot* begin.
	15 December	"Extract from *Watt*" published in *Merlin*.

jeudi [3 January 1952]   Ussy

Cher Vieux

Ta bonne lettre ce matin.[1] Nous sommes partis sans enthousiasme, presque pas exprès, espérant vaguement qu'un changement
d'air etc. Je t'en fous. J'ai le coeur qui chaque nuit dévale les précipices
en marche arrrière [sic], comme lorsque j'avais 20 ans, suivi de cau-
chemars en famille torrentiels de larmes avec des coups de poing aux
visages des chers disparus, de quoi se réveiller frais et dispos à faire
joujou avec l'anthracite américain à 20.000 balles la tonne et bluté à
50% d'adamantins cailloux.[2] Dans les intervalles Moustiques de
Faulkner, avec une préface de Queneau à faire dégobiller une
autruche, mais digne du texte, ou bien l'espoir quot[id]iennement
déçu de voir un jour atteindre l'anus les grattages du Baron de la
Meffraie.[3] Enfin, aujourd'hui, dans Combat, un très joli petit poème
de Thomas, et l'autre jour, avant le départ peut-être, la Musique pour
cordes, célesta et percussion de Bartok, écrite en Suisse après sa fuite,
absolument extraordinaire.[4] Nous avons écouté le concerto pour 2
pianos, très dodécaphonisant, à moins que ce ne fût un autre.[5]

Depuis notre sortie avec Bram il est venu deux fois à la maison,
dont une avec pernoctation, comme disait l'autre. Il est réellement
sérieusement dérangé, on ne sait plus quoi lui dire. Il ne s'agit plus de
son travail, mais plus du tout. Pour l'expulsion, il n'avait pas l'air de
s'en faire. A vrai dire c'est surtout Marthe qui sera sur le pavé. Si cela
avait pour effet de les séparer pendant quelque temps, ce ne serait
peut-être pas si mauvais.[6]

Pensant à Riopelle je me dis qu'il lui faudra un drôle de coup de
reins pour se sortir de là.[7]

Je suis tombé enfin, avant le départ, dans les 120 Journées, sur le
passage du soleil, inexactement donné si j'ai bonne mémoire. J'ai
marqué l'endroit et te montrerai ça à notre retour. Moins renversant

que la première fois, entrevu à l'ombre des pages non coupées, mais quand même, au milieu de tous ces étrons et rectums ganahuchés, le bienvenu.[8]

C'est probablement Char qui m'a saboté auprès de la Princesse Caetani (?), non pas que j'en coule particulièrement.[9] Mais son sale fric aurait fait bien Rue de la Gaîté. Jamais bu un Beaujolais, ni mangé un chateaubriand, comme ceux des Iles Marquises. Paie-toi ça, un soir de cafard, et ensuite (sans garantie) les trois faibles femmes d'en face.[10]

Travail néant. L'ancre tient bon et à chaque soubresaut s'enfonce un peu plus dans la vase. Si ça continue il va falloir trouver un autre passe[-]temps.

Affectueusement, cher Georges, et à bientôt, dans une 10aine de jours, si on tient le coup.

s/ Sam

TLS; 1 leaf, 1 side; Duthuit collection. *Dating*: Henri Thomas's poem in *Combat*.

Thursday [3 January 1952]   Ussy

My dear Georges,

Your welcome letter this morning.[1] We left unenthusiastically, almost inadvertently, hoping vaguely for a change of air etc. Some hope. My heart falls backwards down precipices every night, as it did when I was twenty, followed by nightmares, back in the family, floods of tears, fists swinging into the faces of the dear departed: just the thing to help you wake up fresh and bright to play little games with American anthracite at 20,000 francs a ton, and with a 50% sieving of adamantine chippings.[2] In between times Faulkner's *Moustiques*, with a preface by Queneau that would make an ostrich puke, but worthy of the text, or else the hope, daily dashed, of seeing the Baron de la Meffraie's scratchings reach his anus.[3] But then, today, in *Combat*, a very prettily turned little poem by Thomas, and the other day, before we left perhaps, the Music for strings, celesta and percussion by Bartok, written in Switzerland after his escape: absolutely extraordinary.[4] We listened to the concerto for two pianos, very dodecaphonical, unless it was some other one.[5]

Since our outing with Bram he has been to the house twice, once with pernoctation, as the man said. He is genuinely, seriously unhinged: it's hard to know what to say to him. It's not about the work any more, not at all. As for the expulsion, he seemed unconcerned. In actual fact it's Marthe above all who will be on the heap. If the outcome was that they would be separated for a while, it might not be too bad a thing.[6]

About Riopelle I can't help thinking that he'll really have to put his back into it if he's to get out of that.[7]

And then, before we left, I happened, in the *120 Journées*, on the sun passage, inaccurately given if I remember aright. I've marked the place and will show it to you on our return. Less staggering than the first time, glimpsed in the half-light of uncut pages, but all the same, amid all those turds and sucked rectums, very welcome.[8]

It was probably Char who spoiled my chances with Princess Caetani (?); not that I feel the loss all that much.[9] But her filthy lucre would have come in handy in the Rue de la Gaîté. Never drunk a Beaujolais, or eaten a Chateaubriand, like the ones in the Iles Marquises. Treat yourself to these, some evening when you're feeling low, and afterwards (no guarantees) to the *Trois faibles femmes* opposite.[10]

Work nil. The anchor is firmly in, and with each lurch sinks a little deeper into the mud. If it goes on like this I shall have to find another pastime.

Fondest regards, my old friend, till we see each other again – in ten days or so, if we hold out.

Sam

---

1   Duthuit's letter to SB has not been found.

2   The central heating boiler and the stove in SB's Ussy house were both fueled by coal at this time.

3   William Faulkner's 1927 novel *Mosquitoes* was published as *Moustiques* (1948) by Editions de Minuit, in a translation by Jean Dubramet and with an introduction by Raymond Queneau.

SB alludes to René de Solier's novel *La Meffraie* (1951), in which the Baron de la Meffraie, a repugnant and idle man living in the Paris suburbs, beset by mania concerning his own face and body, indulges in his passion for scratching himself and being scratched by his she-cats; his scratching, while it reaches his posterior, never quite reaches his anus.

4   "Un poème inédit de Henri Thomas," *Combat* 3 January 1952: 7.
SB listened to Béla Bartók's *Music for Strings, Celesta and Percussion*, BB 114, Sz. 106, on radio Paris-Inter on Monday 24 December 1951. The concert was broadcast as part of the "Gravures Précieuses" series.

5   Bartók's music was as yet little known in France. Nothing resembling his *Concerto for Two Pianos* was broadcast in the "Gravures précieuses" series by the date when SB writes to Duthuit, nor on any other radio channel, leaving it uncertain which piece or broadcast SB is referring to.

6   A little more than two weeks later, on 19 January, Marthe Arnaud wrote of her precarious situation in the house she was renting with Bram van Velde, in a letter to Jacques Kober: "voilà qu'on veut nous flanquer dehors en plein hiver et à la veille ou au milieu de l'expo de Bram, parce que ces messieurs-dames veulent tout à coup habiter eux-mêmes ce logis qui a été à l'abandon pendant des années" (now it appears they want to throw us out just before or in the middle of Bram's exhibition, just because these fine folk suddenly want to live in the place themselves, when it's been derelict for years) (Kober, *Bram van Velde et ses loups*, 27).

7   Duthuit had been a friend and supporter of the Quebecois painter Jean-Paul Riopelle (1923–2002) since first viewing his work more than one year previously, and had been enthusiastic about Riopelle's exhibition at the Studio Fachetti which had taken place in December 1951 – a show that had been a complete commercial flop (Hélène de Billy, *Riopelle: la biographie* [Montréal: Editions Art Global, 1996] 89–95). Referring to this precise period, when speaking on television in 1968, Riopelle remarked:

> "Les gens qui connaissaient ma peinture et qui l'appréciaient, qui voyaient une possibilité, n'avaient pas les moyens de me faire vivre. Pour eux, il s'agissait tout simplement de m'aider en me disant que si j'avais besoin de quelque chose ... Mais, comme vous dites, il faut de la couleur et il en faut beaucoup, surtout de la façon dont je peins. Je n'avais ni atelier ni galerie, et je venais de faire une exposition où je n'avais rien vendu." (Robert Bernier, with collaboration of Guy Patenaude, François-Marc Gagnon, and Monique Brunet, *Jean-Paul Riopelle: des visions d'Amérique* [Montréal: Les Editions de l'Homme, 1997] 86–87.) (The people who knew and who appreciated my painting, who saw a possibility, weren't rich enough to keep me alive. For them, it was just a question of helping me out, saying that if I needed anything ... But, as you say, I need colours, and lots of them, especially the way I paint. I had neither studio nor gallery, and had just put on an exhibition where I hadn't sold a thing.)

8   The sun's sudden appearance may have been evoked by the opening lines of the poem by Henri Thomas which SB has admired: "Le soleil d'automne entre dans ma chambre. / Charlatan subtil, doux bonimenteur." (The Autumn sun comes into my bedroom. / Subtle charlatan, gentlest of hucksters.)
SB is almost certainly referring to one of two passages in the Marquis de Sade's *120 Journées de Sodome*. The first occurs at the end of the sixth day: "Il est plus que vraisemblable que l'Aurore aux doigts de rose, en entrouvrant les portes du palais d'Apollon, les eût trouvés plongés dans leur ordure, bien plutôt comme des pourceaux

que comme des hommes" (It is very probable indeed that rosy-fingered Dawn, opening the gates of Apollo's palace, would have found them lying still plunged in their excrements, rather more after the example of swine than like heroes) (Sade, *Œuvres*, I, ed. Michel Delon, Bibliothèque de la Pléiade [Paris: Gallimard, 1990] 142; *The 120 Days of Sodom and Other Writings*, ed. and tr. Austryn Wainhouse and Richard Seaver [New York: Grove Press, 1987] 343). The second occurs at the end of the twenty-fourth day: "et la blonde Aurore étant venue, comme disent les poètes, ouvrir les portes du palais d'Apollon, ce dieu, assez libertin lui-même, ne monta sur son char azuré que pour venir éclairer de nouvelles luxures" (and fair-haired Aurora having come, as the poets say, to fling open the gates of the palace where dwelt Apollo, that god, somewhat a libertine himself, only mounted his azure chariot in order to bring light to shed upon new lecheries) (*Œuvres*, I, 246; *The 120 Days of Sodom*, 508).

SB types "ganahuchés" in place of "gamahuchés."

9   Char's widow Marie-Claude Char reports that from 1949 her husband was involved in "une longue et fervente relation amoureuse" (a long and fervent liaison) with Princess Caetani (Marie-Claude Char, *Pays de René Char* [Paris: Flammarion, 2007] 174); while Stefania Valli, more circumspectly, writes of the period of the early 1950s: "seguì una serie de pubblicazioni relative allo scrittore francese René Char, grande amico di Marguerite Caetani e collaboratore di 'Botteghe Oscure' non solo in qualità di autore, ma anche, almeno in qualche occasione, come consulente ed assistente per la sezione francese della rivista" (there followed a series of publications related to the French writer René Char, a close friend of Marguerite Caetani and a collaborator on *Botteghe Oscure* not only in his capacity as author but also, on certain occasions at least, as a consultant and assistant for the French section of the journal) (Stefania Valli, ed., *La Rivista Botteghe Oscure e Marguerite Caetani: La corrispondenza con gli autori italiani, 1948–1960* [Rome: "L'Erma" di Bretschneider, 1999] 11–12).

SB's work sent to Princess Caetani: 9 and 14 June 1951, and 3 July 1951.

10   Aux Iles Marquises was situated at 15 Rue de la Gaîté, Paris 14. *Trois faibles femmes* by Serge Veber, André Homez, and Jean-Jacques Rouff, with music by Bruno Coquatrix, was performed at the Bobino music hall, 20 Rue de la Gaîté, by the Peter Sisters (Mattye, Anne, and Virginia), from 21 December 1951 through April 1952.

THOMAS MACGREEVY
DUBLIN

14/1/52   Paris
My dear Tom

Many thanks for Bartolo and wishes. Ours to you for health and happiness in 1952.[1]

Glad you received the books safely. Don't feel you must read them or, having begun them, finish them. And if you do, don't feel you must write to me about them. They contain passages that are bound to displease you. I know you won't confound the friend with the writer.[2]

Sorry you didn't get over at Xmas. We went to the country and got back yesterday. It was a cold, wet and uncomfortable fortnight. But somehow we feel the better for it. I hope you rested well at Tarbert from Gallery worries and officialdom.[3]

Affectionately, dear Tom.

s/ <u>Sam</u>

TLS; 1 leaf, 1 side; TCD, MS 10402/181.

1   SB may refer to a card with an image of a painting by one of the several Italian artists by the name of Bartolo, among them Matteo di Giovanni di Bartolo (1435–1495), Taddeo di Bartolo (1362/63–1422), Bartolo di Fredi (active 1353–1410).

2   *Molloy* and *Malone meurt.*

On 25 November 1951, Georges Duthuit wrote to his friend Mary Hutchinson* (née Barnes, 1889–1977) about SB's self-deprecation following the success of *Molloy* which was "déconcertant pour Sam qui s'imagine 'ne pas avoir écrit un mot qui ne soit destiné à être désagréable' [...] Le second volume de la suite de trois ouvrages projetés vient de sortir: Malone meurt. Il y a là aussi des choses très bonnes." (Disconcerting for Sam, who imagines himself as "not having written a single word that was not bound to be displeasing" [...] The second volume of the planned series of three has just come out: *Malone meurt.* There too there are good things.) (TxU, Hutchinson collection.)

3   Tarbert, Co. Kerry, was MacGreevy's family home; MacGreevy was Director of the National Gallery of Ireland.

MICHEL POLAC, RADIODIFFUSION FRANÇAISE
PARIS

[after 23 January 1952]

Vous me demandez mes idées sur <u>En Attendant Godot</u>, dont vous me faites l'honneur de donner des extraits au Club d'Essai, et en même temps mes idées sur le théâtre.[1]

Je n'ai pas d'idées sur le théâtre. Je n'y connais rien. Je n'y vais pas. C'est admissible.

Ce qui l'est sans doute moins, c'est d'abord, dans ces conditions, d'écrire une pièce, et ensuite, l'ayant fait, de ne pas avoir d'idées sur elle non plus.

C'est malheureusement mon cas.

Il n'est pas donné à tous de pouvoir passer du monde qui s'ouvre sous la page à celui des profits et pertes, et retour, imperturbable, comme entre le turbin et le Café du Commerce.

Je ne sais pas plus sur cette pièce que celui qui arrive à la lire avec attention.

Je ne sais pas dans quel esprit je l'ai écrit.

Je ne sais pas plus sur les personnages que ce qu'ils disent, ce qu'ils font et ce qui leur arrive. De leur aspect j'ai dû indiquer le peu que j'ai pu entrevoir. Les chapeaux melon par exemple.

Je ne sais pas qui est Godot. Je ne sais même pas s'il existe. Et je ne sais pas s'ils y croient ou non, les deux qui l'attendent.

Les deux autres qui passent vers la fin de chacun des deux actes, ça doit être pour rompre la monotonie.

Tout ce que j'ai pu savoir, je l'ai montré. Ce n'est pas beaucoup. Mais ça me suffit, et largement. Je dirai même que je me serais contenté de moins.

Quant à vouloir trouver à tout cela un sens plus large et plus élevé, à emporter après le spectacle, avec le programme et les Esquimaux, je suis incapable d'en voir l'intérêt. Mais ce doit être possible.

Je n'y suis plus et je n'y serai plus jamais. Estragon, Vladimir, Pozzo, Lucky, leur temps et leur espace, je n'ai pu les connaître un peu que très loin du besoin de comprendre. Ils vous doivent des comptes peut-être. Qu'ils se débrouillent. Sans moi. Eux et moi nous sommes quittes.

TLcc; 1 leaf, 1 side [possibly an enclosure]; Fehsenfeld collection. *Dating*: Jérôme Lindon's letter to SB, 23 January 1952, enclosing a letter from Michel Polac. Previous publication, "Who is Godot?" [two letters by Samuel Beckett], tr. Edith Fournier, *The New Yorker* (24 June and 1 July 1996) 156–157; "Un inédit de 1951 [sic]: Beckett 'Je ne sais pas qui est Godot,'" *Le Nouvel Observateur* 24–30 October 1998: 114; Angela Moorjani, "*En attendant Godot* on Michel Polac's Entrée des Auteurs," tr. Moorjani and Ruby Cohn. *Beckett versus Beckett*. Ed. Marius Buning, Danielle De Ruyter, Matthijis Engleberts, Sjef Houppermans, *Samuel Beckett Today/Aujourd'hui*, Vol. VII. (Amsterdam and Atlanta: Rodopi, 1998) 53–54.

[after 23 January 1952]

You ask me for my ideas about *En attendant Godot*, extracts from which you are doing me the honour of putting on at the Club d'Essai, and at the same time for my ideas about theatre.[1]

I have no ideas about theatre. I know nothing about it. I do not go to it. That is allowable.

What is less so, no doubt, is first of all, in these conditions, writing a play, and then, having done so, having no ideas about it either.

This is unfortunately my case.

It is not given to everyone to be able to move from the world that opens under the page to that of profit and loss, then back again, unperturbed, as if between the daily grind and the pub on the corner.

I know no more about this play than anyone who manages to read it attentively.

I do not know in what spirit I wrote it.

I know no more of the characters than what they say, what they do and what happens to them. Of their appearance, I must have indicated the little I have been able to make out. The bowler hats for example.

I do not know who Godot is. I do not even know if he exists. And I do not know if they believe he does, these two who are waiting for him.

The two others who pass through towards the end of each of the two acts, that must be so as to break the monotony.

All that I have been able to understand I have shown. It is not much. But it is enough, and more than enough for me. I shall even say that I could have made do with less.

As for wanting to find in all this a wider and loftier meaning to take away after the show, along with the programme and the choc-ice, I am unable to see the point of it. But it must be possible.

I am no longer part of it, and never will be again. Estragon, Vladimir, Pozzo, Lucky, their time and their space, I have only been able to know a little about them by staying very far away from the need to understand. They owe you an explanation perhaps. Let them get on with it. Without me. They and I have settled our accounts.

---

1 This was a document to be read "on air" as an introduction to a reading of *En attendant Godot* on 17 February 1952, broadcast on RTF's *Entrée des auteurs*. Michel Polac (b. 1930) was a producer. In his letter of 23 January, Lindon introduced Polac and the project to SB:

> Michel Polac [. . .] est un jeune garçon, ancien employé des Editions de Minuit, et je crois qu'il serait très bien que vous puissiez lui donner, dans la mesure de vos moyens, satisfaction.

Je pense d'ailleurs que la présence de Roger Blin, et peut-être la vôtre, serait la meilleure garantie pour cette émission. D'ailleurs il ne s'agit pas, vous le voyez, d'une interview, ni d'une présentation de l'auteur, mais simplement d'une courte introduction pour le texte. (IMEC, Beckett, Boîte 2, S. Beckett, Divers *En attendant Godot*.)

(Michel Polac [. . .] is a young lad, a former employee of the Editions de Minuit, and I think it would be very good if you could accommodate him, as far as you can.

Incidentally, I think that Roger Blin's presence, and perhaps your own, would be the best guarantee for this broadcast. Besides, as you can see, there is no question of an interview, or an introduction to the writer, simply a little introduction for the text.)

Evidently SB attended the recording or heard the tape of the extracts from *En attendant Godot* which was "recorded on 6 February 1952 before a live audience at the Club d'Essai studio," for he wrote to Roger Blin on 8 February 1952: "Bravo et merci à tous" (Bravo, and thanks to all) (IMEC, Blin; Moorjani, "En attendant Godot on Michel Polac's Entrée des Auteurs," 51). Maurice Nadeau introduced SB and the play; Roger Blin read the message from SB. The cast was Lucien-Pierre Raimbourg (1903–1973) as Vladimir, Julien Verdier (1910–1999) as Estragon, Jacques Hilling (1926–1975) as Pozzo, probably Roger Blin as Lucky, Serge Lecointe (b. 1939) as the boy (Moorjani, 47–56 [the fullest history of the broadcast]; Clas Zilliacus, *Beckett and Broadcasting: A Study of the Works of Samuel Beckett for and in Radio and Television*, Acta Academiae Aboensis, Series A, 51.2 [Åbo, Finland: Åbo Akademi, 1976] 117).

Georges Duthuit wrote to Mary Hutchinson on 7 February 1952: "Hier, à la radio, enregistrement lu en petit comité, de la dernière pièce de Beckett: 'En attendant Godot', Godot ne venant naturellement – jamais. Tout a bien marché, la pièce est excellente [. . .] bien que Sam – quel auteur comique, au fond!" (Yesterday, radio recording, with just a few there, of Beckett's latest play: *Waiting for Godot* – Godot of course never coming. Everything went off well, the play is excellent [. . .] although Sam – what a comic writer, when it comes down to it!) (TxU, Hutchinson collection, Beckett.)

BRAM VAN VELDE

[before February 1952, possibly enclosed with 18 January 1952]

"La vie" écrit Pierre Schneider, dans son bel essai sur Corbière, "est une faute d'orthographe dans le texte de la mort."

Il en est heureusement de plus sérieuses.

Celles dont voici les laves.

Balayés les repentirs.

Peinture de vie et de mort.

Amateurs de natron, abstenez.[1]

Voilà, mon cher Bram, ce que ça donne.

Amitiés.

s/ <u>Sam</u>

TLS; 1 leaf, 1 side; Putman collection. *Dating*: possibly enclosed with SB to Bram van Velde and Marthe Arnaud-Kuntz, 18 January 1952, Putman collection. Previous publication, Alphant, Léger, and Szidon, eds., *Objet: Beckett*, [plate 84].

[before February 1952, possibly enclosed with 18 January 1952]

"Life," writes Pierre Schneider in his fine essay on Corbière, "is a spelling mistake in the text of death."

Happily there are others, more serious.

Those of which the living lava traces are here on show.

Contrition swept away.

Painting of life and death.

Those who like their natron should keep away.[1]

Well, Bram my old friend, this is what I've come up with.

All best

Sam

1   SB's text for the invitation to Bram van Velde's exhibition at the Galerie Maeght, 15 February to 10 March 1952.

Pierre Schneider was at this time a doctoral student at Harvard; later, as a critic and art historian, he wrote for *Les Temps Modernes*, *Critique*, *Mercure de France*, and *l'Express*. The line "La vie est une faute d'orthographe dans le texte de la mort" appears in Schneider's essay "Voix vive, lettre morte" (*Les Lettres Nouvelles* 1.1 [March 1953] 40), which SB may have read before publication. The essay was republished as "Voix vive, lettre morte: Tristan Corbière," in Pierre Schneider, *La Voix vive* ([Paris: Editions de Minuit, 1953] [199]–253).

AIDAN HIGGINS

GREYSTONES, CO. WICKLOW

8/2/52   Ussy-sur-Marne

318

Dear Mr Higgins

Thanks for your letter from Isle of Man. I forget Belacqua near Leopardstown. I see the Ballyogan Road and the sun going down in the wrong quarter. Is that the same story? The only ones I remember are Yellow and the one that originally appeared in Titus's This Quarter, Dante & the L.[1] The Envoy extract is from near the beginning, first "appearance" of Watt, and the other from somewhere near the end.[2] I am touched by the pertinacious interest you seem to take in my work and am sorry you can't read Molloy & Malone. If you feel like trying I shall be glad to send them to you.[3] The third, L'Innommable, due out probably in the spring, seems about the end of the jaunt as far as I am concerned, there being nobody left to utter and, independently perhaps, certainly superfluously, nothing left to utter about. These are hindrances to one deficient in the professional outlook. I used to think all [t]his work was an effort, necessarily feeble, to express the nothing. It seems rather to have been a journey, irreversible, in gathering thinglessness, towards it. Or also. Or ergo. And the problem remains entire or at last arising ends. Forgive these personal considerations, about no one.

With which rays of sunshine I am

Yours sincerely

s/ Sam. Beckett

TLS; 1 leaf, 1 side; TxU, Beckett collection.

1   The letter from Aidan Higgins* (b. 1927) has not been found.
The story that Higgins has mentioned is "Walking Out," from *More Pricks Than Kicks* (1934). The Ballyogan Road passes south of Leopardstown.
Also collected in *More Pricks Than Kicks* are the stories "Yellow" and "Dante and the Lobster," the latter of which appeared in *This Quarter* 5.2 (December 1932) 222–236, edited by Edward W. Titus (1870–1952; Profile, I).

2   "An Extract from Watt," *Envoy*, 11–19; the extract differs from the published edition of *Watt* (Paris: Olympia Press, 1953) 16–24. A second selection, "Extract from Watt," appeared in *Irish Writing* 17 (December 1951) 11–16.

3   *Molloy* and *Malone meurt* were not available in English.

JACOBA VAN VELDE

19/2/52   Paris
Chère Tony
          Votre lettre ce matin. Je viens de vous envoyer Malone. Oui,
j'ai envoyé les deux livres à Bob. Il y a des mois de ça.[1] Il ne m'en a pas
accusé réception. C'est sans doute moi qui exagère en me disant
qu'il aurait pu. Ca ne m'intéresse pas de savoir ce qu'on pense
du travail, mais j'aime autant ne pas avoir à me demander, de
temps en temps, à propos d'un envoi, s'il ne s'est pas égaré. Enfin
tout ça n'a pas beaucoup d'importance. L'Innommable doit paraître avant l'ete [*for* l'été]. On a donné des extraits de Godot à la
radio, avec Blin, bien secondé. Il espère pouvoir le monter bientôt.
Tout dépend si l'aide à la première pièce est accordée ou non. La
pièce paraîtra en librairie au moment de la représentation.[2] Je n'ai
rien pu faire depuis L'Innommable, c'est la fin des haricots. Vous
comprendrez peut-être pourquoi en le lisant. Je gigote, mais sans
résultat. Si je pouvais me résoudre à abandonner, ça vaudrait
mieux. J'y arriverai peut-être. Le vernissage de l'exposition Bram
chez Maeg[h]t a eu lieu vendredi dernier. Formidable.[3] Bram en
effet ne va pas très bien, Geer non plus, Lisl non plus, nous non
plus, quelle bande de crevés. Bram et Marthe sont en effet mean-
cés [*for* menacés] d'expulsion de leur petit logement à la campagne.
Marthe n'a plus son appartement à Paris, mais Bram a toujours son
atelier. Pour le moment ils s'accrochent.[4] Le directeur du Musée
d'Art Moderne d'Amsterdam est passé chez Maeght hier et veut
monter l'exposition à Amsterdam. Le critique Charles Estienne est
enthousiasmé, paraît-il. Il est temps.[5]
          Bon courage, ma chère Tony. Amitiés.
          s/ Sam

TLS; 1 leaf, 1 side; BNF 19794/15.

19/2/52   Paris

Dear Tony

Your letter this morning. I've just sent you *Malone*. Yes, I did send the two books to Bob. Months ago.[1] He hasn't acknowledged them. Perhaps I'm being unduly fussy if I consider that all the same he might have. I'm not interested in knowing what people think of the work, but I'd rather not have to wonder, every so often, whether something I've sent has got lost. Anyway, none of that really matters. *L'Innommable* is to come out before the summer. They did a broadcast of extracts from *Godot* on the radio, with Blin, well supported. He hopes to be able to put it on soon. It all turns on whether the financial assistance for the first play is forthcoming or not. The play will be in the bookshops as soon as it opens.[2] I haven't been able to do anything since *L'Innommable*. It's the bottom of the barrel. Perhaps you'll understand why when you read it. I turn and twist, but to no purpose. If I could make the decision to give up, it might be better. Perhaps I will. The private view for Bram's exhibition chez Maeght took place last Friday. Tremendous.[3] Yes, Bram is not very well, neither is Geer, nor Lisl, nor are we: what a bunch of cripples. And indeed Bram and Marthe are faced with being thrown out of their little place in the country. Marthe no longer has her Paris flat, but Bram still has his studio. For the moment they are hanging on.[4] The Director of the Amsterdam Museum of Modern Art called at the Maeght yesterday, and wants to put the exhibition on in Amsterdam. The critic Charles Estienne is all excited about it, apparently. Not before time.[5]

Cheer up, my dear Tony. Yours ever

Sam

1   In his letter to Jacoba van Velde of 11 June [1951], SB asks for the address of Bob Clerx, husband of Jacoba, so that he can send him *Molloy* (BNF 19794/16). *Malone meurt* may have been the other book sent to him.

2   RTF production of *En attendant Godot*: see [after 23 January 1952], n. 1. Blin's attempt to secure a government subvention for the production of a first play: 4 August 1951, n. 7.

3   The opening of the Bram van Velde exhibition at the Galerie Maeght took place on 15 February 1952. The director of the Stedelijk Museum from 1945 to

1963 was Willem Sandberg (1897–1984). Bram van Velde's work was included in a collective exhibition that opened there on 27 February 1953, Elf Tijdgenoten uit Parijs (Eleven Contemporaries from Paris); Bram van Velde did not have a solo exhibition at the Stedelijk Museum until the retrospective held from 21 December 1959 to 1 February 1960 (Stoullig and Schoeller, eds., *Bram van Velde*, 242, 245).

4   Geer and Lisl van Velde.
Bram van Velde and Marthe Arnaud, Saint-Brice-sous-Forêt: 3 December 1951, n. 1.

5   The art critic Charles Estienne (1908–1966) had written enthusiastically of Bram and Geer van Velde's painting ("Deux peintres hollandais de Paris: les frères Van Velde," *Combat* 4 June 1948: 2), but he did not publish a review of the exhibition in 1952.

JEROME LINDON, EDITIONS DE MINUIT
PARIS

le 26 février 1952   Ussy-sur-Marne
                                                     Seine-et-Marne

Mon cher Jérôme

Merci de la bonne nouvelle que vous êtes le premier à nous annoncer.[1]

Je crois bien que votre Godot est une première version. J'y ai fait pas mal de changements voici bientôt un an, avant que Blin propose la pièce pour l'aide à la première. C'est cette version corrigée que Blin a fait taper pour la commission et pour ses comédiens qui est la bonne, ou presque, car je vois encore quelques petites coupures à faire. Je vais écrire tout de suite à Blin pour qu'il m'en envoie un exemplaire et vous aurez le texte définitif la semaine prochaine.[2]

Il va falloir que je relise Molloy (ce que je n'ai pas fait depuis sa parution) avant la réimpression. Comme je ne l'ai pas ici, voulez-vous m'en envoyer un exemplaire?[3]

J'en suis au quatrième faux départ. Encore quelques pages et ça rentrera gentiment sous terre. Monsieur Micha m'écrit pour comparer Molloy au Roman de la Rose.[4]

Nos bonnes amitiés à Annette et à vous-même.[5]
                    s/ Sam. Beckett

PS Tentative de réflexion faite, ça irait beaucoup plus vite si vous demandiez vous-même à Blin de vous passer un de ses exemplaires et que vous me l'envoyiez en même temps que Molloy. Excusez-moi de vous demander tant de choses.

TLS; 1 leaf, 1 side; Minuit collection; IMEC, Beckett, Boîte 1, S. Beckett, Correspondance 1946–1953.

26th February 1952   Ussy-sur-Marne
                                                Seine-et-Marne

My dear Jérôme

Thank you for the good news, which you are the first to tell us.[1]

I'm inclined to think that your *Godot* is an early version. I made a fair few changes just about a year ago, before Blin put the play up for the first play grant. It is this corrected version, which Blin has had typed for the Commission and for the actors, that is the right one, or almost right, since I can still see a few small cuts to be made. I shall write to Blin straight away asking him to send me a copy, and you will have the definitive text next week.[2]

I shall have to re-read *Molloy* (something I have not done since it came out) before the reprint. As I haven't got it here, would you send me a copy?[3]

I am on to my fourth false start. A few pages more and it will be quietly buried. Monsieur Micha writes to me comparing *Molloy* to the *Roman de la rose*.[4]

Our warm wishes to Annette and yourself.[5]

                    Sam. Beckett

PS On pre-mature reflection, things would go much faster if you were yourself to ask Blin to send you one of his copies and you sent it on to me together with the *Molloy*. Forgive me for asking you for so many things.

1 Roger Blin's application for the subvention for *En attendant Godot* had been successful. In January 1952, Blin had received a letter from Georges Neveux (1900–1982) who was a member of the committee to determine the subventions; he promised that he would fight for it (Blin and Peskine, *Roger Blin*, 84; Aslan, *Roger Blin*, 23).

2　While the play was in rehearsal, and even later, SB and Roger Blin continued to make changes to the script. The first edition of *En attendant Godot* (published on 17 October 1952) preceded production. The original AMS of *En attendant Godot* is held in the Bibliothèque Nationale de France (BNF, Reserve MY-440, microfilm R202751).

3　*Molloy* was reprinted in May 1953.

4　SB's "false start" has not been identified.
On 31 January, SB replied to a letter from René Micha (1913–1992), the editor of the works of Pierre-Jean Jouve, saying that the only clarifications he could give about his own work were biographical and bibliographical (sold by Lame Duck Books, Cambridge, MA; current owner unknown).

5　Annette Lindon (née Rosenfeld, b. 1927), married to Jérôme Lindon.

GEORGES NEVEUX
PARIS

28-2-52　　　　　　　　　　　　　　　　　　Ussy-sur-Marne
Cher Monsieur
　　　Je sais par Roger Blin que c'est grâce à vous que Godot a eu l'aide à la première pièce.[1] Laissez-moi vous dire combien je suis heureux d'avoir eu un tel défenseur et croyez, cher Monsieur, à ma reconnaissance émue.
　　　　　　　　　　　　　　　　Samuel Beckett

ALS; 1 leaf, 1 side; SACD, Fonds Georges Neveux.

28-2-52　　　　　　　　　　　　　　　　　　Ussy-sur-Marne
Dear M. Neveux
　　　I know from Roger Blin that it is thanks to you that *Godot* got the First Play Grant. Let me tell you how glad I am to have had a defender like you. I am much moved by this.
　　　　　　Yours in gratitude
　　　　　　Samuel Beckett

1　The subvention, for which Georges Neveux had been an enthusiastic advocate: 4 August 1951, n. 7.

JEROME LINDON, EDITIONS DE MINUIT
PARIS

2/3/52   Ussy-sur-Marne
Mon cher Jérôme

Je vous renvoie aujourd'hui Molloy et Godot.

Molloy: une dizaine de petites corrections qui n'affectent pas la composition.[1]

Godot: pas grand'chose non plus. J'aurais voulu remplacer "la maison de correction" (p. 4 de votre exemplaire à vous) par le nom d'une maison de correction connue, et ne trouve pas. Vous pourriez peut-être m'aider (je n'insinue rien). Si vous trouvez, corrigez vous-même. Sinon, il n'y a qu'à laisser.[2] J'aurais dû demander à Blin de corriger les indications scéniques du point de vue de la terminologie théâtre. Mais s'il est trop pris, ou si c'est trop pressé, je pense qu'elles peuvent aller telles quelles. L'exemplaire que vous aviez est celui à envoyer à l'imprimeur, quoique j'aie fait les mêmes changements à celui de Blin.[3]

Je ferai sans doute un saut à Paris, seul, vers la fin de la semaine, et ferai l'impossible pour passer vous voir aux Editions.

Ci-joint un mot d'Amérique reçu avant-hier.[4]

Amitiés de nous deux à vous deux.[5]

　　　　s/ Sam. Beckett

TLS; 1 leaf, 1 side; Minuit collection.

2/3/52   Ussy-sur-Marne
My dear Jérôme

I am today returning *Molloy* and *Godot*.

Molloy: ten or so small corrections that do not affect the composition.[1]

Godot: not much either. I would have liked to replace "reformatory" (p. 4 of your copy) by the name of a well-known one, and cannot find

any. Perhaps you could help me (no insinuations). If you find anything, make the correction yourself. If not, just leave it.[2] I ought to
have asked Blin to correct the stage directions from the point of
view of theatre terminology. But if he has too much on, or if it is too
urgent, I think they can go in as they stand. The copy that you had
is the one to send to the printer, although I have made the same
changes on Blin's.[3]

I shall very probably get up to Paris, on my own, towards the end
of the week, and will do everything possible and impossible to get
round to see you at the Editions.

Enclosed a note from America received the day before yesterday.[4]

All good wishes from the two of us to the two of you.[5]

Sam. Beckett

1 The corrections to *Molloy* have not been documented; collation of the first and
second editions may reflect more than the changes discussed here.

2 In the first impression of *En attendant Godot* (1952) "la maison de correction" is
replaced by "la Roquette," a large Paris prison (16). In the TMS of *En attendant Godot* in
the Morgan Library, the replacement is made to the script, although not in SB's hand
(MA 5071.1, p. 6).

3 It would seem that the markings made on the TMS by SB and Blin were
identical; but, as noted in 26 February 1952, n. 2, further changes were made in
later rehearsals.

4 The letter from America has not been identified.

5 The closing line is handwritten.

MANIA PERON
PARIS

2.3.52   Ussy
Chère Mania

Mille remerciements.

"Toute imparfaite qu'elle fût" est selon moi une grave imperfection et j'ai laissé l'indicatif.[1]

J'ai également corrigé Godot, mais là nous aurons les épreuves.

Bêché toute la journée, moins de lombrics que l'année dernière.

A bientôt

Affectueusement

Sam

ALS; 1 leaf, 1 side; *env to* Madame Péron, 69 Rue de la Tombe-Issoire, PARIS 14me; *pm* 4-3-52, La Ferté-sous-Jouarre; TxU, Lake collection, Beckett.

2.3.52   Ussy

Dear Mania

A thousand thanks.

"Toute imparfaite qu'elle *fût*" is in my view a serious imperfection, and I have left the indicative.[1] I have also corrected *Godot*, but there we shall have the proofs.

Digging all day long. Fewer earthworms than last year.

Till soon

Love

Sam

---

1 Mania Péron has been reading the first edition of *Molloy*.
"Toute imparfaite qu'elle *fût*" (imperfect as it was). In *Molloy*, the sentence appears as: "Mais ma solution à moi, toute imparfaite qu'elle était, j'étais plutôt content de l'avoir trouvée tout seul, oui, assez content" (121).

JEROME LINDON, EDITIONS DE MINUIT
PARIS

Samedi 15-3-52   Ussy

Mon cher Jérôme

Merci de votre lettre. Ça m'est égal que Godot soit renvoyé à la rentrée ou à l'hiver prochain, ou au printemps suivant, ou à la rentrée suivante. Je l'ai déjà dit à Tsingos ne voulant pas que Roger se sente obligé de monter Godot avant La Parodie.[1] Elle m'a répondu que c'est Roger qui tient absolument à monter la pièce tout de suite. Le fait est qu'il a trop de travaux sur les bras et que le seul dont il puisse se décharger sans blesser les susceptibilités est le mien. Qu'il en profite, je ne demande pas mieux, et qu'il ne se crève pas à vouloir faire l'impossible. Même si tout se présentait bien, côté salle, ce qui est loin d'être le cas, j'ai l'impression que c'est trop pour un seul homme, Godot et La Parodie coup sur coup. Mais allez lui faire admettre cela. En tout cas si les circonstances l'obligent finalement à laisser tomber Godot pour le moment, qu'il ne se fasse surtout pas de mauvais sang pour moi, ça m'est égal, et qu'il ne pense pas un seul instant à sacrifier la pièce d'Adamov plutôt que la mienne, puisque à Adamov ça ne serait pas égal du tout. Et encore une fois je suis d'accord à l'avance avec tout ce que vous déciderez, aussi bien pour le lieu que pour le moment de la réalisation. Voilà, mon cher Jérôme. Et laissez-moi vous dire encore combien nous sommes touchés, Suzanne et moi, par la part que vous prenez à toute cette histoire et par le mal que vous vous donnez pour que tout marche le mieux possible. Si vous avez besoin de moi à Paris, n'hésitez pas de me faire signe.

Pardonnez mon abominable écriture, la seule vue de ma machine à écrire me donne la nausée.

Nos meilleures amitiés à vous deux.

s/ Sam

ALS; 3 leaves, 3 sides; Minuit, and IMEC, Beckett, Boîte 1, S. Beckett, Correspondance 1946–1953.

Saturday 15-3-52   Ussy

My dear Jérôme

Thank you for your letter. It does not matter to me if *Godot* is put off to the autumn, or next winter, or the following spring, or the autumn after that. I have already said as much to Tsingos, not wanting Roger to feel obliged to put on *Godot* before *La Parodie*.[1] She replied that it was Roger who wants at all costs to put it on at once. The fact is that he has too many works on his hands, and the only one that he can unload without treading on anyone's toes is mine.

Let him take full advantage of that, nothing could please me more, and let him not kill himself trying to do the impossible. Even if everything was looking good on the theatre front, which is far from being the case, I have the feeling that *Godot* and *La Parodie* one on top of the other is just too much for one man. But try getting him to admit that. In any case, if circumstances finally force him to drop *Godot* for the moment, let him not start worrying about me. I do not mind. And let him not think, even for a moment, of sacrificing Adamov's play rather than mine, since Adamov *would* mind. And once again I agree in advance to anything you decide, whether about place or timing of production. There, my dear Jérôme. And let me say again how touched Suzanne and I are by all that you are doing in this whole affair, and the trouble that you are taking to see that everything goes off as well as possible. If you need me in Paris, do not hesitate to get in touch.

Forgive my dreadful handwriting. The mere sight of my type-writer makes me feel sick.

Our very best wishes to you both.

Sam

---

1   Roger Blin was directing Adamov's play *La Parodie*, in which he played the role of the Employé; it opened on 5 June 1952 at the Théâtre Lancry (Blin and Peskine, *Roger Blin*, 76, 305).

The actress Christine Tsingos* (1920–1973) and her husband – the painter, set designer, and architect Thanos Tsingos (1914–1965) – owned the Théâtre de la Gaîté (although, as Knowlson explains, Roger Blin was the titular owner of the French license), where Blin proposed to produce *En attendant Godot*. Christine Tsingos was not enthusiastic, possibly because there was no role for her in the play (Knowlson, *Damned to Fame*, 348; Blin and Peskine, *Roger Blin*, 81).

MANIA PERON
PARIS

28/3/52   Ussy
Chère Mania

Très important. Voulez-vous demander à un collègue mathé-maticien compréhensif et indulgent combien de chiffres comportera le résultat de la multiplication 1 x 2 x 3 x 4 etc. jusqu'à 1000

(1000 étant le dernier multiplicateur et le produit de tous les nombres de 1 à 999 le dernier multiplicande). S'il y a moyen d'obtenir le résultat exact (mais là je sens que je délire) sans trop de fatigue, en employant par exemple des logarithmes ou une machine à calculer, je suis acheteur. Mais en tout cas combien de chiffres en tout, je m'en contenterai.[1]

Affectueusement

s/ Sam

TLS; 1 leaf, 1 side; *T env to* Madame Péron, 69 Rue de la Tombe-Issoire, Paris 14me; *pm* 29-3-52, La Ferté-sous-Jouarre; TxU, Lake collection, Beckett.

28/3/52   Ussy

Dear Mania

Very important. Would you ask an understanding and indulgent maths colleague how many digits there would be in the result of multiplying 1 x 2 x 3 x 4 etc. up to 1,000 (1,000 being the last multiplier and the product of all the numbers from 1 to 999 being the last multiplicand). If there is any way of obtaining the exact result (but here I have the feeling that I am raving) without too much drudgery, by using for example logarithms or a calculator, I'm all for it. But in any event how many figures overall, I'll be satisfied with that.[1]

Love

s/ Sam

1   SB wrote to Jérôme Lindon on 19 March, "Le travail en cours s'est arrêté comme prévu. Je recommence" (The work in progress has come to a stop as predicted. I am starting again) (IMEC, Beckett, Boîte 1, S. Beckett, Correspondance 1946–1953). SB's need for the solution to this mathematical puzzle may have been prompted by this unidentified piece.

MANIA PERON

PARIS

28.3.52   Ussy

Ma chère Mania

Merci de votre lettre bleue.[1]

Bram est cinglé. Tata à lier. Violette à biner.[2]

"He was not laughing, the poor wretch" est juste; ajouter <u>was</u>, c'est de la folie furieuse.[3]

"He had given up" – beaucoup mieux que "he had given it up".[4]

"Sa destinée était faite" – difficile à traduire. On ne peut pas dire "drawn out for him" à mon avis. "Drawn out" ne peut signifier, au figuratif, que "protracted" – traîné en longueur. Le sens en est en effet "it was all over". "His destiny was at an end, accomplished, achieved". J'aimerais assez, quoique ça fasse un peu étrange, "his destiny was <u>done</u>". "His course was run", pas mal non plus. Non, non, ne me remerciez pas.[5]

Je suis pris d'un tel dégoût pour tout ce que je fais que je ne sais plus à quel saint me vouer.

Je ne sais pas quand nous rentrerons. Pour la pièce, rien de fait encore. Pas question du Babylone en tout cas.[6]

Les épreuves de <u>Godot</u> vont probablement tomber pendant votre absence. J'essaierai d'en avoir 2 jeux, pour que ça aille plus vite.

Il neige. Les ouvriers agricoles baisent les vaches, juchés sur le tabouret à traire à 3 pattes. Mauvais pour les vaches, paraît-il. On les appelle "cadets" et on les chasse impitoyablement.

Affectueusement de nous 2.

<u>Sam</u>

ALS; 1 leaf, 2 sides; *env to* Madame Péron, 69 Rue de la Tombe-Issoire, PARIS 14<u>me</u>; *pm* 29-3-52, La Ferté-sous-Jouarre; TxU, Lake collection, Beckett.

28.3.52   Ussy

My dear Mania

Thank you for your blue letter.[1]

Bram is cracked. Tata fit to be tied. Violette to be hoed.[2]

"He was not laughing, the poor wretch" is right; to add "was" is raving madness.[3]

"He had given up": much better than "he had given it up".[4]

"Sa destinée était faite" – difficult to translate. One cannot say "drawn out for him" in my view. "Drawn out" can only mean, figuratively, "protracted" – traîné en longueur. The meaning is "it was all over". "His destiny was at an end, accomplished, achieved." I would quite like, although it sounds a bit odd, "his destiny was done". "His course was run", not bad either. No, no, don't thank me.[5]

I am overcome with such disgust for everything that I do that I no longer know what way to turn.

I do not know when we shall go back. For the play, nothing done yet. No question of the Babylone in any case.[6]

The proofs of *Godot* will probably fall on us in your absence. I shall try to get two sets, so that things can go faster.

It is snowing. The farm-workers are fucking the cows, perched on 3-legged milking stools. Bad for the cows, it seems. They are called "juniors" and are driven away pitilessly.

Love from us 2.

Sam

1   Mania Péron's letter has not been found.

2   Bram van Velde. "Tata": 29 April 1951, n. 1. Violette has not been identified.

3   SB is advising on what appears to be a translation by Péron of Baudelaire's prose poem "Le Vieux Saltimbanque," which contains the phrase "Il ne riait pas, le misérable!" Presumably, Péron has suggested adding a "was," to read: "He was not laughing, was the poor wretch" (Baudelaire, *Œuvres complètes*, I, 296). No record has been found of publication of Péron's translation, which may have been intended for use in her teaching.

4   Further in the same paragraph of Baudelaire's prose poem occurs the sentence, "Il avait renoncé, il avait abdiqué."

5   The same paragraph from "Le Vieux Saltimbanque" ends: "Sa destinée était faite."

6   The Théâtre de Babylone had not yet opened its doors, at 38 Boulevard Raspail, Paris 7, although it would do so in June, under the direction of Jean-Marie Serreau. The difficulties of finding a theatre for *En attendant Godot*: 15 March 1952.

MANIA PERON
PARIS

15.4.52   <u>Ussy</u>
Chère Mania

Merci de vos gentilles lettres. Ici aussi un peu de fièvre aphteuse, mais on est moins vache pour les chiens.[1]

Le nombre de combinaisons possible serait, d'après moi, 51 x 50 x 49 x 48 x 47 etc etc x 3 x 2. Je n'ai pas compris grand'chose aux explications de votre matheuse. Ça ne fait rien, il est dans l'eau, le chef d'oeuvre qui en avait besoin. Merci quand même, à vous et à elle.

Pas encore reçu les épreuves de <u>Godot</u>. Blin n'a pas encore trouvé un théâtre. Vaguement question paraît-il du Monceau, spécialisé dans la caleçon[n]ade. Il est vrai que Estragon perd son pantalon à la fin du deux.[2]

Je ne sais pas quand nous rentrerons. Pas envie de bouger. Temps merveilleux. Aucune nouvelle de personne. Travail néant. Je guette la sortie de mes graines et joue tout seul aux échecs. Suis tout disposé à continuer ainsi jusqu'à l'heure de la connerie suprême.

Bonne fin de vacances à vous tous, rentrez au complet.

        Affectueusement de nous deux

            Sam

Merci beaucoup de vos voeux d'anniversaire. Très touché que vous y ayez pensé.

ALS; 1 leaf, 2 sides; *env to* Madame Péron, Villa "Les Bruyères," La Garenne, ERQUY, Côtes-du-Nord; *pm* La Ferté-sous-Jouarre, 16-4-52; TxU, Lake collection, Beckett.

15.4.52   Ussy
Dear Mania

Thank you for your nice letters. Here too a little foot-and-mouth, but they come down less hard on dogs.[1]

The number of combinations possible would be, according to me, 51 x 50 x 49 x 48 x 47 etc. etc. x 3 x 2. I could not make much sense of your maths friend's explanations. It is no matter: the master-piece that needed it is five fathoms under. Thank you, and her, all the same.

Have still not received the proofs of *Godot*. Blin has still not found a theatre. Some vague talk, apparently, of the Monceau, which spe-cialises in bedroom farce. It is true that Estragon loses his trousers at the end of Act II.[2]

I do not know when we shall go back. No wish to move. Weather marvellous. No news of anyone. Work zero. I watch for my seeds to come up, and play chess on my own. Quite happy to go on doing so till the hour of the farce to end all farces.

Enjoy what is left of the holidays, and come back safe and sound, all of you.

Love from the two of us

Sam

Thank you very much for your birthday wishes. Greatly touched that you should have thought of it.

1 Mania Péron was spending the Easter holidays in Erquy, Brittany, a region where an outbreak of foot-and-mouth disease posed so much of a threat that dogs were being put down to prevent its spread among livestock. The disease spread to mid-July to affect 7 percent of all livestock in France ("Foot-and-Mouth in France," *The Times* 14 July 1952: 6).

2 Lindon wrote to SB on 23 April to say he hoped that SB had received the proofs of *En attendant Godot* (Editions de Minuit).

Lindon wrote of Roger Blin's plans to SB on 24 April: "Pour le moment, il n'envisage plus de monter Godot avant la rentrée, faute de salle, mais voudrait présenter la pièce à la presse, au Babylone, vers le 15–20 mai. D'ici là, je ne désespère pas de trouver une salle." (Editions de Minuit.) (For the moment, he is no longer thinking of putting *Godot* on before the autumn, for want of a theatre, but would like to do a press preview, at the Babylone, round the 15th–20th May. I haven't lost all hope of finding a theatre between now and then.)

The Théâtre Monceau (since 1975, the Théâtre Tristan Bernard) is located at 64 Rue du Rocher, Paris 8.

Estragon's trousers fall when he removes his "belt" so that he and Vladimir should have rope with which to hang themselves (*En attendant Godot* [Paris: Editions de Minuit, 1952] 162; *Waiting for Godot, A Tragicomedy in Two Acts* [New York: Grove Press, 1954] 60).

GEORGE REAVEY
LONDON

2/6/52   Paris

My dear George

Glad to have news of you after so long and to know you far from the miseries of Manchester.[1] I had a letter from your man, Jos. Powers, representing publishers in Chili interested in Molloy. It is good of you to offer to help, but the Editions de Minuit are very good and look after everything.[2]

Poor Gene Jolas died last week, I suppose you know. I hadn't seen anything of him, or of Maria, for a long time. He had a very bad collapse some months ago and was in the country. I understand he suffered horribly for weeks before his death.[3]

Bram had a magnificent show at the Galérie Maeght some months ago. It naturally received no notice. He is well and at present on holiday in Brittany.[4] Geer and Lisl haven't been so grand. I haven't seen much of them. He has great trouble with his eyes, something wrong with the lachrymal ducts, they stream all the time. He was given a big award at the Menton Biennale, 500.000 I think.[5]

I haven't been able to do any work worth talking about for the past two years. Tear up everything. The second play is in rehearsal, producer Roger Blin. Don't know yet when or where it will be put on. Probably in the autumn, at the new Théâtre Babylone, Bd. Raspail.[6] L'Innommable is due out in the autumn.

We spend a good half of our time in the country not far from Paris, on the Marne. Haven't been back to Ireland since summer 1950. Don't think I have any news of anyone you're interested in. Tom MacGreevy very happy and in his element as director of the Dublin National Gallery. If I didn't send you my books, it is because for me the three are one.[7] Shall send you the three together when the Innommable appears. The play is due for publication shortly, all by itself. Shall send.

Sorry I don't know your wife's painting. I saw some reproductions somewhere, but no help. I hope she will exhibit in Paris one of these days. My kind regards to her.[8]

All the best, my dear George. A bientôt j'espère.

s/ SAM

TLS; 1 leaf, 2 sides; TxU, Reavey collection.

1   Reavey resigned from the University of Manchester and moved to London in August 1951 (Bearor, *Irene Rice Pereira*, 236).

2   Joseph Powers has not been identified; there seems not to have been a Chilean publication of *Molloy*, for the only translation of *Molloy* in the Biblioteca Nacional de Chile is dated 1961 (translated by Roberto Bixo). "Chili" is the French spelling of Chile.

3   Eugene Jolas died in Paris on 26 May 1952, from acute nephritis. He and Maria Jolas had been at their home in Chérence, Val-d'Oise, until mid-April; then his health worsened, and they returned to Paris (Betsy Jolas, 6 May 2010).

4   Bram van Velde's exhibition at the Galerie Maeght: 19 February 1952. SB writes "Galérie" for "Galerie."

5   Geer van Velde's award, Menton Biennale: 17 August 1951, and n. 5.

6   Lindon has told SB that the production will take place in the autumn. Although the Théâtre de Babylone was mentioned as the site for a press preview in May, this appears not to have taken place (see 15 April 1952, n. 2).

7   *Molloy, Malone meurt*, and *L'Innommable*.

8   Irene Rice Pereira.

ROGER BLIN

ILE DE BATZ, FINISTERE

2.8.52

Cher vieux – Merci de votre carte. En voici une bien pépère. Salez et iodez-vous à fond, c'est affreux ce qui vous attend. A votre disposition ou non comme et quand vous voudrez. Pourvu que Médina soit de bonne composition. Pozzo ne veut rien vouloir dire, j'ai beau le solliciter.[1] Affectueusement de nous 2. Sam

APCS; 1 leaf, 1 side; "Ussy-sur-Marne, Un bon coin de Pêche"; *pm* [illeg], La Ferté-sous-Jouarre; *to* Roger Blin, Poste Restante, Ile de Batz, Finistère; IMEC, Blin.

2.8.52

    My dear Roger – Thanks for your card. Here is a beauty. Salt and iodize yourself thoroughly: you've no idea what terrible things are in store for you. At your disposal, or not, as and when you wish. So long as Médina is easy to get on with. Pozzo will not say anything – even when I press him.[1] Love from us both. Sam

    1 Ile de Batz, near Roscoff in Brittany. SB refers to the production of *En attendant Godot*, which he expected to take place in the autumn.
    Albert Médina (1930–2009), who worked with Jean-Louis Barrault (1910–1994) at the Théâtre Marigny from 1946 to 1986, was asked to take the role of Pozzo, but he eventually refused it because, he said, he did not "like nor agree with the significance of Pozzo's role, if there was a significance at all" (interviewed by Natalie Frederic, 9 February 2000).

JEROME LINDON, EDITIONS DE MINUIT
PARIS

19-8-52   Ussy
Mon cher Jérôme

    De retour ici aujourd'hui, laissant Suzanne à Paris avec sa mère, je trouve votre lettre du 12. D'où uniquement ce retard à vous répondre.[1]

    Je ne connais pas du tout cette revue. Je ne tiens pas beaucoup à leur donner un extrait de L'Innommable. Et s'agira-t-il là encore d'un inédit, ou d'un livre? Le Calmant est disponible, mais j'aimerais mieux que personne ne le lise jamais. Le mieux serait un de ces derniers petits textes qui ont achevé de me fermer le bec. Est-ce traduit, ou en pidgin, qu'ils voient ça? Paient-ils? En tout cas ne vous en occupez plus que s'ils reviennent à la charge, vous avez assez à faire sans ça.[2]

    Vous verrez sans doute Suzanne très prochainement, quoiqu'il lui soit très difficile de quitter sa mère.

Je ne sais pas très bien quand je rentrerai. J'ai besoin de mille ans de silence, surtout du mien.

Rien de Roger depuis sa carte.[3] C'est la bousculade assurée.

Bien amicalement à vous deux.

Sam

ALS; 1 leaf, 1 side; Minuit collection.

19-8-52   Ussy

My dear Jérôme

Back here today, leaving Suzanne with her mother, I find your letter of the 12th. The one and only reason for my delay in replying.[1]

I do not know this review at all. I have no great wish to give them an extract from *L'Innommable*. And then again, are they thinking of an unpublished piece or a book? "Le Calmant" is available, but I would rather nobody ever read that. The best thing would be one of those last little texts which have finally managed to shut me up. Are they seeing it as something translated, or in pidgin? Do they pay? In any case, do nothing more about it unless they come back to it again: you have enough to do without that.[2]

You will no doubt be seeing Suzanne very soon, although it is very hard for her to leave her mother

I am not very sure when I shall go back. I need a thousand years of silence, my own above all.

Nothing from Roger since his card.[3] That guarantees a mad scramble.

All best to you both

Sam

1 Jérôme Lindon wrote to SB on 12 August to convey a request from *Merlin*, an English-language journal, for an unpublished text (Minuit collection). *Merlin* was edited by Alexander Trocchi* (1925–1984) in Paris. An article on SB was to be published in the next issue (Richard Seaver, "Samuel Beckett: An Introduction," *Merlin* 1.2 [Autumn 1952] 73–79); in the issue following that, *Merlin* wished to publish a work by SB.

2 "Le Calmant": 15 December 1946, n. 6. SB refers to *Textes pour rien*. In the end, an "Extract from Watt" was published in *Merlin* 1.3 (Winter 1952–1953) 118–126.

3 SB refers to the card from Roger Blin to which he responded on 2 August 1952.

JEROME LINDON, EDITIONS DE MINUIT
PARIS

dimanche soir [14 September 1952]
cher ami

Je viens de voir Médina avec Roger. Pas question de le laisser tomber. Je vais le dire demain à France Guy.[1] Je viens de passer au théâtre, mais elle n'est pas là. J'ai dit à la caissière de lui dire que je passerai demain au théâtre à 4 (quatre) heures et qu'elle vous prévienne par téléphone si cela ne lui convient pas. J'aimerais beaucoup vous avoir avec moi. Si cela vous est possible, rendez-vous à trois heures et demie sur le boulevard devant le théâtre. Je sais que j'abuse de votre temps et de votre patience et que vous ne m'en voudrez pas. J'ai dans l'idée une combine susceptible peut-être d'arranger les choses, mais voudrais pas jouer cette carte avant de vous en parler.[2]

Bien amicalement

Sam

ALS, pneu; 1 leaf, 1 side; *to* M. Jérôme Lindon, Editions de Minuit, 5 Rue Bernard-Palissy, PARIS 7ᵉ (*for* 7 Rue Bernard-Palissy, PARIS, 6); *pm* 15-9-52, Paris; IMEC, Beckett, Boîte 2, Dossier France Guy. *Dating*: from pm, Sunday was 14 September 1952.

Sunday evening [14 September 1952]
My dear Jérôme

I have just seen Médina with Roger. No question of dropping him. I shall say so tomorrow to France Guy.[1] I have just been round to the theatre, but she is not there. I told the woman on the desk to tell her that I shall look in at the theatre tomorrow at 4 (four) and that she

12. Jérôme Lindon in the early 1950s, Paris

should let you know by telephone beforehand if that does not suit her. I would love to have you with me. If that is possible for you, meet at half past three on the boulevard in front of the theatre. I know I am making unjustified demands on your time and your patience, and that you will not hold it against me. I have thought up a scheme that just might straighten things out, but would not want to play this card before talking to you.[2]

All best

Sam

1   It is not known whether France Guy (1916–1954), Director of the Théâtre de Poche, had asked that Médina be dropped. France Guy, Roger Blin, and Jérôme Lindon had agreed on 23 July 1952 that the subvention from the Ministère de l'Education Nationale, "pour aider le montage" (in support of the production) of *En attendant Godot*, would be paid to France Guy, that rehearsals would begin on 15 September at the Théâtre de Poche, and that production would open in the autumn season, when the current production, *Uncle Vanya*, finished its run (IMEC, Beckett, Boîte 2, Dossier France Guy). It is clear from Lindon's letter to France Guy on 23 October that Guy had agreed to the choice of actors in September, namely Verdier, Raimbourg, Médina, and Blin.

Since plans had gone forward to publish the text of *En attendant Godot*, there may have been concern about timing the release of the book to coincide with the premiere. As SB wrote to Thomas MacGreevy on 19 September, "There is little chance of Godot's being performed before November. I am just as glad, for it will need all the rehearsing it can get. It is to appear in book form very shortly (a mistake, I think), and I shall send it to you." (TCD, MS 10402/183.)

2   SB's plan to address the difficulties with Guy and the production of *En attendant Godot* at the Théâtre de Poche is not known.

JEROME LINDON, EDITIONS DE MINUIT

PARIS

[on or after 27 October 1952]

Exemplaires signés le 27-10-52[1]

Nadeau

Bataille

Blanchot

Blanzat

Fouchet

Lemarchand, Jacques

Carlier

Hautefeuille

Lambrichs

Neveux

Bachelard

Ionesco
Wahl
Tzara
Adamov[2]

AL list in SB's hand; 1 leaf, 1 side; IMEC, Beckett, Boîte 1, S. Beckett, Correspondance 1946–1953.

[1] "Exemplaires signés le 27-10-52" (Copies signed the 27th October 1952) of *En attendant Godot*.

[2] Those on this list not previously identified: Jacques Lemarchand (1908–1974), theatre critic for *Combat*, and, from 1950, for *Le Figaro*; Gaston Bachelard; Eugène Ionesco.

JACOBA VAN VELDE

25/11/52   6 Rue des Favorites

                                  Paris 15me

Chère Tonny

Merci de votre lettre. Je savais que votre mère était morte et par où vous aviez dû passer.[1] Je connais bien la question. Tous les jours je la connais un peu mieux. Rien à faire, rien à dire, qu'à encaisser, et gare aux insomnies.

Grand vernissage Geer avant-hier chez le Bien Aimé. Par la suite, jusqu'à minuit, et sans doute encore bien après, speech de Vitullo toutes les quinze minutes, de quoi presque aimer la bourgeoisie.[2]

Bram ne fout rien, se promène, gémit et tourne autour du pot. Comme je le comprends. Maeght l'a foutu en l'air, vous le saviez sans doute.[3]

Pour votre boulot je pense tout de suite à Deirdre of the Sorrows (Yeats ou Synge), Manon Lescaut, Aucassin et Nicolette, La Princesse de Clèves, Effie Briest [*for* Effi Briest] de Theodor Fontane (livre peu connu et formidable). Moins abruti je trouverais des centaines d'autres.[4]

Je vais vous envoyer Godot. On répète en ce moment, au Babylone, Bd Raspail. C'est horriblement difficile. On voudrait passer avant la Noël, mais ce ne sera pas prêt. L'Innommable au printemps.

J'en donne un extrait à Paulhan pour sa Nouvelle NRF, dont le 1er numéro est prévu pour janvier.[5]

Et Paolo et Francesca? Et Tristan et Yseult? Merde alors, les grands mamoureux, il n'y a que ça.

> Affectueusement de nous deux
> s/ Sam

TLS; 1 leaf, 1 side; BNF 19794/18.

25.11.52   6 Rue des Favorites
                                             Paris 15me

Dear Tonny

Thank you for your letter. I knew that your mother had died, and what sorts of things you'd had to go through.[1] It's something I'm very familiar with. More familiar every day. Nothing to be done, nothing to be said; nothing but take it, and watch out for sleepless nights.

Great Geer private view yesterday chez the Beloved. Afterwards, till midnight and probably long after, speechifying by Vitullo every quarter of an hour. Enough to make you like the bourgeois, almost.[2]

Bram isn't doing a stroke. Goes for walks, moans, beats about the bush. How well I understand him. Maeght has given him the boot, as you probably knew.[3]

For your own work I think straightaway of *Deirdre of the Sorrows* (Yeats or Synge), *Manon Lescaut*, *Aucassin et Nicolette*, *La Princesse de Clèves*, *Effi Briest* by Theodor Fontane (not well known, tremendous). If I weren't feeling so low I'd come up with hundreds of others.[4]

I'm going to send you *Godot*. It's in rehearsal at the moment, at the Babylone, Boulevard Raspail. It's dreadfully difficult. They'd want to put it on before Christmas, but it won't be ready. *L'Innommable* in the spring. I'm letting Paulhan have an extract for his *Nouvelle NRF*; their first number is due out in January.[5]

What about Paolo and Francesca? And Tristan and Isolde? Hell's bells, there's nothing like them, these Great Loovers.

Love from us both

Sam

---

1   Hendrika Catharina van Velde, mother of Jacoba, Bram and Geer van Velde: 15 December 1946, n. 15.

2   In November 1952, Geer van Velde had his third exhibition at the Galerie Maeght. Brazilian sculptor Sesostris Vitullo (1899–1953) came to Paris in 1925, and worked as a model, as well as in quarries, while he pursued his art; he was a friend of Bram van Velde and Antonin Artaud.

3   Bram van Velde signed a contract in 1947 with the Galerie Maeght and was released from the contract in 1952 (Mason, ed., *Bram van Velde*, 306).

4   *Deirdre* (1907) by W. B. Yeats; *Deirdre of the Sorrows* (1910) by John Millington Synge; *Histoire du chevalier des Grieux et de Manon Lescaut* (1731) by Antoine François Prévost (Abbé Prévost); the anonymous romance, *Aucassin et Nicolette* (thirteenth century); *La Princesse de Clèves* (1678) published anonymously by Madame de La Fayette; *Effi Briest* (1895) by Theodor Fontane. All concern the misfortunes of lovers, as suggested by SB's afterthought, at the close of the present letter, which brings in Paolo and Francesca and Tristan and Isolde.

5   "Mahood," an extract from *L'Innommable*, would be published in the second issue of *NNRF* edited by Jean Paulhan.

CHRONOLOGY 1953

1953	January	Cottage at Ussy completed.
	5 January	Premiere of *En attendant Godot*, Théâtre de Babylone.
	31 January	Boisterous spectators interrupt performance of *En attendant Godot*.
	February	"Mahood," an excerpt from *L'Innommable*, published in the *Nouvelle Nouvelle Revue Française* with unauthorized cuts.
		Alain Robbe-Grillet publishes essay on SB's work in *Critique*.
	by 19 February	SB reads a draft of Elmar Tophoven's German translation, *Warten auf Godot*.
	6 March	Death of Stalin.
	April	Note of apology published in the *Nouvelle Nouvelle Revue Française* for cuts made to SB's "Mahood."
	May	"Trois Textes pour rien [III, VI, X]" published in *Les Lettres Nouvelles*.
	12–26 May	Frank and Jean Beckett visit SB in Paris and Ussy.
	15 May	Offer received from Mrs. Garson Kanin and Thornton Wilder for an English translation and production in the United States of *En attendant Godot*.
	20 May	Publication of *L'Innommable*.
	before 22 May	Barney Rosset, Grove Press, offers to publish English translations of *En attendant Godot*, *Molloy*, *Malone meurt*, and holds an option for *L'Innommable*.
	3 July	"Texte pour rien, XI" published in *Arts-Spectacles*.
	23 July	Armistice signed between Korea and the United States.

345

by 27 July	SB working in Paris with Patrick Bowles on the English translation of *Molloy*.
31 August	Imprint date of *Watt*, Collection Merlin, Olympia Press.
September	Reprint of *En attendant Godot* with cuts and changes made for performance.
	Nadeau publishes essay on *L'Innommable* in *Les Lettres Nouvelles*.
	SB meets Pamela Mitchell for the first time in Paris.
early September	Thomas MacGreevy in Paris.
8 September	SB attends premiere of *Warten auf Godot*, Schlossparktheater, Berlin.
15 September	"Extract from *Molloy*," translated by Patrick Bowles, published in *Merlin*.
25 September	Reprise of *En attendant Godot*, Théâtre de Babylone.
by 31 October	SB works on French translation of *Watt* with Daniel Mauroc.
November	"Texte pour rien, XIII" published in *Le Disque Vert*.
16 November – 12 December	Tour of the Théâtre de Babylone production of *En attendant Godot*: Germany, Italy, and France.
29 November	Opening performance of *Godot*, by prisoners, in Lüttringhausen, in a German translation by one of their number.
14 December	Ethna MacCarthy in Paris.

8/1/53   Ussy

Mon cher Jérôme

Merci de votre gentille lettre. Je n'oublie pas et n'oublierai pas l'énorme part qui vous revient dans toute cette histoire. Sans vous nous n'en serions pas là.[1]

Ravi pour Raimbourg et qu'on ait pigé au moins ça.[2]

Pour la Radio, je regrette, je ne peux pas. A toute demande d'interview, d'où qu'elle vienne, vous pouvez toujours et plus que jamais répondre non.[3]

Pour la Revue de Paris, je ne vois vraiment pas ce que je pourrais leur donner. On verra ça ensemble à mon retour. Je réponds en ce sens à la très gentille lettre de Thiébaut.[4]

J'ai reçu une invitation (2 places) pour le Poche, pour aujourd'hui en huit au choix, de la main même de France, à en juger par les soulignements.[5]

Gabriel Marcel et l'Aurore! C'est bien ma veine.[6]

Puis-je vous demander un service, c'est de m'envoyer une dizaine de programmes. Achetez-les et je vous réglerai ça à mon retour.

Je ne sais quand je rentrerai. Je suis horriblement fatigué et aimerais rester ici un bon moment. Si je dois rentrer ce sera pour très peu de temps. Je vous ferai tout de suite signe.

Encore merci pour tout.

A vous deux de nous deux bien amicalement.

s/ Sam

J'apprends par le Combat d'aujourd'hui que je vais être un des piliers de la nouvelle revue de Nadeau et Saillet. Première nouvelle. Ils ne m'ont rien demandé. Et je me demande avec quoi.[7]

TLS; 1 leaf, 1 side; IMEC, Beckett, Boîte 1, S. Beckett, Correspondance 1946–1953.

8/1/53   Ussy

My dear Jérôme

Thank you for your kind letter. I do not forget and will not forget the great share owed to you in all this. Without you we would not be there.[1]

Delighted for Raimbourg, and that at least they got hold of that.[2]

For the radio, sorry I cannot. To any request for an interview, from wherever it comes, you can always and more than ever say no.[3]

For the *Revue de Paris*, I really do not see what I can give them. We shall look into it together when I am back. I am replying along those lines to Thiébaut's very nice letter.[4]

I have received an invitation (2 seats) for the Poche, for today week anywhere, in the same France's own handwriting, to judge by the underlinings.[5]

Gabriel Marcel and *L'Aurore*! Just my luck.[6]

May I ask you a favour: send me ten or so programmes. Buy them and I shall settle up when I am back.

I do not know when I shall go back. I am dreadfully tired and would like to stay on here for a good spell. If I do have to go back it will only be for a very short time. I shall let you know immediately.

Thank you again for everything.

To both of you from both of us, in friendship.

        Sam

I learn from *Combat* today that I am going to be one of the pillars of Nadeau and Saillet's new review. First I've heard of it. They have not asked me for anything. And what with, I wonder.[7]

1 Lindon's letter of 6 January to SB was about the success of the premiere of *En attendant Godot* at the Théâtre de Babylone on 5 January, which he said exceeded the success of the Générale "auprès de gens de milieux très différents" (among people from very different backgrounds) (IMEC, Beckett, Boîte 1, S. Beckett, Correspondance 1946–1953). The Générale is the final dress rehearsal with an audience.

2 In his letter of 6 January, Lindon wrote that he was happy that Lucien Raimbourg, who played the role of Vladimir in *En attendant Godot*, had received recognition from the critics.

3 Lindon wrote on 6 January that the Section Anglaise de la Radio wanted to interview SB on the following Friday; Jean-Marie Serreau planned to participate in the broadcast.

4   With his letter of 6 January, Lindon enclosed a request from Marcel Thiébaut (1897–1961), Editor of the *Revue de Paris*, for an unpublished piece; Lindon proposed "une des nouvelles" (one of the novellas); neither this enclosure nor SB's reply has been found.

5   France Guy, Director of the Théâtre de Poche, sent congratulations on the opening of *En attendant Godot* (6 January 1953, IMEC, Beckett, Boîte 1, S. Beckett, Correspondance 1946–1953); the note mentioned here has not been found.

6   G[ustave] Joly, "Au Théâtre de Babylone *En attendant Godot* ou Le soliloque du pauvre," *L'Aurore* 6 January 1953: 2; rpt. in *Dossier de presse* En attendant Godot *de Samuel Beckett (1952–1961)*, ed. André Derval (Paris: IMEC et Editions 10/18, 2007) 31–33. In this review Joly names SB as an American novelist, a designation which Jérôme Lindon hastens to correct in his letter to Joly of 7 January (IMEC, Beckett, Boîte 1, S. Beckett, Correspondance 1946–1953).

Philosopher and playwright Gabriel-Honoré Marcel (1889–1973), "En attendant Godot," *Les Nouvelles Littéraires* (15 January 1953) 5; rpt. in *Dossier de presse* En attendant Godot *de Samuel Beckett (1952–1961)*, ed. Derval, 64–65. In his letter of 6 January, Lindon mentioned that his favorable review would be published on the 15th.

7   The announcement of Maurice Nadeau's new journal, provisionally entitled *La Revue des Lettres Françaises*, named Nadeau as Director, Maurice Saillet as Editor in Chief; "Les collaborateurs réguliers seront ... Henri Michaux, Pascal Pia, Michel Leiris – dont on sera content de revoir la signature – et Samuel Beckett" (The regular contributors will be ... Henri Michaux, Pascal Pia, Michel Leiris – whose signature we shall be glad to see reappearing – and Samuel Beckett) ("Bref," *Combat* 8 January 1953: 7). The journal was published as *Les Lettres Nouvelles* from March 1953 to April 1977.

ROGER BLIN
PARIS

9/1/53   Ussy

Mon cher Roger

Bravo à tous. Je suis si content de votre succès à tous.

Ne m'en veuillez pas de m'être barré, je n'en pouvais plus.

Il y a une chose qui me chiffonne, c'est le froc d'Estragon.[1] J'ai naturellement demandé à Suzanne s'il tombe bien. Elle me dit qu'il le retient à mi-chemin. Il ne le faut absolument pas, c'est on ne peut plus hors de situation. Il n'a vraiment pas la tête à ça à ce moment-là, il ne se rend même pas compte qu'il est tombé. Quant aux rires qui pourraient saluer la chute complète, au grand dam de ce touchant tableau final, il n'y a absolument rien à y objecter, ils seraient du même ordre que les précédents. L'esprit de la pièce, dans la mesure où elle en a, c'est que rien n'est plus grotesque que le tragique, et il faut l'exprimer jusqu'à la fin, et surtout à la fin. J'ai un tas d'autres raisons pour vouloir que ce jeu de scène ne soit pas escamoté, mais je vous en fais grâce. Soyez seulement assez gentil de le rétablir comme c'est indiqué dans le texte, et comme nous l'avions toujours prévu au cours des répétitions, et que le pantalon tombe complètement, autour des chevilles. Ca doit vous sembler stupide, mais pour moi c'est capital. Et je vous croyais tous les deux d'accord avec moi là-dessus, quand je vous ai vus samedi dernier après l'incident de la couturière, et que j'emportais votre assurance que cette scène serait jouée comme je la vois.

Bonne continuation et une amicale poignée de main à tous.

s/ Sam

TLS; 1 leaf, 1 side; IMEC, Blin. Previous publication, Alfred Simon, "Tout un théâtre," *Le Magazine Littéraire* 231 (June 1986) 35; Valérie Marin La Meslée, "Samuel Beckett et le froc d'Estragon," *Le Magazine Littéraire* 453 (May 2006) 97 [facsimile]; Alphant, Léger, and Szidon, eds., *Objet: Beckett*, plate 101.

9/1/53   Ussy
Dear Roger

Well done all! I'm so pleased about the success you've had.

I hope you don't mind my having slipped away. I couldn't take any more.

There is one thing that bothers me: Estragon's trousers.[1] Naturally I asked Suzanne if they fall down properly. She tells me that he holds on to them half-way down. This he must not do – it's utterly inappropriate. It wouldn't occur to him at that moment – he doesn't realise they have fallen down. As for any laughs that might greet their falling right down, to the great detriment of that touching final tableau, there's absolutely no objection to them. They'd be of the same order as the earlier ones. The spirit of the play, in so far as it has one, is that nothing is more grotesque than the tragic, and that must be put across right to the end, and particularly at the end. I have lots of other reasons for wanting this business not to be underplayed, but I'll spare you them. But please do as I ask and restore it as it is in the text, and as we had always planned in rehearsal; and let the trousers fall right down, round the ankles. It must seem silly to you, but to me it's vital. And there was I, thinking you both agreed with me, when I saw the two of you last Saturday, after that business in the costume rehearsal, and went away with you assuring me that the scene would be acted the way I see it.

Hope things keep going well. Best wishes to all.

Sam

1   At the end of Act II, the stage directions read: 'Estragon dénoue la corde qui maintient son pantalon. Celui-ci, beaucoup trop large, lui tombe autour des chevilles" (Estragon loosens the cord that holds up his trousers which, much too big for him, fall about his ankles) (*En attendant Godot* [Minuit: 1952] 161; *Waiting for Godot* [Grove: 1954] 60). In an interview with this volume's editors, Jean Martin* (1922–2009), who played Lucky, recalled that SB had attended the "couturière" (dress and technical rehearsal), and that when Estragon's trousers fell down the "costume mistress laughed heartily . . . Sam liked that" (Jean Martin, 1 July 1996).

JEROME LINDON, EDITIONS DE MINUIT
PARIS

samedi 10/1/53   Ussy
Cher Jérôme

J'ai bien reçu votre seconde lettre hier et pense que vous aurez la mienne aujourd'hui.[1]

Je n'ai rien reçu de Roger. Je ne voulais pas rentrer de sitôt, mais je vois qu'il va le falloir. Je serai donc à Paris mercredi prochain et passerai aux Editions un peu après 3 heures. Si Roger pouvait venir également nous pourrions voir le texte ensemble.[2]

Je regrette de n'avoir pu vous prévenir pour la Radio plus tôt. Je n'ai reçu votre première lettre que mercredi soir.[3]

J'ai vu la photo du Figaro Littéraire. Elle est très belle.[4]

Bien amicalement
s/ Sam

TLS; 1 leaf, 1 side; IMEC, Beckett, Boîte 1, S. Beckett, Correspondance 1946–1953.

Saturday 10/1/53   Ussy

Dear Jérôme

I received your second letter yesterday and think that you will get mine today.[1]

I have not received anything from Roger. I did not want to go back so soon, but I see that I shall have to. So I shall be in Paris next Wednesday and will call in at Minuit a little after 3. If Roger could come as well we could look at the text together.[2]

I am sorry not to have been able to warn you about the Radio sooner. I only received your first letter on Wednesday evening.[3]

I have seen the photo in the *Figaro Littéraire*. It is lovely.[4]

All good wishes

Sam

1   SB refers to Lindon's letter of 8 January, in which Lindon apologized for having sent the letter of 6 January to SB's Paris address, rather than to him in Ussy. SB's reply: 8 January 1953.

2   In his letter of 8 January, Lindon wrote that he would like to see SB as soon as possible, "pour quelques retouches éventuelles à faire au texte" (for a few possible small changes to the text) (IMEC, Beckett, Boîte 1, S. Beckett, Correspondance 1946–1953).

3   SB received Lindon's letter of 6 January on the following day; the radio interview was set for Friday 9 January. Lindon's letter of 8 January reiterated the request for an interview by the Section Anglaise de la Radio, and it is this which prompts SB's apology.

4   The photo by Photo Bernand showed all four characters and the tree; it appeared with the review by Jacques Lemarchand, "*En attendant Godot* de Samuel Beckett, au Théâtre de Babylone," *Le Figaro Littéraire* 17 January 1953: 10.

MORRIS SINCLAIR

PARIS

14-1-53   Paris

My dear Sunny

Thanks for your good letter. I'm very glad you were moved by the play. Your reactions are among the very few I care about.

I haven't seen it properly myself yet. I gave up, going mad, the text going on and on in my head day and night, before the first couturière. I hope to work up the courage to go this week.[1]

I think some further cuts might improve matters.[2]

Returning to Ussy very soon. We must arrange a game of chess next time I'm in Paris.

Love to you all

Sam

ALS; 1 leaf, 1 side; Sinclair collection.

1 According to Jean Martin, SB was present at the couturière, but not at the premiere (9 January 1953, n. 1).

2 The rehearsal script of the designer Sergio Gerstein (n.d.) shows that several cuts and additions were made during the rehearsals (Morgan, MA 5071.1). Changes made by SB in rehearsal are recorded in his "prompt copy" given to John Calder and Bettina Jonič (TCD, MS 10495). In the Roger Blin collection at IMEC there is also a marked copy of the text as published in 1952 that shows changes, although its notes are difficult to date. Colin Duckworth compares the original manuscript of *En attendant Godot* (now at the BNF) with the first French edition, the first Faber and Faber edition, and the Grove Press edition (*En attendant Godot: pièce en deux actes*, ed. Colin Duckworth [London: Harrap, 1966]; see 26 February 1952, n. 2).

JEAN WAHL, DEUCALION
PARIS

le 17 janvier 1953   6 rue des Favorites
                                                       Paris 15me

Cher Monsieur

Je m'excuse de ne pas avoir répondu plus tôt à votre si aimable lettre. Je serais heureux de collaborer à votre revue. Les trois textes ci-inclus furent écrits, avec 10 autres de semblable "facture", dont celui de Deucalion, il y a un an peut-être.[1] Depuis je n'ai plus essayé d'écrire. Surtout ne vous croyez pas obligé, du fait de m'avoir demandé ma collaboration, de les accepter. Je trouverai tout naturel que vous les jugiez inutilisables. La seule alternative, malheureusement, est un extrait de L'Innommable, qui ne doit sortir qu'au mois d'avril. Je vous en donnerai un très volontiers, si cela fait mieux votre affaire.

Veuillez faire mes amitiés à Maurice Nadeau et me croire, cher Monsieur, très cordialement à vous.

s/

(Samuel Beckett)

TLS; 1 leaf, 1 side; Clodd collection (Maggs Rare Books, London).

17th January 1953   6 rue des Favorites

Paris 15

Dear Monsieur Wahl

I apologise for not having replied to your very kind letter sooner. I would be happy to contribute to your review. The three texts enclosed were written, with 10 others of similar "construction", including the one in *Deucalion*, perhaps a year ago.[1] Since then I have not tried to write anything more. Above all, do not feel obliged, because of having asked me to contribute, to accept them. I shall find it wholly natural if you judge them unusable. The only alternative, unfortunately, is an extract from *L'Innommable*, which is not due out until April. I shall gladly let you have one if it fits the bill better.

Please give my regards to Maurice Nadeau, and believe me to be
Sincerely yours

Samuel Beckett

1   SB may refer to the "Trois textes pour rien," which were later published in *Les Lettres Nouvelles* 1.3 (May 1953) 267–277; these were numbered as "Textes" III, VI, and X in SB's manuscript of *Textes pour rien*. "Je tiens le Greffe," *Deucalion*, 137–140, was "Texte V."

JEROME LINDON, EDITIONS DE MINUIT
PARIS

3/2/53   Ussy

Cher ami

Voici quelque chose qui m'a tout l'air pour vous. Vous seriez gentil d'envoyer les 3 exemplaires qu'on demande, s'il y a lieu.[1] Pour L'Innommable excusez ma lenteur. J'ai été mal fichu. Suzanne

vous l'apportera cette semaine. J'apprends par Combat que la clownerie énorme cède l'affiche à un spectacle de danse. De mieux en
mieux. Et par Dimanche qu'on s'est bagarré samedi dernier.[2]
Serait-il légitime de voir un rapport entre ces deux nouveautés?
J'espère que les comédiens sont sains et saufs.

    Bien amicalement à vous

        s/ Sam

TLS; 1 leaf, 1 side; IMEC, Beckett, Boîte 1, S. Beckett, Correspondance 1946–1953.

3/2/53   Ussy

My dear Jérôme

    Here is something that has you written all over it. It would be nice
if you would send the 3 copies requested, if need arises.[1] For
L'Innommable, forgive my slowness. I have been in a bad way.
Suzanne will bring it next week. I learn from *Combat* that the great
clowning act is being replaced by a dance performance. Better and
better. And from *Dimanche* that there was fighting last Saturday.[2]
Would it be legitimate to see a relationship between these two
items of hot news? I hope that the actors are safe and well.

    All good wishes

        Sam

1 The letter referred to has not been found, but Lindon's response to SB of
4 February indicates that he has done what was necessary concerning the Société
des Auteurs (IMEC, Beckett, Boîte 1, S. Beckett, Correspondance 1946–1953).

2 The advertisement for *En attendant Godot* at the Théâtre de Babylone announces
the play as "UNE CLOWNERIE ENORME" (a great clowning act) (*Combat* 23 January
1953: 2).

On 2, 3, and 4 February there was a program of dance by "Françoise et Dominique" at
the Théâtre de Babylone. Françoise Dupuy (b. 1930) and Dominique Dupuy (née
Michand, b. 1925) formed the Ballets Modernes de Paris (1951–1979). *En attendant
Godot* returned to the stage on 5 February (*Combat* 2 February 1953: 2).

On 31 January, the performance was interrupted by boisterous spectators described
as "un groupe de spectateurs empanachés, visiblement 'émigrés de quartiers
lointains'" (a group of spectators oddly tricked out, obviously from outlying parts of
the city), causing Roger Blin to drop the curtain before the end of the first act. A
shouting match continued during the intermission; at the beginning of the second act,
the malcontents left en masse ("Manifestations au Théâtre de Babylone," *Le Monde* 1
and 2 February 1953: 6).

ALEXANDER TROCCHI, MERLIN PRESS
PARIS

[on or before 5 February 1953]
Dear Mr Trocchi[1]

Your pneumatique only today in the country.[2] I am not very well and much prefer not to return to Paris for the moment. I propose we postpone our meeting until after your return from London.

I have been thinking over the possibility of <u>Molloy</u> in English and feel that we had far better drop this project for the moment at least.[3] It won't go into English, I don't know why. It would have to be entirely rethought and rewritten which is I fear a job only myself can undertake and which I simply can't face at present. You may of course publish the extract in <u>Merlin</u>, if you still wish to.[4] I am revising the translation which has great qualities.[5] I'm afraid I am making a lot of changes, probably too many. My English is queer.

I can't do much at a time and progress very slowly and don't know when it will be ready. Hardly before the end of this month.

<u>Watt</u> is at your disposal whenever you like. I'll have it round as soon as I get back to Paris.

Wishing you a good trip I am
      Yours sincerely

AL draft; 2 leaves, 2 sides; UoR 2926 [Sam Francis Notebook], 6 verso, 7 verso. *Dating:* from SB to Jérôme Lindon, 5 February 1953.

1 Alexander Trocchi edited *Merlin* from May 1952 to Spring 1955.

2 Trocchi's pneumatique has not been found.

3 A letter from Jérôme Lindon to Trocchi of 11 December 1952 granted the English language rights of *Molloy* to Merlin, with the translation, in principle, to be undertaken by SB (IMEC, Beckett, [Boîte 6, Editions de Minuit / The Olympia Press]).

  SB's struggle with the translation is reflected in his many false starts: he cancels "Trying to reflect on <u>Molloy</u> in English," then inserts and then cancels "Trying to imagine <u>Molloy</u> in English," before settling for the present clause.

4 "Extract from *Molloy*," tr. P[atrick] W. Bowles, *Merlin* 2.2 (Autumn 1953) 88–103.

5 SB makes several false starts: he cancels "In spite of its wants I think it has good" – then inserts and cancels "The translation has great possibilities," before settling for the present sentence.

JEROME LINDON, EDITIONS DE MINUIT
PARIS

5/2/53   Ussy
Mon cher Jérôme

Merci de votre bonne lettre. Je n'ai pas vu la NNRF. Puisque c'est comme ça j'écris à Paulhan pour lui annoncer la fin de ma collaboration.[1]

Suzanne vous aura apporté L'Inno. Il y aura peut-être encore quelques petits repentirs au stade des épreuves, j'ai été trop abruti pour pouvoir tout voir.

La traduction en anglais de l'extrait de Molloy n'est pas bonne. Je suis en train de la réviser et elle pourra quand même passer dans Merlin. Mais j'ai écrit à Trocchi qu'il vaut mieux laisser tomber pour le moment son projet de traduction intégrale. Il faudrait que je le fasse moi-même, très librement, et je n'en ai pas le courage en ce moment. D'une façon générale je sais que je ne supporterai pas mon travail traduit en anglais par un autre. Et réviser, comme j'essaie de le faire en ce moment, me donne encore beaucoup plus de mal que de traduire moi-même, et pour un résultat déplorable.[2] Je crois que c'est dans ce sens qu'il faut répondre aux propositions anglaises et américaines.[3] Qu'on attende que je puisse le faire ou qu'on laisse tomber. D'ailleurs je ne tiens pas beaucoup à ce que tout ça paraisse en anglais.

Merci beaucoup pour les 300.000. Ca m'arrange bien en ce moment.

Bien amicalement à vous deux
s/ Sam

TLS; 1 leaf, 2 sides; IMEC, Beckett, Boîte 1, S. Beckett, Correspondance 1946–1953.

5/2/53   Ussy

My dear Jérôme

Thank you for your good letter. I have not seen the *NNRF*. Since that's how it is, I am writing to Paulhan to declare an end to my collaboration.[1]

Suzanne will have brought you *L'Innommable*. There may perhaps be a few second thoughts at the proofs stage – I've been feeling too knocked about to be able to take it all in.

The English translation of the passage from *Molloy* is not good. I am busy revising it, and, even as it stands, it will do for *Merlin*. But I have written to Trocchi that it would be better if he dropped for now his project of a complete translation. It would have to be myself that did it, very freely, but I haven't the heart for that at the moment. Broadly speaking, I know that I shall not be able to bear my work being translated into English by someone else. And revising, as I'm trying to do right now, is even more trouble than doing my own translating, and for a dire outcome.[2] I think that something along these lines has to be the answer to the English and American proposals.[3] Let them wait till I'm able to do it or let the whole thing drop. In any case I am not particularly keen on seeing all this come out in English.

Many thanks for the 300,000. They are very welcome just now.

    All best to you both
        Sam

1   Lindon's letter to SB of 4 February reported that the extract from *L'Innommable* published as "Mahood" (*NNRF* 1.2 [February 1953] 214–234) suppressed a passage that the Editorial Committee thought compromising (IMEC, Beckett, Boîte 1, S. Beckett, Correspondance 1946–1953).

2   Patrick Bowles* (1927–1995) had translated the selection from *Molloy* that would appear in *Merlin*; SB refers to his letter [before 5 February 1953] to Trocchi.

3   Barney Rosset* (b. 1922), Editor of Grove Press, had contracted to publish *En attendant Godot*, *Molloy*, and *Malone meurt* in English. Rosset wrote to Lindon on 16 January that if Merlin did not hold the publication rights for "Beckett's books," he would "be happy to work with any other British publisher," but that he had "no intention of letting somebody do the translation who did not have the complete approval of Beckett himself" (NSyU).

JEROME LINDON, EDITIONS DE MINUIT
PARIS

9/2/53   Ussy

Cher Ami

Merci de votre lettre avec les deux autres. J'ai répondu en disant que je ne pouvais pas.[1]

Voici la lettre que je voudrais envoyer à Paulhan. Mais je vous la soumets d'abord. Renvoyez-la[-]moi avec vos suggestions.[2] Il faut aussi que je voie la NNRF. Je l'aurai demain. Je ne voudrais évidemment pas lui donner l'occasion, par ma lettre, de m'attaquer. Et en même temps je la voudrais aussi vache que possible. Celle que voici est le fruit de bien de prudence et de sacrifices. Ne la perdez pas, je n'ai pas de copie. Suzanne tique sur le mot escroquerie.[3] Que pourrait-on mettre à sa place?

Suzanne m'a tout raconté sur Godot et le mal que vous continuez à vous donner pour que tout marche le mieux possible. Quel ami vous êtes.

De coeur à vous deux de nous deux.

s/ Sam

TLS; 1 leaf, 1 side; IMEC, Beckett, Boîte 1, S. Beckett, Correspondance 1946–1953.

9/2/53   Ussy

My dear Jérôme

Thank you for your letter with the two others. I have replied saying that I could not.[1]

Here is the letter that I would like to send to Paulhan. But I am submitting it to you first. Send it back with your suggestions.[2] Also I must see the *NNRF*. I shall get it tomorrow. Obviously I would not want to give him an opportunity, through my letter, to attack me. And at the same time I would like it to be as nasty as possible. This one is the outcome of a great deal of caution and concession. Do not lose it,

I have no copy. Suzanne baulks at the word "escroquerie".[3] What might one say instead?

Suzanne has told me all about *Godot* and the trouble you go on taking to see that everything goes off as well as possible. What a friend you are.

Heartfelt wishes to you both from us both.

Sam

1 Lindon's letter mentioned here has not been found, nor the two others.

2 SB's drafted letter to Jean Paulhan has not been found. In his letter to SB of 11 February, Lindon responded:

> Je vous ai dit à quel point ce procédé de la Revue me paraissait incorrect. Je ne sais pas, néanmoins, s'il est tout à fait indiqué d'envoyer à Paulhan votre lettre. Je pense même que sa publication éventuelle pourrait être mal interprétée par bien des gens. (IMEC, Beckett, Boîte 1, S. Beckett, Correspondance 1946-1953.) (I have told you how unacceptably discourteous I found this course of action by the review. Nonetheless, I do not know if it is entirely appropriate to send Paulhan your letter. Indeed I think that it might, should it be published, be taken the wrong way by many people.)

3 "Escroquerie" (swindle, dishonest act).

JEROME LINDON, EDITIONS DE MINUIT
PARIS

11/2/53   Ussy

Mon cher Jérôme

Cette lettre se croisera probablement avec votre réponse à ma dernière.[1] Tant pis.

J'ai eu la NNRF hier. Ce n'est pas quelques phrases qui ont sauté, mais une demi-page à peu près, depuis "La tuméfaction" p. 72 du MS jusqu'à "Un percheron" p. 73. Tout le passage quoi. Trop écoeuré pour lire plus avant, j'ignore ce qu'on a pu couper d'autre. Il faudrait d'ailleurs comparer avec le bon à tirer.[2]

Ca me rend littéralement malade. Une lettre, même cinglante, ne me semble plus suffisante. Il va falloir qu'on se voie bientôt. Est-ce que je peux lui faire un procès? Ou tout au moins l'obliger, sous la menace de poursuites, à publier dans un prochain numéro le passage omis, avec ses excuses? Votre beau-frère avocat est-il suffisament au courant de ces questions pour nous conseiller?[3] Cette affaire dépasse de beaucoup ma personne. Mais même sans ça, et malgré l'horreur que j'ai de la polémique et de la publicité, je ne peux faire autrement que d'aller au bout de cette histoire. D'autre part je ne voudrais absolument pas vous créer des difficultés à vous. Mais je vous sens aussi indigné que moi.

Réfléchissez et dites-moi si je dois rentrer tout de suite. Ca ne m'arrangerait pas en ce moment. Mais rien ne me dérange autant que de laisser cette affaire en suspens. J'aurai la peau de ce salaud, même si je dois y laisser la mienne.

Bien amicalement à vous.

s/ Sam

TLS; 1 leaf, 1 side; IMEC, Beckett, Boîte 1, S. Beckett, Correspondance 1946–1953.

11/2/53   Ussy

My dear Jérôme

This letter will probably cross your reply to my last.[1] Too bad.

I got the *NNRF* yesterday. It is not a few sentences that have gone but nearly half a page, from "La tuméfaction", p. 72 of the ms, to "Un percheron", p. 73. Well, the whole passage dammit. Too disgusted to read on, I do not know what else they may have cut. Moreover, we should compare it with the final proof.[2]

It makes me literally ill. A letter, even a stinger, no longer seems to me enough. We shall have to meet. Can I sue him? Or at least oblige him, on pain of legal action, to publish in one of his next issues the passage omitted, and an apology? Is your barrister brother-in-law well enough up in these matters to advise us?[3] This affair concerns far more than just me. But even without that, and in spite of the horror that I have of polemic and publicity, I have no choice but to see the matter through. On the other hand, I would absolutely not want to create difficulties for you. But I sense that you are as indignant as I am.

Think it over and tell me if I must go back straight away. That would not suit me right now. But nothing is more upsetting than leaving this affair hanging. I'll have the bastard's hide, even if it means losing my own.

All good wishes

Sam

1 Lindon did write a letter to SB on 11 February.

2 The passage rejected by the *NNRF* should have followed "L'obscène protrusion de la langue" (Beckett, "Mahood," 222):

> La tuméfaction de la pine. Tiens, la pine, je n'y pensais plus. Quel dommage que je n'aie plus de bras, il y aurait peut-être quelque chose à en tirer. Non, c'est mieux ainsi. A mon âge, me remettre à me masturber, ce serait indécent. Et puis ça ne donnerait rien. Après tout, qu'est-ce que j'en sais? A force de tractions bien rythmées, en pensant de toutes mes forces à un cul de cheval, au moment où la queue se soulève, qui sait, j'arriverais peut-être à un petit quelque chose. Ciel, on dirait que ça remue. Est-ce à dire qu'on ne m'a pas coupé? Pourtant il me semblait bien qu'on m'avait coupé. Je confonds peut-être, avec d'autres bourses. Du reste ça ne bouge plus. Je vais me concentrer à nouveau. Un percheron. (*L'Innommable* [Paris: Editions de Minuit, 1953] 77.) (The tumefaction of the penis! The penis, well now, that's a nice surprise, I'd forgotten I had one. What a pity I have no arms, there might still be something to be wrung from it. No, tis better thus. At my age, to start manstuprating again, it would be indecent. And fruitless. And yet one can never tell. With a yo heave ho, concentrating with all my might on a horse's rump, at the moment when the tail rises, who knows, I might not go altogether empty-handed away. Heaven, I almost felt it flutter! Does this mean they did not geld me? I could have sworn they had gelt me. But perhaps I am getting mixed up with other scrota. Not another stir out of it in any case. I'll concentrate again. A Clydesdale. (*The Unnamable* [New York: Grove Press, 1958] 62–63.)

In his letter of 11 February, Lindon writes that he could not check the omission precisely because he had neither the proofs of the *NNRF* (in which the cut had not been indicated) nor the final typescript of the novel.

3 Pierre Rosenfeld (1922–2004), a barrister, was the brother-in-law of Jérôme Lindon.

JEROME LINDON, EDITIONS DE MINUIT

PARIS

16/2/53   Ussy

Cher Jérôme

Je reçois à l'instant une lettre de Paulhan dont voici, sans commentaires, la copie:

"Cher Monsieur

Excusez-moi de vous écrire si tard. J'ai été souffrant. Je le suis encore.

J'avais prié notre ami commun Georges Belmont de vous dire que le passage de <u>Mahood</u> en question nous embarrassait un peu. C'est ensuite que tout s'est précipité. Notre Comité de Direction – Malraux, Schlumberger, Caillois – a jugé la publication, en tout état de cause, impossible: de nature à ruiner la Revue, sans le moins du monde nous servir. Je pensais trouver appui chez notre avocat; malheureusement, son avis a été formel: le passage entraînerait pour nous – et pour la <u>nrf</u> du même coup – des poursuites judiciaires, et sans aucun doute une condamnation (alors qu'il avait toutes chances de passer dans un livre inaperçu). Il était trop tard pour vous avertir, le numéro était sous presse. Du moins aurais-je dû dès le lendemain vous écrire. C'est ce retard que je vous prie de pardonner. Je suis votre JP"[1]

J'attends avec impatience de savoir si vous avez jugé bon d'envoyer la lettre que je vous ai soumise. Je répondrai à Paulhan, mais pas avant de m'être calmé encore une fois.[2]

Côté Godot j'ai encore un service à vous demander. C'est de faire retenir deux places au contrôle au nom de Madame Péron pour la matinée de dimanche prochain le 22 et deux autres au nom de Michel Péron pour le jeudi suivant 26.[3]

Nous aimerions ne rentrer que la semaine prochaine. Mais si cette histoire de la NNRF l'exige, je suis prêt à rentrer tout de suite.

Bien amicalement de nous deux à vous deux.

s/ <u>Sam</u>

TLS; 1 leaf, 1 side; IMEC, Beckett, Boîte 1, S. Beckett, Correspondance 1946–1953.

16/2/53   Ussy

Dear Jérôme

I have just received a letter from Paulhan of which this is a copy, without comments:

"Dear Mr Beckett

Forgive me for being so late in writing to you. I have been ill. I still am.

I had asked our common friend Georges Belmont to tell you that the passage in question from 'Mahood' was causing us some difficulty. It was after that that things started to go very fast. Our Editorial Board – Malraux, Schlumberger, Caillois – judged that publication was in any case impossible: such as to ruin the *Revue* without doing us the least good. I thought I might get support from our lawyer. Unfortunately, his judgement was unhesitating: the passage would involve us – and the NNRF by the same token – in lawsuits, and beyond doubt a decision against us (while in a book it had every chance of passing unnoticed). It was too late to warn you; the issue was already printing. I should at least have written to you the next day. It is this delay that I am asking you to forgive.

Yours JP"[1]

I am waiting impatiently to know if you thought it right to send the letter that I had submitted to you. I shall reply to Paulhan, but not until I have calmed down again.[2]

On the *Godot* front, another favour to ask of you. It is to have put aside at the box office two seats in the name of Madame Péron for the matinee next Sunday 22nd, and two others in the name of Michel Péron for the following Thursday 26th.[3]

We would like not to go back until next week. But if this NNRF business demands it, I am ready to leave at once.

All good wishes from us both to you both.

Sam

---

1   On 12 February, Lindon reported that he and Georges Lambrichs had broached the matter with the review and that Paulhan claimed that the decision had been made in his absence, without his being consulted. Lindon added that SB might receive a letter from Paulhan.

Lindon doubted that the NNRF would publish the suppressed passage, and said that doing so would make little sense. He suggested that SB write to Paulhan stating the facts of the case and requesting a statement of the editorial decision to truncate the extract, the exact page of the cut, and the reasons for this.

A copy of Paulhan's letter, dated only "février," can be found (anomalously) in IMEC, Beckett, Boîte 7, S. Beckett, Correspondance 1969–1972; SB's transcription differs in two details: SB capitalizes the first word, "Excusez-moi," and changes "pour vous" to "pour nous."

André Malraux, Jean Schlumberger (1877–1968), Roger Caillois (1913–1978).

2   SB responded to Lindon's letter of 11 February on 13 February: "Votre lettre à l'instant. Si vous approuvez celle ci-jointe vous seriez tout à fait gentil de l'envoyer, recommandée si vous jugez bon." (Your letter this very minute. If you approve the enclosed, do be good enough to send it, recorded delivery if you see fit.) SB added, "Vous avez raison, comme toujours. La fureur noire est mauvaise conseillère." (You are right, as always. Black rage is a poor adviser.) (IMEC, Beckett, Boîte 1, S. Beckett, Correspondance 1946–1953.)

3   Mania Péron and her son Michel Péron. SB wrote to Mania Péron on 12 February:

> Il ne faut absolument pas que vous payiez votre place pour voir Godot. Pareillement pour Michel et Alexis. Il m'est très facile d'avoir des places à l'oeil. Mais comme aux dernières nouvelles il y a encore du monde, je vous demanderai seulement de m'indiquer un peu à l'avance (8 jours) le soir que vous voudrez y aller et de vous contenter de deux places à la fois. (TxU, Lake collection, Beckett.) (You must absolutely not pay for your ticket to see *Godot*. Same for Michel and Alexis. It is very easy for me to get seats for nothing. But as, when I last heard, there are still a fair few people turning up, I shall just ask you to let me know a little ahead of time [a week] which evening you want to go on, and to make do with two seats at a time.)

JEROME LINDON, EDITIONS DE MINUIT
PARIS

17/2/53   Ussy
Bien cher ami

Votre lettre à l'instant. Vous aurez reçu la mienne, avec le supplément d'infamie de Paulhan. Je suis content que vous ayez envoyé mon mot.[1] Je ne pense pas qu'on nous donne cette piètre satisfaction. C'est pour cela qu'il serait peut-être bon, dès à présent, de savoir jusqu'à quel point je suis fondé en droit à l'exiger. Le bon sens ne laisse pas de doute là-dessus, mais je m'en méfie. Si vous voyez votre beau-frère, vous seriez gentil de lui en parler.

Merci infiniment de nous inviter si gentiment pour samedi prochain. Hélas c'est non, mon cher Jérôme, à Annette et vous on peut le dire tout bêtement.[2]

J'attends la traduction allemande.[3] Malheureusement je n'ai pas de Godot ici et ne le sais plus tout à fait par coeur heureusement.

Voulez-vous m'en envoyer un exemplaire? A propos, merci pour Critique. J'ai trouvé excellent l'article de R.-G., de loin le meilleur que j'aie lu. Je vais essayer de lui torcher un petit mot de remerciement. A quand les Gommes?[4]

Sachant que Step n'écrira pas, Suzanne vous demande de nous toucher un mot, dans votre prochaine lettre. Est-ce que Joffe a fait quelque chose?[5]

Bien amicalement à vous deux de nous deux

s/ Sam

TLS; 1 leaf, 2 sides; IMEC, Beckett, Boîte 1, S. Beckett, Correspondance 1946–1953.

17/2/53   Ussy

My dear friend

Your letter just now. You will have had mine, with the supplementary infamy from Paulhan. I am glad that you sent my note.[1] I do not think that we shall get even that small satisfaction. It is for this reason that it would perhaps be good, without further ado, to know how far I am within my rights in demanding it. Common sense leaves no room for doubt on it, but I am wary of that. If you see your brother-in-law, please do talk to him about it.

Thank you so much for so kindly inviting us for Saturday next. Alas it is no, my dear Jérôme, to you and Annette I can just say it without frills.[2]

I am waiting for the German translation.[3] Unfortunately I have no *Godot* here, and I no longer know it by heart – fortunately. Would you send me a copy? By the way, thank you for *Critique*. I found R.-G.'s article excellent, by far the best I have read. I am going to try to scribble him a word of thanks. When is *Les Gommes* due out?[4]

Knowing that Step will not write, Suzanne asks you to let us know about him in your next letter. Is Joffe doing anything?[5]

Our very best wishes from us both to you both.

Sam

1 SB refers to Lindon's letter of 16 February, in which Lindon writes that he has just sent SB's letter of complaint to Paulhan by pneumatique, as well as his own to Paulhan of the same date (IMEC, Beckett, Boîte 1, S. Beckett, Correspondance 1946–1953).

2 In his letter to SB of 16 February, Lindon invites SB and Suzanne Deschevaux-Dumesnil to a dinner party the following Saturday along with about ten other Minuit authors:

> J'ai pensé que cela vous ennuierait, Suzanne et vous, de participer à une manifestation littéraire.
> Il va sans dire cependant, que vous êtes absolument invités, et que votre présence nous ferait à tous un très grand plaisir. Mais votre absence ne nous vexerait pas.
> (I thought that neither you nor Suzanne would enjoy being at a literary event.
> However it goes without saying that you are very definitely invited and that your presence would be a great pleasure for us all, but your absence would not upset us.)

3 Elmar Tophoven* (1923–1989) began his German translation of *En attendant Godot* immediately after he attended the premiere. Lindon's letter of 16 February indicates that he sent the translation that morning under separate cover, that Tophoven translated Adamov's plays, and that this text would be taken by Fischer Verlag, if SB agreed: "L'auteur vous a signalé dans une note à part quelques-unes des difficultés principales qu'il a rencontrées, avec des suggestions pour chacune d'elles, mais je pense qu'il faudrait qu'il puisse vous voir avant de donner un texte définitif" (The author has pointed out, in a separate note, some of the main difficulties he has encountered, with suggestions for each one of them, but I think he would have to come and see you before giving a definitive text).

4 Alain Robbe-Grillet, "Samuel Beckett, Auteur Dramatique," *Critique* 9 (February 1953) 108–114. Robbe-Grillet's novel *Les Gommes* (*The Erasers*) was published by Editions de Minuit on 27 February 1953.

5 Step and Joffe have not been identified. Lindon writes on 18 February 1953: "Pour Step, dites à Suzanne que ça ne semble pas aller très fort bien que Joffe ait été très gentil" (For Step, tell Suzanne that things are not going too well although Joffe has been very kind) (IMEC, Beckett, Boîte 1, S. Beckett, Correspondance 1946–1953).

JEROME LINDON, EDITIONS DE MINUIT
PARIS

19/2/53   Ussy
Mon cher Jérôme
Merci de vos deux lettres, de la traduction et du texte de Godot.[1]
Je ne trouve pas la traduction très bonne. Pas mal de contresens, peu de style. Mais je ne veux pas décevoir le type. Dites-lui donc

seulement, si vous le voyez, qu'il va falloir que nous revoyions ça ensemble. Je crois qu'il y a moyen d'en faire quelque chose de convenable. Ce sera un gros boulot. Je vais d'ailleurs lui écrire en ce sens et nous nous y mettrons dès mon retour.

Je serais heureux de voir les dessins de Mlle Bentin. Mais il ne faut pas qu'elle fasse dépendre son exposition de mes réactions. Ils sont à elle et elle est libre d'en disposer comme elle veut.[2]

Un mot de Roger. Il dit qu'il a déplacé une "roubignolle" à force de gueuler et que Latour a un orgelet.[3]

J'essaie de ne plus penser à l'histoire Paulhan. Je suis persuadé que sa réaction sera mauvaise et qu'il serait utile de savoir dès à présent quels sont nos droits.

Bien amicalement à vous deux

s/ <u>Sam</u>

Les 2 places au nom de Michel Péron sont pr. aujourd'hui en 8 le 26. Pardonnez tous ces emmerdements et ceux à venir.[4]

TLS with AN PS; 1 leaf, 1 side; IMEC, Beckett, Boîte 1, S. Beckett, Correspondance 1946–1953.

19/2/53   Ussy

My dear Jérôme

Thank you for your two letters, for the translation, and for the text of *Godot*.[1]

I find the translation not very good. A fair number of blunders, not much style. But I do not want to disappoint the bloke. Just tell him, if you see him, that we shall have to go over it together. I think that there are ways of making something decent out of it. It will be a big job. And indeed I am going to write to him along these lines, and we shall set to when I am back.

I should be happy to see Mlle. Bentin's drawings. But she must not make her exhibition depend on my reactions. The drawings are hers, and she is free to do what she pleases with them.[2]

A note from Roger. He says he has displaced one of his balls by too much shouting, and that Latour has a stye.[3]

I am trying not to think about the Paulhan business. I am convinced that his reaction will be bad and that it would be useful to know straight away what our rights are.

All good wishes to you both.

Sam

The two seats in the name of Michel Péron are for today week the 26th. Forgive all these bloody nuisances, and the ones to come.[4]

---

1 SB refers to Lindon's letters of 17 and 18 February (IMEC, Beckett, Boîte 1, S. Beckett, Correspondance 1946–1953), and to Tophoven's German translation of *En attendant Godot*.

2 A Mlle. Bentin was sent by Roger Blin to Lindon to present her drawings of *Godot*, and to request SB's permission to exhibit them in a gallery on the Rue de Beaune, Paris (Lindon to SB, 17 February [1953], IMEC, Beckett, Boîte 1, S. Beckett, Correspondance 1946–1953). She has not been further identified.

3 Blin's note to SB has not been found, but SB's response follows below. Pierre Latour (1907–1976) played Estragon.

4 PS: AN in lower left margin. Lindon requested these tickets on 18 February, and on 19 February requested tickets for Eugène Ionesco, Jean Paulhan (neither of whom could attend earlier), and others (IMEC, Beckett, Boîte 2, Dossier France Guy).

ELMAR TOPHOVEN

PARIS

19/2/53   6 Rue des Favorites

                                       Paris 15me

Cher Monsieur

Merci de votre lettre. J'ai lu votre traduction, une fois, trop rapidement. Je serais heureux de vous voir. Il y a d'ailleurs pas mal de choses dont je voudrais vous parler, de mon côté. Je suis à la campagne en ce moment. Dès mon retour à Paris je vous ferai signe. Je vous demanderai, si vous voulez bien, de venir travailler chez moi, à l'adresse ci-dessus. J'ai l'impression que ça va être un assez gros boulot, mais que nous arriverons à quelque chose de bien. Soyez assez gentil de garder mon adresse pour vous.

> Cordialement à vous
> s/ Sam. Beckett
> (Samuel Beckett)

TLS; 1 leaf, 1 side; Tophoven collection.

19/2/53   6 Rue des Favorites
                                                           Paris 15

Dear Mr Tophoven

Thank you for your letter. I have read your translation, once, too rapidly. I should be glad to see you. In any case there are quite a few things of my own that I would like to talk to you about. I am in the country at the moment. As soon as I go back to Paris I shall get in touch. I shall ask you, if you are willing, to come and work here, at the above address. I have the feeling that it will be rather a big job, but that we shall get through to something good. Please be kind enough to keep my address to yourself.

> Yours sincerely
> Sam. Beckett
> (Samuel Beckett)

ROGER BLIN
PARIS

jeudi 19.2.53   Ussy

Mon cher Roger

Merci de ton mot avec les lettres. Les revoici, ça pourrait t'intéresser, ce passionnant point d'histoire théâtrale.[1]

Désolé pour la roubignolle, j'espère qu'elle a regagné sa base. Un peu de massage, peut-être avant de dormir.[2]

J'ai pensé que tu pourrais chantonner l'air de Vladimir en prenant ton élan au I°, qu'en penses-tu? Histoire d'ajouter à la confusion.[3]

J'ai lu une traduction allemande. Pas très bonne.

Nous t'avons entendu dans L'Ecole des Bouffons.[4]

Nous serons à Paris vers la fin du mois probablement, à moins que mes chicots ne m'obligent à rentrer plus tôt.

Amitiés à tous. Bon courage et bonne suite.

    Affectueusement de nous 2

      Sam

ALS; 1 leaf, 1 side; *env to* Monsieur Roger Blin, 264 Rue Saint-Honoré, Paris 1er; *pm* 19-2-53, La Ferté-sous-Jouarre; IMEC, Blin.

Thursday 19.2.53   Ussy

My dear Roger

Thanks for your note with the letters. Here they are back again, this might interest you, an exciting moment in theatre history.[1]

Very sorry to hear about the testicle. Hope it made it back to base. A little massage perhaps before sleep.[2]

It occurred to me that you might hum Vladimir's tune when you really get going in Act I, what do you think? Just to add to the confusion.[3]

I've read a German translation. Not very good.

We heard you in *L'Ecole des Bouffons*.[4]

We'll be in Paris towards the end of the month, probably, unless my stumps make me go back sooner.

All the best to everyone. Keep your courage up, and keep on.

    Love from the 2 of us

      Sam

1   Blin may have sent SB letters that he had received in response to the production of *En attendant Godot* disrupted on 31 January; two letters denouncing the play were published by Michel Polac ("Controverse autour de 'Godot,'" *Arts-Spectacles* 400, 27 February – 5 March: 3). Polac commented: "On a pu apprécier par ailleurs les opinions de Armand Salacrou et Jean Anouilh qui contrastent avec ces lettres" (We have been able to enjoy by the same token the opinions of Armand Salacrou and Jean Anouilh which contrast with these letters). In the same issue of *Arts-Spectacles* were

Salacrou's essay "Ce n'est pas un accident mais une réussite" (1) and Anouilh's essay "Godot ou le sketch des *Pensées* de Pascal traité par les Fratellini" (1).

SB may have sent to Blin a cutting that documented the violent reaction to the play (see 3 February 1953, n. 2).

2   Blin reluctantly assumed the role of Pozzo in the premiere of *En attendant Godot*, as he wrote on 5 January to the actress Delphine Seyrig (1932–1990): "Il se trouve que j'ai été amené à jouer Pozzo!" (As it turns out, I've been talked into playing Pozzo) (Youngerman collection). Seyrig had contributed personal funds as a surety for the production.

3   SB's suggestion refers to the song that Vladimir sings at the opening of Act II of *En attendant Godot*: "Un chien vint dans l'office" (96).

4   *L'Ecole des Bouffons* (1943) by Michel de Ghelderode (1898–1962) was produced for radio, directed by Serge Baudo; Roger Blin performed in the piece which was aired in the series *Soirée de Paris*, on the Chaîne Nationale, RTF, on 15 February 1953 (Roland Beyen, *Ghelderode: présentation, choix de textes, chronologie, bibliographie* [Paris: Seghers, 1974] 108, 203; Anne Pavis, Inathèque de France, 8 February 2010).

MANIA PERON

PARIS

mardi [before 26 March 1953]   Paris

Chère Mania

   Voici une première tranche de l'Innommable. Un coup d'oeil par pitié.[1]

   Venez prendre le thé samedi si vous êtes libre et que ça vous chante. Peut-être que vous pourriez me rapporter les épreuves ce jour-là?

   Donc sauf contre[-]ordre à samedi.

   Affectueusement de nous deux.

       Sam

ALS; 1 leaf, 1 side; *enclosure not extant; AN AH upper right margin* 1953; TxU, Lake collection, Beckett. *Dating*: This letter is prior to SB to Mania Péron, jeudi [26 March 1953] (TxU, Lake collection, Beckett), which indicates that SB is waiting for the rest of the proofs of *L'Innommable*.

Tuesday [before 26 March 1953]   Paris

Dear Mania

   Here is a first chunk of *L'Innommable*. A quick look for pity's sake.[1]

Come and have tea on Saturday if you are free and feel like it. Perhaps you could bring the proofs that day?

So unless I hear from you otherwise, till Saturday.

Love from the two of us.

Sam

1 SB wrote to Mania Péron on 12 February that *L'Innommable* was at the printers: "Je demanderai un double jeu d'épreuves et vous demanderai d'y promener une dernière fois votre oeil de lynx" (I shall ask for a double set of proofs and will ask you to cast your lynx's eye over it one last time) (TxU, Lake collection, Beckett).

JEROME LINDON, EDITIONS DE MINUIT
PARIS

31-3-53   Ussy
Cher Jérôme

Merci de votre mot. La note de la NNRF n'est pas celle que nous avions exigée et je ne suis pas du tout sûr que les choses puissent en rester là. Les "excuses", évidemment, rendent difficile toute continuation sur le plan judiciaire.[1] Mais un exposé détaillé de l'affaire, à paraître dans Combat ou Arts ou Les Lettres Nouvelles, serait peut-être à envisager. J'aimerais avoir votre sentiment là-dessus, et celui de votre beau-frère.[2]

Merci encore de m'avoir prévenu si promptement. Mes amitiés à vous deux.

Sam.

ALS; 1 leaf, 1 side; IMEC, Beckett, Boîte 1, S. Beckett, Correspondance – Divers, 1950–1956.

31-3-53   Ussy
Dear Jérôme

Thank you for your letter. The note in the *NNRF* is not what we had demanded and I am not at all sure that things can be left at that.

The "apology", of course, makes it hard to go on with legal proceedings.[1] But a detailed account of the whole affair, to appear in *Combat*, or *Arts*, or *Les Lettres Nouvelles* could perhaps be considered. I would like to have your view on that, as well as that of your brother-in-law.[2]

Thank you again for having warned me so promptly. My best wishes to you both.

Sam.

1   Lindon wrote to SB on 28 March to say that he had just received the issue of the *NNRF* that published a note of apology (IMEC, Beckett, Boîte 1, S. Beckett, Correspondance 1946–1953). The apology read:

> Après consultation juridique, et afin d'éviter des poursuites, la N.R.F. a dû supprimer, au tirage, treize lignes du texte de *Mahood* (1er février, p. 222, ligne 9).
> Nous nous en excusons auprès de Samuel Beckett. (*NNRF* 1.4 [April 1953] 768.)
> (After legal advice was taken and in order to avoid a lawsuit, the *N.R.F.* had to suppress, at the printing stage, thirteen lines of the text of *Mahood* [February 1st, p. 222, line 9].
> We apologize to Samuel Beckett.)

2   Lindon responded to SB on 8 April:

> Mon beau-frère n'est pas rentré de vacances encore, mais pour ma part, j'envisage difficilement que l'on fasse paraître un exposé de cette affaire dans "Combat" ou "Arts"; par définition, ces journalistes déformeront les faits et leur donneront une signification très différente de la véritable. Quant aux Lettres Nouvelles, cela risquerait de devenir un épisode de la guerre entre les revues. (IMEC, Beckett, Boîte 1, S. Beckett, Correspondance 1946–1953.) (My brother-in-law has not come back from holiday, but I am reluctant to consider the publication by *Combat* or *Arts* of your exposé of this affair. By definition, these journalists will distort the facts and present a meaning very different from the true one. As for the *Lettres Nouvelles*, that would run the risk of becoming an episode in the war between journals.)

MANIA PERON

PARIS

5 avril 1953 [*for* 4 avril 1953]   Ussy

Chère Mania

Je vous envoie aujourd'hui sous pli séparé la suite et fin des épreuves.[1] Vous seriez gentille de me les retourner Rue des Favorites.

Merci de votre lettre. Non, je n'ai pas mis de virgule entre <u>pas</u> et <u>va</u>, j'aime mieux sans.[2] Quant aux subjonctifs, il n'y a pas à tortiller du cul, si l'un est juste l'autre aussi, et merde pour l'indicatif, je les laisse tous les deux.

Je m'excuse de ne pas avoir donné <u>Godot</u> à Alexis et Michel, je croyais l'avoir fait. Je le leur donnerai en même temps que l'<u>Innommable</u>.

J'espère qu'il fait meilleur chez vous que chez nous, mais il y a peu de chances.

Voilà le facteur, je vous quitte.

Affectueusement de nous 2

    <u>Sam</u>

ALS; 1 leaf, 2 sides; *env to* Madame Péron, Villa les Bruyères, La Garenne, ERQUY, Côtes-du-Nord; *pm* 4-4-53, La Ferté-sous-Jouarre; TxU, Lake collection, Beckett. *Dating*: from pm.ed

5 April 1953 [*for* 4 April 1953]   Ussy

Dear Mania

I am sending today under separate cover the next and last part of the proofs.[1] Would you be kind enough to send them back to me at the *Rue des Favorites*.

Thank you for your letter. No, I did not put a comma between "pas" and "va", I like it better without.[2] As for the subjunctives, there is no need to get all het up: if one of them is correct, the other is too, and to hell with the indicative, I shall leave both.

I apologise for not giving *Godot* to Alexis and Michel; I thought I had. I shall give it to them at the same time as *L'Innommable*.

I hope that the weather is better where you are than here, but there is not much chance.

Here is the postman, I must leave you.

Love from us 2.

    Sam

1   Proofs of *L'Innommable*.

2   This construction occurs once in *L'Innommable*: "Se peut-il qu'un jour, premier pas va, j'y sois simplement resté, où, au lieu de sortir, selon une vieille habitude, passer jour et nuit aussi loin que possible de chez moi, ce n'était pas loin" (7).

GEORGE REAVEY

12/5/53   6 Rue des Favorites

                                                    Paris 15me

My dear George

Very glad to have your letter. Forgive my remissness in not replying to your last. Glad to hear you are writing. I haven't seen Botteghe O. Had some unpleasantness with the princess.[1] I don't know where you left off with me. Since the war there have been Murphy in French with Bordas and with Editions de Minuit Molloy (too tired to underline), Malone Meurt and En Attendant Godot. L'Innommable is due out in a few days, also (tiens-toi bien) our old misery Watt with the Merlin juveniles here in Paris who are beginning a publishing business.[2] Shall of course send you L'Inno. and Watt and of course also whatever else what [sic] you want. Since 1950 have only succeeded in writing a dozen very short abortive texts in French and there is nothing whatever in sight.[3] No; I don't seem to have written any criticism apart from the old commissions you mention. Thanks for offer of Echo's Bones, but I still have a whole charnel of them here that you gave me.[4] Haven't seen anyone you know except Tom MacGreevy, now as you probably know Director of the National Gallery in Dublin and I think very happy with that. Hardly ever seen the Van Velde. Geer and Lisl have not been so well, especially Lisl who seems to have some chronic disorder that the doctors can't identify. Geer has les yeux qui foirent dans la sciure, something wrong with the tear ducts. Bram has been turned off by that bastard Maeght, hasn't been able to do any work for a long time and lives God knows how.[5] No, I haven't seen any American writes on me. Had a letter from the Saunders agency asking for a text for New World Writing. Don't feel like trusting the Americans with anything.[6] Haven't been back to Ireldand [sic] since my mother's death in 50 and hope I never shall. I possess two rooms on a remote elevated field beyond Meaux about 30 miles from Paris and hope to live there mostly in the future, watching the grass try to grow among the stones and pulverizing the pretty charlock with Weedone. Tout un programme.[7] Write again soon and tell me what to send you. My very kind regards to Irene.[8]

Ever affectionately yours

Sam

TLS; 1 leaf, 1 side; TxU, Reavey collection.

1   George Reavey published a poem, "The House of Great Longings," in *Botteghe Oscure* 11 (1953) 139–142.
SB's previous exchanges with Princess Caetani: 14 June 1951, and 3 July 1951.

2   *Watt* was with Editions Merlin, whose editorial staff included Alexander Trocchi, Richard Seaver* (1926–2009), Alice Jane Lougee (known as Jane, m. Griscom, b. 1933), Christopher Logue (b. 1926), Austryn Wainhouse (b. 1927), and their co-publisher for *Watt* Maurice Girodias* (1919–1990) of Olympia Press.
Seaver later wrote:

> We published a long excerpt of *Watt* in our next issue – Beckett had dictated which passage we could use … I suspected then, and later confirmed, that in so specifying that passage, Beckett was testing the literary fibre of the magazine, for taken out of context it could have been judged pedantic or wearily over-experimental, which indeed, according to some of our readers' letters, it was. But we didn't care: we had a mission, and Beckett was our leading man ("Richard Seaver on Translating Beckett," in *Beckett Remembering, Remembering Beckett*, ed. James Knowlson and Elizabeth Knowlson [London: Bloomsbury, 2006] 103–104).

"Tiens-toi bien" (hold on to your chair).

3   There were thirteen *Textes pour rien*.

4   *Echo's Bones and Other Precipitates* (1935) had been published by George Reavey's Europa Press.

5   "Geer has les yeux qui foirent dans la sciure" (Geer is having vision problems, as if he had sawadust in his eyes). Following a five-year contract with the artist, Aimé Maeght at the Galerie Maeght in Paris had lost interest in Bram van Velde's work (Stoullig and Schoeller, eds., *Bram van Velde*, 181; Mason, *Bram van Velde*, 306).

6   To this date, there had been no criticism of SB's work in the United States. The first to appear there was by Irish critic Niall Montgomery, who was asked in October 1953 to prepare a study for publication in *New World Writing* (NLI 6475, Lot 7, Idda, now in Miscellaneous, Victor Weybright to Montgomery, 27 October 1953). An extract from *Molloy* was published in *New World Writing* (3.5 [April 1954] 316–323).
New York literary agent Marion Saunders (n.d.).

7   Having had a two-room house built near Ussy-sur-Marne, SB and Suzanne Deschevaux-Dumesnil moved into it in January 1953 (SB to Susan Manning, 16 April 1953, TxU, Beckett collection; Knowlson, *Damned to Fame*, 351). As SB wrote to Mania Péron on 16 February (TxU, Lake collection, Beckett): "La maison n'est pas photo-génique [...] C'est un petit parallelepipède grisatre." (The house is not photogenic

13. Samuel Beckett with his brother Frank and Suzanne
Deschevaux-Dumesnil, at Ussy, 1953

[. . .] It is a little greyish parallelipiped.) SB omits two of the accents in "parallélépipède," and the circumflex in "grisâtre."

In his letter of 16 April to Susan Manning, SB also wrote: "A lot of little things remain to be done and the ground has yet to be enclosed and at least part of it turned into something resembling a garden" (TxU, Beckett collection).

"Weedone" is a commercial herbicide.

"Tout un programme" (A whole programme).

8 Reavey's wife, Irene Rice Pereira.

JEROME LINDON, EDITIONS DE MINUIT
PARIS

<u>Samedi</u> [before 18 May 1953]   <u>Ussy</u>
Cher Jérôme

Merci de votre lettre. Je serai à Paris, et + ou moins libre, à partir de jeudi prochain. Je pourrais rencontrer Kenin vendredi ou samedi. Il faut faire attention avec ces histoires d'adaptation.[1]

Une carte – tenez-vous bien – de Roger et contre-signée par toute la bande! "Rude soireé – mouvements divers. Gagnée au finish." J'ai l'impression qu'il ne marchera pas pour le Théâtre La Bruyère. Trop fatigués tous.[2]

J'espère que vous avez de meilleures nouvelles des <u>Gommes</u>. Bonne poignée de main à l'auteur.[3]

Affectueusement à vous deux et à bientôt

<u>Sam</u>

ALS; 1 leaf, 1 side; IMEC, Beckett, Boîte 1, S. Beckett, Correspondance 1946–1953. *Dating*: from Jérôme Lindon's letter to Denise Tual of 18 May 1953.

Saturday [before 18 May 1953]   Ussy
Dear Jérôme

Thank you for your letter. I shall be in Paris, and more or less free, from next Thursday on. I could meet Kanin on Friday or Saturday. We have to be careful with this adaptation business.[1]

A card – hold on to your seat – from Roger, countersigned by the whole gang! "Rough evening – disturbances. Won at the tape." I have

379

the feeling that he will not be on for the Théâtre La Bruyère. Too tired, all of them.[2]

I hope you have better news of *Les Gommes*. My warm greetings to the author.[3]

Love to you both and till soon.

Sam

1 On 6 May, French theatre producer Denise Tual (1906–2000) wrote to SB that she had seen Roger Blin who had given her SB's address. She introduced American writer and director Garson Kanin (1912–1999), whom SB spells "Kenin," as a friend who was adapting *En attendant Godot* with Thornton Wilder (IMEC, Beckett, Boîte 2, S. Beckett, *En attendant Godot* représentations [2]). On 15 May, Jérôme Lindon wrote to SB that he had received a serious offer for the adaptation of *En attendant Godot* from them (IMEC, Beckett, Boîte 1, S. Beckett, Correspondance 1946–1953). On 18 May, Lindon wrote to Tual to confirm that the option for *En attendant Godot* in English for the United States and Great Britain was available (IMEC, Beckett, Boîte 2, S. Beckett, *En attendant Godot* représentations [2]).

2 Roger Blin had been on tour with *En attendant Godot*, and was expected back in Paris for a reprise, possibly at the Théâtre La Bruyère, according to Lindon's letter of 15 May. On 28 May, Lindon writes to SB that Jean-Marie Serreau is eager to put on a reprise of *En attendant Godot* (Minuit collection).

3 Alain Robbe-Grillet.

ROSICA COLIN
LONDON

May 19th 1953

Editions de Minuit
7 Rue Bernard-Palissy
Paris 6me

Dear Mrs Colin

Thank you for your letter of May 8th.[1]

Re English and American rights of my work in French I think you would be well advised to get in touch with my editor Monsieur Jérôme Lindon at the above address. He knows better than I how things stand. I am not even sure that they are still available.[2]

My few translations of Francis Ponge are unsatisfactory and I do not wish to have them reproduced.[3]

I shall send you in a few days a copy of <u>Transition</u>, Ed. Georges Duthuit, in which you will find, translated by myself, two short extracts from <u>Molloy</u> and <u>Malone Meurt</u>.[4]

Yours sincerely

s/

(Samuel Beckett)

TLS; 1 leaf, 1 side; Rosica Colin collection.

1   On 8 May, London literary agent Rosica Colin* (1903–1983) wrote to SB expressing enthusiasm for *En attendant Godot*, "which strikes me as one of the very best plays possible" (Fehsenfeld collection). While she thought that a club performance would be the only possibility for a production in England, she hoped that she could place the publication rights for the play and for SB's novels in England and the US.

2   In a Gallicism, SB writes "editor" for "publisher."

On 21 May, Jérôme Lindon wrote to the Société des Auteurs et Compositeurs Dramatiques that the rights for *En attendant Godot* were taken in the US and Canada by Grove Press (IMEC, Beckett, Boîte 13, SACD, *En attendant Godot* 1953–1963).

3   Rosica Colin wrote: "I believe that M. Francis Ponge told me at one time that you had translated some of his poems into English," and she asked about these because New Directions were interested in including some of Ponge's poems in their annual anthology. SB had translated several pieces by Ponge for *Transition*, but not poetry (see 27 May 1948, n. 1; 1 March 1949, n. 3, n. 4, n. 5).

SB did review the translations by Pierre Schneider and Richard Wilbur of Ponge's poetry that appeared in *Transition Fifty*, no. 6, 75–86. SB wrote to Marguerite Duthuit-Matisse, "J'aurais besoin, pour pouvoir réviser les poèmes de <u>PONGE</u>, du texte français" (In order to revise the poems of *PONGE*, I would need the French text) (Dimanche [before 20 October 1950], Duthuit collection).

4   Colin also asked if there were any English translations of SB's French books. An extract from *Molloy* and another from *Malone meurt* were published as "Two Fragments," *Transition Fifty* no. 6, 103–106.

JACOBA VAN VELDE

AMSTERDAM

24 juin 1953   Paris

Chère Tonny

Merci de votre lettre. Je suis content que vous vous soyez chargée de la traduction de Godot, je suis sûr que vous ferez ça très bien.[1]

Demandez-moi tout ce que vous voulez à ce sujet. La Roquette, c'est –
ou c'était – une maison de correction pour jeunes délinquants à Paris.
Maintenant je crois qu'il n'y a plus que des femmes. Ca correspond à
Borstal en Angleterre. Si un tel lieu n'existe pas dans votre beau pays,
vous n'aurez qu'à mettre l'équivalent de maison de correction.[2] La
chanson est inspirée par une chanson allemande que j'avais entendue
là-bas en Allemagne, pas à la Roquette:

> Ein Hund kam in die Küche
> Und stahl dem Koch ein Ei.
> Da nahm der Koch ein Löffel
> Und schlug den Hund zu Brei.
>
> Da kamen die anderen Hunde
> Und gruben ihm ein Grab
> Und setzten ihm ein Grabstein
> Worauf geschrieben stand:
>
> Ein Hund kam in die Küche etc.[3]

Je vous envoie du reste par le même courrier le texte allemand
qui est assez fidèle et qui pourra vous aider.[4]

Votre Ms est bien arrivé aux Ed. de Minuit et vous pouvez être
tranquille qu'il sera lu consciencieusement.[5]

Bien amicalement de nous deux

s/<u>Sam</u>

TLS; 1 leaf, 1 side; BNF, 19794/22.

June 24th 1953   Paris
Dear Tonny

Thank you for your letter. I'm glad that you're taking on the translating of *Godot*, I'm sure you'll do it very well.[1] Ask me anything you like
about it. La Roquette is – or was – a reformatory for young delinquents
in Paris. Now I think there are only women. It corresponds to Borstal in
England. If there's no such place in your fair country, you have only to

put in the equivalent of reformatory.[2] The song is inspired by a German song I'd heard there (in Germany, not in La Roquette):

> Ein Hund kam in die Küche
> Und stahl dem Koch ein Ei.
> Da nahm der Koch ein Löffel
> Und schlug den Hund zu Brei.
>
> Da kamen die anderen Hunde
> Und gruben ihm ein Grab
> Und setzten ihm ein Grabstein
> Worauf geschrieben stand:
>
> Ein Hund kam in die Küche etc.[3]

In any case I'm sending you by the same post the German text, which is pretty accurate, and which may help.[4]

Your ms has arrived safely at the Editions de Minuit, and you can rest assured that it will be read conscientiously.[5]

Very best wishes from us both

Sam

---

1   On 29 May, SB wrote to Jacoba van Velde that a theatrical agency in Holland had purchased the rights to *En attendant Godot*: "J'ai pensé que vous pourriez le traduire. Quoique je ne voie pas du tout un Godot intégral sur une scène de chez vous." (It occurred to me that you might translate it. Though I can't imagine an uncut *Godot* being staged in your country.) SB adds that he has talked with Lindon, who will ask that the translation be given to her (BNF, 19794/21). Lindon's letter of 21 May to the Société des Auteurs et Compositeurs Dramatiques gives the Dutch agency as Georges Marton (IMEC, Beckett, Boîte 13, SACD, *En attendant Godot* 1953–1963).

Jacoba van Velde translated *En attendant Godot* into Dutch as *Wachten op Godot* (published in Samuel Beckett, *Wachten op Godot, Eindspel, Krapp's laatste band, Gelukkige dagen, Spel*, Literaire euzenpocket [Amsterdam: De Bezige Bij, 1965]).

2   The prisons of La Roquette, Paris 11, opened in 1830 and closed in 1974; La Petite Roquette became a prison for women in 1932 (France Hamelin, *Femmes en prison dans la nuit noire de l'occupation: le Dépôt, la petite Roquette, le camp des Tourelles* [Paris: Editions Tirésias, 2004] 132). Borstal Prison opened in 1870; it became a detention center for juveniles in 1902. As a model, its name became generic for such reformatories.

3   A literal translation of the song given in German:

A dog came into the kitchen
And stole an egg from the cook.

So the cook took a spoon
And beat the dog to pulp.

Then came the other dogs
And dug him a grave
And set him up a gravestone
On which was written

A dog came into the kitchen etc.

As published in SB's translation (*Waiting for Godot* [Grove Press] 37–38):

A dog came in the kitchen
And stole a crust of bread
The cook up with a ladle
And beat him till he was dead

Then all the dogs came running
And dug the dog a tomb
And wrote upon the tombstone
For the eyes of dogs to come:

A dog came in the kitchen etc.

4   *Warten auf Godot*, tr. Elmar Tophoven (Frankfurt: Suhrkamp, 1953).

5   In his letter of 29 May, SB wrote to Jacoba van Velde about her novel *De grote zalle* (1954), suggesting that she send it to Editions de Minuit (BNF 19794/21). She did so on 8 June 1953 (IMEC, Beckett, Boîte 1, S. Beckett, Correspondance 1946–1953).

BARNEY ROSSET, GROVE PRESS
NEW YORK

June 25th 1953   6 Rue des Favorites
                                                   Paris 15me

Dear Mr. Rosset

Thank you for your letter of June 18th.[1] Above my private address, confidentially. For serious matters write to me here, for business to Lindon, Ed. de Minuit, please.

Re translations. I shall send you to-day or to-morrow my first version of <u>Godot</u>. This text is also in the hands of Mr Harold L. Oram, 8 West 40th Street, New York, who has our authority to treat for the performance rights up till I think November 1st. This translation has been rushed, so that Mr Oram may have something to work on as soon as possible, but I do not think the final version will differ from it very much. I should like to know what date roughly you have in view for publication.[2] Before or after performance in USA (highly doubtful) does not much matter, I think. Here the book appeared before, and sold after, performance.[3]

With regard to the novels my position is that I should greatly prefer not to undertake the job myself, while having the right to revise whatever translation is made. But I know from experience how much more difficult it is to revise a bad translation than to do the thing oneself.[4] That is why I should like to see a few brief specimens of translation before coming to a decision. Trocchi has kindly undertaken to produce three specimens of the first 10 pages of Molloy and Malone. If your Belgian (whose beginning of Godot it would interest me to see) could do a few pages of Molloy I should be very glad too. My idea was that it would be easier to collaborate with a translator living here. In any case it is a job for a professional writer and one prepared to write in his own way within the limits of mine, if that makes any sense, and beyond them too, when necessary.[5] I translated myself some years ago two very brief fragments for Georges Duthuit's Transition. If I can get hold of the number in which they appeared I shall send it to you.[6]

I understand very well your point of view when you question the propriety of the publication in Merlin of Act 1 of Godot and I have no doubt that Trocchi will appreciate it too.[7]

My own copy of my Proust has disappeared and I really do not know where to suggest your looking for one.[8] It is a very youthful work, but perhaps not entirely beside the point. Its premises are less feeble than its conclusions.

With regard to my work in general I hope you realize what you are letting yourself in for. I do not mean the heart of the matter, which is unlikely to disturb anybody, but certain obscenities of form which may not have struck you in French as they will in English, and which frankly (it is better you should know this before we get going) I am not at all disposed to mitigate. I do not of course realize what is possible in America from this point of view and what is not. Certainly as far as I know such passages, faithfully translated, would not be tolerated in England. I think you would do well to talk to Fowlie about this.[9]

Sylvia Beach said very nice things about the Grove Press and that you might be over here in the late summer. I hope you will.[10]

Thank you for your interesting catalogue. I shall certainly ask you for some of your books at a later stage.

Thanking you for taking this chance with my work and wishing us a fair wind, I am

Yours sincerely

s/

Samuel Beckett

TLS; 2 leaves, 2 sides; NSyU. Previous publication, Samuel Beckett, "Letters to Barney Rosset," *The Review of Contemporary Fiction* 10.3 (Fall 1990) 64–65; Samuel Beckett and Barney Rosset, "The *Godot* Letters: A Lasting Effect," *The New Theater Review* [now *Lincoln Center Theater Review*] 12 (Spring 1995) 10–11; Samuel Beckett and Barney Rosset, "Letters [1953-1955]," in *The Grove Press Reader, 1951-2001*, ed. S. E. Gontarski (New York: Grove Press, 2001) 27–28; Barney Rosset, "Remembering Samuel Beckett," in *Not Even Past: Hybrid Histories*, ed. Bradford Morrow, Conjunctions 53 (Annandale-on-Hudson, NY; Bard College, 2009) 11.

1 On 18 June, in his first letter to SB, Rosset wrote that he had received signed contracts from Editions de Minuit for publication by Grove Press of *En attendant Godot*, *Molloy*, and *Malone meurt*, and an option on *L'Innommable*. Rosset wrote: "It is about time that I write a letter to you – now that agents, publishers, friends, etc., have all acted as go-betweens" (NSyU).

2 Harold Leon Oram (1907–1990), theatrical producer and philanthropist, had taken an option on the performance rights of *Waiting for Godot*.

3 *En attendant Godot* was published on 17 October 1952, well before the premiere in Paris.

4 SB had worked on a revision of a translation of *Molloy* by Patrick Bowles, for publication in *Merlin*, 88–103 (see [before 5 February 1953]). He had also worked with Elmar Tophoven on the revision of *Warten auf Godot*, the German translation of *En attendant Godot*.

5 Alexander Trocchi's role in producing three specimens of the opening pages of *Molloy* and *Malone meurt* is uncertain; one specimen was by Patrick Bowles. Trocchi wrote to Barney Rosset on 15 June 1953: "Your main difficulty will be to translate in a way which satisfies Beckett, and without omissions." Merlin intended to publish a Continental edition of the novel in English, and Trocchi was willing to take an option on the Grove translations. He wrote that if Grove could "not produce what is according to Beckett a satisfactory translation – and you shouldn't be over-confident, I know Beckett very well – and we are able to do so, we shall be only too pleased to make it accessible to you" (NSyU).

In his letter to SB of 18 June, Rosset had proposed "A young man, Belgian by birth, who moved to this country some seven years ago":

> He originally wrote in French, but in the last few years he has turned to English, and I find no stiltedness or other problems in his use of our language. Beyond that, he is a great admirer of your work, and he immediately set to work to do a

translation of GODOT when someone told him I might publish it here. Now that you are doing it yourself there is not much future for his work, but I thought that if you were willing I would show you what he did, and it might indicate to you whether or not he could be capable of doing the novels.

The translator has not been identified.

6   SB's translations of excerpts from *Molloy* and *Malone meurt* in *Transition*: 19 May 1953, n. 4.

7   In his letter to SB of 18 June, Rosset wrote: "I explained to Trocchi [...] why I thought it better for MERLIN not to publish the first act in advance of book publication [...] I hope you will join me in this idea. EN ATTENDANT GODOT should burst upon us as an entity in my opinion."

8   Samuel Beckett, *Proust* (1931).

9   Rosset had been a student of Wallace Fowlie (1908-1998) at The New School for Social Research, and he had asked him to propose French authors for Grove Press. Fowlie reports that, in 1953, he wrote to Rosset "about three new French playwrights I urged him to consider publishing in English: Beckett, Ionesco, and Genet. In his answer he said he thought I was somewhat insane to recommend such writers, but just to humor me, he would try publishing Beckett. He soon added the other two." ("A Return Visit to Paris," *The Virginia Quarterly Review* 51.1 [Winter 1975] 81.)

10   SB and Sylvia Beach (1887-1962; Profile, I) met on 23 May 1953, at SB's request; Beach's notes from this meeting suggest that they reviewed the terms of the Grove contract (SB to Sylvia Beach, 22 May 1953, NjP, Beach 186/23). Beach wrote to Barney Rosset on 25 May:

> I saw Mr Samuel Beckett, and learned from him that everything had already been arranged through his agent in New York - apparently the contract was signed, and there was nothing left for me to do but to congratulate him on having such nice publishers, and to bring him your greetings.
> And I congratulate you on having secured Beckett. (NSyU.)

BARNEY ROSSET, GROVE PRESS
NEW YORK

July 18th 1953   6 Rue des Favorites
                                                 Paris 15me

Dear Mr. Rosset

Thank you for your letter of July 13th. I am surprised you [have] not received my translation of Godot which I sent you towards t[he] end of last month. Do you wish me to send you another copy, or [can] you arrange to take a copy of Mr Oram's?[1]

I think I have found a suitable translator here for the no[vel] if I can judge from the specimen he showed me. Unless I prefer [the] translation of your acquaintance, which I have not yet receive[d, I] shall submit to you the specimen in question.[2]

In raising the question of the obscenities I simply wished to make it clear from the outset that the only modifications of them that I am prepared to accept are of a kind with those which hold for the text as a whole, i.e. made necessary by the change fro[m] one language to another. The problem therefore is no more complicat[ed] than this: are you prepared to print the result? I am convinced you will agree with me that a clear understanding on this matter before we set to work is equally indispensable to you, the translato[r] and myself.

Herewith Transition with my translation of fragments from Molloy and Malone.[3]

Yours sincerely

s/

Samuel Beckett

TLS; 1 leaf, 1 page; *torn right edge, obliterating words at right margin*; NSyU. Previous publication, Beckett, "Letters to Barney Rosset," 65–66; Rosset, "Remembering Samuel Beckett," 12–13;

1 A problem had also occurred with mailing of the TMS to Harold Oram in two packets: the first act arrived after the second act (SB to Jérôme Lindon, 9 July 1953, IMEC, Beckett, Boîte 1, S. Beckett, Correspondance 1946–1953).

2 SB refers to Patrick Bowles. In his notes about his meetings with SB to work on the translation of *Molloy*, Bowles wrote that SB chose "my trial pages for the reason that I wasn't a translator, rather than that I was: he wanted a writer rather than a translator" ("'How to Fail,'" *P.N. Review* 96, 20.4 [March–April 1994] 24).

3 "Two Fragments": 19 May 1953, n. 4.

CARLHEINZ CASPARI
BONN

le 25 juillet 1953

6 Rue des Favorites

Paris 15me

Cher Monsieur[1]

Je vous remercie de votre aimable lettre et m'excuse d'avoir tant tardé à vous répondre.

Il m'est très difficile de m'expliquer sur mon travail. Et je ne veux pas influencer votre mise en scène.[2] Je n'essaierai donc pas d'approfondir, ce qu'elles le méritent, les questions que vous soulevez. Du reste, et vous l'avez bien senti, vouloir trop creuser ici ne va pas sans danger. Voici donc, aussi simplement que possible, ma façon de sentir les choses.

Si ma pièce renferme des éléments expressionnistes, c'est bien à mon insu. Je n'ai d'ailleurs, sur ce style, que des notions fort confuses. Ce n'est pas non plus, pour moi, une pièce symboliste, je ne saurais trop insister là-dessus. Il s'agit d'abord et avant tout d'une chose qui arrive, presque d'une routine, et c'est cette quotidienneté et cette matérialité qu'à mon avis il importe de faire ressortir. Qu'à chaque instant des Symboles, des Idées et des Formes se profilent, cela pour moi est secondaire, derrière quoi ne se profilent-ils pas? A les préciser en tout cas on n'a rien à gagner. Les personnages sont des êtres vivants, à peine si l'on veut, ce ne sont pas des emblèmes. Je conçois fort bien votre gêne devant leur peu de caractérisation. Mais je vous engagerai à y voir moins l'effet d'un effort d'abstraction, ce dont je suis peu capable, que le refus d'atténuer tout ce qu'ils ont à la fois de complexe et d'amorphe. Vous verrez d'ailleurs, si je peux en juger d'après notre expérience ici à Paris, des identités se préciser au fur et à mesure de votre travail. Godot lui-même n'est pas d'une autre espèce que ceux qu'il ne peut pas ou ne veut pas aider. Moi-même je le connais plus mal que quiconque, n'ayant jamais su, même obscurément, ce dont j'avais besoin. Si son nom suggère les cieux, c'est seulement dans la mesure où un produit à faire pousser les cheveux peut paraître divin. A chacun de lui donner un visage. D'autres, plus fortunés, y verront Thanatos.

De la mise en scène allemande en général je crains en effet la simplification métaphysique et le recours aux symboles. Le grand mérite de Roger Blin est de les avoir évités et c'est en quoi sa mise en scène, dont naturellement on peut discuter par ailleurs, me paraît exemplaire.

Le temps qui stagne, saute des vies entières, l'espace inparcourable [*for* imparcourable] comme une tête d'épingle, sont peut-être les vrais faux dieux de la pièce, s'il faut absolument qu'elle en ait. Faux trop tard. Les cris qu'ils arrachent, celui-ci à Estragon (pages 99 et 100), celui-là à Pozzo (page 155), sont des abjurations d'immolés.[3] Ce que vous dites à ce sujet est tres beau, mais je n'y avais pas pensé. Et ce que j'en dis moi n'est guère convaincant. De cet aspect de la pièce il en va hélas comme des autres, on n'en peut rien affirmer, sous une forme satisfaisante pour l'intelligence, qu'à condition d'y rajouter, ou d'en retrancher.

Le côté farce me semble indispensable aussi bien du point de vue technique (moyen de détente) que par rapport à l'esprit de la pièce. Donc ni à escamoter ni à exagérer. Ici le malheur est le comble du grotesque et tout acte est clownerie. En rire donc et en faire rire, du malheur et de l'acte, mais pas tout le temps, ce serait trop beau, et toujours plutôt jaune.

De tout ce qui précède et qui me fait l'effet d'un devoir d'écolier, j'ai peur que vous ne tiriez pas grand'chose susceptible de vous aider. N'en tenez compte que dans la mesure où vous y trouverez votre compte. Je suis le premier à en sentir l'inutilité. Sur un travail où il y a si peu de ma tête, ma tête ne trouvera jamais rien qui vaille.

Je vous remercie vivement, ainsi que Herr Rose, de votre aimable invitation.[4] J'aimerais beaucoup être parmi vous le soir de la première, mais je ne sais pas encore si je vais le pouvoir. Je vous tie[n]drai au courant.

J'aimerais mieux, si cela ne vous ennuie pas trop, que votre programme soit sans texte de moi. Pour la photo veuillez vous adresser à mon éditeur, Monsieur Jérôme Lindon, Editions de Minuit, 7 Rue Bernard-Palissy, Paris 6me.

Croyez, cher Monsieur, à mes sentiments très cordiaux.

Samuel Beckett

TLcc; 1 leaf, 2 sides; Fehsenfeld collection. Previous publication, Beckett, "Who is Godot?" *The New Yorker*, 136–137.

25 July 1953   6 Rue des Favorites

                                                 Paris 15me

Dear Mr Caspari[1]

Thank you for your kind letter and I apologise for having taken so long to reply.

I find it very difficult to talk about my work. And I have no wish to influence your production.[2] I shall not therefore go into the questions you raise in the way that they deserve. In any case, and you are well aware of this, the desire to go too deeply in is not without danger. Here, then, as simply as possible, is the way I feel about things.

If my play contains expressionist elements, it is without my knowledge. In any case I have, about this style, only the haziest of notions. Nor is it, for me, a symbolist play, I cannot stress that too much. First and foremost, it is a question of something that happens, almost a routine, and it is this dailiness and this materiality, in my view, that need to be brought out. That at any moment Symbols, Ideas, Forms might show up, this is for me secondary – is there anything they do not show up behind? In any event there is nothing to be gained by giving them clear form. The characters are living creatures, only just living perhaps, they are not emblems. I can readily understand your unease at their lack of characterisation. But I would urge you to see in them less the result of an attempt at abstraction, something I am almost incapable of, than a refusal to tone down all that is at one and the same time complex and amorphous in them. Incidentally, if I may judge from our experience here in Paris, you will see identities shaping up as your work proceeds. Godot himself is not of a different species from those he cannot or will not help. I myself know him less well than anyone, having never known even vaguely what I needed. If his name suggests the heavens, it is only to the extent that a product for promoting hair growth can seem heavenly. Each person is free to put a face on him. Others, more fortunate, will see in him Thanatos.

With German theatre production in general I really do fear metaphysical simplification and recourse to symbols. The great merit of Roger Blin is that he avoided them and it is in this respect that his production, open of course to discussion in other respects, seems to me exemplary.

Time that stands still, that skips over whole lives, space no easier to cross than the head of a pin, these perhaps are the true false gods of the play, if it absolutely has to have some. False too late.

The cries that they wring, the former from Estragon (pages 99 and 100), the latter from Pozzo (page 155), are the abjurings of men sacrificially destroyed.[3] What you say about this is very fine, but it had not occurred to me. And what I have to say is not particularly convincing. On this aspect of the play as also on the others, no clear statement can be made in a form that can satisfy the mind, except by adding things or taking things away.

The farce side seems indispensable to me as much from the technical point of view (comic relief) as for reasons to do with the spirit of the play. Therefore neither to be hurried through nor to be overdone. Here unhappiness is the height of the grotesque and every act is a piece of clowning. Laugh at them then and get them laughed at, at unhappiness and at the act, but not all the time, that would be too good, and always a little reluctantly.

From the preceding, which feels to me like a schoolboy essay, I fear that you will not be able to extract much that might be of assistance to you. Take account of it only in so far as you have a mind to. I am the first to feel its uselessness. Concerning a work in which there is so little of my head, my head will never come up with anything worthwhile.

My grateful thanks to you, as well as to Herr Rose, for your kind invitation.[4] I should very much like to be there, for the premiere, but I am not yet sure if I shall be able to. I shall keep you informed.

I should prefer, if it is not too inconvenient for you, to have no text by me in the programme. For photographs please get in touch with my publisher, Monsieur Jérôme Lindon, Editions de Minuit, 7 Rue Bernard-Palissy, Paris 6me.

Yours sincerely

Samuel Beckett

1 Carlheinz Caspari* (b. 1921), director of the production of *Warten auf Godot* at the Badisches Staatstheater in Karlsruhe, wrote to SB on 12 July 1953. This production was the West German premiere; it opened on 5 September 1953. As SB wrote to Susan Manning on 16 April 1953: "It has been translated into German and has been demanded by various theatres in Germany, where the custom is to have the same play performed in different towns by different companies simultaneously" (TxU, Beckett collection).

2 Caspari later wrote about the production in "Zu Samuel Becketts Theater," *Atoll* 1 (1954) 24–28:

> Da Beckett für mich erreichbar war, fragte ich ihn selbst. Er half mir, indem er mir seine Hilfe versagte … Das Stück Becketts ist unerhört streng und exakt gebaut … Alles darin ist vollkommen klar und plastisch, wenn man sich dem Stück überläßt und nichts darüberhinaus will. (25–27.) (Since Beckett was accessible to me, I asked him directly. He helped me by denying me his help … Beckett's play is constructed in an exceptionally strict and exact way … Everything in it is completely clear and graphic, if one abandons oneself to the play and asks nothing more from it.)

3 SB's page references may be to the TMS of *Warten auf Godot*, translated by Tophoven.

4 The Generalintendant of the Badisches Staatstheater in Karlsruhe from 1953 to 1962 was Paul Rose (1900–1973), in whose name Caspari had invited SB to attend the premiere in Karlsruhe.

MANIA PERON

PARIS

27 juillet [1953]   Paris

Chère Mania

Merci de vos lettres et carte. Le défi de Michel m'honore et je le relève, à condition qu'il me prête une raquette. Je perdrai le premier set, gagnerai le second et mourrai au troisième. Vous viendrez, j'espère, il serait dommage de manquer ça.[1] En attendant j'ai encore fait un abcès dans ce qui me sert de cavité buccale, paradentaire cette fois seulement, quel pot. Nous retournons à Ussy cette semaine. Je me suis laissé dire qu'un journaliste du Figaro Littéraire, chargé d'enquêter sur les écrivains de Seine-et-Marne, avait découvert mon adresse malgré toutes nos précautions et, sa conscience professionnelle l'emportant sur toute considération de sécurité personnelle, menace de me rendre visite. Suivez donc attentivement les faits divers dans les semaines qui viennent, il y aura peut-être deux emmerdeurs en moins dans l'Ile de France.[2] Lu ce qui suit dans les annonces matrimoniales: Brebis galeuse déçue par la vie ép. bouc émissaire ayant eu malheurs.[3] Je commence à traduire Molloy en anglais avec un jeune Sud-Africain. Je fais dans son vase devient I piss and shit in her pot, j'espère que ce n'est pas trop tirer sur la portée de faire.[4] Je vais aller à Berlin pour la première de Godot le

4 septambre [*for* septembre].⁵ J'espère que cette lettre vous aura fait passer un bon moment. Affectueusement de nous 2 à vous tous.

s/ Sam

TLS; 1 leaf, 1 side; TxU, Lake collection, Beckett. *Dating*: mention of *Warten auf Godot* in Berlin, work with Patrick Bowles on translation.

27 July [1953]   Paris
Dear Mania

Thank you for your letters and card. Michel's challenge does me honour, and I accept it, on condition he lends me a racquet. I shall lose the first set, win the second, and die in the third. You will come, I hope – it would be a pity to miss that.¹ Meanwhile I have developed an abscess in what passes for my buccal cavity, just paradental this time, lucky me. We go back to Ussy this week. I have heard that a journalist on the *Figaro Littéraire*, who had been sent out to do a survey of writers in the Seine-et-Marne, had found out my address in spite of all our precautions and, professional conscientiousness carrying the day over all thought of personal safety, is threatening to call on me. So keep a close eye on the crime page in the coming weeks. There may well be two bloody nuisances fewer in the Ile de France.² Read the following in the Personal column: Black sheep disappointed in life would marry scapegoat with troubled past.³ I am beginning to translate *Molloy* into English with a young South African. "Je fais dans son vase" becomes "I piss and shit in her pot." I hope that is not pushing the scope of "faire" too far.⁴ I am going to Berlin for the premiere of *Godot* on the 4th September.⁵ I hope that this letter will have given you a moment's pleasure. Love from us both to you all.

Sam

1   According to Alexis Péron, the tennis match was proposed by Michel Péron, but not played (4 September 2009).

2   The journalist has not been identified, but his unsigned interviews were published as "Six écrivains en quête de vacances," *Le Figaro Littéraire* 8 August 1953: 10; "Les écrivains aussi vont, parfois, en vacances," *Le Figaro Littéraire* 15 August 1953: 1, 10.

3   The source of the advertisement has not been found.
SB omits the cedilla on "déçue."

4   The passage in French from *Molloy* was published unrevised (*Molloy*, tr. Patrick Bowles in collaboration with the author [New York: Grove Press, 1955] 8).

Translating *Molloy* with SB was "slow, painstaking work … It was wrung and thrashed and hammered out. Every day we revised a few pages, pen in hand, but debating virtually every word." ("'How to Fail,'" 24.)

5   Writing to the director Karl Heinz Stroux* (1908–1985) on 24 July, SB accepted his invitation to attend the Berlin premiere of *Warten auf Godot* on 8 September:

> Je suis heureux de pouvoir vous assurer dès maintenant que sauf imprévu j'y serai.
>
> Je pense que vous verrez monsieur Tophoven avant moi. Il connaît admirablement ma pièce et vous en parlerai [*for* parlera], soyez-en sûr, mieux que je ne saurais le faire moi-même. (Stroux collection.)
>
> (I am happy to be able to assure you straight away that, barring unforeseen circumstances, I shall be there.
>
> I think that you will be seeing Mr Tophoven before I do. He has an admirable knowledge of my play, and will talk to you about it, you may be sure, better than I could myself.)

A. J. LEVENTHAL

DUBLIN

August 6th 1953   6 Rue des Favorites

                                        Paris 15me

My dear Con

Thanks for your letter of July 2nd. There is a PTT strike on here, convinced at the moment, and God knows when you will get this, before your departure I hope. Delighted at the prospect of seeing you soon. My plans are roughly as follows: in the country near Paris until 20th inst., then Paris probably until end of month, then Berlin for première of Godot in German Sept 4th. Don't know exactly how long I shall stay in Bocherie, shall certainly do utmost to get back to Paris in time to see you second week Sept if those are still your plans.[1] Nothing much of interest here. Haven't seen anything of note on L'Inno, have the impression it is pretty frigidly received, tant mieux, tant mieux.[2] Inertia, literary, continues, haven't the least desire to put pen to paper, prefer mixing mortar and stretching barbed wire, long may these dispositions continue. Watt is having a difficult birth but is expected out into the dark of day next week, shall keep your copy to put into your hands.[3] Revival of Godot with Blin and Co at Babylone Sept 20th, with slightly changed cast. Have translated it, hurriedly and badly, into English, for possible performance New York.[4] Saw El[l]mann, likable enough in spite of incessant note-snatching. He sent me his Yeats, haven't read it, it looks competent and dull.[5] Arland sent me his great Irishmen, they haven't much greatness left when he's done with them.[6] When you see Ethna thank her for her letter and say I'm writing. Morris Sinclair has now a job with WHO at Geneva, having left UNESCO. Haven't heard how he likes it.[7] John Beckett talks of going to London. I think he'd be well advised.[8] If you see the skip Power would you give him a pound from me, I can let you have it back by cheque on Dublin or in francs here, as you prefer.[9] Write soon and give me a rough date for our meeting in Paris.

Ever yours

s/ <u>Sam</u>

TLS; 1 leaf, 1 side; TxU, Leventhal collection.

1 Leventhal's letter of 2 July has not been found. The strike of the Postes, Télégraphes et Téléphones began on 6 August, and ended on 27 August; regional involvement varied ("Brusque flambée d'agitation sociale: le trafic postal est à peu près paralysé," *Le Monde* 7 August 1953: 1; "Le trafic est redevenu normal à la S.N.C.F., dans les P.T.T. et les transports parisiens," *Le Monde* 27 August 1953: 1).

"Bocherie" (Krautland).

2 *L'Innommable* was published on 20 May 1953; a facsimile of a page from the novel appeared in *Arts-Spectacles* 418, 3–9 July 1953: 5; a mention of it is made in Robert Kemp's column in *Les Nouvelles Littéraires* (23 July 1953) 2.

"Tant mieux" (so much the better).

3 *Watt* was to be published by Olympia Press.

4 There were two changes in the cast when the reprise of *En attendant Godot* opened: Pierre Asso (1904–1974) played Vladimir, and Jean-Jacques Duverger (n.d.), played the boy.

5 Richard Ellmann (1918–1987), working on his biography of James Joyce, met SB on 28 July (Tulsa, Ellmann, Series 1, Beckett interview). Richard Ellmann, *Yeats: The Man and the Mask* (1948).

6 Arland Ussher, *Three Great Irishmen: Shaw, Yeats, Joyce* (1952).

7 Ethna MacCarthy (1903–1959; Profile, I).

Morris Sinclair had worked as a writer and producer for radio broadcasts in German at UNESCO; at the World Health Organization in Geneva, he worked in the Public Information Office from 1952.

8 John Beckett moved from Dublin to London in September 1953 (John Beckett, 23 June 1993).

9   SB's skip when he had rooms in Trinity College, J. Power: 25 January 1931 to McGreevy, n. 9.

BARNEY ROSSET, GROVE PRESS
NEW YORK

September 1st 1953   6 Rue des Favorites
                                                 Paris 15me

Dear Mr. Rosset

Thank you for your letters of August 4th and July 31st both received yesterday only and also for the translation from <u>Godot</u>. It has as you say great merits, but I think all things considered it is better for Bowles to go on with the job he has so well begun. Will you convey my thanks to your translator and my congratulations for his excellent version.[1]

I am glad you liked the specimen from <u>Molloy</u>. Bowles too will be very glad. I hope the question of his remuneration will soon be settled satisfactorily to you both and that we can get seriously to work on this very difficult job.[2]

<u>Watt</u> I believe is now out, but I have not yet seen it. Standards of book presentation are not the same here as with you and the resources of Merlin are very limited. What matters to me is that this work refused by a score of London publishers in the years following the war is at last between boards. A handsomer edition in America would of course give me great pleasure. I am so hopelessly incompetent in these matters that it is better I should not intervene in negotiations with Merlin. I am in advance in agreement with whatever arrangement you come to with them.[3]

It is good news that my translation of Godot meets with your approval. It was done in great haste to facilitate the negotiations of Mr Oram and I do not myself regard it as very satisfactory. But I have not yet had the courage to revise it. (The copy made by the services of Mr Oram contains a number of mistakes.)[4] I understand your point about the Anglicisms and shall be glad to consider whatever suggestions you have to make in this connexion.[5] But the problem involved here is a far-reaching one. Bowles's text as revised by me is bound to be quite unamerican in rhythm and atmosphere and the mere substitution here and there of the American for the English term is hardly likely to improve matters, on the contrary. We can of course avoid those words which are incomprehensible to the American reader, such as skivvy and cutty, and it will be a help to have them pointed out to us. In Godot I tried to retain the French atmosphere as much as possible and you may have noticed that the use of English and American place-names is confined to Lucky whose own name might seem to justify them.[6]

Yours sincerely

s/ Samuel Beckett

TLS; 1 leaf, 1 side; NSyU. Previous publication, Beckett and Rosset, "Letters [1953–1955]," 31–32; Rosset, "Remembering Samuel Beckett," 14–15.

1   With his letter to SB of 31 July, Rosset encloses "the fragment of *Godot* translated by the man here" (NSyU); the translator has not been identified: 18 July 1953, n. 5.

2   Rosset sent a contract for the translation of *Molloy* to Bowles on 10 August; on 25 August, Bowles requested a higher fee for the translation, noting that the ten-page sample that he and SB had done together was the eighth draft (McM, Samuel Beckett Collection, Collection Merlin, 3.18).

3   Rosset wrote to SB and to Alexander Trocchi on 4 August to say that he had seen corrected proofs of *Watt* through the Marion Saunders Agency. Rosset assured SB that Grove Press would "undertake to copyright" *Watt*, and would make arrangements with Merlin about co-publication (NSyU). *Watt* was published by Olympia Press on 31 August 1953.

4   In his letter of 31 July, Rosset wrote that he had received SB's translation of *Godot*: "I like it very much, and it seems to me that you have done a fine job. The long speech by Lucky is particularly good and the whole play reads extremely well."

5   In his letter of 31 July, Rosset observes that "neutralization of the speech away from the specifically English flavor might have the result of enhancing the French original for an American reader." Rosset's letter of 4 August 1953 makes mention of the words "skivvy" and "cutty" in SB's translation of *En attendant Godot*.

6   Place names in Lucky's speech: English place names, Peckham, Fulham, Clapham (*Waiting for Godot*, 28–29) replace French place names, real and imaginary, Seine-et-Oise, Seine-et-Marne, Marne-et-Oise (*En attendant Godot*, 59, 61). Connemara in the English edition (29) replaces Normandie in the French (61).

MAURICE NADEAU

PARIS

le 5 septembre 1953

6 Rue des Favorites
Paris 15me

Mon cher Maurice Nadeau

J'ai lu avec émotion votre article sur L'Innommable dans Les Lettres Nouvelles.[1] Dans un moment où mon travail ne valait plus rien. A vous lire l'envie renaît d'essayer encore. Elle n'ira peut-être pas loin. Mais comprenez ce que cela signifie pour moi et la mesure de ce que vous me donnez. Le il a été devient il sera, avec moi jusqu'à la fin. Je ne peux même plus vous remercier. Je peux seulement vous envoyer mon affectueuse amitié.[2]

s/

Samuel Beckett

TLS; 1 leaf, 1 side; Nadeau. Previous publication, Nadeau, *Grâces leur soient rendues*, 366.

5th September 1953   6 Rue des Favorites
                                                    Paris 15

My dear Maurice Nadeau

I was greatly moved to read your article on *L'Innommable* in *Les Lettres Nouvelles*.[1] In a time when my work no longer had any value. Reading you, the desire to try again reawakens. Perhaps it will not go far. But do understand what that means for me, and the scale of what you are giving. The "he was" becomes "he will be", with me to the end. I can no longer even thank you. I can only send you my affectionate friendship.[2]

s/

Samuel Beckett

1   Maurice Nadeau, "La 'Dernière' Tentative de Samuel Beckett," *Les Lettres Nouvelles* 1.7 (September 1953) 860–864.

2   Nadeau closes his review of *L'Innommable* by saying of SB:

> Au regard de ce qu'il espérait, sans illusion et fuyant la duperie, Samuel Beckett a sans doute échoué une fois de plus et sans qu'on croie possible, de sa part, une nouvelle tentative. Au regard de ce que nous attendions de lui après *Murphy*, *Molloy* et *Malone meurt*, cette tentative s'inscrit parmi le[s] plus audacieuses et les plus éclairantes qui aient jamais existé, illustrant en termes d'épure la quête nécessaire de l'identité de la parole avec l'être, la vie, la réalité, et nous donnant le sentiment que cette identité deviendra possible. (In respect of what he hoped for, free of illusion and with his back turned on deception, Samuel Beckett has

doubtless failed yet again, without, one might think, the possibility of a new venture on his part. In respect of what we expected from him after *Murphy*, *Molloy* and *Malone meurt*, this venture must count among the boldest and the most illuminating ever, illustrating in terms of a blueprint the necessary search for the identity of speech with being, life, reality, and giving us the feeling that this identity will become possible.)

KARL HEINZ STROUX
BERLIN

le 13 septembre 1953   6 Rue des Favorites
                                     Paris 15me

Cher Monsieur Stroux

Merci de votre gentil mot reçu à l'hôtel la veille de mon départ.[1]

J'espère que vous ne m'en voulez pas trop de mon pauvre discours de l'autre jour et que vous en aurez mis, pour les pardonner, les maladresses et les énormités sur le compte de mon mauvais allemand. Je ne peux ouvrir la bouche sans perdre la tête, mais en français j'aurais pu tout de même vous dire tout cela plus simplement et surtout plus gentiment. Que vous voyiez la pièce un peu autrement que moi, c'est votre droit le plus strict, ma façon de voir n'est pas forcément la bonne. De toute manière je n'avais pas à intervenir là-dedans. Et les brèves heures passées auprès de vous, je les aurais mieux employées à vous exprimer, à vous et à vos comédiens, mon admiration et ma reconnaissance.[2] Mais aux écorchés la sagesse est difficile.

A vous-même donc, cher Monsieur Stroux, ainsi qu'à Messieurs Schieske, Hessling, Franck et Maurer, une chaleureuse poignée de main et mes remerciements émus. J'espère vous savoir très bientôt tout à fait remis et de nouveau sur la brèche.[3]

Mes respectueux hommages à Madame Stroux.

                     Votre dévoué

    s/

              Samuel Beckett

TLS; 1 leaf, 1 side; Stroux collection.

13th September 1953 6 Rue des Favorites
Paris 15

Dear Mr Stroux

Thank you for your kind note, received at the hotel the day before
I left.[1]

I hope that you will not hold against me too much my wretched
speech the other day, and that you will, in order to excuse them, have put
down my awkwardnesses and blunders to my bad German. I cannot open
my mouth without losing my head, but in French I could at least have
said it all for you more simply and most of all in a nicer way. That you
should have a different view of the play from mine is your perfect right;
my view is not necessarily the correct one. In any case I had no business
getting into that. And the few hours with you would have been better
spent in expressing, to you and your actors, my admiration and gratitude.[2] But behaving well doesn't come easily to the very thin-skinned.

To yourself then, and also to Messrs Schieske, Hessling, Franck
and Maurer, my warm greetings and my deeply felt thanks. I hope to
hear very soon that you are wholly recovered and back on the job.[3]

My respects to Madame Stroux.

Yours most sincerely
s/
Samuel Beckett

1 Stroux's note to SB has not been found.
SB left for Berlin on 7 September and returned to Paris on or before 12 September (SB
to Thomas MacGreevy [7 September 1953], TCD, MS 10402/187; Knowlson, *Damned to
Fame*, 695, n. 48).

2 Stroux had fallen from the stage shortly before the premiere at the
Schlossparktheater in Berlin and broken a vertebra. Eva Stroux reported that her
husband "was forced to do the last week of rehearsals lying flat in bed and was only
able to polish the dialogues"; she recalled that SB spent "nearly four hours with my
husband" at the hospital discussing the play, and that he admitted that his views of the
play might have changed since he was now working on a new play (Eva Stroux, 19
November 1993 and 31 January 1994).
Generalintendant Boleslaw Barlog (1906–1999) recounts of Stroux: "Ich nahm ihm die
letzten Proben ab, ganz in seinem Sinne, ohne etwas hinzuzufügen" (I stood in for him in
the last rehearsals, fully in line with his thinking, without adding anything). Barlog also
recalls: "Bei der ersten 'Godot'-Premiere war es uns, wenn ich mich recht erinnere, zum

einzigen Mal gelungen, Beckett zum Verbeugen vor das Publikum zu bringen. Die verschämten, todunglücklichen Bewegungen, die er dabei machte, offenbarten dem Publikum, auf eigenartige Weise, den weltabgewandten Charakter dieses Dichters." (Boleslaw Barlog, *Theater lebenslänglich* [Munich: Knaur, 1981] 109.) (At the premiere of Godot, we succeeded, if I remember correctly, for the only time, in getting Beckett to bow before the audience.) The awkward, painfully unhappy movements with which he did so, in a strange way, conveyed to the audience the withdrawn character of this poet.)

3   Alfred Schieske (1908–1970), Vladimir; Hans Hessling (1903–1995), Estragon; Walter Franck (1896–1961), Pozzo; Friedrich Maurer (1901–1980), Lucky.

BOLESLAW BARLOG

BERLIN

le 13 septembre 1953   6 Rue des Favorites

                                        Paris 15me

Cher Monsieur Barlog

Ce petit mot pour vous dire, ainsi qu'à tous vos camarades, combien j'ai été touché par votre grande gentillesse envers moi pendant mon séjour à Berlin.

J'ai chargé Monsieur Stroux de transmettre, aux acteurs qui ont si vaillamment défendu ma pièce, mes amitiés et ma reconnaissance. Voulez-vous en dire autant de ma part à Monsieur Karl Gröning que dans l'affolement de la première j'ai négligé de féliciter.[1]

Mes hommages à Madame Barlog.

Bien cordialement à vous

s/ Samuel Beckett

Samuel Beckett

TLS; 1 leaf, 1 side; Stiftungsarchiv der Akademie der Künste (Berlin).

13 September 1953   6 Rue des Favorites

                                        Paris 15

Dear Mr Barlog

This little note to let you and all your friends and colleagues know how touched I was by your great kindness to me during my stay in Berlin.

I have charged Mr Stroux with passing on my warm wishes and my gratitude to the actors who so valiantly took up the cause of my play. Please say as much on my behalf to Mr Karl Gröning whom I failed to congratulate, in the mad scramble of the premiere.[1]

My respects to Madame Barlog.[2]

With all good wishes

Samuel Beckett

1   Karl Gröning (1897–1980) designed the set and costumes for the production.

2   Herta Berlog (née Schüster).

JACOBA VAN VELDE

<table>
<tr><td>13/9/53</td><td>6 Rue des Favorites</td></tr>
<tr><td></td><td>Paris 15me</td></tr>
</table>

My dear Tonny

Thanks for your letter of 10th inst. and for previous one. I would have replied before now but had to go to Berlin for the première of Godot in German at the Schlosspark-Theater. It wasn't very good, not to be compared with Paris performance, but was well received. Glad you are pleased with your translation. I don't know Dutch well enough to appreciate your version of the Dog Song. Do you know the melody? If not I can send it. Sorry if Lindon wrote rather brusquely. I got the wind up when you spoke about "having to cut".[1]

I am willing to considerer [sic] whatever modifications you deem absolutely unavoidable for the performance or publication in Holland.[2] But some things simply can't be changed. And I prefer no publication and no performance to those of a text that no longer makes sense.

I hear Bram is in Venice, enthusiastic. I saw Lisl's sister Moidi in Berlin where she seems very comfortably installed.[3]

All the best, dear Tonny.

s/ Sam

TLS; 1 leaf, 1 side; BNF 19794/23.

1 Jacoba van Velde's letters to SB have not been found. She had written to him on 2 September, concerned that some passages would have to be cut for the play to be presentable in Holland. Jérôme Lindon wrote to her on 8 September, to remind her that the contract for translation called for "une traduction 'intégrale'" (an unedited translation), and that SB would have to approve any modifications in the text (IMEC, Beckett, Boîte 2, S. Beckett, Représentations *En attendant Godot* [2]).

The lyric in Jacoba van Velde's Dutch translation differs from that in the French original (55):

> Een hond stal eens een biefstuk
> Al in een slagerij.
> De slager was heel woedend
> En sloeg de hond tot brij.

> De andere honden die dit zagen
> Hebben hem vlug begraven.
> Ze gaven hem een kruis heel wit
> En daarop was te lezen dit:

> Een hond stale eens een biefstuk
> Al in een slagerij.
> De slager was heel woedend
> En sloeg de hond tot brij.

> De andere honden die dit zagen

2 The Dutch translation by Jacoba van Velde first printed in the collection *Wachten op Godot, Eindspel, Krapp's laatste band, Gelukkige dagen, Spel* (1965) shows only a few small cuts from the first French edition of *En attendant Godot* (1952; page references are to this edition): "On portait beau alors" (13), "mon cochon!" and "la gigue" (65), in addition to name changes, missing stage directions, and some changes of emphasis. Cut from the Dutch translation is the passage: "Estragon – Avec Bim. / Vladimir. – Et Bom. / Estragon. – Les comiques staliniens" (56), which is also cut in later French editions and the Grove Press edition. One large cut, beginning with Pozzo's line, "Attendez! . . ." and continuing through Pozzo's line, "Je suis fatigué" (67-70), is also made in the Grove Press edition (28).

3 Bram van Velde had gone to Italy with Jacques Putman (1926-1994); a photo of them in Venice can be found in Stoullig and Schoeller, eds., *Bram van Velde*, 182.

The writer Anna Marie Jokl (known as Moidi, 1911-2001), sister of Geer van Velde's wife Lisl, lived in Berlin.

MANIA PERON
PARIS

mercredi [16 September 1953]   Paris

Chère Mania

Merci de votre mot.

Hélas pas question de tennis en ce moment. Je suis dans la merde jusqu'à la fontanelle: répétitions tous les jours (reprise le 25), traductions de tous les côtés, gens à voir, je ne m'en sors pas. Vous ferai signe quand tout ça se sera calmé.[1]

> Affectueusement de nous
>
> <u>Sam</u>

A Berlin ça a été mal joué mais bien reçu, j'aurais préféré le contraire, si c'est ça le contraire.[2]

ALS; 1 leaf, 1 side; *env to* Mme Péron, 69 Rue de le Tombe-Issoire, PARIS 14°; *pm* 16-9-53, Paris; TxU, Lake collection, Beckett.

Wednesday [16 September 1953]　　　　　Paris

Dear Mania

Thank you for your note.

Alas tennis out of the question at the moment. I am in the shit fontanelle deep: rehearsals every day (reprise the 25th), translations on all sides, people to see, I can't keep up. Will let you know when it has all calmed down.[1]

> Love from us both.
>
> Sam

In Berlin it was badly acted but well received. I would have preferred the opposite, if it is the opposite.[2]

1 SB was assisting with the rehearsals for the reprise of *En attendant Godot*, in part because new actors were playing the roles of Vladimir and the boy (see 6 August 1953, n. 4).

Thomas MacGreevy had been in Paris, and Suzanne Deschevaux-Dumesnil's mother Jeanne Fourniols had been visiting.

2 *Warten auf Godot* at the Schlossparktheater, Berlin.

PAMELA MITCHELL

NEW YORK

September 26th 1953　　　　　　　　6 Rue des Favorites

　　　　　　　　　　　　　　　　　　Paris 15me

My dear Pamela[1]

Last night over at last and safely. The first act went well, the second less well, the new Didi forgetting his lines all over the place, with me sweating in the back row. The audience didn't seem to mind. The lighting was bad too. It will be better next week. The new Pozzo gave it up finally as a bad job and Blin had to play. The Rossets were there and Pat Bowles. The new programme wasn't ready, I'll send it when it is.[2] I had a good evening with the Rossets, they turned out very nice. We dined at the Escargot where you and I were. I look forward to having good news of your flight home and then of the Giant. I shall see Lindon next Monday and get him moving on the letter he promised you, if he hasn't sent it already.[3]

Those were good evening[s] we had, for me, eating and drinking and drifting through the old streets. That's the way to do business. I'll often be thinking of them, that is of you. Remember me kindly to HJO.[4] Write me sometime and happy days.

s/   Sam

TLS; 1 leaf, 1 side; UoR, BIF, MS 5060.

1   Pamela Winslow Mitchell* (c. 1922-2002) worked for Harold L. Oram who had taken an option on *En attendant Godot*; she met SB in Paris while representing Oram in the negotiations.

2   The reprise of *En attendant Godot* opened on 25 September. Lucien Raimbourg was replaced by Pierre Asso in the role of Vladimir.

According to Jérôme Lindon's letter to SB of 27 August, Blin had considered Jacques Hilling (1926-1975) for the role of Pozzo. That Hilling rehearsed the part is implied by SB's letter to Pamela Mitchell of 25 November: "You probably caught your pneumonia that afternoon in the Babylone when you borrowed Hilling's coat" (UoR, BIF, MS 5060). However, the program lists Roger Blin as Pozzo.

3   Barney Rosset and his wife, Charlotte (née Eckert, known as Loly, b. 1923), (Rosset, "Remembering Samuel Beckett," 15). L'Escargot Montorgueil, 38 Rue Montorgueil, Paris 1.

No letter from Lindon to Pamela Mitchell or Harold Oram has been found.

4   SB mistakenly writes "HJO" for "HLO." Harold Leon Oram was the producer for *Take a Giant Step* by Louis Peterson which opened at the Lyceum Theatre in New York on 24 September (Brooks Atkinson, "First Night at the Theatre: Louis Peterson's 'Take a Giant Step' is the Story of an Adolescent Negro," *The New York Times* 25 September 1953: 16).

THOMAS MACGREEVY
DUBLIN

27/9/53   6 Rue des Favorites

My dear Tom

Glad to have your letter and know you safely home and your sister better. I was out early the morning of your departure and not back to lunch, so did not get your telegram and went to the Invalides. But Suzanne was waiting for me there with the news you had driven to Le Bourget. I was only sorry not to have a last glimpse of you, until the next time, which will I hope be soon.[1] Suzanne's mother is gone and she is beginning to feel better. The 1st of Godot, 2nd series, went off all right last Friday night, Blin playing Pozzo after all and Raimbourg's successor adequate but leaving me wishing for Raimbourg. The play he left us for, a new one by Salacrou, is going badly and poor Lucien getting no notice at all. I think he may soon be back with us and the old team whole again for the tour of the provinces, Switzerland, Milan and Germany.[2] I'm very tired and jumpy, we were rehearsing up till the end all afternoon and evening up to midnight. I'm working too with the English translator of Molloy, every morning, and soon will be with the German translator, and this will go on for years, until 1955 anyway, an indigestion of old work with all the adventure gone.[3] I tell me take art easy, but nothing will come any more, all contracted and unhappy about it. Last night a marvellous Bérénice on the air, with Barrault Antiochus. There too nothing happens, they just talk, but what talk, and how spoken.[4] There is the country to go to, but I often wish there was not, it's a burden, a house and garden, if Suzanne wasn't there I'd get rid of it. Perhaps it's only a mauvais moment à passer.[5] The whiskey you brought is marvellous, a little more and I'd go all assiduous Rue Paul Valéry.[6] Shall soon be writing to Jack Yeats, with the new programme that might amuse him.[7] In the meantime fondly to him. And kindest remembrance to your sister and nieces.

Love ever *and from Suzanne*[8]

s/ Sam

TLS; 1 page, 1 side; TCD, MS 10402/188.

1   MacGreevy had been in Paris in early September before SB left for Berlin (SB to MacGreevy, Monday [7 September 1953], TCD, MS 10402/187), "on his way back from Strasbourg and Grünewald" (SB to George Reavey, 29 September 1953, TxU, Reavey collection). Les Invalides was (and remains) a terminus for bus connections to Paris airports; Le Bourget, an airport to the northeast of Paris. It is not known to which of MacGreevy's sisters SB refers.

2   The reprise of *En attendant Godot* opened on 25 September.

Lucien Raimbourg, the original Vladimir, was playing in Armand Salacrou's *Les Invités du Bon Dieu* at the Théâtre Saint-Georges. The play's knockabout style suited Raimbourg's talent, but Raimbourg does not receive a mention in the review by Robert Kemp ("'Les Invités du Bon Dieu,'" *Le Monde* 25 September 1953: 13). Jean-Marie Serreau took up the role of Vladimir in the Théâtre de Babylone tour of *En attendant Godot* in Germany, Milan and Switzerland from 16 November through 12 December 1953 (IMEC, Beckett, Boîte 2, S. Beckett, *En attendant Godot*, Dossier France Guy).

3   Patrick Bowles, English translator of *Molloy*; Erich Franzen* (1892–1961), German translator of *Molloy*.

4   SB adapts a line from W. B. Yeats's poem "Down by the Salley Gardens": "She bid me take life easy" (*The Poems*, I, 2nd edn., ed Richard J. Finneran, The Collected Works of W. B. Yeats [New York: Scribner, 1997] 18).

Jean Racine's *Bérénice* (1670) was broadcast on RTF on 26 September, with Jean-Louis Barrault as Antiochus.

5   SB refers to his two-room cottage at Ussy.

SB cancels "moment" and writes "mauvais moment" (a bad patch).

6   SB humorously imagines himself becoming an habitué of L'Etoile de Kléber, the famous "maison close" at no. 4 Rue Paul Valéry, which opened in 1941. During the War years the brothel had been home to Edith Piaf, and it later served as a meeting-place for artists and entertainers (Nicole Canet, *Maisons closes 1860–1946: bordels de femmes, bordels d'hommes* [Paris: La Galerie Au Bonheur du Jour, 2009] 59).

7   The new program of *En attendant Godot*.

8   Suzanne Deschevaux-Dumesnil adds by hand: "and from Suzanne."

SERGIO GERSTEIN

PARIS

3-10-53   Paris

Mon cher Sergio

Je viens de terminer m[a] lecture de votre pièce.¹ Il faudrait qu'on se voie pour en parler. Mais je m'en vais pour quelque temps. A mon retour on reparlera de tout ça. Ça m'a vraiment intéressé.

Grande habileté scénique, comme je pouvais m'y attendre. Langue un peu molle par endroits. Peut-être aussi tendance à vouloir trop dire. Je ne sais pas, j'ai horreur de critiquer. Resserré, simplifié, plus claquant dans l'expression, ça gagnerait peut-être. Une lecture ne suffit pas, mais vous en avez peut-être besoin. Nous en reparlerons. Bon courage et à bientôt.

Sam. Beckett

ALS; 1 leaf, 1 side; Morgan, MS 5071.5.

3-10-53   Paris
My dear Sergio

I have just finished my reading of your play. We should get together to talk about it, but I'm going away for a while. We'll talk about it again on my return. It really interested me. Great sense of theatre, as I might have expected. Language a little slack here and there. Perhaps also a tendency to try to say too much. I don't know, I hate being critical. Tightened up, simplified, sharper in expression, it might be the better for that. One rehearsed reading isn't enough, but maybe you need it. We'll talk about it again. Bon courage, and till soon.

Sam. Beckett

1   The play by Sergio Gerstein, designer for the Théâtre de Babylone production of *En attendant Godot*, has not been identified.

JACOBA VAN VELDE

14/10/53
Chère Tonny

Merci du MS. Je vous le renverrai la semaine prochaine.[1]

Le texte allemand, ainsi que la deuxième impression du texte français, tient compte des quelques changements et coupures survenus au cours des répétitions. Il précise en outre quelques jeux de scène trouvés pendant le travail. Il est donc plus conforme au spectacle tel qu'on l'a donné à Paris que la première impression française parue bien avant la représentation. Je crois que vous auriez intérêt à suivre cette version très légèrement modifiée, mais ce n'est pas indispensable. Les changements en question ont été en fonction de la mise en scène et des acteurs de Roger Blin.[2] Dans une autre mise en scène et avec d'autres acteurs ils ne s'imposeraient peut-être pas de la même façon. Quoique à mon avis la pièce y gagne. Vous pourriez peut-être les indiquer au metteur en scène hollandais, en lui laissant le soin de les adopter ou non, comme il veut.[3]

Nous sommes à la campagne et ça ne va pas fort. A mon retour à Paris la semaine prochaine je vous enverrai L'Innommable.

Existe-t-il une reproduction du paysage de Hercules Seghers au Musée d'Amsterdam (il n'y en a qu'un paysage)? Je vous serais très reconnaissant de me l'envoyer, si ça existe.[4]

Voilà, ma chère Tonny, bon courage. C'est plutôt de l'héroïsme qu'il nous faudrait.

Amitiés de nous deux

s/ <u>Sam</u>

TLS; 1 leaf, 1 side; BNF 19794/35.

14.10.53

Dear Tonny

Thank you for the ms. I'll send it back to you next week.[1]

The German text, like the second impression of the French text, takes into account some changes and cuts made in rehearsal. It also specifies certain bits of business we hit on as the work proceeded. It is therefore more in line with the performance as it was given in Paris than is the first French edition, which came out well before the performance. I think you would do well to follow this very slightly modified version, but it's not vital. The changes are bound up with Roger Blin's production and cast.[2] In another production, and with other actors, they would not perhaps be so clearly appropriate. Although in my view the play is the better for them. Maybe you could point them out to the Dutch director, and leave it to him to decide whether to take them on or not.[3]

We are in the country, and things are not going well. When I return to Paris next week I'll send you *L'Innommable*.

Is there in existence a reproduction of the Hercules Seghers landscape in the Amsterdam Museum (there's only one landscape)? I'd be very grateful if you could send me one, if it does exist.[4]

Well, that's it, dear Tonny. Keep your spirits up. It's heroism, rather, that we'd need.

Best wishes from us both

s/ Sam

1 SB had requested a copy of Jacoba van Velde's Dutch translation *Wachten op Godot* in his letter to her of 29 September 1953 (BNF 19794/24).

2 The Dutch translation follows the first French edition (1952), with some variations (see 13 September 1953 to Jacoba van Velde, n. 2). The acting script of *En attendant Godot* at the Morgan Library records changes made during rehearsal, by SB, Blin, and Gerstein; some of these, in SB's hand, reflect changes made prior to the publication of the first French edition (MA 5071.1; for SB's prompt copy, see also 14 January 1953, n. 2).

3 *Wachten op Godot* was first produced in Arnhem by the Toneelgroep Theater on 6 March 1955 in a private performance, directed by Roger Blin, with Richard Flink, Gerard Hartkamp, Johan Walhain, Bernard Droog, and Martine Grefcoeur (Hans van Maanen, "The Theatre System of the Netherlands," in *Theatre Worlds in Motion: Structures, Politics and Developments in the Countries of Western Europe*, ed. Hans van Maanen and S. E. Wilmer [Amsterdam–Atlanta: Rodopi, 1998] 419; Ton Verbeeten, *Toneelgroep Theater 1953–1988: 35 Jaar Wachten op Godot* [Arnhem: Toneelgroep Theater, 1988] 133; Dirk van Hulle indicates that Karen-Else Sluizer played the boy: "Beckett's Reception in the Low Countries," *The International Reception of Samuel Beckett*, ed. Mark Nixon and Matthew Feldman [London: Continuum, 2009] 193).

4 Hercules Seghers, *River Valley* (c. 1626, Rijksmuseum, Amsterdam, no. SK-A-3120).

BARNEY ROSSET, GROVE PRESS
NEW YORK

October 27th 1953 · · · · · · · · · · · · 6 Rue des Favorites
· Paris 15me

My dear Barney

Thank you for your letter of Oct 19th. If I had known a little earlier I would have come up for the day to wish you a fair wind. But as it was there was literally not time.[1]

I know you will do all you can to help with Godot in New York. Your 1% seems what they call here dérisoire.[2]

Sorry you weren't at the Babylone last night when I am told the audience expelled manu militari an indignant female heckler. "Conasse, va te coucher." They are playing on to Nov 8th, then going on tour, in Germany mostly.[3]

Work with Pat Bowles proceeds apace, i.e. about a page an hour. Yesterday we did the unpleasant Ruth or Edith idyll which I fear may shake you in English.[4]

With my kind remembrance to Loly I am,

Yours very sincerely

s/ <u>Sam Beckett</u>

TLS; 1 leaf, 1 side; AN by Loly Rosset on the letter: "Told him about publ of Godot in Spring with NAL Nov 5 Loly"; NSyU. Previous publication, Beckett and Rosset, "Letters [1953–1955]," 34.

1 The Rossets left Paris on 12 October (SB to Rosset, 14 October 1953, NSyU).

2 Rosset's contract with Editions de Minuit of 2 June 1953 necessitated his approval, as well as a small payment to him for productions in the United States and North America (NSyU).
"Dérisoire" (laughable).

3 "Manu militari" (by main force). "Conasse, va te coucher" (Stupid bitch, just go home).
The tour of the Théâtre de Babylone production began on 16 November in Saarbrücken, Germany, and ended on 10 December in Chaumont, France (IMEC, Beckett, Boîte 2, S. Beckett, *En attendant Godot*, Dossier France Guy).

4 The Ruth or Edith idyll: "It was she made me acquainted with love ..." (Beckett, *Molloy* [New York: Grove Press, 1955] 75–79).

PAMELA MITCHELL

NEW YORK

1.11.53 [*for* 31 October 1953]   6 rue des Favorites

Paris 15°

My dear Pamela

Horribly sorry to hear you are ill. Write soon that it's all over.

I'm writing this at 10 o'clock in the morning in a café in Montparnasse. I'm as dull as ditchwater and can hardly hold the pen. Nobody can read my writing but it's the best I can do. I went to Godot last night for the first time in a long time. Well played, but how I dislike that play now. Full house every night, it's a disease. No news from H.L.O. and his option expires to-day.[1] It's cold and bright and I wish I were on the banks of the Marne. Another fortnight and I shall. Another fortnight of translating Molloy and Watt and rehearsing with the touring cast.[2] What will you do when you leave hospital? Convalesce in Massachusetts before going back to the good works? Have they filled you full of penicilline? Wish I could think of something likely to amuse you but can't. Have to go down now to that bloody theatre and encourage the new Pozzo.[3] Pen drying up too, like myself. Are there any French books you'd like me to send you? Ce serait avec joie.[4] Or fashion rags? Let me know. Let me know above all that you're better and the fever gone.

    Love

    Sam

ALS; 1 leaf, 1 side; *env to* Miss Pamela Mitchell, 229 East 48th Street, New York, N.Y., U.S.A.; *pm* 31-10-53, Paris; UoR, BIF, MS 5060. *Dating*: from postmark.

1 SB canceled "paper" and inserted "pen."
SB refers to Harold L. Oram's option on the production rights of *Waiting for Godot* in the United States.

2 The touring cast consisted of Jean-Marie Serreau as Vladimir, Pierre Latour as Estragon, Jean Martin as Lucky, Albert Rémy (1915–1967) as Pozzo, and Albert Duby as the boy (Federman and Fletcher, *Samuel Beckett*, 57).

3 Pamela Mitchell's home town was Worcester, Massachusetts. SB adds an "e" to "penicillin," as occurs in French.
The "new Pozzo" was Albert Rémy.

4 "Ce serait avec joie" (I'd be delighted to do it).

C. G. BJURSTRÖM
PARIS

le 4 novembre 1953   6 Rue des Favorites
                                                       Paris 15me
Cher Monsieur[1]

Je regrette vivement que je n'aie pu passer chez vous prendre le café l'autre jour. Je ne disposais vraiment pas d'assez de temps entre mes deux rendez-vous.

Pompier et mimi: en argot, délices érotiques accordés, dans l'amour hétérosexuel, par la rencontre de la bouche femelle avec le sexe male, et inversement, piètre définition.[2]

Spécificité du langage des primitifs: nous en avons justement parlé l'autre jour, et je vous ai donné l'exemple de tous les mots en gaélique pour licou, selon l'animal, alors qu'il n'y en a pas un seul pour le terme vague et général bête, au lieu de jument, cheval, demi-sang, pouliche, etc.[3]

En effet c'est moi qui détiens les droits et je vous les donne bien volontiers.[4]

Merci encore de tout le mal que vous vous êtes donné.

            Bien cordialement à vous
            s/
                Samuel Beckett

TLS; 1 leaf, 1 side; NLS.

4th November 1953   6 Rue des Favorites
                                                       Paris 15
Dear Mr Bjurström[1]

I very much regret that I was not able to come and have coffee with you the other day. I really did not have enough time, between my two appointments.

Pompier and *mimi*: in argot, erotic pleasures produced, in hetero-sexual lovemaking, by contact between the female mouth and the male sex, and conversely; a poor definition.[2]

Specificity of primitive peoples' speech: we did indeed talk about this the other day, and I gave you the example of all the Gaelic words for *halter*, according to the animal, whereas there is no single word for the vague, general *animal*, instead of mule, horse, half-breed, filly, etc.[3]

It is indeed I who have the rights, and I gladly give them to you.[4]

Thank you again for all the pains you have taken.

> With best wishes
>
> s/
>
> Samuel Beckett

1   Swedish translator and literary critic Carl Gustaf Bjurström* (1919–2001), who introduced SB's work to Sweden, was translating "L'Expulsé." SB responds to Bjurström's letter of 31 October 1953 (NLS).

2   Bjurström was working with the French text of "L'Expulsé" published in *Fontaine* 10.57 (December 1946 – January 1947) 685–708. He asks about the phrase "pompier et mimi n'existeront bientôt plus que dans la musique de Chopin" (pompier et mimi will soon not exist anywhere outside the music of Chopin) (*Fontaine*, 696). This passage is cut (following "Je ne vis personne à genoux") in Beckett, "L'Expulsé," *Nouvelles et Textes pour rien* (Paris: Editions de Minuit, 1955) 25.

SB omits the circumflex on the a in mâle.

3   "Et on nous parle de la spécificité du langage des primitifs" (*Fontaine*, 701; Minuit, 31) ("And they talk to us about the specificity of primitive peoples' speech" (Beckett, *Stories and Texts for Nothing* [New York; Grove, 1967] 20).

4   Because "L'Expulsé" had as yet been published only serially, the rights remained with SB.

RICHARD SEAVER
PARIS

12/11/53
6 Rue des Favorites
Paris 15me

My dear Seaver

Completely forgot yesterday when making our appointment that I had one already the same day and same hour with Daniel Mauroc to work on Watt.[1] So I'm afraid we'll have to leave The Expelled until I get back from the country about the middle of next month.[2]

> Yours sincerely
>
> s/ Sam. Beckett
>
> Samuel Beckett

TLS; 1 leaf, 1 side; TxU, Seaver collection.

1 French playwright, poet, and translator Daniel Mauroc (1926–2007) had published *Contre-amour* (1952) with Editions de Minuit. In 1950, he founded the journal *Janus: Cahiers de la Jeune Poésie Française et Américaine.*

Mauroc undertook the French translation of *Watt* with SB's assistance or supervision. On 27 October, SB writes to Pamela Mitchell that he is "Up to my eyes helping with translations, Molloy into English, Watt into French." On 12 January 1954, SB writes to Mitchell that he has the "French translation of <u>Watt</u> to correct" (UoR, BIF, MS 5060).

It is not clear for whom the translation of *Watt* was being prepared; Collection Merlin had negotiated with Editions Plon to publish *Watt* in French, an arrangement which Editions de Minuit eventually challenged (Lindon to SB, 13 October 1953; SB to Lindon, 14 October 1953 [IMEC, Beckett, Boîte 1, S. Beckett, Correspondance 1946–1953]; Lindon to Alexander Trocchi, 30 October 1953 [McM, Beckett Collection, Collection Merlin, 3.16], and IMEC-Samuel Beckett, Boîte 6, Editions de Minuit / The Olympia Press).

2 Richard Seaver had already translated SB's "La Fin" ("The End") when he was asked by SB to translate "L'Expulsé." Long after, he described the request in the following terms:

> When we had finally finished "The End" to his satisfaction, Beckett asked me – to my surprise but none the less pleasure, for a vote of confidence from him restored in large measure the humbling experience of our joint endeavour – if I would translate another story, "L'Expulsé" ... I hesitated. "Are you sure you wouldn't prefer to do it yourself?" I ventured. "Not at all," he said. "I couldn't ... I simply couldn't. No, it's a great help, Dick, believe me." So I said I would, and did. ("Richard Seaver on Translating Beckett," 106.)

A. J. LEVENTHAL

DUBLIN

17/11/53   6 Rue des Favorites

                                        Paris 15me

My dear Con

I have received a letter from one Alan Simpson representing the Pike Theatre Club, 18A Herbert Lane, asking for permission to present Godot. Before committing myself I should very much like to know what you think of them and also if you would eventually consent to supervise the production. I would not come over myself and it would be a great relief to feel you were there with your knowledge of the theatre and understanding of the play.[1] I have translated the text myself, pretty literally, and am now beginning to revise it for publication in New York next Spring. Shall send you the MS as soon as ready if you are interested in taking on this probably thankless job.[2]

Ethna is still here with the Précigout and having a pretty wretched time. We had dinner together yesterday. If she can stick it out here long enough I think there is a good chance that things will straighten themselves or something else turn up. But it is likely to drag on for a long time.[3]

Shall write a longer letter when I get your reply to this.

Yours ever s/ <u>Sam</u>[4]

Ethna tells me you are preparing a lecture on the modern French theatre. I suggest you should write to Roger Blin (metteur en scène et Pozzo de Godot), saying you are an old friend of mine and asking him whatever you feel like asking him. Address: 264 Rue Saint-Honoré, Paris 1er. You should not omit Adamov and Ionesco, especially the latter, the first volume of whose theatre is now available in book form. I can have him send it to you if you wish. When is your lecture? Martin (Lucky) may be going to Dublin next month and would give you the lowdown on the whole situation. A very nice fellow into the bargain.[5]

TLS; 1 leaf, 2 sides; TxU, Leventhal collection.

1 Alan Simpson* (1920–1980) and his wife Carolyn Swift* (1923–2002) founded the Pike Theatre Club in Dublin.

2 The draft translation had been accepted by Grove Press with a request to remove the English idioms. SB sent the draft translation to Peter Glenville on 7 September: "This very hurried translation needs to be revised. But as it stands it will give you an idea of what you are up against" (TxU, Glenville collection).

3   Ethna MacCarthy was in Paris to complete examinations, professional and physical, for a position with the World Health Organization in Geneva (for further detail see 14 December 1953 to Thomas MacGreevy).
"The Précigout" has not been identified.

4   "Yours ever" is handwritten.

5   Leventhal's lecture has not been identified. It was not published; Leventhal wrote the column "Dramatic Commentary" for *Dublin Magazine* from 1943 to 1958, largely on Dublin productions.
"Metteur en scène et Pozzo de Godot" (Director and Pozzo of *Godot*).
Arthur Adamov.
The first collection of Eugène Ionesco's plays, *Théâtre I* (Paris: Arcanes, 1953), included *La Cantatrice chauve*, *La Leçon*, *Jacques ou la soumission*, and *Le Salon de l'automobile*; the latter two were radio plays. A larger collection, published in 1954, added *Les Chaises*, *Victimes du devoir*, *Amédée ou Comment s'en débarrasser*, and omitted *Le Salon de l'automobile* (*Théâtre I* [Paris: Gallimard, 1954]).

ALAN SIMPSON

DUBLIN

17/11/53   c/o Editions de Minuit
                                                      7 Rue Bernard-Palissy
                                                      Paris 6

Dear Mr Simpson

Thank you for your letter. I think you had better read the play before we go any further. I have translated it myself into English, as literally as I could, and am now revising this translation for American publication in the Spring. Frankly I cannot see how an integral performance would be possible in Dublin, even in such a theatre as yours, because of certain crudities of language if for no better reason. These remain in the English version and I would not consent to their being changed or removed.[1]

Tell me more about your activities up to date. If finally you feel you can undertake to put on the play as it stands there should be no difficulty about permission, from us here and from whoever acquires the English rights.

You will receive the French text in a few days. Don't bother about payment.

                                      Yours sincerely
                                      s/
                                      Samuel Beckett

TLS; 1 leaf, 1 side; *A corr, black ink, AN by Alan Simpson, lower right margin, blue ink:* "21/11/53 Wrote thanking him giving details & sending circular. AS"; TCD 10731/1.

1   SB refers to his English translation, *Waiting for Godot*, prepared for Grove Press. SB's *More Pricks Than Kicks* had been banned in Ireland in 1935, and more recently *Watt* had been banned as well (SB to Thomas McGreevy, 7 May 1936, n. 3; Gerry Dukes, "Englishing *Godot*," in *After Beckett / D'Après Beckett*, ed. Anthony Uhlmann, Sjef Houppermans, and Bruno Clément, *Samuel Beckett Today/Aujourd'hui*, XIV [Amsterdam and New York: Rodopi, 2004] 526–527).

The Pike Theatre operated as a club theatre.

LOLY ROSSET, GROVE PRESS
NEW YORK

20/11/53   6 Rue des Favorites
                                            Paris 15me

My dear Loly

Many thanks for your letter of November 5th. Thank you also for the two books arrived the other day.[1] I am glad you have decided to bring out Godot in the Spring. As you say there is no point in waiting for the performance. I am beginning now to revise my translation and hope to let you have the definitive text next month. As you have probably heard from Pat Bowles we have now finished translating the first part of Molloy. I leave it to you to judge the result, I am beyond doing so. I don't think it stinks too much of a translation, but it certainly doesn't take kindly to English. The dernière at the Babylone was last Sunday week, now the little company is in Germany.[2] No news yet. I think there is increasing resistance to the play in Germany. I'm just as glad. Have been up to my eyes all this time in translations and am now in the country unsuccessfully recovering. Watt in French is something horrible.[3] Have you read The Catcher in the Rye by Salinger. Bowles lent it to me and I liked it very much indeed, more than anything for a long time.[4] I'll write again when I'm less tired, less stupid and less gloomy.

Friendly greetings to you both.

s/ Sam. Beckett

TLS; 1 leaf, 1 side; NSyU. Previous publication, Beckett, "Letters to Barney Rosset," 66; Beckett and Rosset, "Letters [1953–1955]," 34–35.

1   The letter from Loly Rosset to SB of 5 November has not been found, nor is it known what books had been sent to him by Grove Press.

2   The final night of *En attendant Godot* at the Théâtre de Babylone took place on 8 November; the tour in Germany: 27 September 1953, n. 2.

3   Translations of *Molloy* and *Watt*: 12 November 1953, n. 1.

4   J. D. Salinger, *The Catcher in the Rye* (1951). SB was reading the Signet first paperback edition (1953), published by New American Library.

PAMELA MITCHELL
NEW YORK

25/11/53   6 Rue des Favorites
                                              Paris 15me

My dear Pamela

I was worrying and it was a relief to get your letter to-day and to know you were out of hospital and well enough at least to smoke, drink and feel an aversion to work. That my last wretched letter helped the penicilline is nice to hear but hard to believe.[1]

Here I am back in the Marne mists with piles of texts to revise and nothing in my head but false teeth. The holes are ready but no trees as yet. A <u>negundo panaché</u> is a kind of maple with green and white leaf, very elegant. They'll probably all die long before the Spring to judge by the look of the holes.[2] I was kilt entirely co-translating in Paris, 8 stupid hours daily, and the result not very satisfactory. Wish I could discover why my cursed prose won't go into English. Now revising English Godot for publication by Grove in the Spring. Brandel introduced me to a Chantilly American L.L. Lawrence who seems tempted to invest money in a New York production. Can't take to Brandel.[3] Saw Lindon a few days ago when he told me Oram had written to say he was abandoning. I think he is well advised. Remember me to him very kindly.[4] It seems a London West End production is now pretty well certain, producer Peter Glenville whom I have met. Very willowy and gentlemanly, can't imagine him consenting to farts and erections.[5] They finished at the Babylone a fortnight ago. Now they are on tour in Germany. A card from Lucky from Frankfurt yesterday saying they had had 18 curtains at Darmstadt! Darm funny Stadt that must be.[6] Read a very good novel by a young American J. D. Scalinger, The Catcher in the Rye, a Signet Book, best thing I've read for years, think you would like it too.[7] Going out suddenly now for no reason to do some digging.

That was a mistake, what is not?

Wonder what job you'll be put on next, now that Godot is off the list of good works. What news of the Giant?[8] Nothing much doing in Paris. O'Neill's Desire under the Elms is flopping.[9] The Merlin crowd are battling along, a new Merlin is just out or just due after great difficulties with the printer, an English inebriate living in Majorca[.][10] Pat Bowles is pleasant to work with and we finished translating the first half of Molloy, of which an extract is to appear in next issue of New World Writing I think. Also with Seaver whom I don't think you met, an American, translated an old short story, one of the very first efforts in French.[11] Sick and tired of the sight of myself in print – and otherwise. When I'm here never want to leave the place and when in Paris wish I was rid of it, I must have told you that before. Have to be back in Paris early next month for a painter friend's vernissage and to start on the miserable Moran and get on with the wretched Watt.[12] Seriously contemplating shamming sick (if necessary) and lolling on here well into the New Year.

Write soon again that you're feeling better than before you fell ill and not killing yourself for Oram Inc.

Love

s/ Sam

You probably caught your pneumonia that afternoon in the Babylone when you borrowed Hilling's coat. All Godot's fault again. Or walking back in the rain from the Iles Marquises to your hotel.[13]

TLS; 1 leaf, 1 side; UoR, BIF, MS 5060.

14. Samuel Beckett digging at Ussy.

1   Pamela Mitchell wrote to SB on 16 November, saying: "staggered into work for a couple of hours today for the first time [...] I am sure it is commiseration as much as penicillin which cures me, so your note was especially appreciated" (UoR, BIF, MS 5060).

2   SB had had several teeth pulled.
SB had prepared to plant trees around the cottage at Ussy.

3   The producer to whom SB refers was probably Marc Brandel (né Marcus Beresford, 1919–1994), actor and screen-writer active in New York in the early 1950s. SB wrote to Jérôme Lindon on 17 November: "Conversation hier avec Brandel et Lawrence tout ce qu'il y a de vague" (Conversation yesterday with Brandel and Lawrence, all very vague) (IMEC, Beckett, Boîte 1, S. Beckett, Correspondance 1946–1953).
L. L. Lawrence (known as Laudy, 1899–1988), European representative for MGM Studios (1947 to 1957); his home was Green Lodge, in Chantilly, where he bred and raced horses. SB reports to Mitchell on 21 December: "Brandel introduced me to a nice American millionaire called Lawrence, lives at Chantilly not far from Paris. He liked the play and was considering putting money in a N.Y. production. That was some time ago. Since when no word from either of them" (UoR, BIF, MS 5060).

4   Pamela Mitchell's employer Harold L. Oram had taken an option to produce *Waiting for Godot* in the United States. Mitchell replied to SB on 24 November: "I feel very badly about the upshot of negotiations between HLO & Lindon on *Godot* – from every possible angle. Although I haven't much influence, keep thinking that if only I hadn't gone & fallen ill when I did maybe I could have done something" (UoR, BIF, MS 5060). SB wrote to Mitchell on 21 December 1953: "It appears Oram jibbed at Rosset's 1%, but I imagine that was just an excuse" (UoR, BIF, MS 5060).

5   London actor, director, and producer Peter Glenville (1913–1996) had been negotiating for British rights to *Waiting for Godot* with Dorothy Kitty Black* (1914–2006), then an agent with Curtis Brown.

6   Jean Martin played Lucky in the Théâtre de Babylone production on tour. The production played in Darmstadt on 18 November. An advance article mentions Martin's creation of this role, and compares the Blin production to the Berlin premiere (Kuno Epple, "Wir warten auf 'Godot,'" *Darmstädter Echo* 14 November 1953: 11). No review of this production has been found; Martin's card to SB has not been found.

7   *The Catcher in the Rye*: 20 November 1953, n. 4. SB types "Scalinger" for "Salinger."

8   *Take a Giant Step* closed in New York on 28 November 1953: 26 September 1953, n. 4.

9   Critical disdain for the French revival of Eugene O'Neill's *Desire under the Elms* was nearly universal (Lewis W. Falb, "The Critical Reception of Eugene O'Neill on the French Stage," *Educational Theatre Journal* 22.3 [December 1970] 399, 402). Robert Kemp wrote: "Je ne me laisserai pas troubler ... Mais en vérité j'ai du chagrin" (I am not going to let it affect me ... But the truth is that I feel real sadness); he contrasts the care taken over the production with the unacceptability of the play, as compared with the admirable *Mourning Becomes Electra* ("'Le Désir sous les ormes' à la Comédie des Champs-Elysées," *Le Monde* 11 November 1953: 9). The play ran from 5 November to 19 December.

10   *Merlin* published an "Extract from *Molloy*," 88–103.

11   From the first half of *Molloy*, a portion appeared as "Molloy," *New World Writing*, 316–323.
SB had been working with Richard Seaver on a translation of "L'Expulsé," written early in 1946.

12 "Moran" refers to the second part of *Molloy*.
Henri Hayden's exhibition of recent works opened in December 1953 at the Galerie Suillerot (Jean Selz, *Hayden* [Geneva: Editions Pierre Cailler, 1962] 34).

13 Jacques Hilling: 26 September 1953, n. 2.

JEROME LINDON, EDITIONS DE MINUIT
PARIS

1.12.53   Ussy
Mon cher Jérôme
 Merci de votre lettre. Nous avons été déçus de ne pas vous voir dimanche. Tâchez de venir dimanche prochain, nous y serons encore.[1]
 Pour le Renaudot c'est hélas non sur toute la ligne. Je ne perticiperais [*for* participerais] pas aux réjouissances et je ne donnerais d'interview ni aux Nouvelles Littéraires ni à personne. Si l'attribution de ce prix dépend de singeries pour ne pas dire de marchandages pareils, merde. Je suis aussi moche qu'un autre, vous le savez bien, il y a simplement des choses que je ne peux pas faire, non pas parce que je les trouve moches, mais parce que c'est plus fort que moi. Je suis désolé encore une fois du tort que je vous fais, à vous qui avez tant fait et qui faites tant tous les jours pour moi. Vous voyez, les mochetés dans mes cordes, je ne les rate pas.[2]
 Nous sommes ravis de ce que vous êtes arrivé à faire pour ce pauvre Straram.[3] C'est formidable. Pourvu que ça ne vous retombe pas sur le coin de la gueule.
 Je pense aussi qu'on devrait laisser les droits américains à Albery et Glenville.[4]
 Bravo aussi pour Bordas.[5]
 Venez dimanche. Les arbres sont en place, à part un négundo et le prunus dont vous avez creusé le trou.
 Bien amicalement de nous deux à vous deux.
  s/ <u>Sam</u>

424

TLS with *AN* corrections; 1 leaf, 1 side; IMEC, Beckett, Boîte l, S. Beckett, Correspondance 1946–1953; *A* draft, "Sam Francis Notebook," UoR, BIF, MS 2926, 37 verso.

1.12.53   Ussy

My dear Jérôme

Thank you for your letter. We were disappointed not to see you on Sunday. Try to come next Sunday, we shall still be here.[1]

For the Renaudot, alas it is no all along the line. I would not take part in the celebrations and I would not give an interview, not to the *Nouvelles Littéraires*, not to anyone. If the award of this prize depends on antics not to say hagglings like this, to hell with it. I am as nasty a piece of work as the next man, as you know, just that there are things that I cannot do, not because I find them nasty, but because it is something stronger than me. I am really sorry once again for the harm I do you, you who have done so much and go on doing so much every day for me. You see, any little nastinesses in my power, I never miss them.[2]

We are delighted with what you have managed to do for poor Straram.[3] It is tremendous. So long as it does not all come crashing down on you.

I think too that we ought to leave the American rights with Albery and Glenville.[4]

Bravo too for Bordas.[5]

Do come on Sunday. The trees are in place, except a negundo and the prunus that you dug the hole for.

All best from us both to you both.

        Sam

1   SB responds to Lindon's letter of 30 November (IMEC, Beckett, Boîte 1, S. Beckett, Correspondance 1946–1953). SB had hoped to see Lindon on Sunday 29 November (SB to Jérôme Lindon, 26 November 1953, IMEC, Beckett, Boîte 1, S. Beckett, Correspondance 1946–1953).

2   In his letter of 30 November, Lindon had outlined the possibility that, with the backing of jury members Maurice Nadeau and Claude-Edmonde Magny (1913–1966), SB might be awarded the Prix Renaudot for *L'Innommable*. Lindon wrote also of French journalist and film critic Georges Charensol (1899–1995), co-founder of the Prix Renaudot, who had inquired as to SB's willingness to attend the prize ceremony and to be interviewed for *Les Nouvelles Littéraires*, of which he was Director.

In a second letter dated 1 December, SB wrote to Lindon:

> Pour les réjouissances, si c'est plus facile pour vous, dites que je suis souffrant et ne peux pas quitter la campagne en ce moment, c'est ailleurs un peu vrai.
> Pour l'interview, pas de changement, je n'en donne jamais.
> Bien malheureux de toute cette histoire. (IMEC, Beckett, Boîte 1, S. Beckett, Correspondance 1946–1953.)
>> (For the celebrations, if it is easier for you, say I am not well and cannot come up from the country for the moment. It is actually not untrue.
>> About the interview, no change. I never give them.
>> Really miserable about this whole affair.)

3   At the end of September 1953, the French writer Patrick Straram (1934–1988) had importuned passers-by "while brandishing a knife," and was hospitalized in the psychiatric hospital of Ville-Evrard (Guy Debord and Alice Debord, *Guy Debord, Correspondance, I, juin 1957 – août 1960* [Paris: Fayard, 1999] 377, n. 7.) As Lindon explains in his letter to SB of 30 November, he met Straram, his wife, and his social worker, arranged to have him released from the hospital, and found a small job for him: "Je pense pouvoir lui procurer un travail plus important dans le courant de la semaine" (I think I will be able to get him a more serious job some time next week) (IMEC, Beckett, Boîte 1, S. Beckett, Correspondance 1946–1953).

4   In his letter of 30 November, Lindon wrote that agreement had been reached with Peter Glenville and producer Donald Albery* (1914–1988) regarding an option for the production of *Waiting for Godot*. He asked if SB agreed that it would be better to leave the United States rights to Glenville and Albery.

5   In his letter of 30 November, Lindon wrote that he had reached an agreement about *Murphy* with Pierre Bordas; this was confirmed in Pierre Bordas's letter to SB on 1 December which asked SB to countersign the terms of their arrangement (IMEC, Beckett, Boîte 1, S. Beckett, Dossier Murphy 1946–1957).

NIALL MONTGOMERY

DUBLIN

2.12.53   6 rue des Favorites

Paris 15

Dear Niall

Very impressed by your report and touched by the enormous trouble you have taken.[1]

I learned a lot about myself I didn't know & hadn't suspected.

I emerge more organized than I am.

I am too tired and stupid to write intelligently and know it; no good putting it off till I'm less tired and stupid.

The heart of the matter, if it has one, is perhaps rather in the Naught more real than nothing and the ubi nihil vales, already in Murphy – I imagine so.[2]

Watt is long before the French writings, having been finished in 45.[3]

Yellow is not a novel, but one of the stories in More Pricks.

I can't remember ever having written on Dante. Dante and the Lobster is another story in More Pricks.[4]

Proust is a long essay (30,000 words) published by Chatto & Windus in the Dolphin series 1930 I think.[5]

I haven't the Proust myself, nor More Pricks – and they can't be had.

I'll send you all the French works and Echo's Bones not suitably inscribed but inscribed.[6]

The errors in Watt are genuine coquilles.[7]

I don't remember either having translated any Rimbaud other than the Bateau Ivre which has never been printed anywhere.[8]

Again all my thanks. You're one of the few reading critics.

Remember me kindly to your wife. Mais oui, sans faute, à un de ces jours.[9]

     Sam

May I keep yr. Ms. or do you want it back?[10]

ALS; 1 leaf, 1 side; NLI, Accession 6475, Lot 7, Box Gregory, with T transcription (not wholly accurate) which is also in Lot 5, box d.

1   On 27 October, Niall Montgomery was asked by Victor Weybright (1903–1978), Chairman and Editor of The New American Library, to write an article on SB's work for *New World Writing*. Montgomery wrote to SB to ask his permission, to which SB replied on 2 November: "Should be delighted if you would write about me. Don't let our friendship deter you" (NLI, Accession 6475, Lot 7 IDDA [now Miscellaneous]).

2   SB refers to *Murphy* (1957) 246. The phrase in *Murphy* is taken from Geulincx, "Ubi nihil vales" (Where you are worth nothing) (see 16 January [1936] to Thomas McGreevy, n. 5).

3   *Watt*: 10 May 1945, 25 May 1945.

4   "Yellow," *More Pricks Than Kicks* (London: Chatto and Windus, 1934) 227–252; "Dante and the Lobster," *More Pricks Than Kicks*, 1–20. SB forgets to mention his 1929 essay "Dante… Bruno. Vico.. Joyce."

5   *Proust*, The Dolphin Books (London: Chatto and Windus, 1931).

6   SB's published works in French at this time: *En attendant Godot, Malone meurt, Molloy, L'Innommable,* as well as poetry and extracts in journals. *Echo's Bones and Other Precipitates* (Paris: Europa Press, 1935). With the letter to SB of 28 November 1953, Montgomery sent a copy of his essay; he said that he had borrowed SB's books from Frank Beckett (NLI, Accession 4675, Lot 7 IDDA [now Miscellaneous]).

7   Montgomery, "No Symbols Where None Intended," *New World Writing* 5 (1954) 324–337. Montgomery notes an error in the text of *Watt* (p. 335, n. 38).
    "Coquilles" (typos).

8   Montgomery takes his title, "No Symbols Where None Intended," from the end of *Watt* (New York: Grove Press, 1959) 330. SB's translation of Rimbaud's *Le Bateau ivre*: 13 [September 1932], n. 9, and 28 November 1937 [for 1936], n. 20, both to Thomas McGreevy.

9   "Mais oui, sans faute, à un de ces jours" (Yes, definitely, let's get together one of these days). Montgomery's wife, Rosanna (née Hopkins, known as Hop).

10   A PS placed in upper right margin of the letter.

ROBERT PINGET
PARIS

5 décembre 1953   Editions de Minuit
Cher Monsieur
    Merci de votre gentille lettre. J'ai beaucoup aimé Mahu. Je n'ai pas encore lu le Renard. Je suis content que Alain Robbe-Grillet écrive sur vous.[1]
    Je suis tout le temps ou presque à la campagne en ce moment. Je vous ferai signe un de ces jours et nous boirons un pot ensemble. Ne soyez pas intimidé, il n'y a vraiment pas de quoi, vous verrez.[2]
            Bien cordialement à vous
                Sam. Beckett

ALS; 1 leaf, 1 side; *env to* Monsieur Robert Pinget, 4 Rue de l'Université, Paris 7°; *pm* 5-12-53, Paris; Burns Library, Pinget-Beckett Letters.

5 December 1953   Editions de Minuit
Dear Mr Pinget

Thank you for your kind letter. I greatly enjoyed *Mahu*. I have not yet read *Le Renard*. I'm glad Alain Robbe-Grillet is writing about you.[1]

I'm in the country all or nearly all the time at the moment. I'll get in touch with you one of these days and we can have a drink together. Don't feel intimidated, there's really no cause, you'll see.

Most cordially yours

Sam Beckett

1   Robert Pinget* (1919–1997) had published *Mahu ou le matériau* in 1952 with Laffont and *Le Renard et la boussole* in August 1953 with Gallimard.

Alain Robbe-Grillet, "Un roman qui s'invente lui-même," *Critique* 10.80 (January 1954) 82–85.

2   Pinget had requested a meeting with SB through Jérôme Lindon (Lindon to SB, 30 November 1953 [IMEC, Beckett, Boîte 1, S. Beckett, Correspondance 1946–1953]).

C. G. BJURSTRÖM

PARIS

le 14 décembre 1953   6 Rue des Favorites

                                                         Paris 15°

Cher Monsieur

Merci de votre lettre du 12 décembre. Je suis heureux que votre article doive paraître si prochainement. D'accord pour un des trois textes des Lettres Nouvelles, à votre choix, je n'ai pas de préférence.[1] Je vous signale à tout hasard que le treizième et dernier de ces petits textes, fait voici un an à peu près, et depuis lequel plus rien, vient de paraître dans le Disque Vert.[2]

A votre disposition si vous avez besoin d'autres textes courts pour joindre à L'Expulsé.[3]

Merci encore de l'intérêt que vous portez à mon travail et du mal que vous vous donnez pour le faire connaître en Suède.

Bien cordialement à vous

s/

Samuel Beckett

TLS; 1 leaf, 1 side; NLS.

14th December 1953   6 Rue des Favorites

                                                          Paris 15

Dear Mr Bjurström

Thank you for your letter of the 12th December. I am very pleased that your article is to appear so soon. Agreed for one of the three texts in *Les Lettres Nouvelles*, your choice, I have no preference.[1] I should point out to you, just in case, that the thirteenth and last of these little texts, written about a year ago, since which time nothing more, has just appeared in *Le Disque Vert*.[2]

Am at your disposal if you need other short texts to put in with "L'Expulsé".[3]

Thank you again for the interest you are taking in my work and the trouble to which you are putting yourself to get it known in Sweden.

    With all good wishes

      Samuel Beckett

---

1 C. J. Bjurström's "Samuel Beckett," *Bonniers Litterära Magasin* 23.1 (January 1954) 27-33.

SB refers to "Trois textes pour rien," 267-277; although numbered I, II, III, these were 'Textes pour rien" III, VI, and X.

Bjurström's translation of the second "Texte" of those published in *Les Lettres Nouvelles* ("Texte pour rien, VI") appeared in *Bonniers Litterära Magasin* 23.1 (January 1954) 24-26.

2 The thirteenth text of *Textes pour rien* was published as "Texte pour rien," *Le Disque Vert* 4 (1953) 3-5. *Le Disque Vert*, an avant-garde literary monthly, was launched in Brussels by Franz Hellens (1881-1972), and ran from 1922 to 1934. A new series was launched in July 1941, but only one issue was published. In December 1952, an hors série issue appeared, followed by a new series (nos. 1-6, 1953-1954) edited by Hellens and René de Solier (1914-1974).

3 Bjurström's translation of "L'Expulsé" appeared much later as "Utkastad" in *Samuel Beckett Knivavnej: Prosastycken 1946-66* (Stockholm: Almquist & Wiksell, 1969) 9-25, and as part of his Swedish translation of the collection of Beckett's works published as *No's Knife* (London: Calder, 1967).

BARNEY AND LOLY ROSSET, GROVE PRESS
NEW YORK

14/12/53   6 Rue des Favorites
                                          Paris 15°

Dear Barney and Loly

Sorry for the no to design you seem to like. It was good of you to consult me. Don't think of me as a nietman.[1] The idea is all right. But I think the variety of symbols is a bad mistake. They make a hideous column and destroy the cohesion of the page. And I don't like the suggestion and the attempt to express it of a hierarchy of characters. A la rigueur, if you wish, simple capitals, E. for Estragon, V. for Vladimir, etc., since no confusion is possible, and perhaps no heavier in type than those of the text. But I prefer the full name. Their repetition, even when corresponding speech amounts to no more than a syllable, has its function in the sense that it reinforces the repetitive text. The symbols are variety and the whole affair is monotony.[2] Another possibility is to set the names in the middle of the page and text beneath, thus:

ESTRAGON

I'd rather he'd dance, it'd be more fun.

POZZO

Not necessarily.

ESTRAGON

Wouldn't it, Didi, be more fun?

VLADIMIR

I'd like well to hear him think.

ESTRAGON

Perhaps he could dance first and think afterwards, if it isn't too much to ask him

But personally I prefer the Minuit composition. The same is used by Gallimard for Adamov's theatre (1st vol. just out).[3] But if you prefer the simple capitals it will be all right with me.

Could you possibly postpone setting of galleys until 1st week in January, by which time you will have received the definitive text? I have made a fair number of changes, particularly in Lucky's tirade, and a lot of correcting would be avoided if you could delay things for a few weeks.

I was annoyed by NWW's horrible montage. The excerpt is always unsatisfactory, but let it at least be continuous. I don't mind how short it is, or with how little beginning or end, but I refuse to be short-circuited like an ulcerous gut.[4]

Molloy hasn't advanced much further. I am tired and most of the time in the country. But part 2 will go faster. And there does not seem to be any great hurry.

Signed yesterday for London West End production within 6 months, producer probably Peter Glenville. Oram as you probably know has renounced.[5]

The tour of Babylone Godot mostly in Germany (including the Gründgens theatre in Düsseldorf), but also as far as the Milan Piccolo, seems to have been successful. They are opening again here day after to-morrow for a month or 6 weeks, then off on tour again.[6] Marvellous photos, unposed, much superior to the French, were taken in Krefeld during actual performance. One in particular is fantastic (end of Act 1, Vladimir drawing Estragon towards wings, with moon and tree). It is the play and would make a remarkable cover for your book. I shall call at the theatre this afternoon before posting this and add address of photographer in case you are interested in purchasing the set.[7]

Best wishes for Xmas and the New Year.

s/ Sam

Samuel Beckett

FOTO DÖNITZ

KREFELD

WINNERTZHOF 20

GERMANY[8]

TLS with pencil AN; 1 leaf, 2 sides; NSyU. Previous publication, Beckett, "Letters to Barney Rosset," 67; Beckett and Rosset, "Letters [1953–1955]," 35–36; Rosset, "Remembering Samuel Beckett," 14–15.

1   SB had been sent a trial page set-up for *Waiting for Godot* and responded to Grove Press in a telegram that was received on 14 December: "NO SORRY WRITING" (NSyU). "Nietman," based on Russian "niet" (no).

2   No copy of the trial layout has been found. "A la rigueur" (just about possible).

3   The Editions de Minuit text indents each new speech from the left margin, preceded by the speaker's name in capital letters. If the speech continues beyond one line, subsequent lines carry over flush with the left margin.
The style finally adopted by Grove Press presents each speaker's name in capital letters in a column flush with the left margin, and each speech as a second column that is flush with the right margin.

4   SB refers to the presentation of the excerpts from *Molloy* in *New World Writing* in which there is no indication that the text is not continuous ("Molloy," 316–323). In his letter to Barney Rosset of 4 November, SB asked "Any idea why they don't want the first 13 pages?" (NSyU).

5   The contract with Peter Glenville (as director) and Donald Albery (as producer) gave a six-month option (extendable for a further six months) for a London West End production of *Waiting for Godot* (IMEC, Beckett, Boîte 5, S. Beckett Correspondance 1962–1968, Curtis Brown 1957 [*for* 1952–1957]).

6   The Théâtre de Babylone production of *En attendant Godot* toured in Germany from 16 to 25 November (Saarbrücken to Stuttgart). The tour gave one performance in Düsseldorf on Sunday 22 November, at the Schauspielhaus which is on a square now named for the German actor and director Gustav Gründgens (1899–1963). SB explained to Loly Rosset at Grove Press: "No, Gründgens has not produced or played in Godot and does not intend to. He simply invited the Babylone players to his theatre in Düsseldorf. I have just been sent his book: Wirklichkeit des Theaters with preface by my German publisher Peter Suhrkamp" (29 December 1953, NSyU).
The touring company performed at the Schauspielhaus in Zurich, Switzerland, and then at the Piccolo Teatro in Milan on 30 November, before returning through cities in France.
En attendant Godot re-opened at the Théâtre de Babylone on 17 December and played there through 1 April 1954.

7   The image described here, of the production when it played in Krefeld, was used on the cover of Grove's first edition of *Waiting for Godot*.

8   The "Foto Dönitz" address is handwritten.

THOMAS MACGREEVY
DUBLIN

December 14th 1953   6 Rue des Favorites
                                       Paris 15°

My dear Tom

Delighted to get your letter. It was good of you to write again before I had properly replied to your last.

Poor Pikelny did not do much good in London. Read was in America and though I had a friendly letter from his secretary saying that the necessary would be done, nothing seems to have been done. However he made his expenses and came back Burtonized from head to foot.[1]

I did not expect anything very penetrating from Niall. What impressed and touched me was the trouble he seemed to have taken and the evidence of at least having read the books, no easy or pleasant matter as you know.[2] I had a friendly but rather dull article also in the TCD Icarus by one Sebastian Ryan, animadverting with some violence on Thersites, who sneered painstakingly at Godot without having either read or seen it.[3]

Delighted to hear that we are going to see JBY in Paris at last. I suppose I may announce it now?[4] Duthuit will certainly write at length, probably in the Lettres Nouvelles and in the Cahiers d'Art perhaps too. I'll try and do something myself somewhere, in Arts possibly, but shall have to be in better form than I am now. I am very tired and stupid, more and more so in spite of my often resting in the country, and I feel more and more that I shall perhaps never be able to write anything else. Niemand wandelt unbestraft on the road that leads to L'Innommable.[5] I can't go on and I can't get back. Perhaps another play some day.

I understand how you feel about America. Once you get started you'll be all right. You'll probably see George Reavey. He wrote me recently about Dylan Thomas's death, which seems to have been a very sinister business.[6]

Poor Ethna MacCarthy is here battling with World Health Organization which has treated her shamefully. She signed her contract, liquidated her affairs in Dublin, arrived in Geneva and was turned down there on the strength of a scandalously severe medical examination. She has succeeded in obtaining a counter-examination by a UNESCO doctor, but I fear it will be a prejudiced one. It means my remaining in Paris until the thing is decided one way and another, this week I hope, and I am longing for Ussy.[7]

The Babylone Godot is back from tour, in Germany mostly, though they played also at the Piccolo in Milan. They are opening again here for a month or six weeks day after to-morrow, then going on tour again. I signed yesterday for a London West End production within 6 months, producer probably Peter Glenville. I have nearly finished revising my English version, just the second act to type. I don't think it can do any good in London. But then I didn't think it could do any good here.

Suzanne sends her love. She is well, but having trouble with her eyes and teeth. Poor Frank is laid up, dizzy attacks, low blood pressure, heart tired, I don't like it at all. He has been prescribed a fortnight's complete rest. Jean wrote reassuringly, but too obviously so to reassure me. I should have though[t] he had high rather than low pressure. He takes that old office too much to heart, like Father. Fortunately he has had the sense to take a partner.[8] Fortunately Jean is quite well again and able to look after him.

I shall write to Jack Yeats for Xmas, I feel criminal not having written to him for so long. In the meantime give him my very affectionate greetings.

I advised Ethna to go and see the Cremins. They were very nice to her but I'm afraid not much help.[9]

We do hope you will come in February. A Yeats exhibition without you wouldn't be right.

Kindest regards to your sister and nieces. And much love from us both.

Ever

s/ Sam

TLS; 1 leaf, 2 sides; TCD, MS 10402/190.

1 SB had called MacGreevy's attention to the London exhibition of Polish-born French painter Robert Pikelny (1904–1986) that began on 28 October at the Renel Gallery, 40–41 Burlington Arcade. SB hoped that MacGreevy might encourage a mention from Eric Newton (1893–1965); however, at this time Newton, who had been Art Critic for *The Sunday Times*, did not hold a regular reviewing position. It appears that SB had written as well to Herbert Read, although this letter has not been found.

"Burtonized" refers to Montague Burton, the men's clothing store.

2   SB refers to Niall Montgomery's article in *New World Writing* (see 2 December 1953).

3   In his essay, Sebastian Ryan (1932–1994) wrote:

> The only comment in Ireland that I saw was that of a certain "Thersites," who, fearing that the smallest suspicion of prejudice should enter into his comments, scrupulously avoided either reading or seeing the play … he proceeded to some irrelevant and vulgar sneers, and concluded by giving Beckett a patronizing slap on the back for successfully putting over an Irish joke on the French ("Samuel Beckett," *Icarus* 3 [November 1953] 79–86).

Ryan refers to a column in the book section of *The Irish Times* signed "Thersites": "Not having read or seen the play, I have, of course, no competence to pass a judgment on it" ("Thersites," "Private Views," *The Irish Times* 21 February 1953: 6). "Thersites" was a pen name of Thomas Woods (who also wrote as Tom Hogan, 1923–1961); Woods was with the Department of External Affairs and was Ireland's Permanent Representative to the Council of Europe.

4   The projected first Paris exhibition of the painting of Jack B. Yeats.

5   "Niemand wandelt unbestraft" (No one wanders unpunished), a slight variation from Goethe's original (see 27 May 1948, n. 3).

6   Reavey wrote to SB from New York toward the end of November:

> I was about to write some three weeks ago when suddenly Dylan Thomas went into a coma and what ensued was a series of grisly and ghastly events which might be out of Poe, with a band of pseudo literary gangsters trying to put their hands on his papers, certify Mrs Thomas to Bellevue, etc. etc. I was finally up to my neck in it and had to get British Consul to intervene [. . .] Dylan of course died and the coma has never been properly explained. (TxU, Reavey collection.)

Bellevue is a hospital in New York.

Dylan Thomas, a close friend of Reavey, died in New York on 9 November 1953, aged thirty-nine, while on a lecture tour in the United States.

7   The documentation concerning MacCarthy's effort to obtain an appointment with the WHO has not been found.

8   Ian McMillan was taken on as a partner in Beckett and Medcalf; the firm was sold to him in 1954, and he continued to run it under that name (Edward Beckett, 24 June 2010).

9   Cornelius Christopher Cremin (1908–1987), First Secretary of the Irish Legation in France (1937–1943) and Ambassador to France in the Irish Legation in Paris (1950–1954), and his wife Patricia Josephine Cremin (née O'Mahony, 1913–1971).

PATRICIA HUTCHINS (MRS R. GREACEN)

December 18th 1953   6 Rue des Favorites
                                                      Paris 15°

Dear Mrs. Greacen[1]

As a result of erratic hitherandthitherings in the Ile de France and unredirected mail I received only today your letter of December 2nd.[2] I fear you must have thought me very discourteous and greatly regret having missed you again on your way through Paris.

The only time I remember having met Pound was one evening at dinner with the Joyces in the Trianons, Place de Rennes. He was having great trouble with a fond d'artichaud and was very aggressive and disdainful.[3]

I may be in London round about April and perhaps we could meet then. In the meantime if there are any particular questions you wish to ask me about Joyce I suggest your doing so by letter, though my memories of that time are increasingly confused.

> Yours sincerely
> s/ Sam. Beckett
> Samuel Beckett

TLS; 1 leaf, 2 sides; *AN by Patricia Hutchins, ink lower left corner, side 2*: "Wrote 1-4-54"; TCD, MS 4098/8.

1 Patricia Hutchins (1911–1985) was married to Robert Greacen (1920–2006); in her publications she usually used her maiden name.

2 Hutchins's letter of 2 December has not been found.

3 SB writes "artichaud" for "artichaut" (artichoke). Aux Trianons, a restaurant in Place de Rennes (now Place du 18 juin 1940).

SB told Hugh Kenner (1923–2003) that he had met Ezra Pound in 1929 while at dinner with James Joyce. In a letter to Kenner, SB recalls: "My memory is of the Trianon restaurant and I can still see the artichoke's heart evading his fork while he inquired cuttingly what epic I was engaged on at the moment" (19 September 1968, TxU, Kenner collection). As told by Kenner, Pound "came upon Joyce holding court and was enraged by what he took to be a climate of sycophancy. Of one slim youth he enquired, in withering tones, whether he might be writing an *Iliad*, or would it be a *Divina Commedia*." Kenner added: "One should not say such a humiliating thing to anyone ... but it is especially regrettable that he should have said it to Sam Beckett" (*The Pound Era* [Berkeley: University of California Press, 1971] 396, 584, n. 396).

CHRONOLOGY 1954

1954	12 January	SB attends Cirque Medrano with Jean Martin to see Buster Keaton perform.
	20 January	Correcting proofs of *Waiting for Godot* for Grove Press. Reviewing Trino Martínez Trives's translation *Esperando a Godot*. Refuses to allow *Mercier et Camier* to be published by Editions de Minuit.
	23 January – 17 February	Reviews German translation of *Molloy* by translator Erich Franzen in a series of letters.
	February	Jack B. Yeats exhibition, Galerie Beaux-Arts, Paris.
	25 February	Blin's production of *Warten auf Godot* opens in the Schauspielhaus, Zurich.
	March	"Extract from *Molloy*" published in *The Paris Review*.
		SB asks Jacques Putman, Georges Duthuit, and Pierre Schneider to contribute short essays on the painting of Jack B. Yeats for *Les Lettres Nouvelles*.
	13 March – 7 May	Battle of Dien Bien Phu, climactic confrontation between the French and the Viet Minh.
	April	"Molloy," an excerpt from *Molloy*, published in *New World Writing*.
		SB's "Hommage à Jack B. Yeats" published in *Les Lettres Nouvelles*.
	14 April	SB responds to the objections of the Lord Chamberlain's Office to text of *Waiting for Godot*.
	May	Pamela Mitchell in Paris.
		Two sonnets by Miguel de Guevara, translated by SB for the *Anthology of Mexican Poetry*, published in *Hermathena*.
	27 May	SB leaves for Dublin to be with Frank Beckett who is gravely ill.

439

23 June	Objections of the Lord Chamberlain's Office to the text of *Waiting for Godot* resolved.
12 July	SB has begun the English translation of *Malone meurt*.
20 July	France and Vietnam agree to a ceasefire, marking end of the French Indochina War.
end of August	*Waiting for Godot*, translated by the author, published by Grove Press.
Summer–Autumn	"The End," translated by Richard Seaver in collaboration with the author, published in *Merlin*.
7 September	SB correcting proofs of Pablo Palant's Spanish translation *Esperando a Godot*.
13 September	Death of Frank Beckett.
24 September	SB meets Donald Albery, Peter Glenville, and Sir Ralph Richardson in London on his way from Dublin to Paris.
26 September	SB in Ussy.
15 October	*Watt* banned in Ireland.
1 November	Algerian War begins (la Toussaint Sanglante).
19 November	SB returns to Paris after nearly two months in Ussy.

le 9 janvier 1954   6 Rue des Favorites
                                                    Paris 15me

Cher Monsieur Suhrkamp

Merci de votre lettre du 5 janvier et de vos voeux. A vous les miens, de coeur.[1]

J'ai été naturellement déçu que votre projet des trois textes en un seul volume ne puisse se réaliser. Mais je comprends fort bien vos raisons et je m'y rends.[2] J'ai tout d'abord songé à vous proposer un titre général (qui resterait à trouver) pour les trois livres et qu'à chacun soit affecté un numéro d'ordre. Mais à bien y réfléchir ce travail ne constitue un tout fermé que dans la mesure où l'on tient pour chose acquise l'impossibilité de continuer. C'est bien hélas mon sentiment, mais on ne sait jamais. De même qu'on peut en situer le point de départ dans Murphy.

Je suis heureux que la traduction de Monsieur Franzen vous plaise à ce point. J'attends avec impatience de pouvoir la lire. Je conçois fort bien qu'il renonce à aller plus loin. Pour la suite Monsieur Tophoven me semble tout indiqué en effet.[3]

J'ai vu Monsieur Lindon aujourd'hui. Il a bien reçu votre lettre et vous enverra incessamment les critiques dont vous avez besoin. Sur Molloy Maurice Nadeau et Georges Bataille me paraissent les meilleurs. La critique d'ensemble de Nadeau (je ne me rappelle plus où) m'a plu également. Mais la chose capitale, pour moi, est la récente chronique de Maurice Blanchot sur L'Innommable, dans la NRF. Mais vous saurez vous-même, mieux que moi, faire le choix qui s'impose.[4]

Je suis flatté que vous envisagiez de me consacrer le prochain numéro de votre Morgenblatt. Je viens de lire, avec un réel plaisir, votre Weg zu Proust.[5]

441

Croyez, cher Monsieur Suhrkamp, à mes sentiments d'amitié
et d'estime.

s/

Samuel Beckett

TLS; 1 leaf, 1 side; Fehsenfeld collection.

9th January 1954   6 Rue des Favorites
                                              Paris 15

Dear Mr Suhrkamp

Thank you for your letter of the 5th January, and for your wishes.
My own to you, warmly.[1]

Naturally I was disappointed that your plan to publish the three
texts in a single volume could not be carried through. But I quite
understand your reasons, and defer to them.[2] I did at first think of
suggesting to you an overall title (still to be found) for the three books,
with each having its number in the sequence. But on further reflection, this work is a complete whole only in so far as one takes for
granted the impossibility of going on. That, alas, is my feeling, but
one never knows. Just as one might locate the point of departure
in *Murphy.*

I am glad that you like Mr Franzen's translation so much. I am
impatient to be able to read it. I can well imagine that he does not
want to go any further. For what follows, Mr Tophoven does indeed
seem the right man.[3]

I saw Monsieur Lindon today. He has received your letter, and
will shortly be sending you the reviews that you need. On *Molloy*
Maurice Nadeau and Georges Bataille seem to me the best. I also
liked Nadeau's general critique (I forget what in). But the big thing,
for me, is the recent piece by Maurice Blanchot on *L'Innommable*,
in the *NNRF*. But you will know better than I the right choice to
make.[4]

I am flattered that you are thinking of devoting the next issue of
your *Morgenblatt* to me. I have just read, with real pleasure, your *Weg
zu Proust.*[5]

442

With my warmest good wishes
Samuel Beckett

1   In his letter of 5 January, Peter Suhrkamp* (1891–1959) sent greetings for the New Year which he hoped would be productive for their work together (Suhrkamp).

2   Peter Suhrkamp had hoped to publish the German translations of *Molloy*, *Malone meurt*, and *L'Innommable* in a single volume. Erich Franzen, the translator of *Molloy*, was not in a position to translate the other novels. In his letter of 5 January, Suhrkamp noted that it would be helpful to publish *Molloy* quickly in order to take advantage of the interest stimulated by the productions of *Warten auf Godot*.

3   In his letter of 5 January, Suhrkamp wrote: "Ich arbeitete sie in der Festzeit durch und mir scheint, dass sie ihm ungewöhnlich gut gelungen ist. Sie wirkt nicht wie eine Übersetzung und hat meines Erachtens vor allem den Sprachrhythmus getroffen." (I worked through it over the holidays, and it seems to me that he managed it exceptionally well. It does not seem like a translation and, to my mind, captures especially the rhythm of the language.)

4   Suhrkamp wrote in his letter of 5 January that he wished to prepare a Samuel Beckett special edition of the *Morgenblatt für Freunde der Literatur*, the house journal of Suhrkamp Verlag. In it he would publish "die grösseren und wesentlicheren Kritiken und Aufsätze, die in Paris über Sie erschienen sind" (the longer and more important reviews and articles published in Paris about you), especially related but not limited to *Molloy*. He intended to ask Elmar Tophoven to translate these.

Maurice Nadeau, "Samuel Beckett, ou: En avant, vers nulle part!"; Maurice Nadeau, "Samuel Beckett, l'humour et le néant," *Mercure de France* 312 (1 August 1951) 693–697. Georges Bataille, "Le silence de Molloy," *Critique*, 387–396. Maurice Blanchot, "Où maintenant? Qui maintenant?" *NNRF* 2.10 (October 1953) 678–686.

5   The *Morgenblatt für Freunde der Literatur* 5 (1954), was devoted to SB. The Proust special issue of the *Morgenblatt für Freunde der Literatur* 4 (1953), published Peter Suhrkamp's essay "Mein Weg zu Proust" (1–2).

PAMELA MITCHELL
NEW YORK

12.1.54   <u>Paris</u>
My dear Pamela

Glad to have your 2 letters and to hear about all your diversions. I am stuck here until end of this week at latest I hope. Then a few days only at Ussy. Then perhaps to Zurich with old <u>Godot</u> and thence to Geneva to see friends.[1] But more likely shall renounce at last minute.

Nice Xmas card from H.L.O. That was nice of him.[2]

Yes, I'm gloomy, but I always am. That's one of the numerous reasons you shouldn't have anything to do with me. More than gloomy, melancholy mad.

Can't write a word, its awful. I'll have to write something on Jack Yeats who is having a big exhibition here next month – his first in Paris. I'm looking forward to it enormously, haven't seen anything since 1950. But dreading having to write about it.

What do you mean by "doubt that it was mittens". Please elaborate. Don't forget you're addressing yourself to 10 stone (approx.) of professional stupidity.[3]

Read 2 plays in MS by Alberti and Ionesco. Neither comes off exactly.[4] Saw the Spanish translator of mine. Esperando G! Now it has to be shown to the Bishop of Madrid![5] It's still going here, and is to carry on till mid February. Last time I went I ended up under the seat, moaning. The trousers didn't come down at end. Technical accident. That finished me.

Continue to gallivant. Hope you enjoyed Sleepy Hollow and that the ice wasn't too thin.[6]

German translation of Molloy coming in. English do. to get on with with Bowles. French translation of Watt to correct. Spanish translation of Godot to decipher. Proofs of English do. coming in. German Malone to begin. Article on Yeats. J'y laisserai la peau et les os. Ce sera toujours ça.[7]

Ate canard à l'orange at the Iles Marquises, under the trout aquarium. Why don't you take up your quarters at the Montalembert?[8]

Love and succedanea[9]

Sam

Going to Cirque Médrano this evening with Lucky, to see Buster Keaton.[10]

ALS; 3 leaves, 3 sides; UoR, BIF, MS 5060.

1 SB may be referring to Pamela Mitchell's letter of 24 November 1953 and her undated letter before 12 January 1954 (UoR, BIF, MS 5060). Roger Blin directed the French production of *En attendant Godot* at the Schauspielhaus in Zurich from 25 January 1952, and then directed *Warten auf Godot* there with Erwin Parker, Walter Richter, Fred Tanner, and Wolfgang Wahl in the cast. The German production opened

at the Schauspielhaus on 25 February 1954 (SB to Pamela Mitchell, 28 February 1954, UoR, BIF, MS 5060; "Französisches Theater: 'En attendant Godot,'" *Neue Zürcher Zeitung* 27 January 1954: 8; "Zürcher Kalendarblatt," *Neue Zürcher Zeitung* 24 February 1954: n.p.).

2 Harold L. Oram.

3 In her undated letter before 12 January 1954, Pamela Mitchell wrote: "As for Mr. Swift's cold hands, wonder what Stella thought? Doubt that it was mittens" (UoR, BIF, MS 5060).

4 It is not known which plays SB may have read by Eugène Ionesco and Rafael Alberti (1902–1999). Ionesco's *Amédée ou comment s'en débarrasser* (*Amédée, or How to Get Rid of It*) was published in 1954. Alberti wrote *El adefesio* (1944; *The Disaster*); his later play was *Noche de guerra en el Museo del Prado* (1956; *A Night of War in the Prado Museum*).

5 Trino Martínez Trives (d. 2009) saw *En attendant Godot* when it opened in Paris and prepared the Spanish translation (Trino Martínez Trives, "Mi versión de *Esperando a Godot* y su estreno en España," *Primer Acto: Revista Española del Teatro* 1 [April 1957] 15–16; Samuel Beckett, *Esperando a Godot*, tr. Trino Martínez Trives, *Primer Acto: Revista Española del Teatro* 1 [April 1957] 21–45). SB omits the "a" in *Esperando a Godot*.

6 In her undated letter before 12 January, Mitchell describes her holiday activities and her plan to go to "'Sleepy Hollow' country near Tarrytown on the Hudson for skating on a remote lake."

7 *Molloy* was translated into German by Erich Franzen; *Molloy* was translated into English by Patrick Bowles with SB; *Watt* was translated into French by Daniel Mauroc, but not published (see 12 November 1953, n. 1, and Daniel Mauroc to SB, 7 September 1968, IMEC, Beckett, Boîte 4, S. Beckett Correspondance 1967–1968). The German translation of *Malone meurt* was by Elmar Tophoven.

"J'y laisserai la peau et les os. Ce sera toujours ça." (It will be the death of me. Well, that's always something.)

8 When Mitchell was last in Paris on behalf of Harold L. Oram, she stayed at the Hôtel Montalembert, Paris 7 (Knowlson, *Damned to Fame*, 361).

9 "Succedanea" (Lat., and the like).

10 SB went with Jean Martin (Lucky) to the Cirque Medrano, located at 63 Boulevard Rochechouart, to see the variety program of clowns and musical acts that included an exclusive performance by Buster Keaton with his wife Eleanor Keaton (née Norris, 1918–1998). The program opened on 8 January 1954 (Cirque Medrano 1954 program, www.takkinen.se/BusterKeaton/, accessed on 20 January 2010).

JEROME LINDON, EDITIONS DE MINUIT
PARIS

20/1/54   Ussy

Mon cher Jérôme

Merci de votre lettre et d'avoir envoyé les coupures. Le vieux Peter sera content et vous les renverra sûrement au complet.[1]

445

Pour M. & C[.] je suis désolé que vous preniez ça au sérieux. Je ne pourrais vraiment pas supporter que ce texte soit divulgué de mon simili-vivant. Il peut toujours avoir sa place, si vous y tenez, dans un volume à intituler <u>Merdes Posthumes</u>, avec tous les faux départs par exemple (pas à confondre avec les textes pour rien) et ceux à venir (j'en ai déjà un autre en bonne voie). L'idée de <u>Watt</u> déjà m'empourpre jusqu'aux os. Si on le réservait aussi pour les M.P?[2]

Je corrige les épreuves de <u>Godot</u> en anglais. Elles sont excellentes. La traduction espagnole est exécrable, pleine de fautes et d'ommissions. Il va falloir que je revoie le mec avant son départ à la fin du mois.[3]

Le 2me négundo est en place depuis hier. Ayant vu l'autre prunus, invisible à dix pas, que l'architecte veut m'offrir, j'ai commandé pour le trou creusé par vous un marronnier rouge. J'ai trouvé le cèdre faisant avec la terre un angle de 30°. Le vent. Il va sûrement crever.

Je serai encore là dimanche. Si ça vous dit de venir . . .

Meilleures amitiés à tous les deux[4] s/ <u>Sam</u>

TLS; 1 leaf, 1 side; IMEC, Beckett, Boîte 1, S. Beckett, Correspondance – Divers, 1950–1956.

20/1/54   Ussy

My dear Jérôme

Thank you for your letter and for sending the cuttings. Old Peter will be pleased and will certainly return them all.[1]

For *Mercier et Camier* I am very sorry that you are taking it seriously. I really could not bear it if that text were released in my imitation lifetime. It can always take its place, if you really want it, in a volume to be entitled *Posthumous Droppings*, together with all the false starts for example (not to be confused with the texts for nothing) and those still to come (I already have another one well on the way). The idea of *Watt* already makes me go purple right down to the bones. What about keeping it too for the *PD*?[2]

I am correcting the proofs of *Godot* in English. They are excellent. The Spanish translation is execrable, full of mistakes and omissions. I shall have to see the bloke before he leaves at the end of the month.[3]

The 2nd negundo has been in place since yesterday. Having seen the other prunus, invisible at ten feet, that the architect wants to offer me, I have ordered for the hole dug by you a red horse chestnut. I found the cedar standing at an angle of 30°. The wind. It is bound to die.

I shall still be here on Sunday. If you feel like coming . . .

All best to you both.[4] Sam

1   Peter Suhrkamp requested French reviews of *Molloy* to consider for publication in the Beckett special issue of the *Morgenblatt für Freunde der Literatur* 5. In his letter to SB of 19 January, Lindon reported that he had sent all the reviews to Suhrkamp.

2   Lindon wrote to SB: "J'ai lu Mercier et Camier que je trouve rudement bon. Verriez-vous un inconvénient à ce que nous signions dès maintenant un contrat pour ce livre qui paraîtrait après Watt?" (I've read *Mercier and Camier*, which I thought just great. Would you see any reason why we shouldn't sign a contract straight away, so that this book could come out after *Watt*?) (IMEC, Beckett, Boîte 1, S. Beckett, Correspondance – Divers, 1950–1956.)

3   Trino Martínez Trives: 12 January 1954, n. 5.
SB adds an extra "m" to "omissions."

4   The closing line is handwritten.

BARNEY ROSSET, GROVE PRESS
NEW YORK

22/1/54   6 Rue des Favorites
                                          Paris 15
                                          Ussy-sur-Marne[1]

My dear Barney

Thanks for your letter received to-day. The galleys have just gone off, by air mail. I found them quite excellent and nine tenths of the corrections are author's pentimenti. In my letter to Mr. Turner I made one or two suggestions regarding set-up. But I leave it entirely to you to adopt them or not.[2]

The photo that so impressed me is of the very end of Act 1 – the tree, the moon and Vladimir drawing Estragon after him, all very spectral. You can't mistake it.[3]

I don't know what the Lindon business is about, it's the first I've heard of it. I'll find out next week when I get back to Paris. There must certainly be some misunderstanding. Lindon appreciates perfectly that L'Innommable cannot appear prior to or independently of Molloy and Malone. As far as I remember you have no contract with us so far covering L'Innommable, and I imagine this is what he must be driving at. I'll let you know as soon as I get it clear.[4]

My convention with Merlin concerns Molloy only and I do not intend to extend it to the other works for the moment.

Have just read the Spanish so-called translation of Godot. Bad. German ditto of Molloy is coming in for revision (pretty shaky from the extracts I have seen) and I begin on Malone in German with the translator of Godot, in Paris fortunately. Then there's Bowles. Sick of all this old vomit and despair more and more of ever being able to puke again.[5]

By the way, 2 ms in L'Innommable, in case you have to use the French title anywhere. It's a mistake the French themselves sometimes make.

I hope to enjoy some day your East Hampton hospitality. Who knows.[6]

With best wishes to you both

yours

s/ Sam Beckett

TLS; 1 leaf, 2 sides; NSyU. Previous publication: Beckett, "Letters to Barney Rosset," *The Review of Contemporary Fiction*, 68.

1　SB handwrites: "Ussy-sur-Marne."

2　SB replies to Barney Rosset's letter of 16 January 1953 [*for* 1954] (NSyU). Rosset knew that the proofs had been sent to SB, but he had not himself seen them.

Howard Turner (b. 1918), Office Manager at Grove Press from 1953 to autumn 1955.

3　Rosset wrote that he hoped Grove had selected the correct photo for the cover image of *Waiting for Godot*. They had.

4 Rosset wrote that Lindon "seems to be pressing me to go ahead with l'INNOMMABLE now, and not to wait for the completion of MOLLOY and MALONE MEURT."

5 On 21 January 1954, SB wrote to A. J. Leventhal that the Spanish translation by Trino Martínez Trives was "full of mistakes & omissions and unjustifiable liberties" (TxU, Leventhal collection). SB expects Franzen's translation of *Molloy* into German; he intends to work with Tophoven on the German translation of *Malone meurt*; and he continues to collaborate with Patrick Bowles on the English translation of *Molloy*.

6 Barney and Loly Rosset had just moved to a new home in East Hampton, Long Island.

PETER SUHRKAMP, SUHRKAMP VERLAG
FRANKFURT

le 23 Janvier 1954   6 Rue des Favorites Paris
                                            15°

Cher Dr Suhrkamp

Merci de votre lettere [*for* lettre] du 19 courant. Vous aurez maintenant reçu les extraits de presse. J'espère que vous y trouverez de quoi alimenter votre bulletin.

J'ai regardé la liste des passages litigieux fournie par le Dr Franzen. Il a mal compris un certain nombre de choses. Qu'il ne voie pas là l'ombre d'un reproche, ce sont des passages très peu clairs. J'attends d'avoir lu son texte en entier (je ne l'ai pas encore reçu) pour vous adresser des éclaircissements susceptibles de l'aider.[1]

En effet, ça m'intéresserait vivement de lire l'article de Günther Anders et je vous remercie d'avoir fait le nécessaire pour qu'on me l'envoie.[2]

Recevez, cher Dr Suhrkamp, l'assurance de mes sentiments amicaux et dévoués.

Samuel Beckett

TLcc; 1 leaf, 1 side; Suhrkamp and Fehsenfeld collection.

23rd January 1954   6 Rue des Favorites Paris
15°

Dear Dr Suhrkamp

Thank you for your letter of 19th January. By now you will have received the press cuttings. I hope that you will find in them something for your bulletin.

I have looked at the list of unresolved passages from Dr Franzen. He has misunderstood a certain number of things. Let him not see in that even the shadow of a reproach; these are very obscure passages. I shall wait till I have his whole text (I have not yet received it) before sending you clarifications that may help him.[1]

I would indeed be greatly interested to read the article by Günther Anders, and thank you for arranging for it to be sent to me.[2]

Believe me to be

    Yours sincerely

    Samuel Beckett

---

1 In his letter to SB of 19 January, Peter Suhrkamp indicated that he had not yet received the reviews from Editions de Minuit, and that he was sending a carbon copy of Erich Franzen's German translation of *Molloy*, as well as Franzen's list of translation problems (this list appears with SB's response of 28 January 1954, below).

2 Günther Anders, "Sein ohne Zeit: Zu Becketts Stück *En attendant Godot*," *Neue Schweizer Rundschau* 9 (January 1954) 526–540.

ERICH FRANZEN
MUNICH

28th January 1954   6 Rue des Favorites
Paris 15°

Dear Dr Franzen

Herewith suggestions bearing on your list of queries. I hope you will find them of some help. The German is of course quite tentative and intended only to serve as a point of departure for yours.

The complete text has arrived and I am reading it. Even a rapid collation with the original will take longer than I thought, at least a fortnight I am afraid. I am noting in red ink on the MS itself such variants as occur to me. I think you will agree this is the simplest method.

My impression so far is of a quite excellent translation.

Yours sincerely

s/

(Samuel Beckett)

1) <u>non-sens cul et sans issue.</u> Cul is here used as adjective.	eine [*for* ein] unflätiger (widerwärtiger) auswegloser Unsinn[1]
2) <u>a vant [for avant] le fracas des colles</u>	bevor der unauflösbare Lärm ausbricht/bevor der Lärm ausbricht, der keine Antwort duldet.[2]
3) <u>poliment perplexe</u>	in meinem offenbar erstaunten Inneren[3]
4) <u>mimétique</u>	Chamäleon[4]
5) <u>coup de gueule</u>	Schrei[5]
6) <u>comme d'ordures de saints le</u> [*for* la] <u>flamme</u> = comme la flamme est peuplée d'ordures et de saints.	manchmal ausgefüllt, wie das Sc[h]mutz brennende Heilige umhüllende (an Heiligen auflodernde) Feuer.[6]
7) <u>Trahissons, trahissons la traître pensée</u>	Betrügen wir, betrügen wir, das trügerische Denken[7]
8) <u>et le monde meurt aussi, lourdement, lâchement nommé</u>	die mit Namen feige belastete Welt abstirbt / die Welt abstirbt, feige mit Namen belastet[8]
9) <u>la longue sonate des Cadavres</u>	die lange Sonate der Leichen[9]
10) <u>si vous vous en connaissez</u>	wenn Ihr [*for* ihr] von solchen Leuten Kenntnis habt[10]

451

11) proprement ineffable etc.

ja, ganz unaussprechlich war sie,
die Bedürfnislosigkeit an der
ich zu Grunde ging[11]

12) Je m'entends dicter etc.

und höre von einer erstarrten
Welt reden, die etc./und die
Stimme einer erstarrten, aus
dem Gleichgewicht geratenen
Welt, dringt auf mich ein[12]

13) pour vous livrer etc.

um euch den tiefsten Grund meines
Entsetzens zu enthüllen[13]

14) questions de basse pointure

hoch über allem primitiven
Suchen nach der richtigen
Schuhnummer[14]

15) oscillant en rase-mottes

dicht über dem Erdboden
einherschwankte[15]

16) autant de tarauds etc

lauter Löcher in dem Fass der
Geheimnisse[16]

17) m'étendre sur lui

mich näher mit ihm zu befassen[17]

18) les souris etc

Das Lächeln etc ... aber man
braucht ein wenig Abstand
dazu[18]

19) innombrable

vielfältiges[19]

20) à ce point de vue etc.

Und in dieser Hinsicht war mir
meine Unterlegenheit, in [for
im] Vergleich zu meinen
anderen Bekannten (meine[n]
anderen Bekannten gegenüber),
sehr deutlich bewusst[20]

TLS; 1 leaf, 1 side; *enclosure*, 2 leaves, 2 sides: typed list of suggestions responding to the questions posed by Franzen sent to SB with Peter Suhrkamp's letter of 19 January 1954; Mannheimer collection. Previous publication, "Samuel Beckett and Erich Franzen:

Correspondence on Translating MOLLOY," *Babel* 3 (Spring 1984) 23–35. The carbon copy of the TMS with SB's markings has not been found.

1 Because this letter deals with language issues of French to German, and not of either language to English, exceptionally, no translations are given in the notes. The French and the German suggestions are, in any case, "notes towards" a translation. Page references are given for the passages at issue in the French original (Minuit), the English translation by Patrick Bowles with the author (Grove), and the final German text as translated by Erich Franzen (Suhrkamp). A full account is given by Franzen in "Samuel Beckett and Erich Franzen," *Babel*, 23–35.
Minuit, 17; Grove, 16; Suhrkamp, 21–22.

2 Minuit, 20; Grove, 19; Suhrkamp, 26.

3 Minuit, 20; Grove, 18; Suhrkamp, 26.

4 Minuit, 43; Grove, 39; Suhrkamp, 59.

5 Minuit, 39; Grove, 35; Suhrkamp, 53.

6 Minuit, 40; Grove, 36; Suhrkamp, 55.

7 Minuit, 40; Grove, 36; Suhrkamp, 55.

8 Minuit, 46; Grove, 41; Suhrkamp, 63.

9 Minuit, 46; Grove, 41; Suhrkamp, 63.

10 Minuit, 50; Grove, 45; Suhrkamp, 69.

11 Minuit, 50; Grove, 45; Suhrkamp, 69–70.

12 Minuit, 59; Grove, 53; Suhrkamp, 82.

13 Minuit, 89; Grove, 79; Suhrkamp, 124.

14 Minuit, 87; Grove, 78; Suhrkamp, 122.

15 Minuit,101; Grove, 89; Suhrkamp, 141.

16 Minuit, 192; Grove, 170; Suhrkamp, 267.

17 Minuit, 246; Grove, 217; Suhrkamp, 342.

18 Minuit, 255; Grove, 226; Suhrkamp, 355.

19 Minuit, 262; Grove, 232; Suhrkamp, 365.

20 Minuit, 263; Grove, 233; Suhrkamp, 366.

ROGER BLIN
ZURICH

7.2.54   Paris
Cher Roger,

Content d'avoir de tes nouvelles. Ça ne doit pas être commode pour toi. Tu finiras par savoir l'allemand. J'espère que ça t'intéresse quand

453

même et que le changement t'a fait du bien. Il y a peu de chances que je vienne à Zurich. Mais il est possible que Suzanne y aille, elle a envie de bouger.[1]

Suis passé très tard au théâtre l'autre soir, à temps pour apprécier Lucien Raimbourg au comble de sa composition, buste parallèle au sol et guibolles bloquées. Il n'y a plus beaucoup de monde à présent. Et Amédée est loin d'être prêt. Faudrait que Jean s'arrête lundi.[2]

Dommage que tu ne sois pas là pour l'exposition gratis & formidable. J'y ai rencontré Rivoallan plus libé barbu que jamais.[3]

Suis allé voir La Soirée des Proverbes, sur invitation, ce qui m'a empêché de partir avant la fin.[4]

As-tu vu Giorgio Joyce? Et ce sculpteur Lipsi que tu connais je crois. Son adresse à tout hasard:

Zürichstrasse 36

Goldbach

Zürich[5]

Je travaille tous les jours avec Tophoven, à corriger la traduction allemande de Molloy. Abrutissant au possible.

Pedimus de tes nouvelles bientôt.[6]

Affectueusement de nous deux

Sam

ALS; 2 leaves, 2 sides; IMEC, Blin.

7.2.54   Paris

Dear Roger

Glad to hear from you. It can't be all that easy for you. You'll end up knowing German. I hope all the same that it interests you, and that the change is doing you good. There's not much chance of my coming to Zurich. But it may be that Suzanne will go; she's keen to get away.[1]

Looked in at the theatre the other evening, in time to enjoy Lucien Raimbourg at the high point of his performance, torso parallel to the stage, legs blocked rigid. Not all that many people now. And *Amédée* is a long way from being ready. Jean would have to stop on Monday.[2]

Pity you're not here for the tremendous – and free – exhibition. I met Rivoallan at it, more the bearded liberator than ever.[3]

Went to see *La Soirée des proverbes*, by invitation, which stopped me from leaving before the end.[4]

Have you seen Giorgio Joyce? And that sculptor Lipsi whom I think you know. His address, just in case:

Zürichstrasse 36

Goldbach

Zürich[5]

I'm working every day with Tophoven, correcting the German translation of *Molloy*. Utterly mind-numbing.

More news soon, pedimus.[6]

Love from us both

Sam

1 Blin directing *Warten auf Godot* at the Schauspielhaus in Zurich: 12 January 1954, n. 1.

2 Lucien Raimbourg returned to play his original role as Vladimir in January 1954 ("Nouvelles," *Le Monde* 8 January 1954: 8). Jean Martin played Lucky.

Eugène Ionesco's play *Amédée, ou Comment s'en débarrasser* (1954; *Amédée, or How to Get Rid of It*).

3 SB refers to the recently opened exhibition of paintings by Jack B. Yeats at the Galerie Beaux-Arts, in the Hôtel de Wailly, 57 Rue La Boétie, in an extended space that fronted on the interior courtyard of 140 Rue du Faubourg Saint-Honoré, Paris 8 (Joseph Baillio, "Wildenstein, Paris, New York and Old Master French Art," in *The Arts of France from François 1er to Napoléon 1er* [New York: Wildenstein, 2005] 23).

Anatole Rivoallan (1886–1976) was a specialist in Irish literature and a translator.

4 *La Soirée des proverbes* (1954) by Georges Schehadé (1905–1989), with music by Maurice Ohana (1914–1992), had been selected by Jean-Louis Barrault to open his Petit Théâtre Marigny on 30 January 1954. Schehadé's play was published in *Les Lettres Nouvelles* 1.9 (November 1953) 1126–1161.

5 Giorgio Joyce lived in Zurich. Polish-born French sculptor Morice Lipsi (1898–1986).

6 "Pedimus" (Lat., we beg).

ERICH FRANZEN

MUNICH

February 8th 1954   6 Rue des Favorites

Paris 15°

Dear Dr Franzen

I am sending you to-day c/o Suhrkamp Verlag the first part of your text with my corrections and suggestions. These latter are made with all the due humility of one whose German is very imperfect.[1]

I like your translation very much indeed.

The second part will follow in a few days.

> Yours very sincerely
>
> s/
>
> Samuel Beckett

?TLS; 1 leaf, 1 side; original not consulted. Previous publication, "Samuel Beckett and Erich Franzen" *Babel*, 26.

1 The carbon copy of this section of the manuscript marked by SB has not been found.

BARNEY ROSSET, GROVE PRESS
NEW YORK

February 11th 1954   6 Rue des Favorites

Paris 15e

My dear Barney

Thanks for your friendly and understanding letter of Feb. 5th. You will have seen mine to Mr Turner thanking him for the jacket. The Dönitz photo makes a marvellous front to the book. If the little changes can't be made, no matter.[1]

I don't make a cent of additional income out of the translations, except that of Godot. I'm compelled to do it by a foolish feeling of protectiveness towards the work. Am just finishing revision of German Molloy, well done I think, but with many mistakes and an irritating way of turning the unusual into the usual so that it won't read like a translation! Also beginning to work on Malone with German translator of Godot, a very nice man who lives here. Had the Spanish Godot too, that was awful.[2]

I thought myself of trying again in English, but it's only evading the issue like everything else I try. If there was a head and a rock I'd rather beat that against this than start the old fake stravaguing again in another proxy. It's hard to go on with everything loathed and repudiated as soon as formulated, and in the act of formulation, and before formulation. I'll soon be assembling a queer little book for Lindon, three longish short stories, the very first writing in French and of which one at least seems to me all right, and the thirteen or fourteen very short abortive texts (Textes pour Rien) that express the failure to implement the last words of L'Innommable: "il faut conti-nuer, je vais continuer." He also wanted to publish Mercier et Camier, the first "novel" in French and of which the less said the better, but I had to refuse.[3] At the moment I have a "man" crawling along a corridor in the rock in the dark, but he's due to vanish any day now.[4] Of course there's no reason why it would start now or ever for that matter. I'm horribly tired and stupefied, but not yet tired and stupefied enough. To write is impossible but not yet impossible enough. That's how I cod myself these days.

All the best to you both.

s/ Sam. Beckett

TLS; 1 leaf, 1 side; NSyU. Previous publication, Beckett, "Letters to Barney Rosset," *The Review of Contemporary Fiction*, 68–69.

1   On 5 February, Barney Rosset had written sympathetically about SB's difficulty in starting new work: "Maybe the trying is what does the stopping" (NSyU).

SB's letter to Howard Turner has not been found.

2   Rosset had written on 5 February: "All of this translating – it is nice for us, and it means some additional income for you – but it must surely inhibit new feelings from rising to the surface."

Erich Franzen's translation of *Molloy*; Elmar Tophoven's German translation of *Malone meurt*; Trino Martínez Trives's Spanish translation *Esperando a Godot*.

3   SB refers to *Nouvelles et Textes pour rien*. There were thirteen texts in *Textes pour rien*. The final words of *L'Innommable*: "il faut continuer, je ne peux pas continuer, je vais continuer" are translated by SB as "you must go on, I can't go on, I'll go on" (Beckett, *L'Innommable*, 213; Beckett, *The Unnamable* [Grove Press] 179).

SB's refusal to publish *Mercier et Camier*: 20 January 1954.

4   The text by SB has not been positively identified. A much revised draft of a prose work in French dates from this period: "16.1.54, 17.1.54" (TCD, MS 4662, 6r–12r; "Cumulative TCD Catalogue," in Matthijs Engelberts, Everett Frost, and Jane Maxwell, eds., *Notes Diverse Holo: Catalogues of Beckett's Reading Notes and Other Manuscripts at Trinity College Dublin, with Supporting Essays*, Special Issue, *Samuel Beckett Today/Aujourd'hui* 16 [2006] 184); it is cursorily described as illegible by Cohn in *A Beckett Canon*, 209–210.

ERICH FRANZEN
MUNICH

17th February 1954   6 Rue des Favorites
                                                         Paris 15°
Dear Dr Franzen

1) This passage is suggested (a) by a passage in the Ethics of
Geulincx where he compares human freedom to that of a man, on
board a boat carrying him irresistibly westward, free to move eastward
within the limits of the boat itself, as far as the stern; and (b) by Ulysses'
relation in Dante (Inf. 26) of his second voyage (a mediaeval tradition) to
and beyond the Pillars of Hercules, his shipwreck and death. I do not
understand very well your difficulty in reconciling this passage with
"Das ist eine grosse Freiheit für jemanden etc." I imagine a member of
the crew who does not share the adventurous spirit of Ulysses and is at
least at liberty to crawl homewards (nach Osten) along the brief deck.[1]

2) Coenesthésie or cénesthésie has nothing whatever to do with
kinesthésique. The OED definition is: "the general sense of existence
arising from the sum of bodily impressions." Henle: "c'est le chaos
non débrouillé des sensations qui de tous les points du corps sont sans
cesse transmises au sensorium." Wundt: "wir rechnen zur Klasse der
Gemeinempfindungen alle Empfindungen[,] die einen ausschliesslich subjektiven Charakter bewahren und dadurch wesentlich
Bestandteile des Gemeingefühls bilden". I do not see why you cannot
use Coenesthesis or Gemeinempfindung or Gemeingefühl if you prefer. They are the corresponding German philosophical terms.[2]

3) Obviously a Neigung cannot have Bewusstsein. But neither can a
disposition se savoir velléitaire. Perhaps the absurdity is less tolerable
in German than in French and if you prefer to circumvent it in the way
you suggest, do so by all means. I do hope you appreciate that at least
three quarters of my interventions are suggestions of the most tentative kind and that you are absolutely free to adopt or reject them.[3]

4) I prefer Gegend to Gebiet precisely because it is vaguer (limits
never determined by Molloy) and somehow less administrative. Gebiet is
a Moran word, not a Molloy word. But here again the choice lies with you.[4]

You will I hope by now have safely received Part II which I sent directly to your Munich address.

Do not hesitate to call on me if you think I can be of any further help to you.

Yours sincerely

s/ Samuel Beckett

Thank you also for your letter of Feb. 10th. Your remarks on my work interest me greatly and I look forward to reading your introduction in the Merkur.[5]

TLS; 1 leaf, 1 side; Mannheimer collection. Previous publication, "Samuel Beckett and Erich Franzen," *Babel* 28.

1 SB responds to Franzen's letter of 12 February ("Samuel Beckett and Erich Franzen," *Babel*, 27–28).

SB notes a passage from Geulincx's annotations to his *Ethics*: "Just as a ship carrying a passenger with all speed towards the west in no way prevents the passenger from walking towards the east, so the will of God, carrying all things, impelling all things with inexorable force, in no way prevents us from resisting His will (as much as is in our power) with complete freedom" (Arnold Geulincx, *Ethics, with Samuel Beckett's Notes*, ed. Han van Ruler, Anthony Uhlmann, and Martin Wilson, tr. Martin Wilson [Leiden and Boston: Brill, 2006] 182, 317).

In his letter of 12 February, Franzen said that he did not understand SB's correction: "entlang der kurzen Brücke nach Osten zu schlichen (schleichen?)" (to creep along the short bridge eastward). "I do not understand the meaning of this, especially not in connection with the following 'Das ist eine grosse Freiheit für jemanden, der nicht die Seele eines Pioniers hat'" (That is a great freedom for someone who does not have the soul of a pioneer) ("Beckett and Franzen," *Babel*, 27).

2 SB cites Friedrich Henle (1809–1885), a German anatomist and pathologist who defines "coenaesthesis" or "general sensibility" as "C'est le chaos non débrouillé des sensations qui de tous les points du corps sont sans cesse transmises au sensorium" ("It is the not yet unravelled chaos of the sensations incessantly transmitted from every point of the body to the sensorium") (Friedrich Henle, *Allgemeine Anatomie* [1841] 728, cited in Théodule-Armand Ribot, *Les Maladies de la personnalité* [Paris: Felix Alcan, 1885] 23; Théodule-Armand Ribot, *Diseases of Personality*, ed. Daniel N. Robinson, Significant Contributions to the History of Psychology 1750–1920 [Washington, DC: University Publications of America, 1977] 19–20).

SB also cites Wilhelm Maximillian Wundt (1845–1920), an important figure in early experimental psychology: "wir rechnen zur Klasse der Gemeinempfindungen alle Empfindungen[,] die einen ausschliesslich subjektiven Charakter bewahren und dadurch wesentlich Bestandteile des Gemeingefühls bilden" (we include, in the class of common sensations, all sensations that retain an exclusively subjective nature, and, through this, essentially form components of the common feeling) (Wilhelm Wundt, *Grundzüge der physiologischen Psychologie*, II [Leipzig: Wilhelm Engelmann, 1902] 42). SB's citation of the German varies slightly from the original.

In citing Henle and Wundt, it is most likely that SB took the quotations from a philosophical dictionary (one such as André Lalande, *Vocabulaire technique et critique de la philosophie*, I, Société Française de Philosophie [Paris: Librairie Félix Alcan, 1928] 110).
"Coenesthesis/ Gemeinempfindung" (common sensation).
"Gemeingefühl" (common feeling).
In his letter of 12 February, Franzen wrote, "Your correction: 'Coenesthesis/ Gemeinempfindung.' Neither term can be used in German, nor do I know what they mean." After receiving the present letter from SB, Franzen replied on 18 February, explaining further:

> Regarding "Coenesthésie", I simply cannot use the term "Gemeingefühl" (or Gemeinempfindung) for these reasons: first, Hitler's propaganda monopolized the term; second, nobody remembers Wundt's psychology; and third, if such terms which you intend to bear a special meaning, but which to Germans indicate something general (Hitler's Gemeingefühl), are used, the blame will be on the translator. (This last point I have to consider in many instances, where I would prefer to simply stick to your words . . .) ("Samuel Beckett and Erich Franzen," *Babel*, 29.)

3 "Neigung" (inclination) cannot have "Bewusstsein" (consciousness).
"Se savoir velléitaire" (know itself to be indecisive).

4 "Gegend" (area, without specific borders, as in geographic or topographic space); "Gebiet" (area, with borders and limits, often abstracted, as in political jurisdiction or professional expertise).
SB canceled "Malone" and replaced it with "Molloy."

5 In his letter to SB of 10 February 1954, Franzen wrote:

> I am sure you realize that I have to try to make also the somewhat obscure sentences sound well in German. That is to say, I will have to avoid participles and constructions which in German would make the impression of being clumsy, while in French they may even be poetic. ("Samuel Beckett and Erich Franzen," *Babel*, 26.)

Franzen also wrote of how much he admired "the daring and power of your thinking which does not shy from confronting the ultimate consequences of your approach." He regretted that he was not qualified to translate *Malone meurt* and *L'Innommable*, explaining that he would need to consult SB in Paris; this, in view of his modest fee for translations, he could not afford to do.
Franzen's introduction to excerpts from Molloy: "Samuel Beckett: *Molloy*," *Merkur* 8 (March 1954) 239–241.

HANS NAUMANN

MAINZ

le 17 février 1954   6 rue des Favorites
                                                    Paris 15°

Cher Monsieur

Merci de votre lettre du 15 février et de votre travail sur les Irlandais que j'ai lu avec beaucoup d'intérêt.[1]

Je ne demande qu'à vous aider, quoiqu'il me soit très difficile, pour ne pas dire impossible, de parler de moi et de mon travail.

Mes rapports avec Joyce. J'ai fait sa connaissance en 1928, année de mon arrivée à Paris comme lecteur d'anglais à l'Ecole Normale Supérieure. Nos rapports ont été d'ordre purement amical. Je n'ai jamais été son secrétaire. Nous avons très peu parlé lit[t]érature, il n'aimait pas cela, moi non plus. Nous sortions souvent ensemble. Il était pour moi d'une gentillesse et d'une générosité extrêmes. Il me passait un bouquin de temps en temps en me demandant d'y jeter un coup d'oeil et d'y relever les passages susceptibles de l'aider pour la rédaction de Finnegans Wake. J'ai quitté l'Ecole en 1930 (je n'ai jamais été chargé de cours à la Sorbonne sauf, très brièvement, d'un cours de langue anglaise). A partir de ce moment-là jusqu'à mon retour à Paris en 1937 pour m'y installer définitivement, je n'ai plus revu Joyce que fort irrégulièrement. Je l'ai vu pour la dernière fois à Vichy en 1940. Je le considère toujours comme un des plus grands génies littéraires de tous les temps. Mais je crois avoir senti de bonne heure que la chose qui m'appelait et les moyens dont je pouvais disposer étaient pratiquement à l'opposé de sa chose et de ses moyens à lui. Il a eu une très forte influence morale sur moi. Il m'a fait entrevoir, sans le vouloir d'ailleurs le moins du monde, ce que peut signifier: être artiste. Je pense à lui avec une admiration une affection et une reconnaissance sans bornes.[2]

Jusqu'en 1945 j'ai écrit en anglais. Voici la liste de ces écrits.

Whoroscope (poème), Hours Press, Paris. 1930

Proust (essai), Chatto & Windus, London. 1931

More Pricks than Kicks (nouvelles), Chatto & Windus, London. 1934

Echo's Bones & Other Precipitates (poèmes), Hours Press, Paris. 1935

Murphy (roman), Routledge, London. 1938

Watt (roman), Editions Merlin, Paris. 1953[2]

Depuis 1945 je n'écris plus qu'en français. Pourquoi ce changement? Il ne fut pas raisonné. Cela a été pour changer, pour voir, pas plus compliqué que cela, apparemment au moins. Rien à voir en tous cas avec les raisons que vous suggérez. Je ne considère pas l'anglais comme une langue étrangère, c'est bien ma langue. S'il en est une qui m'est parfaitement étrangère, c'est le gaélique. Vous pouvez me ranger dans la triste catégorie de ceux qui, s'ils devaient agir à bon escient, n'agiraient jamais. Ce qui n'empêche pas qu'il puisse y avoir, à ce changement, des raisons urgentes. Moi-même j'en entrevois plusieurs, maintenant qu'il est trop tard pour revenir en arrière. Mais j'aime mieux les laisser dans l'ombre. Je vous donnerai quand même une piste: le besoin d'être mal armé.[3]

Proust. Un court essai sur lui (30.000 mots) a été mon premier ouvrage en prose. Il m'avait été commandé par les éditions Chatto & Windus pour leur série de Dolphin Books. Je m'y suis attaché à suivre les différentes étapes de son expérience clef depuis la madeleine trempée dans l'infusion jusqu'aux pavés de la cour de l'hôtel Guermantes. Depuis cette époque je ne l'ai guère relu. Il m'impressionne et m'agace. Je supporte mal sa manie, entre autres, de vouloir tout ramener à des lois. Je crois que je le juge mal.[4]

Kafka. Je n'ai lu de lui, hormis quelques textes courts, que les trois quarts environ du Château, et cela en allemand, c'est à dire en en perdant beaucoup.[5] Je m'y suis senti chez moi, trop, c'est peut-être cela qui m'a empêché de continuer. Cause instantanément entendue. Je ne me rappelle plus ce que Nadeau à [sic] dit à ce propos.[6] Je me rappelle avoir été gêné par le côté imperturbable de sa démarche. Je me méfie des désastres qui se laissent déposer comme un bilan.

Je n'essaie pas d'avoir l'air réfractaire aux influences. Je constate seulement que j'ai toujours été un piètre lecteur, incurablement distrait, à l'affût d'un ailleurs. Et je crois pouvoir dire sans esprit de paradoxe que les lectures qui m'ont le plus marqué sont celles qui m'y ont le mieux renvoyé, à cet ailleurs.

Je ne connais les travaux ni de Picard ni de Parain. Parmi les livres que j'ai explorés pour Joyce il y avait Beiträge zu einer Kritik der Sprache de Fritz Mauthner qui m'a très fortement impressionné. J'ai souvent eu envie de le relire. Mais il semble introuvable.[7]

De l'Irlande enfin il m'est tout à fait impossible de parler avec retenue. J'ai horreur de ce romantisme-là. Et je n'ai pas eu besoin de boire de la fontaine magique pour supporter de ne pas y vivre.[8]

Je crains que cette lettre ne puisse vous servir à grand'chose. Je vous demanderai en tout cas de bien vouloir la considérer comme confidentielle, autrement dit de ne pas la citer. Si vous avez d'autres questions à me poser comportant des réponses précises, je suis à votre d[i]sposition. Mais quant à dire qui je suis, d'où je viens et ce que je fais, tout cela dépasse vraiment ma compétence.

Croyez, cher Monsieur, à l'assurance de mes sentiments les meilleurs.

Samuel Beckett

TLcc; 2 leaves, 2 sides; Fehsenfeld collection.

17th February 1954   6 Rue des Favorites
                                  Paris 15me

Dear Mr Naumann

Thank you for your letter of 15th February and your piece on the Irish which I read with great interest.[1]

I shall be only too glad to help you, although it is hard, not to say impossible, for me to talk about myself and my work.

My dealings with Joyce. I met him in 1928, the year I came to Paris as lecteur d'anglais at the Ecole Normale Supérieure. Our dealings were entirely those of friends. I was never his secretary. We very seldom talked literature, he didn't like doing it, neither did I. We often went out together. He showed me the greatest kindness and generosity. He would hand me a book from time to time and ask me to have a look at it and pick out passages that might help him with the writing of *Finnegans Wake*. I left the Ecole in 1930 (I never held a lecturing post at the Sorbonne, except, very briefly, on an English language course). From then until I came back to settle in Paris for good in 1937, I had only very occasional meetings with Joyce. I saw him for the last time in Vichy in 1940. I still think of him as one of the greatest literary geniuses of all time. But I believe I felt very early on that the thing that drew me and the means I could call on were virtually the opposite of his thing and his means. He had a very strong moral influence on me. He gave me, without in the least wishing to do so, an insight into what the words "to be an artist" mean. I think of him with unqualified admiration, affection, and gratitude.[2]

Up until 1945 I wrote in English. Here is a list of these writings.

Whoroscope (poem), Hours Press, Paris. 1930

Proust (essay), Chatto & Windus, London. 1931

More Pricks than Kicks (stories), Chatto & Windus, London. 1934

Echo's Bones & Other Precipitates (poems), Hours Press, Paris. 1935

Murphy (novel), Routledge, London. 1938

Watt (novel), Editions Merlin, Paris. 1953[2]

Since 1945 I have written only in French. Why this change? It was not deliberate. It was in order to change, to see, nothing more complicated than that, in appearance at least. In any case nothing to do with the reasons you suggest. I do not consider English a foreign language, it is my language. If there is one that is really foreign to me, it is Gaelic. You may put me in the dismal category of those who, if they had to act in full awareness of what they were doing, would never act. Which does not preclude there being urgent reasons, for this change. I myself can half make out several, now that it is too late to go back. But I prefer to let them stay in the half-light. I will all the same give you one clue: the need to be ill equipped.[3]

Proust. A short essay on him (30,000 words) was my first prose work. It had been commissioned by Chatto & Windus for their series of Dolphin Books. I concentrated on following the different stages of his key experience from the madeleine dipped in tisane to the cobble-stones in the courtyard of the Guermantes' great house. Since that time I have hardly looked at him. He impresses and irritates me. I find it hard to bear his obsessive need, among others, to bring everything back to laws. I think I am a poor judge of him.[4]

Kafka. All I've read of his, apart from a few short texts, is about three-quarters of *The Castle*, and then in German, that is, losing a great deal.[5] I felt at home, too much so – perhaps that is what stopped me from reading on. Case closed there and then. I can't remember now what Nadeau said in this connection.[6] I remember feeling disturbed by the imperturbable aspect of his approach. I am wary of disasters that let themselves be recorded like a statement of accounts.

I am not trying to seem resistant to influences. I merely note that I have always been a poor reader, incurably inattentive, on the look-out for an elsewhere. And I think I can say, in no spirit of paradox, that the reading experiences which have affected me most are those that were best at sending me to that elsewhere.

I do not know the work of either Picard or Parain. Among the books that I explored for Joyce there was *Beiträge zu einer Kritik der Sprache* by Fritz Mauthner which greatly impressed me. I have often wanted to re-read it. But it seems impossible to find.[7]

On Ireland, finally, it is utterly impossible for me to speak with moderation. I loathe that romanticism. And I had no need to drink at the magic fountain to be able to bear living outside it.[8]

I fear this letter may be of little use to you. I shall ask you in any event to be good enough to treat it as confidential, in other words not to quote from it. If you have other questions to ask, questions to which there are precise answers, I am at your disposal. But as for saying who I am, where I come from and what I am doing, all that is quite beyond me.

Yours sincerely

Samuel Beckett

---

1 Hans Naumann (n.d.), a translator and editor of French and Irish literature, wrote a long letter to SB on 15 February 1954 saying that he had responded immediately to *Molloy* in 1951, and had telegraphed Editions de Minuit to obtain the option for German publication (Fehsenfeld collection). He was asked by Suhrkamp to translate the articles of Nadeau, Bataille, and Blanchot (see 9 January 1954, n. 4). In a letter of 1 November 1960, Elmar Tophoven wrote to Max Niedermayer* (1905–1968), founder of Limes Verlag: "Soviel ich weiss, ist Dr. Naumann einer der Entdecker Becketts. Jedenfalls hatte er Dr. Peter Suhrkamp schon früh auf Beckett aufmerksam gemacht." (As far as I know, Dr Naumann was one of Beckett's discoverers. At any rate, he brought Beckett to the attention of Dr Peter Surhkamp very early.) (Deutsches Literaturarchiv Marbach, Limes Verlag collection, Tophoven). It is not known what piece on the Irish Naumann had sent to SB.

Naumann wrote, "Je m'explique: est-il juste, d'après vous, de chercher dans votre oeuvre une tradition irlandaise (malgré l'expression en langue française)" (Let me make myself clear: would it be right to try to find in your work the presence of an Irish tradition [in spite of its being expressed in French]?). Naumann sent SB an essay written for Radio Frankfurt, asking him to look it over, "et de faire des remarques si vous le trouvez faux" (and to comment if you think it mistaken).

2   SB's last meeting with Joyce was on 12 June 1940, as he and Suzanne Deschevaux-Dumesnil made their way south from Paris; Joyce arranged a loan for them from Valery Larbaud.

Echo's Bones was published by Europa Press.

3   In his letter to SB, Naumann wrote:

> Les motifs du changement de langue, quels sont-ils? Je vois un motif tout à fait extérieur. Dans l'impossibilité de lancer une oeuvre littéraire écrite en langue irlandaise au-delà les frontières du petit pays vous vous trouvez, certes, dans la nécessité de choisir une langue étrangère, ou le français ou l'anglais; vous choisissez le français. Mais il doit y avoir quand même une raison plus profonde. Est-ce que vous croyez que la culture française est un fonds plus adéquat pour l'oeuvre? (Just what are the motives for the change of language? I can see one entirely external motive. Given the impossibility of launching an Irish-language work beyond the borders of that small country, you find yourself forced to choose a foreign language: either French or English; you choose French. But there must all the same be a deeper reason. Do you think that French culture is a more adequate base for your work?)

4   SB had not been commissioned by Chatto and Windus to write *Proust*, but submitted it for consideration as a Dolphin Book (see Thursday [? 17 July 1930] to Thomas McGreevy, n. 8).

5   Franz Kafka, *Das Schloss* (1927; *The Castle*). Naumann asked: "Est-ce que l'oeuvre de Kafka a jamais joué un rôle dans votre vie spirituelle" (Has the work of Kafka ever played a part in your spiritual life).

6   SB's writing is linked to Kafka in several early essays by Maurice Nadeau, for example when he writes: "L'aventure, contée avec verve et toute pleine d'un humour quelque peu kafkéen ..." (Adventure, told with verve, rich in a slightly Kafkaesque humour) ("Samuel Beckett ou: En avant, vers nulle part!" *Combat* 12 April 1951: 4). Elsewhere, Nadeau writes: "Rien n'est sûr, sauf le vide et l'erreur, sauf cette course imbécile que tout homme semble condamné à fournir pour rien et qui ressemble quelque peu, comme chez Kafka, à l'effet d'on ne sait quelle malédiction divine" (Nothing is sure but emptiness and error, nothing but this idiotic race that every man seems condemned to engage in for no gain and which seems rather, as in Kafka, to be the effect of some divine curse) ("Samuel Beckett, l'humour et le néant," *Mercure de France*, 694). Nadeau further connects SB with Kafka: "Samuel Beckett ou le droit au silence," *Les Temps Modernes*, 1273-1282, and "La 'Dernière' Tentative de Samuel Beckett," *Les Lettres Nouvelles*, 860-864.

7   Naumann asks about SB's familiarity with the work of Max Picard (1888–1965) and Brice-Aristide Parain (1897–1971), both of whom discuss "silence." Naumann mentions Picard's book *Hitler en nous* (1942; *Hitler in Ourselves*), and Parain's *Recherches sur la nature et les fonctions du langage* (1942; Research into the Nature and Functions of Language) as well as his essays, *L'Embarras du choix* (1947; An Embarrassment of Riches).

SB refers to *Beiträge zu einer Kritik der Sprache*, 3 vols. (1901–1902; *Contributions to a Critique of Language*) by Fritz Mauthner (1849–1923).

8   SB may be referring to the central image of W. B. Yeats's *At the Hawk's Well*.

SB writes "boire de" where one would expect "boire à."

GIAN RENZO MORTEO
TURIN

[after 20 February 1954]
Monsieur[1]

En attendant Godot est mon unique pièce. Les droits pour l'Italie sont toujours disponibles. Je vous autorise par la présente à la traduire pour la revue Questioni.[2]

biographie

1906	Né à Dublin de parents irlandais.
1923–27	Etudes à Trinity College, Dublin.
1928–29	Lecteur d'anglais à l'Ecole Normale Supérieure, Paris.
1930–32	Lecteur de français à Trinity College, Dublin.
1937	S'installe définitivement à Paris.
1945	Commence à écrire en français.

bibliographie

Ouvrages en anglais

1935 [sic]	Proust (Essai) dans: Chatto & Windus, London etc. etc.

Ouvrages en français

1951	Molloy roman
1952	Malone meurt roman
1952	En attendant Godot pièce
1953	L'Innommable roman

Veuillez agréer, etc.

AL draft; 1 leaf, 1 side *on* Dr. Gian Renzo Morteo to SB, 20 February 1954; IMEC, Beckett, Boîte 2, S. Beckett, Edition En attendant Godot 1946–1957.

[after 20th February 1954]

Dear Dr Morteo[1]

Waiting for Godot is my only play. The rights for Italy are still available. I hereby authorise you to translate it for the review *Questioni*.[2]

biography:

1906	Born in Dublin of Irish parents.
1923–27	Studied in Trinity College Dublin.
1928–29	English-language lecteur, Ecole Normale Supérieure, Paris.
1930–32	Lecturer in French, Trinity College Dublin.
1937	Finally settled in Paris.
1945	Began to write in French.

bibliography:

Works in English

1935 [sic]   *Proust* (Essay) in: Chatto & Windus, London etc. etc.

Works in French

1951	*Molloy*	novel
1952	*Malone Dies*	novel
1952	*Waiting for Godot*	play
1953	*The Unnamable*	novel

Yours sincerely etc.

---

1 Gian Renzo Morteo (1924–1989) was a scholar and translator of French drama; from 1954 to 1958, he was affiliated with the journal *Il Dramma*, and from 1955 collaborated with the publisher Einaudi on the series Collana di teatro, eventually preparing numerous volumes; along with his translations into Italian of the work of Adamov, Claudel, Duras, Molière, Schehadé, Tardieu, Vitrac, and Ionesco, he is known for his study *Il teatro popolare in Francia* (1960).

2 *Questioni*, a bimonthly journal of arts and letters; it was founded as *Galleria Arti e Lettere* in 1953, directed by Mario Lattes and Oscar Navarro, but changed its name to *Questioni* in 1954.

Morteo wrote the introduction to "Il Teatro 'nuovo' francese," a special issue of *Questioni* 1.3–4 (July–August 1954) 3–11. This issue published plays by Jean Tardieu, Eugène Ionesco, Arthur Adamov, and Georges Schehadé in French. SB is mentioned only in passing in Morteo's introduction. There is no evidence that he undertook a translation of *En attendant Godot*.

JACQUES PUTMAN

PARIS

Samedi [? mars 1954]

Cher Jacques

J'ai beaucoup aimé votre travail sur Yeats. Vous serait-il possible d'en tirer, ou d'en faire, une page, une page et demie, pour qu'on puisse le présenter, avec les textes très courts de Duthuit, Schneider et moi-même, au[x] Lettres Nouvelles? Il paraît que Saillet dispose de très peu de place pour ce genre d'exercice.[1]

Pourriez-vous me rejoindre lundi prochain un peu avant 3 heures au petit tabac Rue de la Boétie je crois où nous allions après l'exposition? Ensuite nous pourrions passer chez Duthuit essayer d'arranger ça. J'y serai de toute manière.

Amitiés

Sam Beckett

ALS; 1 leaf, 1 side; Porte collection. *Dating*: *AN AH* "March"; prior to the publication of Samuel Beckett, Pierre Schneider, and Jacques Putman, "Hommage à Jack B. Yeats," *Les Lettres Nouvelles* 14 (April 1954) 619–621; Beckett's contribution is reprinted in Beckett, *Disjecta*, 148.

Saturday [? March 1954]

Dear Jacques

I greatly enjoyed your work on Yeats. Would it be possible for you to take out of it, or make it into, a page or a page and a half so that we could present it to *Les Lettres Nouvelles*, along with the very short texts by Duthuit, Schneider and myself? It appears that Saillet has very little space at his disposal for this kind of thing.[1]

Could you join me on Monday next a little before 3 at the little bar-tabac, in the Rue de la Boétie I think, where we went after the exhibition? Then we could go along to Duthuit's to try to set things up. I shall be there in any case.

All best

Sam Beckett

1 SB was organizing publication of critical response to the Jack B. Yeats exhibition in Paris that took place at the Galerie Beaux-Arts in February 1954. Maurice Saillet, Editor of *Les Lettres Nouvelles*, had agreed to include these short essays in the April issue.

THOMAS MACGREEVY

DUBLIN

1.3.54   Paris

My dear Tom

Glad to know you safe home.

Went to Wildenstein's for the 5th or 6th time last Thursday closing day. Waddington was there and seemed quite pleased about everything.[1] As you will have heard the purchase of the Musée d'art moderne of Music in a Marshy Place is, if not yet official, almost a certainty. Though the attendance was not so big and the reactions of critics not so important as we had hoped, nevertheless the word has got round, the work is being talked about and in my own small circle all those whose opinion I value are enormously impressed.[2] Bram van Velde, the most difficult and critical of painters, went at least 10 times and is quite bouleversé. I never saw him in such a state about any living artist. Duthuit also was very enthusiastic and such young violently uncompromising & personal painters as Francis and Riopelle. Also the young critic Pierre Schneider.[3] The best article I saw was by the "Pèlerin Passionné" in Peintre.[4] I have arranged for a little group of Hommages to appear in the April number of the Lettres Nouvelles, the most enterprising literary monthly we have here now. There will be Duthuit, Schneider, perhaps Jacques Putman (a young writer friend of Bram's) and myself. Short texts. I have dreadful difficulty with this form of writing, it is real torture, and spent days before the blank sheet before I could do anything, and the result is no more than the most clumsy of obeisances.[5] But I hope the bowing down is what matters. To prove or defend or describe or situate seem to me all equally superfluous in the presence of such an achievement. Tell Jack Yeats that he has lit a fire that will spread. What we should aim for now is another exhibition next year, in the Musée d'art moderne. Wildenstein's was not the right place.

Thanks for joint card with Frank and Alan. Were you lunching at the airport? The day after you left, I had the Gazette sent to you and hope you received it safely.[6] Suzanne went to Zurich for the première of Godot in German there. Guest producer Roger Blin. She stayed 3 days and seems to have enjoyed herself. Giorgio gave her a great welcome.[7]

It was good being with you again even though too briefly. Perhaps I shall be over in May. Frank writes in better form, but still seems far from his old self. My affectionate remembrance to JBY.

Love ever

Sam

ALS; 2 leaves, 2 sides; *env to* Thomas MacGreevy, Esq, 24 Fitzwilliam Place, Dublin, IRLANDE, *pm* 1-3-54, Paris; TCD, MS 10402/191.

1 The Galerie Beaux-Arts, site of the Jack B. Yeats exhibition, was under the management of the Wildenstein family (Ay-whang Hsia, Wildenstein and Co., Inc., 26 January 2010). Georges Wildenstein (1892–1963) was Editor-in-chief of *Gazette des Beaux-Arts*; his son Daniel Wildenstein (1917–2001) administered the *Gazette* and research projects of the Wildenstein Institute.

Victor Waddington (1907–1981), Jack B. Yeats's Dublin dealer.

2 *Music in a Marshy Place* (Pyle 1133, entitled *Entertainment in a Marshy Woodland*; Musée National d'Art Moderne, *Divertissement dans un bois marécageux*, AM 3300 P) (Pyle, *Jack B. Yeats: A Catalogue Raisonné of the Oil Paintings*, II, 635).

SB wrote to Susan Manning on 6 April: "His exhibition here did not make the stir it should have" (TxU, Beckett collection).

3 Bram van Velde; "bouleversé" (overcome).

American artist Sam Francis (1923–1994); Jean-Paul Riopelle; Pierre Schneider.

4 Le Pèlerin Passionné, "Les Métamorphoses de Jack B. Yeats," *Le Peintre* (15 February 1954) 8; the unidentified writer signs with the title of Jean Moréas's book written in 1891. This essay contrasted Yeats with the Fauves and the Impressionists: "La couleur est pourtant son unique véhicule" (Yet colour is his only vehicle). The writer notes that, although Yeats's point of departure is fable, his paintings are not illustrations or narratives: "Peintre de métamorphoses, Yeats a le pouvoir de ressusciter les choses inanimées. Ses figures se dissolvent dans l'ambiance aérienne. Ses

paysages émettent un fluide magique." (Yeats, painter of metamorphoses, has the power to resuscitate inanimate objects. His figures dissolve in the ambient air. His landscapes emit a magic fluid.)

5 Beckett, Schneider, and Putman, "Hommage à Jack B. Yeats," *Les Lettres Nouvelles*, 619–621. Duthuit's contribution was not published.

6 MacGreevy's card, co-written with SB's brother Frank Beckett and (probably) Alan Thompson, has not been found.

7 *Warten auf Godot*, directed by Roger Blin at the Schauspielhaus, Zurich: 12 January 1954, n. 1.
Giorgio Joyce.

GEORGES DUTHUIT

2/3/54   Paris
Cher Vieux
    Merci de ta lettre. Il ne faut pas prendre trop au sérieux mes idées fixes, visions fixes et balbutiements d'affolé. Il n'y a pas de litige entre nous. Il y a simplement peut-être que nous n'arrivons pas à dégager, avant d'essayer d'en parler, ce dont il s'agit. Il y a à cela visiblement trop de raisons pour que j'aie le courage de les aborder. Je crois finalement que nos préoccupations sont de deux ordres très différents et comme séparées par une zone d'ombre où, exilés l'un et l'autre, nous trébuchons vainement vers un point de rencontre. Ayant cru discerner chez Yeats la seule valeur qui me demeure encore un peu réelle, valeur que je ne veux plus essayer de cerner et dont les si respectables considérations de pays et de facture ne peuvent rendre compte, je deviens littéralement aveugle pour tout le reste.[1] C'était déjà la même chose quand il s'agissait de Bram.[2] Ce n'est donc pas avec moi qu'on puisse parler art et ce n'est pas là-dessus que je risque d'exprimer autre chose que mes propres hantises. Sur Yeats, après des heures et des journées littéralement suppliciées, j'ai pondu une petite page la plus minable qui soit, irritée et lasse, tout le contraire de ce que j'aurais tellement voulu. Même pour ce grand vieillard que j'aime et vénère je n'aurai pas été foutu de m'oublier un peu.[3] Je ne sais pas si la fin de ta lettre signifie que tu renonces à écrire quelques lignes sur lui. Avoir à le craindre me rend très triste, et je le suis déjà assez.[4]

Affectueusement et à vendredi.

    s/ Sam

TLS; 1 leaf, 1 side; Duthuit collection.

2/3/54   Paris

Dear old friend,

    Thank you for your letter. You must not take too seriously all my idées fixes, visions fixes and madman's babblings. There is no serious dispute between us. All there is, perhaps, is that we are not managing to get clear, before trying to talk about it, what is at issue. Visibly there are too many reasons for that for me to have the courage to start on them. In the end, I think that our preoccupations are of two very different orders as if separated by a zone of shadow where, exiled from each other, we vainly seek a meeting point. Having thought I had detected in Yeats the only value that remains at all real for me – a value which I no longer want to try to pin down closely, and which cannot be accounted for by the so very respectable considerations of country and workmanship – I become literally blind to all the rest.[1] That was how it was already when we were talking about Bram.[2] So I am not someone to talk art with, and on that subject I am not likely to utter anything other than my own obsessive concerns. On Yeats, after hours and days of literal torture, I produced one little page of the most wretched kind, irritated and weary, the very opposite of what I would so much have liked to say. Even for that great old man whom I love and venerate I could not damned well manage to forget myself a little.[3] I do not know if the last part of your letter means that you are giving up your idea of writing something on him. Having to fear that you are saddens me, and I am sad enough already.[4]

    Affectionately and see you on Friday.

    Sam

1 Exhibition, Peinture, by Jack Yeats at the Galerie Beaux-Arts, Paris.

2 Bram van Velde.

3 SB's section in "Hommage à Jack B. Yeats" opens:

> Ce qu'a d'incomparable cette grande œuvre solitaire est son insistance à renvoyer au plus secret de l'esprit qui la soulève et à ne se laisser éclairer qu'au jour de celui-ci.
>
> De là cette étrangeté sans exemple et que laissent entière les habituels recours aux patrimoines, national et autres. (619.)
>
> (What is beyond compare in this great, solitary work is its insistence on reaching back into the most secret parts of the mind that bears it up, and on letting in no light that does not come from there.
>
> Hence this unexampled strangeness, forever proof against the usual invokings of patrimonies, national and other.)

After dismissing attempts to find parallels for Yeats's work, SB goes on: "L'artiste qui joue son être est de nulle part. Et il n'a pas de frères" (619). (The artist who risks his whole life does not belong anywhere. And he has no brothers). SB ends his homage: "S'incliner simplement, émerveillé" (620) (Stand simply, head bent, in wonder).

4 Duthuit's letter to SB has not been found. On 15 April, SB reported to Thomas MacGreevy:

> I am sending you by same post copy of Lettres Nouvelles which you may have already seen with our hommages. Duthuit's though written and good did not unfortunately appear because of a row he had with Saillet as a result of which he withdrew the text and refused all future collaboration. Without going into it I must say he was very badly treated and could hardly do otherwise. Of my own hommage I can only report what I said to you already, that it is nothing more than an obeisance, and a clumsy one. I cannot write that kind of thing and I only hope JBY will not be too disappointed and that he was not looking forward to a weightier text. (TCD, MS 10402/192.)

Maurice Saillet: 8 January 1953, n. 7.

EDOUARD COESTER
PARIS

le 11 mars 1954   6 Rue des Favorites
                                                   Paris 15me

Cher Monsieur[1]

C'est seulement avant-hier, après une absence de plus d'un mois, que j'ai trouvé dans ma boîte aux lettres à la campagne, où pendant tout ce temps elle était restée en souffrance, votre émouvante lettre du 4 février. Vous avez dû me trouver très grossier.[2]

Je ne sais trop quoi vous dire au sujet de votre projet. Je me suis déjà formellement opposé à toute musique de scène (Werner Egk avait envisagé d'en composer une).[3] Ce serait là, pour moi, un très pénible contresens. Il en serait tout autrement d'une musique inspirée par la pièce et je serais très flatté par toute initiative en ce sens. Mais en disant cela je pensé [*for* pense] à une musique purement instrumentale, sans voix. Pour être tout à [fait] franc, je ne crois pas que le texte de <u>Godot</u> puisse supporter les prolongements que lui conférerait forcément une mise en musique.[4] La pièce comme tout dramatique, si, mais pas le détail verbal. Car il s'agit d'une parole dont la fonction n'est pas tant d'avoir un sens que de lutter, mal j'espère, contre le silence, et d'y renvoyer. Je la vois donc difficilement partie intégrante d'un monde sonore.

Mais ce drame que vous semblez avoir si bien senti, si vous jugiez bon de le traduire, si librement que ce soit, en musique pure, voilà qui m'intéress[er]ait beaucoup et me ferait un grand plaisir. Et p[o]ur ne parler que du silence, n'attend-il pas toujours son musicien?

Je serais en tout cas heureux de savoir où vous en êtes et que vous ne m'en voulez pas trop de ma discourtoisie bien involontaire.

Croyez, cher Monsieur, à mes sentiments très cordiaux.

Samuel Beckett

TLcc; 1 leaf, 1 side; Fehsenfeld collection. Previous publication, Samuel Beckett, *Lettres à un musicien* (privately printed by Michel Archimbaud [?2007]).

11th March 1954   6 Rue des Favorites
                                   Paris 15me

Dear Monsieur[1]

It was only the day before yesterday, after more than a month's absence, that I found in my letter-box in the country, where it had lain all this time unopened, your moving letter of 4th February. You must have thought me very rude.[2]

I hardly know what to say to you about your project. I have already publicly expressed my opposition to any stage music (Werner Egk had thought of writing some).[3] For me that would be an awful mistake. A very different case would be music inspired by the play and I would be greatly flattered by any venture in that direction. But, in saying that, I have in mind instrumental music, no voices. To be quite frank, I do not believe that the text of *Godot* could bear the extensions that any musical setting would inevitably give it.[4] The piece as a dramatic whole, yes, but not the verbal detail. For what is at issue is a speaking whose function is not so much that of having a meaning as of putting up a struggle, poor I hope, against silence, and leading back to it. I find it hard to see it as an integral part of a sound-world.

But this drama which you seem to have felt so keenly, if you thought fit to translate it, however freely, into pure music, that would interest me a great deal and give me great pleasure. And then what about silence itself, is it not still waiting for its musician?

I would in any event be glad to know the present position and that you do not hold my wholly involuntary rudeness too much against me.

With best wishes

Samuel Beckett

1   Edouard Coester* (1905–2001) studied both literature and law, and had a successful career as a lawyer. Under the pseudonym of Edmond Costere, he was a composer and published musicologist.

2   In his letter to SB of 4 February, Coester wrote:

> L'audition, puis la lecture de EN ATTENDANT GODOT m'ont profondément atteint, par certaines résonances qui me semblent aller jusqu'à la racine de l'être.
>
> Etant musicien, et compositeur, cette émotion s'est résolue en musique, et j'ai composé sous cette inspiration quelques pièces [...] qui s'efforcent de traduire tel ou tel de vos personnages, ou tels ou tels de leurs actes ou de leurs paroles.
>
> Sur ces données, j'ai commencé à mettre en musique les premières pages, chant et orchestre réduit. Mais je me suis arrêté, car je voudrais avoir votre accord. (Fehsenfeld collection.)
>
> (Hearing, then reading *En attendant Godot* have affected me deeply, through certain resonances which seem to me to go to the very root of being.
>
> Being a musician and a composer, this emotion took on musical form, and, under this inspiration, I composed several pieces [...] which strive to convey this character or that, this act or that of theirs, or of their words.
>
> On the basis of these, I have begun to put the opening pages to music, for voice and small orchestra. But I stopped, for I would want to have your agreement.)

3   Werner Egk (1901–1983), German composer and conductor of the Berlin Staatsoper from 1936 to 1940. Neither Egk's request nor SB's response has been found.

4   Coester explained: "Il ne s'agirait nullement dans mon esprit d'une simple musique de scène, mais d'une oeuvre chantée de bout en bout (sauf sans doute la

grande tirade de Lucky), car la moindre des paroles de vos personnages suffit à déclencher une multitude de sentiments et de pensées" (There would never be any question in my mind of mere background music, but of a work sung from start to finish [apart no doubt from Lucky's tirade], for the slightest of your characters' words sets off a host of feelings and thoughts).

EDOUARD COESTER

PARIS

le 23 mars 1954   6 Rue des Favorites
                                                      Paris 15°

Cher Monsieur

Merci de votre lettre. Vous parlez en musicien, moi en écrivain, je crains que les deux positions ne soient inconciliables.[1] Je suis trop sensible à la musique et sait [*for* sais] trop bien ce qu'elle fait aux textes pour pouvoir consentir à y exposer le mien. Je ne tiens pas du tout à avoir raison et développer ce point de vue ne servirait à rien. Le travail fait, on fait ce qu'on peut pour le protéger. Si je m'y prends mal, tant pis pour lui et pour moi.

Je suis désolé d'avoir à vous répondre ainsi. Je ne peux pas faire autrement.

Cordialement à vous.

Samuel Beckett

TLcc; 1 leaf, 1 side; Fehsenfeld collection.

23 March 1954   6 Rue des Favorites
                                                     Paris 15me

Dear Monsieur Coester

Thank you for your letter. You speak as a musician, I as a writer, I fear that our two positions are irreconcilable.[1] I am too sensitive to music, and too well aware of what it does to texts to be able to allow mine to be exposed to it. I have no strong wish to be right, and for me to develop this point of view would be useless. Once the work is done,

one does what one can to protect it. If I go about that the wrong way, so much the worse for it and me.

I am very sorry to have to reply to you in this way. I cannot do otherwise.

Yours sincerely
Samuel Beckett

---

1 Coester had appealed to SB to reconsider. He wrote on 18 March:

> C'est sur un tout autre plan que se pose la question que je vous soumettais: le plan musical. Et vous l'avez si bien compris, que vous admettez, vous souhaitez même, qu'une sorte de fresque symphonique vienne traduire, en une musique purement instrumentale, la pièce envisagée comme un tout dramatique.
>
> Mais cette fresque musicale, dont j'ai esquissé les éléments, perd tout son sens sans le soutien des paroles: Elle n'est alors que musique pure, où l'imagination de l'auditeur erre à sa fantaisie; et le message humain qu'elle portait en elle s'abolit.
>
> De message humain, qui est votre oeuvre, ne croyez-vous pas que les musiciens y ont droit eux aussi, et dans leur domaine? (Fehsenfeld collection.)
>
> (The question I was putting belongs on a quite different level: the musical level. You yourself have understood this so well that you can allow, even wish that some sort of symphonic fresco might, in a purely instrumental work, realise the play imagined as a dramatic whole.
>
> But this musical fresco, the elements of which I have sketched in, loses its whole meaning without the support of the words. It is then no more than pure music, in which the audience's imagination roams free, while the human message that it bore is lost.
>
> When it comes to the human message, which your work is, do you not think that musicians too have a right to it, and in their own field?)

Coester then proposed several musical alternatives, and asked SB to meet him to discuss them.

ALAN SIMPSON
DUBLIN

9.4.54   Paris
Dear Mr Simpson

Thank you for your letter of March 27th.[1]

As far as I remember (I have not the contract here) Albery Productions have acquired British Empire rights, and option on American rights. I don't know how this affects your position. You'll have to get it clear with Curtis Brown.[2]

No requests for modifications of any text have yet been made.[3]

I think the simplest thing [is] for you to postpone your production until after London production. I hope this does not mean too great an upset to your plans.[4]

As to the propriety of first production in English being in Dublin, I'm afraid I have no feeling about that at all.[5]

> Yours sincerely
>
> Sam. Beckett

ALS; 1 leaf, 1 side; TCD, MS 10731/9.

1   In his letter of 27 March, Alan Simpson appealed to SB (TCD, MS 10731/8). He was upset that Kitty Black had written on 23 March to say that Donald Albery and Peter Glenville, who held the contract for *Waiting for Godot*, did not wish to authorize a production in Dublin before their own performance in London had opened.

In the remaining notes to this letter, references are to Simpson's letter of 27 March.

2   Simpson argued that ownership of the English and American rights should have no effect upon Irish production rights, unless SB had granted them world English language rights.

3   Simpson pointed out that it was unlikely that an uncut production could be performed in England, except in club conditions, because of censorship.

4   Simpson had originally proposed to present *Waiting for Godot* from 26 April, but delay over permissions made that improbable.

The original of the present letter has a hole punched at the point in the sentence where "is" would be.

5   Simpson mentioned that he had spoken to the actor Cyril Cusack (1910–1993) about the matter: "he thought that it would be fitting for the first production in English to be in Dublin."

BARNEY ROSSET, GROVE PRESS
NEW YORK

21-4-54

6 Rue des Favorites
Paris

My dear Barney

Thanks for your letter. Sorry <u>Godot</u> is postponed to the autumn. I'm sure I'll be very pleased with the book. The Ed. de Minuit are also doing a reimpression with photos.[1]

We were all set for a London West End performance until the Lord Chamberlain got going. His incriminations are so preposterous that I'm afraid the whole thing is off. He listed 12 passages for omission! The things I had expected and which I was half prepared to amend (reluctantly), but also passages that are vital to the play (first 15 lines of Lucky's tirade and the passage end of Act I from "But you can't go barefoot" to "and they crucified quick") and impossible either to alter or suppress.[2] However Albery (the theatre director) is trying to arrange things in London. I am to see him this week-end and all is not yet definitely lost. It would be a pity, as there was talk of Alec Guinness for the role of Estragon.[3]

With regard to translation I fear I have been very remiss. The revision of the German Molloy finished me.[4] I have not seen or heard from Bowles for a long time. I revised the first few pages of Part II of Molloy and that was our last contact. With the delayed appearance of Godot I suppose there is no great hurry about Molloy. Sometimes I feel the only alternative is to wash my hands of it entirely or to do it entirely myself.

Received New World Writing with Niall Montgomery. Witty specification.[5]

Hope indeed I shall be in the States some day if only in order to take advantage of your hospitality. Am buried in the Ile de France at the moment and find it no better or worse than anything else.[6]

Shall let you know how the London affair works out.

With best wishes to you both,

Yours ever

Sam Beckett

ALS; 2 leaf, 2 sides; NSyU. Previous publication, Beckett, "Letters to Barney Rosset," *The Review of Contemporary Fiction*, 69–70; Beckett and Rosset, "Letters [1953–1955]," *The New Theater Review*, 37–38.

1   In April 1954, Editions de Minuit reprinted *En attendant Godot* in a second edition with four plates from the German tour by the Théâtre de Babylone (Federman and Fletcher, *Samuel Beckett*, 57–58).

2   Rosset mentioned a reference in the press to the forthcoming production of *Waiting for Godot* in London (Sam Zolotow, "'Magic and Loss' Arrives Tonight," *The New York Times* 9 April 1954: 21).

The Lord Chamberlain's Office was charged with issuing theatre licenses in London, from 1737 to 1968. In effect his Office acted as a censor for the theatre.

On 1 April, Donald Albery wrote to SB to enclose a copy of a letter of 31 March from the Lord Chamberlain's Office calling for twelve deletions in the text of *Waiting for Godot* before a license could be granted. Albery advised proposing "alternative dialogue if an omission matters to the play," adding "it is surprising how near and how strong you can make the alternative. The fact that you have agreed to alter something seems to be more important than the alteration itself" (BL, Lord Chamberlain's Plays Correspondence, 1955/6597 [hereafter LCC Corr.]; TxU, Albery collection).

The Lord Chamberlain's Office requested changes to the first lines of Lucky's speech (from "Given the existence as uttered forth" through "and who can doubt it will fire the firmament"), and called for omission of the lines at the end of Act I beginning "But you can't go barefoot," through "And they crucified quick" (Beckett, *Waiting for Godot* [Grove Press], 29, 36).

3 SB wrote to Albery on 14 April:

> I am prepared to try and give satisfaction to the Lord Chamberlain's Office on ten of the twelve points raised. This is for me a big concession and I make it with the greatest reluctance. Were it not for my desire to be agreeable to Mr. Glenville and yourself, I should simply call the whole thing off without further discussion.
>
> But two of the passages condemned, those namely numbered 5 and 6 on the list, are vital to the play and can neither be suppressed nor changed. I cannot conceive in what they give offence and I consider their interdiction wholly unreasonable. I am afraid this is quite final. (TxU, Albery collection.)

SB and Albery met to discuss the changes requested on the weekend of 24–25 April 1954. For items 5 and 6 see 23 June 1954, n. 3.

4 SB's work with Erich Franzen on the German translation of *Molloy*: 28 January 1954, 17 February 1954.

5 Montgomery, "No Symbols Where None Intended," *New World Writing*, 324–337.

6 Although SB gives his address on this letter as from Paris, he is in Ussy-sur-Marne.

JACQUES PUTMAN
PARIS

7.5.54

Mon cher Jacques

Je n'ai pas votre adresse à la campagne.

Je viens de recevoir une lettre de Jack Yeats, très touché par vos petits textes. En voici un extrait:

"I will be very much obliged if you could convey to the Editor of 'Les Lettres Nouvelles' that I have received great happiness in the articles of Monsieur Schneider and of Monsieur Putman and in their open hearted wide thinking understanding of the headlands where I wish to move."[1]

    A bientôt j'espère

       Amitiés

       <u>Sam. Beckett</u>

ALS; 1 leaf, 1 side; Porte collection.

7-5-54

My dear Jacques

    I haven't got your country address.

    I have just had a letter from Jack Yeats, much touched by your little texts. Here is an extract:

    "I will be very much obliged if you could convey to the Editor of *Les Lettres Nouvelles* that I have received great happiness in the articles of Monsieur Schneider and of Monsieur Putman and in their open hearted wide thinking understanding of the headlands where I wish to move."[1]

    Till soon, I hope.

       Best wishes

       <u>Sam. Beckett</u>

1   Beckett, Schneider, and Putman, "Hommage à Jack B. Yeats," 619–621. Maurice Saillet was Editor of *Les Lettres Nouvelles*.

DONALD ALBERY

LONDON

23-6-54   Shottery

                                Killiney

                                C$^{\underline{o}}$ Dublin[1]

Dear M$^{\underline{r}}$ Albery,

    Thank you for your letters of June 16$^{\underline{th}}$ and 22$^{\underline{nd}}$.[2]

    Referring to your schedule I propose the following adjustments:

1. Replace <u>fly</u> by <u>coat</u>. The rest unchanged.
2. Replace <u>pubis</u> by <u>stomach</u>.
3. Read:

   > Estragon What about hanging ourselves?
   > Vladimir Hmm …
   > (He whispers to Estragon)
   > Estragon No!
   > Vladimir With all that ensues, etc.

4. Replace <u>arse</u> by <u>backside</u>.
5. Replace <u>Fartov</u> by <u>Popov</u>.
7. Replace <u>piss</u> by <u>do it</u>.
8. Replace <u>foetal</u> by <u>crouching</u>.
10. Replace <u>farted</u> by <u>belched</u>.

   (This passage, leading up to Estragon's <u>fausse sortie</u> top of p. 31 cannot simply be deleted).

11. Replace <u>privates</u> by <u>guts</u>.[3]

I am sorry you are having all this trouble.

I shall be seeing the Pike Theatre people here next week. As proprietor of British rights I am not sure that you can restrain them from putting on the play here before the London performance. My own feeling is that they should not, and if that is your feeling too I shall of course not consent to their doing it. Perhaps you would let me have a note stating your objections to this project.[4]

I hope you have by now received from New York the three other copies of the book.[5]

I look forward to hearing from you soon that you have been able to engage Alec Guinness and establish an approximate date for opening.

> Yours sincerely,
> Sam. Beckett

ALS photocopy; 2 leaves, 2 sides; TxU, Albery collection; TL copy, 1 leaf, 2 sides; TxU, Glenville collection.

1   SB left for Dublin on 27 May 1954. The evening before, he wrote to Pamela Mitchell: "I have very bad news of my brother this evening. I am leaving here early tomorrow morning and, if I can get a place, Paris for Dublin to-morrow" (UoR, BIF, MS 5060; Pilling, *A Beckett Chronology*, 124). Frank Beckett was suffering from lung cancer.

2   No letter from Donald Albery to SB dated 16 June 1954 has been found; however, SB may refer to a copy of the letter sent by Albery to Norman Gwatkin (d. 1971), Assistant Comptroller, Lord Chamberlain's Office, of that date. In it, Albery outlines the changes that have been agreed by SB, Albery, and Charles D. Heriot (d. 1972), Senior Examiner, Lord Chamberlain's Office. Albery's letter to SB of 22 June 1954 encloses the response of the Lord Chamberlain's Office to his letter of 16 June.

3   Albery's letter of 16 June summarized the changes that Albery proposed during a meeting with Heriot who had attended a reading of the play. Based on Heriot's report of the reading, objections 5 and 6 were removed and those passages allowed to stand. Objection 5 contained the beginning of Lucky's speech: "Given the existence as uttered forth" down to "and who can doubt it will fire the firmament." Objection 6 covered from "But you can't go barefoot" down to "and they crucified quick" (Norman Gwatkin to Albery, 29 April 1954 [BL, LCC Corr., 1955/6597; photocopy, TxU, Albery collection]).

The page numbers below refer to a typescript of *Waiting for Godot*. The Lord Chamberlain's objections are stated first; the agreed changes follow. SB's letter responds to these points, but omits numbers 6 and 9 since further action is unnecessary.

Act I

1.   Page 2: "You might button it all the same". "True" (he buttons his fly). Cut as required by the Lord Chamberlain.
2.   Page 3: "His hand pressed to his pubis" to be changed to "His hand pressed to his stomach" or deleted.
3.   Page 9: Lord Chamberlain's requirement to be complied with by deleting the following: "It'd give us an erection". "An erection"; leaving the following: "What about hanging ourselves?" Vladimir whispers to Estragon. "With all that ensues. Where it falls mandrakes grow. That's why they shriek when you tear them up. Did you not know that?"
4.   Page 27: "on his arse" to be changed to "on his backside".
5.   Page 40: The paragraph originally objected to to stand but "Popov" to be substituted for "Fartov".
6.   Page 52: The Lord Chamberlain withdraws his objection.

ACT II

7.   Page 3: "You see you piss better [w]hen I'm not there" to be changed to "You see you do it better when I'm not there".
8.   Page 16: The Lord Chamberlain's cut to be made as required. [This was "he resumes his foetal posture".]
9.   Page 20: The Lord Chamberlain withdraws his previous objection to the words "Gonococcus! Spirochaete!"
10.   Page 30: "Who farted" to be changed to "Who did that?" [This is rejected by the Lord Chamberlain's office; no reference to the breaking of wind was allowed. SB notes that without this, Estragon's "fausse sortie" (feigned exit) would not be motivated.]
11.   Page 38: "and the privates" to be changed to "and the guts".
12.   Page 54: It is agreed that Estragon will be well covered when his trousers fall. (BL, LCC Corr., 1955/6597; TxU, Albery collection.)

4   Alan Simpson and Carolyn Swift, Pike Theatre. That a London performance should take precedence over the Dublin performance: 9 April 1954.

5   SB had asked Barney Rosset to send Albery copies of *Waiting for Godot* in his letter of 11 June 1954 (NSyU).

PATRICIA HUTCHINS (MRS R. GREACEN)
LONDON

25-6-54   Dublin

Dear Mrs Greacen

Thank you for your letter and article which I have read with great interest.[1] I fear I have no recollection of that note to Joyce and can shed no light on it. The words are certainly infinitive and substantive. My writing then was no better than now.[2]

In 1940 I was for a few days with the Joyces at their little hotel at Vichy and saw them leave for St. Gérand. It was the last time I saw him.[3] I was with them at St Gérand the Easter of the previous year, 1939.[4] If I remember anything likely to be of use to you shall let you know. At the moment am staying here with my brother who is ill and likely to be here for some time yet.

Wishing you bonne chance

I am

> Yours sincerely
>
> Sam. Beckett

ALS; 1 leaf, 1 side; TCD, MS 4098/11.

1 Patricia Hutchins Greacen wrote to SB on 19 June indicating her plans to be in Paris to "help Stuart Gilbert with the notes of the collection of Joyce's letters which he is editing" (TCD, MS 4908/10). The article she sent to SB concerned Joyce at Saint-Gérand-le-Puy; it may have become a portion of her book *James Joyce's World* (London: Methuen, 1957).

2 Hutchins wrote: "I seem to be one of Joyce's recording devils and possessed now by his own love of detail." She asked SB about his note to James Joyce to confirm her reading of the words "substantive" and "infinitive" (see [26 April 1929] to James Joyce). She indicated that in her article on Joyce's correspondence, she wished to "reproduce a few letters"; in the end, Joyce's letter to SB was not among them ("James Joyce's Correspondence," *Encounter* 7.2 [August 1956] 49–54; Hutchins published SB's letter to Joyce in *James Joyce's World*, 169).

3 SB's last meeting with Joyce: 17 February 1954, SB to Hans Naumann, n. 2.

4 SB had been with the Joyces and Maria Jolas at Saint-Gérand-le-Puy during the Easter holidays of 1940, not 1939 (see 1 April 1940, SB to Maria Jolas, n. 1).

DONALD ALBERY
LONDON

July 4th 1954   Shottery,
                                                 Killiney,
                                                 Co. Dublin,

Dear Mr. Albery,

Thank you for your letter of June 28th. I have seen the Pike Theatre people and explained our point of view. They now seek permission to put on the play in their tiny theatre here one week after London opening. I do not think there can be any objection to this. But I await your assent – at your earliest convenience – before giving them mine.

I have been thinking over your project of a pre-London showing in Dublin. My feeling is that this would be ill-advised. I am very poorly thought of in this town and even a first-class performance of Godot here is likely to provoke very hostile reactions. Indeed I find myself wondering if it would not be preferable, in the case of this play, to forget any form of provincial tour and present it directly in London.

If Alec Guinness's uncertainty as to his commitments is to hold us up much longer, I think we should decide to look for someone else.

Yours sincerely,
SAM BECKETT

TL copy; 1 leaf, 1 side; TxU, Glenville collection.

BARNEY ROSSET, GROVE PRESS
NEW YORK

12.7.54   SHOTTERY,
                                                 KILLINEY,
                                                 CO. DUBLIN
                                                 Dalkey 262

Dear Barney

Thanks for your letters of June 8th and – this morning – July 7th.

I am afraid my brother is not going to recover. I must stand by here as long as I am need[ed]. Probably for some months longer.[1]

It is better that Bowles shd. finish Molloy. I am waiting for him to send me more pages to revise.

I have begun to translate Malone.

Thanks for sending copies of Godot to Albery. Things are being held up because of Guinness and his complicated commitments.[2]

No, there are no compensations for me in this country, on the contrary. And as so shortly to be the only survivor of my family I hope never to have to return.[3]

Best wishes to you both

Yrs.

Sam. Beckett

ALS; 1 leaf, 1 side; letterhead; NSyU.

1   In his letter of 7 July, Rosset sent his wishes that Frank Beckett would "make a good recovery."

2   SB refers to the London production of *Waiting for Godot*. On 28 June, Donald Albery wrote to SB that the film commitments of Alec Guinness were uncertain: he might be free in October or November, but if not, then there would be considerable delay (TxU, Albery collection).

3   SB wrote to Pamela Mitchell on 23 June:

> Never felt less like writing and I haven't felt like it for years, and never so revolted at the thought of the work done. Sometimes feel like letting myself be sucked in by this exquisite morass, just lie down and give up and do nothing more. Always felt that temptation here but never so strong as these last weeks. The old Irish slogan "Die in Ireland". It's a dangerous place to come back to for any other purpose. (UoR, BIF, MS 5060.)

JEROME LINDON, EDITIONS DE MINUIT
PARIS

12.7.54   Dublin

Cher Jérôme

J'ai signé et vous retourne ci-joint le contrat pour l'Italie. Félicitations et merci d'avoir si bien mené cette affaire.[1] Suzanne m'a envoyé votre catalogue. Là encore j'ai été très touché par la façon dont vous présentez mes ouvrages.

Ca fait je crois plus de 6 semaines que je suis ici et toujours pas question de repartir. L'état de mon frère n'a pas visiblement évolué pendant tout ce temps, mais peut toujours s'aggraver brutalement d'un instant à l'autre. J'ose à peine m'éloigner de la maison.

J'ai vu Simpson du Pike Theatre. Je lui ai dit qu'il ne doit pas monter Godot ici avant la présentation Albery. Il demande l'autorisation de le monter 8 jours après la première de Londres. Albery veut bien. Nous attendons l'accord de Glenville. Quant à Guinness, les pourparlers continuent.[2]

Si la dernière impression de Godot est prête, je veux dire celle avec photos, vous seriez gentil de m'envoyer quelques exemplaires, mettons 4.[3]

J'ai commencé à traduire Malone. Ça me donne beaucoup moins de mal que la révision Bowles.

Merci encore, cher Jérôme, pour tout ce que vous faites.

Bien amicalement à vous deux

Sam

ALS; 1 leaf, 2 sides; IMEC, Beckett, Boîte 1, S. Beckett, Correspondance – Divers, 1950–1956.

12.7.54   Dublin

Dear Jérôme

I have signed and enclose herewith the contract for Italy. Congratulations, and thanks too for having handled this business so well.[1] Suzanne has sent me your catalogue. There too I was greatly touched by the way you present my works.

I have been here more than 6 weeks now, and still no question of getting away. My brother's condition has not noticeably developed in all that time, but may still take a sharp turn for the worse from one moment to the next. I hardly dare venture out of the house.

I have seen Simpson of the Pike Theatre. I told him that he is not to put on *Godot* here before the Albery launch. He is asking for permission to put it on a week after the London premiere. Albery is willing. We are still waiting for Glenville's agreement. As for Guinness, talks are continuing.[2]

If the latest impression of *Godot* is ready, I mean the one with photos, I would be grateful if you could send me a few copies, say 4.[3]

I have started to translate *Malone*. It is giving me far less trouble than revising Bowles.

Thank you again, dear Jérôme, for everything you are doing.

Warmest good wishes to you both

Sam

1 Lindon sent the contracts for production rights in Italian with Luciano Mondolfo (1910-?) with his letter of 9 July 1954 (IMEC, Beckett, Boîte 1, S. Beckett, Correspondance - Divers, 1950-1956). SB drops the circumflex in "Jérôme" in the greeting of this letter.

2 SB wrote to Alan Simpson of the Pike Theatre in Dublin on 9 July, quoting from a letter that he had received from Donald Albery: "'I will consult Peter Glenville about the Pike Theatre doing the play one week after the London Opening. I personally have no objection but I must, as a matter of convention, ask him too'" (TCD, MS 10731/11; Albery's letter to SB has not been found).
  The date of the London production hinged on securing the services of Peter Glenville and Alec Guinness.

3 SB refers to the second edition of *En attendant Godot*, with illustrations, published by Editions de Minuit in April 1954.

PAMELA MITCHELL
PARIS

25.7.54   [Dublin]

Mouki. Thanks for your good letters. I can't do any more than scribble a few lines. Not much change here, though I suppose a big one compared to when I arrived over 2 months ago. It may well drag on for 2 more if not longer. I am wanted in London re Godot and may be obliged to dart over for 24 hours. I hope not. Guinness is out, can't wait indefinitely on his good pleasure, or for a gap in his endless commitments. Producer Glenville too seems up to his eyes in more lucrative undertakings and perhaps we'll have another producer. In any case have told them to get on with it with whatever people available and to hell with stars.

If the play can't get over with ordinarily competent producing and playing then it's not worth doing at all.[1]

Don't be killing yourself in that foolish office if half-a-day's work is a possibility and enough to keep you going. One can really do with very little money living as you are now.

[. . .]

If you see those <u>Merlin</u> bastards kick them in the pants for me, they'll understand why.[2]

    Love

      <u>Sam</u>

ALS; 1 leaf, 2 sides; UoR, BIF, MS 5060.

1 On 21 July, Albery wrote to SB that he had been able to get Alec Guinness and Peter Glenville to make a decision, and he forwarded to SB a letter from Guinness (which has not been found); on 24 July, Glenville wrote to SB that Guinness was enthusiastic about the play, but unable to set a date, and so they had decided to go ahead without him (TxU, Glenville collection).

2 SB's complaints about Merlin are detailed in his letter to Mitchell of 19 August 1954.

PETER GLENVILLE

LONDON

July 28th 1954   SHOTTERY,

                                  KILLINEY,

                                CO. DUBLIN.

My dear Peter Glenville

Many thanks for your letter of July 24th.

I think my last letter to Donald Albery makes my position quite clear. Frankly I was beginning to wonder whether, under the pressure of other commitments, your own inclination was not to relinquish the direction of <u>Godot</u>. I am very happy to see from your letter that this is not so and that you look forward to getting things moving early next year. I personally am very willing in that case to have the option extended for another 6 months.[1] You will of course have to consult my publisher, M. Jérôme Lindon, who I feel sure will have no objection to offer.

I should like nothing better than to come to London and talk the whole thing over with Donald Albery and yourself. Unfortunately my brother is so gravely ill and in such need of my presence that anything like a definite appointment is out of the question at the moment. But you may rely on my doing my utmost to put in a brief appearance in London towards the end of next month.

I should be grateful if you would agree in principle to production by the Pike Theatre here one week after the London opening.

> With best wishes I am
> > yours very sincerely
> > > Sam. Beckett

ALS; 2 leaves, 2 sides; letterhead; TxU, Glenville collection.

1   SB refers to his letter of 4 July to Donald Albery. On 24 July, Glenville wrote to SB that since he was not free to direct *Waiting for Godot* until mid-December, he had been prepared to give up the role of director (suggesting Tyrone Guthrie as a replacement) in the interests of doing the play by December with Sir Ralph Richardson; however, when it became clear that Richardson was unavailable until the new year, Glenville instead proposed that SB agree to a further option of six months (TxU, Glenville collection).

JEROME LINDON, EDITIONS DE MINUIT
PARIS

29-7-54

> SHOTTERY,
> KILLINEY,
> CO. DUBLIN.
> DALKEY 262

Cher ami

Albery et Glenville me demandent un prolongement de 6 mois de l'option, afin que celui-ci, pris par d'autres obligations jusqu'au mois de décembre, puisse mettre en scène. J'ai donné mon accord en disant qu'il lui faudrait évidemment obtenir également le vôtre.[1]

Guinness est dans l'eau. Mais il est fortement question maintenant de Sir Ralph Richardson, qui vient de lire et d'approuver la pièce. Lui non plus ne sera libre qu'au mois de janvier prochain.

Ici les choses suivent leur cours.

Amitiés

       <u>Sam</u>

ALS; 1 leaf, 1 side; Minuit.

29-7-54   SHOTTERY,

                                      KILLINEY,

                                      CO. DUBLIN.

                                      DALKEY 262

My dear Jérôme

Albery and Glenville are asking me for a 6-month extension of the option, so that the latter, caught up in other obligations until December, can start producing. I have given my agreement, telling him that of course he must have yours as well.[1]

Guinness has gone for a burton. But now there is much talk of Sir Ralph Richardson, who has just read and approved the play. He too will not be free till next January.

Here things are taking their course.

    All best

       Sam

1 Lindon wrote to Kitty Black at Curtis Brown about the option; her reply on 6 August indicated that "the plan at present is to do the play with Sir Ralph Richardson some time in the New Year. Sir Ralph was very excited about the play, and I know Mr. Beckett was delighted with this casting" (IMEC, Beckett, Boîte 5, S. Beckett, Correspondance 1962–1968, Curtis Brown 1957 [for 1952–1957]).

PAMELA MITCHELL

PARIS

<u>19.8.54</u>   <u>Dublin</u>

Dear Pamela

Thanks for all your letters and news of your doings. Do not get silly ideas into yr head about hurting. It is I the hurter of the two.[1]

Merlin did not send me a copy of their review with my story nor was I given the opportunity of correcting proofs of same nor have they paid me a penny of what they owe me. None of this has the slightest importance.[2]

News out of the blue this morning from Buenos Ayres of a Spanish translation of <u>Godot</u> with threat of proofs to follow. But I simply can't face that. Shall simply have to send them back uncorrected and à la grâce de Dieu. No importance either.[3]

Here the damnable round continues. Complications are beginning and God knows for what atrociousness we are bound.

See nobody and have long since lost all desire to.

Fortunately there is plenty to do, more than ever, and fortunately the nights are still long and fairly good with the old sea still telling the old story at the end of the garden. My room has a French window out to the garden and I can slip out of an evening and prowl without disturbing anyone.

Here are a few books you could read, if you have not already:

<u>Sartre:</u>	<u>La Nausée</u>
<u>Malraux</u>	<u>La Condition Humaine</u>
<u>Julien Green</u>	Léviathan
<u>Céline</u>	<u>Voyage au Bout de la Nuit</u>
<u>Jules Renard</u>	Journal
<u>Camus</u>	<u>L'Etranger</u>[4]

Love

<u>Sam</u>

ALS; 1 leaf, 2 sides; *env to* Mademoiselle Pamela Mitchell, 4<u>bis</u> Rue de la G<u>de</u> Chaumière, Paris 6<u>me</u>, FRANCE; *pm* [2]0-__-__; Dun Laoghaire; UoR, BIF, MS 5060.

1 On 6 August, SB wrote to Mitchell: "And most evenings the walk along the beach, or over the hill to the mountain view, but not this evening. Should have made quite a good butler, no, too much responsibility, but a superior kind of house-boy, a head house-boy, no, just an ordinary house-boy. Soon the leaves will be turning, it'll be winter before I'm home, and then? It'll have to be very easy whatever it is, I can't face

any more difficulties, and I can't bear the thought of giving any more pain." (UoR, BIF, MS 5060.)

2 SB's story "The End" was translated by Richard Seaver in collaboration with the author (*Merlin* 2.3 [Summer–Autumn 1954] 144–159).

3 *Esperando a Godot*, the translation by Argentine playwright, director, and critic Pablo Palant (1914–1975), was published by Editorial Poseidon in Buenos Aires in 1955. The title page indicates that the translation was "revised by the author."
"A la grâce de Dieu" (in God's hands).

4 Jean-Paul Sartre, *La Nausée* (1938; *Nausea*). André Malraux, *La Condition humaine* (1933; *Man's Fate*). Julien Green, *Léviathan* (1929; *The Dark Journey*). Louis-Ferdinand Céline, *Voyage au bout de la nuit* (1932; *Voyage to the End of the Night*). Jules Renard, *Journal* (1935). Albert Camus, *L'Etranger* (1942; *The Outsider*; *The Stranger*).

JACOBA VAN VELDE

20.8.54

SHOTTERY,
KILLINEY,
CO. DUBLIN.
DALKEY 262

Chère Tonny

Content d'avoir de vos nouvelles. Vous pouvez avoir confiance en Tophoven. Très consciencieux et ne demandant pas mieux que de se faire aider par l'auteur. Brave type par-dessus le marché, ce qui ne gâte rien.[1]

Ici ça va on ne peut plus mal. On dit ça en sachant qu'on n'a encore rien vu. Je ne sais pas combien peu de temps ça va se traîner encore. Pas plus de deux mois, je pense. Peut-être bien avant.

Je crois que vous êtes mal renseignée sur Godot. Encore plus mal que moi, ce qui n'est pas peu dire. Aux dernières nouvelles il n'était plus question de Guinness, trop pris par d'autres engagements et on parlait de Ralph Richardson. Rien en tout cas avant le Nouvel An, sauf imprévu.[2]

Content que Bram ait repris le travail. Vu hier une toile de Geer à la galerie Waddington. Un type que je connais s'y intéresse beaucoup et ça ne m'étonnerait pas qu'il l'achète. Je l'ai encouragé comme il fallait.[3]

Ma vie ici – rien, mieux vaut ne pas en parler. Ça finira comme tout le reste et le chemin sera à nouveau libre qui va vers la seule fin qui compte.

J'essaie de réviser l'affreuse traduction qu'on a faite de Molloy. Un cauchemar, encore un. Je commence moi-même la traduction de Malone.

Affectueusement à vous tous

Sam

ALS; 1 leaf, 2 sides; letterhead; BNF 19794/29.

20.8.54

SHOTTERY,
KILLINEY,
CO. DUBLIN.
DALKEY 262

Dear Tonny

Glad to hear from you. You can trust Tophoven. Very conscientious, and more than happy to let himself be helped by the author. Nice man into the bargain, which does no harm.[1]

Here things are as bad as they could be. We say that, even though we know that we've seen nothing yet. I don't know how long it will drag on. Not more than two months, I think. Maybe much before.

I think you're misinformed about *Godot*. Even more than I am and that's saying something. The last I heard was that Guinness was out of the running, too busy with other engagements, and that there was talk of Ralph Richardson. In any case, nothing before the New Year unless something turns up.[2]

Very glad Bram has got back to work. Yesterday saw one of Geer's paintings in the Waddington Gallery. A fellow I know is very interested, and I wouldn't be surprised if he bought it. I made all the right encouraging noises.[3]

My life here – nothing; better not mentioned. It will end like everything else, and the way will again be free that goes towards the only end that counts.

I am trying to revise the frightful translation that's been done of *Molloy*. A nightmare, one more. I myself am starting on the translation of *Malone*.

Love to you all

Sam

1 SB recommends Elmar Tophoven's German translation *Warten auf Godot* as Jacoba van Velde prepares the Dutch translation of *En attendant Godot*.

2 An announcement of a London production of *Waiting for Godot* had appeared in *Le Monde* on 10 July 1954 ("Nouvelles des Lettres," 8): "Traduite en anglais sous le titre *Waiting for Godot*, cette même pièce sera représentée, l'année prochaine, à Londres et à New-York. Elle aura pour principaux interprètes Alec Guin[n]ess et Ralph Richardson." (Translated into English under the title *Waiting for Godot*, this same play will be performed next year in London and New York. The cast will be led by Alec Guinness and Ralph Richardson.)

3 Bram van Velde had gone through a period of withdrawal from painting (Kober, *Bram van Velde et ses loups*, 20–21, 30).

The Waddington Galleries no longer possess sales records of the Victor Waddington Gallery in Dublin for this period, hence neither the painting nor the potential buyer has been identified (Louise Shorr, Waddington Galleries, 21 November 2008).

BARNEY ROSSET, GROVE PRESS
NEW YORK

August 21st 1954

SHOTTERY,
KILLINEY,
CO. DUBLIN.
DALKEY 262

My dear Barney

Thank you for your letter.

Re. Molloy: I am slowly and with great difficulty continuing the revision of Bowles's text. The last pages he sent me bring us up to p. 208 of the book. I expect the next 100 will be to the end. When he last wrote he was in Spain. He seems to be having bad health. I am sorry for all this delay, it has really been from every point of view an unsatisfactory job. When the revision is finished and clean copy made by Bowles we shall have to go through it rapidly again. I really do not think you can count on having our final version much before November. I have so much to do here that an hour's continuous work is exceptional.

R[e] Godot. I know nothing about acquisition of American rights by Guinness. The United Kingdom rights have, as you know, been acquired jointly by Albery and Glenville and they also have option on American rights. Or had, when I last heard from them. There was much talk of Alec Guinness for the London production and he seemed very keen himself. But he was so tied up with other theatre and film commitments that he finally renounced. All this shilly-shally has delayed things in London and there was even some doubt as to whether the director of production would be available (Glenville). Last news from Albery was that the play wd. be produced by Glenville in a West End theatre in first quarter of 1955, probably with Ralph Richardson as Estragon or Vladimir. Knowing how keen Alec Guinness was to play it wd. not surprise me if he had acquired American rights. I think I shd. not rely too much on Mme. Sundstrom's assertions.[1] Your group in New York should write to Albery and find out exactly how things stand. You know his address: Donald Albery, New Theatre, St. Martin's Lane, London W.C. 2.[2]

I am completely out of touch with everything connected with my work. I have not even seen a copy of German Molloy. Out of the blue the other day came news from Buenos Ayres of a Spanish edition of Godot.[3] Lindon in the great kindness of his heart is dealing with everything himself and I must say I am grateful to him. You know, Barney, I think my writing days are over. L'Innommable finished me or expressed my finishedness.

Here the situation progresses slowly from bad to worse. I think 2 months at the outside will see it out. Perhaps not so much. My only interest in life at the moment is to keep on my feet until it is over.

With kindest remembrance to you both,

Yours

Sam Beckett

P.T.O.

So far as I know it is an understood thing that Merlin and Grove editions of *Molloy* shd. be instantaneous. Bowles mentioned it in his last letter. I wd. advise you however to obtain a written assurance, for what such things are worth – from Merlin to that effect.

ALS; 3 leaves, 4 sides; letterhead; NSyU.

1 In his letter of 18 August 1954, Rosset wrote that Jacqueline Sundstrom (b. 1917), an actress, director, and translator associated with the Théâtre de Babylone, had conveyed the information that Alec Guinness had bought the English performing rights to *Waiting for Godot* (NSyU).

2 The New York group interested in producing *Waiting for Godot* was Proscenium Productions, composed of Sybil Trubin (b. 1925), Robert E. Merriman (1916–1983), and Warren Enters (b. 1922); they had leased the Cherry Lane Theatre in Greenwich Village (Louis Calta, "Tour is Planned by 'Fifth Season,'" *The New York Times* 29 September 1954: 24). Rosset assured SB that the group was "professional"; their first season was honored with a special Tony Award in 1955 for "consistently good work by an off-Broadway group" ("'The Desperate Hours' Receives Perry Award," *The New York Times* 28 March 1955: 24).

3 *Molloy* translated into German by Erich Franzen was published by Suhrkamp on 24 May 1954 (Peter Suhrkamp to SB, 25 May 1954, Deutsches Literaturarchiv, Marbach, Suhrkamp archives).
Esperando a Godot translated by Pablo Palant: 19 August 1954, n. 3.

ALEXANDER TROCCHI
PARIS

Aug. 27th 1954

SHOTTERY,

KILLINEY,

CO. DUBLIN.

DALKEY 262

Dear Mr Trocchi

I have received, not from you, a copy of the latest issue of Merlin.[1]

My text is full of errors. Why did you not send me proofs? If, in this instance, circumstances had prevented me from correcting them, and they would not have, at least you would have done what it was incumbent on you to do. Are you too forgetting, in the fuss of editing, the needs of writers?[2]

15. Alexander Trocchi

I am still waiting for you to begin payment of royalties you owe me.[3]
I begin to weary of your treatment of me.[4]

If we cannot have ordinarily correct relations, it is better we
should have none at all.

Yrs. sincerely
Sam. Beckett

ALS; 1 leaf, 1 side; letterhead; McM, Samuel Beckett Collection, Collection Merlin, 1.22.

1   *Merlin* 2.3 (Summer–Autumn 1954).

2   "The End," translated by Richard Seaver with the author, 144–159.

The draft of Trocchi's reply, dated 30 August, attempts to answer SB's complaint about the errors and the lack of proofs:

> As far as your text in the current issue of Merlin is concerned, the decision to use it here and not in the next number was a sudden one, and I had Seaver's assurance that the text in manuscript had been passed by you. Let me say that I am fully satisfied that Seaver told the truth on this point [...] As for the proofs themselves, the circumstances under which Merlin was printed this time made it almost impossible to send them to you, and our own check against the manuscript was so thorough that we were confident you would be well-satisfied. I'm very sorry you're not. (McM, Samuel Beckett Collection, Collection Merlin, 1.22).

3   Trocchi had written to SB on 31 July about the royalties owed to him by *Merlin*:

> I hear through Austryn Wainhouse who bumped into Mr. Lindon a few days ago that you are surprised at not having received royalties promised you by us.
> The whole thing is not difficult to explain. The money would have been paid to you precisely on those dates indicated in my letter of 29 May had you been in Paris or had you left instructions how we were to get the money to you in Ireland. (McM, Samuel Beckett Collection, Collection Merlin, 1.22.)

SB responded on 3 August, by sending his Paris bank account information to Trocchi (McM, Samuel Beckett Collection, Collection Merlin, 1.22).

Trocchi addresses the matter of payment in his letter to SB of 30 August 1954: "As you know, it has been Girodias of Olympia Press who has handled the sale and accounts of Watt [...] I can give you my assurance that 85,000 francs will be paid into your Paris account by the end of this week."

4   Trocchi closes his letter to SB of 30 August: "That you were able to get so many recriminations on one small page does credit to your literary ability but says little for what I believed was our friendship. I really am more sorry than I can say that you felt obliged to adopt the tone you did in your letter."

PAMELA MITCHELL
PARIS

27.8.54

Dear Pamela

Many thanks for Merlin. "The End", for want of proof correcting, is full of ridiculous mistakes. Have written a stinker to Trocchi. Fed up with them.[1]

I'm not bothering about Godot in London. They are now trying to engage Ralph Richardson. I'd feel worse if they were rehearsing now and I couldn't be there to be a nuisance to them.[2]

Here things drag on, a little more awful every day, and with so many days yet probably to run what awfulness to look forward to. Delighted to hear you are enjoying just being in Paris, the air, the people, the sights and food and drink. I'd give a large slice of my uncertain expectations for a bottle of Invalides Beaujolais, for consumption on the spot.[3] And I suppose when I do get it there'll be some other misery to spoil it. The first bottle anyway.

So it goes, with great ungratitude for such a great thing as to be able to rise and move from one's place, if only a few sad steps.

> Love
> Sam

ALS; 1 leaf, 1 side; UoR, BIF, MS 5060.

1 Responding to SB's complaint about not having received a copy of *Merlin*, Mitchell sent him one from Paris.

2 Possible casting of Sir Ralph Richardson in *Waiting for Godot*: 29 July 1954, n. 1, and 20 August 1954, n. 2.

3 SB refers to the restaurant Chez Françoise at the Aérogare des Invalides. On 28 February 1954, he wrote to Mitchell: "Had lunch the other day at the restaurant of the Invalides airstation. That's where we should have dined your last evening [...] Excellent Beaujolais and the best coffee in Paris" (UoR, BIF, MS 5060).

BARNEY ROSSET, GROVE PRESS
NEW YORK

17-9-54

SHOTTERY,
KILLINEY,
CO. DUBLIN.
DALKEY 262

My dear Barney

Thanks for yours of the 12th. Very sorry to hear of the death of your father so young. He was lucky to go quick.[1] Frank my brother died finally here in his home 4 days ago. I have been here now coming on to 4 months. I am going back to Paris next week so in future write me there.[2]

Yes, Albery is very slow and vague, but I think he will do a good job in London when the time comes, early next year, probably.[3] I have finished revision of Molloy up to p. 209 and am waiting for Bowles to send me from there to end. Si ça ne dépendait que de moi you'd have the finished article next month. I'll chivvy Patrick when I get back to civilization. Make yr. mind easy the authorised version will go to you & them simul et semel whatever that means. I used to know.[4]

Re future work, I feel very doubtful, though sometimes have premonitions of a brief & final haemorrhage prior to what condolers call the higher life. Can't do anything about it in any case. So tired now that all I can visualize is return to the valley of the Marne and cower till the first cuckoo.

I hear yr. Godot is on the market and a few copies here with Hodges & Figgis.

Will you debit me a copy in favour of

> Dr Alan Thompson
> 24 Fitzwilliam Place
> Dublin[5]

With best wishes to you both,

Yrs. ever

Sam

ALS; 1 leaf, 2 sides; letterhead; NSyU.

1   On 12 September, Barney Rosset wrote of the death of his father, Barnet Rosset, who died suddenly on 4 September (NSyU; "Barnet Rosset Dies; Headed Trust Company," *Chicago Daily Tribune* 6 September 1954: C6).

2   Frank Beckett died on 13 September.

3   Rosset wrote on 12 September: "We have advised the Americans who are interested in producing Godot to contact Albery directly. He wrote us a curiously vague letter but I hope that something eventually happens to let Vladimir and Estragon stroll on a New York stage. We need them."

4   "Si ça ne dépendait que de moi" (If it depended just on me).
"Simul et semel" (Lat., at one and the same time).

5   Hodges and Figgis, a leading Dublin bookstore, now at 56–58 Dawson Street.

JEROME LINDON, EDITIONS DE MINUIT
PARIS

le 14 octobre 1954   Ussy-sur-Marne
Mon cher Jérôme

Merci de votre lettre avec lettres jointes. Elles sont en effet très émouvantes et j'y répondrai sans tarder. Je ne sais qui a pu dire que je devais partir en Rhénanie, il n'en a jamais été question. Mais j'espère un jour pouvoir aller les voir.[1]

J'ai envoyé c/o Ed. de M. une autre lettre pour Mondolfo ainsi que sa traduction avec mes observations. Elle est assez quelconque.[2]

Pour les formules de demande d'exonération d'impôts, aussitôt reçues je les ai remplies en partie, signées et envoyées à Claude Schulmann pour qu'il achève de les remplir.[3] Je crois vous l'avoir écrit au moment de le faire. Il devait vous les retourner et, si j'ai bonne mémoire, il m'a écrit l'avoir fait. Etes-vous bien sûr de ne pas les avoir aux Editions? Si en cherchant encore vous ne les trouve[z] toujours pas je téléphonerai à Schulmann.

Ici ça commence à aller un peu mieux. Je n'ai toujours pas envie de bouger.

Bien amicalement de nous deux à vous deux.

s/ Sam

TLS; 1 leaf, 1 side; IMEC, Beckett, Boîte 1, S. Beckett, Correspondance – Divers, 1950–1956.

14th October 1954   Ussy-sur-Marne
My dear Jérôme

Thank you for your letter, with enclosed letters. They are indeed very moving, and I shall answer them straight away. I do not know who can have said that I was to leave for the Rhineland. There has never been any question of that. But I do hope to go and see them one day.[1]

I have sent c/o the Editions another letter for Mondolfo as well as his translation with my comments. It is pretty ordinary.[2]

As for the requests for tax exemption, the minute I received them I filled part of them in, signed them and sent them on to Claude Schulmann for him to complete.[3] I think I wrote to you about it as I did it. He was to send them back to you, and, if I remember aright, he wrote to say that he had. Are you quite sure that you have not got them at the Editions? If you do not find them when you have another look, I shall telephone Schulmann.

Here things are beginning to go a little better. I still have no wish to move.

Best wishes to both of you from both of us.

Sam

1   An announcement in *Le Figaro Littéraire* on 10 July 1954, "Nouvelles des Lettres," states: "De Noël à Pâques, l'adaptation allemande de la pièce de Samuel Beckett, *En attendant Godot*, a été représentée ... par des prisonniers devant leurs co-détenus de la prison de Lüttringhausen" (8). (From Christmas to Easter, the German translation of Samuel Beckett's play, *En attendant Godot*, has been performed ... by prisoners in front of their fellow inmates at the Lüttringhausen prison.)

With his letter of 12 October, Lindon sent two cuttings (Hugo F. Engel, "Das Drama von Warten auf Gott," *Illustrierte Woche* 30 [24 July 1954] 812–813, and Helmut Ollesch, "Sie warten hinter Gittern: Strafgefangene in Lüttringhausen spielen Samuel Becketts Stück um Godot," *Der Weg* 16/17 [1954] np), and two letters from the prison at Lüttringhausen. One was dated 1 October 1954 from "un Prisonnier" (Karl-Franz Lembke [1903–?]), and the other was dated 3 October 1954 from Ludwig Manker (1898–1985), the chaplain of Zuchthaus Remscheid-Lüttringhausen from 1948 to 1961 (IMEC, Beckett, Boîte 1, S. Beckett, Correspondance – Divers, 1950–1956).

The prisoner describes how he received a copy of the play in July 1953, began to translate it, searched for his actors among the prisoners, and how the curtain went up on 29 November 1953: "Votre Godot ce fut un triomphe, le délire!! – Votre Godot ce fut 'Notre' Godot, à nous! bien à nous!" (Your Godot was a triumph, something wild! – Your Godot was "Our" Godot, ours, our very own!). The prisoner invites SB to see the production in a private performance in the prison.

Chaplain Manker wrote, in his uncertain French: "J'admire le courage d'avoir osé à dire la vérité vraie de la situation réelle de l'humanité d'aujourd'hui [...] Nos hommes l'ont acceptée comme étant leur pièce à eux et moi je garde l'arbre qui fut utilisé sur la scène chez moi à la sacristie car il m'est devenu l'arbre de vie." (I admire the courage of having dared to tell the real truth about the real situation of humanity today [...] Our men accepted it as their play, and I am keeping the tree that was used on the stage, now in my room in the sacristy, for it has become for me the tree of life.) And he writes, "Car moi aussi, je dois me demander souvent 'Est-ce-que j'ai dormi pendant que les autres souffraient?'" (For I too must often ask myself: Did I sleep while others suffered?).

Pastor Peter Schippel, who witnessed a performance in 1954, remembered: "daß während der Aufführung die Wände transparent wurden. Schließlich war die ganze

Justizvollzugsanstalt ein 'Warten auf Godot'. In gewissem Sinne auch die Welt, in die wir zurückkehrten." (During the performance the walls became transparent. In the end, the whole prison was a 'Waiting for Godot.' In a certain sense, so was the whole world to which we returned.) (Pastor Hans Freitag, 26 February 1997, enclosing the recollections of Pastor Peter Schippel, 21 January 1997.)

2 *Aspettando Godot*, the Italian translation of *En attendant Godot* by Luciano Mondolfo, was produced at the Teatro di Via Vittoria, Rome, from 22 November 1954 to 7 January 1955 (Annamaria Cascetta, *Il tragico e l'umorismo: studio sulla drammaturgia di Samuel Beckett*, Storia dello spettacolo [Florence: Le lettere, 2000] 297; R. Rad, "'Aspettando Godot' di S. Beckett al Teatro di Via Vittoria," *Il Giornale d'Italia* 24 November 1954: 5). The Biblioteca e Raccolta Teatrale del Burcardo in Rome holds two typescripts of this translation, annotated by Mondolfo (C76:5 and C76:6).

3 Claude Schulmann, an accounting consultant for Editions de Minuit.

KARL-FRANZ LEMBKE
LÜTTRINGHAUSEN, GERMANY

[on or after 14 October 1954]
Mon cher Prisonnier

Je lis et relis votre lettre.

Godot est de 48 ou 49, je ne me rappelle plus. Mon dernier ouvrage, de 50. Depuis rien. C'est vous dire qu'il y a longtemps que je suis sans mots. Je ne l'ai jamais regretté autant qu'aujourd'hui, où j'en ai besoin pour vous.

Depuis longtemps déjà, un peu au courant de cette extraordinaire histoire de Lüttringhausen, je rêve souvent à celui qui, dans sa cage, a lu, traduit, fait jouer ma pièce. De ma vie d'homme-écrivain il ne m'est jamais rien arrivé de pareil. Emu comme je le suis on fait facilement des phrases, mais d'un [? boniment] peu à vous dès que je ne suis plus le même et ne pourrai plus être le même après ce que vous avez fait vous tous. Là où depuis toujours et pour toujours je tourne en rond, tombe et me relève, il ne fait plus tout à fait noir ni tout à fait silencieux.

Que vous m'ayez ainsi réconforté, je n'ai que cela à vous offrir comme réconfort. Moi qui suis ce qu'on appelle libre d'aller et venir, de me taper la cloche et de faire l'amour, je n'aurai pas la fatuité de vous adresser des paroles de sagesse. A ce que ma pièce a pu vous apporter je ne trouve à ajouter que ceci, l'énorme don que vous m'avez fait en l'acceptant.

AL draft; 1 leaf, 1 page; TCD, MS 4662, 13v [letter sent has not been found].

[on or after 14 October 1954]
My dear Prisoner
    I read and re-read your letter.
    Godot is from 48 or 49, I can't remember. My last work is from 50. Since then, nothing. That tells you how long I have been without words. I have never regretted it so much as now, when I need them for you.
    For a long time now, more or less aware of this extraordinary Lüttringhausen affair, I've thought often of the man who, in his cage, read, translated, put on my play. In all my life as man and writer, nothing like this has ever happened to me. To someone moved as I am, phrases come easily, but from a sloppy way of talking, not at all your style, given that I am no longer the same, and will never again be able to be the same, after what you have done, all of you. In the place where I have always found myself, where I will always find myself, turning round and round, falling over, getting up again, it is no longer wholly dark nor wholly silent.
    That you should have brought me such comfort is all that I can offer you as comfort. I, who am what is called free to come and go, to gorge myself, to make love, I shall not be fatuous enough to dispense to you words of wisdom. To whatever my play may have brought you, I can add this only: the huge gift you have made me by accepting it.

BARNEY ROSSET, GROVE PRESS
NEW YORK

18/10/54   Ussy-sur-Marne
My dear Barney
    Thank you for your letter of Sept. 28th. Yes, I am now mercifully and unbelievably back in France, in the country, with no

more than a glimpse of Paris on the way here. Tired, inert and of a stupidity hitherto unequalled even by me and with no other desire than to potter about in my walled field until the black oxen come home.

I stopped off in London on my way through, saw Glenville and Albery and had a highly unsatisfactory interview with SIR Ralph Richardson who wanted the low-down on Pozzo, his home address and curriculum vitae, and seemed to make the forthcoming of this and similar information the condition of his condescending to illustrate the part of Vladimir. Too tired to give satisfaction I told him that all I knew about Pozzo was in the text, that if I had known more I would have put it in the text, and that this was true also of the other characters. Which I trust puts an end to that star. Indeed the whole set up is unsatisfactory, with Glenville going to Hollywood to make a film, and I think the whole West End attitude to the play all wrong. However Albery is a very nice chap and I suppose knows his business and his public. I shall not however consent to a further extension of their option if they fail to put on the play within the contracted time. I also told Richardson that if by Godot I had meant God I would [have] said God, and not Godot. This seemed to disappoint him greatly.[1]

Bowles too is hopeless. No acknowledgement of my last corrections and no sign of the concluding pages. I do not even know where he is. I wish as heartily as you that it was finished and out of the way. Yes, I have begun Malone, child's play after the Bowles revision, and I look forward to getting on with it rapidly when my false teeth resume their cerebration. You may draw up a translator's contract on the model of Bowles's, I don't hold with it but I'll sign it. And I do appreciate that in taking on me you are taking on a pretty pickle. I thoroughly approve of your project of a lower-priced book.[2]

I was obli[g]ed to write a stinker to Trocchi from Dublin on the occasion of his last Merlin with text of mine full of absurd mistakes because they did not send me proofs.[3] Most extraordinary thing for one writer to do to another. So for the moment we are not on speaking terms.

With best wishes to you both,

Yours

s/ <u>Sam</u>

TLS; 1 leaf, 1 side; *AN AH, upper right margin: 6 rue des FAVORITES, PARIS 15*; NSyU. Previous publication, Beckett, "Letters to Barney Rosset," *Review of Contemporary Fiction*, 70–71; [incorrectly dated as October 10th 1954], Beckett and Rosset, "The *Godot* Letters: A Lasting Effect," *The New Theater Review* [now *Lincoln Center Theater Review*], 11.

1   SB was in London on 24 September when he met Donald Albery, Peter Glenville, and Sir Ralph Richardson (Albery to SB, 22 September 1954, TxU, Peter Glenville collection). SB cancels "Estragon" and inserts "Vladimir" when writing about the role envisaged for Richardson.

In his letter of 14 October, SB describes Richardson's questions in his letter to Mary Manning Howe (Profile, I): "Wanted the low-down on POZZO, his home address, family background & <u>curriculum vitae</u>. As I know nothing of these matters we parted coldly. Have heard nothing since but presume he is out" (TxU, Beckett collection). SB also writes to Susan Manning, on 18 October: "He asked a lot of stupid questions I was too tired to answer. There are no answers to such questions but less tired I could have found some. He is not definitely out, as far as I know. I wish he were, he is not the man for the play, and I do not think the W.E. is the place for it either." The option held by Albery and Glenville on the play was valid through 31 December 1954 (TxU, Glenville collection).

2   Rosset wrote to Trocchi on 28 September, proposing that Merlin cooperate with Grove on the typesetting of *Molloy*, and indicating that Grove planned to publish, both from the same sheets, a cloth-bound and "a paper bound book" (McM, Samuel Beckett Collection, Collection Merlin, 1.25).

3   SB's letter to Trocchi: 27 August 1954.

MAURICE NADEAU

PARIS

19/10/54   6 Rue des Favorites

Paris 15°

Cher Maurice Nadeau

Je m'excuse d'avoir tant tardé à vous répondre. J'ai passé quatre mois affreux à Dublin et viens seulement de rentrer, moins vif que mort.

Si j'avais le moindre inédit potable je m'empresserais de vous le donner. Or je n'ai toujours rien. <u>Watt</u> ne vaut rien et en français moins que rien. Je regrette de l'avoir fait éditer et ne me pardonne pas de l'avoir laissé traduire.[1]

Je me sens plus loin que jamais de pouvoir écrire. Non che la speme il desiderio è morto. Ou presque. Si jamais ça me reprend, aux L.N. la primeur, c'est-à-dire à vous. Car je n'oublie pas.[2]

Croyez, cher Maurice Nadeau, à ma fidèle amitié.

s/

Samuel Beckett

TLS; 1 leaf, 1 side; Nadeau. Previous publication, Nadeau, *Grâces leur soient rendues*, 367.

19/10/54   Rue des Favorites

Paris 15

Dear Maurice Nadeau

I am sorry for having been so slow in replying. I have spent four dreadful months in Dublin and have just come back, more dead than alive.

If I had the slightest piece of half-decent unpublished work I would send it to you there and then. But I still have nothing. *Watt* is worthless, and in French worth less. I regret having given it to a publisher, and cannot forgive myself for having let it be translated.[1]

I feel I am further than ever from being able to write. Non che la speme il desiderio è morto. Or almost. If it ever comes back, the first to have it will be *Les Lettres Nouvelles*, that is, you. For I do not forget.[2]

I am, dear Maurice Nadeau,

Yours most sincerely

Samuel Beckett

1   SB, although having undertaken revision of a French translation of *Watt*, preferred not to have it published (see 12 November 1953, 20 January 1954).

2   "Non che la speme il desiderio è morto" (Not only hope, desire is dead). The line is from an 1833 poem "A se stesso" ("To Himself") by Giacomo Leopardi (*Selected Prose and Poetry*, ed. and tr. Iris Origo and John Heath-Stubbs, Oxford Library of Italian Classics [London: Oxford University Press, 1966] 280–281). SB writes "morto," where the original reads "spento" (snuffed out).

EDITH GREENBURG, INDIANA UNIVERSITY PRESS
BLOOMINGTON, INDIANA

November 18th 1954   6 Rue des Favorites
                                                      Paris 15°

Dear Miss Greenburg

Thank you for your letter of October 18th, also for MS of anthology and copy of The Cross and the Sword.[1]

I have no doubt there is much in my translation that leaves a great deal to be desired and much that calls for revision. This unfortunately I shall not be able to undertake for a very considerable time, because of other commitments.[2]

If you wish to publish this text in the near future I suggest that you modify it as you see fit and that I withdraw my name as translator. Or else that only those poems which you are prepared to accept in their present form be signed by me and the others by their emendator. Either of these solutions is acceptable to me.

If on the other hand you prefer to wait for my revised text, I cannot promise to let you have it before the autumn of next year at the earliest. It is only fair you should know this.

I shall not return the MS before hearing from you.

> Yours sincerely
> s/
>   Samuel Beckett

TLS; 1 leaf, 1 side; IUP; copy, InU, Lilly, IUP MSS II, Box 12.

1 On 18 October 1954, Edith R. Greenburg, Associate Editor of Indiana University Press, wrote to SB sending to him a marked copy of the TMS of his translations of the *Anthology of Mexican Poetry* that he had done for UNESCO in 1950 (see 27 [February 1950], n. 5). With this letter, Greenburg sent SB *The Cross and the Sword*, Robert Graves's translation of *Enriquillo* by Manuel de Jesús Galván (1834–1910); it was published in the UNESCO Collection of Representative Works series by Indiana University Press in 1954.

2 SB had been surprised to receive a letter from Sally Konitzky of Indiana University Press, dated 26 March 1954, that informed him of their plans to publish the *Anthology of Mexican Poetry*; SB replied to Konitzky on 6 April 1954:

> More than four years ago I was commissioned by UNESCO to do this translation and, so great was the urgency then, given four months in which to complete it. I

have had no news of it since and had not the slightest idea that you were undertaking its publication. Have you acquired the rights from UNESCO, or are you acting as UNESCO's publisher? I should be greatly obliged if you would let me know what exactly the position is.

I trust I may count on your sending me proofs. (IUP; copy, InU, Lilly, IUP MSS II, Box 12.)

In her letter to SB of 18 October, Edith Greenburg wrote that there were "a number of spots that seemed to us awkward or infelicitous or somewhat more florid than the Spanish seemed to require" (IUP). She asked him to look over the marked passages and queries.

JEROME LINDON, EDITIONS DE MINUIT
PARIS

18/11/54   Ussy
Mon cher Jérôme

Je crois qu'on aurait tort d'empêcher des groupements de jeunes de monter Godot pour un nombre limité de représentations et dans des conditions à définir. Je serais donc plutôt d'avis que nous donnions notre accord de principe à cette jeune compagnie de Toulouse.[1] Il faudrait évidemment qu'ils obtiennent l'accord de Roger, peut-être aussi du Babylone, même s'il n'existe plus.[2] Comme on ne peut contrôler chaque mise en scène il semble injuste de laisser à l'étranger le monopole du massacre. Voilà mon point de vue. Mais à vous de décider.

Nous rentrons demain ou samedi. Donc à très bientôt.

Bien amicalement à vous deux.

s/ Sam

TLS; 1 leaf, 1 side; IMEC, Beckett, Boîte 1, S. Beckett, Correspondance – Divers, 1950–1956.

18/11/54   Ussy
My dear Jérôme

I think it would be wrong to prevent groups of young people from putting on *Godot*, for a limited number of performances and with certain provisos. So my view would be on the whole that we should give our agreement in principle to this young Toulouse company.[1] They would of course have to get Roger's agreement, maybe that of the Babylone too, even if it no longer exists.[2] As we can't keep an eye on every production, it seems unfair to leave the monopoly of botch-ups to foreigners. That is my point of view. But the decision is yours. We are going back tomorrow or on Saturday. So till very soon.

Warmest greetings to you both

Sam

1   On 17 November, Lindon had asked SB how to respond to the request of the Comédiens-Troubadours, Toulouse, who wished to produce *En attendant Godot*. Lindon was concerned: "Nous n'avons aucune garantie que ce sera fait convenablement" (We have no guarantee that it will be done properly) (IMEC, Beckett, Boîte 1, S. Beckett, Correspondance – Divers, 1950–1956).

2   Lindon wrote to Blin on 26 November, to ask him if he knew the Comédiens-Troubadours, and whether he would approve (IMEC, Beckett, Boîte 1, S. Beckett, Correspondance – Divers, 1950–1956).
The Théâtre de Babylone announced their autumn program in September 1954: Eugène Ionesco's *Victimes du devoir* (*Victims of Duty*) and Bertolt Brecht's *L'Exception et la règle* (*The Exception and the Rule*) would begin on 20 September, with performances of Strindberg's *Mademoiselle Julie* starring Eléonore Hirt on Wednesdays ("Brecht, Ionesco, Strindberg au Théâtre de Babylone," *Le Monde* 18 September 1954: 9). Although Geneviève Latour and Florence Claval indicate that Jean-Marie Serreau ceased his active involvement with the Théâtre de Babylone in September 1954, the program of Serreau's group seems to have continued into November 1954 (Geneviève Latour and Florence Claval, eds., *Les Théâtres de Paris* [Paris: Bibliothèque Historique de la Ville de Paris, 1991], 257). Daily advertisements for *Victimes du devoir* continue through 31 October 1954; *Mademoiselle Julie* is advertised through 11 November 1954.

BARNEY ROSSET, GROVE PRESS
NEW YORK

24/11/54   6 Rue des Favorites
                                              Paris 15°

My dear Barney

Thanks for your letters. I thought you would like to know that I have finished revising Bowles's text and have sent it to him to type out clean.[1] Then I go through it rapidly once again and then off it goes to you. Bowles wrote me that the Merlin people, or rather Gerodias who is now in charge of the collection, are agitating to get hold of the text.

I wrote Bowles that there was no question of releasing it until I had gone through it all again. Have you come to an understanding with them about simultaneity of publication here and in America? Am I at liberty to hand them over the text the day it leaves here for New York? Or do you wish me to hold it up until it is in your hands? Let me know your views on this.[2] Nothing further from London.[3] A letter from New York from one Sadoff of the Actors Studio asking for permission to do Godot. All I can do is to refer him to Albery who seems set on a Broadway production and so is not likely to be helpful.[4] Shall get on now with Malone. Six months should do it.

    Best wishes to Loly and yourself,

      s/ Sam

    Samuel Beckett

TLS; 1 leaf, 1 side; NSyU.

1   With his letter of 27 October, Rosset sent the contract for the translation of *Malone meurt*; his letter of 28 October asked about the translation of *Molloy*, adding that the news from Austryn Wainhouse was that Bowles had sent the final corrections to SB.

2   SB frequently writes "Gerodias" or "Gérodias" rather than "Girodias"; this will not be further noted.

Because of an agreement between Merlin and Grove to release jointly the English translation of *Molloy*, respectively in Europe and the United States, SB is concerned about how this should be done.

3   The option held by Albery and Glenville ended at the close of the year.

4   Fred Sadoff (1926–1994) of The Actors' Studio in New York. Lee Strasberg was the Director (1951–1982) of this theatre workshop formed to encourage continuing development of professional actors and to experiment with new forms of theatre. Method acting is its hallmark.

BARNEY ROSSET, GROVE PRESS
NEW YORK

December 7th 1954   6 Rue des Favorites
                                     Paris 15me

My dear Barney

    Thanks for your letters of November 27th and December 1st. Herewith <u>Malone</u> contract duly signed.[1]

I have seen Bowles. He has finished typing out clean the revised text of <u>Molloy</u> and I am at present giving it a final go-through. It will certainly go off to you next week. I am not satisfied with it but have reached the stage when I simply do not see it any more.[2]

Agreed about the <u>bon à tirer</u> not to be given to Gerodias before you. I think you would be better advised to set the book independently, even though it prove a little more expensive.[3]

When we get <u>Molloy</u> off to you I shall get on with <u>Malone</u> of which I have already translated about 60 pages.

An ultimatum has gone off to Albery and Glenville to get on with the job or abandon their option (and their deposit).[4]

With best wishes to Loly and yourself I am

Yours very sincerely

s/ Sam.

Samuel Beckett

TLS; 1 leaf, 1 side; enclosure: signed contract for translation of *Malone Dies*, date-stamped received Dec 10, 1954; NSyU.

1   Rosset's letter to SB of 27 November crossed in the mail with SB's to him of 24 November, as Rosset noted in his letter of 1 December (NSyU). The Grove contract for *Malone Dies* was with SB as translator.

2   SB later wrote to Pamela Mitchell: "Putting the finishing daubs at last to Bowles's <u>Molloy</u>, that makes about the 10th re-reading and it has my soul drowned in vomit. I am absurdly and stupidly the creature of my books and *L'Innommable* is more responsible for my present plight than all the other good reasons put together" (27 December 1954, UoR, BIF, MS 5060).

3   On 1 December, Rosset wrote to SB that he had not heard from Merlin or Maurice Girodias as to how they wished to work with Grove Press; Rosset indicated that he preferred to use photographic offsets rather than printed sheets imported from France. Rosset warned SB not to "allow printing to go ahead [with Merlin] before you have given your final o.k. on page proofs," and not to do so "before you do to us" (NSyU).

"Bon à tirer" (passed for press).

4   On 2 December 1954, Jérôme Lindon asked Kitty Black to insist that Albery and Glenville confirm their intention to produce *Waiting for Godot* (IMEC, Beckett, Boîte 5, S. Beckett Correspondance 1962–1968, Curtis Brown 1957 [for1952–1957]).

CHRONOLOGY 1955

1955	13 January	SB gives Patrick Bowles final text of translation of *Molloy*; Bowles sends to Rosset on 23 January.
	27 January	Pamela Mitchell sails from France to New York.
	31 January	SB writing a new play.
	7 February	Working on second act of the new play.
	March	Collection Merlin / Olympia Press publish *Molloy*.
	6 March	Opening of Blin's production of *Wachten op Godot*, Toneelgroep Theater, Arnhem.
	13 March	SB completes draft of new play. Revises texts written between 1945 and 1951 to be published as *Nouvelles et Textes pour rien*.
	27 March	Delivers manuscript of *Nouvelles et Textes pour rien* to Editions de Minuit.
	April	State of emergency declared in Algeria.
	15 April	SB is witness at the wedding of Stephen Joyce and Solange Raytchine in Paris.
	May–June	"Deux Textes pour rien [I, IX]" published in *Monde Nouveau/Paru*.
	28 May	*Esperando a Godot* performed in Madrid, despite ban on publicity and public performance.
	June	Widespread strikes in France.
	week of 5 June	SB meets in Paris the American painter Joan Mitchell (former wife of Barney Rosset).
	28 June	Attends opening of Alan Schneider's production of Thornton Wilder's *The Skin of Our Teeth*, Théâtre Sarah Bernhardt, Paris.
	August	*Molloy* published by Grove Press.
	3 August	Opening of *Waiting for Godot*, Arts Theatre, London, directed by Peter Hall.

18 August	SB completes draft of his translation of *Malone meurt.* Has written a mime scenario for Deryk Mendel.
7 September	Extract from *Watt* broadcast on the BBC Third Programme.
12 September	*Waiting for Godot* transfers to the Criterion Theatre, London.
October	"Trois poèmes" ("Accul," "Mort de A.D.," and "vive morte") published in *Cahiers des Saisons*, a Minuit journal previously entitled *84: Nouvelle Revue Littéraire.*
8 October	SB spends several days with Giorgio and Asta Joyce in Zurich. Visits Joyce's grave.
28 October	Opening of *Waiting for Godot* at the Pike Theatre, Dublin. Composer John Beckett working in Paris with Deryk Mendel on music for a mime (*Acte sans paroles*).
November	"Henri Hayden, homme-peintre" published in *Arts-documents* (Geneva).
3 November	SB meets Donald Albery in Paris.
15 November	Imprint date of *Nouvelles et Textes pour rien.*
from 26 November	SB discusses *Waiting for Godot* with Alan Schneider in Paris.
early December	SB and Schneider attend several performances of London production of *Waiting for Godot.* SB meets German actress Elisabeth Bergner in London.
8 December	SB attends 100th performance of *Waiting for Godot* in London.

16. Roger Blin on the set of August Strindberg's *La Sonate des spectres*, 1949

ROGER BLIN
ARNHEM, HOLLAND

29.1.55   6 rue des Favorites
                                           Paris 15e

Bien cher Roger

Merci de ta carte. J'ai vu Tonny hier soir et ai été navré d'apprendre par elle que tu es souffrant. Une hernie, m'a-t-elle dit. J'espère que ce n'est pas grave et que tu vas vite t'en remettre. Laisse-toi soigner

surtout et ne t'acharne pas à cause de la pièce.[1] Il paraît que tu seras
ici pour quelques jours au début de février. Fais-moi signe. Je serai
peut-être à Ussy mais je rappliquerai et nous passerons j'espère une
soirée ensemble.

Je suis trop fatigué et trop triste pour pouvoir t'écrire une lettre qui
vaille la peine. Le dernier travail est au point mort, mais je n'aban-
donne pas. Il y a là une pièce quelque part, mais comme on est faible!
Et les instants de force on les use à des conneries. Si jamais j'y arrive
ce sera je crois grâce à toi. Je n'ai jamais pu te dire mon amitié, ni te la
montrer.

Donne de tes nouvelles, des bonnes.

Bien affectueusement de nous 2

Sam

ALS; 1 leaf, 1 side; *env to* Monsieur Roger Blin, Hotel Carnegie, ARNHEM, HOLLANDE,
pm 30-01-55, Paris; IMEC, Blin.

29.1.55   6 Rue des Favorites
                                               Paris 15

My dear Roger

Thank you for your card. I saw Tonny yesterday, and was really
sorry to learn from her that you're not well. Hernia, she said. I hope
it's not serious, and that you'll soon be over it. Above all, allow
yourself to be looked after, and don't work too hard on the play.[1]
Apparently you'll be here for a few days in early February. Let me
know. I may be in Ussy, but I'll dash back, and I hope we'll be able to
spend an evening together.

I'm too tired and too sad to be able to write a proper letter. The
latest work has ground to a halt, but I'm not giving up. There's a
play there somewhere, but how weak one is! And then one uses up
the moments of strength on silly things. If I ever get there, it will be
thanks to you. I've never been able to put into words how fond I am of
you, or show it.

Let's have some news from you, good news.

Much love from both of us

Sam

1   Blin was directing *Wachten op Godot* in Arnhem, with Dutch actors (see 14 October 1953, n. 3; Blin and Peskine, *Roger Blin*, 103–104).

On 21 January, SB wrote to Jacoba van Velde that he had received a card from Roger Blin from Honfleur, on the Normandy coast: "Il a l'air content des acteurs et des premières répétitions" (He seems pleased with the actors and the first rehearsals) (BNF 19794/30).

BARNEY ROSSET, GROVE PRESS
NEW YORK

31.1.55   6 Rue des Favorites

                                                         Paris 15°

My dear Barney

Thanks for your letter and – in advance – for the copies of G. not yet arrived. I should be grateful if you would debit me with a further copy in favour of

Pamela Mitchell
229 E. 48 Street
New York City[1]

Saw Bowles yesterday. He sent you the MS on 23rd of this month, so you must have received it shortly after having sent your last letter to me. Hope you will not be too disappointed by our united labours. The same day he gave Gérodias his copy. It appears G. is writing to you about the possibility of sharing blocks.[2]

Godot in English, latest edition: Guinness finds himself unexpectedly free, a film-making having been postponed, and the New Theatre ditto, as a result of two successive flops, hence hopes of an immediate production with Guinness in London.[3] Further: Wallach, of T Williams Teahouse fame, wants to do the play in New York, this with blessing of Albery & Co, and with or without Guinness. Note: next week all this will be changed.[4]

I am struggling with a new "play" in French, so have dropped Malone for the time being. If you could give me some idea when you would like to have the English MS of <u>Malone</u>, that would help me to bestlay my plans.

Bien amicalement à tous les deux.

s/ Sam

Samuel Beckett

TLS; 1 leaf, 1 side; NSyU.

1   Pamela Mitchell sailed for New York on 28 January (SB to Pamela Mitchell, 29 January 1955, UoR, BIF, MIS 4660).

2   The English translation of *Molloy* by Patrick Bowles and SB was sent to Grove Press on 20 January. SB writes Gérodias instead of Girodias.

3   The two previous plays at the New Theatre had not been "flops": *I Am a Camera* by John van Druten enjoyed a long run through 1954, and *The Night of the Ball* by Michael Burn opened on 12 January and continued into March 1955.

4   Kitty Black's letter to Lindon of 19 January 1955 reports interest in the play by Eli Wallach (b. 1915), who played in *The Rose Tattoo* (1951) by Tennessee Williams and in *Teahouse of the August Moon* on Broadway in 1953 (in a stage adaptation by John Patrick [1905–1995] of a novel by Vern Sneider [1916–1981]).

ALAN SIMPSON

DUBLIN

February 7th 1955   6 Rue des Favorites

                                                    Paris 15°

My dear Alan Simpson

        Thank you for your letter. Donald Albery has now got rid of the star-obsessed Glenville and acquired for himself exclusively a further six months option on <u>Godot</u>. He says, as usual, that he will now press forward with production, and perhaps he will, with only himself to please. In any case I am afraid we must stick to our agreement with him not to produce in Dublin before the London opening. In other words I cannot give you formally permission at this stage to open at the Pike on April 23rd, though it is quite possible you may be able to do so. I think your best course would be to hold your horses until we get a definite date from Albery and in the meantime get on with something else. Sorry for all this mess.[1]

Glad to hear of your success with "The Q.F.". Remember me to the new O'Casey.[2]

Yours sincerely

s/ Sam. Beckett

Samuel Beckett

TLS; 1 leaf, 1 side; TCD, MS 10731/13.

1   The agreement to allow production of *Waiting for Godot* one week following the London premiere: SB to Lindon, 12 July 1954.

2   The Pike Theatre had produced *The Quare Fellow* by Brendan Behan (1923–1964) from 19 November to 18 December 1954. The new play by Sean O'Casey was *The Bishop's Bonfire*, to be produced at the Gaiety Theatre in Dublin from 28 February ("Date fixed for Mr. Sean O'Casey's New Play," *The Times* 18 January 1955: 5; "Mr. Sean O'Casey's New Play," *The Times* 1 March 1955: 6).

PAMELA MITCHELL

NEW YORK

7.2.55   Paris

Pamela – Nothing from you yet. In yesterday's paper I saw a photo of the Liberté struggling towards berth through Hudson ice. Which must mean you were days overdue and had a bad crossing. I hope you found my letter on arrival and perhaps also the Grove Godot which I asked Rosset to send you.[1] News from London is bad, Guinness seems definitely out of the question and Glenville now will not produce unless he has him or a star of comparable magnitude! Albery wants a new contract in his name alone, which he can have if he coughs up another £250. But I think it is more likely we shall have done with these gentlemen and let Wannamacker have it if he still wants it.[2] Struggling gloomily with Act II of the other, making blunders all the way that I have not much hope of retrieving. An occupation, but not a pleasant one. Saw Roger Blin yesterday evening, here for a few days from Holland. It appears the play has been violently attacked by the Roman Catholic press in Holland, that the municipality of Arnhem got the wind up and were on the point of banning the production, saying it was a homosexual work because Gogo says to Didi, "Tu vois, tu pisses mieux quand je ne suis pas là"! But they seem to have been calmed by the threat of the players' director to resign if the play was banned and rehearsals continue.[3]

I wonder what you have found at the office on your return. Here everything is as bloody as can be. I haven't been to the country. The central heating is off to-day for chimney-sweeping and I'm shivering. I've given up bothering about the old heart and when it hurts me in the street I quicken my step. I've been reading in your grand Baudelaire and in the Holy Bible the story of the Flood and wishing the Almighty had never had a soft spot for Noah. And there's no 4 bis and no you.[4]

17. Pamela Winslow Mitchell. From the Vassar College yearbook, *The Vassarion*, 1943

That's the way with it.

    Love

      <u>Sam</u>

ALS; 2 leaves, 2 sides; *env to* Pamela Mitchell, 229 E. 48<u>th</u> Street, New York 17, N.Y., U.S.A., *upper left corner* <u>Air Mail</u>, *verso* S. Beckett, 6 Rue des Favorites, Paris 15°; *pm* [7-2-55], Paris; UoR, BIF, 5060.

1 Pamela Mitchell sailed from Le Havre on 28 January, on the *Liberté*; the ship arrived on time in New York on 3 February, but it could not dock for two hours because of ice on the Hudson River (Wayne Phillips, "Zero Weather Numbs City on Coldest Day in 7 Years," *The New York Times* 4 February 1955: 1 [with photo]; "Shipping Mails," *The New York Times* 3 February 1955: 49). The newspaper in which SB saw the picture has not been found.

2 See 7 February 1955 to Alan Simpson. SB canceled "fame" and wrote "magnitude!" American film actor and director Sam Wanamaker (1919–1993) sent a telegram to SB on 20 December 1954, asking if the production rights of *Waiting for Godot* were free for England and the United States (IMEC, Beckett, Boîte 5, S. Beckett, Correspondance 1962–1968, Curtis Brown 1957 [*for* 1952–1957]). SB misspells "Wanamaker."

3 In Arnhem, *Wachten op Godot* was performed privately, not to the general public, to avoid the "reactions of an unprepared audience" (Jeanne van Schaik-Willing, "Wachten op Godot," *De Groene Amsterdammer* [6 March 1955] np).

"Tu vois, tu pisses mieux quand je ne suis pas là" ("You see, you piss better when I am not there") (*En attendant Godot* [Minuit], 99; *Waiting for Godot* [Grove], 38).

4 Pamela Mitchell had been abroad for six months on a leave of absence from her position with Harold Oram.

Mitchell's apartment in Paris had been at 4 bis Rue de la Grande Chaumière, Paris 6.

PAMELA MITCHELL

NEW YORK

Feb 17th 1955   Ussy-sur-Marne

Pamela

    Many thanks for 5000, glad they were of use, there was no hurry, your credit didn't need them to be good. So sorry to hear of your mother's illness and hope she is well over the op and the outlook good. Tu n'avais pas besoin de ça. It would have been easier if you had found an account waiting for you at Oram Inc. but I've no doubt you'll find something in a very short time and perhaps of a more interesting nature.[1] I am here alone in the country, arrived to-day and walked the three miles from the station in the sun and the cold. There were days in Paris towards the end of your stay when I wondered if I would ever be able to get over that piece of ground on my feet in this life again. I have looked at my trees, the negundo, prunus and limes are actually budding, the chestnut too, and the cedar hangs on to its needles. The "lawn" is white, the house warm and I have the Telefunken for company. Nothing to eat in the house till to-morrow, but tea, wine and tordboyaux, so I'm all right.[2] News of Godot: the star-haunted Glenville has taken himself off thanks be to Christ and the Albery has acquired – for another 250 pounds advance on royalties – for himself alone a further 6 months option for U.K. and U.S.A. and talks almost seriously of getting the play on in London in April. This arrangement had hardly been signed when I had a letter from one Kerz (decorator) of the New Repertory Theatre, N.Y. asking for permission to put on the play on Broadway with Buster Keaton, Marion Brando, Cox and Allen! It was bitter to have to say no. Imagine Keaton as Vladimir and Brando as Estragon! The others I know nothing of.[3] The percentage for UK and the States is appallingly low compared to Paris, starting at 5% (Paris 12% all over) of gross receipts, this including my fee as translator! This seems pure robbery to me, but apparently it's normal. When Lindon gets his whack out of this there won't be much left for oursins, Beaujolais, niece and nephew.[4] The losing battle with my maniacs continues, I have A out of his armchair flat on his face on the stage at the moment and B trying in vain to get him back. I know at least I'll go on to the end before using the waste-paper basket.[5] I have been lousy and miserable and so nervous that the bawls are out of me, in the house and in the street, before I can stop them. Hope I'll calm down here a bit. Have decided not to go to Holland after all. Did I tell you the play was nearly banned there after an onslaught from the R.C. press? Wouldn't surprise if it was yet.[6] There is an exhibition in a few days of poems-engravings, or if you like engravings to poems. Bill Hayter asked me for a text and I gave him the following, written a couple of years ago:

> je voudrais que mon amour meure
> qu'il pleuve sur le cimetière
> et les ruelles où je vais
> pleurant celle qui crut m'aimer

Haven't yet seen what he has made of it. He has an exhibition at the moment in the Rue La Boétie, interesting. He has lived a good deal in New York, perhaps you know his work.[7] Haven't got in touch with your man yet, for want of an occasion, but he may come in useful later on.[8] Rosset has at last received MS of Molloy and I suppose the proofs will soon be upon me. The moquette is down and the doors back and I'm 50 dollars the poorer and no happier, though it's always a pleasure to get rid of 50 dollars.[9] Yes, the Seat of the Scornful was good though the scene in the piscine with the lights out seemed just waste of time. Am now reading La Maison Biscornue which is very tired Christie.[10] Have been reading in your big magnificent Zingarelli with much satisfaction and wishing he was more explicit about the difference between the s's of cosa and rosa and the zz's of mezzo and pazzo.[11] Seem to have forgotten more Italian than I thought. Paris is lonely, and Montparnasse in particular, without you and I feel remorseful that I didn't give you a better time that last fortnight? Make up for it some day. Je t'embrasse bien fort.[12]

Sam

Will you tell me if this letter is sufficiently stamped?[13]

ALS; 1 leaf, 2 sides; *T env to* Pamela Mitchell, 229 E. 48th Street, New York 17, N.Y., U.S.A., *upper left* Par Avion, Air Mail; *pm* 18-2-55, La Ferté-sous-Jouarre; *pm* 28-2-55, New York *postage due*; UoR, BIF, MS 5060.

1   Pamela Mitchell's adoptive mother was Marion Bunker Winslow Mitchell (n.d.). "Tu n'avais pas besoin de ça" (You didn't need this). Mitchell had apparently returned to New York to find that Harold Oram had no assignments for her.

2   Telefunken, here a German brand of radio.
"Tord-boyaux" (rotgut).

3   Kitty Black requested a new option on *Waiting for Godot* for an additional six months in the name of Donald Albery on 31 January 1955, to which Jérôme Lindon agreed on 8 February (IMEC, Beckett, Boîte 5, S. Beckett, Correspondance 1962–1968, Curtis Brown 1957 [*for* 1952–1957]).
The letter to SB from theatrical designer and producer Leo Kerz (1912–1976) has not been found. Kerz and Hardy William Smith (1916–2001, life partner of Peter Glenville) were Managing Directors of the New Repertory Theatre. Their plans were still tentative in January: Kerz said "there still were pieces that had to be fitted into place" but that there was a possibility of *Waiting for Godot* being performed with Alec Guinness (Lewis Funke, "News and Gossip Gathered on the Rialto: New Repertory Theatre May Still Make Debut This Season," *The New York Times* 9 January 1955: 11).

The cast mentioned to SB consisted of Buster Keaton, Marlon Brando, Wally Cox (1925–1973), and Steve Allen (1921–2000). SB types "Marion" for "Marlon."

SB wrote to Pamela Mitchell on 23 February: "Wrote to Kerz I wished I could give him permission to play it in a stable, with Brando & Keaton" (UoR, BIF, MS 5060). SB's letter to Kerz has not been found.

4   "Oursins" (sea urchins).

5   SB wrote to Barney Rosset on 11 February, referring to the play as "my two old men in a dead world" (NSyU).

6   Blin's production in Arnhem was to open on 6 March.

7   Stanley William Hayter had an exhibition of paintings at the Galerie Denise René, from 4 February to 2 March. Hayter had a further exhibition, Engravings, Etchings and Lithographs, at St. George's Gallery Prints in London from March through April; the catalogue for this exhibition does not list any work that illustrated SB's poem (Herbert Edward Read, *Exhibition of Engravings, Etchings and Lithographs* [London: St. George's Gallery Prints, 1955]). Hayter also published illustrations of poems in *Poétique de la danse: avec des poèmes de Euripide, Kabir, Tagore, W. von der Vogelweide, Góngora, Schiller ...*, ed. Jean-Clarence Lambert (Paris: Falaize, 1955); Beckett's poem was not in this collection. SB translates this poem as:

> I would like my love to die
> and the rain to be raining on the graveyard
> and on me walking the streets
> mourning her who thought she loved me
> (Samuel Beckett, *Selected Poems: 1930–1989*, 61).

8   The person whom Mitchell suggested SB should contact has not been identified.

9   SB had carpets fitted, which required removal and rehanging of the doors.

10   John Dickson Carr, *The Seat of the Scornful* (1943). Agatha Christie, *La Maison biscornue* (1951; *Crooked House*, 1949).

11   Nicola Zingarelli, ed., *Vocabolario della lingua italiana* (Bologna: Nicola Zanichelli, 1954) (Mark Nixon, BIF, confirms that SB owned this edition, 30 November 2008). The discussion of the pronunciation of these consonants is on an unnumbered page under the heading "Avvertenze."

12   "Je t'embrasse bien fort" (Big kiss).

13   The PS is inserted perpendicularly to the text in the right margin. The envelope of this letter was marked "insufficient postage."

JEROME LINDON, EDITIONS DE MINUIT
PARIS

le 19 février 1955   Ussy-sur-Marne

Cher Jérôme

Ci-joint une lettre que j'ai reçue du fils Baeza et copie de ma réponse. Je ne sais pas si j'ai dit ce qu'il fallait. Vous seriez infiniment gentil de lui mettre un mot en lui disant ce que vous en pensez. Désavouez-moi si j'ai dit des conneries.[1]

Ici tout est blanc et les arbres ont le culot de bourgeonner. Une carte de Roger, les godasses de van Gogh! Tout se présente bien, sauf le public.[2]

Bien amicalement à Annette et à vous-même.

s/ Sam

Enclosure: F E R N A N D O   B A E Z A ,   M A D R I D

le 19 février 1955   6 Rue des Favorites
                                                        Paris 15°

Cher Monsieur

J'ai bien reçu votre lettre du 14 courant. Il est exact que nous avons un contrat avec M. Martinez, qu'il a versé un à-valoir et que j'ai revu rapidement avec lui la traduction de <u>Godot</u>.[3] Il me semble néanmoins que les accords passés avec lui ne sont en rien incompatibles avec l'autorisation que je vous ai donnée de monter la pièce dans un cercle fermé, devant un public d'invités et pour un nombre restreint de représentations, et c'est bien dans cet esprit que j'ai accédé à votre demande. Je pourrais évidemment, conformément aux termes de notre contrat avec M. Martinez, lui interdire de présenter ma pièce autrement qu'intégralement, mais je ne tiens pas à aller jusque-là, vu le mal qu'il s'est donné et les difficultés qu'il a dû surmonter. J'ai vraiment l'impression qu'il se méprend sur la nature du spectacle que vous vous proposez de présenter et qu'il vous sera possible de parvenir à un arrangement à l'amiable avec lui.[4] En tout état de cause il n'est pas question que vous me versiez le moindre à-valoir, puisque votre entreprise n'a rien de commercial.[5] J'ai eu sans doute tort de ne pas prévenir M. Martinez au moment d'approuver votre projet, mais je n'en voyais pas l'utilité. Envoyez, si vous jugez bon, copie de cette lettre à M. Martinez. Je suis persuadé qu'il acceptera que la pièce soit présentée d'une part par lui, avec certaines coupures, devant son public payant, et de l'autre par vous, intégralement, pour vos invités. Et s'il devait vous gagner de vitesse, votre travail ne perdrait pour autant rien de sa raison d'être, étant donné le décalage entre les deux textes, sans parler de la différence d'interprétation.

Le texte des Editions Poseidon n'est pas celui de M. Martinez.[6]

Comme je ne suis pas à Paris en ce moment je ne peux pas discuter de tout cela avec mon éditeur, M. Lindon. Mais je vais lui communiquer votre lettre en le priant de bien vouloir vous donner son opinion, bien plus autorisée que la mienne, sur vos droits et ceux de M. Martinez et sur la meilleure suite à donner à cette affaire.[7]

Rappelez-moi, je vous prie, bien amicalement au souvenir de Monsieur votre père et croyez-moi cordialement à vous.

Samuel Beckett

TLcc; 1 leaf, 1 side; *enclosure* Fernando Baeza to SB, 19 February 1955 [1 leaf,1 side]; IMEC, Beckett, Boîte 1, Correspondance – Divers, 1950–1956.

19th February 1955   Ussy-sur-Marne
Dear Jérôme

Enclosed a letter I have received from Baeza junior and a copy of my reply. I don't know if I said the right kind of thing. It would be really kind of you if you would drop him a line saying what you think. Disown me if I've talked rubbish.[1]

Here all is white and the trees have the cheek to start budding. A card from Roger – Van Gogh's boots! Everything is looking good, except the public.[2]

All good wishes to Annette and yourself.

Sam

Enclosure: F E R N A N D O   B A E Z A ,   M A D R I D
19th February 1955   6 Rue des Favorites
                                             Paris 15

Dear Mr Baeza,

Received your letter of the 14th. You are correct in saying that we have a contract with M. Martinez, that he made an advance payment, and that I had a quick look over the translation of *Godot* with him.[3] Nevertheless, it seems to me that the agreements that we have entered into with him are in no way incompatible with the authorisation that I gave you to put on the play in a private club, in front of an invited audience, and for a limited number of performances, and it was with this in mind that I agreed to your request. I could of course, in line with the terms of our contract with M. Martinez, forbid him to put on my play in anything other than its complete form, but I have no wish to go as far as that, in view of the trouble he has taken and the difficulties he has had to overcome. I really do have the impression that he misunderstands the nature of the performance that you are proposing to put on, and that you will be able to reach an amicable agreement with him.[4] In any event there is no question of your having to send me any advance payment, since there is nothing commercial about your venture.[5] No doubt I was wrong not to warn M. Martinez when I gave my approval to your project, but I saw no point in doing so. Do, if you see fit, send a copy of this letter to M. Martinez. I feel sure that he will accept that the play can be staged, on the one hand by him, with certain cuts, in front of his paying public, and on the other hand by you, in its full version, for an invited audience. And if he were to get going ahead of you, your work would lose none of its raison d'être on that account, given the difference between the two texts, not to mention the difference of interpretation.

The Editions Poseidon text is not the text that M. Martinez has.[6]

As I am away from Paris at the moment, I am unable to discuss all this with my publisher, M. Lindon. But I shall pass on your letter to him and ask him to be kind enough to give you his opinion, which has far more authority than mine, on your rights and those of M. Martinez, and on the best way to proceed in this matter.[7]

Please remember me to your father, and believe me to be
Yours sincerely
Samuel Beckett

1   Fernando Baeza (1920–2002) wrote to SB on 14 February. He was the son of Ricardo Baeza whom SB had known at UNESCO when he worked with Octavio Paz on the *Anthology of Mexican Poetry*.

2   Roger Blin's card to SB has not been found.

3   In his letter of 14 February, Fernando Baeza wrote that the Madrid production of *Esperando a Godot*, for which SB had given permission to his father in a letter of 24 November 1954, had been postponed to the end of March while he and his father sought actors capable of doing justice to the work. They were using a translation prepared by the Ultraist poet Rafael Lasso de la Vega (1890–1959), Marqués de Villanova; Ricardo Baeza had revised this translation.

Now, Fernando Baeza reported, their plans were upset because Trino Martínez Trives had announced that he had a contract to produce the play in his own translation, which had been approved by SB, and that he challenged the right for another production to be done at the same time in Madrid.

4   Baeza felt that a rush to be the first to produce the play would be detrimental, leading him to confront SB:

> Ou bien M. Martínez monte la pièce comme il l'entend, avec certaines coupures qu'il considère inévitables à fin d'obtenir la permission de la censure pour des représentations "à guichet ouvert", ou bien je continue avec mes efforts pour la présenter dans son intégrité au public lettré de Madrid dans l'Institut de Boston, institution culturelle qui jouit d'un statut spécial en raison de son origine étrangère. (IMEC, Beckett, Boîte 1, S. Beckett, Correspondance – Divers, 1950–1956.)

> (Either M. Martínez puts on the play as he intends, with certain cuts which he thinks inevitable in order to obtain the censor's permission for open performances, or I carry on with my attempt to present the uncut text to the educated Madrid public in the Boston Institute, a cultural institution which enjoys special status because of its foreign origins.)

5   In order to document his rights, Fernando Baeza asked for a contract, for which he provided a model, and expressed his willingness to pay a fee.

6   *Esperando a Godot*, tr. Pablo Palant, revised by the author (see 19 August 1954, n. 3).

7   No letter from Jérôme Lindon to Fernando Baeza has been found.

PAMELA MITCHELL
NEW YORK

13.3.55   Ussy-sur-Marne

Poor Pamela you are having a hideous time and I can't help or I don't see how. I wonder would Rosset be able to do anything, it would be no harm to try him. If you decide to I'll write to him. Let me know. It's good news at least that your mother is better and that your friends are a help. Thanks for the theatre news. Nothing further from London, I don't even know if the money has arrived.[1] Of course I don't get it all, one half. I was invited to Holland all expenses paid to see their Godot but didn't go. Suzanne went.[2] I am in lousy form, all alone in the country, and the old heart knocking hell out of me nightly and like an old stone in the day. Don't seem to care much. Yes, I finished the play, but it's no good and I have to begin all over again.[3] At the moment struggling to prepare old texts to make a little book for Lindon, the first written in French 1945 and the last 1951! Depressing hair-raising job. Wish I had never consented, though some of the little Textes pour Rien of 1951 are all right I think.[4] Another week should see it out. Then there is the translation of Malone to get on with. Molloy at least finished and done with, i.e. page proofs corrected, you'll get a copy in due course. Am writing to Combat to-day to abonner you, so happy to be able to do something.[5] In Paris had been doing nothing but wine and dine and gamble at a queer variation of roulette invented by Henri Poincaré called "Multicolor", don't remember if I told you about it. Didn't lose much. Bitterly cold here. The old typewriter has just given up the ghost and don't know if I can get it mended at La Ferté. Grand boil on my stiff neck to add to the gaiety. Too much Beaujolais at the Iles. Saw Carpentier there one evening.[6] Trees surviving, even the two apples showing shy signs of life. Shall soon have to buy a mechanical scyther-mower, never get round the grass otherwise. Visited by partridges now daily, about midday. Queer birds. They hop, listen, hop, listen, never seem to eat. Wretched letter, forgive me. Hope you can read it all the same. Write me with better news soon, and in better form. Much love.

 Sam

ALS; 2 leaves; 2 sides; UoR, BIF, MS 5060.

1 Mitchell had asked about SB's share of the fee paid by Albery for extending his option on *Waiting for Godot* (see 7 February 1955 to Mitchell).

2 *Wachten op Godot* opened on 6 March in Arnhem.

3 With regard to his drafted play, on 23 February, SB reported to Mitchell, "I don't disown it – yet" (UoR, BIF, MS 5060).

4 *Nouvelles et Textes pour rien.*

5 "To abonner you" (take out a subscription for you).

6   Aux Iles Marquises: Thursday [3 January 1952], n. 10.
SB is probably referring to French boxing champion Georges Carpentier (1894–1975)
who held European and World titles from 1911 to 1914 and 1919 to 1922.

PAMELA MITCHELL
NEW YORK

26/3/55   Paris
Pamela
    Glad to have your letter and to feel you in better form. Hope in
your next to hear you are casée in a nice cushy. Back in Paris till end of
month with avalanches of people on top of me. Then towards middle
of April they begin again. Have to be witness of Joyce's grandson
Stephen getting married here on 15th, thank God its only the
Mairie, but with reception afterwards. God help me and my dirty
old brown suit.[1] Have nearly finished book of white-haired texts for
Lindon.[2] Have pulled the flush on A and B and have to start all over
again, if anything. All I want is to sit in the country watching my trees
being hopeful or pulled along by the faucheuse-tondeuse yet to be
acquired.[3] Rosset keeps writing fussy letters about Molloy proofs.[4]
News from London scant and depressing. The old carcass up and
down, one day dying and the next lepping.[5] Yes, I remember Turner
being pleased with Godot proofs, I didn't understand why, I could
never correct proofs, or only with emblems that I thought intelligible
to none but me. He must be a remarkable man.[6] Extraordinary
heat-wave here all of a sudden the hottest since 1880[7] [...]
        Love
            s/ Sam

TLS; 1 leaf, 1 side; UoR, BIF, MS 5060.

1   "Casée" (well settled).
SB was witness at the marriage of Stephen Joyce (b. 1932) and Solange Raytchine
(n.d.) on 15 April, in Paris. SB types "its" for "it's."

2   *Nouvelles et Textes pour rien* which SB described to Barney Rosset as "3 nouvelles
from 1945, i.e. before Molloy, and 13 Textes pour Rien, very short from 1951, i.e. after
L'Innommable [...] The Textes pour Rien are I think quite untranslatable" (NSyU).

3   "Faucheuse-tondeuse," a mechanical scyther-mower.

4   Barney Rosset wrote to SB on 2 March and 17 March about the proofs (NSyU).

5   On 22 March, the contract for the license for London production of *Waiting for Godot* was sent for SB's signature (IMEC, Beckett, Boîte 5, S. Beckett Correspondance 1962–1968, Curtis Brown 1957 [*for* 1952–1957]).

6   Howard Turner, Office Manager, Grove Press.

7   *Le Monde* indicates that the temperature reached 25° C, the highest March temperature since 1873 ("Prévisions météorologiques," *Le Monde* 27–28 March 1955: 10).

CYRIL CUSACK

10 May 1955   6 Rue des Favorites
                                     Paris 15me

Dear Mr Cusack

Thanks for your letter of May 6th. I am sorry we did not succeed in even having a talk on the phone while you were in Paris. I only got your second note on the Thursday afternoon in the country and could not have reached Paris in time to see you. I left my telephone number with your hotel and they should have been able to give it to you.[1]

The Arts Theatre production is news to me. I hope you will be able to take part. By all means do it in Gaelic in Dublin if you think it worth while. Why parts in English?[2] In any case you have my permission, and most cordially, but you will have to write to my publisher, M. Jérôme Lindon, Editions de Minuit, 7 Rue Bernard-Palissy, Paris 6me, for his. A mere formality. The business end too is entirely in his hands.

Yes indeed, I hope we shall meet next time you are in Paris.

        Yours sincerely
        s/ Sam Beckett

TLS; 1 leaf, 1 side; Cusack collection.

1   On 6 April, SB had written to Cyril Cusack in reply to his request for permission to perform *Waiting for Godot* in Dublin. SB told him that Albery had the London option and that the Pike Theatre was authorized to present the play in Dublin (Cusack collection).

2   Peter Hall (b. 1930), whom Albery had appointed to direct *Waiting for Godot* at the Arts Theatre Club, London, had offered Cusack the part of Vladimir.

Cusack proposed a "bi-lingual adaptation for production at the Abbey Theatre." His idea was to set the scene "in bleakest Connemara," and, "as is the familiar pattern in Gaeltacht areas," that Vladimir and Estragon should be conversant in both Gaelic and English, speaking Gaelic between themselves, and English with Pozzo and Lucky. He continued:

> I had approached Donald Albery with a view to obtaining his permission to operate a production of "GODOT" in Dublin and in English [. . .] Albery refused to let "GODOT" be done in Dublin until such time as he might give permission, at which I lost my temper and came out with: "Alright, then I'll do it in Irish!" (Cyril Cusack, 4 August 1992.)

BARNEY ROSSET, GROVE PRESS
NEW YORK

June 5th 1955   6 Rue des Favorites
                                                          Paris 15me

Dear Barney

Thanks for your letter and enc. I have not seen latest issue of Merlin so know nothing of the text you refer to.[1] I hear, indirectly of course, that <u>Godot</u> is due in London at the Arts Theatre early in August. Not a word from Albery for months past. In any case his option expires in August and, if he does not do his stuff, will certainly not be renewed.[2] In Madrid, in spite of whole-hearted official opposition (prohibition to announce performance in the press and of every form of publicity whatsoever), they have at last succeeded in doing the play once, in a remote theatre, with great success I am told, and hope to get permission for further performances.[3] I received a letter from your friend Joan Mitchell staying at the Montalambert and hope to make her acquaintance this week.[4] Have been very tired and doing no work. But <u>Malone</u> is well advanced and will be finished before the sere and yellow.[5]

Best wishes to you both.

Yours
s/ <u>Sam</u>
Samuel Beckett

TLS; 1 leaf, 1 side; NSyU.

1   In his letter of 19 May, Rosset asked SB what he thought of *The New Tenant*, a play that had appeared in *Merlin*; SB assumed that Rosset was referring to the most recent

issue of *Merlin*, which he had not seen. In fact, Eugène Ionesco's play *Le nouveau locataire*, translated by Donald Watson as "The New Tenant," had appeared nearly a year earlier (2.3 [Spring/Summer 1954] 172–191), in the issue that had also published SB's "The End" (tr. Richard Seaver with the author, 144–159).

2   Alan Simpson wrote to SB on 14 May that he had seen in *The Stage* that *Waiting for Godot* was to open on 3 August at the Arts Theatre Club (TCD, MS 10731/15). SB replied: "With regard to the date, I have not been notified by Albery [. . .] In fact I did not even know that he had decided on the Arts Theatre Club" (20 May 1955, TCD, MS 10731/16).

3   Antonia Rodríguez-Gago reports that the production by Trino Martínez Trives was "refused a license by the censors," but it was performed on 28 May at the University of Madrid ("Beckett in Spain: Madrid [1955] and Barcelona [1956]," in *Waiting for Godot: A Casebook*, ed. Ruby Cohn [London: Macmillan, 1987] 45). Martínez Trives's history of the performance was published as "Mi versión de *Esperando a Godot* y su estreno en España," *Primer Acto*, 15–16.

4   American artist Joan Mitchell was Barney Rosset's first wife; they were married from 1949 to 1952 (Klaus Kertess, *Joan Mitchell* [New York: Harry N. Abrams, 1997], 179–180). The Hôtel Montalembert (which SB types as "Montalambert") is at 3 Rue de Montalembert, Paris 7.

5   SB had promised to deliver his translation of *Malone meurt* by autumn; he adapts a line from Shakespeare's *Macbeth*: "My way of life / Is fall'n into the sere, the yellow leaf" (V.iii.22–23).

PATRICK WALDBERG

PARIS

29/6/55   6 Rue des Favorites
                                           Paris 15me

Mon cher Patrick

Je suis désolé, incapable de rien faire en ce moment, non che la speme il desiderio è morto, il ne faut pas compter sur moi pour ton 1er numéro. J'ai bien encore 1 ou 2 Textes pour Rien inédits que je te donnerais avec joie s'ils pouvaient faire l'affaire, mais je ne vois pas comment.[1] Sur Bram bramant en effet il y aurait beaucoup à dire, mais moi je ne peux pas, je n'ai même pas été foutu d'aller à son exposition. J'espère beaucoup que tu le diras toi.[2] Ne m'en veuille pas, cher Patrick, et crois-moi ton ami.

s/ Sam

TLS; 1 leaf, 1 side; Doucet, Waldberg, MS 41684.

29/6/55   6 Rue des Favorites
                                                Paris

My dear Patrick

I am really sorry, can't manage anything at the moment, not just the hope but the *desire* is dead; you mustn't count on me for your 1st number. I do still have 1 or 2 unpublished *Textes pour Rien* which I would gladly let you have if they would do, but I don't see how they could.[1] On Bram, the belling Bram, there would indeed be much to say, but I can't do it. I couldn't even get myself to his exhibition. I hope very much that you might say it.[2] Don't be angry with me Patrick, and believe me to be your friend

                                         Sam

1   It is not certain that the art journal that Waldberg was planning ever came to anything.
"Non che la speme il desiderio è morto" (see 19 October 1954, n. 2).

2   The Galerie Michel Warren had put on an exhibition of Bram van Velde's work in May. Patrick Waldberg did write on Van Velde, but his essay was not published until 1958. In it, Waldberg acknowledged the importance of SB for Van Velde, quoting the artist: "'I awaited each of Beckett's visits with intense eagerness, and I shook with emotion when I showed him my canvases. He spoke of my painting as no one had ever spoken before; his presence was stimulating to me'" ("Bram van Velde," *Apollo* 398 [April 1958] 130–134).

DAVID HAYMAN
PARIS   .

July 22nd 1955   6 Rue des Favorites
                                                Paris 15me

Dear Mr Hayman

I have finished reading your thesis and am leaving it in to-day with your publisher Rue Cardinal-Lemoine.[1]

I do not agree that I am particularly qualified to give an opinion on what you have written. I am quite out of touch with Joycian exegesis and it is a very long time since I last returned to the texts. And to have known him as well as I did is of little help in a matter of this kind. So do not take too seriously the few very vague and general remarks I have to offer you.

I have first to congratulate you on what seems to me a very ingenious and thorough piece of work. You have not altogether dispelled my scepticism as to the importance of Mallarmé to Joyce, but you have taken it down a great number of pegs.

I prefer the fourth chapter to the third.[2] I think perhaps you derive Joyce's use of the technique of suggestion too directly and exclusively from the Symbolists and Mallarmé. The device after all is as old as writing itself. The <u>Divine Comedy</u> is full of it. And one can well imagine the effect on Joyce, when he read it in Dublin as a very young man, of the <u>Vita Nuova</u> and its systematic trivalence, literal, allegorical and anagogical.[3] Writing this I remember once quoting to Joyce Leopardi's <u>E fango è il mondo</u>, to which his instantaneous and sole reaction consisted in seizing on the association <u>Il mondo – immonde</u>.[4] This is beside the point, but the anecdote may amuse you. And perhaps suggest to you an exagmination of how in Joyce the form of judgement more and more devoured its gist and the saying of all the saying of anything, in a way more consistent with Bruno's identification of contraries than with the intellectualism of Mallarmé.[5]

In your identification in F.W. of Mallarmean elements the palpable hits fall thick and fast.[6] Perhaps here too sometimes you seem rather to strain the point and solicit your texts, but I think you could hardly have done otherwise. For you had not only to resist the special pleading to which all thesis is an invitation, but at the same time texts into which almost anything may be read. And I think you are greatly to be praised for having kept it all as quiet as you have done. But it might be worth considering, in the published version, to <u>nuancer</u> here and there, or in a postscript. Unless of course you quite disagree, and perhaps very rightly, with what I have said.[7]

Finally let me congratulate you again on your handling of a horribly difficult job and wish you much success and happiness as a writer and as a teacher in the years to come.

With very kind regards to your wife I am[8]
Yours sincerely
s/ Sam. Beckett
Samuel Beckett

TLS; 1 leaf, two sides; TxU, Beckett collection.

1   David Hayman (b. 1927) had given SB a copy of his doctoral thesis, *James Joyce et Stéphane Mallarmé: Une étude d'influence*, submitted to the Faculté des Lettres at the Sorbonne in 1955, and published in two volumes in 1956 as *Joyce et Mallarmé* by Lettres Modernes (which had its seat at 73 Rue du Cardinal Lemoine, Paris 5). Hayman went on to publish numerous further works, on Joyce among others, and to become Professor of Comparative Literature at the University of Iowa, later at the University of Wisconsin-Madison.

2   Chapters 3 and 4 constitute the bulk of the thesis: Chapter 3 is entitled "La Suggestion: théorie et pratique"; Chapter 4 is entitled "Les Eléments Mallarméens dans l'oeuvre de Joyce."

3   The text most often referred to in discussion of allegory in the *Divine Comedy* is Dante's "Epistle to Can Grande della Scala," Epistola XIII, 20–25. SB's "trivalence" is surprising in relation to *Vita Nuova*, as it omits the fourth, moral or tropological, sense. *Vita Nuova* itself contains no explicit discussion of allegory, and SB may have had in mind the passage discussing the subject in the *Convivio* – though here again four rather than three "sensi" or valences are invoked (Dante, *Convivio*, II, I, 3–9).

4   SB's quotation is from the poem "A se stesso" ("To Himself") by Giacomo Leopardi: "Amaro e noia / La vita, altro mai nulla; e fango è il mondo" ("Boredom and bitterness / Is life; and the rest nothing; the world is dirt") (*Selected Prose and Poetry*, 280–281). "E fango è il mondo" served as an epigraph to SB's first published book, *Proust* (1931).
SB picks up on what he sees as Joyce's characteristic preference for form over content, although in fact the chime that Joyce notices links to Leopardi's thought by way of "fango," since "immonde" means "filthy, foul."

5   In his 1929 essay "Dante... Bruno. Vico.. Joyce." SB wrote in the following terms of what he called the "identified contraries" of Giordano Bruno:

> There is no difference, says Bruno, between the smallest possible chord and the smallest possible arc, no difference between the infinite circle and the straight line. The maxima and the minima of particular contraries are one and indifferent. Minimal heat equals minimal cold. Consequently transmutations are circular. The principle (minimum) of one contrary takes its movement from the principle (maximum) of another. Therefore not only do the minima coincide with the minima, the maxima with the maxima, but the minima with the maxima in the succession of transmutations. Maximal speed is a state of rest. The maximum of corruption and the minimum of generation are identical: in principle, corruption is generation. And all things are ultimately identified with God, the universal monad, Monad of monads. (*transition* 16–17 [June 1929] 244; Beckett, *Disjecta*, 21 [In *Disjecta*, as unwonted "one" is inserted before "another" in this passage].)

6   By "FW" SB intends James Joyce's *Finnegans Wake*.
SB cites "palpable hit" from *Hamlet* V.ii.280.

7   "Nuancer" (widen your perspective a little).
As published, Hayman's book contains no postscript, but in its "avant-propos" the author thanks SB, along with others "qui eurent l'obligeance de lire et de critiquer notre manuscrit avant sa publication" (who were kind enough to read and criticise our manuscript before publication) (I, 6).

8   SB had met Hayman's wife Loni Goldschmidt (b. 1930) when Hayman hand-delivered his thesis to him (Hayman, 17 January 2010).

PAMELA MITCHELL
NEW YORK

18/8/55   6 Rue des Favorites
                                                Paris 15°

Pamela

Glad to have news of you after so long with the good photo. I thought you had given me up as a bad job and how wise you were, the job being worse than ever. Very pleased to hear the hospital job is turning out so well and that you have not to assist at panhysterectomies and cranioclasms.[1] You deserve something upholstered after the rotten time you had and all the knocking at wrong doors. I hope you have sidestepped Connie and Diana. What news of your mother after her op?[2] I have nothing of much interest to tell you. I am at Ussy nearly all the time and hope to continue so. Godot opened in London at the Arts Theatre on August 3rd. Violently attacked by the daily rags but a lot of space and serious criticism in Times, Observer, Sunday Times, New Statesman and Nation, and a few of the other less never never shall be publications.[3] I did not and shall not go over to be crucified by the production, though it seems now (to judge by the little I have been able to glean) a fairly good production. They plan to run at the Arts until end of this month only. I think, though I don't know, not having been told, that the Arts production is in the nature of a try-out (in place of the usual pre-westend provincial tour) and that the play may be transferred to a larger theatre later on, this ingenuous theory being based on nothing more serious than the assumption that Albery and Co would like to get their money back and if possible a little over. They have been markedly unfriendly to me throughout, leaving me in the dark as to their plans and not consulting me at any stage, though their contract specifies they must, about cast, settings and so on. Further propositions from N.Y., including one from the Théâtre du Lys, which of course I cannot take up as Albery has a further six months within which to present the play in the States.[4] I am really very tired of Godot and the endless misunderstanding it seems to provoke everywhere. How any thing so skeleton simple can be complicated as it has been is beyond me. People are never happy unless they are digging.[5] Molloy in English has appeared in Paris but not due from Grove until next month or October, I forget. I shall tell them to send you a copy then. I have just finished translating Malone myself, first draft. Have to revise, retype it and get it off to Rosset by end of October. Here at Ussy I wage bitter and shamefaced warfare on the moles, my strategy being based on the fact, or more likely the myth, that they are haemophile, even the molesses. Have discovered a good Italian illustra[t]ed weekly called Oggi and am recovering my Italian. Glad you are getting Combat regularly. I'll renew it when it runs out, they'll probably notify me. Would you not like the Officiel de la Mode and get the low-down on the Y line or whatever it is?[6] Am writing this sitting out in a three-walled shed eating green-gages from neighbour's garden. Misty and grey, but pleasant. I have to go to Paris to-morrow for 24 hours, reluctantly. Have done nothing more with the play I used to blather to you about, but have written a ten-minute scenario for a mute white clown, gruesomely gloomy, for possible production at the Fontaine des 4 Saisons at the end of the year. With the help of the bad winter weather and lucid intervals permitting I may have another shot at A and B soon.[7] The book for Lindon is all ready and is due to mount the scaffold in a month or so.[8] Rosset is a proud father of a Peter Michael. I met his ex-wife here, by name Mitchell(!), at the Montalembert(!), stood her two stiff and rapid Scotch and Perrier in the dive next door, and that was the end of that, there's only one Mitchell. Went one evening with friends to the Air France restaurant and wolfed the usual ham and spinach after a Pernod at the bar.[9] The old heart seems a bit more lively, though still intermittently leadenly uproarious, to judge by the way my bicycle climbs the local inclines. I have cancer of the broncus about twice a month, then it passes. What the hell, for Chrissake, as your man says.

      Ever   Sam

TLS; 1 leaf, 2 sides; UoR, BIF, MS 5060.

1   Mitchell had taken a position as a fundraiser for the Hospital of Special Surgery (part of Columbia University).

2   Connie and Diana have not been identified.

3   On 11 August, SB wrote to Thomas MacGreevy thanking him for reviews of *Waiting for Godot*, saying: "The shop-keepers seem to be making mince-meat of Godot, though I really do not know much about it all. I did not go over for the opening and shall not during the run" (TCD, MS 10402/196). As Kitty Black wrote to Jérôme Lindon on 5 August, the play had had a "very mixed reception" on its opening night, 3 August: "all praise the acting and production but were very much less enthusiastic about the text" (IMEC, Beckett, Boîte 5, S. Beckett, Correspondance 1962–1968, Curtis Brown 1957 [*for* 1952–1957]).

Reviews in the dailies included: W. A. Darlington, "An Evening of Funny Obscurity," *Daily Telegraph* 4 August: 8; David Lewin, "Nothing happens, it's awful (it's life)," *Daily Express* 4 August 1955: np; Milton Shulman, "Duet for Two Symbols," *Evening Standard* 4 August 1955: 6; Cecil Wilson, "The Left Bank Can Keep It: This is Tedious," *The Daily Mail* 4 August 1955: 8; Anthony Hartley, "Theatre," *The Spectator* 12 August 1955: 222.

What SB called "serious criticism" included: "Arts Theatre, 'Waiting for Godot,'" *The Times* 4 August 1955: 11; Harold Hobson, "Tomorrow," *The Sunday Times* 7 August 1955: 11, and "Samuel Beckett," *The Sunday Times* 14 August 1955: 11; Kenneth Tynan, "New Writing," *The Observer* 7 August 1955: 11; T. C. Worsley, "The Arts and Entertainment: Cactus Land," *The New Statesman and Nation* 13 August 1955: 194; Philip Hope-Wallace, "Theatre," *Time and Tide* 36 (13 August 1955): 1045; *Punch* (10 August 1955) 169. Harold Hobson* (1904–1992) urged: "Go and see 'Waiting for Godot.' At the worst you will discover a curiosity ... at the best, something that will securely lodge in a corner of your mind for as long as you live" ("Tomorrow," 11).

4   SB wrote to Howard Turner at Grove Press on 2 August, "I have already to my extreme mortification been obliged to turn down most interesting propositions from New York, including one to present the play on or off Broadway with Buster Keaton and Marlon Brando!" (NSyU; see 17 February 1955, n. 3).

The managing directors of the off-Broadway Theatre de Lys, Carmen Capalbo (1925–2010) and Stanley Chase (né Stanley Cohen, b. 1928), wrote to SB on 26 July 1955 wishing to produce *Waiting for Godot* in their Autumn season; SB referred them to Donald Albery (SB to Stanley Chase, 8 August 1955, CLU, Stanley Chase Papers). SB types "Théâtre du Lys."

5   SB wrote to Mary Manning Howe on 18 August: "How anything so skeleton simple can be made so complicated is beyond me. Like a lot of seaside brats digging for worms people are" (TxU, Beckett collection).

6   The Italian weekly *Oggi Illustrato* covered national news; it was established in 1945. *Combat* was a daily newspaper that SB read regularly. *L'Officiel de la Mode* is a French fashion magazine. Christian Dior's new silhouettes included the Y-Line, featuring v-shaped collars and large stoles.

7   SB had written to Mitchell on 18 April 1955: "A and B are not defunct, but sleeping, sleeping sound. One of these days I hope to kick them into better groans and howls than the ones you know" (UoR, BIF, MS 5060). SB canceled "Godot" and wrote "A and B."

SB's scenario was *Acte sans paroles*, written for the dancer and mime artist Deryk Mendel* (b. 1921). The Fontaine des Quatre Saisons was a Cabaret-Theatre at 59 Rue de Grenelle, Paris 7.

8   *Nouvelles et Textes pour rien.*

9   In his letter to SB of 27 July, Howard Turner of Grove Press reported that the Rossets had had a son, Peter Michael, four weeks before (NSyU).

SB refers to Chez Françoise at the Aérogare des Invalides.

JEROME LINDON, EDITIONS DE MINUIT

PARIS

le 19 août 1955   Ussy-sur-Marne

Cher Jérôme

Voici un casse-tête pour la vôtre. J'aimerais, si vous êtes d'accord, et si cela [ne] crée pas de difficultés avec la Société des A.D., que l'on puisse dire oui à ces gens-là.[1]

Merci de votre lettre et félicitations de votre nouvelle paternité.[2] Les oreilles sont importantes, c'est d'elles que la beauté part, gagnant de proche en proche.

Godot à Londres, situation confuse, en ce qui me concerne. Dans les jours suivant la première, couacs furieux des canards quotidiens. Mais le dimanche critiques longues et (pour les boutiquiers) sérieuses, dans l'Observer et le Sunday Times. Bonne critique également dans l'hebdomadaire New Statesman & Nation. Et deuxième article dans le Sunday Times sur l' "humour" de la pièce. Presse irlandaise haineuse à l'extrême. Pozzo et Lucky bons, m'a-t-on écrit, V. et E. moins. Décor mauvais. Ils doivent arrêter un peu avant la fin du mois. J'ignore quelles sont les intentions de Albery, à supposer qu'il puisse en avoir. Nouvelles propositions de NYC (et une de Belfast!).[3]

Achevez de bien vous reposer, l'hiver s'annonce dur.

Bien amicalement de nous deux à vous deux.

Sam

TLS; 1 leaf, 1 side; IMEC, Beckett, Boîte 2, S. Beckett, Représentations *En attendant Godot* (2).

19th August 1955   Ussy-sur-Marne

Dear Jérôme

Here is a brain teaser to tease yours. I should like us, if you are in agreement, and if it does not create difficulties with the Société des Auteurs Dramatiques, to say yes to these people.[1]

Thank you for your letter, and congratulations on your new fatherhood.[2] The ears are important, for it is from there that beauty starts, moving ever outwards.

Godot in London: situation confused, as far as I am concerned. In the days following the premiere, furious wailings from the dailies. But on Sunday, long and (for shopkeepers) serious reviews, in *The Observer* and *The Sunday Times*. Good review too in the weekly *New Statesman and Nation*. And second article in *The Sunday Times* on the "humour" of the play. Irish press hate-filled in the extreme. Pozzo and Lucky good, someone wrote, V. and E. less. Set bad. They are to stop by the end of the month. I do not know what Albery's intentions are, supposing that he has any. New proposals from NYC (and one from Belfast!).[3]

Go on having a good rest right to the end; looks like being a hard winter.

All best from both of us to both of you.

Sam

1   SB had received a letter dated 7 August 1955 from Alfred Mesquita (1907–1986), Founder and, from 1948 to 1969, Director of the Escola de Arte Dramatica de São Paulo, Brazil; Mesquita requested permission to translate and produce *En attendant Godot* at his school. The translation was prepared by Luiz de Lima. SB replies on 19 August that, if it were entirely his decision, he would grant these rights, but that he is uninformed about the negotiations that have already taken place. SB indicates that he has asked

543

Jérôme Lindon to deal with the matter when Lindon returns to Paris. Although Mesquita may have considered doing a Portuguese translation, SB mentions the Spanish translation by Pablo Palant (*Esperando a Godot*) that has already been published (IMEC, Beckett, Boîte 2, S. Beckett, Représentations *En attendant Godot* [2]).

2   A son, Mathieu, was born to Annette and Jérôme Lindon in Caen.

3   Reviews of *Waiting for Godot*: 18 August 1955, n. 3. SB's "humour" is discussed in Harold Hobson's second piece in *The Sunday Times* ("Samuel Beckett," 14 August 1955: 11). The Dublin reviews sent to SB by Thomas MacGreevy have not been identified; the author of the one that appeared in the unsigned "London Letter" of *The Irish Times* seemed baffled by the play: "Either it has suffered terribly from the channel crossing, or there is a profound difference of opinion between London and Paris as to what constitutes an interesting evening" (6 August 1955: 7).

AIDAN HIGGINS
LONDON

August 30th 1955   6 Rue des Favorites
                                          Paris 15°

Dear Mr Higgins

Thanks for your letter. I am sorry you are having such a difficult time. I hope it is not sad all the time. I know very little about the Arts Theatre production of <u>Godot</u>, only what John has told me, and I was glad to have your impressions. I think they under-rehearsed and started badly. The set seems all wrong from the little I have heard.[1] I did not know I had doctrines, but I wouldn't know.[2] I know more or less what you mean, and it doesn't matter much what you call them. I don't know what you mean by helping people, what has writing to do with that? I can't help you with Moran, must one have reasons for these things? It was always submission with me, until I overdid it, with <u>L'Innommable</u>, I mean beyond the joke.[3] I have just finished translating, very badly, without the help of Bowles (yes, South Africa), <u>Malone</u>. I shall be very glad to send you a signed copy of <u>Molloy</u>, when the American edition comes out, in a month or so.[4] I have a little book due here soon, odds and ends, the first and last work in French, from 1945 and 1950.[5] I don't suppose you want it in French, if you do let me know. Since 1950 I haven't been able to do anything. Sorry to have such a reduced picture of Arland, is his fly still stained with I suppose urine?[6] Curious effect on homespun. What news of your man Parsons?[7]

    Yours sincerely

      s/ Sam Beckett

TLS; 1 leaf, 1 side; TxU, Beckett collection.

1 SB had been told about the production of *Waiting for Godot* by his cousin John Beckett. Aidan Higgins had attended the opening night on 3 August with John Beckett and his companion Vera Slocombe (née Nielsen, c. 1913 – c. 2005, m. John Beckett 1961–1969).

2 In his lengthy account of the play, Higgins wrote on 29 August to Arland Ussher:

> A saturation play. Written after a second Fall done, performed by the Lord's anointed. Falling first from Grace and then from History. The world is depopulated in the play. The remnants (two tramps, a landlord and his menial) are trying to remember the past. I hesitate to say archetypes, but four archetypes remain. The past looms up through the darkness. It is sententious. It is doctrinaire. It is also tremendous. [. . .]
>
> The doctrine is obvious enough in the written text [. . .] The un-named country is a desolate Ireland, though only one of the characters (Estragon) is authentic. The Landlord and his Grief (Lucky) supply a key. Amen. (TCD, MS 9331–9041/1498.)

3 Aidan Higgins's letter to SB has not been found, so his question about Moran in *Molloy* is not known.

4 Higgins had asked SB if Patrick Bowles was South African. Higgins had known someone who had attended Rhodes University in South Africa with a Patrick Bowles, and he wondered if they were one and the same (interview with Aidan Higgins).

5 *Nouvelles et Textes pour rien.*

6 Arland Ussher.

7 Although Aidan Higgins indicated to the editors that this was D. J. Parsons, it seems more likely that it was John Desmond Parsons (1907–1968), a graduate of TCD in 1929, with whom SB and Higgins had both played golf at Greystones (Aidan Higgins; Dolores Pocock, Alumni Office, TCD).

JEROME LINDON, EDITIONS DE MINUIT
PARIS

le 24 septembre 1955   Ussy-sur-Marne
Cher Jérôme

    Ci-joint lettre reçue ces jours-ci de Londres rapport à une édition éventuelle en Angleterre de mes romans, et ma réponse, que je termine en leur disant de se mettre en rapport avec vous pour les questions de copyright, etc. J'aurais pu leur dire de s'adresser directement à Merlin, mais je préfère de beaucoup, avec mon indifférence coutumière au travail que je vous donne, que cela passe par vous. Je ne connais pas les Edts. Gordon Fraser. On dirait une marque d'automobile.[1]

Un mot de Peter Hall, metteur en scène de Godot à Londres, me disant qu'au Criterion cela marche "gentiment". Par le même courrier des amabilités de Curtis Brown en personne, m'offrant de me loger chez lui si je veux aller à Londres et désireux de faire éditer mes écrits à Londres.[2] Mon ami Leventhal, ayant vu le spectacle au Criterion, m'écrit qu'il est totalement différent de celui de Paris qu'il avait vu deux fois, beaucoup plus public et qu'il m'aurait certainement déplu. Le plateau notamment, si mes soupçons sont corrects, doit ressembler à un paysage de Salvator Rosa. Je l'ai échappé encore plus belle que je ne croyais.[3]

Ci-joint également la lettre de Topolski avec son adresse.[4]

Merci encore une fois et meilleur[e]s amitiés de nous deux à vous deux.

s/ Sam

Enclosure: B O R I S   F O R D ,   G O R D O N   F R A S E R ,   L O N D O N

September 24th 1955   6 Rue des Favorites
                                                  Paris 15me

Dear Mr Ford

Thank you for your letter of September 15th.

There are three novels of which I believe United Kingdom rights are available.

1. Murphy, originally published I think in 1937 and so long out of print that even Routledge can hardly claim it for their own.[5]

2. Watt, continental edition 1953 by Olympia Press, Paris (collection Merlin).

3. Molloy, translated from original French by Patrick Bowles, continental edition by Olympia Press, Paris (collection Merlin), American edition by Grove Press, New York, both this year.

English translations by myself of my novels Malone Meurt and L'Innommable will appear in due course in American and continental editions by Grove Press and Olympia Press respectively.

I am passing on your letter to my Paris publisher, Monsieur Jérôme Lindon, Editions de Minuit, 7 Bernard Palissy, Paris 6me. If you are interested in pursuing the matter you should apply to him for information regarding copyright and such matters, of which I can give you no coherent statement.

Yours sincerely

Samuel Beckett

TLS; 1 leaf, 1 side; enclosures from Boris Ford, Gordon Fraser Gallery, 15 September [1955] and from Feliks Topolski, *Topolski's Chronicle*, London, 16 August 1955, and SB to Boris Ford, Gordon Fraser, London, 24 September 1955 (TLcc; 1 leaf, 1 side; IMEC, Beckett, Boîte 1, S. Beckett, Correspondance – Divers, 1950–1956).

24th September 1955   Ussy-sur-Marne
Dear Jérôme

Enclosed letter received recently from London about a possible edition of my novels in England, and my reply, which I end by telling them to get in touch with you on matters of copyright etc. I could have told them to go direct to Merlin, but far prefer it, with my customary indifference to the work that I give you, to go through you. I am not familiar with Gordon Fraser Editions. They sound like a brand of car.[1]

A note from Peter Hall, director of *Godot* in London, telling me that at the Criterion it is going "nicely". By the same post polite remarks from Curtis Brown in person, offering to put me up if I want to go to London, and keen to have my writings published in London.[2] My friend Leventhal, having seen the performance at the Criterion, writes that it is totally different from the Paris one, which he had seen twice, much more public, and that I would certainly have disliked it. The stage in particular, if my suspicions are correct, must look like a landscape by Salvator Rosa. I had an even luckier escape than I knew.[3]

Enclosed also Topolski's letter with address.[4]

Thank you again, and all best from us both to you both.

Sam

1   Boris Ford (1917–1988), Editor at Gordon Fraser, London, wrote to SB on 15 September 1955. Ford wrote that Gordon Fraser (1911–1981) had "introduced Christmas Cards in good taste and at a reasonable price. Before the war he was [with] the Minority Press in Cambridge [...] and since the war he was until last year Head of Broadcasting at UNESCO. I am, amongst other things, Editor of the Pelican Guide to English Literature in umpteen volumes" (IMEC, Beckett, Boîte 1, S. Beckett, Correspondance – Divers, 1950–1956).

2   Peter Hall's letter to SB has not been found. *Waiting for Godot* opened at the Criterion Theatre, in London's West End, on 12 September 1955.

The letter written before 24 September 1955 from Spencer Curtis Brown (1906–1980) to SB has not been found.

3   A. J. Leventhal wrote later: "The London production differed from the Paris one ... in so far as the stage was less bleak and that our withers were not wrung so intensely" ("Dramatic Commentary," *Dublin Magazine*, 31.1 [January–March 1956] 52–54).

The set designs by Peter Snow (1927–2008) are discussed by Katharine Worth in *Samuel Beckett's Theatre: Life Journeys* ([Oxford: Clarendon Press, 1999] 26–28). Along with the tree, the backdrop depicted backlit spiky plant silhouettes. Leventhal had described the set design of the Théâtre de Babylone production: "Godot has a bare classical stage. The direction reads simply: *A country road. A tree*" ("Mr. Beckett's *En attendant Godot*," *Dublin Magazine* 29.2 [April–June 1954] 11).

The landscapes of Salvator Rosa (1615–1673): 8 September 1934 to Thomas McGreevy, and n. 12.

4   Polish-born British painter and chronicler Feliks Topolski (1907–1989), who published *Topolski's Chronicle* (1953–1979 and 1982–1989), wrote to SB on 16 August that he would like to publish *Waiting for Godot* "either in the shape of a larger issue of my broadsheet with my sketches of the production; or, [...] in book form, again with my drawings" (IMEC, Beckett, Boîte 1, S. Beckett, Correspondance – Divers, 1950–1956).

5   *Murphy* was published in 1938.

ROBERT PINGET

LONDON

le 28 septembre [1955]   6 Rue des Favorites
                                                        Paris 15me

Mon cher Robert Pinget

Merci de votre gentille lettre et de m'avoir envoyé le programme que je n'avais pas vu. Si elle est juste, l'idée que peu à peu grâce à des lettres comme la vôtre je me fais de la mise en scène londonienne, je ne suis pas d'accord. Mais c'est peut-être eux qui ont raison.[1]

Content que vous vous plaisiez à Londres. J'ai essayé, pendant deux ans, il y a très longtemps, dans World's End, plus loin que Chelsea.[2]

J'espère apprendre bientôt que vous avez un job à votre convenance et que Gallimard consent à vous foutre la paix.[3]

> Amitiés.
>
> s/ Sam. Beckett

J'ai perdu votre adresse. J'envoie donc c/o Eds. de Minuit.[4]

TLS; 1 leaf, 1 side; Burns Library, Pinget-Beckett Letters.

28 September [1955]   6 Rue des Favorites
                                       Paris 15

Dear Robert Pinget,

Thank you for your kind letter, and for sending me the programme, which I had not seen. If it is accurate, the idea which I am gradually forming of the London production, thanks to letters like yours, I don't agree with. But perhaps it's they who are right.[1]

Glad you are enjoying London. I tried, for two years, a very long time ago, in World's End, farther out than Chelsea.[2]

I hope to be hearing soon that you have a job that suits you, and that Gallimard agrees to stop hounding you.[3]

Best wishes

Sam. Beckett

I have lost your address, so am sending this c/o Eds. de Minuit.[4]

1   Pinget's letter to SB has not been found.

2   SB lived in London in 1934 and 1935. World's End refers to the district in London SW round the pub of that name, where SB lived at 34 Gertrude Street.

3   Pinget held various temporary jobs during the nine months he lived in London (Léonard A. Rosmarin, *Robert Pinget* [New York: Twayne Publishers, 1995] x).
Pinget had published *Le Renard et la boussole* with Gallimard in 1953. His next text, entitled *Forêt de Grance*, was rejected later that year by Raymond Queneau at Gallimard;

it was published with the title *Graal flibuste* by Editions de Minuit in 1956, which, thereafter, was Pinget's publisher. Pinget's move from Gallimard to Editions de Minuit was difficult; SB wrote to Pinget on 20 September: "Jérôme Lindon m'a parlé des incroyables exigences de Gallimard rapport à vous. C'est insensé. Ça doit pouvoir s'arranger." (Burns Library, Pinget-Beckett Letters.) (Jérôme Lindon has told me of the incredible demands Gallimard are facing you with. It's lunacy. There must be a way of straightening it all out.)

4 Handwritten PS.

JEROME LINDON, EDITIONS DE MINUIT
PARIS

1.10.55   Ussy

Cher Jérôme

Ci-joint seconde lettre de Curtis Brown où il revient à la charge. J'avais répondu à sa première, où il me me [sic] proposait ses services comme agent littéraire, en lui disant, sans entrer dans le détail, qu'en effet j'avais plusieurs livres dont les droits étaient disponibles pour le Royaume Uni, que de vagues pourparlers étaient en cours en vue de leur publication à Londres et qu'à l'occasion nous pourrions avoir recours à ses bons offices. Mais, comme vous voyez, il ne se décourage pas pour si peu.[1]

Les livres en question sont:

Murphy (réédition à laquelle Routledge ne pourrait décemment s'opposer). Encore faut-il en trouver un exemplaire.

Proust (même remarque, mais Chatto and Windus).

Watt (accord à obtenir de Merlin).

Molloy (accord à obtenir de Merlin et sans doute aussi de Grove Press, du fait qu'elle a acheté la traduction).

Sans parler de Malone, que j'ai presque fini de traduire, et de L'Innommable, que je traduirai sans doute l'année prochaine.

Si nous nous entendons avec les Edns Gordon Fraser, inutile évidemment de passer par Curtis Brown.

D'autre part il se peut que ça ne marche pas avec les Eds Gordon Fraser ou qu'elles ne veuillent pas s'engager pour tous les livres disponibles, mais seulement pour un ou deux. En prévision de quoi nous aurions peut-être intérêt à autoriser d'ores et déjà Curtis Brown à se mettre en branle.[2]

D'autre part encore il peut y avoir d'autres demandes d'autres maisons d'édition rendant inutiles les services d'un agent à Londres.

Je m'en remets entièrement à vous pour la marche à suivre.

Je vais répondre à Curtis Brown que je vous ai communiqué sa lettre en vous priant de bien vouloir vous mettre en rapport avec lui.[3]

Je sais bien que Watt et Molloy ne sont pas entièrement vos oignons, mais je n'ai vraiment pas le courage de discuter le coup avec les gens de Merlin.[4]

Les nouvelles de Godot au Criterion, quoique maigres, sont bonnes. On m'annonce un chèque de 25.000 frs pour la lecture de Watt à la BBC il y a trois semaines.[5]

Rien de Mendel. J'espère pouvoir rester ici encore quelque temps.

Bien amicalement[6]   s/ Sam

TLS with AN and A corrections; 1 leaf, 1 side; Minuit.

1.10.55   Ussy

Dear Jérôme

Enclosed a second letter from Curtis Brown, back at it again. I had replied to his first, in which he proposed his services as literary agent, telling him, without going into details, that I did indeed have several books the rights of which were available for the United Kingdom, that vague discussions were going on about their publication in London and that we might occasionally have recourse to his good offices. But, as you see, it takes more than that to discourage him.[1]

The books in question are:

Murphy (reissue to which Routledge could not decently object). Even then we have to find a copy.

Proust (same remark, but Chatto and Windus).

Watt (agreement to be obtained from Merlin).

Molloy (agreement to be obtained from Merlin and no doubt also from Grove Press, since it has bought the translation).

Not to mention *Malone*, which I have almost finished translating, and *L'Innommable*, which I shall no doubt translate next year.

If we reach agreement with Gordon Fraser Ltd., obviously no point in going through Curtis Brown.

On the other hand it may be that things won't work out with Gordon Fraser or that they won't want to take on all the available books, but only one or two. In anticipation of which, we would perhaps be wise to give permission here and now to Curtis Brown to get going.[2]

On the other hand again, there may be other requests from other publishers making the service of a London agent unnecessary.

I am relying entirely on you about what direction to take.

I am going to reply to Curtis Brown that I have passed this letter to you asking you to be kind enough to get in touch with them.[3]

I am well aware that *Watt* and *Molloy* are not entirely your affair, but I really haven't the courage to argue the toss with the Merlin people.[4]

The news of *Godot* at the Criterion, although scant, is good. I am told of a cheque for 25,000 francs for the reading of *Watt* on the BBC three weeks ago.[5]

Nothing from Mendel. I hope to stay on here a little longer.

All the best[6]

Sam

1   Spencer Curtis Brown wrote to SB on 27 September, asking if he might represent SB's novels in London: "If you have some odd novels lying around do please send them over. I would be immensely curious to read them, and very probably we could find a publisher for them [. . .] If you are having vague negotiations about them, perhaps you will let me know what publishers have already seen them or have wanted to see them" (IMEC, Beckett, Boîte 5, S. Beckett Correspondance 1962–1968, Curtis Brown 1957 [sic]).

2   Boris Ford's inquiry on behalf of Gordon Fraser: SB to Jérôme Lindon, 24 September 1955.

3   No letter from SB to Curtis Brown on this matter has been found, and none may have been written, since, on 4 October, Lindon wrote to SB: "En tous cas, je pense que dans l'immédiat, nous n'avons aucune raison de céder l'option à Curtis Brown" (In any case, I think that right now we have no reason to yield the option to Curtis Brown) (Editions de Minuit collection).

2 October 1955, Barney Rosset

4 Merlin published both *Watt* and *Molloy* in English, and they held the Continental rights in English for these novels.

5 An extract from *Watt* was read by John Holmstrom, the announcer of the BBC Third Programme, on 7 September 1955, as an "interlude of prose" (Louise North, BBC Written Archives, 11 May 2010).

6 The last line of the letter and its closing are handwritten.

BARNEY ROSSET, GROVE PRESS
NEW YORK

October 2nd 1955   6 Rue des Favorites
                                                    Paris 15me

My dear Barney

Thanks for your letter and clipping. Now revising, laboriously, my translation of <u>Malone</u>, and hope to get down to the final typing this month. This time you'll have the text before Merlin.[1] Godot is going well at the Criterion from all I hear. In the Sunday Times of yesterday week the enclosed very moving tribute, Hobson's third performance on me in the same paper in the space of 4 or 5 weeks. You are welcome to keep the cuttings, good, bad and indifferent I prefer not to have them.[2] I know nothing of Albery's plans for New York. If any more producers apply to you please tell them there is no good in writing to me, that Albery is the man, New Theatre, Saint-Martin's Lane; London. After the London surprise and with the existing interest in NY I think our chances there are pretty good.[3]

All the best to all three

s/ Sam

TLS; 1 leaf, 1 side; NSyU.

1 With his letter of 24 September, Rosset sent SB the first review of *Molloy* (Vivian Mercier, "Beckett and the Search for Self," *The New Republic* 132 [19 September 1955] 20–21).

2 Harold Hobson's third mention of *Waiting for Godot*, a paragraph in his column in *The Sunday Times* on 18 September, indicates that Hugh Burden (1913–1985) has succeeded Paul Daneman (1925–2001) as Vladimir: "The echoing duets between Estragon and Vladimir fall with the old satisfying music, and Mr. Timothy Bateson's bravura piece of stuttering fantasy is as haunting as ever" (11). Bateson (1926–2009) played Lucky.
SB canceled "always throw them away" and wrote "prefer not to have them."

3   As it happened, this became a moot point, for Donald Albery sent a contract dated 3 October 1955 to Michael Myerberg* (1906–1974) for the production rights in the United States.

H. O. WHITE

TRINITY COLLEGE, DUBLIN

3-10-55   6 rue des Favorites
                                                Paris 15°

My dear HO White[1]

Very many thanks for sending me cutting from Sunday Times. It is a most touching and courageous tribute and I read it with emotion. I have not had many defenders, but the few I have had (among whom I make bold to number yourself) do not fall to the lot of many writers.[2]

Wishing you a pleasant and successful term I am

Yours very sincerely

Sam. Beckett

ALS; 1 leaf, 1 side; *env to* Professor H.O. White, 39 Trinity College, Dublin, IRLANDE, *pm* Paris 3-10-55; TCD 3777/13.

1   Herbert Martyn Oliver White* (popularly known as HO, 1885–1963), Professor of English, Trinity College Dublin.

2   It is not certain what cutting from *The Sunday Times* had been sent to SB by H. O. White, possibly one of the three articles by Harold Hobson; Hobson's piece "Samuel Beckett" addressed objections to the play and was warm in its praise of it (14 August 1955: 11).

GIORGIO AND ASTA JOYCE

ZURICH

13.10.55   6 Rue des Favorites
                                                Paris 15me

Bien chers amis

Arrived safely in Paris in warm summery weather after a perfect flight. Piles of letters and botherations that I hardly feel equal to facing at the moment, but must. All I want is to disappear into the country, but no chance of that before a week at the earliest. Suzanne is in good form and saw plenty of friends during my absence. She sends you her love. Even my bad memory will never forget the week with you and all your kindness and patience with a "sullen silent sot, always dreaming and never thinking", though dreaming is too good a word for it.[1] Our drives and evenings at the Grill and Giorgio and Hans there at the Flughaven until the end, none of that will go from me.[2] No news of Stephen, I thought Suzanne might have seen him, but she had not. When I get some of this mess out of my way I'll make him a sign and offer them a fish soup, which she likes, at the Iles Marquises, I remember it was there he asked me to be his témoin.[3] It appears there were second proofs of my book which I should have been here to correct and that my publisher was upset, but understanding.[4] I have to see him to-morrow, about that and a million other things, and Roger Blin, about a projected revival of Godot with Jean Vilar at the Chaillot.[5] What I should like to feel sure of now is that Asta will not leave me for months without a few lines of news. Too tired and stupid now for more. Remember me to the Baur au Lac and believe as I do that we shall soon be together again, in Paris or Zurich or elsewhere, ce n'est pas le vide qui manque.[6]

Love to you all

s/ Sam

SUZANNE VERY TOUCHED BY YOUR PRESENT OF CHOCOLATE.[7]

TLS, with APS; 1 leaf, 1 side; Zurich James Joyce Foundation.

1   SB traveled to Zurich to visit Giorgio Joyce and his wife Dr. Asta Jahnke Joyce (née Osterwalder, m. Joyce 1954, 1917–1993). SB refers to himself in words from George Farquhar's *The Beaux' Stratagem*, II.i, when Mrs. Sullen advises: "if you ever marry, beware of a sullen, silent Sot, one that's always musing, but never thinks" (*The Beaux' Stratagem*, ed. Charles N. Fifer, Regents Restoration Drama Series [Lincoln: University of Nebraska Press, 1992] 27).

2   SB refers to the Grill Room in the Baur au Lac Hotel, located at the upper end of Bahnhofstrasse, close to Lake Zurich. Giorgio and Asta used to go there for a drink (Hans Jahnke in conversation with Ursula Zeller, Zurich James Joyce Foundation). Asta's son, Hans Jahnke (1944–2010), was with Giorgio at the "Flughaven" (airport) when SB left; SB types "Flughaven" for "Flughafen."

3   "Témoin" (witness). SB recollects his role in the wedding of Stephen and Solange Joyce.

4 SB refers to the second proofs of *Nouvelles et Textes pour rien*.

5 The first Théâtre National Populaire (known as the TNP) used the Palais du Trocadéro from 1920 until 1934, when the building was razed and a new complex, the Palais de Chaillot, was built for the International Exhibition in Paris (1937); the larger auditorium in the new building was used from 1953 to 1972 by the TNP; as its head, Jean Vilar had artistic direction of the Théâtre de Chaillot (www.encyclopedia.com/doc/1O79-ChaillotPalaisde.html, accessed on 4 June 2010).

6 "Ce n'est pas le vide qui manque" (There is no shortage of gaps).

7 The PS is handwritten in block capital letters.

ROGER BLIN
PARIS

17-10-55   6 rue des Favorites
                                              Paris 15e
Cher Roger

Te serait-il possible de passer chez nous demain mardi vers 4 heures? Je voudrais te montrer le scénario Frollo et te demander conseil.[1] Si cela te convient mieux qu'on se retrouve ailleurs, fais-moi savoir par pneu où et quand. Si je n'ai rien de toi je t'attendrai ici vers quatre heures.

Bien amicalement de nous deux à vous deux
Sam

ALS Pneu; 1 leaf, 1 side; *env to* Monsieur Roger Blin, 264 Rue Saint-Honoré, Paris 1ᵉʳ, *upper left corner*: Pneumatique; *pm* 17-10-55, Paris; IMEC, Blin.

17.10.55   6 rue des Favorites
                                              Paris 15e
Dear Roger

Could you possibly call in on us tomorrow Tuesday at about 4? I'd like to show you the Frollo scenario and ask your advice.[1] If it would suit you better to meet somewhere else, let me know by pneumatique where and when. If I don't hear from you I'll expect you here about 4.

All the best from both of us to both of you.

Sam

1   SB refers to *Acte sans paroles*, the first mime written for Deryk Mendel; Mendel's performance character was a clown figure named "Frollo."

JEROME LINDON, EDITIONS DE MINUIT
PARIS

18.10.55   Ussy
Cher Jérôme

J'ai trouvé ici votre lettre dont la dernière phrase m'a profondément touché. Vous êtes le seul éditeur français qui, il y a cinq ans, ait voulu de moi. A qui donc la dette de reconnaissance?[1]

Par contre aucune trace des épreuves. Mystère.[2]

Comme je n'ai fait que "réviser" la traduction de Molloy faite par Bowles, je n'ai reçu aucune rémunération de Merlin.

Bien amicalement et à bientôt.

s/ Sam

TLS; 1 leaf, 1 side; Minuit collection.

18.10.55   Ussy
Dear Jérôme

I found your letter here. The last sentence touched me deeply. You are the only French publisher who, five years ago, wanted anything to do with me. Whose is the debt of gratitude?[1]

By contrast no trace of the proofs. Mystery.[2]

As I did no more than "revise" the translation of *Molloy* done by Bowles, I have received no remuneration from Merlin.

All best and till soon.

Sam

1   SB refers to Lindon's letter of 4 October about *Nouvelles et Textes pour rien*; it closes with: "Je viens de relire (et même, pour La Fin, de lire pour la première fois) tout le

livre. C'est je crois le plus beau, avec L'Innommable. Quelle reconnaissance je vous devrai toujours de m'avoir permis d'être votre éditeur: quoi qu'il arrive, j'aurai au moins été cela." (Minuit.) (I have just re-read [and even, for "La Fin," read for the first time] the whole book. It is, I think, the finest, with *L'Innommable*. How grateful I shall always be to you to have allowed me to be your publisher: whatever happens, I shall at least have been that.)

2   Second proofs of *Nouvelles et Textes pour rien* were sent in the same post as the letter but did not arrive. In his letter of 4 October, Lindon asks SB to reconsider the title of the book.

MANIA PERON

PARIS

Mardi [? after 18 October 1955]

Ma chère Mania

Chauvet m'a rejoint. Très gentil. Il m'a dit que ma phrase est correcte telle quelle, c'est à dire avec *à qui*. Il m'a cité d'autres cas où il faudrait *de*. Il n'a pas su très bien m'expliquer ça. Je crois que l'éloignement du complément du groupe verbal y est pour beaucoup. Selon lui c'est une question d'usage impossible à présenter sous forme de règle. Il m'a accompagné jusqu'à ma porte et a été on ne peut plus aimable. Merci de l'avoir lancé à mes trousses.[1]

J'ai adopté beaucoup de vos suggestions ma[i]s pas toutes. Pour *malinement*, j'ai l'autorité de Rimbaud.

> Elle était fort déshabillée
> Et de grands arbres indiscrets
> Aux vitres penchaient leur feuillée
> Malinement, tout près, tout près.
>
> (Comédie en 3 Baisers)[2]

Il s'en sert aussi à un autre endroit.[3] Il est évident que *malignement* veut dire tout autre chose.[4]

Je ne saurai jamais assez vous remercier de tout le mal que vous vous êtes donné. Vous devez être bien fatiguée, presque autant que moi. Demain le cadavre s'en va, indifférent, vers les noirs bataillons.[5]

Bien affectueusement de nous deux. Passez quand le coeur vous en dira.

s/ Sam

TLS; 1 leaf, 1 side; TxU, Lake collection, Beckett. *Dating:* on 18 October 1955, SB expected to have received second proofs of *Nouvelles et Textes pour rien*, but had not; this letter mentions returning these proofs.

Tuesday [? after 18 October 1955]

My dear Mania

Chauvet got hold of me. Very nice man. He told me that my sentence is correct as it stands, that is with "à qui". He quoted other instances to me where it would have to be "de". He was not able to give me a very good explanation. I think that the distance of the object from the noun phrase has a lot to do with it. According to him, it is a question of usage, impossible to present in the form of a rule. He came back with me right to my door, and was exceptionally pleasant. Thank you for sending him after me.[1]

I have taken up many of your suggestions but not all. For "malinement" I have Rimbaud's authority.

> She was barely dressed
> And great trees, indiscreet
> Bent their foliage against the window
> Slyly, in close, in close.
> (Play in 3 Kisses)[2]

He uses it somewhere else as well.[3] Obviously "malignement" means something very different.[4]

I shall never be able to thank you enough for all the trouble you have taken. You must be very tired, almost as much as I am. Tomorrow the corpse moves off, indifferent, towards the black battalions.[5]

Much love from us both. Come over when you feel like it.

Sam

1 Between 1923 and his retirement in 1937, Paul Chauvet (1877–?) had taught English at the Lycée Buffon, where Mania Péron also taught. The evaluations of the Inspecteurs d'Académie declare him to be highly qualified – over-qualified indeed for the level of his pupils – and criticize him for being too indulgent to his pupils, leading

them to take advantage of him. (Centre d'Accueil et de Recherche des Archives Nationales, Fonds de l'instruction publique, F/17/24571.)

Given the widely divergent meanings and implications of "à qui" and "de qui," it is hard to imagine what rule SB can have been seeking.

2 Three very similar versions exist of the one Rimbaud poem: in two of them, "Comédie en trois baisers" (which SB cites here) and "Première soirée," Rimbaud uses the word "Malinement" (twice in each poem); in the third version, "Trois baisers," in the same places he uses "Malignement" (*Œuvres complètes*, 67–70).

3 Rimbaud uses the word "malinement" in line 8 of his poem "La maline" (*Œuvres complètes*, 110).

4 "Malinement" occurs in SB's "Textes pour rien, II": "Arrivé au bord de la falaise il se jette, on dirait follement, mais non, malinement, comme une chèvre, en brusques lacets vers la grève" (*Nouvelles et Textes pour rien*, 127) ("When it comes to the top of the cliff it springs, some might think blindly, but no, wilily, like a goat, in hairpin zigzags towards the shore") ("Text for Nothing 2," *Stories and Texts for Nothing*, 83). This text was initially drafted in French from 4 to 6 February 1951 (TxU, Beckett collection, Works, 5.7, notebook 1).

The associations of "malignement," much the more common form, are hardly ever pleasant (at best "cunningly"), whereas "malinement" can suggest far less objectionable artfulness. Rimbaud's poem "La maline" illustrates this: its servant-girl's ruse is so transparent as to be touching. SB's backing away from "follement" to "malinement" in "Textes pour rien, II" follows the same direction, as can be seen from his rejection of Mania Péron's suggested emendation.

5 SB speaks of returning the corpse of his finished book – the proofs of *Textes pour rien* – using a term from Baudelaire's poem "Une Charogne" ("Carrion") in which the poet, out walking, comes across a rotting corpse:

> Les mouches bourdonnaient sur ce ventre putride,
> D'où sortaient de noirs bataillons
> De larves, qui coulaient comme un épais liquide
> Le long de ces vivants haillons.
> (Flies kept humming over the guts
>   from which a gleaming clot
> of maggots poured to finish off
>   what scraps of flesh remained.)

> (*Œuvres complètes*, I, 31; *Les Fleurs du mal: The Complete Text of The Flowers of Evil*, 35.)

NIALL MONTGOMERY
DUBLIN

November 2nd 1955   6 Rue des Favorites
                                               Paris 15me

Dear Niall

It did my old pinking heart a power of good to have your warm and affectionate letter. They seem to have done a good job in the Pike, though Simpson writes that he is not pleased with his Estragon and confessing to having made minor improvements in the text. The reviews I have seen seem hardly less foolish if less venomous than usual. The whole affair is so simple, no symbols where none intended.[1] I'm afraid I won't be able to get over to see it and you all, you all and it. But perhaps next year, Con has his hooks in me for the Scholard's Dinner, our last chance probably.[2] If I do, and the family dying dead, it's the quare times we'll be having. I'm in toothless twyminds at the moment about proceeding to Broadway where it opens in January and this old hag invited expenses paid.[3] Looking forward rather to assisting at a revival in a Rhineland penitentiary by a group of thieves, embezzlers, assassins and sexual aberrants, I'm told they had the gaolers in tears.[4] I had a good week in Zurich with Giorgio Joyce seeing the ways the father went and where they ended.[5] Laburnum tendrils how are you. No I have not yet meet [sic] the O'Briens, Desmond Ryan has great accounts of them and wants to arrange it, but I have a phobia about Irish officials. I'm glad Curran went and admitted there might be something, remember me warmly to him.[6] John Beckett is here for a week, we are trying to do something together, tell you about it another time, I'll be sorry to see him go.[7] No news of Deirdre. Morris very prosperous at WHO, hardly ever see him now.[8] I met Sheila Murphy at a party at Ryan's, depressed at the thought of going home.[9] Enclosed a letter might divert you, typical of many, tear it up and keep the stamps.[10] I saw some of Mercier's stuff, very gratifying I'll be bound.[11] What about your own play, don't mind its going yellow, my first is mahogany, do another.[12] Have a little book coming out here very soon, first and last gasps in French, 1945 and 1950, if I forget to send it write demanding, but I won't.[13] Very tired, stupid, dirty, old and willless, all systems capital S, and somewhere the vague wish I could mind.

      Affectionately to you all.

        s/ Sam

Tante belle	Pinget seems to have got bogged in
cose to	London, he'll probably be over
JBY.[14]	in Dublin later on.[15]

TLS, with AN; 1 leaf, 1 side; *AN AH* RECD 5 NOV '55; NLI, Accession 6475, Lot 7, Box Gregory.

1   Austin Byrne (n.d.) played Estragon in the Pike Theatre production.
It is uncertain which of the Dublin reviews SB may have seen of the Pike Theatre production which opened on 28 October 1955. The one in *The Irish Times* commented: "Mr.Beckett, using none of the accepted dramatic conventions and defying most of them . . . has produced a statement of such terrifying and compelling intensity that 2 1/2 hours in the Pike last night seemed to pass in ten minutes." The review also praised the acting, saying that Dermot Kelly (Vladimir) was "superbly dextrous in walking the tight-rope between farce and tragedy, without over balancing," that Nigel Fitzgerald kept "his Pozzo just the right side of overplaying," and that "Donal Donnelly's Lucky is frighteningly heart-rending and his speech a 'technical *tour-de-force*'" (K., 'Waiting for Godot' by Pike Theatre Company," *The Irish Times* 29 October 1955: 8).
"No symbols where none intended" was the title of Montgomery's essay on SB (see 2 December 1953, n. 8).

2   At Trinity College Dublin, in 1926, SB was awarded a Foundation Scholarship (commonly known as Schol.). Scholars are invited to the Scholars' Dinner every tenth anniversary of their year of election; SB would attend with Leventhal, who was elected to Schol. in 1916. "Scholard" – SB makes play with an uneducated local version of "Scholar."

3   SB makes play with a phrase from the Shem episode in James Joyce's *Finnegans Wake*, "you have become of twosome twiminds" (James Joyce, *Finnegans Wake* [New York: Viking Press, 1969] 188).
In his letter of 25 October, Barney Rosset conveyed Michael Myerberg's invitation to SB to come to New York, saying that "Garson Kanin might be the director and [. . .] that Kanin wants you to be here to advise him" (NSyU).

4   The production of *Warten auf Godot* by prisoners at Lüttringhausen: 14 October 1954, n. 1.

5   SB spent a week in early October with Giorgio and Asta Joyce (see 13 October 1955). James Joyce lived in Zurich from 1915 to 1920 and briefly again from 1940 until his death in 1941. He is buried there.

6   "Laburnum tendrils" is a phrase from James Joyce's poem "Alone," which appeared in *Pomes Penyeach*: "The shore-lamps in the sleeping lake / Laburnum tendrils trail" ([Paris: Shakespeare and Company, 1927] [11], lines 3 and 4).
Conor Cruise O'Brien (1917–2008) was Counsellor in the Irish Embassy in Paris from 1955 to 1956, and a member of the Irish Delegation to the United Nations from 1955 to 1960; his first wife was Christine (née Foster, m. 1939–1959).
Journalist and author Desmond Ryan (1893–1964) had lived in Ireland and more recently in Paris, where he frequently hosted gatherings of Irish friends.
Constantine Curran (1883–1972) was a lawyer and a historian of art and architecture; he was part of a Dublin circle that included W. B. Yeats, G. W. Russell (known as AE), and James Stephens; he had been a close friend of James Joyce.

7   John Beckett and Deryk Mendel had worked together to coordinate music and movement in SBs mime for Mendels character, Frollo, *Acte sans paroles*.

8   Deirdre Sinclair Morrow: 21 October 1945, n. 6. Morris Sinclair and his work at the WHO: 6 August 1953, n. 7.

9 Sheila Murphy (1898–1983), Irish diplomat, was a First Secretary in the Department of External Affairs in 1948 and later served as First Secretary in the Irish Legation in Paris (1956–1961), as well as on the Irish Delegation to the United Nations General Assembly (1956).

10 The letter that SB sent on to Montgomery has not been identified.

11 SB had seen Vivian Mercier's essay "Beckett and the Search for Self" (see 2 October 1955, n. 1). He may also have been aware of Mercier's review of *Waiting for Godot*: "A Pyrrhonian Eclogue," *Hudson Review* 7.4 (Winter 1955): 620–624. A further study by Mercier, "Godot, Molloy et Cie," appeared in *The New Statesman and Nation* 50.1291 (5 December 1955): 754.

12 Montgomery's play has not been identified.

13 *Nouvelles et Textes pour rien*, published by Editions de Minuit on 15 November.

14 Handwritten PS. "Tante belle cose" (All good things). JBY: Jack B. Yeats.

15 Handwritten PS. Robert Pinget: 28 September [1955], n. 3.

A. J. LEVENTHAL
DUBLIN

5-11-55   Paris
My dear Con

Many thanks for letter with press cuttings. The Pike seems to have made a gallant shot at it. I think your D.M. article has helped many people. I had letters from Simpson and Niall Montgomery.[1] I understand the "big" Dublin theatres are very riled. Tant mieux.[2] I saw Albery here this week. He hopes to continue at the Criterion for some time. The Arts Theatre metteur en scène, Peter Hall, has been invited to direct production on Broadway. We don't know yet if he can get away (opening January). I am invited all expenses paid by the producer Michael Myerburg, but presume I won't go.[3]

I met the McCabes at a party at Desmond Ryan's [. . .][4]

I am hoping to go to the Rhineland, more precisely to the Lüthringhausen penitentiary to see a last performance of this fucking play by and for the prisoners if permission can be obtained for them to do it again.[5]

John Beckett has been over for a week, working with Frollo on music for our little turn. He has begun a very good job. They greatly enjoyed their evening with you and Ethna.[6]

Remember me to HO.[7]

Yours ever

Sam

ALS; 1 leaf, 1 side; TxU, Leventhal collection.

1 *Waiting for Godot* opened at the Pike Theatre in Dublin on 28 October. A. J. Leventhal wrote on the Paris production in "Mr. Beckett's *En attendant Godot*," *Dublin Magazine*, 11–16. It is not known what cuttings Leventhal had sent (see 2 November 1955, n. 1).

Writing about the production at the Pike Theatre to his friend John Sweeney in Boston, Niall Montgomery commented: "Con Leventhal acted as godotfather – he was the liaison with Sam" (30 October 1955, NLI, Accession 6475, Lot 7, Personal Correspondence, Alex).

2 SB wrote to Alan Simpson on 4 November:

> I saw Donald Albery yesterday. I put it up to him that the British Empire rights as acquired per contract by him might be construed as not extending to the Republic of Ireland. He said at once they certainly would not in the absence of the additional clause "and Eire" usual in such contracts since 1949. He assumed it figured in mine. If it did not (it does not) it was a regrettable omission on their part. In a sense he seemed rather relieved, having received letters from Dublin's "big" theatres abusing him for having consented to your doing the play and to which he can now retort that he had no say in the matter. The question therefore no longer arises of his issuing you with a licence or of your owing him royalties. (TCD, MS 10731/23.)

3 Peter Hall was "metteur en scène" (director) of the Arts Theatre production that transferred to the Criterion Theatre on 12 September 1955 (see 10 May 1955, n. 2). SB writes "Myerburg" for "Myerberg."

4 The McCabes have not been identified. Desmond and Mary Ryan's home in Paris was a gathering place for Irish friends.

5 SB writes "Lüthringhausen" for Lüttringhausen.

6 John Beckett and Vera Slocombe had had dinner with Leventhal and Ethna MacCarthy in London.

7 H. O. White.

THOMAS MACGREEVY

DUBLIN

November 6th 1955   6 Rue des Favorites
                                                   Paris 15me

My dear Tom

Thanks for your good letter. My work and what was ever left of
me before and after that could by none be so gently and understand-
ingly uttered as by you, I know that. I am only sorry they pestered you
with it.[1]

Can't get a verse of Milton out of my mind: "Insuperable height of
loftiest shade."[2]

John Beckett has been over from London getting some music
down for a sketch I have done for a clown. He has gone back now
and I miss him.

I am still being pressed to go to London to see the production. It
would be less perilous now than some months ago.[3] Also invited to
New York by American producer, all expenses paid, in January probably. I think it would be a mistake to accept.

Did George Reavey send you his poems? There was at least one
extraordinarily good one, I thought.[4]

Niall wrote me a most touching and affectionate letter after
having seen the play at the Pike. He said poor Con Curran s'est
dérangé and said kind things.[5]

Jean writes cheerful and courageous.[6] They have not yet succeeded in working out what her income will be.

I met Sheila Murphy at a party at Desmond Ryan's, depressed at
having to return to Dublin. She painted me a gloomy picture of Nuala
and her parents.[7]

I may be over next year, for the Scholards' Dinner. But I hope we
shall see you here before then.

Things are not very grand with me. It is time now I made big
changes in my way of living, but I doubt if I have the energy. My little
book of odds and ends is due now very soon.[8]

I spent a week at Zurich with Giorgio and his German wife, saw the father's haunts and ways and where they ended, in the woods above the town.

Very affectionately, dear Tom, from us both.

s/ Sam

Poor Adrienne Monnier committed suicide.[9]

TLS; 1 leaf, 1 side; TCD, MS 10402/197.

1   MacGreevy's letter to SB has not been found, nor is it known who had troubled MacGreevy for a comment on SB's oeuvre.

2   SB's Gallicism, "verse," picks up the French "vers" – a single line of poetry.
SB quotes from John Milton's description of the Garden of Eden as Satan approaches it: "over head up grew / Insuperable highth of loftiest shade, / Cedar, and Pine, and Firr, and branching Palm" (John Milton, *Paradise Lost*, ed. Barbara K. Lewalski [Malden, MA: Blackwell Publishing, 2007] Book IV, lines 137–139).

3   In his letter to Barney Rosset of 26 October, SB says that Harold Hobson had told him that *Waiting for Godot* was doing well in London (NSyU).

4   In his letter to Reavey of 22 October, SB thanks Reavey for his recent collection of poems, *Colours of Memory*, and tells him that the poem "Never," in particular, is "unforgettably beautiful and poignant" ([New York: Grove Press, 1955] 56; TxU, Reavey collection).

5   Niall Montgomery: see 2 November 1955.

6   Jean Beckett, widow of Frank Beckett.

7   Nuala Costello (1907–1984; Profile, I); her parents were Thomas Costello and Evelyn Costello (née Drury). SB cancels "the Costello" and inserts "Nuala."

8   *Nouvelles et Textes pour rien.*

9   Adrienne Monnier (1892–1955), close friend of the Joyces and proprietor of the Paris bookshop La Maison des Amis des Livres, had been seriously ill since 1950; on 18 June 1955, she took an overdose of sleeping pills (Noel Riley Fitch, *Sylvia Beach and the Lost Generation: A History of Literary Paris in the Twenties and Thirties* [New York: W. W. Norton, 1983] 410–411).
SB's PS is handwritten.

BARNEY ROSSET, GROVE PRESS
NEW YORK

November 12th 1955

6 Rue des Favorites
Paris 15me

My dear Barney

Thanks for your letters and Myerburg news. I am very touched by his offer to pay my expenses to go to New York. As he has not written to me personally I leave to you the conveyance of my very warm thanks. I do not want to say definitely yes or no just now, gored insufficiently by the old horns. I suppose it will alas be no as usual. If it were just to give the director of production a hand, without getting in his way, or letting him get in mine, and then exemption from inter-views, journalists, fool answers to fool questions and kindred miseries, then I would consider going very seriously. But it is obvious I cannot accept such a generous offer and then not do what is expected of me. If there is one thing I cannot do it is talk about my work, or "explain" it, except perhaps over the third bottle with an indulgent friend. That, my dear Barney, is roughly how I feel about it at the moment.[1]

The prospect of a cheaper edition of the play pleases me greatly. If such an article were available in London and Dublin at the moment, I think the sales would probably be considerable.[2] So far as I know still no complaints from Piccadilly and Albery, when I saw him here was it last week, was optimistic about further prospects. He told me that Peter Hall, who directed in London, had been invited to direct New York production, but might not be able to get away. No news since.

You will be glad to hear that the typing of final version of Malone Dies is now proceeding apace. I think I can safely say you will have it by the end of the month, or very little later.

Salutations to Loly and the hopeful.

> Yours
> s/ Sam

Many thanks for sending books.

I saw Patrick Bowles yesterday. Will you not send him a few copies of *Molloy*? He devours them![3]

TLS with AN PS; 1 side, 1 leaf; NSyU. Previous publication, Beckett and Rosset, "The *Godot* Letters: A Lasting Effect," *The New Theater Review*, 11–12.

1   Rosset's most recent letter, that of 3 November, reported that, pending signing of contracts, Myerberg expected *Waiting for Godot* to open in Miami on 3 June 1956, and to make two further stops on its way to New York. SB writes "Myerburg" for "Myerberg."

2   In his letter of 3 November, Rosset said that if the production went well, he would print a $1 paperback edition of the play.

3   The books sent to SB by Grove have not been identified.
The PS is handwritten.

BARNEY ROSSET, GROVE PRESS
NEW YORK

November 20th 1955   6 Rue des Favorites
                                      Paris 15me

Dear Barney

Thanks for your letters. Malone is responsible for tardy reply. I look forward to meeting Schneider next Saturday. I saw his *Skin* here at the last festival. I did not much like it. If I feel he is amenable to my distant cerebrations and that there is really a chance of my helping him, and the play, then I'm your man, now that I know myself absolved by Myerberg from performing apery.[1]

I have seen photos of the Criterion set-up, all wrong I think. I suppose Sch[n]eider will pause in London to see the production. I feel rather glad now that Hall is not available for USA.[2]

Thanks for Bowles['s] Molloys. I shall hand them over as soon as they arrive.[3]

Malone will be off to you this week, probably Thursday or Friday.

If I come to New York will you have any dollars for me? In any case do not send the second whack of my translator's emoluments until I know where I am.

            Best wishes to you all.

                s/ Sam

I certainly do not feel like taking on the Innommable at the moment.

TLS; 1 leaf, 1 side; NSyU.

1   Rosset sent a telegram on 14 November to ask SB if he would meet Alan Schneider* (1917–1984), who had been chosen to direct the New York production of

Waiting for Godot; he was to be in Paris on 26 November. In his letter of 15 November, Rosset introduced Schneider to SB:

> He directed the Paris performance of Wilder's SKIN OF OUR TEETH, which was put on a few months back. [...] I hope he will turn out to be somebody you like and that he will make you inclined to come here and help put the play together. Myerberg assures me that you would not be bothered by journalists, fool questions, and etc. (NSyU.)

Alan Schneider's production of Thornton Wilder's *The Skin of our Teeth* was performed in the Theatre of Nations Festival in Paris, from 28 June 1955. Schneider directed a cast that included Helen Hayes and Mary Martin. Playwright William Saroyan (1908–1981) had advised Myerberg: "The producer of The Skin of Our Teeth is the man to do Waiting for Godot" (Saroyan to Myerberg, 12 November 1955, WHS, Myerberg collection, 102/11/1).

2   The set design of the London production: 24 September 1955, n. 3.

3   In his letter of 15 November, Rosset indicates that he has sent off three copies of *Molloy* for Patrick Bowles, care of SB, "because I am afraid maybe his address has changed."

ALAN SIMPSON, PIKE THEATRE
DUBLIN

November 20th 1955   6 Rue des Favorites
                                      Paris 15me

Dear Alan

Thanks for letter and photographs and to your players for their autographs which I shall treasure. I liked particularly that of Vladimir looking at the boot as if it were an early 17th century skull.[1] I'm afraid I'm very bad about photographs. I'm not due another until 1960, when my identity card will have to be renewed. I should be interested to read The Q. F., but fear not the slightest chance of getting it done here. In any case I couldn't take on the job of translating it, being up to my eyes translating myself.[2] I suggest you have a look through the theatre of Arthur Adamov and Eugène Ionesco (Con Leventhal has them both). La Leçon or Les Chaises of Ionesco. They have not been done in English as far as I know.[3] Latest news of NY is that Alan Schneider (who directed I think not happily Wilder's Skin) is to be director of production. I am to see him here next Saturday and may go back with him or after him to give a hand if I feel he is the kind of man to whom my kind of hand can be given. The producer is Michael Myerberg and he plans, I am told, to open in Miami, of all ridiculous places, on Jan 3rd and thence proceed by stages (c'est le cas de le dire) to NY where opening is scheduled for Jan 22nd approx.[4] Myerberg first invited Arts Theatre director Peter Hall to do the job for him, but he could not get away. I am rather glad, having seen photos of Criterion set-up and heard echoes of their Anglican fervour especially in Act II. In London day after to-morrow they are doing a debate on the play at the Institute of Contemporary Arts which may perhaps help it into the Christmas business.[5]

Best wishes to you all and good continuation.[6]

> Yours
>
> s/ Sam

TLS; 1 leaf, 1 side; *A corr ink, pencil markings in AH*; TCD 10731/25.

1   The cast of the Pike Theatre *Waiting for Godot*: Dermot Kelly (Vladimir), Austin Byrne (Estragon), Nigel FitzGerald (Pozzo), Donal Donnelly (Lucky), Seamus Fitzmaurice (Boy). The photograph of Vladimir inspecting the boot (Carolyn Swift, *Stage by Stage* [Dublin: Poolbeg, 1985] image [8]).

2   The Pike Theatre had enjoyed a very successful run with Brendan Behan's play *The Quare Fellow*; Simpson had asked SB if a French production might be possible.

3   Arthur Adamov's plays had been collected in two volumes: *La Parodie, L'Invasion, La grande et la petite manœuvre, Le Professeur Taranne*, and *Tous contre tous* in *Théâtre I* (Paris: Gallimard, 1953); *Le Sens de la marche, Les Retrouvailles, Le Ping-Pong* in *Théâtre II* (Paris: Gallimard, 1955).
   Eugène Ionesco's plays: 17 November 1953. Ionesco's plays *La Leçon* (*The Lesson*) and *Les Chaises* (*The Chairs*) were not published in translation until 1958.

4   Myerberg's plans for *Waiting for Godot* in the United States: SB to Barney Rosset, 20 November 1955, n. 1. "C'est le cas de le dire" (appropriately enough).

5   SB had received Lucas's letter of 16 November by this time (see 22 November 1953 [*for* 1955] to Cyril Lucas, n. 1, below).
   On 22 November, there was a discussion of *Waiting for Godot* at the Institute of Contemporary Arts, with Peter Hall, Harold Hobson, David Paul, Toni del Renzio, Tony Richardson, and John Whiting, chaired by David Sylvester. Its intent was announced by the November *Bulletin of the Institute of Contemporary Arts* (2):

> It is perhaps the only play for years of genuine originality. The richness and unfamiliarity of the play is such that what is needed is (1) some analysis of the play's impact on London audiences compared with (2) a backgrounding in the intellectual scene of Paris (where Beckett lives), and (3) comment on the

attitudes symbolized by the play. A discussion has been arranged that will cover a part of these requirements.

6 "Good continuation" is a Gallicism (bonne continuation), intending "hope things keep going well."

A. J. LEVENTHAL
DUBLIN

22-11-55   6 Rue des Favorites
                                           Paris 15me

My dear Con

Many thanks for your letter of Nov. 7th and forgive delay in replying. I have been, with breakneck dedication, getting final version of <u>Malone</u> off my pigeon chest for Grove Press.

Hayden's exhibition closes to-day. He has had an excellent press but no sales so far.[1] The names and addresses you ask for are:

> BRAM VAN VELDE
> c/o JACQUES PUTMAN
> 3 RUE DE L'ISLY
> PARIS 8
> GEER VAN VELDE
> 30 BD DE LA VANNE
> CACHAN, SEINE

Simpson sent me photos of Pike production. Hard to tell from them. Vladimir has the perfect gob for the part.[2]

I am to see here next Saturday American director of N.Y. production one Alan Schneider. He directed Wilder's <u>Skin</u> which I saw here at dramatic festival this summer and did not much like. When I have seen him I shall decide whether or not to accept producer Myerberg's invitation to go over. They plan, I am told, to open at Miami (!) on January 3rd and thenceforward by, I hope, easy stages (cas de le dire) to Broadway where opening scheduled for Jan. 22nd approx.[3]

Advance copies of my Nouvelles & Textes pour gar nix have arrived and your copy will get off to you this week. The nouvelles are uninteresting. But I think the Textes were worth publishing.[4]

John was over for a week and got down some good music. Mendel promises to do the job very well. We hoped to have it done in the next musical at the Royal Court Theatre, Sloane Square, but it was too late.[5]

Hope soon to hear you are snug in the Rubrics. Is the date of next year's Scholard's Dinner fixed. I should be glad to know it if it is, as I am concerned with the possibility of fitting it in with the Lords Test Match against the Australians.[6]

What news of Ethna, I have none. I suppose my fault for not writing. John & Vera greatly enjoyed their dinner with you in London.[7]

Kind remembrance to HO. I am thinking of taking two of the Merlin lads to a meal chez Marius this evening.[8]

Toute mon amitié[9]

Sam

ALS; 2 leaves, 2 sides; TxU, Leventhal collection.

1 Henri Hayden's exhibition of recent works at the Galerie Suillerot, Paris.

2 Dermot Kelly (Vladimir): 20 November 1955 to Alas Simpson, n. 1.

3 "Cas de le dire" (appropriately enough).

4 *Nouvelles et Textes pour rien* was published on 15 November. SB's plays with the title "Textes pour gar nix" (Texts for nothing at all). "Gar nix" (Ger. colloq., from "gar nichts," nothing at all).

5 John Beckett was working with Deryk Mendel on SB's *Acte sans paroles*. Information about the intention to produce the mime at the Royal Court Theatre in London has not been found. A musical sing-along program, *Let's Make an Opera*, was performed there in December; a review produced by Laurier Lister (1907–1986), *Fresh Airs*, opened there on 12 January 1956. Lister's review seems the most likely potential venue for SB's mime.

6 The Rubrics is a row of red brick buildings facing Library Square, on the eastern side, in Trinity College Dublin; they were built c. 1700.
Scholars' Dinner is held on Trinity Monday. In 1956, that fell on 25 June. The Test Match at Lord's against Australia was scheduled for 21–26 June 1956.

7   Ethna MacCarthy. John Beckett and Vera Slocombe.

8   H. O. White, Leventhal, and SB dined out together when White visited SB in Paris in September 1955 (SB to H. O. White, 28 September 1955, TCD, MS 3777/12).
Le Petit Marius, 6 Avenue George V, Paris 8.

9   "Toute mon amitié" (fondest wishes).

CYRIL LUCAS
LONDON

22-11-53 [*for* 1955]   6 rue des Favorites
                                                         Paris 15°

Dear Mr Lucas

You are perfectly right.

"Miséricorde" in Paris was a scarcely intelligible scarcely audible ejaculation.

That is how "Christ etc" should be uttered.

It is largely I suppose the fault of my bad translation.

I am afraid the London production tends throughout toward this redemptive perversion.[1]

This helps to account for its success.

     Yours sincerely
     Samuel Beckett

ALS; 1 leaf, 1 side; env to Cyril Lucas Esq, 14 Sussex Mews East, London W.2, Angleterre; pm 22-11-55, Paris; UoR, BIF, MS 5149. *Dating*: from Lucas to SB, 16 November 1955 and 28 November 1955.

1   Cyril Lucas (b. 1926). Lucas wrote to SB on 16 November:

> Each time that I have seen your admirable play, I was worried by one line. It is Vladimir's reply to the Boy's "I think it is white, Sir" – "Christ have mercy on us". The line is given such emphasis and spoken with such fervour that the Christians have seized it as if it were the key that unlocks the whole of the play. Mr. Hobson for example, has declared it to be the most beautiful line in "Godot" [. . .] I turned to the French text and found the less committal, unparticularised and entirely comprehensible "Miséricorde", which confirmed my impression that your intention has been distorted. I draw your attention to this only because I think it is a pity – in so far as this has any meaning at all – that your audiences should be led deliberately to misunderstand "Godot", rather than merely fail to understand as would otherwise be, and, indeed, has anyway proved to be, the case. (UoR, BIF, MS 5149.)

The line referred to here is in Act II (*Waiting for Godot* [Grove Press], 59; *En attendant Godot*, 159).

Harold Hobson wrote: "When Vladimir is told by a young boy at the end of the play that the Godot for whom he has been vainly waiting all his life has a white beard, his awed exclamation, 'Christ have mercy upon us,' is the most solemn thing heard in our comic theatre for many years" ("Samuel Beckett," *The Sunday Times* 11 August 1955: 11).

ALAN SCHNEIDER

NEW YORK

December 14th 1955   6 Rue des Favorites

Paris 15me

My dear Alan

Herewith some notes I have sent to Peter Hall, and letter with afterthoughts. I thought you might like to have them.[1]

It was finally decided in London that a new production during performance was not feasible.[2]

I got back here last Sunday. I have decided not to go to the States. Having worked with you so pleasantly and, I hope, profitably, in Paris and London, I feel my monster is in safe keeping. All I ask of you is not to make any changes in the text without letting me know. If their way of speaking is not the American way it simply cannot be helped. Not, as you know, that I am intransigent about changing an odd word here and there or making an odd cut. But do please let me have the opportunity of protesting or approving.[3]

It appears my publisher has been making things difficult. We have done all in our power to cawm him and I do hope peace now reigneth.[4]

I hear there was talk in your papers of Wilder coming to our rescue with an adaptation of my play. This would make me laugh if it was not prohibited.[5]

All the best, Alan. Let me have your news.

                Yours

          s/ Sam

          Sam Beckett

Enclosure: PETER HALL, LONDON

December 14th 1955   6 Rue des Favorites
                                            Paris 15me

Dear Peter Hall

Herewith a few notes, depressingly inadequate.

When Lucky dances a third time instead of thinking he should begin exactly the same movements as the first two times, and at the same place, and then get to his thinking place under Pozzo's orders.

The correct lighting in both acts is:

1) Unvarying evening light up to boy's exit.
2) Then suddenly darkness.
3) Then suddenly moonrise and moonlight till curtain.

I don't suppose this can be done without serious disturbance. But it seems to me you could have the moon rise, through an arc of 90° i.e. from horizon to zenith. This should last about 10 seconds. Vladimir watches it in silence. I do feel this is important and need not upset anything.

Important also to get Pozzo to vary his tone.

With best wishes to you all,

Yours sincerely

Samuel Beckett

8   AP-PALLED More emphatic.

9   and the other . . . damned. He should take longer to find the
        word.

     or thereabouts. Give more irony to this parenthesis,
     suggestion being they were keeping out of trouble.

11   But what Saturday? etc. Much slower and more broken. Pause
                          after each question. Each question a
                          banderilla. Let each day sink in
                          before passing on to next.

     DON'T TELL ME More anguished.

12   If it hangs you it'll hang anything better than … it'll hang
     you.

13   Long embarrassed silence after horse.
     I'm hungry. More violent.

14   Ti-ed. Two syllables.
     For the moment. Longer pause before.

17   Oh I say … It's the chafing. A little too fast. More value to 5
     successive it's. A trifle effeminate etc. A little too fast.

18   Basket. Immediately upon Can't you see he wants to rest?
     Lucky should not grab at bones. Bateson knows about this.

19   One should feel that Estragon's Ah that's better is an echo of
     Pozzo's, p. 18.

21   Not Well, that's what I think but Well, that's that, I think.

22   The tears of the world etc. Much more lyrical.
     Swine. Meaning Lucky.

24   You missed a treat. Addressed to Vladimir.
     Black night. Better than Darkest night.
     Ask me again. Much more an aside.
     Whip should crack here and elsewhere as indicated. It was
     mute throughout.

25   What is your name? – Adam. Why omitted? Good? Fair? etc.
     Cascando of tones from hopefulness to gloom.

26   Lucky dances for Pozzo who should not turn his back, but
     manifest his disgust.

27   My left lung etc. Much hoarser, followed by series of feeble
     coughs.
     But my right lung etc. More ringing.
     Wait.Wait. Longer. Parody of anguished concentration.
     Wait.

28   Lucky's speech. Wastes and pines more emphatic.

29

31 <u>Adieu</u>. Pronounce adioo.

33 Correct boy's <u>sirs</u>.

34 <u>In the loft</u>. Simply. No pointing to heaven.[6]
<u>Not really</u>. Ironic. Grock's <u>Sans blââââgue</u>.[7]

----->

37 Song. Air herewith. Vladimir should advance to extreme
front, parody attitude of amateur cantatrice and sing with
exaggerated feeling. What stops him is the word tomb. He
broods on death.

38 <u>What a day</u>. Out of a silence.

39 Full value to silence between Estragon's <u>We are happy</u> and
<u>What do we do now</u> etc.

40 <u>Say something</u>. Anguished. Full value to preceding silence.

41 <u>Say anything</u>. Do. Do.
<u>This is awful</u>. Do. Do.
<u>What is terrible is to have thought</u>. Accent on have.

42 They concentrate bare-headed. Longer. More parodic. Same
effect as in Act I when Vladimir, Estragon and Pozzo
concentrate.
<u>We spent blathering about nothing in particular</u> better than
<u>We spent talking</u> etc.

44 <u>Not sufficiently</u> better than <u>Not enough</u>.

45 Vladimir's walk in his shirt-sleeves should last longer. The coat
should fall to the ground when Estragon wakes with a start.
<u>Don't tell me</u>. More vehement.

47 Vladimir should inspect audience at much greater length
before saying <u>Well I can understand that</u>. All this passage
played too fast.

48 Strict symmetry of position when watching out. Vladimir was too far from wings. Burlesque peering from under eye-screening hands.

49 Long silence before <u>How time flies etc.</u> <u>Let's just do the tree.</u> Sketch herewith. It is the hands pressed together as though in prayer that produces Estragon's <u>Do you think God sees me.</u>

53 <u>We are men.</u> Very solemn.

55 <u>7 o'clock ... 8 o'clock.</u> More hesitation and separated by longer inspection of the sky.
Much longer silence before Estragon's <u>Expand.</u>
<u>Don't question me.</u> More vehement.
<u>It's indescribable ... There's a tree.</u> Suggest all three totter round, where they stand, in a full circle.[8] Lines to be spoken as they do so or when they come back to their original position.

56 Estragon's <u>exactly.</u> Ironical.
<u>Make sure he's alive ... if he's dead.</u> Not enough made of this.

57 <u>They give birth etc.</u> Much more lyrical.
<u>Don't tell me.</u> More vehement.

58 Not <u>The air is full of cries</u> but <u>The air is full of our cries.</u>
Correct boy's <u>sirs.</u>
Full value to silences throughout dialogue between boy and Vladimir.

59. <u>Two other ... men.</u> Long hesitation before <u>men.</u>
<u>Christ have mercy on us.</u> Almost unintelligible ejaculation. Keep hat on.
From now on to curtain dead numb tone for Vladimir.
<u>Everything's dead but the tree.</u> Dead numb tone.

TLS; 1 leaf, 1 side; enclosure: SB to Peter Hall, 14 December 1955 (TLS; 1 leaf, 1 side) and T enclosure (3 leaves, 3 sides); Burns Library, Schneider-Beckett Collection. Previous publication: Samuel Beckett and Alan Schneider, *No Author Better Served*, ed. Maurice Harmon (Cambridge, MA: Harvard University Press, 1998) 1–5.

Note: the numbers refer to page numbers in the Grove edition.

1   SB attended the London production with Alan Schneider at the end of November and in early December, seeing five performances together (Schneider, *Entrances*, 224–225). Schneider indicated that, when they were backstage one evening, "I had to prevent Sam firmly from giving out an array of written notes to the actors" (Alan Schneider, "Working with Beckett," in *Samuel Beckett: The Art of Rhetoric*, ed. Edouard Morot-Sir, Howard Harper, and Dougald McMillan III, North Carolina Studies in the Romance Languages and Literatures Symposia, no. 5 [Chapel Hill: University of North Carolina, Department of Romance Languages, 1976] 278); Alan Schneider to Michael Myerberg. Thursday night [December 1955], UCSD, Alan Schneider Collection, MSS 103/11/10).

2   Peter Hall's production of *Waiting for Godot* continued at the Criterion Theatre until 24 March 1956.

3   SB returned to Paris on Sunday 9 December.

4   Rosset had been concerned about his percentage of royalties on productions in the United States.

5   Schneider sailed to Europe on the S. S. *Independence* on which Thornton Wilder was a fellow-passenger. Given that they had already worked together on *The Skin of Our Teeth*, and in view of Wilder's early interest in the play, the two discussed *Waiting for Godot* in detail (*Entrances*, 222–223). Arthur Gelb reported in *The New York Times*: "Thornton Wilder is lending Director Alan Schneider a helping hand in deciphering the puzzling dialogue and plot of Samuel Beckett's 'Waiting for Godot'... Mr. Wilder, who has seen the play several times in London and Paris, and Mr. Schneider are now aboard the same Europe-bound ship" ("2 New Musicals Advancing Plans," 25 November 1955: 37).
The possibility of Thornton Wilder's "adapting" *En attendant Godot* had been voiced in very early negotiations with Garson Kanin (see [before 18 May 1953], n. 1). Now much closer to production, Rosset reports again that "Thornton Wilder was going to write an adaptation of your play and that that would be the one to be put on [on] Broadway" (6 December, NSyU).

6   The line from page 34 is a handwritten addition by SB.

7   SB refers to an element of the comic routine of the Swiss clown, Grock (né Charles Adrien Wettach, 1880–1959), namely, to drawing out the vowel sound in a word. "Sans blâââgue" for "sans blague" (no kidding).

8   There is a handwritten addition following "full circle," not in SB's hand: "to look at the place."

ROBERT PINGET
LONDON

14 décembre 1955   6 Rue des Favorites
                                                     Paris 15me

579

Mon cher Robert Pinget

Ca me fait beaucoup de peine de vous savoir tellement embêté. Je suis moi-même à un tel point fatigué et débordé en ce moment que je ne puis m'engager à comparer les deux textes, le vôtre et celui que vous propose Robbe-Grillet, afin de pouvoir vous conseiller en connaissance de cause.[1] Du reste cela ne servirait à rien, ces causes-là on ne les connaît jamais. Il faut que vous vous décidiez tout seul, en vous disant autant que possible que quoi qu'on fasse on est sûr de le regretter. Je ne connais que trop bien ce que vous éprouvez devant un dilemme pareil. J'ai toujours été intransigeant et je l'ai quelquefois regretté. Dites oui ou non et débarrassez-vous de cette histoire. Survivre, je sais que la question n'est pas là et que ce n'est pas un argument. Mais pouvoir continuer à crier en est peut-être un, pour ceux qui ne savent se taire. Il faut voir tout ça d'un peu haut. Les histoires qu'on vous supprime, vous vous en servirez par la suite. J'espère que vous sentez combien je suis gêné.

Je viens de passer quelques jours à Londres. Je n'ai pas pu vous joindre. Je n'ose pas vous envoyer un chèque sans votre accord. Mais si 20 livres peuvent vous servir à quelque chose, elles sont à vous. Faites-le moi savoir. Et ne m'en veuillez pas de ne pouvoir vous pousser à faire ce que moi je ferais probablement, et probablement à tort, à votre place. Ce n'est pas une simple dérobade.

Bien amicalement à vous

s/ Sam. Beckett

TLS; 1 leaf, 1 side; Burns Library, Pinget-Beckett Letters.

14th December 1955   6 Rue des Favorites
                                             Paris 15

Dear Robert Pinget,

It really saddens me to know that you're having such a bad time. I myself am so tired and so overworked just now that I can't undertake to compare the two texts, yours and the one that Robbe-Grillet is proposing, so as to give you advice based on an informed inside

18. Robert Pinget

view.[1] In any case it would get us nowhere: those sorts of insides we can never view. You must make up your own mind, telling yourself as much as possible that whatever one does, one is bound to regret it. I am only too familiar with what you are going through, faced with a dilemma of this kind. I have always been uncompromising, and I have sometimes regretted it. Say yes or no and be shot of the whole business. Surviving – I know that that's not the point, and that it's not an argument. But perhaps being able to go on shouting is, for those who cannot keep silent. You must take a longer view of it all. The stories that they're turning down you will be able to use later. I hope you can feel how hard I am finding this.

I have just spent a few days in London. I couldn't get through to you. I don't dare send you a cheque without your agreement. But if 20 pounds would be of any use to you, they're yours. Let me know. And don't hold it against me that I can't push you into doing what I would probably do, probably wrongly, in your place. It's not just evasion.

All good wishes

Sam. Beckett

1 Pinget's novel *Graal Flibuste* was published by Editions de Minuit in 1956. However, this edition and that published in 1963 by Editions 10/18 were incomplete texts: "the changes in the text of *Graal Flibuste* in the definitive 1966 edition [Editions de Minuit] restore short segments of this work that Pinget had reluctantly deleted before its first publication" (Robert M. Henkels, Jr., *Robert Pinget: The Novel as Quest* [University, AL: The University of Alabama Press, 1979] 4). Robbe-Grillet brought Pinget's work to the attention of Jérôme Lindon; it is not known what role he played with regard to initial cuts to *Graal Flibuste*, but he supported Pinget's requests for their restoration in the third edition (Henkels, *Robert Pinget*, 231).

PAMELA MITCHELL
NEW YORK

16.12.55   6 Rue des Favorites
                                            Paris 15me

Pam

Thanks for your letter of end October. Forgive delay in replying. I was hoping to be able to say à bientôt. But I have decided not to go to NY after all, though invited by Godot producer Myerberg.[1] Perhaps later on, quietly, under my own feeble steam, if the play takes on. I am just back from a rather hectic time in London. I went there with Alan Schneider, director of American production, to work with him, and we did so, I think to some purpose. A pleasant easy man, with I thought the right ideas, and the right reaction to the London production, we got

on well together, to my huge relief, and he didn't mind my saying I had
not liked his Wilder's Skin. The play is doing well at the Criterion,
Piccadilly, and we had a great party in the theatre for its 100th there,
buckets of champagne and a powerful crowd. They were all very nice to
me in London, critics and journalists included, they left me alone. Only
one newspaper man, who talked to me more about himself than about
me.[2] A good few old friends too. I am glad to be back in Gerard's Vale.[3]
Going to the country to-morrow to escape the festivities and try and
work. Rosset has been making trouble about USA production, but I
think all is well now. He has received my translation of Malone and has
it with the printer already. I hope you got Molloy. There are exciting
plans for my mime, here and in London, but so far nothing definite. My
London cousin came over and did the music.[4] Enough about me, too
much. Glad your job is turning out so acceptable and that your mother
is back to health. I suppose you'll be going to Worcester for Xmas.[5]
Nothing much happening here, except general elections beginning of
next month, if they can be called something.[6] The Nouvelles et Textes
pour Rien are out, but not worth sending. Tired and stupid beyond
belief. Glad Ray Sugar pulled it off, do you remember his photos in the
Iles Marquises?[7] I sometimes pass by the Gde Chaumière and think of
the happy hours and the sad ones. So it goes in the world, in the fairy-
tale's closing words.[8]

    Much love.   s/Sam

TLS; 1 leaf, 1 side; UoR, BIF, MS 5060.

1 "A bientôt" (till soon).

2 The hundredth performance of *Waiting for Godot* at the Criterion Theatre took
place on Thursday, 8 December 1955. SB attended. The journalist has not been
identified.

3 SB plays with the name Rue de Vaugirard, a long Parisian street near his home,
which passes Luxembourg Gardens and runs into the Boulevard St. Michel in the Latin
Quarter. The Old French name for this area was Val Girard.

4 John Beckett.

5 Mitchell's home town was Worcester, Massachusetts.

6   A general election was held in France on 3 January 1956.

7   Boxer Sugar Ray Robinson (1921–1989) regained the world middleweight title on 9 December in Chicago by knocking out Carl "Bobo" Olson (1928–2002). At the Iles Marquises, photographs of the famous adorned the walls.

8   Mitchell rented an apartment at 4 bis Rue de la Grande Chaumière from July 1954 through January 1955.

SB refers to the common German saying "So geht es in der Welt" (So it goes in the world).

BARNEY ROSSET, GROVE PRESS
NEW YORK

December 17th 1955   6 Rue des Favorites
                                                       Paris 15me

Dear Barney

Thanks for various letters and catalogue and books for Bowles.[1]

I have been so upset by all this business that I preferred to defer writing. I am now given to understand, through the vehicle of Mr Spencer Curtis Brown's churlish English, that I am the guilty one. This does not surprise me. I am ordering sackcloth and ashes.[2]

I have just written to Myerberg, in reply to his letter just received, that I have decided not to accept his generous invitation.[3] I am very tired and good for nothing but my hole in the Marne mud, whither I go this morning. Perhaps later, when the dust settles, if any is raised, I shall go under my own wheezy steam.

Glad you liked my Malone. Pleased also that the cheap Godot is on its way. I can't imagine any photo I'd like better than the one you have.[4]

I greatly enjoyed working with Alan Schneider in London. He strikes me as a good man, though I did not much like his Wilder's Skin.

Myerberg says they are opening in Miami Jan 3rd as planned. He also speaks of performance in Washington circa Jan 16th. I thought they had planned to go to Philly. When I told Kenneth Tynan in London that we had Lahr and Ewell he folded up with joy.[5]

Shall write less surlily after a few days retreat. In the meantime my warm greetings to Loly, the hopeful and yourself and to Grove Press and all its works for a happy Xmas and a prosperous New Year.

Yours

s/ Sam

TLS; 1 leaf, 1 side; NSyU. Previous publication, Beckett and Rosset, "The *Godot* Letters: A Lasting Effect," *The New Theater Review*, 12.

1 Rosset had written a series of letters to SB (29 November, 6 December, 7 December, and an undated letter) during this period. All of them touched on the issue of honoring Rosset's contracted right to 10 percent royalties on any production of *Waiting for Godot* in the United States, as well as the need for his permission for performance (NSyU).

SB had received a Grove Press catalogue and copies of *Molloy* on behalf of Patrick Bowles.

2 On 12 December, Spencer Curtis Brown wrote to Rosset outlining the option that was prepared by Curtis Brown for Albery's signature, and Albery's subsequent leasing of the option for performance of *Waiting for Godot* in the United States; he said that neither Albery nor Myerberg was aware that Rosset should have a right in such an agreement, something that SB "should have asked officially" (NSyU).

3 SB's letter to Michael Myerberg has not been found.

4 Rosset's letter of 7 December reported that Myerberg had requested that the Grove Press paperbound edition have a photograph of the American actors on the cover (NSyU).

5 Kenneth Tynan, Drama Critic for *The Observer*. Bert Lahr (1895–1967), Estragon; Tom Ewell (1909–1994), Vladimir.

ALAN SCHNEIDER

NEW YORK

december 27th 1955   6 Rue de Favorites

                                               Paris 15me

Dear Alan

Very glad to have your letter. I much appreciate your having found the time, in the stress of rehearsal, to write to me at such length and I am very interested by all you tell me.[1] There is no point in my commenting from here on your problems, if anyone can solve them you can. Very pleased by your remarks on your Vladimir, he is the spirit of the play and his wrongness in London was little short of disastrous.[2] Not much point either in my adding at this stage to the suggestions I made in London. But one or two things occur to me that may help your actors. If you feel they won't you needn't mention them. One has to do with Pozzo. He is a hypomaniac and the only way to play him is to play him mad. The difficulty always experienced by actors with this role (apart from its mechanics which are merely complicated) results I think from their efforts to clarify it and to give it a unity and a continuity which it simply cannot receive. In other words they try to establish it from without. The result at the best is lifelessness and dul[l]ness. Pozzo's sudden changes of tone, mood, behaviour, etc., may I suppose be related to what is going on about him, but their source is in the dark of his own inner upheavals and confusions. The temptation is to minimize an irresponsibility and discontinuity which should on the contrary be stressed. The uniformity of Peter Bull in London was unbearable.[3] Such an understanding of the part is perhaps a lot to ask of an actor, but I am convinced it is the only proper one and, what is more, the only possibly effective one. Played in any other way Pozzo is just dead, artificial and tedious. The other point is simply that Estragon is inert and Vladimir restless. The latter should be always on the fidget, the former tending back to his state of rest. On[e] should hear Vladimir's feet. But I think we talked this over in London.

I am not coming to the States just now because I am tired and cannot face the fuss. If I don't get away by myself now and try to work I'll explode, or implode. So I have retreated to my hole in the Marne mud and am struggling with a play. Later on, if Godot makes any dollars, and when the dust settles, if any is raised, I'll come along under my own wheezy steam. In all I have had one brief letter from Myerberg. I have written him that I cannot get away at present. The Wilder story came from my NY publisher. I don't know where he saw it, or how crooked.[4]

Why the platform? Is it just rising ground?[5]

Good of you to send me a list of your changes. If I had not met you I'd be on a hot griddle![6]

I saw Kenneth Tynan in London before I left. When I told him you had Ewell and Lahr he folded up with speechless joy.

Warm greetings to you all. Et courage! On les aura![7]

Yours

s/ Sam

TLS; 1 leaf, 1 side; Burns Library, Schneider-Beckett Collection. Previous publication, Alan Schneider, "Beckett's Letters on *Endgame*: Extracts from His Correspondence with Director Alan Schneider," *The Village Voice* 19 March 1958: 8, 15; Beckett and Schneider, *No Author Better Served*, 6–7.

1   Schneider's letter to SB has not been found.

2   Tom Ewell played Vladimir in Schneider's production. Paul Daneman initially played the role in Peter Hall's production at the Arts Club Theatre in London; he was succeeded by Hugh Burden.

3   Peter Bull (1912–1955) played the role of Pozzo in the London production.

4   SB's letter to Myerberg has not been found. "The Wilder story": SB to Alan Schneider, 14 December 1955, n. 5.

5   Although no platform is required by the text, Schneider envisioned "a sort of platform with a rather interesting tree in front of a sky-drop" (Schneider to Thornton Wilder, 20 January 1956, UCSD, MS 103/5/2).

6   The list of Schneider's changes has not been found.

7   "Et courage! On les aura!" (And courage! We'll get the so-and-sos!)

CHRONOLOGY 1956

1956 3 January   Opening of *Waiting for Godot*, Coconut Grove Playhouse, Miami, directed by Alan Schneider.

      13 January   *Molloy* banned in Ireland.

      21 January   SB declines to be proposed for election to the Irish Academy of Letters.

      10 February   *Waiting for Godot* published by Faber and Faber, in expurgated version.

      27 February   SB begins translation of *L'Innommable*.

      April   Extract from *Malone Dies* published in *Irish Writing*.

      19 April   Opening of *Waiting for Godot* at the John Golden Theatre, New York, directed by Herbert Berghof.

      May-June   SB revises new play for Marseille Festival in August.

      1 June   Declines request by Cyril Cusack to write a tribute to George Bernard Shaw.

      14 June – 23 September   Reprise of *En attendant Godot*, Théâtre Hébertot, Paris.

      21 June   SB invited to write a radio play for the BBC.

      25 June   Makes acquaintance of Avigdor Arikha at home of Alain Bosquet.

      July   Writing *All That Fall* for the BBC.

      8 July   SB learns that *Fin de partie* and *Acte sans paroles* will not be produced in Marseille Festival.

      18–28 July   Alan Schneider in Paris.

      21 July   SB accepts proposal by Limes Verlag to publish his collected poems in German with French and English originals.

      26 July   Suez Canal nationalized by Egypt.

August	*Waiting for Godot* published in *Theatre Arts* (New York).
11 August	SB meets Goddard Lieberson, Columbia Records, who brings him test recording of *Waiting for Godot*.
September	"L'écriture est gravure" by Jean Wahl, translated by the author with the assistance of SB as "The Word is Graven," published in *Verve* with Marc Chagall's "Illustrations for the Bible."
7 September	Extract from *Watt*, the BBC Third Programme.
27 September	SB sends *All That Fall* to the BBC.
October	*Malone Dies* published by Grove Press.
	Fin de Partie in rehearsal at the Théâtre de l'Œuvre, Paris.
23 October – 10 November	Popular uprising against Hungarian Communist Government crushed by Soviet armed intervention.
29 October	Suez War begins. The attempt by British, French, and Israeli troops to wrest control of the Canal from Egypt is abandoned after international pressure. Ceasefire on 6 November.
November	"Yellow" published in *New World Writing*.
11 November	John Calder Ltd. proposes to publish SB's three novels in a single volume in Great Britain.
28 November	SB "pre-rehearsing" *Fin de partie* with Jean Martin and Roger Blin.

ALAN SCHNEIDER
MIAMI

SCHNEIDER=
    COCOANUT [sic] GROVE PLAYHOUSE MIAMI
PARIS   1956 JAN 3
CROSSING EVERYTHING HEART IN MIAMI SUCCESS TO YOU ALL
        SAM[1]

Telegram; 1 leaf, 1 side; Burns Library, Schneider-Beckett Collection; photocopy, UCSD: Schneider. Previous publication, Beckett and Schneider, *No Author Better Served*, 8.

1 Telegram sent by SB on the opening of *Waiting for Godot* in Miami. Alan Schneider describes the audience, the performance (which started nearly an hour late), and the reviews in *Entrances*, 232–233.

CYRIL LUCAS
LONDON

January 4th 1956   6 Rue des Favorites
                                         Paris 15me

Dear Mr Lucas

    Forgive my having delayed so long in replying to your letter of last November.[1] The position with regard to my translated work is the following.

    My original intention was to find a translator for all my books written in French, as I was very loath to take on the job myself. Patrick Bowles made quite a good fist at Molloy, but the revision of his text gave me so much trouble that I felt it would be simpler to do the following translations myself. I finished Malone Meurt some months ago and it will be published shortly by the Grove Press, New York. I am

591

now faced with L'Innommable. I feel here again that the simplest thing is for me to translate it myself, though I do not intend to take it on for the moment. I am by no means a good translator, and my English is rusty, but I simply happen to be able still to write the queer kind of English that my queer French deserves.

With regrets, yours sincerely

s/ Samuel Beckett

TLS; 1 leaf, 1 side; *T env to* Cyril Lucas Esq, 14 Sussex Mews, London W2, Angleterre; pm 4-1-56, Paris; UoR, BIF, MS 5149.

1 On 28 November 1955, Lucas wrote to thank SB for his letter of 22 November. He remarked: "I see that you have recently allowed another hand to translate 'Molloy.' I wonder whether you might allow me to attempt 'Malone' or 'L'Innommable', entirely subject to your approval." (UoR, BIF, MS 5149.)

BARNEY ROSSET, GROVE PRESS
NEW YORK

January 6th 1955 [*for* 1956]   6 Rue des Favorites
                                                 Paris 15me

Dear Barney

Many thanks for Twain and greetings.[1]

Enclosed letter I have sent to the director of the Pike Theatre in Dublin where Godot is now playing. The takings will be minute.[2]

I asked Jérôme Lindon to-day to write to Curtis Brown requesting them to remit to you directly from now on your 10% of sums due to us on Albery productions and also to calculate arrears due to you and to pay them off as soon as possible. He is doing this.[3]

A cable from Alan Schneider from Miami this morning telling me of unfavourable reception there. I think this was to be expected and is not to be taken too much to heart.[4]

I accept without any question your computation of what remains due to me on my translation of Malone and should be glad if you would let me have same when convenient.

I am in the throes of an even worse play.

Thanks for cover. Only regret is that you did not quote Harold Hobson's name. Our debt to him in London is very great. I suppose it is too late now.[5]

Kindest regards to Loly.

Yours ever

s/ Sam

TLS; 1 leaf, 1 side; *enc* TLcc, 1 leaf, 1 side, SB to Alan Simpson, 6 January 1956; Grove, NSyU. *Dating*: from SB letter to Alan Simpson regarding Barney Rosset's portion of royalties due for English translation of *Waiting for Godot*. Previous publication, Beckett and Rosset, "The *Godot* Letters: A Lasting Effect," 12–13.

1 *Puddn'head Wilson* by Mark Twain was published by Grove Press in 1955; this is probably the book sent to SB.

2 SB enclosed his letter of 6 January to Alan Simpson, the Pike Theatre, Dublin (TCD, MS 10731/28).

3 On 3 January, Kitty Black wrote to Jérôme Lindon asking SB to indicate the percentage due to Rosset so that they could pay him directly; in his letter of 6 January, Lindon conveyed this to SB (IMEC, Beckett, Boîte 5, S. Beckett Correspondance 1962–1968, Curtis Brown 1957 [*for* 1952–1957]).

4 Reaction to the play in Miami began before the curtain fell: "Many left after the first act," Jack Bell wrote: "I've never seen a fine cast try so hard with so little, and wind up with so-so-nuthin'" ("The Town Crier," *The Miami Herald* 5 January 1956: 2A). Herb Rau wrote "The new Grove Playhouse is a smash hit, but what was presented on its stage last night was a smash flop" ("Theater is a Hit But 'Godot' Isn't," *Miami Daily News* 4 January 1956: 7B).

On 5 January, Myerberg withdrew the play from its New York engagement and announced that the production would end in Miami on 14 January (Sam Zolotow, "Play by Beckett to Close on Road," *The New York Times* 6 January 1956: 20).

5 SB refers to the cover of the paperback edition of *Waiting for Godot*.
The reviews of Harold Hobson: 18 August 1955, n. 3, and 2 October 1955, n. 2.

ALAN SCHNEIDER

MIAMI

January 11th 1956   6 Rue des Favorites

Paris 15me

My dear Alan

Many thanks for your letter received this morning. What a hell of a time you have had, with everybody and everything, you must be in tatters.[1] It is easy for me here. Success and failure on the public level never mattered much to me, in fact I feel much more at home with the latter, having breathed deep of its vivifying air all my writing life up to the last couple of years. And I cannot help feeling that the success of Godot has been very largely the result of a misunderstanding, or of various misunderstandings, and that perhaps you have succeeded better than any one else in stating its true nature. Even with Blin I never talked so unrestrainedly and uncautiously as with you, probably because it was not possible at that stage.[2] When in London the question arose of a new production, I told Albery and Hall that if they did it my way they would empty the theatre. I am not suggesting that you were unduly influenced by all I said or that your production was not primarily your own and nobody else's, but it is probable our conversations confirmed you in your aversion to half-measures and frills, i.e. to precisely those things that 90% of theatre-goers want. Of course I know the Miami swells and their live models can hardly be described as theatre-goers and that their reactions are no more significant than those of a Jersey herd and I presume their critics are worthy of them.[3] It is of course impossible for me to judge, with so confused a situation and so many factors operating of which I know nothing, but I think if Myerberg had maintained his programme, instead of caving in the way he has, he would perhaps not have had reason to regret it.[4] My New York publisher Rosset is now very set on giving the play a Lys Theatre production, Capalbo and Chase being apparently very keen.[5] But from what you tell me Myerberg retains the rights, though his contract with Albery was for a Broadway production, so I suppose the usual disputes will arise. For the moment all I can say and all I want to say is that this Miami fiasco does not distress me in the smallest degree, or only in so far as it distresses you, and that the thought has not crossed my mind that you are in any way to blame. On the contrary I thank you more warmly than ever for your faith in the play and for the way you have laboured, in an impossible set-up, to present it as we agree it should be presented, and I send you my affectionate friendship and esteem.

> s/ Sam
> Sam Beckett

I am writing an even worse affair and have got down the gist of the first act (of two).

TLS; 1 leaf, 1 side; Burns Library, Schneider-Beckett Collection. Previous publication, Beckett and Schneider, *No Author Better Served*, 8–10.

1   Schneider's letter to SB has not been found. However, Schneider described the production and the opening in some detail in his letter of 20 January to Thornton Wilder. Of Bert Lahr and Tom Ewell, he wrote:

> I had two stars, who were friends but really unable to share the play between them. Bert had taken the job under the impression that he was the comic and Tommy the straight man; he was terribly surprised and hurt to discover that this was just not the case. Tommy had taken the job realising Bert's technique and background, but thinking that the two of them would find a way of working together. They couldn't and didn't.

The opening night of *Waiting for Godot* was also the opening night of the Coconut Grove Theatre in Miami; the play had been billed "The laugh sensation of two continents." Schneider continues to Wilder:

> Almost an entirely invited audience, previously wined and dined in the theatre's ultra plush-plush dining room. Much standing around in minks and much flashbulb shooting of society shots. We could hardly drive them into the theatre, finally did about 9:20. When they got seated, they wouldn't stop talking, even when the house lights were down some 5 minutes [. . .] Well, the show wasn't too bad, but the audience walked out in droves both before and during the intermission. As you know, they not only didn't like it, they hated it. (UCSD, Schneider MS 103/5/2.)

2   In the same letter to Wilder, Schneider recounts his conversations with SB about *Godot* when the two attended performances of the Peter Hall production of the play in London together:

> both of us taking copious notes, and then talking them over the next day [. . .] In London and especially after seeing the play, he seemed to me to mellow and change completely [. . .] he began to open up about the play, to explain it in the most illuminating terms, and in specific terms. We would be watching the performance, and he would lean over to me and say in a whisper that I felt could be heard onstage: "'It's ahl wrang'" then the next day he would explain with great clarity and usually theatrical wisdom what he meant. (UCSD, Schneider MS 103/5/2.)

3   Walter Winchell panned the play, calling it a "great bore" and "vulgar" ("Walter Winchell of New York," *Daily Mirror* 6 January 1956: 10). In *Variety*, the review (signed "Lary") described the play as "a wearisome two-acter, aimless in plotting, devoid of

excitement, an impossible guessing game containing little to keep the theatre-goer interested" ("Waiting for Godot," 11 January 1956: 75).

4   Myerberg's original intention was to follow the two-week run in Miami with a week in either Philadelphia or Boston before opening in New York (Arthur Gelb, "Play by Beckett Due on Broadway," *The New York Times* 14 November 1955: 32); SB understood his plan to be "Boston-Washington-Philade[l]phia" (SB to Barney Rosset, 17 January 1956, NSyU). By 6 January, the New York production at the Music Box Theatre had been canceled, and by 9 January, Myerberg announced he would recast the play, retaining only Bert Lahr in the eventual Broadway production (Zolotow, "Play by Beckett to Close on Road," *The New York Times* 6 January 1956: 20; Arthur Gelb, "Drama Fete Picks Artistic Leader," *The New York Times* 9 January 1956: 20).

5   Interest of the Theatre de Lys in producing *Waiting for Godot*: 18 August 1955, n. 4.

ALEC REID

DUBLIN

January 17th 1956   6 Rue des Favorites

Paris 15me

Dear Alec Reid[1]

Thanks for your letter and article. I think you have done a good job and made the best of my splutterings.[2] The few comments hereinafter are not the sole that occur to me, but there is no getting straight so crooked an affair within the limits at your disposal. The trouble about my little world is that there is no outside to it. Aesthetically the adventure is that of the failed form (no achieved statement of the inability to be). I am glad you saw the Criterion production. We had a glorious fiasco in Miami, all the swells and their live models sweeping out in droves.

Best wishes to your wife and yourself.

Yours sincerely

s/ Sam. Beckett

Samuel Beckett

1. Whoroscope and Proust belong to the ENS years, More Pricks to the TCD ones. But unimportant.

2. Association with réseau 1941. On the trot from 1942.

3. Nouvelles et Textes pour Rien.

4. L'Innommable.

5. "Birth and Death are sufficiently exciting for me." Joyce to Colum. A very unsartrian remark.[3]

6. Suggest: "between the nought than which nought is more of Democritus and etc."[4]

6A. Perhaps better: falsified.

7.   "   "   precarious.[5]

8. Cf. 4.

TLS; 1 leaf, 1 side; Reid collection.

1   Alec Reid (né Frederick Alexander Reid, 1921–1986), graduate of Trinity College Dublin, teacher, drama critic, and later author of *All I Can Manage, More Than I Could: An Approach to the Plays of Samuel Beckett* (1968).

2   Signed with the pseudonym Michael George, the article by Alec Reid on which SB comments is "Samuel Beckett," *Irish Tatler and Sketch* 65.5 (February 1956) 19, 40.

3   Reid's published essay adopts SB's suggestions and corrections, here numbered 1–5. ENS refers to the Ecole Normale Supérieure.

4   Reid writes: "There is a fundamental difference between nought, a definite entity, and nothing, an abstract conception" (19).

5   Reid writes: "The more consciously the form is developed, as in Kafka, the more the content, the emotional unknowingness, falsified; conversely, the more precarious the form, the nearer it approaches to disintegration, the truer is the emotional content" (19).

SEUMAS O'SULLIVAN
DUBLIN

January 21st 1956   6 Rue des Favorites
                                     Paris 15°

Dear Seumas[1]

I am very touched and flattered by your wishing to propose me for election to the Irish Academy of Letters.[2]

To my deep regret I have to tell you that I could not accept membership.

I should be distressed if you were to think of me, because of this, as unfriendly or systematically aloof.

I could not belong and I could not be a credit to any academy.

It is not with a light heart that I forgo the honour, or the chance of the honour, of joining a company of writers presided by you.

Please give my very warm regards to Stella.[3]

With best wishes

> Your friend
>
> s/ Sam
>
> Samuel Beckett

TLS; 1 leaf, 1 side; InU, Starkey.

1 Seumas O'Sullivan (pseud. of James Starkey; 1879–1958; Profile, I), Editor of *Dublin Magazine.*

2 The Irish Academy of Letters was formed in 1932.

3 Artist Estella Solomons (1882–1968; Profile, I), married to Seumas O'Sullivan.

A. J. LEVENTHAL

DUBLIN

26.1.56   6 Rue des Favorites

Paris 15me

Dear Con

Many thanks for Dublin Magazine and your letter yesterday. Also for your Calais message. I liked greatly your article in the DM and was very touched by its closing judgement. I cannot see any more than you in what the play is particularly Irish. However if it suits Cusack to think so by all means let him do so. There are some Irishisms in the translation liable to mislead. I was very interested by Ruddy's journal, I think it was well worth publishing and I hope there will be more.[1]

To my regret and embarrassment I had to reply to Seumas that I could not accept membership of the Irish Academy of Letters.[2] I hope he will not be offended nor think of me as arrogant and upstage. The thought of academies has always made me feel sick and the thought of Ireland more and more so. If I had accepted and been elected we should all have regretted it.

I could not face the States. Godot was a glorious fiasco at Miami. (Cocoanut [sic] Grove Playhouse!).[3] Situation now very confused and nothing definite about NY production. But I think Broadway is off. Albery wants to bring Criterion production to NY. I think he will have trouble with "Equity", whatever that is. I am seeing him here this week.[4]

Very pleased by your reaction to Nouvelles et Textes, alias First and Last gasps. Afraid for me that is the Endstation. I am struggling with another old 2 acter, but don't believe in it and have really no interest. Shall soon have the NY proofs of Malone and I suppose then I might as well get on with L'Inno as sit looking out of the window, indéfénestrable.[5]

Was amused by Ruddy's reference to the Norwegian painter Diriks. Hayden knew them well and has often told me about them. The son is a doctor-amateur painter in Montparnasse, treats all the rapins buckshee.[6]

It is good news they have a better Lucky in Herbert Lane. Mr Hugh Burden-Vladimir has also been got rid off [sic] in London, by a merciful bout of sciatica, and I understand his successor is good.[7]

All the best. Come to Paris soon.

Ever

s/ Sam

TLS; 1 leaf, 1 side; TxU: Leventhal collection.

1 A. J. Leventhal's "Dramatic Commentary" included a review of *Waiting for Godot* at the Criterion Theatre in London and the Pike Theatre in Dublin (*Dublin Magazine*, 52–54). Its closing judgement: "The Pike Theatre Club must be congratulated on their enterprise in mounting possibly the most important drama of this century" (53). Leventhal comments on the Irish accents of Vladimir and Estragon, pointing out that "the author had in mind a universal rather than a regional application of his vision of mankind in perpetual expectation" (52), and that the characters' names derive from different nationalities. Leventhal records the inclination to claim the play as Irish: "It is understood that there is a proposal to translate the play into Irish which would assist in bringing about a general acceptance here of that theory" (52).

Cyril Cusack in relation to an English and Gaelic translation of the play: 10 May 1955, n. 2.

In the same issue of *Dublin Magazine* is Leventhal's edition of "Extracts from the Unpublished Memoirs of the late T. B. Rudmose-Brown" (30–51).

2 Seumas O'Sullivan: 21 January 1956.

3   Rosset, who had talked with Myerberg, explained to SB in his letter of 23 January that "he might lose Schneider who would perhaps have to go off on another project," and that the "cast faded away" (NSyU).

4   Donald Albery wrote to Barney Rosset on 16 January that he had been advised by Tennessee Williams and others to bring the English production to New York (NSyU). Rosset disagreed, arguing for an Off-Broadway production at the Theatre de Lys (Rosset to Kitty Black, 17 January 1956, NSyU).

Equity is the professional actors' union.

5   "Indéfénestrable." SB adds an unwarranted accent to the second "e" in "Indéfenestrable" (not even capable of being thrown out through it).

6   The painter Karl-Edward Diriks (1855–1930), whose son Dyre Diriks (1894–1976) was a doctor who lived in Montparnasse; although he did not begin painting until 1932, Dyre Diriks became Secretary of the Salon d'Automne and exhibited his work in the Salon des Indépendants (Emmanuel Bénézit, *Dictionnaire critique et documentaire des peintres, sculpteurs, dessinateurs et graveurs de tous les temps et de tous les pays*, III, 3rd edn. [Paris: Librairie Gründ, 1976] 592–593).

7   The Pike Theatre production had five different actors in all who successively played the role of Lucky, as Carolyn Swift recounts: Chris McMaster (b. 1925) replaced Donal Donnelly (1931–2010) on 2 January; four weeks later Brendan Matthews (n.d.) took up the role, followed by John Corish (n.d.) and Gilbert McIntyre (n.d.) (*Stage by Stage*, 187–188).

Hugh Burden left the cast of the Criterion Theatre production, and was replaced by "an understudy" for two weeks until the role was taken up by William Squire (1916–1989) (*The Times* 1 December 1955: 8; Kitty Black to Jérôme Lindon, 3 January 1955 [*for* 1956], IMEC, Beckett, Boîte 5, S. Beckett Correspondance 1962–1969, Curtis Brown 1957 [*for* 1952–1957]).

BARNEY ROSSET, GROVE PRESS
NEW YORK

February 2nd 1956   6 Rue des Favorites
                                                                 Paris 15°

Dear Barney

Thanks for your letters, cheque and cuttings.

In presenting the play on Broadway, as he now seems resolved to do, Myerberg is simply carrying out his contract. You and Alan Schneider say he is making a mistake. You may be right. On the other hand the event may prove him right. In any case what can we do about it? Nothing. I am naturally disturbed by the thought of a new director of production. And still more so by the menace, hinted at in one of your letters, of unauthorized deviations from script. This we cannot have at any price and I am asking Albery to write Myerberg to that effect. I am not intransigent, as the Criterion production shows, about minor changes, if I feel they are necessary, but I refuse to be improved by a professional rewriter. Perhaps it is a false alarm. I do hope so.[1]

Albery's idea of exporting his show was function of his conviction that Myerberg would not proceed with production. I think Schneider is over critical of the London production.[2] I did not agree with it, but I could see it had many good things and much fine acting. The Gogo was by far the best I had seen.[3] But I too naturally want an original American production and would be against any initiative from London of a nature to jeopardize it.

I suppose you have heard that all editions of Molloy have been banned in Ireland.[4]

I do not like the places the new play is taking me now. But there is not much I can do about that either.

Kind regards to Loly.

Yours ever

s/ Sam

TLS; 1 leaf, 1 side; NSyU.

1   SB is responding to Rosset's letter of 27 January (NSyU).
In his letter to SB of 13 January, Rosset had written that a journalist who was writing a story on Tom Ewell had asked Grove for a copy of the play: "He said the Myerberg office would not let him see it, saying that it was going to be changed ???????" (NSyU). SB's letter to Donald Albery has not been found. On 6 February, Rosset writes: "Myerberg once told me on the phone that he considered the translation to be a poor one and that he would like to have Thornton Wilder redo it. I think it entirely possible that he may be messing around with it but I also think that a word from Albery would stop him from doing anything without your permission." (NSyU.)

2   As Rosset summarized his discussion in his letter of 27 January to SB, Schneider thought that the London production was "inferior to American standards," "lacked clarity," and was "without redeeming elements such as lyricism or humor" (NSyU).

3   Peter Woodthorpe played Estragon in the London production; SB congratulated him with "'Bloody marvellous!'" when he saw the performance (Knowlson, *Damned to Fame*, 376).

4   *Molloy* was prohibited in Ireland on 13 January 1956, and the prohibition published officially in the Irish State gazette, *Iris Oifigiúil*, on 20 January; the prohibition was not revoked until 1967 (Kay M. Power, Office of the Censorship of Publications, Dublin; "'Daily Sketch' Banned with 77 Books," *The Irish Times* 21 January 1956: 9).

BARNEY ROSSET, GROVE PRESS
NEW YORK

Feb 22nd 1956   6 Rue des Favorites
                                                 Paris 15me
Dear Barney
   Your letter of 17th this morning. By all means a paper bound
edition, I am all for cheaper books. Looking forward to getting the
galleys. I gave an extract to Irish Writing, a Dublin quarterly, and
when preparing it found myself making a good few changes. I hope
you do not mind if this time my corrections are more numerous than
heretofore.[1] Looking forward also to copies of cheap Godot. I hear from
Faber their bowdlerized edition is going like mad.[2] No news from Albery,
Schneider or Myerberg. Shall be seeing Kitty Black here this week. Have
finished the play to my great dissatisfaction, especially with Act 1.[3] Am
letting it cool off and have begun to translate L'Inno. The beginning goes
well enough but I am getting into very choppy water now.[4] To[-]night
they are celebrating the 100th of Godot at the Pike, Dublin. In London
they push gallantly forward towards the tourist business.
                     With kindest regards to Loly,
                          Yours ever
                            s/ Sam

TLS; 1 leaf, 1 side; NSyU.

1   SB refers to a paperbound edition of *Molloy*.
The extract to which SB refers is "Malone Dies: From the Author's Translation of
Malone Meurt," *Irish Writing* 34 (Spring 1956) 29–35.

2   Grove Press published a $1 paperbound edition of *Waiting for Godot*.
A "Publisher's Note" tipped into the Faber first edition (1955) reads: "When *Waiting
for Godot* was transferred from the Arts Theatre to the Criterion Theatre, a small
number of textual deletions was made to satisfy the requirements of the Lord
Chamberlain. The text printed here is that used in the Criterion Theatre production"
(London: Faber and Faber, 1955).

3   The manuscript at this stage may be what is described by Admussen as "C_1 (OU)
and C_2 (TCD)" (Act I and Act II of *Fin de partie, The Samuel Beckett Manuscripts*, 51).
A notebook which includes a first draft of *Fin de partie* "II" is "dated 16.2.56" (TCD,
MS 4663; "Cumulative TCD Catalogue," 187; see also S.E. Gontarski, *The Intent of*

Undoing in Samuel Beckett's Dramatic Texts [Bloomington: Indiana University Press, 1985] 25–54).

4 This mention of a translation of *L'Innommable* predates the extant manuscripts of the English translation (TxU, Beckett collection, Works 5.9: "The Unnamable" "Started February 1957"; Lake, ed., *No Symbols Where None Intended*, 62; Admussen, *The Samuel Beckett Manuscripts*, 86).

CHARLES MONTEITH, FABER AND FABER
LONDON

February 27th 1956   6 Rue des Favorites
                                            Paris 15

Dear Mr Monteith[1]

Many thanks for your letters and Times Lit. Sup. Forgive my having been so slow about replying.[2]

It is good news your Godot is doing well. My only regret is that it is not complete. Some passages are quite meaningless because of the holes. They could have been bridged with a little rewriting. Well, there it is.[3]

Afraid my memoirs are unlikely. J'ai moins de souvenirs que si j'avais six mois.[4]

> With best wishes,
> Yours sincerely
> s/
> Samuel Beckett

TLS; 1 leaf, 1 side; Faber, 17/50.

1 Charles Monteith* (1921–1995), Editor, Faber and Faber.

2 G[eorge] S[utherland] Fraser (unsigned, like all *TLS* reviews at the time), "They Also Serve," *Times Literary Supplement* 2815 (10 February 1956) 84. A photograph of the London production of *Waiting for Godot* appears on the first page.

3 Charles Monteith wrote to SB on 16 February to inform him that *Waiting for Godot* "is selling fast and exciting much interest and discussion everywhere" (Faber, 17/50). The cuts in the Faber and Faber edition: 22 February 1956, n. 2.

4 "J'ai moins de souvenirs que si j'avais six mois" (I have fewer memories than if I were six months old). SB adapts "J'ai plus de souvenirs que si j'avais mille ans," the opening line from Baudelaire's poem "Spleen" ("Souvenirs? / More than if I had lived a thousand years") (*Œuvres complètes*, I, 73; *Les Fleurs du mal: The Complete Text of The Flowers of Evil*, 75).

ROBERT PINGET
LONDON

8.3.56   Paris

Cher Robert Pinget

    Merci de votre gentille lettre. Avec les Edts de Minuit ça s'arrangera sûrement. Les papiers ne valent rien, il n'y a que la confiance de vrai, dans ces histoires-là, et avec Jérôme elle est en lieu sûr. Mais je n'ai pas de conseils à donner, ayant toute ma vie déconné.[1] Je retrouve dans votre lettre quelque chose de Mahu et regrette que vous n'ayez pas plus de temps à vous, pour travailler. Mais peut-être travaillez-vous quand même. Moi j'essaie encore, par petites rafales d'automne, il y a six ans que ça dure.[2] Je suis souvent à la campagne. Le long froid a tué mon cèdre, je pense aux mimosas et pleure jaune. J'ai entendu, Salle Gaveau, Fischer-Dieskau chanter le Voyage d'Hiver. Merveilleux.[3] Je vais planter trente arbores vitae et un cyprès bleu, hier j'ai creusé quinze trous. Je suis allé beaucoup au théâtre, histoire de me prouver que j'étais à Paris, Le Personnage Combattant, Les Bas Fonds, Les Chaises reprises par Mauclair.[4] J'irai peut-être à Londres au mois de juin, voir le test match à Lords entre l'Angleterre et l'Australie. Allez faire un tour à Kew, je pense que ça vous plairait.[5] Ne vous désespérez pas, branchez-vous bien sur le désespoir et chantez-nous ça.

                                Votre ami
                                s/ Sam. Beckett

TLS; 1 leaf, 1 side; Burns Library, Pinget-Beckett Letters.

8.3.56   Paris

Dear Robert Pinget,

    Thank you for your kind letter. The Editions de Minuit will deal with it all, for certain. Bits of paper are worth nothing: only trust is genuine, in matters like this, and with Jérôme it is in safe hands. But I have no advice to give you, having blundered all my life.[1] I find something of Mahu in your letter, and am sorry that you haven't more time for yourself, to do your work. But perhaps you are working all the same. I am still trying to, in little autumnal gusts: six years, that's been going on.[2] I am often in the country. The long cold spell has killed my cedar. I think of the mimosas and have a little cry. I heard Fischer-Dieskau in the Salle Gaveau singing *Winterreise*. Marvellous.[3] I am going to plant thirty arbores vitae and a blue cypress; yesterday I dug fifteen holes. I went to the theatre a good deal, by way of proving to myself that I was in Paris: *Le Personnage combattant, Les Bas-fonds*; *Les Chaises* revived by Mauclair.[4] Perhaps I'll go to London in June to see the Test Match at Lord's between England and Australia. Do go and have a look round Kew: I think you'd like it.[5] Don't lose heart: plug yourself into despair and sing it for us.

>Your friend
>Sam. Beckett

1   Pinget's novel *Le Renard et la boussole* had been published by Gallimard, which held the option on his future books. His next novel, *Graal Flibuste* was published by Editions de Minuit, with whom Pinget agreed to publish henceforth (see 28 September [1955], n. 3; Robert Pinget, Madeleine Renouard, *Robert Pinget à la lettre: entretiens avec Madeleine Renouard* [Paris: Belfond, 1993] 245–246).

2   "Mahu" is a character in Pinget's novel *Mahu; ou, le matériau* (1953; *Mahu or The Material*).

3   Dietrich Fischer-Dieskau performed Schubert's *Die Winterreise*, op. 89, at the Salle Gaveau on 27 February.

4   *Le Personnage combattant* (1955; The Fighting Character) by Jean Vauthier (1910–1992) is a play for two voices and sound; it was created by Jean-Louis Barrault at the Petit Théâtre Marigny from 1 February. Maxim Gorki's *Les Bas-fonds* (The Lower Depths), directed by Sacha Pitoëff (1920–1990), was performed at the Théâtre de l'Œuvre from 21 February. Jacques Mauclair (1919–2001) directed and performed in a revival of Eugène Ionesco's *Les Chaises* (The Chairs) with the premiere of Ionesco's *L'Impromptu de l'Alma, ou Le Caméléon du berger (Improvisation, or The Shepherd's Chameleon)* at the Studio des Champs-Elysées from 15 February.

5   The Test Match between England and Australia: 22 November 1955, n. 6. Kew Gardens.

PAMELA MITCHELL
NEW YORK

12-3-56   6 rue des Favorites
                                           Paris 15e.

Pam

So glad to have your letter after so long. I find it increasingly difficult to write – even letters. Good for nothing but doddering about my place in the country, where I am at the moment. The cold was desperate all last month and I think has killed the cedar, though there are still traces of green in the burnt needles that make me hope it will recover. Have been digging holes for new plantations and hope to get them down this week – including a blue cypress! Gave up my dream of a golden yew on being informed its maximum rate of growth was one inch a year. I did not realize your Nantucket place had been sold and understand how much you must miss it.[1] I have written another 2 act play but don't like it and shall probably throw it away.[2] Apart from that no work. The mime has not yet been performed but will be I hope this year, perhaps at the Marseille Festival in August.[3] Godot coming to an end in Dublin and plodding on in London bravely towards what the producer calls the "tourist business".[4] Situation in N.Y.C. quite confused. I suppose Myerberg will do something before July rather than forfeit his rights and advance on royalties.[5] Rosset has done a cheap edition and the London edition (Faber) is, I am told, selling well. I may go to London in June to see some cricket with an old T.C.D. crony.[6] Just possible also I may go to Dublin in May, but when it comes to the point I shall probably funk it. I have corrected proofs of Malone for Rosset and the book should be out soon. Don't buy a copy for God's sake and don't even read the one I'll have sent to you. My God how I hate my own work. Have started the impossible job of translating L'Innommable and gave it up the other day in loathing. Shall be fifty (50) in a month's time and can well believe it. 18.000 days and not much to show for them. Better stop before I start. No news anyway. Just jog along, on the flat of my back 15 hours of the 24. Often think of our brief times together. Cold comfort. Forgive wretched letter. At least it's a sign of life. Write again soon. Love

Sam

ALS; 1 leaf, 2 sides; *env to* Miss Pamela Mitchell, 229 E. 48th Street, New York 17, N.Y., U.S.A., *upper left* Par avion, Air mail; *pm* 12-3-56, Paris; UoR 5060.

1 The address of Pamela Mitchell's Nantucket house has not been located. From the 1920s, the Mitchell family had a summer home, Stonewall Cottage, on Conanicut Island in Narragansett Bay, Rhode Island, where Mitchell lived from 1980 to her death in 2002 (Elizabeth Connelly, "Curator's Comments," *Heritage* [Jamestown Historical Society] Spring 2002: 6; Rosemary Enright, Jamestown Historical Society, 3 May 2010; Linwood M. Erskine, Jr., 14 May 2010).

2 The theatrical work in progress: 22 February 1956, n. 3.

3 *Acte sans paroles* was proposed for the Marseille Festival de l'art d'avant-garde, 4–14 August 1956, to be held on the roof of the Cité Radieuse designed by Le Corbusier.

4 The Pike Theatre production of *Waiting for Godot* was transferred to the larger Gate Theatre from 12 to 17 May (Alan Simpson, *Beckett and Behan and a Theatre in Dublin* [London: Routledge and Kegan Paul, 1962] 86–88).

The London production continued at the Criterion Theatre through 24 March, while Donald Albery was trying to find another theatre to extend the run (Kitty Black to Barney Rosset, 13 March 1956, NSyU).

5 Michael Myerberg's option required a Broadway production each year.

6 Test match at Lord's in London: 22 November 1955, n. 6.

BARNEY ROSSET, GROVE PRESS
NEW YORK

March 15th 1956   6 Rue des Favorites
                                              Paris 15me

Dear Barney

Many thanks for your letter, dollar Godots and Inno contract which signed herewith.[1] Molloy, Malone, L'Inno and Godot and Nouvelles et Textes pour Rien have been sent to your man Rexroth. I didn't think the French Murphy would interest him and no copy in English is to be had.[2] Godot is finishing both in Dublin and in London where business has fallen in the last few weeks. Albery is trying to find another theatre, as he thinks it is a seasonable slump.[3] I have just

607

been reading Italian proofs of Godot for Einaudi, not a brilliant job, but faithful enough.[4] I have not looked at the new play for some weeks now nor, I confess, pursued struggle with L'Inno. But have dug fifty-six large holes in my "garden" for reception of various plantations, including 39 arbores vitae and a blue cypress. Stuck in Paris with a Dublin visitor for the moment, but hope soon to be back in the oxygen.[5] I like the new Godot very much and am glad to hear sales are satisfactory. I quite like the idea of the London director for New York. I talked with him in London and gave him notes and I think he is now in a position to do a rather better production.[6] Regarding publication of novels in U.K. Lindon has not the slightest objection to your initiating negotiations, but there is some copyright difficulty owing to the Molloy rights having been acquired by the Merlin group and subsequently transferred to the Olympia Press. We are now trying to recover some rights from Girodias who has behaved badly over both Watt and Molloy. I know Lindon has also negotiations on hand in view of UK publication. And I hear from a friend in Dublin that Macmillan are also interested. As long as you keep in touch with Lindon all will be well, and if you would like a fuller account of the Girodias business just ask him.[7] By the way I have given an extract from Malone to "Irish Writing", a Dublin 3-monthly to which I have formerly contributed.[8] The position with regard to Godot Dublin royalties is that they pay them in a lump at the end of the run, i.e. in a fortnight or 3 weeks, and remit to you your 10% at the same time. They will not amount to much, 80 or 90 pounds at the most I imagine. I had a letter from Mr Desmond Smith asking me to explain the play to him. Canadians are queer that way.[9] Greetings to Loly and Peter and all the best to all in the Grove.

Yours ever

s/ Sam

I am not sure that an integral publication in Theatre Arts Magazine would help your sales. But I leave it to you to do what you judge best.[10]

TLS; 1 leaf, 1 side; NSyU.

1   SB responds to Rosset's letter of 8 March, in which Rosset indicates that he will prepare the contract for SB as translator of *L'Innommable* (NSyU).

2   SB inserts <u>Nouvelles et Textes pour Rien</u> in left margin.
Rosset had written to SB on 8 March that poet, critic, and literary translator Kenneth Rexroth (1905–1982) planned to write an essay on SB for *Nation* and wished to build a Beckett library. In his essay, Rexroth called *Molloy* "the most significant ... novel published in any language since World War II" ("The Point is Irrelevance," *Nation* 182.15 [14 April 1956] 325).

3   London and Dublin productions of *Waiting for Godot*: 12 March 1956, n. 4. Albery appears not to have arranged another London theatre to continue production.

4   Carlo Fruttero translated the play as *Aspettando Godot*, published in Einaudi's series, Collezione di teatro (Turin: G. Einaudi, 1956).

5   In his letter of 15 March, SB mentions to Susan Manning that Thomas MacGreevy is visiting in Paris for a few days (TxU, Beckett collection).

6   SB refers to the paperbound edition of *Waiting for Godot*.
In his letter of 8 March, Rosset asked what SB thought of the idea of Peter Hall directing *Waiting for Godot* in New York.

7   Jérôme Lindon, for *Molloy*, and SB, for *Watt*, had initiated a suit against Girodias, publisher of Olympia Press (Lindon to SB, 27 February 1956, IMEC, Beckett, Boîte 1, S. Beckett, Correspondance – Divers, 1950–1956; SB to Paul Rosenfeld, 29 February 1956, IMEC, Beckett, Boîte 6, Editions de Minuit / The Olympia Press).
The friend in Dublin who suggested that Macmillan was interested has not been identified.

8   "Malone Dies" in *Irish Writing*: 22 February 1956, n. 1. *Irish Writing* had also published an "Extract from Watt" (see 4 August 1951, n. 3).

9   Desmond Smith (b. 1927), originally a news and current affairs television producer for the Canadian Broadcasting Corporation and subsequently a television producer in the United States, wrote to SB before 4 February to inquire about Canadian production rights for *Waiting for Godot*; SB advised him to contact Rosset, which he did on 4 February.

10   In his letter of 8 March, Rosset mentioned that *Theatre Arts* magazine wished to "reprint the whole text" of *Godot* in an issue in the summer ("Waiting for Godot" [unabridged], *Theatre Arts* 40.8 [August 1956] 36–61 [although consecutively numbered, the order of the pages is incorrect in this publication]).
The PS is handwritten.

DESMOND SMITH
TORONTO

April 1st 1956   Rue des Favorites
                                           Paris 15me

Dear Mr Smith

Thank you for your letter of March 5th.[1]

I understand from Mr Rosset that Mr Myerberg is opposed to your presenting the play in Canada prior to the New York production. I am sorry to hear this. However you will not have long to wait now.[2]

I am afraid I am quite incapable of sitting down and writing out an "explanation" of the play. I think the simplest thing would be for you to send me a list of queries. My answers to some of these might cover a lot of ground. The trouble with most commentators is their failure to see the wood for the trees. Do try and see the thing primarily in its simplicity, the waiting, the not knowing why, or where, or when, or for what. If there are obscurities of detail their elucidation will never be in terms of a system of symbols. It is not in any sense a symbolic work. The point about Pozzo, for example, is not who he is, or what he is, or what he represents, but the fact that all this is not known, so that for a moment he can ever [sic] be confused with Godot. It is essential he should not be specified. It might even be said that he does not know himself who or what he is, and it seems to me that it is only out of a great inner dereliction that the part can be played satisfactorily. Confusion of mind and of identity is an indispensable element of the play and the effort to clear up the ensuing obscurities, which seems to have exercized most critics to the point of blinding them to the central simplicity, strikes me as quite nugatory.

There were, I thought, good things in the London production, in particular some good playing by Estragon and Lucky, but the set was quite wrong, and the timing, which is all important, I mean the giving full value to the silences.[3]

I am not at all sure that the author's views are without danger for the director of production. Perhaps a wrong production, wrong for me, but with the coherence of your purely personal experience of the work, is to be preferred to one in which you try to combine with your own ideas others springing from a quite different conception. Nor is the author necessarily right. However if you feel like running the risk send along your questionnaire and I'll do my best to answer it. At least I can help you with difficulties in the script, if you have encountered any such.[4]

With regard to rights of my next play, I am not at all sure that there will be a next. In any case you would have to apply to my publisher here, Monsieur Jérôme Lindon, Editions de Minuit, 7 Rue Bernard-Palissy, Paris 6me.

Yours sincerely

s/

Samuel Beckett

TLS; 1 leaf, 2 sides; sold by Swann Gallery, current owner unknown. Previous publication, Beckett, "Who is Godot?" *The New Yorker*, 136–137.

1 Desmond Smith's letter to SB of 5 March has not been found. Having seen the play in London, Smith thought he might produce *Waiting for Godot* at the Crest Theatre in Toronto (Desmond Smith, 27 September 1995).

2 *Waiting for Godot* opened on 19 April at the John Golden Theatre, New York.

3 The London production: 24 September 1955, n. 2, and 14 December 1955 to Peter Hall. It was transferred to the Criterion Theatre on 12 September 1955, where Beckett saw it with Alan Schneider.

4 Since the opportunity to produce the play did not develop, Smith did not send a questionnaire to SB.

NANCY CUNARD

April 5th 1956   6 Rue des Favorites

                                  Paris 15me

Bien chère Nancy

Your card direct and then letter via not i migliori fabbri safely arrived. I am so glad you saw the play and that it wound its way to you, but the French production was more like what I wanted, nastier. My translation is no great shakes either and I have a copy of the French edition for you, on your way through here, if you would like it, though reading plays is a bore.[1] I still have Negro snug on my shelves, unlike most of what I once had, and even a few Whoroscopes.[2] I have a tight cottage now in the spinachy Seine-et-Marne and am there as much as I can. But I shall not fail to be in Paris round about the 20th and hope you will keep an evening free for me. The dog is duller than ever but its friends know it doesn't mind if they get up and go away. I wish I had a copy of your Norman Douglas and look forward to your Moore. If you are organizing subscriptions for your A.A. Ivories put me down.[3]

Much love, dear Nancy.

s/ Samuel

TLS; 1 leaf, 1 side; TxU, Cunard collection. Previous publication, Anne Chisholm, *Nancy Cunard: A Biography* (New York: Alfred A. Knopf, 1979) 305.

1 Nancy Cunard (1896–1965; Profile, I). Cunard's card and letter to SB have not been found. It is not known who conveyed Cunard's card to SB. With "i migliori fabbri" (the better craftsmen) SB adapts T. S. Eliot's assessment of Ezra Pound from Eliot's dedication to *The Waste Land* ("Il miglior fabbro"); this assessment itself adapts Guido Guinizzelli's expression of admiration for Arnaut Daniel in Dante's *Purgatorio* (*La Divina Commedia, Purgatorio*, XXVI, line 117).

2 SB contributed translations to *Negro, Anthology Made by Nancy Cunard, 1931–1933*, ed. Nancy Cunard (London: Published by Nancy Cunard at Wishart and Co., 1934). Cunard had published SB's *Whoroscope* (Paris: Hours Press, 1930).

3 Nancy Cunard wrote a memoir of Norman Douglas (1868–1952), *Grand Man: Memories of Norman Douglas, with Extracts from his Letters, and Appreciations by Kenneth Macpherson, Harold Acton, Arthur Johnson, Charles Duff, and Victor Cunard and a Bibliographical Note by Cecil Woolf* (London: Secker and Warburg, 1954). Cunard's book *GM: Memories of George Moore* (London: Hart-Davis, 1956) had not yet been published.
Cunard had begun a project on "Ivories of Ancient Africa" to be called *The Ivory Road*, for which she intended to visit "museums, galleries and private collections"; Cunard accumulated nearly seven hundred pages of notes and manuscript, but the project was not completed (Chisholm, *Nancy Cunard*, 303–304; TxU, Cunard collection).

MAURICE GIRODIAS, THE OLYMPIA PRESS
PARIS

le 7 avril 1956   6 Rue des Favorites
                                    Paris 15me

Monsieur

Je vous accuse réception de votre lettre du 19 mars et du chèque de 5000 francs qui y était joint. Je me permets de vous signaler que par lettre du 29 mai 1954 "Merlin" m'annonçait le versement de 15.000 francs correspondant à des droits d'auteur de 20% sur le prix des exemplaires de luxe de WATT. Pourriez-vous envisager le règlement du solde prévu?[1]

L'ouvrage étant épuisé, voudriez-vous me dire également à quelle date vous envisagez de le réimprimer? Jérôme Lindon me dit que vous lui avez parlé de le faire dès cet été. Je pense qu'il faudrait, dans ce cas, établir un contrat direct entre nous.[2]

Croyez, Monsieur, à l'expression de mes sentiments distingués.

Samuel Beckett

TLcc; 1 leaf, 1 side; copy enclosed with SB to Lindon, 7 April 1956; IMEC, Beckett, Boîte 6, Editions de Minuit / The Olympia Press.

7th April 1956   6 Rue des Favorites
                                                         Paris 15

Dear Mr Girodias

I acknowledge receipt of your letter of 19th March and of the cheque for 5,000 francs enclosed with it. May I remind you that in a letter dated 29th May 1954 "Merlin" informed me that there would be a payment of 15,000 francs, corresponding to royalties of 20% of the cost of *Watt* in the de luxe edition. Might you consider passing on the balance?[1]

As the work is now out of print, could you also tell me when you are planning to reprint it? Jérôme Lindon tells me that you have spoken of doing so no later than this summer. In that case, I think that a direct contract should be drawn up between us.[2]

Yours sincerely

Samuel Beckett

1   Girodias's letter to SB of 19 March has not been found. The letter of 29 May 1954 was written by Alexander Trocchi on behalf of Collection Merlin; it gave the schedule of payments for *Watt*, including that for thirty copies of the deluxe edition of *Watt* (McM, Collection Merlin, 1/22).

2   Girodias responded to SB on 2 May saying that he intended to reprint *Watt* in the summer, that the date and price of publication would depend on possibilities of sales in the United Kingdom and the United States, and that a contract for the edition should be prepared when these were clear (IMEC, Beckett, Boîte 6, Editions de Minuit / The Olympia Press).

BARNEY ROSSET, GROVE PRESS
NEW YORK

April 7th 1956   6 Rue des Favorites
                                                         Paris 15me

Dear Barney

Thanks for your letters, cheque, cutting, Mexican documentation, contract and Danish letter. Also for article on 3d Opera.[1] I shall tell Irish Writing to send you a copy.[2] The books as they stand in English are I think unpublishable in the UK, where there is some kind of official Public Morals organisation that has all the publishers terrified with the threat of action for obscenity.[3] The skirmish with Girodias is dying away into a recognition of his rights. There is talk of his doing a reimpression of WATT this summer. You could put my old ECHO'S BONES on your list if you want to, I have scores of copies alying [sic] about my place here.[4] I was impressed by the Mexican photos. Their whole procedure seems highly irregular, they don't seem even to have used the Poseidon translation. I'll get Lindon to write to them, but I don't imagine we shall get much change out of them.[5] Japanese translation and performance are in the air, it would be a great relief to see the play in Japanese.[6] I have not yet reshouldered the great dead weight of the other play, but have made a little further headway with L'INNO. All my trees are down in the cold ground where I shudder to think what is happening to their roots. I have been in Paris the past week trotting a niece around to respectable entertainment and return to Ussy this evening.[7] Not more than mildly curious about Godot at the John Golden, I hope you and Loly at least will not be too disappointed.[8] I wrote to Smith asking for a list of queries and telling him there were no symbols in the work as far as I knew, but that I was always open to correction.[9] I don't think the MORE PRICKS stories are worth bothering about, except perhaps YELLOW, but I leave you free to do as you please with them. I don't possess a copy of the work myself. No news from the Pike since they completed their tour, if they have done so, but what little money there is should soon be available. They wound up with a week at the Gate Theatre, to what effect in the way of business I have not heard.[10] I suppose the Criterion production will also be going on tour, but I have heard nothing about this either. All the best to you and Loly and the young 'un.

Ever

s/ Sam

TLS; 1 leaf, 2 sides; NSyU.

1   With his letter of 26 March, Rosset sent SB the review by Brooks Atkinson that lauded the production of Brecht's *Threepenny Opera* by Carmen Capalbo and commented on the suitability of the space of the Theatre de Lys (NSyU; "Songs and Cynicism: 'The Threepenny Opera' A Triumph of Style," *The New York Times* 11 March 1956: 129). Rosset also sent a column announcing that Myerberg's production of *Waiting for Godot* would open on 16 April with Bert Lahr and E.G. Marshall (1914–1998), with the "possibility" that Herbert Berghof would direct (Sam Zolotow, "'Affair of Honor' will open April 4," *The New York Times* 13 March 1956: 39).

Salvador Novo (1927–1975) directed his own translation of *Esperando a Godot* at the hundred-seat Teatro La Capilla, in the Coyoacan district of Mexico City, from 28 June 1955; the actors were Carlos Ancira (Vladimir), Mario Orea (Pozzo), Raúl Dantes (Lucky), Antonio Passy (Estragon), and Didier Alexander (boy) ("Preview for July," *Mexico/This Month* [July 1955] np; *Excelsior* 28 June 1955: 22A, and 25 July 1955: 25A. Arturo Diaz, Coordinator of Documentation, Biblioteca de las Artes, Centro Nacional de las Artes [CENART], and Rodolfo Obregón, Director, Centro de Investigación Teatral "Rodolfo Usigli," Instituto Nacional de Bellas Artes [CITRU/ INBA]).

The contract and the Danish letter have not been identified.

2   The excerpt from *Malone Dies* in *Irish Writing*: 22 February 1956, n. 1.

3   Rosset wrote in his letter to SB of 26 March that Hamish Hamilton refused *Malone Dies*, expecting there to be "a censorship problem."

4   *Echo's Bones and Other Precipitates* (1935).

5   The Poseidon translation, *Esperando a Godot*: 19 August 1954, n. 3. The Teatro la Capilla had not requested production rights from Grove Press or from Editions de Minuit but, as SB later wrote to Rosset: "Apparently the Mexican production was in order and a contract signed with the Society of Dramatic Authors here to which I have the good fortune to belong" (19 April 1956, NSyU). The specific photographs of the production that were sent to SB have not been identified.

6   *Waiting for Godot* was translated into Japanese by Shinya Ando (1927–2000) as *Godō wo machinagara* (Tokyo: Hakusuisha, 1956).

7   Caroline Beckett had been visiting Paris.

8   Myerberg's Broadway production at the John Golden Theatre was to open on 16 April, but this was deferred to 19 April, according to the advertisement in *The New York Times* (8 April 1956) np.

9   Desmond Smith.

10   The Pike Theatre production of *Waiting for Godot* at the Gate Theatre: 12 March 1956, n. 4. The Pike tour began during the week of 18 March with performances in Dundalk, Navan, and Drogheda; it resumed on 1 April in Cork, followed by a "couple days each" in Clonmel, Waterford, and Carlow (Swift, *Stage by Stage*, 196–201; Simpson, *Beckett and Behan and a Theatre in Dublin*, 88–92).

CHRISTIAN LUDVIGSEN
HELLERUP, DENMARK

April 23rd 1956   6 Rue des Favorites
                                                  Paris 15me

Dear Mr Ludvigsen

Thank you for your letter of April 19th. I am glad that all the trouble you have taken as translator and animator has not been in vain and that it has brought you some pleasure and satisfaction. My sincere thanks and congratulations.[1]

Since Eleuthéria was announced as due for publication I have changed my mind and decided it can be neither produced nor published as it stands.[2] I may try to revise it some day, but I think this is unlikely.

It is good of you to offer to send me photographs of the Aarhus Theater production. I should be very interested to see them.

> With best wishes,
> Yours sincerely
> s/
> Samuel Beckett

TLS; 1 leaf, 1 side; *env to* Chr. Ludvigsen, C.V.E. Knuthsvej 18 a, Hellerup, Danemark; *pm* 23-4-56, La Ferté-sous-Jouarre; Ludvigsen collection.

1   Christian Ludvigsen* (b. 1930) translated *En attendant Godot* into Danish as *Vi venter på Godot* (Fredensborg: Arena, 1957); thanks to his persistence, the play had its Danish premiere on 10 April at the Århus Theater.

2   The first edition of *Malone meurt* (1951) announces the forthcoming SB publications: "A paraître, *L'Innommable*, roman. *Eleuthéria* (pièce en 3 Actes)" [4].

CHRISTIAN LUDVIGSEN
HELLERUP, DENMARK

1.5.56   Paris

Dear Mr Ludvigsen

Many thanks for the cuttings and for the trouble you took to translate them. I am pleased by the reception the play seems to have had at Aarhus.[1] Let people laugh by all means, and then be reminded it is no laughing matter. I'm afraid the only photo available is the one you mention. It can always be had from my French publisher if required.[2]

> With best wishes yrs sincerely,
>
> Samuel Beckett

ALS; 1 leaf, 1 side; *env to* Chr. Ludvigsen, C.V.E. Knut[h]svej 18a, Hellerup, Danemark; *pm* 2-5-56, Paris; Ludvigsen collection. Previous publication, Chr[istian] Ludvigsen, *Det begyndte med Beckett: min egen teaterhistorie,* Aktuelle teaterproblemer (Aarhus: Institut for Dramaturgi, 1997) 41 [facsimile and transcription].

1   It is not known which cuttings about the premiere of *Vi venter på Godot* Ludvigsen had sent.

2   At this time there were two standard photos of SB: the first appeared on the back cover of the first trade edition of *Molloy,* and was taken by an unnamed photographer in 1951 (see 10 April 1951, n. 2); the second was taken by Boris Lipnitzki in 1956 (François-Marie Banier, *Samuel Beckett,* Portraits d'auteur [Paris: Marval, 1997] 10–13).

GEORGE REAVEY

NEW YORK

15 5 55 [*for* 15 May 1956]   Paris

Dear George

Glad to have news of you. Very sorry to hear of upheaval. Hope all is for the best.[1] It is good of you to invite me and if I went to NY there is nowhere I should like better to hide. But I am not going. Pas folle à ce point, la guêpe.[2] I am plunged up to ears, nose and throat in sudden and urgent work, with concomitant panic. I remember at Portora a long weedy amiable hank called Pierre, is that the man?[3] So glad to hear of the success of your poems. I sold 30 <u>Echo's Bones</u> 5 bob apiece to the famous Jake Schwartz better know[n] as the Great Extractor. I feel part of this sum is due to you. We'll fix that when next you are over. I am sending some more to Barney suggesting he should sell them at a dollar.[4] Saw both Geer and Bram lately, they both have good pictures in the Salon de Mai. And the sister Tonny (Jacoba)'s book is doing well in the French translation.[5] I saw McAlpine & his wife in London, on the eve of their return to Tokio, where they are doing culture at the British Embassy.[6] I sometimes run into Hayter in the Select. He has a good painting in the Salon and his wife Helen a powerful wood.[7]

All the best, cher vieux.

Sam

ALS; 1 leaf, 1 side; TxU, Reavey collection.

1   Irene Rice Pereira left Reavey in December 1955, and by 2 March 1956 the couple had signed a separation agreement (Bearor, *Irene Rice Pereira*, 237).

2   "Pas folle à ce point, la guêpe" (not all that many flies on me).

3   Pierre from Portora Royal School has not been identified.

4   Reavey's collection of poems, *Colours of Memory*, was published in 1955 by Grove Press; his poem "Inward" was published in *The Palate* 35.1 (Winter 1955) [30].

Reavey had published SB's poems, *Echo's Bones and Other Precipitates*, in 1936.

Jacob Schwartz (n.d.), a books and manuscripts dealer, formerly a dentist in Brooklyn, earned his nickname "for his uncanny ability to separate authors from their literary material" (Carlton Lake, "Ed the Collector, Jake the Dentist and Beckett: A Tale that Ends in Texas," *The New York Times* 6 September 1987: BR2; Nicholas A. Basbanes, *A Gentle Madness: Bibliophiles, Bibliomanes and the Eternal Passion for Books* [New York: Holt, 1999] 317).

5   Bram van Velde exhibited *Composition* (1955, no. 180) and Geer van Velde exhibited *Composition* (no. 191) in the Salon de Mai (*XIIe Salon de Mai, Musée d'Art Moderne de la Ville de Paris, du 5 au 27 mai 1956* [Paris: Salon de Mai, 1956]).

Jacoba van Velde's novel *La grande salle*, tr. Maddy Buysse (Paris: Julliard, 1956).

6   William and Helen McAlpine lived in Tokyo from 1953 to 1960; he worked with the British Council in cultural programing, aiding students who wished to study in England. They both gave radio talks, and hosted artists on tour in Japan (Harry Johnson, 29 January 2006).

SB uses the then current French spelling of "Tokyo."

7   In the Salon de Mai, Stanley William Hayter exhibited two engravings, *La noyée* (no. 23) and *Femme accroupie* (no. 24), and one painting, *Orage* (no. 82). American sculptor Helen Phillips (1913–1995, m. to Hayter 1940–1970) exhibited a sculpture, *Arbre de vie* (no. 19 ter), and two engravings, *Virgo* (no. 31) and *La Promenade* (no. 32) (*XIIe Salon de Mai* [1956]; "Helen P. Hayter, 81, Sculptor, Is Dead," *The New York Times* 1 February 1995: D21).

BARNEY ROSSET, GROVE PRESS
NEW YORK

15.5.55 [*for* 15 May 1956]   Paris or rather Ussy

Dear Barney
Thanks for avalanche of cuttings. No one tells me how the play is doing, I mean box-office. A letter from Reavey in which he mentions it has been extended for a fortnight. Is there any talk of resumption in the Fall? Enclosed a document quite incomprehensible to me, is it a joke? Please enlighten.[1] Up to my gills in sudden urgent work, a mime and an act (the 2 acts compressed) for the Marseille Festival in August, and full of panic and doubt. Both as black as ink. I nearly have them, not quite, and I feel in my grandeur like Marcel at the end of the Temps Retrouvé, afraid to take a fiacre. Godot is rollicking beside this awful thing, Gott hilfe mir, ich kann nicht anders.[2] Received an application from USA for the amateur rights, I suppose I shove it on to Kitty Black.[3] All the best, dear Barney and Loly, cross everything and write soon.

s/ Sam

TLS; 1 leaf, 1 side; NSyU. *Dating*: Rosset's letter to SB of 18 May 1956 responds to SB's questions (NSyU).

1   It is not known what reviews SB was sent; press response to *Waiting for Godot* had been abundant, including Brooks Atkinson, "Theatre: Beckett's 'Waiting for Godot': Mystery Wrapped in an Enigma at Golden," *The New York Times* 20 April 1956: 21; Brooks Atkinson, "'Godot' is No Hoax: Eccentric Drama has Something to Say," *The New York Times* 29 April 1956: 129.
   Box office receipts were published in *Variety* for the first full week of the production ("B'way Up; Godot $15,300 . . .," 2 May 1956: 71).
   The play was extended twice, from 12 to 26 May, and on 30 May for fourteen additional performances; it closed on 9 June (Arthur Gelb, "Miss Coco Back on Stage June 11," *The New York Times* 7 May 1956: 30; [advertisement], *The New York Times* 30 May 1956: 11; [advertisement], *The New York Times* 9 June 1956: 14).
   Rosset apologized for sending papers not intended for SB (Rosset to SB, 18 May 1956).

2   Theatrical work in progress and *Acte sans paroles*, Marseille: 12 March 1956, n. 3. The compression of two acts into one is described by Admussen as draft G, *Fin de partie* (OSU, Spec. rare, MS Eng 29; *The Samuel Beckett Manuscripts*, 53).
   As it dawns on him that he is carrying within him the literary work he has for so many years hoped to produce, in the final pages of Proust's *A la recherche du temps perdu*, the narrator (Marcel) is stricken by anxiety that he might not live long enough to complete it, imagining his death in an accident. SB misremembers slightly, as it is in an automobile, not a fiacre, that the narrator imagines himself coming to an untimely end:

> Je savais très bien que mon cerveau était un riche bassin minier, où il y avait une étendue immense et fort diverse de gisements précieux. Mais

aurais-je le temps de les exploiter? J'étais la seule personne capable de le faire. Pour deux raisons: avec ma mort eût disparu non seulement le seul ouvrier mineur capable d'extraire ces minerais, mais encore le gisement lui-même; or, tout à l'heure quand je rentrerais chez moi, il suffirait de la rencontre de l'auto que je prendrais avec une autre pour que mon corps fût détruit et que mon esprit, d'où la vie se retirerait, fût forcé d'abandonner à tout jamais les idées nouvelles qu'en ce moment même, n'ayant pas eu le temps de les mettre plus en sûreté dans un livre, il enserrait anxieusement de sa pulpe frémissante, protectrice, mais fragile. (Marcel Proust, *Le Temps retrouvé*, *A la recherche du temps perdu*, IV, ed. Jean-Yves Tadié, Bibliothèque de la Pléiade [Paris: Gallimard, 1989] 614.) (I knew that my brain was like a basin of rock rich in minerals, in which lay vast and varied ores of great price. But should I have time to exploit them? For two reasons I was the only person who could do this: with my death would disappear the one and only engineer who possessed the skill to extract these minerals and – more than that – the whole stratum itself. Yet presently, when I left this party to go home, it only needed a chance collision between the cab which I should take and another car for my body to be destroyed, thus forcing my mind, from which life instantly would ebb away, to abandon for ever and ever the new ideas which at this moment, not yet having had time to place them within the safety of a book, it anxiously embraced with the fragile protection of its own pulpy and quivering substance.) (Marcel Proust, *Time Regained*, *In Search of Lost Time*, VI, tr. Andreas Mayor and Terence Kilmartin, revised D. J. Enright [New York: Modern Library, 1993] 514.)

"Gott hilfe [*for* helfe] mir, ich kann nicht anders" (God help me, I cannot do otherwise).

3 It is not known who had requested amateur production rights from SB.

BARNEY ROSSET, GROVE PRESS
NEW YORK

26.5.56   sub arbore vitae
Cher vieux Barney

Yours of 22nd this day and let me hasten before all else to say that few things would give me more pleasure than to see you in Paris next month, this month or any month, with I hope Loly on your arm, and with my ill-gottens to buy for us spirals of apéritifs and bring you to Bobino and supper with buckets of Beaujolais and Sancerre at the ever satisfactory Marquesas. So do write soon and confirm this good news.[1]

Many thanks for letters, cuttings, accounts and cover of Malone which pleases me much.[2] The picture is now much clearer in my mind and having unfathomable confidence in everyone (less tiring) have no doubt my bank account will put on a little weight in the ful[l] ness of time.

Have been and still am working like mad (for me) to get ready an evening's rollicking entertainment for the Marseille Festival in August, to be held on the roof of Le Corbusier's Cité Lumineuse! A mime, of which there exists two versions, a simple and a double, choice not yet established, with music by my cousin, to be followed (says he hopefully) by a long one-acter, aliter the 2 acts you've been hearing about zusammengeschmozzled together. This latter hairandroofraiser is not yet in the bag, but I'm stuffing away at it and anyway there's no drawing back now.[3] Not a tap done on L'Inno needless to say. Latest news of Godot revival here that the Théâtre Hebertot is definite and June 15th likely. Original cast except for Pozzo now sought actively. I hear (but of course neither from Albery nor Black) that the English provinces have it coming.[4] I received my copy of Irish Writing and wrote to White the editor to remind him to send you yours.[5] Not a word from the Pike and devil the sight or sign of royalties, so I'll have to get after them soon, which I was hoping not to have to do. I gave a brief text "From an Abandoned Work" in English to another little Dublin review and shall have it sent to you in due and proper course.[6] Congrats on Yellow ingenuities, of course Chatton & Windup have long since forfeited all rights. But I should have liked its date indicated. Smeraldina is a sad old affair "done long ago and ill done", what plot are you hatching for her? Re Moore a priori I'd say no, unless as Myerberg would say there's dough in it.[7] What I would love you to do is that most moving and beautiful novel Theodor Fontane's Effi Briest which I'm sure Loly knows and of which I know of no English version, that is if you have a first-rate translator up your sleeve. I read it for the fourth time the other day with the same old tears in the same old places.[8]

But of all that and much else when we meet. Let me know a little in advance so that I can brush the weeds off my trousers and buy a clean collar.

Ever

s/ Sam

TLS; 1 leaf, 1 side; Burns Library, Rosset-Beckett Collection.

1 Bobino, a music-hall theatre at 20 Rue de la Gaîté; the restaurant Aux Iles Marquises was located across the street.

2 The cover of the paperbound edition of *Malone Dies* was a graphic design in orange, white, and black.

3 SB's *Acte sans paroles* is a mime for one actor, whereas *Acte sans paroles II* has two actors. *The Sunday Times* of 17 June described *Acte sans paroles* as depicting "the difficulties confronting an agitated man in coping with a number of refractory inanimate objects." The article continues:

> Beckett was then asked if he could provide a play for the festival. At first, Beckett said he could not possibly tie himself down to producing anything in time. Second thoughts, however, dwelt upon the work he had in hand, and now the playwright has reshaped a piece, unsatisfactory to him in its two act form, into a long one-act play to run for about an hour. (*Sunday Times* Correspondent, "Waiting for Beckett: Two New Works," 17 June 1956: 10.)

"Cité Lumineuse": SB's play on "Cité Radieuse."

"Zusammengeschmozzled" is SB's portmanteau, combining "zusammen" (together) with "geschmolzen" (mingled).

4 The revival of *En attendant Godot* with the original cast (except that Albert Rémy initially replaced Roger Blin as Pozzo) at the Théâtre Hébertot opened on 14 June and ran to 23 September. SB omits the acute accent on "Hébertot."

A tour of the Criterion Theatre production of *Waiting for Godot* was announced for Harrow, Cambridge, Blackpool, Bournemouth, and Brighton ("'Waiting for Godot' to Tour," *The Times* 17 May 1956: 3).

5 An excerpt from *Malone Dies* published in *Irish Writing*: 22 February 1956, n. 1. SB's letter to Seán J. White has not been found.

6 "From an Abandoned Work" was published in *Trinity News* 3.17, 7 June 1956: 4.

7 Rosset had interested *New World Writing* in "Yellow" from *More Pricks Than Kicks*, published by Chatto and Windus in 1934. In his letter of 22 May to SB, Rosset indicates that his staff were typing out "The Smeraldina's Billet Doux," another story from *More Pricks Than Kicks*; it was published in *Zero Anthology*, 8, ed. Themistocles Hoetis (New York: Zero Press, 1956) 56–61.

In this letter, Rosset wrote, "We have been foozling with the idea of re-publishing George Moore. Two possible volumes are the novel THE LAKE and the group of stories THE UNTILLED FIELD. And what would be your opinion."

8 Loly Rosset was German.

CYRIL CUSACK
DUBLIN

June 1st, 1956   Paris
Dear Cyril Cusack,

You ask me for a tribute to G. B. S., in French, for your souvenir programme.[1]

This is too tall an order for me.

I wouldn't write in French for King Street.

I wouldn't suggest that G. B. S. is not a great play-wright, whatever that is when it's at home.

What I would do is give the whole unupsettable apple-cart for a sup of the Hawk's Well, or the Saints', or a whiff of Juno, to go no further.[2]

Sorry.

    s/ Samuel Beckett

?TLS; 1 side, 1 leaf; text as published in the program of *Androcles and the Lion* (see n. 1 below).

1   With Cusack Productions' performance of *Androcles and the Lion* by George Bernard Shaw at the Gaiety Theatre in Dublin (2–7 July 1956), a program honoring the latter's centenary was prepared by Cyril Cusack.

2   W. B. Yeats, *At the Hawk's Well* (1916); John Millington Synge, *The Well of the Saints* (1905); Sean O'Casey, *Juno and the Paycock* (1924).

THOMAS MACGREEVY
DUBLIN

4-6-56   Ussy-sur-Marne
Bien cher Tom

Many thanks for card from Holland.[1] Forgive my slowness in writing. I have [been] up to my eyes & rather in a panic preparing a "spectacle" for the Marseille Festival d'Avant-Garde in August – the mime with music by John Beckett and a longish one-acter. Have done all I can do for the moment and am taking a breather, but unfortunately have to toil back to Paris to-morrow where <u>Godot</u> is being revived next week at the Théâtre Hébertot in Blin's <u>mise en scène</u> and with the original cast. All I feel like is staying on here in the quiet and the great air. I hope I'll be able to get back in about ten days. The Marseille affair is going to be difficult to realise and I rather dread the coming months. But I say to myself too that if I hadn't these things to goad me on I'd give way very soon to a kind of pottering inertia.

I hope your meeting went off better than you expected and that your way is clearer. Suzanne and I often think of our evenings with you and look forward to more of them soon. Suzanne met Mihailovici and Monique at a concert last week and we shall probably be dining with them this week. He is having an opera performed at the Théâtre des Champs-Elysées next Saturday and we shall certainly go to that.[2] I don't think I have been to a concert since you left.

Morris Sinclair, wife & children were here a fortnight ago, all in good form. Ralph Cusack is expected at the end of this week. They seem to be settling in at Spéracèdes. He gave me an immense MS to read, full of good elements but very messy.[3] My American publisher also due in Paris this week. A letter from George Reavey, announcing his separation from the Pereira and inviting me to stay with him in New York. Thank God I had the sense not to go there.

I read <u>Andromaque</u> again with greater admiration than ever and I think more understanding, at least more understanding of the chances of the theatre to-day.[4]

I hear from Cyril Cusack that Liam O'Brien is translating <u>Godot</u> into Irish. Feel unexpectedly pleased about this.[5]

With Jean I am at least 3 letters behindhand, but shall get one off to her to-day. They all seem in excellent form, though finances as nebulous as ever. A letter from Alan after a long silence.[6] Nancy Cunard sent me her book on Douglas. I feel we would not have got on. Very snarky about Lawrence & Aldington.[7]

Suzanne is tired, but otherwise in good form. She sends you her love. And I send you mine. And affectionate greetings to JBY.[8]

Write soon. Ever

Sam

ALS; 2 leaves, 2 sides; TCD, MS 10402/199.

1 Thomas MacGreevy's card to SB has not been found.

2 Marcel Mihalovici (1898–1985) and his wife the pianist Monique Haas (1906–1987) were friends of Thomas MacGreevy. Mihalovici's opera *Phèdre* (1949) was performed at the Théâtre des Champs-Elysées on Saturday, 9 June. SB writes "Mihailovici" for Mihalovici.

3 Morris and Mimi Sinclair, with their children Frank and Anne, lived in Geneva. Ralph Cusack and Nancy Sinclair now lived in the south of France at Spéracèdes. Cusack's manuscript was of his book *Cadenza: An Excursion* (1958).

4 SB had attended a performance of Racine's *Andromaque* with MacGreevy in June 1948 (see 8 July [1948], n. 5).

5 Cyril Cusack's letter to SB has not been found. Professor of Romance Languages at University College, Galway, Liam O'Brien (Liam Ó Bríain, 1888–1974) translated *Waiting for Godot* into Gaelic as "Ag fanacht le Godó" (NLI, Abbey Theatre Playscripts, TMS).

6 Jean Beckett.
Alan Thompson's letter to SB has not been found.

7 In *Grand Man: Memories of Norman Douglas*, Nancy Cunard records her own memories, portions of Douglas's letters, and also recollections of him offered by his friends. Douglas comments of D. H. Lawrence's style: "diffuseness is a fault of much of his work" (47). In a letter to Cunard published in the book, Charles Duff recalls that Douglas had said that Lawrence "'never recovered from the shock of puberty, never outgrew it, remained a frustrated schoolboy right to the end and persuaded himself – and how many others! – that he was a pioneering genius in a *terra incognita*'" (247).
Cunard reprints a letter from Douglas to an unnamed American magazine written to dispute remarks made by Aldington about Douglas in his book *Life for Life's Sake*, in which he comments also on Aldington's caricature of him in another book (176–177). Cunard recounts a row she had with Aldington over a payment of royalties (97).

8 Jack B. Yeats.

NANCY CUNARD

6-6-56   Paris
Bien chère Nancy

Many thanks for Uncle Norman which I am reading with avidity, more I confess for what it tells of you than of what it tells of him.[1]

Shall be seeing Desmond Ryan and Ralph Cusack this week-end and, since they are going your way, shall give them to take you two copies of poor Echo's old bones.[2]

Have just succeeded in grinding out of my gritty old maw "per lungo silenzio. . fioco" the one-act howl for Marseille and am not a pretty sight as a result.[3] On top of which the resuscitation of <u>Godot</u> next week at the Hébertot. I wish I were next November looking out of my window in the country at the leaves falling.

The great Avulser continues with his chits and bits. At the thought of him in Brighton I sometimes stop in the street and have a good incomprehensible laugh.[4]

> much love
> Samuel

ALS; 1 leaf, 1 side; TxU, Cunard collection.

1 Cunard, *Grand Man: Memories of Norman Douglas*.

2 Desmond Ryan and Ralph Cusack were traveling to the south of France; Cunard had asked if SB had any copies of *Echo's Bones and Other Precipitates*.

3 SB refers to *Fin de partie* with words from Dante's *Inferno*, I.63: "per lungo silenzio [parea] fioco" (seemed weak from long silence) (Dante, *The Divine Comedy*, I, *Inferno*, 25).

4 SB refers to the book and manuscript dealer Jake Schwartz who lived in Brighton, East Sussex.

NINO FRANK

PARIS

17 juin 1956   6 Rue des Favorites
                                                      Paris 15°

Cher Nino Frank

Votre si gentille lettre m'a fait grand plaisir.[1] Merci de tout coeur.

La scène du veston est conforme au texte qui avait paru en librairie avant les représentations au Babylone. J'en serais incapable aujourd'hui.[2]

Je suis heureux que vous soyez si bien rétabli. Je repars à la campagne ces jours-ci, mais serai très souvent à Paris dans les mois qui viennent. Ça me ferait plaisir de vous revoir tous les deux. Quels sont vos projets pour les vacances? Je vous téléphonerai à tout hasard un de ces jours.

> Bien amicalement
> Sam. Beckett

ALS; 1 leaf, 1 side; TxU, Beckett collection.

17 June 1956   6 Rue des Favorites
                                                Paris 15

Dear Nino Frank

Your very nice letter gave me great pleasure.[1] Warmest thanks.

The jacket scene is in line with the text that had been out in the bookshops before the performances at the Babylone. I would not be capable of it now.[2]

I am glad that you have recovered so well. I am going back to the country any day now, but will very often be in Paris in the coming months. I would really enjoy seeing the two of you again. What are your plans for the holidays? I shall telephone you on the off chance one of these days.

> All good wishes
> Sam. Beckett

1   Nino Frank (1904–1988), literary and film critic who had translated "Anna Livia Plurabelle" into Italian with Joyce. His letter to SB has not been found.

2   SB refers to the scene from Act II of *En attendant Godot* in which Estragon sleeps and Vladimir removes his jacket and places it over Estragon's shoulders (*En attendant Godot* [1952] 119).

ALAN SCHNEIDER
NEW YORK

June 21st 1956   Paris

Dear Alan

Many thanks for your letter. Look forward greatly to seeing you end July.[1] I had a letter from MM announcing reopening in October.

I have no clear picture of the production. Much seems to get across, but to the exclusion of too much else, probably. Revival here in second week at the Hébertot, a fine theatre. Slow start, but improving now.[2] Have at last written another, one act, longish hour and a quarter I fancy. Rather difficult and elliptic, mostly depending on the power of the text to claw, more inhuman than Godot. My feeling strong, at the moment, is to leave it in French for a year at least, so tired by Godot and all the misunderstanding.[3] I'm in a ditch somewhere near the last stretch and would like to crawl up on it. They kill me, all the translating and silly fuss. Hope you are pleased with your Trip to B.[4] A big success for you would give me more pleasure than I can tell you. All the best, Alan. Et à bientôt.

    Ever

      s/ SAM

TLS; 1 leaf, 1 side; Burns Library, Schneider-Beckett Collection. Previous publication, Beckett and Schneider, *No Author Better Served*, 11.

1 Schneider's letter to SB has not been found. Schneider would see *En attendant Godot* on 20 July and have dinner with SB on 23 July (WHS, Alan Schneider, series 7, box 2).

2 Michael Myerberg wrote to SB on 8 June: "If it is at all possible, we would like to have you present at our Fall opening, which will probably be on October 15, 1956" (NSyU). SB's reply has not been found.

The revival at the Théâtre Hébertot was pronounced "definitive" by Harold Hobson, who wrote: "'En attendant Godot' is as unforgettable as a knife twisted in the ribs. It is only a few hours since I saw the performance and the wound is still in my entrails" ("A Revelation," *The Sunday Times* 15 July 1956: 4).

3 *Fin de partie.*

4 Schneider directed Horton Foote's *The Trip to Bountiful* at the Arts Theatre Club in London; it opened on 4 July.

MAURICE NADEAU

PARIS

Lundi 25-6-56

Cher ami

    C'est encore plus mauvais que je ne croyais.[1]

    Il va falloir trouver autre chose.[2]

Amitiés et à bientôt
Sam Beckett

ALS; 1 leaf, 1 side; enclosed with TMS of *Eleutheria*; Nadeau.

Monday 25-6-56
Dear Maurice Nadeau
  It's even worse than I thought.[1]
  We'll have to find something else.[2]
  All best and till soon
    Sam Beckett

1 SB refers to the typescript of *Eleutheria* from 1947 which was enclosed.

2 Nadeau had asked for a submission for *Les Lettres Nouvelles* where SB later published dramatic works (Maurice Nadeau, 12 July 2010).

H. O. WHITE
TRINITY COLLEGE, DUBLIN

July 2nd [1956]   Paris
Dear Ho
    Thanks for your letter of June 11th and forgive delay in replying. I have laid your idea in my stony ground. The cinema was killed in the cradle and if ever there is an Elijah to lie himself down on the corpse I won't be there to profit by it.[1] Trinity News made a great hames of my text with their unspeakable paragraphs and varsity punctuation. I asked them either not to print it at all or to print it as it stood and above all to send me proofs. Well I suppose I should be used to being improved behind my back and to the horrible semi-colons of well brought-up young blue pencils, mais ce n'est pas ça qui vous encourage à recommencer.[2] I had a nice letter from Henry Richmond asking me to perform before the Society in November and was sorry I had to refuse.[3] Look forward to seeing you in September. The other day on the green gallant's bridge I ducked in out of a flurry of rain to the tabac when

prior to Marius we foregathered with Con and hoped we would be there together again, letting our old engines turn off before setting off along the quays and night's young thoughts (Con's).[4]

Ever

s/ Sam

TLS; 1 leaf, 1 side; *env to* Professor H.O[.] White, Trinity College, Dublin, Irlande, CD; *pm* 2-7-56, La Ferté-sous-Jouarre; TCD, MS 3777/14. *Dating*: from pm.

1 Despite SB's early enthusiasm about cinema (see 2 March 1936 to Sergei Eisenstein), he felt the novelty of sound and technicolor "swamped" the possibilities that were emerging in black-and-white and silent film (see 6 February 1936 to Thomas McGreevy).

2 "Hames" (Ir. colloq., anything botched).
"From an Abandoned Work": 26 May 1956, n. 6.
"Mais ce n'est pas ça qui vous encourage à recommencer" (but it's not the kind of thing would encourage you to do it again).

3 Francis Henry Arthur Richmond (b. 1936), a student of Modern Languages at Trinity College Dublin and also a former pupil of Portora Royal School, recalls SB's warm response, but did not keep the letter (F. H. A. Richmond, March 2010).

4 SB recollects dinner with A. J. Leventhal (see 22 November 1955, n. 8). "Green gallant's bridge" refers to the Pont Neuf. SB's allusion is to the Square du Vert Galant, the tip of the Ile de la Cité where the bridge crosses it.

NANCY CUNARD

4.7.56   Paname[1]

Bien chère Nancy

Forgive delay in answering your letter of June 20th. I have been moidered with one silly thing after another. It seems unlikely now that the new play will be performed at the Marseille Festival which has been announced from 4th to 14th August. Impossible to get anything definite out of the organizers, no contracts for actors, no information about theatre and equipment, so rather than have the play bungled I think we shall withdraw it. Just possible the mime may be given alone. But I rather hope not. The mime is still in Florence and not due back till the end of this week, which leaves us really too little time. Indeed it would not surprise me if the whole Festival were to be called off, or at least the theatre section. From my own point of view it would be much better to keep both mime and play intact for presentation in Paris in October or November, which I think would be quite possible. Shall let you know how things turn out.[2]

Schwartz is becoming rather a nuisance, soon he will be sending me his toilet-paper to inscribe. But he's the kind of play-boy you can't be really annoyed with.[3] Glad you had a good party with Ralph and Desmond.[4] Saw Barry of BBC TV who is interested in the mime (and why not?) and am told Gielgud wants a play for 3rd Programme. Never thought about Radio play technique but in the dead of t'other night got a gruesome idea full of cartwheels and dragging feet and puffing and panting which may or may not lead to something.[5]

Back in the spinach after three tiring weeks in Paris and feel a little less pins screaming in an old cushion. No post last two days, the postman having gone to do battle in Algeria and there being none to replace him. Vive la pagaille![6]

Eating fresh pineapple for the first time in my life with ferocious enjoyment. There's news for you. Have just read Perlès his rather silly Mon Ami Henry Miller. References to Lowenfels and Sam Putnam. Shock to learn Miller is 70.[7] Aspettando Godot is out from Einaudi with a foolish preface by the translator.[8]

> Much love
> s/ Samuel

TLS; 1 leaf, 1 side; TxU, Cunard collection. Previously published, Lake, ed., *No Symbols Where None Intended*, 93, 97.

1   "Paname" is a French slang term for Paris.

2   This was the first Festival de l'art d'avant-garde in Marseille. It was announced by Bernard Chochoy, Secrétaire d'Etat à la Reconstruction, on 6 July, to celebrate Le Corbusier's "Cité Radieuse." There were to be lectures on painting, theatre, cinema, architecture, dance, and music, as well as performances. The entire Festival was organized and its theatrical offerings directed by French director Jacques Polieri

(b. 1925). The only dramatic performance (repeated five times) was a double bill of plays by Eugène Ionesco (*La jeune fille à marier* and *Les grandes chaleurs*) and by Jean Tardieu (*Le Guichet, Le Sacre de la nuit, Monsieur Moi,* and *La Sonate et les trois messieurs*) (Michel Corvin, *Festivals de l'art d'avant-garde: Marseille, Nantes, Paris 1956–1960* [Paris: Somogy Editions d'Art, 2004] 35, 103, 105, 116–117).

3   Jake Schwartz often asked SB to sign the manuscript drafts that he sold to him and to make fair copies of manuscripts with which SB was unwilling to part (an example being the fair copy of *En attendant Godot* made for Schwartz [Lake, ed., *No Symbols Where None Intended*, 66]).

4   Ralph Cusack and Desmond Ryan and their plan to visit Cunard: 6 June 1956, n. 2

5   When BBC Radio Drama and BBC Television Drama became separate departments in 1952, Val Gielgud (1900–1981) continued as Head of Radio Drama, and Michael Barry (1910–1988) became Head of Television Drama. At the time when Barry showed interest in SB's mime, Gielgud expressed interest in a radio play by SB.

Cecilia Reeves (née Hunt, m. Gillie, 1907–1996) in the Paris office of the BBC was asked to contact SB: she wrote on 21 June to the Head of Drama (Sound):

> I have written to Beckett asking if he would write a piece for Third and if he could let us have a text of "la Fin du Jeu". He is, as you know, an elusive character and spending much of his time outside Paris, and our mutual contact Desmond Ryan has already gone South.
>
> He has however reacted amiably to a suggestion that his mime piece "Soif" which is also to be given at Marseille should be considered for Television so I imagine that his former rather hostile attitude to radio in general is improving. (BBC WAC, RCONT I / Samuel Beckett Scriptwriter / I [1953–1962].)

"La Fin du Jeu" is Reeves's approximation of the title of SB's piece.

SB replied to Reeves on 4 July, mentioning his conversation with Michael Barry: "I should like very much to do a radio play for the Third Programme, but I am very doubtful of my ability to work in this medium. However since our conversation I have, to my surprise, had an idea which may or may not lead to something." (BBC WAC, RCONT I / Samuel Beckett Scriptwriter / I [1953–1962].)

6   "Vive la pagaille!" (Here's to mess and confusion!)

7   Alfred Perlès, *Mon Ami Henry Miller: An Intimate Biography* (London: N. Spearman, 1955); *Mon Ami Henry Miller*, tr. Anne Bernadou (Paris: René Julliard, 1956).

Samuel Putnam; Walter Lowenfels (1897–1976). Henry Miller was in fact sixty-five.

8   Beckett, *Aspettando Godot*, translated by Carlo Fruttero.

AIDAN HIGGINS ESQ
LONDON

6-7-56   Ussy-sur-Marne

Dear Aidan –

Glad to have your letter and to hear about your plans. I think the Marseille thing is off, I hope so. Probably Paris in October instead, in a proper theatre and time to prepare.[1] I know nothing about a new edition of Murphy. The Yanks want the Proust but I hesitate. Shall be sending you Malone.[2] Suppose you are glad to be getting shut of London. Queer the way you all go to Ireland when you get a holiday. Piss on the White Rock for me and cast a cold eye on the granite beginning on the cliff face. Never been so miserable as on that strand, not even at Shankill, no solution and it unrealisable but just to walk out into the sea and not come back.[3] Have been asked to write a Radio Play for the 3ʳᵈ and am tempted, feet dragging and breath short and cart wheels and imprecations from the Brighton Road to Foxrock Station and back, insentient old mares in foal being welted by the cottagers and the devil tattered in the ditch – boyhood memories. Probably won't come to anything.[4] You must be tired trying one to read and two to make some sense of this so shall close. Drop me a line from the Igo Inn or from the pub in Killiney Village where Whelan is to be met if care not taken or from the sinister Silver Tassie in Loughlinstown where dear old Jordans, the prettiest pub on the Bray road once stood.[5]

Remember me to Jill.[6]

Yours ever

s/ Sam

ACS; 1 leaf, 2 sides; *env to* Aidan Higgins Esq, 18a Belsize Lane, LONDON N.W. 3, Angleterre; *pm* 6-7-56, Paris; TxU, Beckett collection.

1 Festival de l'art d'avant-garde, Marseille: 12 March 1956, n. 3, and 4 July 1956, n. 2.

2 *Murphy* was not published by Grove Press until 1958. Rosset had asked if they could publish *Proust*. *Malone Dies* was now available in English (Grove Press, 1956).

3 Higgins had begun to work with John Wright's Marionettes in London, rehearsing for what would be a two-year tour in Yugoslavia, Germany, Holland, and then Africa. Before leaving London to begin the tour, Higgins took a holiday in Ireland, from 20 July (Higgins to Arland Ussher, 2 May 1956, TCD, MSS 9331 – 9041/1512).

Whiterock is on Killiney strand. At Whiterock, there is an outcrop of rocks revealing the granite of Killiney Hill. Shankill is another stretch of strand, further south on Killiney Bay.

"Cast a cold eye" is from the final stanza of "Under Ben Bulben" by W. B. Yeats; the words are carved on his gravestone in Drumcliff Churchyard.

4   SB's childhood home, Cooldrinagh, was on the Brighton Road in the suburb of Foxrock; the Foxrock station on the Harcourt Street rail line into Dublin was slightly less than a mile to the west of Cooldrinagh.

5   The Igo Inn is located in Ballybrack. The Druid's Chair Pub in Killiney Village is on Killiney Hill Road. SB probably refers to Seán Ó Faoláin (né John Francis Whelan, 1900–1991), who lived in Kilmacanogue (see 16 January 1936 to Thomas McGreevy, n. 4). Jordan's pub was on the Bray Road in Loughlinstown near Killiney, where The Silver Tassie now stands.

6   Jill Higgins (née Anders, b. 1930).

HELMUT CASTAGNE, S. FISCHER VERLAG
FRANKFURT

le 14 juillet 1956   6 Rue des Favorites
                                                            Paris 15me

Cher Monsieur

Merci de votre lettre du 9 juillet.[1]

En effet, ma nouvelle pièce, en un acte, précédée d'un mime assez court également de moi, devait être présentée au Festival de Marseille le mois prochain.

Malheureusement nous avons été obligés d'annuler ce spectacle, les arrangements ayant été conclus trop tard pour nous permettre de le préparer de façon convenable.

Je pense que nous le monterons à Paris au mois d'octobre ou de novembre.

Je n'aurai le texte définitif de la pièce, dont j'ignore encore le titre, qu'après un certain nombre de répétitions. Il va sans dire que je vous l'enverrai, dès sa parution aux Editions de Minuit.

Je profite de cette occasion pour vous parler de K.-F. Lembke. C'est lui, vous vous en souvenez peut-être, qui avait monté Godot à la prison de Lüttringhausen. Il répète la pièce en ce moment à Wuppertal, en vue d'en donner quelques représentations au Kirchentag de Frankfurt le mois prochain.

Je tiens beaucoup à ce qu'il puisse mener à bien ce projet et je compte sur l'amabilité du Fischerverlag pour lui accorder les facilités dont il a besoin.[2]

Je désirerais également lui faire parvenir la somme de RM 200 (deux cent[s]). Je ne peux pas lui envoyer l'argent directement de Paris sans avoir obtenu au préalable une autorisation de l'Office des Changes, ce qui est long et aléatoire. Je me suis donc demandé s'il vous serait possible de lui envoyer cette somme, en la déduisant naturellement des droits d'auteur actuellement à mon com[p]te chez vous, ou à venir. Si cela vous gêne le moins du monde n'hésitez pas à me le dire, je comprendrai très bien. Mais si au contraire vous estimez la chose faisable vous nous rendriez, à Lembke et à moi-même, un très grand service. Son adresse: K.-F. Lembke, Wuppertal-Barmen, Brombergerstrasse 71.[3]

A moi aussi ça me ferait grand plaisir de vous revoir. J'espère que vous viendrez à Paris un de ces jours.

Croyez, cher Monsieur, à mes sentiments très amicalement dévoués.

s/

Samuel Beckett

TLS; 1 leaf, 1 side; S. Fischer Verlag.

14th July 1956   6 Rue des Favorites

           Paris 15

Dear Mr Castagne

Thank you for your letter of 9th July.

Yes indeed, my new one-act play, preceded by a fairly short mime, also by me, was to have been staged at the Marseille Festival next month.[1]

Unfortunately, we were forced to cancel this performance, the arrangements having been settled too late to allow us to prepare properly.

I think that we shall put it on in Paris in October or November.

I shall only have the final text of the play – title still unknown – after a certain number of rehearsals. Needless to say, I shall send it to you as soon as it comes out in the Editions de Minuit.

I am taking advantage of this chance to talk to you about K.-F. Lembke. He it was, you will remember, who had staged *Godot* in Lüttringhausen Prison. Just now he is rehearsing the play in Wuppertal, with a view to staging a few performances at the Frankfurt Kirchentag next month.

It is very much my wish that he should carry this project through, and I am counting on the good nature of Fischer Verlag to grant him the facilities he needs.[2]

I should also like to put his way the sum of RM 200. I cannot send the money directly from Paris without obtaining authorisation beforehand from the Office des Changes, which is long and uncertain. So I have been wondering if it would be possible for you to send him this sum, deducting it of course from royalties, present or future, in my account with you. If that causes you the least concern, do not hesitate to tell me. I shall understand perfectly. If on the other hand you think it feasible you would be doing both Lembke and me a great favour. His address: K. F. Lembke, Wuppertal-Barmen, Brombergerstrasse 71.[3]

I too would very much like to see you again. I hope that you will come to Paris one of these days.

Yours sincerely

Samuel Beckett

1 Helmut Castagne (n.d.), Head of Drama at Fischer Verlag until September 1956, wrote to SB on 9 July: "es ist in Deutschland bekannt geworden, dass für ein Festival in Marseille Einakter vorbereitet werden. Sie haben also doch wieder etwas für das Theater geschrieben!" (S. Fischer Verlag archive.) (It has become known in Germany that one-act plays are being prepared for a Festival in Marseille. So you have written something for theatre again after all!") Castagne asks if SB would send a copy and if he would be willing to allow S. Fischer Verlag to publish the plays.

2 Karl-Franz Lembke's production in the prison at Lüttringhausen of his German translation, *Man wartet auf Godot*: 14 October 1954, n. 1.

The Evangelische Kirchentage, an annual assembly of Protestant Church laity, encouraged exchanges of ideas among parishioners through performances, workshops, and meetings. The event was to be held in Frankfurt on 8–12 August. SB uses an Anglicism drawing on the English word "facilities." French had no such all-purpose word at that time.

3   Jutta Reigers, Helmut Castagne's secretary, confirmed on 19 July that S. Fischer Verlag had arranged for 200 DM (not RM as SB indicates in his letter) to be sent to Lembke from SB's account, and had approved several performances of Lembke's translation by the "Spielschar der Landstrasse Wuppertal." The Program of the Deutsche Evangelische Kirchentage lists eight (Frau Dr. Stache, Evangelisches Zentralarchiv in Berlin, 8 March 1988; Hans Freitag, 6 February 1996).

MAX NIEDERMAYER, LIMES VERLAG
WIESBADEN, GERMANY

le 21 juillet 1956   6 Rue des Favorites
                                                          Paris 15me

Cher Monsieur

Merci de votre aimable lettre du 17 courant, avec le bel article d'Albrecht Fabri.[1]

Je suis tout à fait d'accord avec les conditions que vous me proposez.

Il va sans dire que vous êtes libre de cho[i]sir votre traducteur ou vos traducteurs. J'aimerais seulement que soient confiés à K.-F. Lembke quelques poèmes faciles et à Elmar Tophoven, avec qui je peux travailler sur place, les plus obscurs.[2]

J'aurai peut-être, si vous le permettez, deux ou trois poèmes à ajouter à ceux que vous avez déjà.[3]

Laissez-moi vous dire enfin combien je suis heureux que ce petit recueil paraisse chez vous.

Croyez, cher Monsieur, à mes sentiments très cordialement dévoués.

    s/

    Samuel Beckett

TLS; 1 leaf, 1 side; PSt, Allison-Shelley Collection.

21st July 1956   6 Rue des Favorites
                                                 Paris 15

Dear Mr Niedermayer

Thank you for your kind letter of the 17th, with the fine article by Albrecht Fabri.[1]

I agree entirely with the conditions you propose.

It goes without saying that you are free to choose your own translator or translators. I should just like K.-F. Lembke to be entrusted with a few easy poems, and Elmar Tophoven, with whom I can work on the spot, with the more obscure.[2]

I shall perhaps have, if you are willing, two or three poems to add to those that you already have.[3]

May I finally say how happy I am that this little collection is appearing in your imprint.

                          Yours sincerely
                          Samuel Beckett

---

1 Max Niedermayer, director of Limes Verlag, proposed to publish a collection of SB's poetry by presenting each poem in its original language with the German translation on the facing page. Niedermayer initially approached Beckett about the project through Elmar Tophoven, who reported to him on 21 November 1955: "Er ist grundsätzlich nicht dagegen" (He is not opposed in principle to it) (Deutsches Literaturarchiv Marbach, Limes Verlag collection, Tophoven).

It is not known what essay by Albrecht Fabri (1911–1998) was sent by Niedermayer to SB; Limes Verlag later published Fabri's *Variationen: Essays* (1959).

2 Niedermayer does take up SB's suggestion that Karl-Franz Lembke translate some of the poems, asking, in his letter of 25 July, that SB and Elmar Tophoven select the poems for Lembke to translate (Schiller-Nationalmuseum, Deutsches Archiv, Marbach).

Tophoven declined to translate poems originally written in English, and so Eva Hesse (b. 1925) was asked to translate these; she was noted as a translator of twentieth-century American poets.

Lembke's involvement as a translator ended abruptly when it later came to Niedermayer's attention that the Wiesbaden performances of *Godot* to be directed by Lembke did not take place because he had embezzled the funds of his young performers (Niedermayer to Tophoven, 26 September 1956, Deutsches Literaturarchiv Marbach, Limes Verlag collection, Tophoven).

3 Three groups of SB's poems are included in *Gedichte*: those from *Echo's Bones and Other Precipitates*, written 1933–1935 (with which is grouped "Cascando"); those from 1937–1939; and those from 1948–1949.

ROSICA COLIN
LONDON

July 26th 1956   6 Rue des Favorites
                                                  Paris 15me

Dear Mrs Colin

    Thanks for your letter of July 20th.

    I prefer not to figure in Who's Who.

    I was in communication with the Braille organisation months ago and naturally gave them permission (signing a form to that effect) to do Godot, and also what I think they call a general permission.[1]

    With best wishes I am

        Yours sincerely

        s/

        Samuel Beckett

TLS; 1 leaf, 1 side; Rosica Colin collection.

1 Colin reported in her letter to SB of 20 July that Faber and Faber had been approached by St. Dunstan's (an organization established in 1915 to provide books in Braille, later founding training centers for the blind), which wished to reproduce *Waiting for Godot* in Braille.

THOMAS MACGREEVY
DUBLIN, IRELAND

30.7.56   Ussy sur Marne

Bien Cher Tom –

    I should have written long ago. You know how it is. I am overwhelmed with silly requests and letters most of which I feel I have to answer. Till I hate the sight of pen and paper. Preparing the revival at the Hébertot was also wearing, and finishing the new play for the Marseille Festival where finally it will not be presented, the organisers having completed their arrangements too late for sufficient rehearsal. Preferable in any case to have the première in Paris, I don't know when, or where, with the little mime. We spend all the time we can in the country, but I have always to be dodging up to Paris to see this one or that one. Fortunately there is a good train up early in the morning and one back late in the evening, giving one a full day in Paris. But there is not much peace any more. A very moving letter from JBY in prompt reply to one from me, written with tears, feeling it was perhaps goodbye. Niall wrote me he was feeling miserable. You have been wonderful with him all these years, no one ever had such a friend as he in you.[1]

Nothing really of interest to tell you. We both keep well enough, Suzanne because she takes care of herself and I quite undeservedly. My American publisher was over and gave us a very handsome electrophone gramophone, with a pile of microgrooves.[2] We hope this week to acquire Dichterliebe sung by Souzay and the Winterreise with Fischer-Dieskau. Suzanne is crazy about Ich grolle nicht and Ich habe im Traum geweint.[3] I hope things in the Gallery are not too difficult and that you will be over with us in Paris for part of your holiday. The Germans are doing my poems, in English and French original and German translation. I wasn't too keen, but am tired of saying no to everything. Am also letting the New York publisher do the Dolphin Proust, the rights of which have reverted to me from our old friends Shaton and Windup. I should be translating L'Innommable, but it's an impossible job. Nothing from Ireland except from Jean and family who seem all right. Edward passed his entrance to Columba's with very good marks.[4] Sorry to be such a very dull dog. Much love from us both

SAM

ALS; 1 leaf, 2 sides; TCD, MS 10402/200.

1   None of the letters mentioned here (SB to Yeats, Yeats to SB, Montgomery to SB) has been found. SB responded to Montgomery's letter and news: "Have written a sad note to Jack. Hope it's not goodbye yet. Yes, Tom is a wonder" (23 July 1956, NLI, Accession 6475, Lot 5, Box d).

2   Barney Rosset's gift of a record player was manufactured by Ducretet-Thomson in Paris.

3   French baritone Gérard Souzay (1918–2004) recorded Robert Schumann's song cycle *Dichterliebe*, op. 48, on a Turnabout/Vox recording (THS 611116) in 1956; it

includes "Ich grolle nicht" (I'll not complain) and "Ich hab' im Traum geweinet" (In dream I wept). Fischer-Dieskau recorded Schubert's *Winterreise* in 1955.

4   Jean Beckett; Edward Beckett. St. Columba's College, Rathfarnum, Co. Dublin, a well-considered public school.

19. Barney Rosset, 1956

BARNEY ROSSET, GROVE PRESS
NEW YORK

August 1st 1956   Paris

Dear Barney

Glad to have your letter of July 25th. Of course I shall give you all help I can with the readings programme.[1] With regard to choice of texts, do you want me to make suggestions? I am quite happy to leave it to you. But go canny on the early stuff. From Murphy for example I thing [sic] the best would be the chapter on M's mind, "Amor intellectualis etc." However I won't go into this aspect of it unless you ask me to. With regard to some readings in French, I have approached Martin and Blin with the suggestion that the former should record Lucky's speech and the latter a passage from L'Inno or a Texte pour Rien. They would both be very glad to do this, and no doubt would do it without payment if necessary, but I feel they should be paid something.[2] I play with the idea of doing a short text in English and another in French myself. I think I'll have at least a shot at it, and then withhold it if too awful. It was all very well for Joyce with his fine trained voice, but when you have a gasp-croak like mine you hesitate.[3] No difficulty about the actual recording, on a tape-recorder, Blin and Martin know all about that. But it could not be done before the first week of September. As I see the meeting is not to be held before October 23rd, this should be time enough. With regard to your presentation I am not worrying, you are as well able as any and better than most to say what little there is to say about me. But needless to say any help or information I can give you are unreservedly at your disposal. As to an inédit, I fear there is really nothing, unless you might mean by that a passage from my translation in progress (?) of L'Inno. I recall now there is a fairly recent text in English – "From an Abandoned Work" – which has only appeared – quite lately – in one of the TCD magazines. I'm afraid I have left it in the country, but I'll send it along next week. I might choose it for my own reading. It's not too bad, I think, and in any case you might get some USA periodical to use it. I think we should leave Fin de Partie alone till after Paris production. Tell the Poetry Center how pleased I feel, and how honoured. And let me have your reaction to all of above, particularly with ref to choice of texts and what dollars I can offer to Blin and Martin.

It's good of you to want to do the Proust. I'm not sure that you are well advised. It's a very juvenile affair. We'll need the date of composition plain and large. I'd be grateful if you'd notify the publishing houses that approached me on the subject, the names of which I gave you, that you're taking up your option on the book, as I told them you might.[4]

I shall be seeing Myerberg here Sunday or Monday, on his way through from Nice to London. Somehow am not looking forward to it. Saw Alan Schneider (quite recovered from Miami and with incredible stories of First-Banana Lahr) and his wife and had a pleasant evening together. He got quite a good press for his recent Arts Theatre Production, something Bountiful – Back to Bountiful? Schneider seems to have a great graw for you.[5] Was rehearsing this morning the new Vladimir, Chevallier, the 3rd since opening at the H. It was he created Les Chaises at the Little Lancry 3 years ago. I think he will be good. We are also at our 3rd Pozzo and second boy who has to play in long trousers his legs are so bandy. When he makes a mistake in his text his alcoholic father comes rushing from the wings and hits him with a bottle, screaming "Schwein[e]hund".[6] I am battling slowly up the steep dull hill of the 3rd Radio script, something may come of it if I'm not careful. Nothing up to date about where or when the mime and act. I understand Godot is scheduled to run walk or crawl till last week of September here. Glad domestic situation is settled to both your satisfactions. The Limes Verlag trilingual edition of poems is in train. Fischer has done the handsome thing about permission for the ex-convict to present Godot at the Frankfurter Kirchentag next month.[7] It is cold and wet and the fireman having left on his annual jaunt to the Riviera we shall have no hot water till August is out. I feel as old as the House of Usher.[8] The electrophone dispenses its balm. This week we get the Dichterliebe and Winterreise.[9] Such are our transports. All the best from us both. And to Loly. Ever

s/ Sam

TLS; 1 leaf, 2 sides; Burns Library, Rosset-Beckett Collection. *AN AH* upper right margin: Alvin Epstein, 25 Indian Road, New York City 34, Williams 2-2743.

1   Rosset's letter to SB of 25 July has not been found. The proposed reading was to be held at the Poetry Center of the 92nd Street YM-YWHA, New York, on 23 October.

2   SB suggests reading from Chapter 6 of *Murphy*. It is not known if the readings in French by Jean Martin and Roger Blin materialized; readings from *Waiting for Godot* were given by Alvin Epstein (b. 1925) and E. G. Marshall, members of the Broadway cast ("'Godot' Dramatic Reading with Comments here, Tues.," *The 'Y' Bulletin* 53.3, 17 October 1956: 1).

3   It is unlikely that SB's proposal to record an English and a French text came to anything.

4   SB refers to inquiries from "the Beacon Press and the New York University Press, both wanting to do an American edition of my Proust" (SB to Barney Rosset, 8 July 1956, Burns Library, Rosset-Beckett Collection).

5   Jean Schneider (née Eugenia Muckle, b. 1923).
Alan Schneider's production of Horton Foote's *The Trip to Bountiful* and his evening with SB in Paris: 21 June 1956, n. 4, and n. 1. Of the critical reception of the play, Schneider notes that "Kenneth Tynan and Harold Hobson, each gave us a flattering paragraph" (*Entrances*, 238).
"Graw" (Gaelic, fondness).

6   Paul Chevalier (n.d.) was the third actor to play Vladimir (following Lucien Raimbourg and Jean-Marie Serreau) in the revival of *En attendant Godot* at the Théâtre Hébertot. Albert Rémy was the first Pozzo, followed by Roger Blin, and then Jean Bolo (1920–1962). The boy was played by Didier Bouillon (b. 1947), who wore short trousers for the performance; the second actor in the role has not been identified (Geneviève Latour, 2 June 2010; Marion Tricoire interview with Danielle Mathieu-Bouillon, 2 and 17 June 2010; Antoine Andrieu-Guitrancourt and Serge Bouillon, *Jacques Hébertot le magnifique (1886–1970): une vie au service du théâtre et des beaux-arts en quatre chroniques* [Paris: Paris bibliothèques / Fondation Hébertot, 2006] 245).
SB writes "Chevallier" for "Chevalier." Ionesco's *Les Chaises*, Théâtre Lancry (opened 22 April 1952).

7   Limes Verlag's proposal: 21 July 1956, n. 1.
S. Fischer Verlag's permission: 14 July 1956, n. 3

8   SB alludes to Edgar Allan Poe's story, 'The Fall of the House of Usher' (1839).

9   Rosset's gift of an electrophone, and SB's intent to acquire these recordings: 30 July 1956, n. 2 and n. 3.

KITTY BLACK, CURTIS BROWN
LONDON

August 10th 1956   6 Rue des Favorites
                                              Paris 15me

Dear Kitty

Thanks for your letter. I do not think you are correctly informed. There is no need for a further "acting edition" of <u>Godot</u>. Faber did <u>not</u> publish the complete text (my grievance). Their edition respects all the LC's cuts. Their text is the text used in the Criterion production and their edition is the acting edition. It could be played by a Sunday School without risk of prosecution. Their publisher's note at my request (slip on page five of book) states this quite clearly.[1]

   All the best.

   Yours ever

   s/ Samuel Beckett

TLS; 1 leaf, 1 side; IMEC, Beckett, Boîte 5, S. Beckett Correspondance 1962–1968, Curtis Brown 1957 [*for* 1952–1957].

1 On 2 August, Kitty Black wrote to SB that Samuel French was prepared to publish an acting edition "which is essential if the amateurs are to do the play since Faber published the complete text without the Lord Chamberlain's cuts. Nobody therefore can perform the Faber edition without running the risk of prosecution!" (IMEC, Beckett, Boîte 5, S. Beckett, Correspondance 1962–1968, Curtis Brown 1957 [*for* 1952–1957]).

BARNEY ROSSET, GROVE PRESS
NEW YORK

Aug 30th [1956]   Paris or rather Ussy

Dear Barney

 Here goes though still deep in drain to try and reply coherently to your last.

Suggestions for readings:

More Pricks	Dante & the L. or better still nothing.
Proust	Pages 1–7 i.e. to first pause and Leopardi again.
Murphy	Amor Intellectualis
Echo's Bones	Exeo in a Spasm
Molloy	End of Part 1
Malone	Beginning
L'Inno	If Blin does not record then extract from unpublished translation which I am sending under separate cover together with 3 poems in French for Epstein and "From an Abandoned Work."
Godot	If Martin does not record then perhaps nothing.
Watt	Beginning of Part III
Textes pour R	If I do not record, then nothing.

It goes without saying that these are mere suggestions and that you are perfectly free to discard them.[1]

Do not count too much on our recordings here. Blin is still away, Martin is going to Berlin and I am at Ussy feeling lousy and dreading the thought of the whole thing.

TCD equals Trinity College, Dublin. They made a balls of the text.[2]

Biographical notes OK.[3]

Thanks for accounts. I suppose it has all gone to Lindon who has been away all August. None has come to me directly.

Many thanks for brochure. You certainly do me proud.[4]

I saw Lieberson of Columbia Rdgs who gave me the Godot record. I find it quite good, as a record, expecially Act 1 where Pozzo is remarkable. The sound element (finger on cords of grand piano blown up through micro) is hardly disturbing, except perhaps at end of 1st act. Some changes and interpolations annoyed me mildly especially at beginning of Act II. I thought Vladimir very wooden and did not at all agree with Epstein's remarkable technical performance in the tirade. The boy I thought very good.[5] I spent a rather dismal evening with Myerberg (nice man) and his lady friend. I mentioned to him that I thought Godot by an all negro cast would be interesting. He said he had had the same idea but was nervous about telling me, fearing I wd not like it. The October reprise, he said, wd be with Golden cast if Lahr was available. I had a letter from him some days ago in which he says that Lahr is not available, having signed on for a musical, and that he is getting going with preparations for performance with all negro cast. This pleases me, rightly or wrongly, much.[6]

Fin de Partie or whatever it is called has been roneotyped and submitted to Hébertot. We do not think he will take it. If he does it will not be played before end of year, as Hébertot has already announced an Italian play to follow Godot which is to run to the end of September at least. If Hébertot does not accept there is talk of a new theatre of 500 seats at the Alliance Française, Bd Raspail. The mime with its stage requirements rather complicates things. Shall let you know as soon as I do myself, i.e. in course of next month I hope. We were well out of Marseille by all accounts.[7] Myerberg, to whom I talked about Fin de Partie, is also asking for MS. I do not intend to send it at the moment. Enquiries also from Germany from the Berlin Schillertheater and Stroux (Gründgens's successor at Düsseldorf, who made such a mess of Godot at the Berlin Festival 3 or 2 years ago).[8]

Distressed to feel you unsettled and unhappy. The trouble with palliatives is they become the whole of life. But I can suggest nothing better. At least you have a Peter Michael and a tennis-court.[9]

Haven't made much progress with 3rd programme script. Not interested.

Lieberson, thanks to you, also brought me Anna Livia record which I am very glad to have. I have an appointment with him on his way back through Paris next Monday, but am so loath to return to Paris at the moment that shall probably cancel it.[10]

All the best, dear Barney, from us both, and happier days.

s/ Sam

A brilliant if one-sided thesis on me in German from NIKLAUS GESSNER, Zurich University, Switzerland. "Die Unzulänglichkeit der

Sprache". Am sure he'd send it to you gladly if you're interested. Write to him direct.[11]

TLS; 2 leaves, 2 sides; NSyU.

1 The program of the readings at the Poetry Center on 23 October: 1 August 1956, n. 2.
"Dante and the Lobster," *More Pricks Than Kicks*, 9–22.
Proust, 1–7.
"Exeo in a Spasm" is the first line of "Enueg I," *Echo's Bones and Other Precipitates* [12–15].
The three French poems have not been identified.
The final script for the reading has not been found.

2 SB refers to publication of "From an Abandoned Work" (see 26 May 1956, n. 6).

3 Rosset's biographical notes have not been found.

4 The particular Grove Press brochure of recent publications has not been identified.

5 Goddard Lieberson* (1911–1977), President of Columbia Records (1956–1966, 1973–1975), met SB on 11 August in Paris (SB to Lieberson, 8 August 1956, CtY, Gilmore, MSS 69). He brought with him the "tests of the records" of *Waiting for Godot* made with the cast of the Broadway production, with Kurt Kazar (1913–1979) as Pozzo, E. G. Marshall as Vladimir, Alvin Epstein as Lucky, and Luchino Solito de Solis (b. 1944) as the boy (Columbia O2L-238 [1956]; re-released as Caedmon TRS 352 [1971]; Lieberson to SB, 2 August 1956, CtY, Gilmore, MSS 69).
Lieberson wrote about the sounds added to the recording:

> It seemed to me that in recording *Waiting for Godot*, another dimension was occasionally called for to sustain moods or atmosphere which had been created on the stage through visual means … I have used invented sounds of a more or less abstract nature created by myself with the electronic assistance of our valued engineer, Mr. Fred Plaut. (Jacket copy, Columbia O2L-238.)

6 Michael Myerberg's friend has not been identified. Myerberg's plan for an October reprise of *Waiting for Godot* with the original Broadway cast had to be changed when Bert Lahr signed a two-year contract to play in a musical version of *Grand Hotel* (Sam Zolotow, "Bert Lahr Signed for 'Grand Hotel,'" *The New York Times* 10 August 1956: 10).

7 Jacques Hébertot (né André Daviel, 1886–1970) directed the theatre bearing his name; he was considering SB's new play following the successful reprise there of *En attendant Godot*. *Acte sans paroles* required sufficient vertical height in the flies for a weight-bearing rope to be suspended and withdrawn.
L'abisso (1948) by Silvio Giovaninetti (1901–1962), in a translation by Giuseppe Attinelli, *Au-delà du mur*, was performed at the Théâtre Hébertot from 27 September to 22 October 1956.

8 In a letter of 16 August, Elmar Tophoven, as requested by SB, informed Jérôme Lindon that Albert Bessler of the Schillertheater in Berlin and Karl Heinz Stroux, Director of the Düsseldorfer Schauspielhaus, were interested in producing *Fin de partie* (Editions de Minuit). Stroux directed *Warten auf Godot* at the Schlossparktheater in Berlin in 1953; he succeeded Gustav Gründgens as director of the Düsseldorfer Schauspielhaus in 1955.

9 Peter Michael, Barney Rosset's son. There was a tennis court on Rosset's property in the Hamptons.

10 The recording of Anna Livia Plurabelle that Lieberson brought to SB was the pressing made in 1951 (from the recording that Joyce made at the Orthological Institute in Cambridge, UK, in 1929); it included presentations from the 1951 meeting of the James Joyce Society held at Gotham Bookmart in New York (*Meeting of James Joyce Society*, Folkways Records [FP/ 93/4, 1955]; Damien Keane, 12 April 2010).
SB wrote to Lieberson on 31 August that he would not be able "to keep our appointment" (CtY, Gilmore, MSS 69).

11 Niklaus Gessner's thesis was published as *Die Unzulänglichkeit der Sprache: eine Untersuchung über Formzerfall und Beziehungslosigkeit bei Samuel Beckett* (Zurich: Juris Verlag, 1957). Rosset requested a copy, which Gessner sent on 17 September (NSyU).
The PS is handwritten.

AVIGDOR ARIKHA
PARIS

4.9.56   Ussy

Cher AA[1]

Merci de votre lettre.[2] Je suis très touché que la petite pièce vous accompagne ainsi. Le problème du titre me tracasse toujours. J'ai l'impression qu'il faut éviter le mot "Fin".[3]

Lindon a été absent de Paris tout le mois dernier et je n'ai pas pu lui reparler de votre projet. Mais je lui en avais déjà parlé. Il est maintenant rentré et vous pourriez aller le voir de ma part. Téléphonez-lui aux Editions de Minuit, BAB 34.97.[4]

Je suis sérieusement fatigué et voudrais rester à la campagne. Mais cela ne sera pas possible et je pense être à Paris vers la fin de la semaine prochaine. Je vous ferai signe. J'aimerais beaucoup voir votre travail.

Bien amicalement à vous.

s/

Sam Beckett

Je n'ai pas votre numéro de téléphone[.]

Merci de vos cartes du Nord.[5]

TLS; 1 leaf, 1 side; Arikha. Previous publication, facsimile and transcription, Atik, *How It Was*, 8–9.

4.9.56   Ussy

Dear AA[1]

Thank you for your letter.[2] I am greatly touched that the little play stays with you like that. The problem of the title is still giving me trouble. I have the impression that I must avoid the word "End".[3]

Lindon has been away from Paris all last month, and I haven't been able to say anything more to him about your project. But I had already spoken of it. He is back now, and you could go and see him, mentioning me. Phone him at the Editions de Minuit, BAB 34.97.[4]

I am really very tired and would like to stay on in the country. But it won't be possible, and I think I'll be in Paris towards the end of next week. I'll get in touch. I would very much like to see your work.

All the best

s/

Sam Beckett

I do not have your telephone number.

Thank you for your cards from the North.[5]

---

1 SB had made the acquaintance of the painter Avigdor Arikha* (1929–2010) on 25 June at a dinner at the home of Alain Bosquet, days after attending a performance of *En attendant Godot* at the Théâtre Hébertot; after the play Arikha had spoken enthusiastically about what he had seen to the man seated next to him in the café, only later to discover that his interlocutor was the play's author. To Alain Bosquet, in a letter of 2 July, SB wrote that he was "très heureux de rencontrer Avigdor Arikha que j'ai trouvé fort sympathique" (happy to have met Avigdor Arikha, whom I greatly took to) (the letter was sold by G. Morssen, Paris; current owner unknown).

2 Arikha's letter to SB has not been found.

3 SB showed Arikha the manuscript of what was to be become *Fin de partie* when Arikha visited him in Ussy.

4 Earlier in the year, Arikha had been taken on by his first dealer, the Francis Matthiesen Gallery in London. Arikha proposed to Matthiesen to make a book of text and etchings using SB's *Textes pour rien*, and SB spoke to Lindon about this. The project

came to nothing, owing, according to Arikha, mainly to his own procrastination (10 October 2009).

5   PS is handwritten.

GODDARD LIEBERSON
NEW YORK

7-9-56   Ussy-sur-Marne

Dear Mr Lieberson

Many thanks for your letter. I am very pleased and flattered to hear of Stravinsky's interest in my play. I shall not fail to get in touch with him on his way through Paris in November.[1]

I look forward to having the definitive Godot recording. I should not think there will be any difficulty with the customs.[2]

It will not be long, I hope, before you are in Paris again. In the meantime, do not hesitate to call on me if I can be of any service to you here.

With my very kind regards to Mrs Lieberson and thanking you again for your kindness, I am[3]

Yours sincerely
Sam. Beckett
6 Rue des Favorites
PARIS 15me

ALS; 1 leaf, 2 sides; CtY, Gilmore, MSS 69.

1   Lieberson's letter to SB has not been found. Robert Craft, Stravinsky's personal assistant and assistant conductor, said that he had given Stravinsky SB's essay on Joyce in 1950, and that the composer had read *En attendant Godot* in French well before he saw the play in New York in the 1957 revival (Robert Craft, 24 November 1997).

On 13 September, Lieberson wrote to Stravinsky, quoting from SB's letter and saying: "I have told him, as you instructed me, that you would be staying at the Plaza Athénée [. . .] If by any chance, you change your plans, please let me know, so that I can write to him" (Paul Sacher Stiftung, Stravinsky).

2   The "definitive" recording of *Waiting for Godot*: 30 August [1956], n. 5.

3   Brigitta Lieberson (née Hartwig, 1917–2003), a ballerina and musical theatre dancer who used the stage name Vera Zorina.

651

AVIGDOR ARIKHA

PARIS

mercredi [19 September 1956]

Cher Arikha

Je suis à Paris jusqu'à samedi. Je serai à la Brasserie Zeyer, près de chez vous, après-demain Vendredi à 4 heures (quatre).[1] J'espère que vous pourrez m'y rejoindre et ensuite me montrer votre travail. Inutile de confirmer si cela vous convient.

Amitiés

Sam Beckett

ALS, pneu; 1 leaf, 2 sides; *to* Monsieur Avigdor Arikha, 10 Villa d'Alésia, PARIS 14°; *pm* 19-9-56, Paris; Arikha. *Dating*: from pm.

Wednesday [19 September 1956]

Dear Arikha

I am in Paris until Saturday. I shall be in the Brasserie Zeyer, near where you live, on Friday, the day after tomorrow at 4 (four).[1] I hope you will be able to join me and then show me your work. No need to confirm if that suits you.

All good wishes

Sam Beckett

1 The Brasserie Zeyer is situated at 234 Avenue du Maine, Paris 14. It was upon leaving this establishment that SB was stabbed on 6 January 1938 (see 12 January 1938 to Thomas McGreevy).

ROBERT PINGET

PARIS

23-9-56   Ussy

Cher ami –

Nous venons seulement de recevoir votre lettre, restée ici toute la semaine en souffrance. Je ne savais donc pas, lors de notre soirée ensemble, que vous aviez lu HAAM et vous avez dû trouver étrange que je ne vous en aie pas parlé. Je suis très content, mais vraiment, que cela vous ait plu et – surtout – fait rire.[1] Lui rallonger le vieux balai, à ce cher balayeur, c'est bien ma dernière chance.

> Bien amicalement de nous deux
> Sam Beckett

APCS; 1 leaf, 1 side; "Ussy-sur-Marne, Vue générale"; *env to* Monsieur Robert Pinget, 4 Rue de l'Université, PARIS 7me; *pm* 24-9-56, La Ferté-sous-Jouarre; Burns Library, Pinget-Beckett Letters.

23-9-56   Ussy
Dear Robert Pinget,

We have just received your letter, which has been waiting for us here for a week, uncollected. So I didn't know, when we had our evening together, that you had read HAAM, and you must have found it odd that I didn't talk about it. I'm very pleased, really very pleased that it gave you pleasure and – most of all – made you laugh.[1] Lengthening my old road-sweeper's broom: that's about my last chance.

> Best wishes from us both
> Sam Beckett

1 "HAAM" was SB's current title for the play which was finally called *Fin de partie*. SB and Pinget may have met on Sunday 26 August or during the second week in September.

BARNEY ROSSET, GROVE PRESS
NEW YORK

23.9.56   6 Favorites, Paris
Dear Barney

Thanks for your letters of 11th and 17th inst.

I would not consent to a film being made of Godot. For television rights in USA I should have thought it was you or Myerberg. If in doubt write to Lindon. He has all the contracts and something resembling a head on his shoulders, which has long ceased to be my case.

Thanks for cuttings. Gratified by the kind words.[1]

Pleased that you should contemplate an edition of Murphy. I consider that Routledge has no further rights whatsoever. I have probably lost original contract with them. I am in the country, but shall look for it when I get back, and also consult the Bordas contract, now transferred to Eds de Minuit. But whatever Routledge's rights may have been 20 years ago they have certainly lapsed by now, after the long silence and failure to reedit.[2]

I shall finish the piece for the BBC this week. You will in due course receive a copy. <u>From an A.W.</u> is original English (most!).[3] The new play, which in the end I shall probably just feebly label <u>HAAM</u>, seems likely to be accepted by Hébertot, together with the mime. Godot finishes to-day. Next week an Italian play at the Hébertot which does not seem likely to run for long. Then, i.e. early November probably, mime and Haam, we hope. Shall let you know as soon as things are definite and rehearsal in progress. Martin certain for Clov and Blin probable for Haam. French edition simultaneous with production.[4]

By all means give them a few yelps from Whoroscope if you think it a good thing.[5]

Amitiés

s/ Sam

Production rights in Australia still available as far as I know. Curtis Brown would be the man for that.

TLS; 1 leaf, 1 side; NSyU.

1 Rosset may have sent the following to SB: Arthur Gelb, "'Godot' to Return with Negro Cast," *The New York Times* 13 September 1956: 40; "Books Today," *The New York Times* 15 September 1956: 28; William Barret, "Real Love Abides," *The New York Times* 16 September 1956: BR 3.

2 SB employs the Gallicism for republish or reissue ("rééditer").

3 *All That Fall*. "From an Abandoned Work."

4 Jean Martin as Clov; Roger Blin as Hamm. The Italian play: 30 August [1956], n. 7.

5 Rosset had asked if SB wanted *Whoroscope* included in the readings planned for the Poetry Center at the 92nd Street YM-YWHA in New York.

GODDARD LIEBERSON
NEW YORK

September 23rd 1956   6 Rue des Favorites
                                   Paris 15me

Dear Mr Lieberson

Many thanks for your letter and enclosure.[1] It is good of you to offer to send me cuttings as they appear. But you must not go to this trouble, as the Grove Press keeps me well supplied.

You are perfectly at liberty to make any statement you wish about our meeting in Paris. It is extremely delicate on your part to feel I might have some objection to this, but I have absolutely none. What I don't feel equal to is the interview – and "explaining" my work.

You may also quote me as saying that I appreciate your reasons for introducing a musical element into your Godot recording and consider you have done it with success and discretion.[2]

Thank you for writing to Stravinsky. The simplest thing would be for him to let me know, a little in advance, when and where it would be convenient for him to see me. He is very welcome to my address.[3]

At the moment I feel that even the negro production of Godot, the thought of which pleases me immensely, will not key me up to New York. But this is not to be relied on, as I do on impulse the little I succeed in doing.

With kind regards to Mrs Lieberson I am

Yours sincerely

s/

Samuel Beckett

TLS; 1 leaf, 1 side; CtY, Gilmore, MSS 69.

1   Lieberson wrote to SB on 17 September (CtY, Gilmore, MSS 69). It is not known what Lieberson enclosed, possibly one of those reviews mentioned in 23 September 1956 to Barney Rosset, n. 1.

2   Lieberson wrote to SB: "I have also been asked what you thought of the music that was added to GODOT which, as you know, was an attempt at and [sic] abstract solution to the problem rather than a literal one" (17 September 1956, CtY, Gilmore, MSS 69).

3   Lieberson's letter to Stravinsky: 7 September 1956, n. 1.

JOHN MORRIS, BBC
LONDON

September 27th 1956   6 Rue des Favorites
                                       Paris 15me

Dear Mr Morris

Herewith the script we spoke of in Paris.[1]

It calls for a rather special quality of bruitage, perhaps not quite clear from the text.[2]

I can let you have a note on this if you are interested in the script for the Third Programme.[3]

With best wishes,

Yours sincerely

s/

Samuel Beckett

TLS; 1 leaf, 1 side; BBC WAC, RCONT I / Samuel Beckett / Scriptwriter / File I (1953–1962); A draft, UoR, BIF, MS 1227/7/7/1, 3 recto.

1 Charles John Morris* (1895–1980), Controller of the BBC's Third Programme, met SB in Paris on 18 July (John Morris to SB, 11 July 1956, BBC WAC, RCONT I / Samuel Beckett / Scriptwriter / File I [1953–1962]). SB sent the script of *All That Fall* with the present letter.

2 "Bruitage" (sound effects). Among those in *All That Fall* are animal noises, bird song, footsteps, musical passages, a motorcar, a train, and rain.

3 Morris was enthusiastic about the radio play but asked SB for a note on his ideas for the sound effects in his reply of 5 October. SB, on 18 October, continued to express concern:

> I find it difficult to put down my thoughts about the bruitage. And I am not sure that what I want to say is worth saying. I feel it might be no more than an amateur's statement of what is common radio practice. For the moment I think I had better hold my peace. By far the best would be for us to meet, or for me to meet the bruiteur, before production, and talk it over. (BBC WAC, RCONT I / Samuel Beckett / Scriptwriter / File I [1953–1962].)

Morris wrote to SB the next day that the producer of *All That Fall*, Donald McWhinnie* (1920–1987), would be in Paris on 22 October to meet SB and discuss the radio play (BBC WAC, RCONT I / Samuel Beckett / Scriptwriter / File I [1953–1962]).

PAMELA MITCHELL
NEW YORK

September 28th 1956   6 rue des Favorites
                                                             Paris 15°

Pam –

It is good to have news of you after so long. Your job doesn't sound very exciting. How are things with Harold these days? No chance of your returning?[1] But I suppose you are more interested in my news than in comments on yours. Nothing much to tell, drooling along in the same old way, between Paris & Ussy, where I am at the moment and hope to be more and more, though it is often deadly, especially between spasms of writing. There is plenty to be done out of doors, but I do it badly and don't always feel up to it. The new play is now as final as possible before rehearsal. There were 3 versions in 2 acts before it finally boiled down to one longish act, well over an hour playing time in any case. The A & B you know are now HAAM & CLOV and are assisted by a moribund Darby & Joan amputated at the groin and living in garbage-cans. That's the lot. Not sure yet of the title – probably just <u>HAAM</u> – a label, like the novels.[2] I don't know what to think of it, i.e. I have thought and go on thinking everything of it, from the best to the worst. Don't know really till I start hearing it and looking at it – not of course even then. I don't know yet where or when it will be played, very possibly at the Hébertot Theatre up in Montmartre on the B^{d} des Batignolles, and opening before Xmas, but nothing signed so far. It was there <u>Godot</u> has played all summer, closing last Sunday. <u>HAAM</u> would be supported by the mime I think you know about – a 20 minute affair with one dancer and objects coming down from the skies (flies) and music by my young cousin John Beckett. I hope all will be definite and under way in the course of next month. I don't think of translating the play at the moment, in fact I feel it is not for export at all. Roger Blin will be the metteur en scène & possibly play Haam. Jean Martin (Lucky) is certain for Clov. I have also just finished a longish radio script for the BBC 3rd

programme, at their invitation, but am not at all sure they will accept it, written directly in English. Nothing left now but to resume losing battle with <u>Innommable</u> translation.[3] Rosset was over and I saw a lot of him. Also Myerberg, with whom I spent an evening, and Lieberson president of Columbia records who brought me his recording of the Broadway <u>Godot</u> which I liked well enough. I am very pleased at thought of Negro production by Myerberg in November, but am afraid it will not screw me up and over the pond. I feel I shall never move out of the Ile de France again. But whatever I do I do on impulse and suddenly, so what I feel now does not mean very much. I don't want you to forget me, but I think it would be the best thing for you. I'm over, as sure as if they were on their way to measure me for the box. I wish you were happy, you have all the equipment for happiness – it seems to me. All the mad things I wish – and the sad things I know.

Cheerful correspondent I am.

Much love

Sam

ALS; 2 leaves, 2 sides; *env to* Pamela Mitchell, 229 E. 48th Street, New York 17, N.Y., U.S.A.; *pm* 28-9-56, La Ferté-sous-Jouarre; UoR, BIF, MS 5060.

1   Mitchell currently worked in fundraising for the Hospital of Special Surgery, Columbia University; she had been working for theatrical producer Harold L. Oram when she first met SB.

2   Referring to what he will eventually entitle *Fin de partie*, SB mentions the characters Nell and Nagg for the first time. Darby and Joan typified an old and happily married couple.

3   Of translating *L'Innommable*, SB says: "Un supplice – et qui ne peut rien donner" (Torture – and nothing can come of it) (SB to Jacoba van Velde, 27 September 1956, BNF 19794/42).

ALAN SCHNEIDER

NEW YORK

October 15th 1956   6 Rue des Favorites

Paris 15°

Dear Alan

Many thanks for your card from the ruins of the Moira where as a Trinity scholard I ate large steaks copiously hawked upon by the consumptive grillman, and for your letter with photos and cutting. Miami looks good to me, Ewell in particular. Delighted that Bountiful went so well at the Olympia. I wonder did you put your nose into the Dolphin – gone to hell too I'm told.[1]

I don't in my ignorance agree with the round and feel Godot needs a very closed box. But I'd give it to you with joy if I were free to do so. So all you want – all! – is the OK from MM and Rosset.[2]

I liked Myerberg. He has great charm. We had a rather dismal evening together in that filthy famous joint La Pérouse.[3] I'm very pleased at the thought of the all black production and hope it comes off. I also met Lieberson of Columbia Records complete with Godot recording. Another very pleasant man.

Have begun work on the new play with Blin and Martin (Lucky)[.] A very long one act, over an hour and a half I shd think. We hope to have the Hébertot but it is not yet quite definite. With the desert mime to follow as last straw.[4] I feel at the moment strongly disinclined to translate the play. I am panting to see the realisation and know if I am on some kind of road, and can stumble on, or in a swamp.

Best of luck with Swollen Feet and the Arena.[5] Come back both of you to Paris soon.[6]

Yours ever

s/ Sam

TLS; 1 leaf, 1 side; Burns Library, Schneider-Beckett Collection. Previous publication, Beckett and Schneider, *No Author Better Served*, 11–12.

1 Schneider had been in Dublin for performances of *The Trip to Bountiful* at the Olympia Theatre, from 20 to 25 August. He wrote of the reception to the play in a letter to Thornton Wilder on 16 September: "They said we compared favorably in play and production to the great days of the Abbey" (CtY, Beinecke, YCAL MSS 108, series I/54/1515/Schneider).

Schneider stayed at the Moira Hotel and Restaurant, 15 Trinity Street (Schneider, *Entrances*, 239). Schneider's letter to SB with photos and cutting has not been found, but these seem to have included photos of the Miami production of *Waiting for Godot*, in which Tom Ewell played Vladimir.

The Dolphin Hotel and Restaurant, Essex Street.

2   Schneider wrote to Thornton Wilder about his growing interest in the possibilities of "the open stage" (the focus of his Guggenheim Fellowship in Europe during the summer of 1956):

> When I see the Brecht company or the Piccolo Teatro of Milan [...] they ignore the proscenium tho they don't destroy it. They "open" it up in another way, physically and psychologically; and a special kind of theatricality [...] comes flying out to the audience [...] I have been rather overwhelmed by the work of the Berliner Ensemble. (16 September 1956, CtY, Beinecke, YCAL MSS 108, Series I/50/Schneider; Schneider, *Entrances*, 238.)

Schneider's forthcoming engagement with the Arena Stage (see n. 5, below) offered an opportunity to direct "in the round" (Schneider, *Entrances*, 239).

Referring to Michael Myerberg and Barney Rosset, SB adds a handwritten exclamation mark to "All!"

3   Opened in 1776, the restaurant Lapérouse is located at 51 Quai des Grands Augustins, Paris 6.

4   The provisional title for *Acte sans paroles* had been *Soif* (Cohn, *A Beckett Canon*, 218).

5   Schneider was to direct Walter Kerr's adaptation of *Oedipus the King* for the television program *Omnibus* in December (Schneider, *Entrances*, 242). Schneider was also directing Arthur Miller's *A View from the Bridge* that opened at the Arena Stage in Washington, DC, on 7 November.

6   SB had met Alan Schneider's wife Jean in Paris when they had dinner on 23 July.

NANCY CUNARD

<u>17.10.56</u>   <u>Paris</u>

Bien chère Nancy

The Whoros go back to you to-day, duly signed.[1]

Glad you enjoyed your trip, and that you have a liking for Ralph. I am ordering your G.M.[2] We are having trouble finding a theatre here for the new play.[3] You have to go waving million franc notes which we wouldn't even if we could. However we'll find a barn somewhere some day.

I'd like to see your notes on Joyce.[4]

There's an error in the poem, but I didn't like to correct it. <u>Who's</u>? That? Hals? Should be <u>Who's that</u>? Hals?[5]

Much love
     Samuel

ALS; 1 leaf, 1 side; TxU, Cunard.

1   SB's poem *Whoroscope* was published by Cunard's Hours Press in 1930.

2   Through SB, Cunard had met Ralph Cusack (see 6 June 1956, n. 2). Cunard, *GM: Memories of George Moore.*

3   The Théâtre Hébertot had declined *Fin de partie* and *Acte sans paroles.*

4   Cunard's notes on Joyce may have related to her attempt to write an autobiography in 1956; some of her memories of Joyce from 1930–1931 are recorded in Anne Chisholm's biography (*Nancy Cunard*, 306–307; 148).

5   SB refers to line 27 of *Whoroscope*. This correction is indicated in a copy of the poem annotated by SB and owned by Georges Belmont.

A. J. AND ETHNA LEVENTHAL
DUBLIN

18-10-56   Paris/Ussy
Bien chers Con & Ethna
     Glad to have news of your safe arrival and hope to hear soon you have hung the pot-hanger with all due solemnity and jollity.[1]
     I had a note some time ago from MacDonagh asking me to meet him for lunch between 11:45 and 12:15 at the Falstaff. As I was in the country and could not get up to town in time, nor let him know, I rang up the Falstaff on the morning in question a little before 12. No one in the bar. Five minutes later. Still no one. Five minutes later. Still no one. I described our man and left a message for him to ring me up at Ussy. No ring. From which I suppose I am to conclude that either (1) He turned up but did not get my message, or (2) He turned up and got my message but preferred not to ring, or (3) He did not turn up at all. I am sorry for this imbroglio and not to have seen him again. Will you explain if you see him and lui faire mes amitiés.[2]
     We have failed to get the Hébertot and now trying elsewhere. The possibilities the Oeuvre, Petit Marigny and Studio des Chs. Elysées.[3] I

661

have started work on the play with Blin and Martin. Uphill work. I have added two passages = approx. 10 minutes, one for the old couple in the bins, the other for Hamm & Clov just before the end.[4] I hear such interesting accounts of the New Watergate Theatre Club at the Comedy in Panton St. that I'm tempted to try them with a translation at an early date.[5]

I had a very pleasant lunch, Sancerre et Fleurie aidant, chez Marius with H.O.'s nephew Eric Keown and his cartoonist Roland [for Ronald] Searle. Should not have thought it was possible to work for Punch and be so entertaining.[6]

A note from Sean whom I suppose you have seen.[7]

The Radio Script has been accepted by the 3rd who ask for more. Perhaps some form of collaboration with John would be possible there.[8]

Not knowing what wedding present to give you I enclose a cheque. Please forgive indelicacy of this proceeding. It is the most sensible way of doing it. With it again all my most affectionate voeux de bonheur.

With the pounds that remain after Power donation would you send me Nancy Cunard's book on George Moore (forget what publisher) and give the change (if any) to Power.[9]

Love to you both and write soon.

Sam

ALS; 1 leaf, 2 sides; TxU, Leventhal collection.

1 Ethna MacCarthy and A. J. Leventhal had married on 25 August and returned home. SB borrows and anglicizes what the French would have said for "arranged a house-warming" (pendu la crémaillère).

2 Donagh MacDonagh (1912–1968), author of three volumes of poetry, the play *Happy as Larry* (1946), and co-editor, with Lennox Robinson (1886–1958; Profile, I), of *The Oxford Book of Irish Verse: XVIIth Century – XXth Century* (1958).
The Falstaff, a bar at 42 Rue du Montparnasse, Paris 14. "Lui faire mes amitiés" (give him my regards).

3 The Théâtre de l'Œuvre, 55 Rue de Clichy, Paris 9. The Théâtre du Petit Marigny, a studio space in the Théâtre Marigny, Paris 8 (from 1953 to 1956, contracted to the Compagnie Renaud-Barrault) (Latour and Claval, eds., *Les Théâtres de Paris*, 170). The Studio des Champs-Elysées, 15 Avenue Montaigne, Paris 8.

4   The passages added to *Fin de partie* for Nell and Nagg and at the end for Hamm and Clov are included in the manuscript notebook "Eté 56" (UoR, BIF, MS 1227/7/7/1; Mary Bryden, Julian Garforth, and Peter Mills, eds., *Beckett at Reading: Catalogue of the Beckett Manuscript Collection at The University of Reading* [Reading: Whiteknights Press and the Beckett International Foundation, 1998] 35–36).

This is the first spelling as "Hamm" in SB's letters; the previous spelling, indeed the provisional title of the play, was "Haam." The change in this name and the designation of the other characters as Clov, Nell, Nagg, first appear in what Admussen describes as the draft G typescript of *Fin de partie* (OSU, Spec. rare, MS Eng 29, undated; Admussen, *The Samuel Beckett Manuscripts*, 52).

5   The New Watergate Theatre, which occupied the former Comedy Theatre, Panton Street in London's West End, was unusual because it was an 850-seat house exempt from rulings by the Lord Chamberlain's Office. Donald Albery was one of its directors. (British Library Theatre Archive Project, Kate Harris interview of Anthony Field, 14 March 2007; www.bl.uk/projects/theatrearchive/field.html, accessed on 21 November 2008.)

6   "Fleurie" is a cru of Beaujolais.

Eric Keown (1904–1963), Dramatic Critic of *Punch*, and Ronald Searle (b. 1920), cartoonist for *Punch*, had lunch with SB at the restaurant Chez Marius, where SB occasionally took Keown's uncle, Trinity College Dublin Professor H. O. White. An image of SB drawn by Ronald Searle at this lunch is reproduced on the cover of the *McMaster University Library Research News* (2.4 [October 1973]) and in Russell Davies, *Ronald Searle: A Biography* (London: Sinclair-Stevenson, 1990) 121; the original is in the McMaster University Library Samuel Beckett collection.

7   Seán O'Sullivan's note to SB has not been found.

8   John Beckett.

9   "Voeux de bonheur" (Wishes for your happiness).

The "Power donation": 6 August 1953 mentions one such remembrance. SB asks for Nancy Cunard's *GM: Memories of George Moore*.

THOMAS MACGREEVY
DUBLIN

oct 18th 1956   Ussy

Bien cher Tom

It was good of you to write so quickly and with such affection. I feel more and more the sullen silent sot, always brooding and never thinking, of the somebody's Revenge by Marston is it, and wonder how even old friends can put up with it.[1] It is not easy to get through the ages from self so estranged and one overdoes the lair. After you left I ran into Jean Martin off to Zurich to play with the Barrault company and then it was the sad familiar trek home by the Invalides and François Xavier and the hideous Rue Lecourbe.[2] We got here last night and shall stay a brief week. We have failed to get the Hébertot for the new show and now must tout round elsewhere – Studio des C.-E., Petit Marigny, Oeuvre, etc. Theatre directors expect you to arrive with your text under one arm and millions of franc notes under the other and this now seems to be an established practice. With Godot after all we had a state grant of 750.000, and now nothing but a gloomy graceless act, a complicated mime and nos beaux yeux. However my publisher's energy and faith will I have no doubt do the trick somewhere.[3] Arrived to-day a little new Erard to replace our old Frankfurt casserole and Suzanne is happy.[4] Everything is drenched and dripping and without definite work on the stocks there does not seem much point in this deep silence and emptiness. I should be getting on with my translation of the Innommable, but it requires much courage. Glad you had such an entertaining reception on your arrival and that you get such fun from the infant. Suzanne has her eyes out on stalks for amusing bootees. I hope to hear soon the move is safely over and good news of the catalogues. I forgot to ask after Wallace and Hickey, remember me kindly to them.[5] Love to Alan and Niall and JB, he is never far from me – a light.[6]

Love ever, dear Tom, from us both, and don't stay too long away.

s/ Sam

TLS; 1 leaf, 1 side; TCD, MS 10402/201.

1 Although SB refers to *Antonio's Revenge* (1600) by John Marston, the phrase "sullen silent sot" is from George Farquhar's *The Beaux' Stratagem* (see 13 October 1955, n. 1).

2 Jean Martin was performing in Georges Schehadé's play *Histoire de Vasco* that opened at the Théâtre Sarah Bernhardt in Paris on 1 October, and at the Schauspielhaus in Zurich on 15 October.

SB describes the walk from the Aérogare des Invalides to his apartment via the Saint-François-Xavier church.

3 The grant awarded to *En attendant Godot*: 4 August 1951, n. 7.

"Nos beaux yeux" (our sweet selves).

Jérôme Lindon wished to publish the play simultaneously with its production.

4 SB refers to an Erard piano that replaced a German one ("Frankfurt casserole") (interview with Edward Beckett).

5 Robert, the son of MacGreevy's niece Elizabeth and her husband Nicholas Ryan, was born in 1956.

Thomas MacGreevy moved from 24 Fitzwilliam Place to 94 St. Stephen's Green in early 1957.

In 1956, MacGreevy published *Catalogue of Pictures of the Italian Schools* (Dublin: Stationery Office, 1956), and in 1957 he published *Dutch Pictures: 17th Century* (Curaçao, 1957) (Leah Benson, Libraries and Archives, NGI, 22 April 2010).

Wallace was an employee of the National Gallery; he has not been further identified.

Tim Hickey, who worked at the National Gallery of Ireland, visited Paris in October 1952 with his son Vincent (d. 1981). At MacGreevy's request, SB showed them the city; as SB wrote to MacGreevy on 7 October 1952:

> I met them at the Aérogare Sunday and brought them to their hotel [. . .]. Sunday afternoon we took a long walk across the Luxembourg Gardens, down to Notre-Dame, through the Ile de la Cité, Louvre, Tuileries and Champs-Elysées. Hickey was bouleversé. Yesterday we had lunch together and went to the Louvre where we spent a couple of hours. They will go back alone to-morrow. We dined at the Coupole and went to the pictures. This morning they did a round Paris tour. I called for them at their hotel and we lunched again together. This afternoon and evening they are off on their own. They have got the hang of the place (especially Vincent) and can manage the tube on their own. They will probably do an excursion to Versailles with the same organization as their Paris tour this morning. I'll be seeing them every day and they have my address if they need me. I'm fond of Hickey and it doesn't seem any trouble giving them a hand. (TCD, MS 10402/185.)

"Bouleversé" (overwhelmed).

Tim Hickey wrote to MacGreevy: "Mr Beckett is an Angel. I shall never forget him. He brought us all over the Louvre, in fact he brought us all over the city. Not only is he teaching us its history he is also teaching us French [. . .] I will never, never, be able to repay him for what he is doing to make our stay here happy and interesting." (7 October [1952], TCD, MS 10402/184.)

6 Alan Thompson, Niall Montgomery, and Jack B. Yeats.

EDITH GREENBURG, INDIANA UNIVERSITY PRESS
BLOOMINGTON, INDIANA

October 20th 1956   6 Rue des Favorites
                                     Paris 15°

Dear Miss Greenburg

Thank you for your letter of October 11th.

I am overwhelmed with work and simply see no possibility of revising my translation of the Mexican Anthology.[1]

This translation was approved by UNESCO in the Spring of (I think) 1950. It was commended with particular warmth by Señor Baeza, under whom I worked.

Of course it is imperfect, like all translations. But it is the best I can do.[2]

With all due respect to your corrector, I am afraid I could not consent, under any circumstances, to the publication of a text signed by me, with the mention "revised by Mr Gerald Brenan".[3]

I suggest therefore:

1) That you publish with my signature the texts that you are prepared to accept without any correction whatever.

2) That you publish with your corrector's signature the texts corrected by him – and no matter how small the correction.

3) That I refund to UNESCO Publications, if they judge fit, a proportion of my emoluments corresponding to the texts now considered unsatisfactory, though approved at the time of their submission.[4]

If this revision had been asked of me six years ago, when the work was fresh in my mind and literary drudgery still my principal occupation, no difficulty would have arisen.

I should have written this letter to you two years ago and I apologize for not having done so. I still thought then that I would have the leisure one day, and the courage, to go back over this old labour. I hope you will understand my position and not think me unreasonable.

I shall post the MSS to you in a day or two, by registered air mail.

Yours sincerely

s/

Samuel Beckett

TLS; 1 leaf, 1 side; IUP; copy, InU, IUP MSS II, Box 12.

1   Edith Greenburg wrote to SB on 11 October to remind him that she had written him in 1954 to request revisions of his translation of the *Anthology of Mexican Poetry* (see SB to Edith Greenburg, 18 November 1954, and n. 1): "You wrote us at that time that your commitments would prevent you from doing any work on this manuscript before the autumn of 1955, and with this understanding we agreed that you would hold our only copy of the manuscript – a carbon copy – until you could get at it" (IUP; copy, InU, IUP MSS II, Box 12).

2   Ricardo Baeza directed the project for UNESCO (see 27 [February 1950], n. 5).

3 Gerald Brenan (né Edward Fitzgerald Brenan, 1894–1987), writer and Hispanist.

4 In the *Anthology of Mexican Poetry*, finally published by Indiana University Press in 1958, SB is named as translator; on the verso of the title page is his statement: "I should like to thank Mr. Gerald Brenan for kindly reading the entire manuscript and for making a number of useful suggestions." A corrected manuscript is held at the Humanities Research Center, University of Texas at Austin (Lake, ed., *No Symbols Where None Intended*, 110). See also UoR, BIF, MS 2926, for SB's notes for the translation.

STEFANI HUNZINGER, S. FISCHER VERLAG
FRANKFURT

le 20 octobre 1956   6 Rue des Favorites
                                                     Paris 15me
Cher Monsieur Hunzinger

Merci de votre lettre du 16 octobre.[1]

Il est exact que j'ai terminé une autre pièce, un seul acte assez long, durée une heure et demie au moins. Mais je ne puis en établir le texte définitif qu'après un certain nombre de répétitions. Celles-ci, je l'espère, vont commencer bientôt, et vous ne tarderez pas à recevoir le manuscrit.

A Paris la pièce sera suivie d'un petit "Acte sans paroles" pour un seul personnage, également de moi, avec musique de mon cousin John Beckett. Durée 20 minutes approx.

J'espère que les Editions de Minuit vous ont envoyé la photo que vous m'aviez demandée. Sinon dites-le[-]moi et je leur rafraîchirai la mémoire.

Croyez, cher Monsieur Hunzinger, à mes sentiments très cordiaux.

s/
Samuel Beckett

TLS; 1 leaf, 1 side; S. Fischer Verlag.

20th October 1956   6 Rue des Favorites
                                                     Paris 15

667

Dear Mr Hunzinger

Thank you for your letter of 16 October.[1]

It is indeed the case that I have finished another play, one single rather long act, lasting at least an hour and a half. But I cannot settle the final text until after a certain number of rehearsals. These will, I hope, start soon, and it will not be long before you have a manuscript.

In Paris the play will be followed by a little "Act Without Words" for one character, also by me, with music by my cousin John Beckett. Lasts 20 minutes approx.

I hope that the Editions de Minuit have sent you the photograph that you asked me for. If not, let me know and I shall jog their memory.

Yours sincerely

Samuel Beckett

1 Stefani Hunzinger* (née Cremer, 1913–2006) wrote to SB on 14 September that she had taken on Helmut Castagne's position at S. Fischer Verlag as of 1 September; she also requested a photograph of SB.

SB mistakes Ms. Hunzinger's gender in the present letter and in the letter he had written on 20 September 1956 to Jérôme Lindon to request that a photo be sent to "le nouveau de chez Fischer" (the new boy at Fischer) (IMEC, Beckett, Boîte 1, S. Beckett, Correspondance – Divers 1950–1956).

MARY HUTCHINSON

LONDON

7-11-56 [*for* 6 November 1956]   Paris

Dear Mary

Do forgive me for not having written long ago to thank you for your letter and notes.[1] There is not much to be said for me as a friend and as a correspondent even less.

I read your notes with great interest and am very touched by the strange effect my work has upon you. I feel more and more something that is almost if not quite loathing for almost everything I have written and simply cannot bear to go back over it and into it. If there is a queer real there somewhere it is the Abderite's mentioned in Murphy, complicated by – ibidem – the Geulincx "Ubi nihil vales etc". I suppose these are its foci and where a commentary might take its rise. But I really do not know myself – and don't want to know – par quel bout le prendre, and can't help anyone.[2]

I have been reading Nancy's "G.M." and found references to "Hutchy" & yourself.[3]

Fin de Partie and Acte sans Paroles face the catcalls at the Théâtre de l'Oeuvre probably next January. I have written a radio script for the 3$^{\underline{rd}}$ to be broadcast probably next January also.

I have not seen Georges and he has not sent me his book. Tant pis, I'll have to buy it.[4]

Hope this reaches you before the hydrogen or uranium or whatever it is gets rid of us.

   Yours ever
   Sam

ALS; 1 leaf, 1 side; *env to* M$^{\underline{rs}}$ Hutchinson, 21 Hyde Park Square, London W.2, Angleterre; *pm* 6-11-56, Paris; TxU, Hutchinson collection.

1 Mary Hutchinson's letter to SB has not been found.

2 SB canceled "everything" and wrote "almost everything."

Mary Hutchinson discussed *Molloy* in her letter to the editor of the *New Statesman and Nation*, and she is unabashed in her admiration of SB: "It is by the control and use of these variations with the whole masterly structure that Samuel Beckett proves himself to be, to my mind, an artist of unique quality and power" ("Samuel Beckett," *New Statesman and Nation* 51 [21 January 1956] 74).

Although there are notes by Hutchinson on SB's work, these are from a later period (TxU, Hutchinson collection). SB refers to "the positive peace that comes when the somethings give way, or perhaps simply add up, to the Nothing, than which in the guffaw of the Abderite naught is more real" (*Murphy* [Grove Press] 246). Geulincx, "Ubi nihil vales": Saturday [on or after 30 April, before 26 May 1949], n. 5.

"Par quel bout le prendre" (where to start).

3 Nancy Cunard describes George Moore's friendship with Mary and her husband St John Hutchinson (1884–1942) (*GM: Memories of George Moore*, 121–125).

4 Georges Duthuit, *Le Musée inimaginable* (Paris: J[osé] Corti, 1956).

"Tant pis" (too bad).

NANCY CUNARD

7.11.56   Paris

Bien chère Nancy

   Glad you got the Whoros safely and that you are off for a jaunt in
the sun.[1] No question of my stirring at the moment, as we shall soon
be rehearsing <u>Fin de Partie</u> and <u>Acte sans Paroles</u> for performance at
the Oeuvre probably in January and it's going to be a terrible job. I
read your GM in an evening with great absorption and pleasure and as
with your ND with more interest for you than for him. I loved the
"Ladies don't move" story. Eppur si muovono.[2] I think your failed
dinner with the Joyces at Fouquet[']s was as usual apropos of Sullivan,
Beecham and your mother. The story Joyce told me was that you told
them you kept the appointment and saw no sign of them – so went.
Delighted to hear you are projecting more memories and with no one
object to tie you down – quasi una fantasia, you'd do that comme
personne.[3] I want to read your Parallax again and the Battersea or
thereabouts gulls skewered to the wind, but can't find it on my
shelves. If you have a spare copy send it along sometime.[4] Not a
mum of his mouth from the GE this long time.[5] The 3rd have taken
the radio script for broadcast to the 4 winds in January. Up to my
palate in teeth misery myself at the moment, have been all my life.
Had a letter from Ralph, his blood pressing hard and gout in a foot and
forbidden to drink a drop of his own wine. Called on Desmond one
afternoon dark and early to find him snug in bed with brandy handy.[6]
Putting down a copper sobbing sycomore, 8 red hawthorn trees and a
cedar of Lebanon.[7] Swing along happy in the south before the hydrogen and uranium get us and write as often as the spirit prompts to
your ever affectionate

        s/ Sam

TLS; 1 leaf, 1 side; TxU, Cunard collection.

   1   SB sent signed copies of *Whoroscope* to Cunard on 17 October (see n. 1). She
planned to travel to Rome (Chisholm, *Nancy Cunard*, 307).

2   SB refers to Cunard's books *GM: Memories of George Moore* and *Grand Man: Memories of Norman Douglas*. Cunard tells the story about a woman who took pointers from a "French cocotte" in order to rekindle her husband's affections: "When she returned she began to put these lessons into practice," only to be told by her husband, "'Dora, *ladies never move*'" (*GM: Memories of George Moore*, 38–39).

"Eppur sì muovono" (yet they do move). SB adapts Galileo's legendary "eppur sì muove."

3   Joyce called on Cunard "to use her influence with her mother to get Sir Thomas Beecham to hear an Irish singer, Sullivan, and have him hired to sing opera in London" (Chisholm, *Nancy Cunard*, 148). Sir Thomas Beecham founded and conducted the Royal Philharmonic Orchestra. Joyce's intense ambition on behalf of John Francis O'Sullivan (1878–1955), a tenor from Cork who studied in France and sang in the Paris Opera, is evident from Nancy Cunard's recollection that Joyce hinted he would reward her help by allowing her to publish some of his writing. Cunard kept Joyce waiting at Fouquet's and stood him up on another occasion as well (Chisholm, *Nancy Cunard*, 148; Ellmann, *James Joyce: New and Revised Edition*, 625–626). Lady Cunard (née Maude Alice Burke, known as Emerald, 1872–1948).

At the end of October 1956, Cunard embarked on writing her memories of writers and artists (Chisholm, *Nancy Cunard*, 305–307). "Quasi una fantasia" (almost a fantasy), as used in describing Beethoven's Piano Sonato no. 14 in C# major.

"Comme personne" (as no one else could).

4   "By the Embankment I counted the grey gulls / Nailed to the wind above a distorted tide" (Nancy Cunard, *Parallax* [London: Hogarth Press, 1925] 11). SB's enthusiasm for the image: Thursday [? 17 July 1930] to Thomas McGreevy, n. 7.

5   "GE" is the Great Extractor, Jake Schwartz: 15-5-55 [*for* 15 May 1956], n. 4.

6   Ralph Cusack; Desmond Ryan.

7   SB planted these trees at Ussy. He links the copper sycamore tree to his poem "Sanies I": "back the shadows lengthen the sycamores are sobbing" (*Echo's Bones and Other Precipitates*, [22–23]).

JEROME LINDON, EDITIONS DE MINUIT
PARIS

11.11.56   Paris

Cher Jérôme

Ci-joint une lettre intéressante de la maison d'édition londonienne John Calder.[1]

Ils proposent de publier M., M.M., et L'I. en un seul volume.

Le rêve, pour mes rhumatismes.

Je leur a[i] répondu en leur expliquant de mon mieux la difficulté en ce qui concerne Molloy et en leur demandant de s'adresser à l'avenir aux Editions de Minuit. En attendant tu serais gentil de leur exposer, mieux que je ne l'ai pu, comment ça se présente pour les droits en Angleterre.[2]

Travaillé hier avec Roger et Jean, celui-là déjà extraordinaire par moments.[3]

Amitiés et à bientôt.

s/ Sam

TLS; 1 leaf, 1 side; enclosure: Pamela Lyon, John Calder, Ltd, London, to SB, 8 November 1956 (TLS; l leaf, 1 side); IMEC, Beckett, Boîte 1, S. Beckett, Correspondance – Divers, 1950–1956.

11.11.56   Paris

Dear Jérôme

Enclosed an interesting letter from the London publishers John Calder.[1]

They are proposing to publish *M.*, *M. M.*, and *L'I.* in a single volume.

A dream, for my rheumatics.

I have replied explaining as best I can the difficulty surrounding *Molloy* and asking them to get in touch from now on with the Editions de Minuit. Meanwhile, perhaps you would be kind enough to explain to them, better than I was able to, how the business of rights stands in England.[2]

Worked yesterday with Roger and Jean, the former extraordinary at moments.[3]

All best and till soon

Sam

1 Pamela Lyon wrote to SB on 8 November indicating that John Calder Ltd. had received a copy of *Malone Dies* from Grove Press and would like to publish "the complete trilogy, in one volume" (InU, Calder; IMEC, Beckett, Boîte 1, S. Beckett, Correspondance – Divers, 1950–1956).

2 On 13 November, Jérôme Lindon wrote to John Calder (b. 1927): "Nous serions très heureux, lui comme moi, que MOLLOY, MALONE MEURT, et L'INNOMMABLE soient publiés par vous en Grande Bretagne en un seul volume. Ce serait même la solution idéale." (We would be very glad, both of us, if *Molloy*, *Malone meurt*, and *L'Innommable* could be published by you in Great Britain in a single volume. Indeed it would be the ideal solution.) (IMEC, Beckett, Boîte 1, S. Beckett, Correspondance – Divers, 1950–1956.)

3 Roger Blin and Jean Martin.

GODDARD LIEBERSON
NEW YORK

November 13th 1956   6 Rue des Favorites
                                      Paris 15me

Dear Mr Lieberson

Safely received yesterday three sets of <u>Godot</u> recording. This is exceedingly generous of you and I send you my warm thanks.[1]

I have written to Igor Stravinsky at the Plaza-Athénée, but I am not at all sure he is in Paris.[2]

You may be interested to know that we are beginning to rehearse my new play, <u>Fin de Partie</u>, opening at the Théâtre de l'Oeuvre probably next January.

With my kind regards to Mrs Lieberson I am
              Yours sincerely
        s/
              Samuel Beckett

TLS; 1 leaf, 1 side; CtY, Gilmore, MSS 69.

1 Recording of *Waiting for Godot*: 7 September 1956, and n. 2.

2 SB's letter to Stravinsky was returned to him (SB to Lieberson, 10 December 1956, CtY, Gilmore, MSS 69).

As Lieberson confirmed to SB on 3 December, Stravinsky had been ill and hospitalized in Munich until 17 November; he traveled from there to Rome on 22 November, and so did not come to Paris as he had planned (see 7 September 1956, n. 1; CtY, Gilmore, MSS 69; Vera Stravinsky, *Dearest Bubushkin: The Correspondence of Vera and Igor Stravinsky, 1921–1954, with Excerpts from Vera Stravinsky's Diaries, 1922–1971*, ed. Robert Craft [London: Thames and Hudson, 1985] 184).

EUGENE IONESCO
PARIS

le 15 novembre 1956   6 rue des Favorites
                                      Paris 15me

673

Mon cher Ionesco

Merci de votre mot.[1]

Je serais très heureux si mon mime pouvait passer avec Les Chaises au Royal Court Theatre. Je viens d'ailleurs de recevoir un mot de Devine.[2]

Comme Lindon a dû vous le dire, c'est très compliqué.[3]

Quand pourrons-nous nous voir? Je quitte Paris aujourd'hui pour quelques jours. Voulez-vous lundi prochain le 19 au Dôme, Montparnasse, à 19 heures? Ne vous donnez pas la peine de confirmer si cela cous convient.

Mes hommages à Madame Ionesco.[4]

Bien amicalement à vous.

s/

Samuel Beckett

TLS; 1 leaf, 1 side; *verso* AN by Ionesco [Latin vocabulary]; BNF, Ionesco COL-166.

15th November 1956   6 rue des Favorites

Paris 15

My dear Ionesco

Thank you for your note.[1]

I should be very happy if my mime could go on with *The Chairs* at the Royal Court Theatre. I have incidentally just received a note from Devine.[2]

As Lindon must have told you, it is very complicated.[3]

When can we meet? I am leaving Paris today for a few days. How about next Monday 19th at the Dôme, Montparnasse, at 7? Don't bother to confirm if that suits you.

My respects to Madame Ionesco.[4]

All good wishes

s/

Samuel Beckett

1   Eugène Ionesco's note to SB has not been found.
On 12 November, Ionesco wrote to George Devine* (1910-1966), Director of the English Stage Company at the Royal Court Theatre in London, about the possibility of SB's "mimodrame," *Acte sans paroles*, appearing on a double bill with his play *The Chairs*. In his letter he mentions having just written a note to SB asking to meet him in order to discuss the matter.

2   Devine wrote to SB on 14 November (TxU, English Stage Company collection).

3   In a letter of 12 November Ionesco reports to George Devine that Jérôme Lindon is hesitant about producing the mime in London before it is staged with *Fin de partie* in Paris, and that Lindon has suggested that the mime should be performed with another play by SB in London (TxU, English Stage Company collection).

4   Rodica Ionesco (née Burileanu, 1910-2004).

JOHN MORRIS, BBC

LONDON

November 16th 1956   Rue des Favorites 6

                                                       Paris 15me

Dear Mr. Morris

Many thanks for your letter. I was very glad to meet Donald McWhinnie, his ideas about the sound agreed with mine and I am sure he will do a very good job. I hope indeed I shall be able to do something else for the Third Programme, possibly with my cousin John Beckett of whom I spoke to you. At the moment I am up to my eyes in the new play and mime opening here at the Oeuvre probably in January.

With best wishes,

Yours ever

s/ Sam. Beckett

TLS; 1 leaf, 1 side; AN *in another hand, ink*: "interoffice 1) Mr. Holme, 2) Mr. Stokes, 3) C.[ontroller] T.[hird] P.[rogramme]"; BBC WAC, RCONT I / Samuel Beckett / Scriptwriter / I (1953–1962).

23 November 1956, Pinget

ROBERT PINGET
PARIS

23.11.56   Paris
Cher ami

Nous avons des places pour le Requiem, jeudi soir.[1]

En attendant venez dîner lundi prochain si vous êtes libre, et que ça vous chante.

Vu Nadeau aujourd'hui. Il est d'accord pour All That Fall. Pour le numéro de février probablement. Quand j'aurai un instant je vous préparerai un texte.[2]

Amitiés de nous deux.

s/ Sam Beckett

TLS; 1 leaf, 1 side; Burns Library, Pinget-Beckett Letters.

23-11-56   Paris
Dear Robert,

We have tickets for the *Requiem*, for Thursday evening.[1]

In the meantime, come and have dinner with us next Monday, if you're free and you feel like it.

Saw Nadeau today. He is on for *All That Fall*. For the February issue probably. When I have a minute I'll get a text ready for you.[2]

Best wishes from us both

s/ Sam Beckett

1   SB saw *Requiem pour une nonne*, an adaptation for the stage of William Faulkner's *Requiem for a Nun* by Albert Camus, at the Théâtre des Mathurins, Paris 8.

2   SB sent the typescript of *All That Fall* to Robert Pinget on 9 December in order to collaborate with him on its translation for publication in *Les Lettres Nouvelles* (Burns Library, Pinget-Beckett Letters).

DONALD MCWHINNIE, BBC
LONDON

November 28th 1956   6 Rue des Favorites
                                           Paris 15me

Dear Mr McWhinnie

An absurdly slight change for page one of script, but towards which I know you will be indulgent. Instead of "all alone in that old crazy house" read "all alone in that ruinous old house."[1]

Write me news when any.

Yours sincerely
s/
Samuel Beckett

TLS; 1 leaf, 1 side; date stamp, 19 NOV 56; BBC WAC, RCONT I / Samuel Beckett / Scriptwriter / I (1953–1962).

1   SB refers to Mrs. Rooney's opening line in *All That Fall*. In his reply to SB on 30 November, McWhinnie agreed to the change (BBC WAC, RCONT I / Samuel Beckett / Scriptwriter / I [1953 1962]).

RICHARD ROUD
LONDON

November 28th 1956   6 Rue des Favorites
                                           Paris 15me

Dear RR

Thanks for your letter. If I had my Proust to my hand, but I haven't, I might recover origin of quote you quote. I think it is probably Francesco de Sanctis, but can't vouch. If it comes back I'll let you know.[1] I think Grove will do an ed. of that old corvée, Shatton and Windup have renounced – c'est la moindre des

677

choses – all rights.[2] Glad to hear you are getting going with free-lancing, anything rather than teaching. Nice of Ionesco. I saw him the other day. Talk of Devine's doing his Chaises with my Acte sans Paroles at the Royal Court, I hope it comes off.[3] Have you read Cioran, I have just his latest [sic], La Tentation d'Exister, great stuff here and there. Must reread his first, Petit Précis de Décomposition.[4] The new play – final version in 1 act of what we talked about, title Fin de Partie – and the mime Acte sans Paroles with music by my cousin John Beckett will face the hyenae at the Théâtre de l'Oeuvre probably first fortnight in January, unless Crommelynck's Chaud et Froid now running there puts on speed unexpectedly. I have begun pre-rehearsing with Blin and Martin with rather gruesome results so far.[5] I have done a longish radio play in English for the 3rd, emission probably January.[6] I shall certainly be here, my remains at least, at Xmas time, and look forward to seeing you. I don't know Arnaud's Aveux.[7] No, the script for the 3rd, All That Fall, cf. Psalms of David 115, is specifically radio, at least I hope so.[8] Blin too is a "gaucher contrarié" and says he has never got over it.[9]

All the best.

Yours ever   s/ Sam Beckett

TLS; 1 leaf, 1 side; T env to Richard Roud Esq, 13 Oakley Street, London S.W. 3, Angleterre; pm illeg., Paris; Smolens.

1   American film critic Richard Roud* (1929–1989) asked about the source of a quotation in SB's Proust (59–60): "Chi non ha la forza di uccidere la realtà non ha la forza di crearla" (Whoever lacks the strength to kill reality lacks the strength to create it). SB correctly identifies the author as Francesco de Sanctis (1817–1883) (Storia della letteratura italiana, II, ed. Niccolò Gallo [Turin: Giulio Einaudi Editore, 1958] 188).

2   Grove Press edition of Proust: 30 July 1956; 1 August 1956, and n. 4.
"Corvée" (drudgery, task). London publishers Chatto and Windus. "C'est la moindre des choses" (It's the least they could do).

3   It is not known how Eugène Ionesco befriended Roud, but Roud lived in the London flat of Ionesco's translator Donald Watson, so they certainly had met (Jean-Yves Mock, 19 June 1996).

4 Emil Michel Cioran, *La Tentation d'exister* (1956; *Temptation to Exist*); *Précis de décomposition* (1949; *A Short History of Decay*).

5 *Chaud et froid, ou L'Idée de Monsieur Dom* (1934; *Hot and Cold or Monsieur Dom's Idea*), a farce by Fernand Crommelynck (1885–1970), opened at the Théâtre de l'Œuvre on 20 November, directed by the author.

6 "Emission," Gallicism for "broadcast."

7 Georges Arnaud (pseud. of Henri Girard, 1917–1987) wrote the play *Les Aveux les plus doux* (performed 1953; published 1954; *Sweet Confession*).

8 "The Lord upholdeth all that fall, and raiseth up all those that be bowed down" (Psalms, 145: 14). SB incorrectly numbers the Psalm as 115.

9 "Gaucher contrarié" (left-handed person forced to become right-handed).

KITTY BLACK, CURTIS BROWN
LONDON

[after 28 November 1956]
Dear Kitty

Thanks for yours of 28<u>th</u>. I quite appreciate that Chairs plus mime are on the short side. On the other hand Chairs & Fin de Partie – which lasts over an hour & a half – would be too long. And on top of that no chance of my finishing the translation for months to come – if I decide it is worth trying. Have to see it here first. The solution might be to add a short act of Ionesco, of A.N. Other, or for me – if Devine likes Act Without Words – to try and extirpate a second from my grizzled matter. Rehearsing here every afternoon with Blin & Martin in the foyer of the Oeuvre, Crommelynck's copious, hideous & immutable set rendering stage unavailable.[1]

No news of anything?

All the best

yrs. ever

AL draft; 1 leaf, 1 side; *on verso* Kitty Black, Curtis Brown Ltd. to SB, 28 November 1956 (TLS; 1 leaf, 1 side); Fehsenfeld collection.

1 The Crommelynck play at the Théâtre de l'Œuvre was *Chaud et Froid, ou L'Idée de Monsieur Dom.*

BARNEY ROSSET, GROVE PRESS
NEW YORK

1.12.56   6 Rue des Favorites
                                           Paris 15me
                                           Ussy

Dear Barney

Very grieved that you are so unhappy, though God knows it is hard to be anything else for more than a few minutes at a time, with the help of dope, or work, or music, or the other. Stick it out for the sake of these. And if you have found someone you'll be all right.[1] These are silly words, but not so silly as the ones they ousted.

Thanks for cheque and account of reading. Thanks for all you did.[2] I am having copies made of ALL THAT FALL (BBC script), emission probably January, and shall send you one together with From An A.W. in the course of next week.[3] I have given final text of the play, Fin de Partie (one time HAAM), and the mime, Acte Sans Paroles, to Lindon and the book will be out in a few weeks, so not worth while sending you MSS before then. Inquiries about both from London and Germany. The mime (applications to Curtis Brown) is free for all at any time, but I see no possibility of an English version of the act for some time – if ever.[4] We are rehearsing as best we can in the foyer of the Oeuvre where we open probably about January 10th. Because of the absence in the Belgian Congo of the man who is playing the mime we shall not be able to get going on it before the last week of December, so that the last three weeks will be an infernal rush.[5] Saunders has sent nothing to me, but she may have to Lindon, I'll ask him next week.[6] When the play gets going I shall retreat here at length and get on with L'Innommable.[7] I shall be delighted to sign as many sheets as you please of Proust and Murphy.[8] I received copies of NWW with Yellow and was sorry they did not specify its date of composition. Perhaps you might make the point in Evergreen, on the occasion of D. & the L. which first appeared I think in 1930 in Edward Titus his This Quarter, Montparnasse.[9] I am tired and depressed with all this fuss of rehearsal and the feeling of barking up the wrong monkey-bread and look forward to the moment when I can dig in again here and see are there any bits left of the solitary worth trying to stick together. Everything here is in a gasoleneless chaos and I am afraid we are going to be stuck for central heating fuel here in the country, though we have enough left for the worst of the winter.[10] Glad to hear of Canada broadcast. I wish Myerb. would make up his mind about NY revival, black or white. Columbia generously sent me 3 sets of Godot recording. C'est assez bien fait mais je trouve que ça ne donne pas grand'chose.[11] Tell Loly I hate being thanked, especially for books, and that she has done just the right thing. I quite understand your not writing. But a few lines in better heart before this hellish year is out would cheer up your always affectionate penman.

    s/ Sam

TLS; 1 leaf, 1 side; Burns Library, Rosset-Beckett Collection.

1   Barney Rosset and Loly Rosset divorced in the following year.

2   SB refers to the reading from his work at the Poetry Center, 92nd Street YM-YWHA, on 23 October. SB's insertion, "Thanks for all you did," following "reading," is typed. Rosset's account of the reading has not been found.

3   SB had already sent Rosset a typescript of "From an Abandoned Work" (see 23 September 1956, n. 3).

4   S. Fischer Verlag's interest in publishing the play: 14 July 1956; George Devine and The Royal Court Theatre's interest in producing the play and the mime: 15 November 1956 and [after 28 November 1956].

SB handwrites and encircles "one time HAAM" in the top margin with a line to "Fin de Partie."

Kitty Black sent George Devine the script of *Acte sans paroles* on 30 November (TxU, English Stage Company collection). Inquiries had been received from Berlin and Düsseldorf (see 30 August [1956] and n. 8).

SB handwrites and encircles "applications to Curtis Brown" in left margin, connecting this with a line to "mime" encircled in the text.

5   Deryk Mendel was on tour in Africa with the modern dance company "Françoise et Dominique"; they visited Angola, and the French and the Belgian Congo (Deryk Mendel).

6   Marion Saunders was the New York agent representing Editions de Minuit; royalties earned in the United States on *Molloy* and *Waiting for Godot* were payable to her (Rosset to Jérôme Lindon, 17 December 1956, IMEC, Beckett, Boîte 1, S. Beckett, Dossier *Murphy* 1956–1957). Rosset wrote to Saunders on 7 December that he had sent her payment on 8 August, but that SB had not received it (IMEC, Beckett, Boîte 1, S. Beckett, Correspondance – Divers, 1950–1956).

7   Although SB had begun the translation of *L'Innommable*, it was "with gruesome results" (SB to Aidan Higgins, 23 November 1956, TxU, Beckett collection).

8   Neither *Proust* nor *Murphy* was published by Grove until 1958.

9   "Yellow" from *More Pricks Than Kicks* was published in *New World Writing* 5.10 (November 1956) 108–119 (see 26 May 1956, and n. 7). SB asked that the date of composition be noted (see 26 May 1956).

"Dante and the Lobster," also from *More Pricks than Kicks*, appeared in *Evergreen Review* (1.1 [December 1957] 24–36). There is no mention of the story's previous publication in *This Quarter*, or of its date of composition.

10   Europe was experiencing an oil shortage, in part due to the Suez Crisis; the Organization for European Economic Cooperation established "a petroleum industry emergency group" to allocate "available supplies between member countries" ("Future of Europe's Oil Supply," *The Times* 1 December 1956: 50). Gasoline rationing was expected to continue for several months. SB writes "gasoleneless" for "gasolineless."

11   Lawrence Hammond at Curtis Brown wrote to Rosset on 15 November that the Canadian Broadcasting Corporation wished to broadcast *Waiting for Godot* (NSyU).

SB refers to Myerberg's proposal for a revival of *Waiting for Godot* with a negro cast in New York.

Goddard Lieberson sent the Columbia recording of *Waiting for Godot* (see 13 November 1956).

"C'est assez bien fait mais je trouve que ça ne donne pas grand'chose" (It is well enough done, but I find it doesn't amount to much).

GEORGE DEVINE, ROYAL COURT THEATRE
LONDON

December 5th 1956   6 Rue des Favorites

                                           Paris 15me

Dear Mr Devine

Thank you for your letter of December 3rd.

I am very glad you like the mime. I realize it adds up with the Chaises to too little time. I rack my brains in vain for 20 minutes more of modern French theatre. Surely Ionesco has a short piece somewhere, or would do one for the occasion. I might be able to manage another mime. This depends a little on when you plan to present this programme. But that would be perhaps too much wordlessness and too much Beckett. Another Ionesco would be preferable.[1] Or would you consider one of Yeats's Plays for Dancers? The Hawk's Well, for example, where there is so much great poetry.[2]

> Yours sincerely
>
> s/
>
> Samuel Beckett

TLS; 1 leaf, 1 side; TxU, English Stage Company collection.

1 In his letter to SB of 3 December, Devine indicated that he liked *Acte sans paroles*, but added: "the problem now is to find one more item of 20 to 25 minutes to make a complete show with LES CHAISES. Have you any ideas – preferably from modern French drama." (TxU, English Stage Company.)

2 W. B Yeats's *Four Plays for Dancers* (1921): *At the Hawk's Well*, *The Only Jealousy of Emer*, *The Dreaming of the Bones*, *Calvary*.

JACOBA VAN VELDE

15.12.56   Paris

Chère Tonny – Je dis Paris, mais je suis à la campagne depuis 2 jours et pour 2 jours encore. Je n'ai pas pu répondre plus tôt à votre bonne lettre, ayant perdu votre adresse à Paris. Je l'ai retrouvée ici . . . Ça n'a pas l'air bien folichon, votre vie là-bas. Je ne connais personne à Rome. Je connaissais l'ambassadeur d'Irlande, mais il est parti.[1] Elle est bien, votre petite tirade sur les gens heureux. Mais est-ce qu'on voudrait en être? J'ai beaucoup répété ces derniers temps avec Blin et Martin. On devait passer, à l'Oeuvre, le 15 janvier. Maintenant c'est remis au 20 février. J'en suis plutôt content. On pataugeait. Et quant au mime, tout reste à faire. Le danseur est au Congo Belge jusqu'au 20 Décembre. D'ici le 20 février on arrivera peut-être à quelque chose. Fin de Partie est très difficile à jouer. J'en ai corrigé les premières épreuves pour Lindon qui veut que la sortie du livre coincide [for coïncide] avec la première. J'essaierai de récupérer une brochure pour vous. Le texte radiophonique, All That Fall, sera diffusée [for diffusé] par le 3me Programme le mois prochain. Robert Pinget est en train de le traduire pour les Lettres Nouvelles. J'ai déjeuné avec Nadeau. On a parlé de vous. Il n'a rien dit de votre nouvelle. Il est très pris par la chose politico-littéraire.[2] Suzanne est tombée, aux 2 Magots, sur Bob et sa vache vrieslandaise, le premier bavard, la seconde mauvaise.[3] J'ai été obligé d'envoyer ballader Jacques Putman, qui me proposait d'organiser une séance avec Blin et Martin pour lire sa pièce. Suis déjà assez emmerdé avec la mienne.[4] Marthe m'invite à dîner avec Bram dans sa cosy case de la Rue Bobillot. J'ai été une fois chez Bram. Seule trace de peinture une grande toile vendue à l'avance à Warren. Pas vu Geer, ni Lisl. Paraît que ça va mal, côté pesetas.[5] J'essaie de traduire L'Innommable. Effroyablement difficile, je n'y arriverai jamais. J'attends de voir jouer ma pièce pour savoir à peu près si je peux continuer dans ce sens-là ou si me suis complètement gouré. Ni l'un ni l'autre, j'ai l'impression déjà, ça va être gai. Vu Ionesco de retour de Londre[s] où on jouait La Leçon et Le Nouveau Locataire. Il est question de donner mon mime là-bas avec les Chaises.[6] Je ne sais qui a donné Fin de Partie à lire en Hollande. Pas moi. Blin sans doute. La moitié du Sélect semble l'avoir lue. Grâce à Martin sans doute.[7] Quels sont vos projets? Rome, puis Paris? Et Fritz, quand rentre-t-il?[8] J'ai vu des Polonais, un directeur de revue et le traducteur de Godot. On le joue à Varsovie le 15 janvier.[9] Et j'ai de bonnes nouvelles de la reprise à New York, avec des noirs (dont un Lucky haut de 2 mètres).[10] A Paris on cherche toujours un petit vieux et une petite vieille pour les poubelles – sans dents autant que possible. Mais avec des jambes qui plient aux genoux. Difficile à trouver. J'ai pensé demander à Marthe. Mais elle est un peu grande.[11] Je donnerais cher (1000 francs) pour que tout soit fini et la pièce en

représentation et moi parti sans les horreurs d'un autre travail.[12]
Quelle vie, où c'est ça le mieux qu'on puisse espérer.

Lundi on vient ici planter des arbres. J'ai préparé les trous. S'il fait
aussi froid que l'année dernière ils créveront [*for* crèveront] tous avant
le printemps. Bientôt on ne pourra plus se chauffer, faute de mazout.
Assez déconné. Faites signe.

Je vous embrasse.

SAM

ALS; 1 leaf, 2 sides; BNF 19794/43.

15.12.56   Paris

Dear Tonny – I say Paris, but I've been in the country for two days,
and will be here for another 2. I couldn't answer your nice letter
any sooner, having lost your Paris address. I've found it here ... Life
where you are doesn't sound wonderful. I know nobody in Rome. I
used to know the Irish ambassador, but he's gone.[1] Really good,
that little tirade of yours about happy folk. But would one want to
be counted among them? I've been involved in lots of rehearsing
recently with Blin and Martin. We were supposed to open, at the
Oeuvre, on the 15th of January. Now it's been put off to the 20th of
February. On the whole I'm glad. It was getting nowhere. And as for
the mime, everything still has to be worked out. The dancer will be
in the Belgian Congo till the 20th of December. Between now and
the 20th of February perhaps we'll get somewhere. *Fin de partie* is
very difficult to act. I've corrected the first proofs for Lindon, who
wants the book to come out the same day as the premiere. I'll try to
get a programme for you. The radio piece, *All That Fall*, will go out
on the 3rd Programme next month. Robert Pinget is translating it
for *Les Lettres Nouvelles*. I had lunch with Nadeau. We talked about
you. He didn't say anything about your short story. He's very much
caught up in things politico-literary.[2] Suzanne ran into, at the
Deux Magots, Bob and his Friesland cow, the former all chat, the
latter all scowls.[3] I had to send Jacques Putman packing, he was all
for organising a session with Blin and Martin to read his play. I've

enough damned trouble with my own.[4] Marthe is inviting me to dinner with Bram in her cosy shack in the rue Bobillot. I've been once to Bram's. Only trace of painting a big canvas sold in advance to Warren. Haven't seen Geer, or Lisl. Seems things are bad on the cash front.[5] I'm trying to translate *L'Innommable*. Horrifyingly difficult. I'll never manage it. I'm waiting to see my play put on so as to know more or less whether I can carry on in that direction, or whether I've gone off the rails entirely. Neither the one nor the other, I have the feeling. That'll be jolly. Saw Ionesco, back from London where they were doing *The Lesson* and *The New Tenant*. There's talk of putting on my mime there, with *The Chairs*.[6] I don't know who gave *Fin de partie* to be read in Holland. Not me. Blin no doubt. Half the Sélect seems to have read it. Thanks to Martin no doubt.[7] What are your plans? Rome, then Paris? And when is Fritz coming back?[8] I've seen some Poles: the editor of a review and the translator of *Godot*. It's going on in Warsaw on the 15th of January.[9] And there's good news of the New York revival, with a black cast (including a 2-metre-tall Lucky).[10] In Paris we're still searching for a little old man and a little old woman for the dustbins – toothless if at all possible – hard to find. But with legs that bend at the knees. I've thought of asking Marthe. But she's a bit tall.[11] I'd give a lot (1,000 francs) for it all to be over, and the play on, and me away without the horrors of another piece of work.[12] What a life, when that's the best that can be hoped for.

On Monday we're coming here to plant trees. I've prepared the holes. If it's as cold as it was last year they'll all be dead before the spring. Soon we'll have no heating, when the oil runs out. Enough of this drivel. Get in touch.

Much love

Sam

1   Jacoba van Velde's letter to SB has not been found. SB knew Denis Devlin who was the Irish Minister to Italy in 1950, before he was posted to Turkey from 1951 to 1957.

2   It is likely that the story by Jacoba van Velde being read by Maurice Nadeau was "Impasse," published by *Les Lettres Nouvelles* 51 (July–August 1957) 31–38.

3   Suzanne Deschevaux-Dumesnil saw Bob Clerx, Jacoba van Velde's second husband, and his companion. Les Deux Magots, 6 Place Saint-Germain-des-Prés, Paris 6.

4   SB writes "ballader" for "balader." Jacques Putman's play has not been identified.

5   Marthe Arnaud. Rue Bobillot, Paris 13. Bram van Velde held two exhibitions, in 1955 and 1957, at the Galerie Michel Warren in Paris.
Geer and Lisl van Velde.

6   Ionesco's *The Lesson* had been performed at the Arts Theatre in March 1955, directed by Peter Hall, but it was *The New Tenant* and *The Bald Prima Donna* that were performed there in November 1956 ("An Apostle of the One-Act Play: London to see Ionesco Fantasy," *The Times* 7 March 1955: 3; "Farcical Theme of Dejection," *The Times* 7 November 1956: 3).

7   Having directed *Wachten op Godot*, the Dutch version of *En attendant Godot*, in Arnhem in 1955, Blin had connections there with the Toneelgroep Theater.
Le Select, a café at 99 Boulevard du Montparnasse, Paris 6.

8   Jacoba van Velde lived with Frederik Carel Kuipers (known as Fritz, 1924–1992).

9   SB met Adam Tarn* (1902–1975) and Julian Rogozinski (1912–1980). Tarn founded the Warsaw drama journal *Dialog* in 1956. Selections from Act I of *En attendant Godot*, translated by Rogozinski as *Czekając na Godota*, were published in *Dialog* 1.1 (May 1956) 89–98. The production was to be directed by Jerzy Kreczmar at the Teatr Współczesny, Warsaw.

10   Myerberg's casting for the reprise of *Waiting for Godot* at the Schubert Theatre in Boston (from 10 January 1957) and the Ethel Barrymore Theatre in New York (from 21 January 1957) included Geoffrey Holder (b. 1930), a dancer born in Trinidad, as Lucky; he was 6 feet 6 inches tall.

11   SB probably refers to Marthe Arnaud.

12   At this time, 1,000 French francs was equivalent to about one pound sterling, and less than three US dollars: not a lot.

DONALD McWHINNIE, BBC
LONDON

December 18th 1956   6 Rue des Favorites
                                                     Paris 15me

Dear Donald McWhinnie

Thanks for your letter with news of progress. On first thoughts, begun this morning when I read your letter, I do not see why the animal utterances by mere humans. I do not think this point arose when we met. I may be quite wrong, but it seems to me a rather gratuitous complication. But then I don't know what is in your mind.

Perhaps your idea is to give them the unreal quality of the other sounds. But this, we agreed, should develop from a realistic nucleus. I think the absurd apropos with which they occur, and their briefness, are enough to denaturalize them. And if not could they not be distorted by some technical means? But perhaps you are thinking of something quite different. If they are badly imitated the result will be atrocious. And if well, what do we gain? Do you lack the recordings of the animals involved? Do not let the above weigh with you unduly. I am simply perplexed and should be grateful if you would let me know a little more fully what is in your mind.[1]

Our opening at the Oeuvre has been postponed to February 20th and I have been wondering all day about going to London for your rehearsals and recording. I have finally decided that I should be very definitely less a help than a hindrance. I am very slow and go wildly and repeatedly wrong before arriving at something that resembles what I want. I'd only bother and upset you all. And I'm not worrying, having talked with you here and felt your feeling for the thing, its ruinedness and stifledness and impudicity.

Finally forgive me if I have to declare myself incapable of writing even a brief occasional piece for Radio Times. My ideas about radio are not even quarter baked and to write about my own work is a thing I simply can't do. I feel miserable about this when I think of the warmth with which John Morris and yourself and the 3rd Programme have received All That Fall. Would an extract from the script itself not be better than nothing?[2]

Thanks for everything and all the best.

Yours ever

s/ Sam. Beckett

TLS; 1 leaf, 1 side; date stamped 21 DEC 1956; BBC WAC, RCONT I / Samuel Beckett / Scriptwriter / File I (1953–1962).

1 Donald McWhinnie replied to SB on 1 January 1957:

I am sorry to disturb you about the animals. Of course, we have realistic recordings, but the difficulty is that it is almost impossible to obtain the right sort of timing and balance with the realistic effects. By using good mimics I think we can get real style and shape into the thing. The other factor is that existing recordings are very familiar to our listeners and I do feel that, without being extreme, we need in this particular case to get away from standard realism. (BBC WAC, RCONT I / Samuel Beckett / Scriptwriter / File I [1953–1962].)

Desmond Briscoe (1925–2006) produced the sound effects for *All That Fall* by enhancing "concrete sources" electronically, and "was one of those whose experiments led to the setting-up of the Radiophonic Workshop in 1958" (Desmond Briscoe and Roy Curtis-Bramwell, *The BBC Radiophonic Workshop: The First 25 Years* [London: BBC, 1983] frontispiece, 18).

2   On 1 January 1957, McWhinnie assured: "Please don't worry about the Radio Times – I have now myself done a very brief piece for them which I hope will meet with your approval" (BBC WAC, RCONT I / Samuel Beckett / Scriptwriter / File I [1953–1962]; Donald McWhinnie, "All That Fall," *Radio Times* [11 January 1957] 4).

JACK YEATS
DUBLIN

December 21st 1956   Paris
Dear Jack Yeats
   This plain card to bring to you, from my heart here, warmest greetings warmest wishes for Xmas and for all the days of 1957.
            Ever your affectionate friend
                    Sam Beckett

ACS; 1 leaf, 1 side; Yeats collection.

JACOBA VAN VELDE

27.12.56   Ussy-sur-Marne
Chère Tonny
   Merci de votre carte. La lettre que je vous ai adressée à Levanto ne semble pas vous être parvenue. J'espère qu'on l'aura fait suivre. Elle en valait la peine.[1]
   Nous sommes ici depuis la veille de Noël et resterons jusqu'au 3 janvier. Puis je reprends les répétitions. Nous devions passer le mois

prochain, mais c'est reculé jusqu'à la fin février. A mon soulagement. La pièce est très difficile à jouer. Je travaille jusqu'à présent avec Blin et Martin seuls. Les 2 vieux des poubelles restent à trouver. Quant au mime, tout reste à faire. Mendel est de retour du Congo Belge, sain et sauf mais très fatigué. Nous n'aurions jamais été prêts pour le 20 janvier. Je serai content – si je vis encore – quand les représentations commenceront. Le texte commence déjà à me scier le crâne, comme celui de Godot vers la fin des répétitions. Qu'est-ce que ça sera d'ici 6 semaines? J'ai corrigé les épreuves pour Lindon. Quand le bouquin sortira je vous enverrai votre exemplaire. A moins de vous le donner de la main à la main, si vous pensez rentrer bientôt. All That Fall passe au 3me Programme le 13 janvier. Et la reprise nègre à New York le 15. Des noirs géants: 1 m 90, 1 m 95 et – tenez-vous bien – 2 m 12 (Lucky)! Rex Ingram (Verts Pâturages) joue Pozzo (120 kilos).[2] J'aimerais voir ça. Mais je n'irai pas. Je n'irai jamais plus nulle part. J'écris un petit acte directement en anglais. Ici rien de mieux à faire.[3] J'ai planté des arbres, dont un cèdre du Liban. Je n'ai vu personne, ni Bram, ni Geer, ni Jacques, ni personne.[4] Quelles nouvelles de Fritz? J'espère qu'il va bientôt rappliquer et que son père finira par cracher de quoi vous installer tous les deux solidement à Paris, si c'est ça que vous voulez.[5] Vivement 57, et 67, et 77, après ça ira, sinon avant. Voilà à quoi vous vous exposez, en me demandant de vous écrire (ce que j'aurais fait de toute façon). Laissez-moi vous souhaiter – en homme bien élevé – beaucoup de bonheur dans cette putain d'année qui vient.

    Affectueusement

    Sam

ALS; 1 leaf, 1 side; BNF, 19794/44.

27.12.56   Ussy-sur-Marne

Dear Tonny

    Thanks for your card. The letter I sent you in Levanto doesn't seem to have reached you. I hope it's been forwarded. It was worth forwarding.[1]

We've been here since Christmas Eve, and will stay on till the 3rd of January. Then I'm going back to rehearsing. We were to have opened next month, but it's been put back to the end of February. To my relief. The play is very hard to act. Up till now I've been working with Blin and Martin only. We still have to find the 2 old people for the dustbins. As for the mime, everything is still to be done. Mendel is back from the Belgian Congo, safe and well, but very tired. We would never have been ready for the 20th of January. I'll be glad – if I'm still alive – when the performances start. Already the text is starting to cut into my brain, as the text of *Godot* did towards the end of rehearsals. What will it be like 6 weeks from now? I've corrected the proofs for Lindon. When the book comes out I'll send you your copy. Unless I can hand it to you direct, if you're thinking of coming back soon. *All That Fall* is going out on the 3rd Programme on the 13th of January. And the Negro revival in New York is on the 15th. Giant black men: 1m 90, 1m 95, and – hold on to your hat – 2m 12 (Lucky)! Rex Ingram (*Green Pastures*) is playing Pozzo (120 kilos).[2] I'd like to see it. But I will not go. I'll never go anywhere again. I'm writing one short act straight into English. Nothing better to do here.[3] I've planted some trees, including a cedar of Lebanon. I've seen no-one, not Bram, not Geer, not Jacques, no-one.[4] Any news of Fritz? I hope he's going to get back soon and that his father will eventually cough up the wherewithal to get the two of you properly housed in Paris, if that's what you want.[5] Let 57 come soon, and 67, and 77. It'll be all right after that, if not before. See what you bring on yourself by asking me to write (I'd have done so anyway). Allow me to wish you – well brought up as I am – much happiness in this bloody awful coming year.

Love

Sam

---

1   Levanto, on the Ligurian coast of Italy. SB refers to his letter of 15 December.

2   In the cast of the 1957 New York production of *Waiting for Godot* were Manton Moreland (1902–1973) as Estragon, Earl Hyman (b. 1926) as Vladimir, Geoffrey Holder as Lucky, and Rex Ingram (1895–1969) as Pozzo. Ingram and Hyman were about 6 feet tall; Holder was taller (see 15 December 1956, n. 10). Both Moreland and Hyman had performed in the film *The Green Pastures* (1936).

3 The short one-acter was "The Gloaming," a dramatic fragment written in English that later became *Rough for Theatre I* (Cohn, *A Beckett Canon*, 236; UoR, BIF, MS 1396/4/6).

4 Bram van Velde, Geer van Velde, Jacques Putman.

5 Fritz Kuipers.

APPENDIX

PROFILES

Donald Albery (1914–1988), London theatre owner and producer, staged *Waiting for Godot* at his Arts Theatre in August 1955 in club conditions, extending the run at his larger West End theatre, The Criterion. To do so required him to mediate between SB and the Lord Chamberlain's Office, which was responsible for censorship. Albery sold the American option on the play to Michael Myerberg, which led, eventually, to the Broadway production of *Godot*. He continued to exercise these contractual rights for several years, with regard to both theatre and film. Albery was knighted in 1977.

Avigdor Arikha (1929–2010), Israeli printmaker, art historian, essayist, painter, and draftsman, was, from 1956 until SB's death in 1989, one of the author's closest and most trusted friends. Arikha was born near Czernowitz in Bukovina. Along with the other Jewish families of the region, he, his sister, and his parents were deported in 1941 toward the Western Ukraine, where the family ended up, after the death of Arikha's father, in a labor camp. Set to heavy manual work in an iron foundry, Arikha owed his survival to a series of drawings he made of atrocious conditions in the ghetto that were transmitted to the International Red Cross, representatives of which succeeded in removing him and his sister from the ghetto and conveying them to Palestine, where they arrived in 1944.

Arikha studied at the Bezalel School of Art in Jerusalem in 1946, then fought and was seriously wounded in 1948 in the Israeli War of Independence. After recuperating, in 1949, he visited Paris for the first time to study at the Ecole des Beaux-Arts. After a further stay in Jerusalem, from 1954 he was again resident in Paris, meeting SB – without at first realizing who he was – in June 1956 after a performance of *En attendant Godot*. He told the editors that his decision to make Paris his permanent home was directly due to the admiration he felt for SB. Through the 1950s and into 1965, Arikha's painting was abstract; after which, following a crisis of faith in such work, he spent nearly eight years working only in black and white (drawings, etchings, lithographs), and exclusively from life. Then and subsequently he made many drawings of SB as well as a series of five sugar-lift aquatints conceived to accompany SB's text *Au loin un oiseau*. From 1973, color re-entered Arikha's work, which continued to be executed rapidly and from life, and which frequently presented – as well as themselves representing – intense acts of observation, often through oil on canvas: still lifes, landscapes, self-portraits. For his portraits, a common subject was his wife, the American poet Anne Atik, a close friend of SB in her own right and the author of a full account of the couple's friendship with him, *How it Was: A Memoir of Samuel Beckett*.

Arikha's work, both in its abstract and its figurative phases, received warm-hearted support from SB, who in 1982 wrote a letter supporting the painter's nomination for a MacArthur Foundation award. The two men would meet regularly, either at Arikha's home near Port-Royal in Paris or in their preferred restaurants and bars. During his periods of residency in New York and Jerusalem, Arikha continued to correspond regularly with SB, the link between the two men being strengthened by, among other shared interests such as music, their fondness for erudition and languages: Arikha described himself (again to the editors) as "fluent in five languages, not including the three I have forgotten." Arikha was an eminent art historian whose oeuvre includes works on Poussin and Ingres, the wide-ranging study *Peinture et regard*, and numerous articles on artists from Caravaggio to Watteau to Cézanne to Giorgio Morandi; he lectured at universities worldwide. His work features in many private and public collections and, since 1972, has been represented by the Marlborough Gallery. Arikha was one of the small handful of SB's friends who attended his funeral in December 1989.

John Stewart Beckett (1927–2007), Irish musician, composer, and conductor, was SB's cousin. He studied music at St. Columba's College in Dublin, the Royal Irish Academy of Music, and the Royal College of Music in London. In 1949, he won a traveling scholarship to study composition at the Conservatoire in Paris under Nadia Boulanger. From 1951 through 1952, he contributed a music column to *The Bell*

(Dublin). In 1960, he founded and served as conductor of London's Musica Reservata, which performed Medieval and Renaissance music. In 1955, SB invited his cousin to Paris to work with performer Deryk Mendel to create music for *Acte sans paroles*. The mime premiered with *Fin de partie* at the Royal Court Theatre in April 1957 as part of a French festival. To open the production, John Beckett composed a prelude for piano, violin, bassoon, and clarinet based on "God Save the Queen" and "The Marseillaise." John Beckett often composed for the BBC, and he did so to accompany Patrick Magee's reading from *Molloy* for the Third Programme in 1957.

SB wrote the radio script *Words and Music* with John Beckett in mind as his creative partner; the play was broadcast in 1962 on the BBC Third Programme. Although John and Edward Beckett composed and performed music for Jack MacGowran's readings of SB's work (*End of Day*) for Claddagh Records in 1966 (accompanied by SB on gong), John Beckett declined later invitations to collaborate with SB, and withdrew his music for *Words and Music*. He continued to contribute music for other BBC productions and for films, notably for Joseph Strick's version of *Ulysses* (1967).

John Beckett was married to Vera Slocombe from 1961 to 1969; following their divorce, his partner was the musician Ruth David, with whom he lived until her death in 1995. In 1973, then teaching at the Royal Irish Academy of Music in Dublin, he initiated and directed what became an annual series of Bach Cantatas in St. Ann's Church, Dublin. He conducted an all-Bach concert in the Promenade series at the Royal Albert Hall (1979). He shared his love of early music with his twin sister Ann; in later years, they spent some time each summer playing in chamber groups together. John Beckett had a special interest in the music of Purcell, Bach, Haydn, and Mahler, and he continued to compose, direct, and present musical programming for BBC Radio 3. He died on his eightieth birthday in London.

Carl Gustaf Bjurström (1919–2001), Swedish literary critic and translator, lived for most of his life in France following study at Uppsala University, and work in Rome where he was attached to the Swedish Legation. He was a regular contributor to many Swedish literary periodicals, as well as to *Dagens Nyheter*, the Stockholm daily newspaper. From 1951 to 1956 he was Director of the Swedish Cultural Institute in Paris. He translated into Swedish works by many French writers including SB, Balzac, Céline, Anouilh, Camus, and Foucault, as well as works of many Swedish writers into French.

Bjurström's essay "Samuel Beckett" introduced SB's work to Swedish readers; it appeared in *Bonniers Litterära Magasin* along with his translation into Swedish of "Texte pour rien, VI." As Bjurström continued to translate SB's prose into Swedish, he stayed in contact with SB, who sent him new short pieces to be included in forthcoming collections. Bjurström's major translations are *Hur det är* (*How It Is*), 1963; *Kniv av nej* (*No's Knife*), 1969; *Avigt & Co.* (a collection of short works including "Premier amour," "Foirades," "Le Dépeupleur," and "Sans"), 1969; and *Mercier och Camier*, 1996.

Dorothy Kitty Black (m. Albertyn, 1914–2006), South African dramatist, translator and theatrical administrator, moved to London before the Second World War. Her career as an agent began in 1937; she worked with H. M. Tennent, and then the Company of Four, where she took part in the production of more than eighty plays at the Lyric Theatre, Hammersmith. Known for her passion for and knowledge of French, she helped translate plays by Cocteau, Anouilh, and Sartre.

In 1953, Black began her work at Curtis Brown Ltd. as the firm's chief play reader. She sold the option for theatrical rights for the first English production of *Waiting for Godot* to Donald Albery and Peter Glenville. Black also negotiated the production rights for *All that Fall, Endgame*, and *Act Without Words*.

After leaving Curtis Brown in 1959, Black was a producer for Granada Television (1961–1963), in the Drama Department at Associated Rediffusion (1963–1966), and was later a house manager for the MacOwan Theatre (1976–1986). Her adaptations and translations included works by Félicien Marceau, Beverley Cross, and Michael Flanders.

Roger Blin (1907–1984), French actor and director, came into prominence as a director of plays by Strindberg, Adamov, Genet, and SB, particularly the premiere of *En attendant Godot* at the Théâtre de Babylone, in which he also played the role of Pozzo. Blin studied with Jean-Louis Barrault, playing in Barrault's productions of *Le Cocu magnifique* (1937; *The Magnificent Cuckold*) and *Numance* (1937; *Numantia*), as well as Raymond Reynal's productions of Synge's *L'Ombre de la vallée* (1941; *The Shadow of the Glen*) and *Le Baladin du monde occidental* (1941; *The Playboy of the Western World*). Blin was a friend of Antonin Artaud, and thought, at one time, to publish his papers. Blin was also active in film, playing in Cocteau's *Orphée* (1949) and in films directed by Marcel Carné. In everyday life Blin suffered from a serious stammer, which left him when he was in a role.

After the War, Blin directed at Christine Tsingos's Théâtre Gaîté-Montparnasse. SB saw his production of Strindberg's *Ghost Sonata* (1949) several times, often finding himself among a very small audience; from that he knew that Blin was dedicated to theatre, and the right director for *En attendant Godot*. Blin was persistent in his efforts to stage *Godot*, and was instrumental in raising funds to produce the play. When the actor playing Pozzo became unavailable, Blin took up the role despite his discomfort as a small man in playing this large and blustering character. Blin's Théâtre de Babylone production toured in Germany, France, and Italy in late 1953, as a result of which Blin was asked to direct *Godot* in German at the Schauspielhaus, Zurich (1954), and in Dutch in Arnhem, Holland (1955). There were Paris revivals at the Théâtre Hébertot (1956), the Théâtre de l'Odéon (1961), and the Théâtre Récamier (1970). Blin created a new mise-en-scène of *Godot* at the Comédie-Française (1978), which was revived at the Odéon (1980).

Blin directed the premiere of *Fin de partie* (1957), first at the Royal Court Theatre, and then at the Studio des Champs-Elysées; later, he directed the German-language premiere at the Fleischmarkt Theater in Vienna (1958). He directed the French premieres of SB's *La dernière bande* at the Théâtre Récamier (1960), and *Oh les beaux jours* with Madeleine Renaud (1963), which opened at the Venice Drama Festival, then in Paris, and later on tour. As a director, Roger Blin also introduced the work of Arthur Adamov and helped to popularize the plays of Jean Genet.

Patrick Bowles (1927–1995), writer and translator, was born in London and raised in Rhodesia. He studied at the Sorbonne and in 1951 became associated with the group of young expatriate writers involved in the journal *Merlin*. For publication by Collection Merlin (in association with Olympia Press), Bowles translated *Molloy* into English in close collaboration with SB. After fifteen months of intense work, the novel was published in 1955, and shortly after by Grove Press, New York. Bowles published his notes about working with SB on the translation in "How to Fail," *P.N. Review* (1994), and in the preface to his translation of *The Visit* by Friedrich Dürrenmatt (1990). Bowles became the Editor of *The Paris Review* (1962–1965), and remained an Advisory Editor for the journal. Bowles published fiction and essays in *Merlin*, *Bookman*, and the *Times Literary Supplement*. He also worked with French radio, Agence France-Presse, and *Le Monde*. Bowles worked as a translator from the French and Portuguese for the World Health Organization, in Brazzaville, Republic of the Congo, where he met his wife, Albertine. Bowles died in Alicante, Spain.

Carlheinz Caspari (b. 1921) worked in the municipal theatre in Cologne. Previously, in France, he had been assistant to Jean Vilar, Jean-Louis Barrault, Jean-Marie Serreau, and Jean Cocteau, and trained as a cinematographer. As he prepared to direct *Warten auf Godot* at the Badisches Staatstheater in Karlsruhe in 1953, he wrote to SB to discuss the play with him. Although Caspari had invited SB to see the production, SB did not attend, but Elmar Tophoven, the German translator of the play, assured Caspari that his production was faithful to SB's intentions. Caspari's essay, "Zu Samuel Becketts Theater," was published in *Atoll* (1954).

Over the course of his career, Caspari worked mainly as a director and writer for television and radio. In 1973, he directed Peter von Zahn's documentary on the Pentagon Papers, *Die geheimen Papiere des Pentagons.* Caspari later directed a film version of Alfred Andersch's play *Der Vater eines Mörders* for German television, winning an award at the 1988 Baden-Baden Television Film Festival.

Edouard Coester (1905–2001) had a long and distinguished career as a French magistrate. He was also a composer and musicologist, and took the pseudonym of Edmond Costere to keep his work in music separate from his legal career. Coester maintained close relationships with many contemporary composers, including Messiaen, Satie, and Jolivet, while publishing on musical harmony. In 1954, Coester wrote to SB requesting permission to set *En attendant Godot* to music, which SB refused.

Rosica Colin (1903–1983) established the literary agency Rosica Colin Limited that represented SB's work in England, along with that of other French writers, such as Beauvoir, Camus, Genet, Ionesco, and Sartre. Born in Romania, Colin moved to Britain in 1939 from Germany. During the War, she worked with Basil Blackwell in Oxford and later for the Romanian section of the BBC. In 1953, she first corresponded with SB about his translation of some poems by Francis Ponge. Jérôme Lindon sent her *Molloy* and *Malone meurt* for which she tried to find a publisher in England. When *Waiting for Godot* was produced at the Arts Theatre in London, she arranged its publication with Faber and Faber (1955), which took an option on SB's future dramatic work, becoming thereby his British publisher for the plays. Against Colin's wishes, Faber published the expurgated text approved by the Lord Chamberlain's Office, a mistake avoided in Faber's publication of *Endgame.* The greater part of her correspondence with SB concerns terms of production and publication of SB's work.

Leslie Herbert Daiken (né Yodaiken, 1912–1964) was SB's student at Trinity College Dublin where he received a BA in 1933, and a B.Litt. in 1942. In London, from 1936 to 1939, he worked for Reuters, and as a publicist and scriptwriter for film and radio. He offered to put SB in touch with Sergei Eisenstein in 1936. Daiken acted on SB's behalf, trying to place *Watt* with a London publisher, and finally leaving it with the literary agents A. P. Watt. In turn, SB suggested that Barbara Bray consider Daiken's radio play *Circular Road* (1959) for production by the BBC.

Daiken married Lilyan Adams in 1944. SB visited them in London and encouraged their visits to Paris. Daiken also kept in touch with SB during the period when Ethna McCarthy was dying of cancer in London.

Daiken contributed poetry and short fiction to *Choice, Dublin Magazine, New Irish Poetry, The New English Weekly*; he edited *Irish Front* with Charles Donnelly and worked on anthologies, such as *Goodbye, Twilight* (1936), and *They Go, the Irish: a Miscellany of War-Time Writing* (1944). Daiken founded the Toy Museum (Trust) of Britain and the British Toymakers' Guild. His later writings include works on the subject of children's games and toys. His film on children's play, *One Potato, Two Potato* (1957), won an award at the 1958 Festival Mondial du Film in Brussels. Daiken was active in Jewish political affairs and retained an interest in Dublin literary matters. After Daiken's death, SB continued to correspond with his daughter, the composer Melanie Daiken.

George Devine (1910–1966), a graduate of Oxford and President of the Oxford University Dramatic Society, invited John Gielgud to direct *Romeo and Juliet*, in which he played Mercutio; he soon joined Gielgud's company at the Queen's Theatre, London. Mentored by Michel Saint-Denis (nephew of Jacques Copeau, who taught at the Vieux-Colombier school in Paris), Devine became actively involved with Saint-Denis's London Theatre Studio, and immersed himself in administration and teaching. He served in India and Burma during World War II, after which he rejoined Saint-Denis at the Old Vic and was made Director of the Young Vic Company.

In 1956, Devine became Artistic Director of the English Stage Company, which he helped to establish at the Royal Court Theatre. From that platform, he applied his considerable energy to creating theatre with broadened artistic scope, wider popular audiences, and new playwrights: a theatre that responded to social and political change. He was an actor–manager immersed in the day-to-day practice of theatre, and committed to encouraging and supporting new writers.

In 1957, Devine was instrumental in bringing the world premiere of *Fin de partie* and *Acte sans paroles* to London before directing the English translation of *Endgame* at the Royal Court in 1958, and playing the role of Hamm. Devine assisted SB in a protracted dispute with the Lord Chamberlain's Office. SB gave Devine and the English Stage Company at the Royal Court Theatre the first option on English productions of his plays, including *Happy Days* (1962) and *Play* (1964). The company also produced *Waiting for Godot*, directed by Anthony Page (1964). When asked, SB offered suggestions for other plays that might be staged by the Royal Court Theatre, notably those by Eugène Ionesco. Devine had announced his plans to leave the Royal Court Theatre in September 1965, when, while acting in John Osborne's *A Patriot for Me* in August, he suffered a heart attack, followed by a stroke.

SB was always grateful for Devine's involvement in his work, calling him "the great inspirer." It was due to Devine that the Royal Court Theatre had priority for SB's plays in London. Although SB began to place his work with other theatres after Devine's death, he remained close to Jocelyn Herbert (1917–2003), Devine's companion, who designed many productions of his work at the Royal Court and in other London venues.

Georges Duthuit (1891–1973) – art historian, essayist, specialist in Byzantine, Oriental, and fauvist art – born in Paris, was orphaned at the age of twelve. From 1910, he came under the decisive influence of the English philosopher of art Matthew Stewart Prichard, who believed that mimetic representational Western art was a falling-off from an ideal of process and oneness, an ideal to be rediscovered in Byzantine art and in the work of certain contemporary painters such as Henri Matisse; to both of these Pritchard introduced him. From 1911 to 1919, Duthuit served in the army, after which he devoted himself to the study of art, publishing articles in journals such as *Action*, *Cahiers d'Art*, *Minotaure*, and *The Listener*. In 1924, he published *Le Rose et le noir (de Walter Pater à Oscar Wilde)*; in 1926, *Byzance et l'art du XIIe siècle*; and in 1936, *Mystique chinoise et peinture moderne*. In 1923, he married Matisse's eldest daughter, Marguerite.

Caught in the United States at the outbreak of the Second World War, Duthuit spent the War years there with his son Claude, participating in radio broadcasts directed at Occupied France; his wife Marguerite worked in the Resistance, was arrested, but escaped while being deported to Ravensbrück Concentration Camp. Upon return to France in 1945, Duthuit formed the project of reviving the journal *transition*, helped by his friends, the journal's founders, Eugene and Maria Jolas; this project brought him into contact, from 1947, with SB.

Tall, athletic, bon-vivant, strikingly handsome, Duthuit was connected with many of the significant painters and writers of the era, in both France and the United States. His friendship with SB has been described by his son Claude as "volcanique." Underpinning it, as well as camaraderie and a sense of being an outsider in post-Occupation France, was a fascination with the possibilities of contemporary art, Duthuit's aesthetic being perhaps even more radical than SB's, in its rejection of the Western mimetic tradition (from the Greeks through Giotto, down through the Italian Renaissance). SB did many translations for *Transition*, translated articles on art by Duthuit, and retranslated Duthuit's *Les Fauves* for its publication as *The Fauvist Painters*. Together, in *Transition*, they published "Three Dialogues" (1949).

From 1953, Duthuit's friendship with SB cooled, for reasons which may be linked to SB's increasing notoriety and independence; this reached the point where the two were no longer on speaking terms. Duthuit found himself ostracized by an influential section of the Paris cultural milieu when he published, in 1956, *Le Musée inimaginable*, viewed as a hostile critique of *Le Musée imaginaire* by André Malraux. Having suffered a crippling stroke in 1963, Duthuit spent his last ten years bed-ridden. From there, a year before his death, he wrote to SB: "Pour me réconforter je me fais faire des lectures de Tolstoï et d'oeuvres de S. Beckett dont la passion et la déréliction ont pour moi des richesses toujours neuves," ending his letter, "Toujours affectueusement" (To comfort myself I arrange to be read to from Tolstoy and works by S. Beckett, whose passion and dereliction hold for me riches continually new . . . Love ever) (Duthuit collection).

Erich Franzen (1892–1961), a German lawyer, literary critic, and writer, translated SB's novel *Molloy* into German. After the First World War, Franzen worked as a general counsel for several firms, and then, in 1926, settled in Berlin where he was a literary critic for the *Frankfurter Zeitung* and several other publications, wrote for radio, and did literary translation. He became a leader in the Schutzbundes deutschen Schriftsteller (SDS) (Defense League of German Writers). Banned by the Nazis from writing in 1934, he emigrated to the United States where he taught Social Psychology at various universities. He returned to Germany in 1951, and in 1954 he became a member of the Deutsche Akademie für Sprache und Dichtung.

Erich Franzen was asked by Suhrkamp Verlag to translate SB's novel *Molloy*. Over the course of several weeks in early 1954, Franzen and SB discussed, by letter, the difficulties in the German translation of the novel. Franzen's translation was praised by critics, but he declined Suhrkamp's invitation to translate *Malone meurt* and *L'Innommable*. A collection of his essays was published in 1966 under the title *Aufklärung* (1966); his correspondence with SB was published in *Babel* in 1984.

Maurice Girodias (1919–1990), publisher and writer, founded Olympia Press. With Merlin Press, he published SB's novel *Watt* and the English translation of *Molloy* (for Continental distribution). Girodias was raised in Paris, where his father Jack Kahane ran the Obelisk Press, which published works forbidden by English censorship laws, including novels by Henry Miller and Anaïs Nin. In March 1938, Kahane asked SB to translate Sade's *Les 120 Journées de Sodome*. After Kahane's death at the outset of the Second World War, Girodias adopted his mother's maiden name, and took over Obelisk Press; he sold the company in 1951, and two years later founded Olympia Press.

Olympia Press was associated with a group of young expatriate writers, many of them affiliated with the literary journal *Merlin*. By publishing pornographic novels in English, Girodias sought to underwrite books of literary merit. Alexander Trocchi and Christopher Logue, publishers of the journal *Merlin*, were allowed their own small series, Collection Merlin, published under the imprint of Olympia. In 1953, they published SB's *Watt*.

Olympia's best-known publications were in the Traveller's Companion Series, which included both erotica and works which were judged too experimental by other publishers. SB's *Molloy, Malone Dies*, and *The Unnamable* were published in this series (1955–1959) along with Vladimir Nabokov's *Lolita*, William Burroughs's *Naked Lunch*, and works by Sade, Georges Bataille, and Raymond Queneau.

Girodias was involved in legal battles over nearly every book he published. The suit by Editions de Minuit and SB over the publication rights of *Watt* and *Molloy* (1957) nearly severed SB's relationship with him. Olympia Press was bankrupt by 1968. Girodias spent the last years of his life in Paris, where he wrote his memoirs, *Une journée sur la terre* (*The Frog Prince*).

Henri Hayden (1883–1970) was a Polish-born French painter, initially associated with the Cubist movement before becoming known as a painter of landscapes and still lifes. As a Jew he fled Paris with his wife Josette during the Nazi Occupation. They made their way to Roussillon where they met SB and Suzanne Deschevaux-Dumesnil, who had also taken refuge in the village. SB and Hayden often played chess together. Hayden's delight in the countryside round Roussillon inspired a series of paintings. SB's friendship with the Haydens continued in Paris after the War. SB admired Hayden's work and wrote "Henri Hayden, homme-peintre" (1952), as well as an anonymous introduction for an exhibition in Paris (1960); these two tributes were collected with a third, "Plus il va, plus c'est beau," and published as *Hayden: Soixante ans de peinture* by the Musée National d'Art Moderne (1968). When working at his cottage in Ussy, SB often visited the Haydens in their country home in nearby Reuil-en-Brie; they continued to play chess together, and SB often drove Hayden around the countryside looking for scenes to paint. SB assisted Hayden and his wife after the painter suffered a heart attack while at his London exhibition in 1965. SB continued to assist his widow after Hayden's death in 1970.

Aidan Higgins (b. 1927), Irish novelist, was born in Celbridge, Co. Kildare, and educated at Clongowes Wood College. He spent long periods in Germany, Spain, and South Africa. In the late 1950s, he traveled in Europe and Africa as a puppet-operator with John Wright's Marionette Company. His best-known novel is *Langrishe, Go Down* (1966). Higgins first contacted SB through SB's cousin John Beckett. SB took an early interest in Higgins's career and recommended that he submit his first collection of stories, *Killachter Meadow* (also known as *Felo de Se*), to John Calder in London. He later recommended the French version of this and *Langrishe, Go Down* to his French publisher, Editions de Minuit. Occasionally, SB offered a detailed response to Higgins's manuscripts. At their first meeting in 1958 at John Beckett's flat in London, SB gave Higgins an inscribed copy of *Textes pour rien*. Higgins has written about his relationship with and admiration for SB in publications that include *Beckett at 60: a Festschrift*, *Hibernia*, and *New Edinburgh Review*. Works from both authors appear in the 1975 collection *Signature Anthology*.

Harold Hobson (1904–1992), British drama critic, graduated from Oxford University in 1928 and began his critical career for the *Christian Science Monitor* in 1931. In 1942, he joined *The Sunday Times* as Assistant Literary Editor, and served as its Drama Critic from 1947 to 1976. Hobson helped record and shape a renewal of British drama, championing new play-wrights such as Howard Brenton, John Osborne, SB, and Harold Pinter. His interest in French theatre was exemplified by his books *The French Theatre of Today* (1953) and *The French Theatre since 1930* (1978). Hobson wrote several enthusiastic reviews of *Waiting for Godot* at the Arts Theatre in 1955; he described the play as a turning point.

Hobson was a member of the board of governors of the National Theatre (1976–1992) and the Critics' Circle, for which he served as President in 1955. Hobson was appointed a Chevalier de l'Ordre de la Légion d'Honneur (1960) and was knighted in 1977.

Stefani Hunzinger (née Cremer, 1913–2006) headed the Theatre Department of S. Fischer Verlag in Frankfurt. Issues regarding publishing and production rights dominate her correspondence with SB, which began in 1956. In 1975, Hunzinger founded her own publishing and production agency, the Stefani Hunzinger Bühnenverlag, in Bad Homburg outside Frankfurt, and continued to represent modern dramatic works in Germany for a quarter-century. She created the double bill of SB's *Krapp's Last Tape* with Edward Albee's *The Zoo Story* in Berlin – the world premiere for the Albee play. From 1970 to 1994, she was Chairperson of the Board of Directors, the Verbandes Deutscher Bühnen- und Medienverlage (Association of German Dramatic and Media Publishers).

Mary Hutchinson (née Barnes, 1889–1977) was a notable British hostess and patron of the arts. Born in India, Mary Hutchinson spent much of her childhood in Italy where she was raised by grandparents. Following school in England, through her cousins Lytton Strachey and Duncan Grant, she made an early connection with the Bloomsbury group. In 1910, she married St. John Hutchinson (1884–1942), a leading barrister who shared her love of art and society. She had lifetime associations with prominent intellectuals, artists, and writers, including Clive Bell, Virginia Woolf, George Moore, T. S. Eliot, Aldous Huxley, Henri Matisse, and SB, to whose work she was introduced by Georges Duthuit, at whose suggestion she read *Molloy* and became fascinated by SB's work.

Hutchinson published only a single volume of her own short stories and essays, *Fugitive Pieces* (1927), but she was a champion of the arts and artists. She launched the literary journal *X* (November 1959 – July 1962), edited by David Wright (1920–1994), to draw attention to international avant-garde artists and writers; SB contributed work of his own and suggested to Hutchinson that she consider that of such emerging writers as Robert Pinget and Aidan Higgins. She was a friend of George Devine and Jocelyn Herbert, and promoted SB's plays at the Royal Court Theatre where Devine was producer. In 1955, SB and Hutchinson began a correspondence which continued to her death and which focused on the progress of SB's writing, translations, and productions, but often contained thoughts on the larger art scene in

Europe as well as news of common friends. She was watching a television production of *Ghost Trio* when she died.

Georges Lambrichs (1917–1992) joined Editions de Minuit in 1945, first as a reader, later becoming Literary Director; he recommended that SB's writing be considered by Minuit. Lambrichs was on the Editorial Board of *84: Nouvelle Revue Littéraire* (1947–1951), edited by Marcel Bisiaux (1922–1990), and published by Minuit. In 1955, he briefly worked for Grasset, and then joined the editorial staff of Gallimard, where in 1959 he founded Le Chemin. This series published over 300 books, including works by Foucault, Butor, Guyotat, Sarraute, and Tardieu, and, in 1967, the journal of the same name. From 1977 to 1987, he directed the *Nouvelle Revue Française*.

Goddard Lieberson (1911–1977) President of Columbia Records, moved with his family from England to New York in 1915. Lieberson's early ambition was to be a pianist and a composer; he attended the University of Washington and the Eastman School of Music. He taught and composed music before joining Columbia Records in 1939 as a studio recording director. His early success and quick rise in the company were marked by his support of Peter Goldberg in the development of the first 33 rpm long-playing record, which led to a dramatic rise in popular music production. He became Executive Vice President in 1949 and President of Columbia Records in 1956. Under his leadership, Columbia Records expanded its catalogue to include country and pop music, as well as show albums such as *My Fair Lady*.

Beginning in 1949, Lieberson recorded classical and modern drama, as well as readings by American and British writers. In 1956, Lieberson recorded the Broadway production of *Waiting for Godot*, and wrote to SB requesting an introduction for the record. SB met Lieberson and his wife Brigitta in Paris in August 1956, and their correspondence remained consistent over the years as they exchanged books and recordings. Lieberson took Igor Stravinsky to see the 1957 New York production of *Waiting for Godot*, and he set up meetings between SB and the composer in Paris in 1962.

Jérôme Lindon (1925–2001) was born and educated in Paris. Following the Fall of France, he volunteered for the French Resistance, although still in his teens. After the War he began to work at Editions de Minuit, a small, formerly clandestine publishing house founded in 1942 by

"Vercors" (pseudonym of Jean-Marcel Bruller, author of *Le Silence de la mer*). Lindon bought the firm in 1948 with money from his family, and moved it from the Boulevard Saint-Michel to its present address, 7 Rue Bernard-Palissy, Paris 6. His publishing strategy was simple and, for the time, breathtakingly bold: to take on and promote a number of writers who were neither well known nor likely ever to be popular successes. The first of these was SB. At the time, Suzanne Deschevaux-Dumesnil was taking the manuscripts of *Molloy*, *Malone meurt*, and *L'Innommable* from one publisher to another, to have them rejected by each in turn. Acting on a suggestion by Robert Carlier, of the Club Français du Livre, she took them to Minuit. Lindon read *Molloy* there and then, and the next day offered SB a contract for all three novels – this at a time when Minuit was struggling financially, something so obvious that SB himself worried whether Lindon's offer might not bankrupt the firm.

It would be difficult to overestimate Lindon's importance for SB. He was as good as his word as far as the publication and promotion of the work were concerned, but, almost as important, he relieved SB of the burdens that most troubled him, acting almost like a personal assistant in everything to do with the management of SB's career: dealing with importunate correspondents, interview seekers, tax problems, legal complications. SB came to depend on him more and more. He was, so to speak, the public face of SB, so that there was nothing surprising in his going to Stockholm to receive the Nobel Prize for Literature on SB's behalf.

Lindon went on to promote the work of authors as different from each other as Nathalie Sarraute, Claude Simon, Marguerite Duras, Alain Robbe-Grillet, Michel Butor, and Robert Pinget. Among the informed, the reputation of Minuit could not have been higher (a special issue of *Yale French Studies* in 1959 was given the playful title "Midnight Novelists").

He was not an easy man: his combination of high principle and autocratic manner saw to that. But he was loyal both to his protégés and to his principles. His stand against torture during the conflict in Algeria brought right-wing attacks on the firm and on his home. Less dramatically, he was a stout defender of authors' rights, and of independent booksellers in their struggle against conglomerate distributors.

At the end of his life he declared that, for him, the reading of *Molloy* was the decisive moment in his life as a publisher. At SB's death in 1989, Lindon became SB's literary executor.

Christian Ludvigsen (b. 1930), a Danish professor, critic, and translator, took an early interest in SB's work. He translated much of *Molloy* in 1952, but could not interest a Danish publisher in the novel. Ludvigsen staged the first Danish production of *En attendant Godot* at the Århus Theater in 1956, and his translation of the play was published the following year. Ludvigsen's correspondence with SB began then and continued for the next fourteen years. SB responded to Ludvigsen's questions with uncharacteristically forthright comments about his work. They met when Ludvigsen visited Paris. Ludvigsen translated and produced most of SB's dramatic work for the Danish stage. He was also involved with Denmark's famed experimental group, the Odin Theater, in Jutland. From 1972 to 1997, Ludvigsen was on the faculty of the University of Århus and chaired the Department of Drama. His autobiography is *Det begyndte med Beckett: min egen teaterhistorie* (1997; It Began with Beckett – My Own Theatre History).

Donald McWhinnie (1920–1987) worked as a scriptwriter and producer at the BBC in the European Division (1945–1949), became Drama Script Editor (1951–1953), and then Assistant Head of Sound Drama from 1953. He directed SB's first radio play *All That Fall* (1957) as well as radio productions of "From an Abandoned Work" (1957) and readings from SB's novels, *Molloy* (1957), *Malone Dies* (1958), *The Unnamable* (1959), for the BBC's Third Programme. He commissioned and produced SB's radio play *Embers* (1959), and produced the radio play *Cascando* (1964); he also directed the BBC Television production of *Waiting for Godot* (1961). McWhinnie's audio experiments led to the formation of the BBC's Radiophonic Workshop.

McWhinnie and SB got on well together, as drinking companions as well as artistic colleagues. McWhinnie directed *Krapp's Last Tape* (1958) at the Royal Court Theatre; with SB, he directed Patrick Magee and Jack MacGowran in *Endgame* at the Aldwych Theatre, London (1965); and he directed the productions of *Play* and *That Time* at the Royal Court (1976). SB worked with McWhinnie as director of *Ghost Trio* when it was broadcast on the BBC in 1976. McWhinnie authored *The Art of Radio* (1959). He directed the premiere of Harold Pinter's *The Caretaker* (1960), Charles Dyer's *Rattle of a Simple Man* (1962), and Bill Naughton's *Alfie* (1963). Among his film credits is *Moll Flanders* (1975).

Jean Martin (1922–2009) performed as Lucky in the first production of *En attendant Godot* (1953). To play the role, Martin consulted a doctor friend, Marthe Gautier, and incorporated the symptoms of Parkinson's disease into his portrayal, to powerful effect. He also created the role of

Clov in *Fin de partie* (1957) at its premiere in French in London and Paris; he read the part of the voice in SB's radio play *Cascando* (1963), and, directed by SB, he played Krapp in *La dernière bande* at the Théâtre Récamier, Paris (1970).

During the 1950s and 1960s, Martin became a close friend to both SB and Suzanne Deschevaux-Dumesnil. SB supported Martin when the actor was banned from work for signing the "Manifeste des 121" in protest against the torture of prisoners in Algeria. In addition to playing many roles from modern French drama, Martin had a successful film career that included *Jamboree* (1957), *The Battle of Algiers* (1965), *My Name is Nobody* (1973), *The Day of the Jackal* (1973), and *Lucie Aubrac* (1999).

Deryk Mendel (b. 1921) is a British dancer and choreographer who trained at Sadler's Wells; he worked in Europe and lives in France. In 1955, Mendel was performing as a mime in a Parisian cabaret, the Fontaine des Quatre Saisons. The act was a success, and so when he was asked to perform another piece featuring the same character (Frollo), he wrote to a number of playwrights, including SB and Ionesco, asking if they would write a short scenario for him. SB was stalled in his writing of *Fin de partie*, and, encouraged by Suzanne Deschevaux-Dumesnil who had seen Mendel in performance, he wrote *Acte sans paroles* for him. Mendel collaborated closely with SB's cousin, John Beckett, whose music was tied to the choreography. The mime was performed in London in 1957 with the French premiere of *Fin de partie* at the Royal Court Theatre. This marked the beginning of a long and fruitful relationship between SB and Mendel.

There followed SB's companion piece, *Acte sans paroles II*, which Mendel performed in 1960. Mendel directed the world premiere of *Comédie* in German (*Spiel*) in Ulm in 1963, as well as the Berlin revival of *Warten auf Godot* (*En attendant Godot*), at the Schillertheater in 1965 (with which SB assisted), and staged *Alle, die da fallen* (*All That Fall*) in 1966. They worked together again on the 1966 television premiere of *He Joe* (*Eh Joe*) in Germany.

Pamela Winslow Mitchell (c. 1922–2002) studied American History at Vassar College; after graduation in 1943, she worked as a civilian with Naval Intelligence during the remaining years of World War II. From the early 1950s, Mitchell worked in New York and Paris with Harold L. Oram, who raised funds for humanitarian causes. Oram became interested in theatrical production, and sent Mitchell to Paris in 1953 to help negotiate the option for the American premiere of *En attendant Godot*.

SB and Mitchell began an affair during this visit to Paris. When Mitchell returned to New York, they corresponded. She moved to Paris in the summer of 1954, but SB had to leave for Ireland in June to be with his dying brother Frank. SB encouraged Mitchell to travel and to pursue other friendships. Mitchell returned to New York at the end of January 1955, and their correspondence continued; in his letters to Mitchell, SB chronicled his struggles with early drafts of *Fin de partie*. Throughout their correspondence, the two suggested and sent each other books to read.

Although they exchanged letters until 1970, the frequency of these diminished considerably after 1956. Mitchell last saw SB in 1964, when he was in New York for the shooting of *Film*. From 1962 to 1980, Mitchell worked in fundraising with the board of The Berkshire Farm for Boys (Canaan, NY), until her retirement as Director of the New York office. She never married.

Charles Monteith (1921–1995) was born in Northern Ireland, and studied at Magdalen College, Oxford. During World War II, he served with the Royal Inniskilling Fusiliers in India and Burma. Although he had qualified as a barrister in 1949, his interests were literary. In 1953, Geoffrey Faber invited Monteith to join Faber and Faber, where he was apprenticed to T. S. Eliot before becoming Commissioning Editor in 1954. His career began well with his backing of William Golding's *Lord of the Flies*. Monteith's success with John Osborne's *Look Back in Anger* spurred Faber and Faber's interest in publishing British playwrights. When the publisher acquired the English publication rights to SB's dramatic and radio works, Monteith was SB's principal editorial contact.

Monteith also worked with Jean Genet, P. D. James, Louis MacNeice, W. H. Auden, Ted Hughes, Seamus Heaney, and his close friend Philip Larkin. He served as Chairman of Faber and Faber between 1977 and 1980 and continued as Senior Editorial Consultant until his death. He was director of the Poetry Book Society (1966–1981), a member of the Literature Panel of the Arts Council of Great Britain (1974–1978), and a member of the Library Advisory Council for England (1979–1981).

Niall Montgomery (1914–1987) studied with Denis Devlin at Belvedere College and University College, Dublin, where he graduated in architecture in 1938. Montgomery met SB through A. J. Leventhal. His father, James, had been on the board of Irish film censors, and he enabled SB to borrow the latest film journals and publications.

Montgomery wrote the first critical study of SB's work published in the United States, "No Symbols Where None Intended," for *New World Writing* (1954). An early admirer of James Joyce, Montgomery published two essays on Joyce's work in the 1960s.

As a practicing Dublin architect, Montgomery helped design the award-winning airport buildings at Collinstown in the late 1930s. His interest in the restoration of Dublin stimulated many of his projects, including the Kilkenny Design Centre. He was President of the Royal Institute of Architects of Ireland in the mid-1970s.

Montgomery published his poetry in journals such as *transition*, *Furioso*, *Envoy*, *The Lace Curtain*, and *The New Mexico Quarterly*. His collected poems were published posthumously as *The Terminal*. He was recognized as a sculptor, and his achievements in the visual arts included a P. J. Carroll Prize in the Living Art Exhibition for the audio-visual work, *The High Contracting Parties* (1973).

Charles John Morris (1895–1980), British writer and broadcaster, came to the BBC as Head of Far Eastern Service in 1943, after extensive experience as a soldier, social anthropologist, and university teacher in Central and Eastern Asia. As the Controller of the BBC's Third Programme (1952–1958), he approached SB about writing a play for radio. Despite initial hesitation, SB responded with the script of *All That Fall*. This began SB's relationship with the BBC: production of radio dramas, readings from his poetry and fiction, as well as recordings of some of his stage productions. Morris helped to develop the BBC Third Programme's reputation as a forum for experimental radio production.

Michael Myerberg (1906–1974) had his first major success as a theatrical producer with Thornton Wilder's *The Skin of Our Teeth* in 1942. In 1955, Donald Albery, the London producer of *Waiting for Godot*, leased the option for the American Broadway premiere to Myerberg, who enlisted Alan Schneider to direct the production. Billed as a "laugh sensation," the play opened in January 1956 at the new Coconut Grove Playhouse in Miami, Florida; the society audience at the premiere walked out in droves. Myerberg changed his tactic when the play came to the John Golden Theatre on Broadway in April 1956, directed by Herbert Berghof; here it was promoted as a play "for discerning intellectuals." Myerberg continued to hold the option for further productions in New York, and staged a revival at the Ethel Barrymore Theatre in 1957, with an all black cast – to SB's great pleasure.

Maurice Nadeau (b. 1911), French literary critic, editor, and publisher, was the author of *Histoire du surréalisme* (1944; *The History of Surrealism*). He was an active Résistant during the War, and from 1947 to 1951 was Director of *Combat*, originally a newspaper of the Resistance. Urged by Tristan Tzara to write about SB's work, Nadeau published "Samuel Beckett ou: En avant, vers nulle part!" (1951), the first review of SB's novel *Molloy*. Nadeau was a literary critic for *L'Express*, *Le Nouvel Observateur*, and *Mercure de France*, where he published the first review of *Malone meurt* in 1952. In the same year he wrote about the three novels (*Molloy*, *Malone meurt*, *L'Innommable*) as a group for *Les Temps Modernes* in the essay "Samuel Beckett ou le droit au silence." Nadeau founded the French literary journal *Les Lettres Nouvelles* in 1953; for its first issue he wrote an article on *L'Innommable*. Through the next decade, Nadeau continued to write on SB's work, with articles on *Fin de partie* (1957) and *Comment c'est* (1961), as well as the essay "Le chemin de la parole au silence" in 1963, in which he traces the role of silence from *Molloy* to *Comment c'est*, declaring that it is impossible to go further than SB had in the search for silence. Nadeau was founding Director of *La Quinzaine Littéraire* (1966–present) which published SB's *Assez* in the first edition. He remains active as its Director and as the head of Editions Maurice Nadeau.

Max Niedermayer (1905–1968) led a printing firm before he founded the Limes Verlag in 1945 in Wiesbaden, Germany. He is perhaps best known for his friendship and correspondence with German poet Gottfried Benn, whose works he published after their initial contact in 1948. In 1959, Limes Verlag published *Gedichte*, the first collection of SB's poems, a project Niedermayer began in 1955 in consultation with Elmar Tophoven. The poems were printed in their original English and French facing the German translations by Eva Hesse (from English) and Elmar Tophoven (from French). *Gedichte* included poems from *Echo's Bones* (1935) as well as those published in Irish, British, and French journals.

Marie Péron (née Lézine-Spiridonof, known as Mania, 1900–1988) was the daughter of a Russian family that emigrated to France when she was five. She taught English at the Lycée Buffon in Paris, and in 1930 she married Alfred Péron, SB's close friend (Profile, I). When Alfred Péron was conscripted in 1938, he asked SB to take care of his family should they need to leave Paris. Alfred Péron was deeply involved with the Resistance Movement in France, and in 1941 he recruited SB to the "Gloria SMH" réseau. In 1942, when her husband was arrested by the Gestapo, Mania Péron warned SB and Suzanne Deschevaux-Dumesnil by telegram. They fled Paris and were hidden for ten days by Nathalie Sarraute, a childhood friend of Mania Péron's (their families had known each other in Russia and later in France). Alfred Péron was sent to the Mauthausen Concentration Camp, and in 1945 he died in transit shortly after his release to the Red Cross. SB remained supportive of his widow and their twin sons, Alexis and Michel.

SB and Mania Péron developed a close working relationship. For some time after the War, they shared a typewriter (typing each other's manuscripts turn and turn about). SB worked in close consultation with her as he prepared his French novels for publication, and he sent the individual *Textes pour rien* to her as each was completed. Throughout the next decade, she would remain the "oeil de lynx" (lynx eye), as he called her in a 1953 letter, to whom he submitted his French writings for scrutiny. In 1958, she published her novel, *Le Caillou*. She remained a close friend and correspondent of SB until her death.

Robert Pinget (1919–1997), novelist and playwright, was born in Geneva, and settled in France in 1951. The course of his dealings with SB is exemplary: a shy and unconfident young man, convinced early of SB's power as a writer, made a timid approach to him. SB read some of his work, recognized his talent and also his disabling unconfidence, offered encouragement. From that the relationship evolved slowly, the older man bringing on the younger one in practical ways (notably pressing his case with Jérôme Lindon, but also suggesting jobs he might take, even offering financial support), and in comments on his work. SB's unshakeable honesty ensured that these were never merely reassuring. Supported in this way, the fledgling Pinget took flight. Their friendship, now easy and adult, grew and lasted. For the Pinget of the writing is a very different person. What SB found in that writing was an acute sensitivity to voice: to the infinite variations of tone and volume that transform speech from blocks of information to idiosyncratic indications of character and feeling. Again, Pinget's favored territory is the *ordinary*, and his favored mode, gossip. SB could see, behind these apparently simple screens, the novelist at work: the gossip which is the manufacture of stories, the ordinary which is the ground where anything may happen. He saw too that Pinget's range went beyond the cosy and engaging to include darker and more troubling elements, as novels such as *Le Libera* (1968; *The Libera me Domine*) or *Fable* (1971) make clear. The nervous young man could invent and populate a huge imaginary provincial world, and the aspiring young writer could go on to collaborate with SB, each translating work by the other: Pinget's *La Manivelle* (1968; translated by SB as *The Old Tune*), and Beckett's *All That Fall* (1957; translated by Pinget as *Tous ceux qui tombent*). In 1966, SB assisted in the production of Pinget's one-act play, *L'Hypothèse*, which appeared on the same bill with *Comédie* (*Play*) and *Va-et-vient* (*Come and Go*) at the Théâtre de l'Odéon. The friendship was made still easier by Suzanne Deschevaux-Dumesnil's fondness for Pinget.

Barney Rosset (b. 1922) bought Grove Press in 1952, and shortly afterwards, on the advice of Wallace Fowlie, his Professor at the New School for Social Research in New York, acquired the North American theatrical and publishing rights to SB's work. Grove published *Waiting for Godot* in 1954, two years before the play's first production in New York. Rosset acted as SB's American publisher and theatrical agent in the US and North America. Grove Press published the journal *Evergreen Review*, in which many of SB's prose writings were published. SB's last work, *Stirrings Still*, was written for Barney Rosset.

Rosset was a champion of the First Amendment in the United States. He took on the challenge of anti-obscenity charges by publishing D. H. Lawrence's novel *Lady Chatterley's Lover* in 1959, and won. Rosset won another highly publicized censorship case over publication of Henry Miller's *Tropic of Cancer* a few years later. Having begun his career in film, Rosset in 1964 commissioned scripts from Eugène Ionesco, Harold Pinter, Marguerite Duras, and Alain Robbe-Grillet; SB's script *Film* was the only one that was produced. SB came to New York for the shooting – his only visit to the United States.

In 1985, Rosset sold Grove Press to Weidenfeld and Getty; Rosset remained for thirteen months as Chief Executive Officer of Grove Press within the larger firm. Afterwards, Rosset started two imprints, Rosset & Co. and Blue Moon Books Inc. In 1988, he was awarded the Publishers' Citation by the PEN American Center (for "distinctive and continuous service to international letters and to the free transmission of the printed word across barriers of ignorance, censorship and repression"), and, in 2008, the Literarian Award for Outstanding Service to the American Literary Community by the National Book Foundation.

Richard Roud (1929–1989) was a writer, film critic, and film festival organizer who helped create a British and American audience for foreign film, especially French Nouvelle Vague cinema. Born in Boston, he studied at the University of Wisconsin, attended the Université de Montpellier on a Fulbright Fellowship, and did graduate work at the Shakespeare Institute at the University of Birmingham. Roud became the Principal Film Critic for *The Guardian* in 1963 and the paper's Roving Arts Critic in 1970. He served as Programme Director for the National Film Festival, London (1959–1967), and the London Film Festival (1960–1969); he is perhaps best known as founder and Director of the New York Film Festival (1963–1987). He also helped to organize film events for the Museum of Modern Art and the Film Society of Lincoln Center. Roud's correspondence with SB from 1955 concerns SB's theatrical productions as well as SB's suggestions for reading. Roud published a number of books on film including *Godard* (1967), *Straub* (1972), and *A Passion for Film* (1983). His awards include the Chevalier de l'Ordre de la Légion d'Honneur (1978), an award from the Theatre Library Association (1984), and another from the National Society of Film Critics (1988).

Alan Schneider (1917–1984), born in Kharkov, Russia, worked primarily in the United States and is best known for interpreting SB's plays. Appointed as director of the American premiere of *Waiting for Godot* by Michael Myerberg, Schneider went to Paris in 1955 to meet SB and to discuss the play. The two men attended the London production several times together. Close consultation with SB was essential to Schneider's preparation for each of the plays in SB's dramatic oeuvre. Together, he and SB went to the premiere of *Comédie* directed by Deryk Mendel in Ulm; they worked closely through each step of the production of SB's *Film* (1964), the first venture for each of them in cinema. When they could not meet to prepare a production, the two exchanged highly detailed letters filled with Schneider's questions and SB's suggestions (published in *No Author Better Served*, 1998).

Although billed as "The laugh sensation of two continents," Schneider's production of *Waiting for Godot* in Miami at the Coconut Grove Playhouse was a commercial flop. Its poor reception cost Schneider his position as director when the play opened on Broadway, but the failure led to a close bond between him and SB. Schneider went on to direct all of SB's work for the stage in the United States, as well as *Film*. He directed the world premiere of *Happy Days* at the Cherry Lane Theatre, New York, in 1961. He also brought *Waiting for Godot*, *Act without Words II*, and *Eh Joe* to television.

Schneider directed the plays of Harold Pinter, Edward Albee, and Joe Orton. He taught directing at The Julliard School in New York and at

Stanford University, and was Professor of Drama at the University of California, San Diego. While directing a play in London, Schneider died after being struck by a motorcycle as he crossed the road to post a letter to SB.

Richard Seaver (1926–2009) was a Fulbright scholar in Paris studying at the Sorbonne when he discovered SB's novels, *Molloy* and *Malone meurt*, in the window of Editions de Minuit. His enthusiastic response to these "two stunning works" is recorded in "Samuel Beckett: An Introduction" in *Merlin*, a small English-language literary journal published in Paris (1952–1955). With SB, Seaver co-translated "La Fin," which was published in *Merlin* as "The End."

Returning to the United States after *Merlin*'s demise, Seaver was Editor of two book clubs owned by George Braziller: the Book Find Club, and the Seven Arts Book Society (1957–1959). He joined Grove Press and the staff of *Evergreen Review* in 1959, thereby continuing his work with SB. He translated more of SB's early fiction: "L'Expulsé ("The Expelled") and "Le Calmant" ("The Calmative"). He edited a collection of Beckett's work, *I Can't Go On, I'll Go On* (1976). Seaver was an Editor at Penguin Books, then at Holt, and finally he established an imprint at Viking called Seaver Books (from 1979). In 1988, with his wife Jeannette Seaver, he began Arcade Publishing, which flourished as a publisher of new voices until his death.

Alan Simpson (1920–1980) co-founded the Pike Theatre in Dublin with his wife Carolyn Swift in 1953. There they presented the plays of Brendan Behan, incurred censorship for their production of Tennessee Williams's play *The Rose Tattoo*, and staged the Irish premiere of *Waiting for Godot*. SB's play opened in November 1955 and ran for six months in their small space, another week at the much larger Gate Theatre in Dublin, and had a successful tour in Ireland. Simpson also directed the first Gaelic-language performances of *Godot*, in Liam Ó Bríain's translation.

SB encouraged Simpson to produce the plays of Eugène Ionesco at the Pike Theatre. In 1958, controversy over censorship in the Dublin International Theatre Festival (An Tóstal) prompted SB to suspend production of his plays in Ireland, and thwarted Simpson's plans to stage *Endgame* and *Act without Words*. After the Pike Theatre closed in 1960, Simpson began working with the Theatre Royal, Stratford East, in London, where he directed *Waiting for Godot* (1961) and played Willie in

Happy Days (1974). He told the story of the Pike Theatre in *Beckett and Behan and a Theatre in Dublin* (1962).

Karl-Heinz Stroux (1908–1985), German film and theatre director and actor, began his career as an actor at the Berlin Volksbühne. In the late 1940s, he served as artistic director at several theatres in Darmstadt, Wiesbaden, and Berlin. From 1951 to 1955, Stroux directed at the Schillertheater and the Schlossparktheater in Berlin under Generalintendant Boleslaw Barlog. Stroux directed *Warten auf Godot* in its premiere in Berlin at the Schlossparktheater (1953), but a fall a week before the opening hospitalized him, leaving Barlog to oversee the final rehearsals. Although critics and audiences were enthusiastic, SB did not care for the production. SB attended the opening in Berlin and afterward visited Stroux in the hospital. He was not critical during their long conversation, but he did tell Stroux that he wanted the audience to flee the theatre in despair.

From 1955 to 1972, Stroux served as Generalintendant at the Düsseldorf Schauspielhaus. He directed SB's *Glückliche Tage* (*Happy Days*) at a small theatre in Düsseldorf in 1961. Stroux worked closely with Eugène Ionesco and Heinrich Böll, and won praise as a director from his actors, who included Bernhard Minetti and Ernst Schröder.

Peter Suhrkamp (1891–1959), German publisher, began his career with S. Fischer Verlag in Frankfurt in the 1930s; in 1936, Suhrkamp was made head of the firm in Germany, while parts of their operation and a portion of their list (some of the most prestigious authors) had to be moved abroad as a result of the Nuremberg Laws. Suhrkamp himself was imprisoned in the Sachsenhausen Concentration Camp in 1944 for his alleged support of resistance elements in Nazi Germany; released in 1945, he reopened the publishing house in October of that year. While he acted as custodial head of S. Fischer Verlag in Germany, Suhrkamp also led his own imprint, Suhrkamp Verlag. In 1950, Suhrkamp Verlag split from S. Fischer Verlag, each allowing its authors to choose their future publishing home.

Early in 1953, Suhrkamp saw Roger Blin's production of *En attendant Godot* in Paris and met SB afterwards. Elmar Tophoven's translation of the play was published by S. Fischer Verlag, but Suhrkamp Verlag moved quickly to become the German publisher of SB's fiction. Suhrkamp Verlag's *Morgenblatt für Freunde der Literatur* devoted an issue to SB's work in May 1954; it included an article by Peter Suhrkamp, "Was ist 'Molloy?'"

which posed the question of how a publisher could discover the originality of a work of art that shatters familiar ideas about beauty and form.

The unique "Suhrkamp-Kultur," a space for conversations about literature, is often considered one of his legacies, and it in turn established Suhrkamp Verlag as a center of intellectual life in
post-War Germany. SB continued to publish with Suhrkamp Verlag
after the death of Peter Suhrkamp.

Carolyn Swift (1923-2002), Irish writer and theatre manager, co-
founded the Pike Theatre with her husband Alan Simpson in 1953, and
introduced Dublin audiences to the work of SB and Brendan Behan. Her
remarkable gusto kept the tiny theatre afloat. After the Pike Theatre closed
in 1960, Swift joined the Drama Department of RTE Television, writing and
adapting plays and series, for both the Drama and the Young People's
Departments. She wrote for RTE's *Sunday Miscellany* and *Appraisal* programs,
was Dance Correspondent for the *Irish Times*, and contributed articles on
theatre, dance, and travel to Irish periodicals and newspapers. Swift authored many children's books (notably the *Robbers* and *Bugsy* series) and
wrote screenplays. Her record of the Pike Theatre is published in *Stage by
Stage* (1985).

Adam Tarn (1902–1975), a major post-War figure in Polish drama, was
the literary manager of several Warsaw theatres. In 1956, he was Editor
of the Warsaw dramatic journal *Dialog*. The journal became the primary
outlet for the increasing experimentation and modernism in Polish
drama, and introduced to Polish audiences the work of SB, as well as
Camus, Dürrenmatt, Ionesco, and Pinter.

Maria Jolas introduced Tarn to SB in 1956. Tarn arranged for SB's
plays to be translated, performed, and published in Poland, beginning
with an abridged version of *Waiting for Godot* in the May 1956 issue of
Dialog. Although he often invited SB to visit Warsaw, the two met only
in Paris. Following the Communist purge of intellectuals in Poland in
1968, Tarn was dismissed from his position at *Dialog*. He emigrated to
Canada. SB did all he could to introduce Tarn to those in Canada who
might be helpful. He also sent several of his new short writings to Tarn,
thinking that he might launch a new drama journal in Canada. This did
not occur, but Tarn continued to publish articles on theatre. He translated *Happy Days* into Polish in 1961 with his wife Mary Tarn. He
returned to Europe and was completing a book on Chekhov's drama
at the time of his death in Switzerland.

Elmar Tophoven (1923–1989) was a German translator of French literature. Beginning in 1949, he lectured first at the Sorbonne, as the first German lektor appointed after the War, and then at the Ecole Normale Supérieure in Paris for twenty-five years. He translated works by Robbe-Grillet, Proust, and Sarraute, as well as most of SB's drama, poetry, and prose. In 1953, he was introduced to SB's work by Arthur Adamov, who took him to the premiere of *Godot* in Paris. Immediately, Tophoven began his translation of the play. He took his draft to Jérôme Lindon three weeks later. Beckett went over the translation with Tophoven, and it was published by S. Fischer Verlag. This set the pattern for Tophoven's future translations of SB's writings; since he lived in Paris, he and SB met regularly to work through the translations.

Erika Tophoven, his wife and fellow literary translator, frequently teamed up with him for translations of SB's English-language works. Tophoven was eager to make the process of translating more visible and collaborative; he shared his notes with students and colleagues, and he explored issues of vocabulary and syntax with other Beckett translators. In his hometown of Straelen in northwest Germany, he founded in 1978 the Europäisches Übersetzer-Kollegium (European College of Translators), a center where translators of literature and non-fiction could work as colleagues rather than in isolation. It served as the model for a number of similar institutions across Europe, including the Collège International des Traducteurs Littéraires (College of Literary Translators) in Arles, France.

Transition (1948–1950), spelled with a capital "T," was the post-War avatar of *transition*, the journal established by Eugene Jolas, Maria Jolas, and Elliot Paul in 1927. Georges Duthuit, who had become close to the Jolases during his War years in the United States, proposed re-launching the journal with himself as Editor and backer, and his wife Marguerite as Administrator. The Advisory Editors for its first issue were: Bataille, Char, Douglas Cooper, Fouchet, Stuart Gilbert, Jolas, Sartre, and Jean Wahl. (From the third issue, David McDowell was added as "Advisory Editor for the U.S.A.") The journal's policy was spelled out in the editorial foreword to its first issue:

> The object of TRANSITION Forty-eight is to assemble for the English-speaking world the best of French art and thought, whatever the style and whatever the application ... contributors are united by a common will to be true to truth, and a common awareness of a new age already kicking in the womb. That age, they hold, will utter a simplification, an astonishing

simplification: whereby science and divination, metaphysics and the arts, all the lusty incompatibilities, will no longer seem apart or out of joint, but fused and re-minted into a wise wholeness.

It is their aim, and the ambition of this paper, to recover somehow the virtue that has gone out of life; to unseal the spirit of festivity; to find again the adjustment, togetherness, at-one-ment of the tavern; to return to the sense of rapture. (5–6)

Four issues were published as *"Transition Forty-Eight"* (though the last of these was printed in 1949), one issue appeared in 1949, and the final issue came out in 1950. The journal's covers were distinguished by specially made designs by Henri Matisse: a cut-out of a mask for nos. 1–4 and 6, and a drawing of faces for no. 5, the "Special Illustrated Art Number."

It was hard to find adequate stock of paper in this period, and distribution of the journal, published by Duthuit's own Transition Press, proved nearly impossible, ensuring that the venture was not financially viable. SB, who published in the journal, was closely involved with Duthuit in the selection of articles for *Transition*, in translating them, and in revising the translations of others.

Alexander Trocchi (1925–1984), Scottish novelist, was born in Glasgow, came to Paris in 1950 on a travel scholarship, and stayed. In 1952, he started the literary journal *Merlin*, which he edited throughout its eleven issues. Writers published in *Merlin* included Sartre, Ionesco, Genet, Eluard, Henry Miller, as well as SB. In its second issue, *Merlin* published Richard Seaver's essay on *Molloy*, and Trocchi asked SB if *Merlin* could publish his stories and extracts from his novels. In 1953, the *Merlin* group (Trocchi, Seaver, Wainhouse, Logue, Bowles, and Lougee) entered into agreement with Maurice Girodias and his Olympia Press to publish books in English under the imprint of Collection Merlin. Their initial publication was the first edition of *Watt*. The series also published *Molloy* in the English translation done by Patrick Bowles with the author. Although relations between Trocchi and SB became strained when SB was not sent proofs or payment, Trocchi was essentially responsible for introducing SB's post-War novels to the English-language literary world.

Trocchi's first mature novel, *Young Adam*, was published by Olympia Press in 1954. During the 1950s, Trocchi acquired a heroin addiction that was to last the rest of his life. After the final issue of *Merlin*, he moved to the United States, where he worked for many years on a barge in New York. From this experience came his novel *Cain's Book*, published by Grove Press in 1960 to critical acclaim. He returned to Britain in 1962, where he became involved in the Situationist International and other counter-cultural projects. He remained in London for the rest of his life, writing much but publishing little.

Christine Tsingos (1920–1973) was a Greek actress, who, with her husband the painter, set designer, and architect Thanos Tsingos, founded the Gaîté-Montparnasse theatre in 1948. As foreigners, she and her husband were not entitled to manage a theatre in France, so they asked Roger Blin to sign the lease and manage the theatre. He did so in hopes of producing his work there. Blin grew acquainted with SB, and made plans to produce *Godot* in 1950, but Tsingos did not like the play and refused to have it in her theatre, perhaps because it lacked a role for her. In 1957, Tsingos played the role of Nell in the premiere (in the original French) of SB's *Fin de partie* at the Royal Court Theatre, London, which Blin directed. When the play was performed in Paris, however, she refused the part, feeling that her reputation in Paris would be damaged by her taking the role of an old woman. Despite this, Tsingos did develop a close friendship with both SB and Suzanne Deschevaux-Dumesnil.

Tsingos reprised her role as Nell in *Fin de partie* at Théâtre 347, Paris (1968), and in Greece. She was much acclaimed in *Happy Days*, which she played in both French and Greek in Athens. Tsingos died of an asthma attack in Greece.

Abraham Gerardus van Velde (1895–1981, known as Bram), the elder brother of Geer and Jacoba van Velde, was born in Zouterowoud, near Leyden. His father abandoned the family in 1903, leaving them in serious financial difficulties. Bram van Velde was apprenticed to a firm of interior decorators, who recognized he had talent and encouraged him to develop it. He lived from 1922 to 1924 in the artists' colony at Worpswede, Germany, and then moved to Paris. His work was presented in the Salon des Indépendants in Paris in 1927. He met Otto Freundlich and discovered Matisse's work at this time. He married the German painter, Lilly Klöker (1896–1936), whom he had met in Worpswede, in 1928. They moved in 1932 to Mallorca; when his wife died, he returned to Paris, staying for a time with his brother Geer. Later he found support in the companionship of Marthe Arnaud (née Kuntz, 1887–1959), formerly a Lutheran missionary in Northern Rhodesia.

SB met Bram van Velde in 1937 through Bram's brother Geer van Velde: the younger brother was a close friend of George and Gwynedd Reavey. Although SB was initially more engaged by Geer's friendship, over time he developed a deeper sympathy for Bram's paintings. SB bought a painting by Bram van Velde (*Sans titre*, also known as *Composition 1937*), and it hung facing his desk where he could see it as he worked. He also owned a gouache (*Sans titre 1939–40*).

SB wrote on both Bram and Geer van Velde's work in two major critical essays, "La Peinture des van Velde ou le monde et le pantalon" (1946) and "Peintres de l'empêchement" (1948); he also wrote short pieces for their exhibitions including "The New Object" (Galerie Maeght, 1948) and "G. et B. van Velde" (1948). In "Three Dialogues," SB's exchanges with Georges Duthuit from 1949, SB notes that Bram van Velde is "the first to admit that to be an artist is to fail, as no other dare fail"; that he accepted "the situation . . . of him who is helpless, cannot act, in the event cannot paint, since he is obliged to paint"; and that he consented to the act "of him who, helpless, unable to act, acts, in the event paints, since he is obliged to paint." In 1975, SB published the prose poem "La Falaise," dedicated "pour Bram."

In 1947, Bram van Velde was given a contract with the Galerie Maeght in Paris. He exhibited his work here in 1948 and 1952, and at the Kootz Gallery in New York in 1948. Sales did not follow, however, and he was dropped by the Galerie Maeght in 1952. There followed a difficult period of inactivity. SB's interest in his work sustained him; Van Velde told Michel Waldberg that SB "spoke of my painting as no one had ever spoken before; his presence was stimulating to me" (1958). After his retrospective at the Bern Kunsthalle in 1958, and with the prospect of another retrospective in Amsterdam in December 1959, he suffered another personal loss when Marthe Arnaud was hit by a car in Paris and died.

Bram van Velde met Madeleine Spierer in Geneva, and she became his companion; he worked there and in Paris until 1977, when he returned permanently to France. From the early 1960s, his work enjoyed successful exhibitions throughout Europe, as well as at the Knoedler Gallery in New York. SB and Bram saw much less of each other. In 1980, his work was again exhibited by the Galerie Maeght. He died at the end of December 1981 in Grimaud, France.

Gerardus van Velde (1898–1977, known as Geer), the younger brother of Bram van Velde, and an older brother of Jacoba, was born in Lisse, near

Leyden. He was apprenticed to a decorating firm in The Hague, fulfilled his military service by working with the Red Cross, and toured Flanders on foot, making money as a painter of interior decorations. He followed his older brother to Paris in 1925, determined to become an artist. Here he met and married Elisabeth Jokl (known as Lisl, b. 1908, m. 1933). He exhibited in the Salon des Indépendants (1926–1930), and in The Hague. Through his friend George Reavey, he met SB in 1937. SB was immediately attracted by Geer van Velde's charisma and dry sense of humor. SB visited Geer's studio often, and they played chess together. SB wrote about the painting of both brothers in "La Peinture des van Velde ou le monde et le pantalon" (1946) and "Peintres de l'empêchement" (1948). Beckett owned two paintings by Geer van Velde, now in a private collection. Although SB would eventually develop a deeper affinity with Bram van Velde, in later years SB and Geer occasionally would see one another in Paris.

Jacoba van Velde (1903–1985), the younger sister of the painters Bram and Geer van Velde, trained in The Hague as a ballet dancer, and in 1922 she was briefly married to the violinist Salomon Polak (known as Harry Polah). She performed as a dancer in France under the name "Pola Maslowa." In 1937, she married Arnold Clerx (1897–1968), a former actor who had established himself in Paris as a writer. When *Murphy* was first published in English, SB gave a copy to Geer, who passed it on to Jacoba, since she was interested in literature. She did not herself get to know SB until after the War, and in 1946 she began to act as his literary agent with Editions Bordas, *Les Temps Modernes*, and others.

In November 1947, when her first story "Evasion" was published in *Les Lettres Françaises*, she concentrated her attention on her own writing. Later, when she returned to Holland, she took on the role of Dutch translator for SB's plays. From 1963 she translated *Molloy*, *Malone meurt*, and *L'Innommable* into Dutch with Fritz Kuipers, who became her companion. She enjoyed international success with her novel *De grote zalle* (1953; *The Big Ward*). SB went through the translations into German and English with her. She published a second novel, *Een blad in de wind* (1961; *A Leaf in the Wind*). She became associated with the Studio company as a dramaturg for French theatre from 1965 to 1971, and wrote some plays herself.

SB and Jacoba van Velde remained close friends for several decades. Their correspondence reflects her translations and her interest in productions of his work. She sought his advice about publication in France and the United States as well as on personal matters. A radio play, *Beckett and Jacoba*, was written by Karlijn Stoffels in 1992.

Jean Wahl (1888–1974), a French philosopher, poet, and literary critic, was born to a Jewish family in Marseille; his father taught English and he was fully bilingual as a child. Wahl's first book was a study that introduced the American philosopher William James to French readers. By 1936, he was a professor at the Sorbonne, where Jean-Paul Sartre was among his students. Wahl became an influential figure in the Existentialist movement, with particular interest in Hegel and Kierkegaard. In 1942, Wahl was among Jews who were arrested by the Gestapo. He was held, interrogated, and tortured at the Drancy Internment Camp, but he managed to escape by hiding in a butcher's truck. With the help of friends he made his way to Marseille, and from there on one of the last refugee ships to the United States. There he taught at Mount Holyoke College, the University of Chicago, and the New School for Social Research. After the War, he resumed his position at the Sorbonne. Wahl was the founder of the Collège Philosophique, as well as the founder and Editor of the philosophical and literary journal *Deucalion*. He approached SB with a request to contribute to the journal, and in 1952 *Textes pour rien* no. V was published as "Je tiens le Greffe." SB assisted Wahl in the translation of his poem "L'écriture est gravure" ("The Word is Graven").

Herbert Martyn Oliver White (1885–1963, popularly known as HO) was a literary scholar who was educated at Trinity College Dublin. He lectured at the Ecole Normale Supérieure, Sheffield University, and Queen's University in Belfast. In 1939, he succeeded W. F. Trench as Professor of English in the Modern Languages department of TCD; his academic specialty was eighteenth-century English poetry. At TCD he established a successful post-graduate school of Anglo-Irish literature. His eccentric manner made him popular among his students. White published *The Works of Thomas Purney* (1933) and was a contributor to *The Review of English Studies*. White supported SB's work with enthusiasm, and suggested that he be awarded an honorary degree by TCD in 1959 – the only such recognition that SB ever accepted. When White visited Paris, SB, often joined by A. J. Leventhal, another TCD alumnus, would make an occasion of it. Three weeks before his death, White attended the 1963 opening of *Oh les beaux jours* in Paris.

BIBLIOGRAPHY OF WORKS CITED

XIIe Salon de Mai, Musée d'Art Moderne de la Ville de Paris, du 5 au 27 mai 1956. Paris: Salon de Mai, 1956.

Ackerley, J. R. *The Letters of J. R. Ackerley.* Ed. Neville Braybrooke. London: Duckworth, 1975.

Admussen, Richard L. *The Samuel Beckett Manuscripts: A Study.* Ed. Jackson Bryer. A Reference Study in Literature. Boston: G. K. Hall, 1979.

Alphant, Marianne, Nathalie Léger, and Amarante Szidon, eds. *Objet: Beckett.* Paris: Centre Pompidou, IMEC-Editeur, 2007.

Anders, Günther. "Sein ohne Zeit: Zu Becketts Stück *En attendant Godot.*" *Neue Schweizer Rundschau* 9 (January 1954) 526–540.

Andrieu-Guitrancourt, Antoine, and Serge Bouillon. *Jacques Hébertot le magnifique (1886–1970): une vie au service du théâtre et des beaux-arts en quatre chroniques.* Paris: Paris Bibliothèques / Fondation Hébertot, 2006.

Apollinaire, Guillaume. "Zone." *Transition Fifty* no. 6 (October 1950) 126–131. Rpt. *Zone.* Dublin: Dolmen Press, 1972.

Arp, Jean. *Jours effeuillés: poèmes, essais, souvenirs, 1920–1965.* Paris: Gallimard, 1966.

On My Way: Poetry and Essays 1912–1947. New York: Wittenborn, Schultz, 1948.

Art impressionniste et moderne: dont un ensemble d'œuvres provenant de l'atelier Degas. Paris: Christie's, 2006.

Aslan, Odette. *Roger Blin and Twentieth-Century Playwrights.* Tr. Ruby Cohn. Cambridge: Cambridge University Press, 1988.

Atik, Anne. *How It Was: A Memoir of Samuel Beckett.* Emeryville, CA: Shoemaker and Hoard, 2005.

"Au pays du matin calme." *Lectures pour Tous, Revue Universelle Illustrée* 9 (June 1904) 752–760.

Baillio, Joseph. "Wildenstein, Paris, New York and Old Master French Art." *The Arts of France from François 1er to Napoléon 1er.* New York: Wildenstein, 2005. 14–48.

Bair, Deirdre. *Simone de Beauvoir: A Biography.* New York: Simon and Schuster, 1990.

Banier, François-Marie. *Samuel Beckett. Portraits d'auteur.* Paris: Marval, 1997.

Barlog, Boleslaw. *Theater lebenslänglich.* Munich: Knaur, 1981.

Basbanes, Nicholas A. *A Gentle Madness: Bibliophiles, Bibliomanes and the Eternal Passion for Books.* New York: Holt, 1999.

Bataille, Georges. *Choix de lettres: 1917-1962.* Ed. Michel Surya. Paris: Gallimard, 1977.

Œuvres complètes. Vol. I. Paris: Gallimard, 1992. 12 vols.

"Le silence de Molloy." Rev. of *Molloy*, by Samuel Beckett. *Critique* 7 (15 May 1951) 387-396.

Baudelaire, Charles. *Les Fleurs du mal: The Complete Text of The Flowers of Evil.* Tr. Richard Howard. Boston: David R. Godine, 1982.

Œuvres complètes. Ed. Claude Pichois. Bibliothèque de la Pléiade. Paris: Gallimard, 1975-1976. 2 vols.

Bauret, Jean-François. *L'Analyse photographique d'un tableau de Bram van Velde.* Fontenay-Mauvoisin: chez l'auteur, 1960.

Bearor, Karen A. *Irene Rice Pereira: Her Paintings and Philosophy.* Austin: University of Texas Press, 1994.

Beckett, Samuel. *Aspettando Godot.* Tr. Carlo Fruttero. Collezione di teatro. Turin: G. Einaudi, 1956.

The Complete Short Prose: 1929-1989. Ed. S. E. Gontarski. New York: Grove Press, 1995.

"Czekając na Godota." Tr. Julian Rogozinski. *Dialog* 1.1 (May 1956) 89-98.

"Dante and the Lobster." *Evergreen Review* 1.1 (December 1957) 24-36.

"Dante... Bruno. Vico.. Joyce." *transition* 16-17 (June 1929) 242-253.

"Denis Devlin." Rev. of *Intercessions*, by Denis Devlin. *transition* 27 (April-May 1938) 289-294.

Disjecta: Miscellaneous Writings and a Dramatic Fragment. Ed. Ruby Cohn. New York: Grove Press, 1984.

Echo's Bones and Other Precipitates. Paris: Europa Press, 1935.

En attendant Godot. Paris: Editions de Minuit, 1952.

En attendant Godot: pièce en deux actes. Ed. Colin Duckworth. London: Harrap, 1966.

"The End." Tr. Richard Seaver with the author. *Merlin* 2.3 (Summer-Autumn 1954) 144-159.

"*Esperando a Godot.*" Tr. Trino Martínez Trives. *Primer Acto: Revista Española del Teatro* 1 (April 1957) 21-45.

"L'Expulsé." *Fontaine* 10 (December 1946-January 1947) 685-708.

"Extract from *Molloy*." Tr. P[atrick] W. Bowles. *Merlin* 2.2 (Autumn 1953) 88-103.

"An Extract from Watt." *Envoy: A Review of Literature and Art* 1.2 (January 1950) 11-19.

"Extract from Watt." *Irish Writing* 17 (December 1951) 11-16.

"Extract from Watt." *Merlin* 1.3 (Winter 1952-1953) 118-126.

Four Novellas. London: John Calder, 1977.

Godō wo machinagara. Tr. Shinya Ando. Tokyo: Hakusuisha, 1956.

L'Innommable. Paris: Editions de Minuit, 1953.

"Je tiens le Greffe." *Deucalion* 36.4 (October 1952) 137–140.

The Letters of Samuel Beckett: 1929–1940. Vol. I. Ed. Martha Dow Fehsenfeld, Lois More Overbeck, George Craig, and Dan Gunn. Cambridge: Cambridge University Press, 2009.

"Letters to Barney Rosset." *The Review of Contemporary Fiction* 10.3 (Fall 1990) 64–71.

"Mahood." *Nouvelle Nouvelle Revue Française* 1.2 (February 1953) 214–234.

"Malone Dies: From the Author's Translation of *Malone Meurt*." *Irish Writing* 34 (Spring 1956) 29–35.

Malone meurt. Paris: Editions de Minuit, 1951.

"Malone s'en conte." *Nouvelle Revue Littéraire* 16 (December 1950) 3–10.

Molloy. Paris: Editions de Minuit, 1951.

Molloy. New York: Grove Press, 1955.

"Molloy." Tr. Patrick Bowles in collaboration with the author. *New World Writing* 3.5 (April 1954) 316–323.

More Pricks Than Kicks. London: Chatto and Windus, 1934.

Murphy. New York: Grove Press, 1957.

Nouvelles et Textes pour rien. Paris: Editions de Minuit, 1955.

"Ooftish." *transition* 27 (April–May 1938) 33.

"Peintres de l'empêchement." *Derrière le Miroir* 11–12 (June 1948) 3, 4, 7.

"La Peinture des van Velde ou le monde et le pantalon." *Cahiers d'Art* 20–21 (1945–1946) 349–356.

"Poèmes 38–39." *Les Temps Modernes* 2.14 (November 1946) 288–293.

Poems: 1930–1989. London: Calder Publications, 2002.

Proust. The Dolphin Books. London: Chatto and Windus, 1931. Rpt. New York: Grove, 1957.

"Quel malheur . . ." *Les Temps Modernes* 71 (September 1951) 385–416.

"Sam over Bram." Tr. Matthijs Engelberts, Ruth Hemmes, and Erik Slagter. *Het Beckett Blad* 11 (Autumn 1996) 19–22.

Selected Poems: 1930–1989. Ed. David Wheatley. London: Faber and Faber, 2009.

"The Smeraldina's Billet Doux." *Zero Anthology*, VIII. Ed. Themistocles Hoetis. New York: Zero Press, 1956. 56–61.

Stories and Texts for Nothing. New York: Grove Press, 1967.

"Suite." *Les Temps Modernes* 1.10 (1 July 1946) 107–110.

"Trois poèmes." *Cahiers des saisons* 2 (October 1955) 115–116.

"Trois poèmes – Three Poems." *Transition Forty-Eight* no. 2 (June 1948) 96–97.

"Two Fragments." *Transition Fifty* no. 6 (October 1950) 103–106.

The Unnamable. New York: Grove Press, 1958.

"Utkastad." *Samuel Beckett Knivavnej: Prosastycken 1946–66*. Tr. Carl Gustaf Bjurström. Stockholm: Almquist and Wiksell, 1969. 9–25.

Vi venter på Godot. Tr. Christian Ludvigsen. Fredersborg: Arena, 1957.
"Waiting for Godot." *Theatre Arts* 40.8 (August 1956) 36–61.
Waiting for Godot, A Tragicomedy in Two Acts. New York: Grove Press, 1954.
Waiting for Godot. London: Faber and Faber, 1955.
Watt. New York: Grove Press, 1959.
"Who is Godot?" Tr. Edith Fournier. *The New Yorker* (24 June and 1 July 1996) 136–137.
"Yellow." *New World Writing* 5.10 (November 1956) 108–119.
[Beckett, Samuel] Andrew Belis, pseud. "Recent Irish Poetry." *The Bookman* 86.515 (August 1934) 235–236.
Beckett, Samuel, and Georges Duthuit. "Three Dialogues: Samuel Beckett and Georges Duthuit." *Transition Forty-Nine* no. 5 (December 1949) 97–103.
Beckett, Samuel, and Erich Franzen. "Samuel Beckett and Erich Franzen: Correspondence on Translating Molloy." *Babel* 3 (Spring 1984) 23–35.
Beckett, Samuel, and Barney Rosset. "The *Godot* Letters: A Lasting Effect." *The New Theater Review* [now *Lincoln Center Theater Review*] 12 (Spring 1995) 10–13.
"Letters [1953–1955]." *The Grove Press Reader, 1951–2001*. Ed. S. E. Gontarski. New York: Grove Press, 2001. 25–38.
Beckett, Samuel, and Alan Schneider. *No Author Better Served*. Ed. Maurice Harmon. Cambridge, MA: Harvard University Press, 1998.
Beckett, Samuel, Pierre Schneider, and Jacques Putman. "Hommage à Jack B. Yeats." *Les Lettres Nouvelles* 14 (April 1954) 619–621.
Beckett, Samuel, Octavio Paz, Eliot Weinberger, and Enrique Chagoya. *The Bread of Days: Eleven Mexican Poets / El pan de los días: once poetas mexicanos*. Afterword by Octavio Paz with Eliot Weinberger. Covelo, CA: Yolla Bolly Press, 1994.
Béhar, Henri. *André Breton: le grand indésirable*. Paris: Calmann-Lévy, 1990.
Belmont, Georges. "Poèmes." *Nouvelle Nouvelle Revue Française* 2.17 (May 1954) 799–802.
Bénézit, Emmanuel. *Dictionnaire critique et documentaire des peintres, sculpteurs, dessinateurs et graveurs de tous les temps et de tous les pays*. 3rd edn. Paris: Librairie Gründ, 1976.
Bernier, Robert, with collaboration of Guy Patenaude, Françoise-Marc Gagnon, and Monique Brunet. *Jean-Paul Riopelle: des visions d'Amérique*. Montréal: Les Editions de l'Homme, 1997.
Bersani, Leo, and Ulysse Dutoit. *Arts of Impoverishment: Beckett, Rothko, Resnais*. Cambridge, MA, and London: Harvard University Press, 1993.
Beyen, Roland. *Ghelderode: présentation, choix de textes, chronologie, bibliographie*. Paris: Seghers, 1974.
Billy, André. *Vie de Balzac*. Paris: Flammarion, 1944. 2 vols.
Billy, Hélène de. *Riopelle: la biographie*. Montréal: Editions Art Global, 1996.

Birksted, Jan K. *Modernism and the Mediterranean: The Maeght Foundation.* Aldershot: Ashgate, 2004.

Bjurström, C. J. "Samuel Beckett." *Bonniers Litterära Magasin* 23.1 (January 1954) 27–33.

Blanchot, Maurice. *Faux pas.* Paris: Gallimard, 1943.

"Où maintenant? Qui maintenant?" Rev. of *L'Innommable*, by Samuel Beckett. *Nouvelle Nouvelle Revue Française* 2.10 (October 1953) 678–686.

Blin, Roger. "Témoignage" in Pierre Mélèse, *Arthur Adamov: textes d'Arthur Adamov, points de vue critiques, témoignages, chronologie.* Théâtre de tous les temps. Paris: Seghers, 1973. 156–158.

Blin, Roger, and Lynda Bellity Peskine. *Roger Blin: souvenirs et propos recueillis.* Paris: Gallimard, 1986.

[Blunden, Edmund Charles]. "Seen from Dublin." Rev. of *Postscript on Existentialism*, by Arland Ussher. *Times Literary Supplement* 2322 (3 August 1946) 367.

Bordas, Pierre. *L'Edition est une aventure.* Paris: Editions de Fallois, 1997.

Boswell, James. *Boswell's Life of Johnson, Together with Boswell's Journal of a Tour to the Hebrides and Johnson's Diary of a Journey into North Wales.* Ed. George Birkbeck Hill. Revised and enlarged L. F. Powell. Oxford: Clarendon Press, 1934. 6 vols.

Bouchet, André du. "Three Exhibitions: Masson – Tal Coat – Miró." *Transition Forty-Nine* no. 5 (December 1949) 89–96.

Bowles, Patrick. "How to Fail." *P.N. Review* 20.4 (March–April 1994) 24–38. Excerpt rpt. as "Patrick Bowles on Beckett in the Early 1950s." *Beckett Remembering, Remembering Beckett: A Centennial Celebration.* Ed. James and Elizabeth Knowlson. New York: Arcade Publishing, 2005. 108–115.

Briscoe, Desmond, and Roy Curtis-Bramwell. *The BBC Radiophonic Workshop: The First 25 Years.* London: BBC, 1983.

Brooke, Peter. *Albert Gleizes: For and Against the Twentieth Century.* New Haven: Yale University Press, 2001.

Browning, Robert. *Robert Browning: The Poems.* Ed. John Pettigrew and Thomas J. Collins. New Haven: Yale University Press, 1981. 2 vols.

Bryden, Mary, Julian Garforth, and Peter Mills, eds. *Beckett at Reading: Catalogue of the Beckett Manuscript Collection at The University of Reading.* Reading: Whiteknights Press and the Beckett International Foundation, 1998.

Buffet, Robert. "Course au trésor." *Qui Détective? Le Magazine de l'énigme et de l'aventure* 142 (21 March 1949) 3–5.

Büttner, Gottfried. *Samuel Beckett's Novel Watt.* Tr. Joseph P. Dolan. Philadelphia: University of Pennsylvania Press, 1984.

Samuel Becketts Roman "Watt"; Eine Untersuchung des gnoseologischen Grundzuges. Heidelberg: Winter, 1981.

Calder, John, ed. *As No Other Dare Fail: For Samuel Beckett on his 80th Birthday by his Friends and Admirers*. Intro. Dougald McMillan. New York: Riverrun Press, 1986.

Campbell, Patrick Gordon. *An Irishman's Diary*. London: Cassell and Company, 1950.

Canet, Nicole. *Maisons closes 1860–1946: bordels de femmes, bordels d'hommes*. Paris: La Galerie Au Bonheur du Jour, 2009.

Carlisle, Norman, and Madelyn Carlisle. "The Big Slot-Machine Swindle." *Reader's Digest* 54 (June 1949) 46–49.

Cascetta, Annamaria. *Il tragico e l'umorismo: studio sulla drammaturgia di Samuel Beckett*. Storia dello spettacolo. Florence: Le lettere, 2000.

Caspari, Carlheinz. "Zu Samuel Becketts Theater." *Atoll* 1 (1954) 24–28.

Cesarani, David. *Arthur Koestler: The Homeless Mind*. New York: The Free Press, Simon and Schuster, 1999.

Chambrun, René de. *Pierre Laval: Traitor or Patriot?* Tr. Elly Stein. New York: Scribner's Sons, 1989.

Chandler, Raymond. *Selected Letters of Raymond Chandler*. Ed. Frank McShane. New York: Columbia University Press, 1981.

Char, René. "The Pulverized Poem." Tr. Eugene Jolas. *Transition Forty-Eight* no. 1 (February 1948) 33–55.

Chisholm, Anne. *Nancy Cunard: A Biography*. New York: Alfred A. Knopf, 1979.

Clair, René. "Sur le problème de Faust." In Jean Marcenac, *La beauté du Diable*. Paris: Les Editeurs Français Réunis, 1950. 45–56.

Cohn, Ruby. *A Beckett Canon*. Ann Arbor: The University of Michigan Press, 2001.
From Desire to Godot: Pocket Theater of Postwar Paris. Berkeley: University of California Press, 1987.

Cointent, Jean-Paul. *Marcel Déat: du socialisme au national-socialisme*. Paris: Perrin, 1998.

Connelly, Elizabeth. "Curator's Comments." *Heritage* [Jamestown Historical Society] (Spring 2002) 6.

Coppée, François. "Un duel au sabre." *Lectures pour Tous, Revue Universelle Illustrée* 9 (June 1904) 739–751.

Corvin, Michel. *Festivals de l'art d'avant-garde: Marseille, Nantes, Paris 1956–1960*. Paris: Somogy Editions d'Art, 2004.

Crowe, Catriona, Ronan Fanning, Michael Kennedy, Dermot Keogh, and Eunan O'Halpin, eds. *Documents on Irish Foreign Policy*. Vol. VII. Dublin: Royal Irish Academy, 2010. 7 vols. 1998– .

Cunard, Nancy. *GM: Memories of George Moore*. London: Hart-Davis, 1956.
Grand Man: Memories of Norman Douglas, with Extracts from his Letters, and Appreciations by Kenneth Macpherson, Harold Acton, Arthur Johnson, Charles Duff, and Victor Cunard and a Bibliographical Note by Cecil Woolf. London: Secker and Warburg, 1954.
Parallax. London: Hogarth Press, 1925.

Dam, René. "Le Disciple." *L'Age Nouveau* 24 (? January 1948) 92–93.

Dante. *The Banquet.* Tr. Christopher Ryan. Saratoga, CA: ANMA Libri, 1989.

Convivio. Ed. Piero Cudini. Milan: Garzanti, 1980.

La Divina Commedia. Comment by Enrico Bianchi. Florence: Adriano Salani, 1927.

The Divine Comedy of Dante Alighieri. Tr. and comment John D. Sinclair. London: John Lane The Bodley Head, 1939–1948, revised 1948. 3 vols.

Davenport, Russell W., with Winthrop Sargeant. "A *Life* Round Table on Modern Art." *Life* (11 October 1948) 56–68, 70, 75–76, 78–79.

Davis, R. J., M. J. Friedman, J. R. Bryer *et al. Samuel Beckett: œuvres et critique franco-anglaise.* Calepins de bibliographie. Paris: Minard, 1972.

De Sanctis, Francesco. *Storia della letteratura italiana.* Ed. Niccolò Gallo. Turin: Giulio Einaudi Editore, 1958. 2 vols.

Debord, Guy, and Alice Debord. *Guy Debord: Correspondance, I, juin 1957 – août 1960.* Paris: Fayard, 1999.

Devlin, Denis. *Collected Poems of Denis Devlin.* Ed. J. C. C. Mays. Dublin: The Dedalus Press, 1989.

Lough Derg and Other Poems. New York: Reynal and Hitchcock, 1946.

"Documents." *Transition Forty-Nine* no. 5 (December 1949) 110–126.

Doshay, Lewis J., and Kate Constable. "Newer Drugs in the Treatment of Parkinsonism." *Neurology* 1 (1951) 68–74.

Dukes, Gerry. "Englishing *Godot*." *After Beckett / D'Après Beckett.* Ed. Anthony Uhlmann, Sjef Houppermans, and Bruno Clément. *Samuel Beckett Today/Aujourd'hui* 15 (2004) 521–532.

Duperray, Eve, Alexandre Didier, and Sandra Chastel, eds. *René Char dans le miroir des eaux.* Paris: Beauchesne, 2008.

Duprey, Jean-Pierre. *Derrière son double.* Preface by André Breton. Paris: Le Soleil Noir, 1950.

Duthuit, Georges. "Bram van Velde ou aux Colonnes d'Hercule." *Derrière le Miroir* 43 (February 1952) 2–4, 8. Rpt. in Georges Duthuit, *Représentation et présence: premiers écrits et travaux (1923–1952).* Intro. Yves Bonnefoy. Paris: Flammarion, 1974. 357–365. Rpt. in Clare Stoullig and Nathalie Schoeller, eds. *Bram van Velde.* Paris: Editions du Centre Georges Pompidou, 1989. 176–179.

"Le Don indien: sur la côte nord-ouest de l'Amérique." *Labyrinthe* 2.18 (April 1946) 9.

Les Fauves. Geneva: Editions des Trois Collines, 1949. Rpt. ed. Rémi Labrusse. Paris: Michalon, 2006.

The Fauvist Painters. Tr. Ralph Manheim. New York: Wittenborn, Schultz, 1950.

"Maille à partir avec Bram van Velde." *Cahiers d'Art* 27.1 (July 1952) 79–81. Rpt. in Claire Stoullig and Nathalie Schoeller, eds. *Bram van Velde.* Paris: Editions du Centre Georges Pompidou, 1989. 180.

Le Musée inimaginable. Paris: José Corti, 1956.

Représentation et présence: premiers écrits et travaux (1923–1952). Intro. Yves Bonnefoy. Paris: Flammarion, 1974.

"Sartre's Last Class (Conclusion)." *Transition Fifty* no. 6 (October 1950) 87–90.

"Sartre's Last Class II." Tr. Colin Summerford. *Transition Forty-Eight* no. 2 (June 1948) 98–116.

Une fête en Cimmérie. Paris: Fernand Mourlot, 1964.

"Vuillard and the Poets of Decadence." *Art News* 53.1 (March 1954) 28–33, 62–63.

[? Duthuit, Georges]. "Notes about Contributors." *Transition Forty-Eight* no. 2 (June 1948) 146–152.

"Notes about Contributors." *Transition Forty-Eight* no. 4 (January 1949) 151–154.

"Notes about Contributors." *Transition Fifty* no. 6 (October 1950) 150–151.

L'Ecole de Paris, 1900–1950. London: Royal Academy of Arts, 1951.

Egger, Anne. *Robert Desnos*. Paris: Fayard, 2007.

Ellmann, Richard. *James Joyce: New and Revised Edition*. Oxford: Oxford University Press, 1982.

Eluard, Paul. "Le travail du peintre – A Picasso." *Poésie ininterrompue*. Paris: Gallimard, 1946. 65–72.

"The Work of the Painter – To Picasso." *Transition Forty-Nine* no. 5 (December 1949) 6–13.

Engel, Hugo F. "Das Drama von Warten auf Gott." *Illustrierte Woche* 30 (24 July 1954) 812–813.

Engelberts, Matthijs, Everett Frost, and Jane Maxwell, eds. "Cumulative TCD Catalogue." *Notes Diverse Holo: Catalogues of Beckett's Reading Notes and Other Manuscripts at Trinity College Dublin, with Supporting Essays*. Special Issue, *Samuel Beckett Today/Aujourd'hui* 16 (2006) 183–199.

Falb, Lewis W. "The Critical Reception of Eugene O'Neill on the French Stage." *Educational Theatre Journal* 22.3 (December 1970) 397–405.

Farquhar, George. *The Beaux' Stratagem*. Ed. Charles N. Fifer. Regents Restoration Drama Series. Lincoln: University of Nebraska Press, 1992.

Federman, Raymond, and John Fletcher. *Samuel Beckett: His Works and His Critics*. Berkeley: University of California Press, 1970.

Fénéon, Félix. "La Grande Jatte: Extracts from the Collected Works of Félix Fénéon." *Transition Forty-Nine* no. 5 (December 1949) 80–85.

Fowlie, Wallace. "A Return Visit to Paris." *The Virginia Quarterly Review* 51.1 (Winter 1975) 80–94.

Franzen, Erich. "Samuel Beckett: *Molloy*." *Merkur* 8 (March 1954) 239–241.

[Fraser, George Sutherland.] "They Also Serve." *Times Literary Supplement* 2815 (10 February 1956) 84.

Gaffney, Phyllis. *Healing Amid the Ruins: The Irish Hospital at Saint-Lô (1945–46)*. Dublin: A. and A. Farmar, 1999.

Gall, Yves Le. "Introduction to Akara." *Transition Forty-Eight* no. 4 (January 1949) 40–41.

Galsworthy, John. *The White Monkey*. New York: Charles Scribner's Sons, 1924.

Genet, Jean. "Thief's Journal (Extracts)." Tr. Bernard Frechtman and Samuel Beckett. *Transition Forty-Eight* no. 4 (January 1949) 66–75.

Gessner, Niklaus. *Die Unzulänglichkeit der Sprache: eine Untersuchung über Formzerfall und Beziehungslosigkeit bei Samuel Beckett*. Zurich: Juris Verlag, 1957.

Geulincx, Arnold. *Ethics, with Samuel Beckett's Notes*. Ed. Han van Ruler, Anthony Uhlmann, and Martin Wilson. Tr. Martin Wilson. Leiden and Boston: Brill, 2006.

Gheerbrant, Alain, and Léon Aichelbaum [interview]. *K éditeur*. Bibliography by Léon Aichelbaum and Raymond-Josué Seckel. Cognac: Le Temps qu'il fait, 1991.

Goethe, Johann Wolfgang von. *Die Leiden des jungen Werthers, Die Wahlverwandtschaften, Kleine Prosa, Epen*. Ed. Waltraud Wiethölter and Christoph Brecht. Frankfurt: Deutscher Klassiker Verlag, 1994. Vol. VIII of *Sämtliche Werke: Briefe, Tagebücher und Gespräche*. Ed. Friedmar Apel, Hendrik Birus, and Dieter Borchmeyer. 39 vols. 1985– .

Gontarski, S. E. *The Intent of Undoing in Samuel Beckett's Dramatic Texts*. Bloomington: Indiana University Press, 1985.

Gontarski, S. E. and Anthony Uhlmann, eds. *Beckett after Beckett*. Gainesville: Florida University Press, 2006.

Gracq, Julien. "Literature Hits below the Belt." Tr. J. G. Weightman. *Transition Fifty* no. 6 (October 1950) 7–26.

"La Littérature à l'estomac." *Empédocle* 7 (January 1950) 3–33.

La Littérature à l'estomac. Paris: José Corti, 1950.

"Mise au point." *Empédocle* 8 (February 1950) 95–96.

Grenier, Roger. *Fidèle au poste*. Paris: Gallimard, 2001.

Gustafson, Donna. "Benjamin Benno." *Benjamin Benno: A Retrospective Exhibition*. Rutgers, NJ: Jane Voorhees Zimmerli Art Museum, 1988.

Hamelin, France. *Femmes en prison dans la nuit noire de l'occupation: le Dépôt, la petite Roquette, le camp des Tourelles*. Paris: Editions Tirésias, 2004.

Hansen, Arlen J. *Expatriate Paris: A Cultural and Literary Guide to Paris in the 1920s*. New York: Arcade, 1990.

Harvey, Lawrence E. *Samuel Beckett: Poet and Critic*. Princeton: Princeton University Press, 1970.

Hayman, Ronald. *Sartre: A Life*. New York: Simon and Schuster, 1987.

Hayter, Stanley William. "The Language of Kandinsky." In Wassily Kandinsky, *Concerning the Spiritual in Art*. Ed. Robert Motherwell. New York: George Wittenborn, 1947. 15–18.

Heed, Sven. *Roger Blin: metteur en scène de l'avant-garde, 1949–1959*. Paris: Circé, 1996.

Heine, Maurice. *Le Marquis de Sade*. Ed. Gilbert Lely. Paris: Gallimard, 1950.

Henkels, Robert M., Jr. *Robert Pinget: The Novel as Quest*. University, AL: The University of Alabama Press, 1979.

Hulle, Dirk van. "Beckett's Reception in the Low Countries." *The International Reception of Samuel Beckett*. Ed. Mark Nixon, and Matthew Feldman. London: Continuum, 2009. 188–208.

Hutchins, Patricia. "James Joyce's Correspondence." *Encounter* 7.2 (August 1956) 49–54.

James Joyce's World. London: Methuen, 1957.

Hutchinson, Mary. "Samuel Beckett." *New Statesman and Nation* 51 (21 January 1956) 74.

Ionesco, Eugène. "The New Tenant." Tr. Donald Watson. *Merlin* 2.3 (Spring/ Summer 1954) 172–191.

Jarry, Alfred. "The Painting Machine." *Transition Forty-Nine* no. 5 (December 1949) 38–42.

Johnson, Samuel. *Lives of the English Poets*. Ed. George Birkbeck Hill. Vol. II. Oxford: Clarendon Press, 1905. 3 vols.

Joly, G[ustave]. "Au Théâtre de Babylone En attendant Godot ou Le soliloque du Pauvre." *Dossier de presse En attendant Godot de Samuel Beckett (1952–1961)*. Ed. André Derval. Paris: IMEC et Editions 10/18, 2007. 31–33.

Joyce, James. *A Portrait of the Artist as a Young Man*. Ed. Chester G. Anderson, and Richard Ellmann. New York: Viking, 1964.

Finnegans Wake. New York: Viking Press, 1969.

Pomes Penyeach. Paris: Shakespeare and Company, 1927.

Kaplan, Steven L. *Le Pain maudit: retour sur la France des années oubliées, 1945–1958*. Paris: Libraire Arthème Fayard, 2008.

Kennedy, Michael. "Denis Ronald McDonald." *Dictionary of Irish Biography*. Ed. James McGuire and James Quinn. Cambridge: Cambridge University Press, 2009. 929.

Kenner, Hugh. *The Pound Era*. Berkeley: University of California Press, 1971.

Kertess, Klaus. *Joan Mitchell*. New York: Harry N. Abrams, 1997.

Knowlson, James. *Damned to Fame: The Life of Samuel Beckett*. New York: Grove Press, 2004.

Knowlson, James, and Elizabeth Knowlson, eds. *Beckett Remembering, Remembering Beckett: A Centenary Celebration*. New York: Arcade, 2006.

Kober, Jacques. *Bram van Velde et ses loups*. Gap: Bartavelle, 1989.

"Le Noir est une couleur." *Derrière le Miroir* 1 (December 1946 – January 1947).

Koestler, Arthur, and Cynthia Koestler. *Stranger on the Square*. Ed. Harold Harris. London: Hutchinson, 1984.

Kundera, Milan. *Testaments Betrayed.* Tr. Linda Asher. London: Faber and Faber, 1995.

Labrusse, Rémi. "Beckett et la peinture: le témoignage d'une correspondance inédite." *Critique* 46.519–520 (August–September 1990) 670–680.

"Extraits de la correspondance entre Georges Duthuit et Samuel Beckett." *Tal-Coat devant l'image.* Ed. Claire Stoullig. Geneva: Musées d'Art et d'Histoire; Colmar: Musée d'Unterlinden; Antibes: Musée Picasso; Winterthur: Kunstmuseum, 1992. 105–112.

"Hiver 1949: Tal-Coat entre Georges Duthuit et Samuel Beckett." *Tal-Coat devant l'image.* Ed. Claire Stoullig. Geneva: Musées d'Art et d'Histoire; Colmar: Musée d'Unterlinden; Antibes: Musée Picasso; Winterthur: Kunstmuseum, 1992. 99–105.

"Samuel Beckett and Georges Duthuit." *Samuel Beckett: A Passion for Paintings.* Ed. Fionnuala Croke. Dublin: National Gallery of Ireland, 2006. 88–91.

Lake, Carlton, ed., with the assistance of Linda Eichhorn and Sally Leach. *No Symbols Where None Intended: A Catalogue of Books, Manuscripts, and Other Material Relating to Samuel Beckett in the Collections of the Humanities Research Center.* Austin: Humanities Research Center, The University of Texas at Austin, 1984.

Lalande, André. *Vocabulaire technique et critique de la philosophie.* Société Française de Philosophie. Vol. I. Paris: Librairie Félix Alcan, 1928. 2 vols.

Latour, Geneviève, and Florence Claval, eds. *Les Théâtres de Paris.* Paris: Bibliothèque Historique de la Ville de Paris, 1991.

Lely, Gilbert. *Vie du Marquis de Sade.* Paris: Jean-Jacques Pauvert, 1965.

Léon, Paul. "Du Palais-Royal au Palais-Bourbon (souvenirs)." *La Nef (Nouvelle Equipe Française)* 2.9 (August 1945) 19–38.

Leopardi, Giacomo. *Selected Prose and Poetry.* Ed. and tr. Iris Origo and John Heath-Stubbs. Oxford Library of Italian Classics. London: Oxford University Press, 1966.

Leventhal, A. J. "Dramatic Commentary." *Dublin Magazine* 31.1 (January–March 1956) 52–54.

"Mr. Beckett's *En attendant Godot*." *Dublin Magazine* 29.2 (April–June 1954) 11–16.

Lindon, Jérôme. "First Meeting with Samuel Beckett." In *Beckett at 60: A Festschrift.* Ed. John Calder. London: Calder and Boyars, 1967. 17–19.

Loustaunau-Lacau, Georges. *"Chiens maudits": souvenirs d'un rescapé des bagnes hitlériens.* Paris: Edition du Réseau Alliance, 1965.

Ludvigsen, Chr[istian]. *Det begyndte med Beckett: min egen teaterhistorie.* Aktuelle teaterproblemer. Århus: Institut for Dramaturgi, 1997.

Maanen, Hans van. "The Theatre System of the Netherlands." *Theatre Worlds in Motion: Structures, Politics and Developments in the Countries of Western*

Europe. Ed. Hans van Maanen, and S. E. Wilmer. Amsterdam-Atlanta: Rodopi, 1998. 407–465.

MacGreevy, Thomas. "Art Criticism, and a Visit to Paris." *The Father Matthew Record* 41.9 (September 1948) 4–8.

Catalogue of Pictures of the Italian Schools. Dublin: Stationery Office, 1956.

"Dante – and Modern Ireland." *The Father Matthew Record* 41.1 (January 1948) 3–4.

Dutch Pictures: 17th Century. Curaçao, 1957.

Jack B. Yeats: An Appreciation and an Interpretation. Dublin: Victor Waddington Publications, 1945.

Pictures in the Irish National Gallery. London: B. T. Batsford, 1945.

McGuire, James, and James Quinn, eds. *Dictionary of Irish Biography*. Cambridge: Cambridge University Press, 2009.

McWhinnie, Donald. "All That Fall." *Radio Times* (11 January 1957) 4.

Maddox, Brenda. *Nora: The Real Life of Molly Bloom*. Boston: Houghton Mifflin, 1988.

Mallarmé, Stéphane. "Edouard Manet." Tr. Samuel Beckett. *Transition Forty-Nine* no. 5 (December 1949) 88.

Œuvres complètes. Ed. Bertrand Marchal. Bibliothèque de la Pléiade. Paris: Gallimard, 2003. 2 vols.

Marcel, Gabriel. "En attendant Godot." *Les Nouvelles Littéraires* (15 January 1953) 5. Rpt. in *Dossier de presse En attendant Godot de Samuel Beckett (1952–1961)*. Ed. André Derval. Paris: IMEC et Editions 10/18, 2007. 64–65.

Marcus, David. *Oughtobiography: Leaves from the Diary of a Hyphenated Jew*. Dublin: Gill and Macmillan, 2001.

Marin La Meslée, Valérie. "Samuel Beckett et le froc d'Estragon." *Le Magazine Littéraire* 453 (May 2006) 97.

Mason, Rainer Michael, ed. *Bram van Velde: 1895–1981. Rétrospective du centenaire*. Geneva: Musée Rath, Musées d'Art et d'Histoire, 1996.

Mercier, Vivian. "Beckett and the Search for Self." *The New Republic* 132 (19 September 1955) 20–21.

"Godot, Molloy et Cie." *The New Statesman and Nation* 50.1291 (5 December 1955) 754.

"Letter from Ireland II." *Horizon* 13.76 (April 1946) 276–285.

"A Pyrrhonian Eclogue." *Hudson Review* 7.4 (Winter 1955) 620–624.

Michaux, Henri. "To Right Nor Left." Tr. Samuel Beckett. *Transition Forty-Eight* no. 4 (January 1949) 14–18.

Milton, John. *Paradise Lost*. Ed. Barbara K. Lewalski. Malden, MA: Blackwell Publishing, 2007.

Molière. *Le Misanthrope*. Ed. Jacques Arnavon. L'Interprétation de la Comédie Classique. Paris: Plon, 1914.

Montgomery, Niall. "No Symbols Where None Intended." *New World Writing* 5 (April 1954) 324–327.

Moorjani, Angela. "*En attendant Godot* on Michel Polac's Entrée des Auteurs."
Tr. Angela Moorjani and Ruby Cohn. *Beckett versus Beckett* Ed.
Marius Buning, Danielle De Ruyter, Matthijis Engleberts,
Sjef Houppermans. *Samuel Beckett Today/Aujourd'hui* 7 (1998) 53–54.

Morand, Paul. "Charles du Bos chez le dentiste." *Opéra* 8.316 (1 August 1951) 1.

Morteo, Gian Renzo. "Introduzione." *Questioni* 1.3-4 (July–August 1954)
3–11.

Murphy, T. E. "Open Every Door." *Reader's Digest* 55 (August 1949) 109–111.
"Ouvrons toutes les portes." *Sélection du Reader's Digest* 3 (October 1949)
1–4.

Nadeau, Maurice. "La 'Dernière' Tentative de Samuel Beckett." *Les Lettres
Nouvelles* 1.7 (September 1953) 860–864.
Grâces leur soient rendues. Paris: Albin Michel, 1990.
"Impasse." *Les Lettres Nouvelles* 51 (July–August 1957) 31–38.
"Samuel Beckett, l'humour et le néant." *Mercure de France* 312 (1 August
1951) 693–697.
"Samuel Beckett ou le droit au silence." *Les Temps Modernes* 7.75 (January
1952) 1273–1282.

Nathan, Monique. "'Les Ambassadeurs' et les Carnets de James." Rev. of *Les
Ambassadeurs*, by Henry James. Tr. Georges Belmont. *Critique* 7.49 (June
1951) 492–498.

National Gallery of Ireland: Illustrated Summary Catalogue of Paintings. Intro.
Homan Potterton. Dublin: Gill and Macmillan, 1981.

[Noel, Lucie] Lucie Léon, pseud. *James Joyce and Paul L. Léon: The Story of a
Friendship*. New York: Gotham Book Mart, 1950.

O'Brien, Eoin. *The Beckett Country: Samuel Beckett's Ireland*, photography David
H. Davison, Foreword James Knowlson, illustrations Robert Ballagh.
Dublin, London: The Black Cat Press in association with Faber and
Faber, 1986.
"Samuel Beckett at Saint-Lô - 'Humanity in Ruins.'" *Journal of the Irish
Colleges of Physicians and Surgeons* 19.2 (April 1990) 138.

O'Farrell, William. *Les Carottes sont cuites*. Tr. Maurice Tourneur. Série Noire.
Paris: Gallimard, 1951.

Ollesch, Helmut. "Sie warten hinter Gittern: Strafgefangene in
Lüttringhausen spielen Samuel Becketts Stück um Godot." *Der Weg* 16/
17 (1954) n.p.

"Ordonnance no. 45-1554, 16 Juil. 1945." *Journal Officiel de la République
Française* (17 July 1945) 4358.

Patri, Aimé. "Discovery of Malcolm de Chazal." *Transition Forty-Eight* no. 3
(October 1948) 5–13.

Patry, Robert. *Saint-Lô, la ville, la bataille: la capitale des ruines / The Capital of
Ruins*. Tr. Eugène Turboult. Saint-Lô: Editions du Syndicat d'initiative de
Saint-Lô, 1948.

Paz, Octavio, ed. *Anthology of Mexican Poetry*. Tr. Samuel Beckett. UNESCO Collection of Representative Works: Latin American Series. Bloomington, IN: Indiana University Press, 1958.

Le Pèlerin Passionné. "Les Métamorphoses de Jack B. Yeats." *Le Peintre* (15 February 1954) 8.

Picabia, Gabrielle. "Apollinaire." *Transition Fifty* no. 6 (October 1950) 110–125.

Pichette, Henri. "APoème 4." *Transition Forty-Eight* no. 2 (June 1948) 24–43.

"Letter – Red." Tr. Jack T. Nile and Bernard Frechtman. *Transition Forty-Eight* no. 2 (June 1948) 5–15.

Pilling, John. *A Samuel Beckett Chronology*. Author Chronologies. Houndsmill, Basingstoke: Palgrave Macmillan, 2006.

Pinget, Robert, and Madeleine Renouard. *Robert Pinget à la lettre: entretiens avec Madeleine Renouard*. Paris: Belfond, 1993.

Ponge, Francis. "Braque, or Modern Art as Event and Pleasure." Tr. Samuel Beckett. *Transition Forty-Nine* no. 5 (December 1949) 43–47.

Œuvres complètes. Ed. Bernard Beugnot. Bibliothèque de la Pléiade. Paris: Gallimard, 1999–2002. 2 vols.

"Poems." Tr. Pierre Schneider and Richard Wilbur. *Transition Fifty* no. 6 (October 1950) 75–86.

Pope, Alexander. *Imitations of Horace, with An Epistle to Dr. Arbuthnot, and The Epilogue to the Satires*. Ed. John Butt. 2nd edn. London: Methuen and Co., 1953.

Prévert, Jacques. "Picasso Goes for a Walk." *Transition Forty-Nine* no. 5 (December 1949) 50–53.

"Preview for July." *Mexico / This Month* (July 1955) np.

Proust, Marcel. *A la recherche du temps perdu*. Ed. Jean-Yves Tadié. Bibliothèque de la Pléiade. Paris: Gallimard, 1987–1989. 4 vols.

In Search of Lost Time. Tr. C. K. Scott Moncrieff and Terence Kilmartin (vols. I–V); Andreas Mayor and Terence Kilmartin (vol. VI). Revised D. J. Enright. New York: Modern Library, 1992–1993. 6 vols.

Pyle, Hilary. *Jack B. Yeats: A Catalogue Raisonné of the Oil Paintings*. London: Andre Deutsch, 1992. 3 vols.

Racine, Jean. *Andromache, Britannicus, Berenice*. Tr. John Cairncross. London: Penguin Books, 1967.

Andromaque. Théâtre complet de Racine. Ed. Maurice Rat. Paris: Librairie Garnier Frères, 1947. [111]–171.

Read, Herbert Edward. *Exhibition of Engravings, Etchings and Lithographs*. London: St. George's Gallery Prints, 1955.

Reavey, George. *Colours of Memory*. New York: Grove Press, 1955.

"Inward." *The Palate* 35.1 (Winter 1955) [30].

Soviet Literature To-day. London: Lindsay Drummond, 1946.

Reavey, George, and Marc Slonim, eds. and trs. *Soviet Literature: An Anthology*. London: Wishart and Co., 1933. Rpt. Westport, CT: Greenwood Press, 1972.

[Reid, Alec] Michael George, pseud. "Samuel Beckett." *Irish Tatler and Sketch* 65.5 (February 1956) 19, 40.

René, Denise. *Denise René, l'intrépide: une galerie dans l'aventure de l'art abstrait, 1944–1978*. Paris: Centre Georges Pompidou, 2001.

Reverdy, Pierre. "Poèmes – Poems." *Transition Fifty* no. 6 (October 1950) 34–65.

Rexroth, Kenneth. "The Point is Irrelevance." *Nation* 182.15 (14 April 1956) 325–328.

Ribot, Théodule-Armand. *Diseases of Personality*. Ed. Daniel N. Robinson. Significant Contributions to the History of Psychology 1750–1920. Washington, DC: University Publications of America, 1977.

Les Maladies de la personnalité. Paris: Felix Alcan, 1885.

Rimbaud, Arthur. *Drunken Boat*. Tr. Samuel Beckett. Reading: Whiteknights Press, 1976.

Œuvres complètes. Ed. André Guyaux and Aurélia Cervoni. Bibliothèque de la Pléiade. Paris: Gallimard, 2009.

Rimbaud: Complete Works, Selected Letters. Tr. Wallace Fowlie. Chicago: University of Chicago Press, 1966.

Robb, Graham. *Balzac: A Life*. New York: W. W. Norton, 1994.

Robbe-Grillet, Alain. "Samuel Beckett, auteur dramatique." *Critique* 9 (February 1953) 108–114.

Rodari, Florian. "Biographie commentée par les textes." *Tal-Coat devant l'image*. Ed. Claire Stoullig. Geneva: Musées d'Art et d'Histoire; Colmar: Musée d'Unterlinden; Antibes Musée Picasso; Winterthur: Kunstmuseum, 1992. 189–225.

Rodríguez-Gago, Antonia. "Beckett in Spain: Madrid (1955) and Barcelona (1956)." *Waiting for Godot: A Casebook*. Ed. Ruby Cohn. London: Macmillan, 1987. 45–46.

Rosmarin, Léonard A. *Robert Pinget*. New York: Twayne Publishers, 1995.

Rosset, Barney. "Remembering Samuel Beckett." *Not Even Past: Hybrid Histories*. Ed. Bradford Morrow. Conjunctions 53. Annandale-on-Hudson, NY: Bard College, 2009. 8–27.

Ryan, John, Valentin Iremonger, and J. K. Hillman. "A Foreword to Our First Issue." *Envoy: A Review of Literature and Art* 1.1 (December 1949) [8].

Saddlemyer, Ann. *Becoming George: The Life of Mrs. W. B. Yeats*. Oxford: Oxford University Press, 2002.

Sade, Marquis de. *The 120 Days of Sodom and Other Writings*. Ed. and tr. Austryn Wainhouse and Richard Seaver. New York: 1987.

The Complete Justine, Philosophy in the Bedroom and Other Writings. Ed and tr. Richard Seaver and Austryn Wainhouse. New York: Grove Press, 1965.

Œuvres. Ed. Michel Delon and Jean Deprun. Bibliothèque de la Pléiade. Paris: Gallimard, 1990–1998. 3 vols.

Saillet, Maurice. "Jean Paulhan et la poésie." *Mercure de France* 302.1015 (1 March 1948) 505–510. Revised and reprinted as "Jean Paulhan et son anthologie." Maurice Saillet, *Billets doux de Justin Saget*. Paris: Mercure de France, 1952. 229–237.

Savane, Paule. *Samuel Beckett à Ussy sur Marne*. Ussy-sur-Marne: Association pour la Sauvegarde d'Ussy, 2001.

Schneider, Alan. *Entrances: An American Director's Journey*. New York: Viking, 1986. "Working with Beckett." *Samuel Beckett: The Art of Rhetoric*. Ed. Edouard Morot-Sir, Howard Harper and Dougald McMillan III. North Carolina Studies in the Romance Languages and Literatures Symposia, 5. Chapel Hill: University of North Carolina, Department of Romance Languages, 1976. 271–289.

Schneider, Pierre. "Introduction to the Works of Francis Ponge." *Transition Fifty* no. 6 (October 1950) 68–74. "Voix vive, lettre morte." *Les Lettres Nouvelles* 1.1 (March 1953) 38–53. Rpt. as "Voix vive, lettre morte: Tristan Corbière." Pierre Schneider, *La Voix vive*. Paris: Editions de Minuit, 1953. [199]-253.

Seaver, Richard. "Richard Seaver on Translating Beckett." *Beckett Remembering, Remembering Beckett*. Ed. James Knowlson and Elizabeth Knowlson. London: Bloomsbury, 2006. 100–107. "Samuel Beckett: An Introduction." *Merlin* 1.2 (Autumn 1952) 73–79.

Selz, Jean. *Hayden*. Geneva: Editions Pierre Cailler, 1962.

Shakespeare, William. *King Lear. The Riverside Shakespeare: The Complete Works*. General and Textual Ed. G. Blakemore Evans, assisted by J. J. M. Tobin. 2nd edn. Boston: Houghton Mifflin, 1997.

Simon, Alfred. "Tout un théâtre." *Le Magazine Littéraire* 231 (June 1986) 35.

Simonin, Anne. *Les Editions de Minuit 1952–1955*. Paris: IMEC, 1994.

Simonin, Anne, and Hélène Clastres. *Les Idées en France 1945–1988: une chronologie*. Le Débat. Paris: Gallimard, 1989.

Simpson, Alan. *Beckett and Behan and a Theatre in Dublin*. London: Routledge and Kegan Paul, 1962.

Staël, Nicolas de, André Chastel, Germain Viatte, Jacques Dubourg, and Françoise de Staël. *Nicolas de Staël*. Paris: Les Editions du Temps, 1968.

Steinegger, Catherine. *La Musique à la Comédie-Française de 1921 à 1964: aspects de l'évolution d'un genre*. Sprimont, Belgium: Mardaga, 2003.

Stephens, James. "A Rhinoceros, Some Ladies, and a Horse." *Irish Writing* 14 (March 1951) 35–42.

Stoullig, Claire, ed. *Tal-Coat devant l'image*. Geneva: Musées d'Art et d'Histoire; Colmar: Musée d'Unterlinden; Antibes: Musée Picasso; Winterthur: Kunstmuseum, 1992.

Stoullig, Claire, and Nathalie Schoeller, eds. *Bram van Velde*. Paris: Editions du Centre Georges Pompidou, 1989.

Stravinsky, Vera. *Dearest Bubushkin: The Correspondence of Vera and Igor Stravinsky, 1921–1954, with Excerpts from Vera Stravinsky's Diaries, 1922–1971*. Ed. Robert Craft. London: Thames and Hudson, 1985.

Suhrkamp, Peter. "Mein Weg zu Proust." *Morgenblatt für Freunde der Literatur* 4 (1953) 1–2.

Surya, Michel. *Georges Bataille: la mort à l'œuvre*. Paris: Librairie Séguier, 1987.

Swift, Carolyn. *Stage by Stage*. Dublin: Poolbeg Press, 1985.

Tardieu, Jean. "Poèmes." *Empédocle* 1.4 (August–September 1949) 53–56.

Thom's Directory of Ireland for the Year 1934. Dublin: Alex. Thom and Co., 1934.

Trives, Trino Martínez. "Mi versión de *Esperando a Godot* y su estreno en España." *Primer Acto: Revista Española del Teatro* 1 (April 1957) 15–16.

Ussher, Arland. "The Meaning of Collaboration." *The Nineteenth Century and After* 140.1333 (July 1946) 330–331.

Vais, Michel. *L'Ecrivain scénique*. Quebec: Presses de l'Université du Québec, 1978.

Valli, Stefania, ed. *La Rivista Botteghe Oscure e Marguerite Caetani: la corrispondenza con gli autori italiani, 1948–1960*. Rome: "L'Erna" di Bretschneider, 1999.

Velde, Jacoba van. *La grande salle*. Tr. Maddy Buysse. Paris: Julliard, 1956.

Verbeeten, Ton. *Toneelgroep Theater 1953–1988: 35 Jaar Wachten op Godot*. Arnhem: Toneelgroep Theater, 1988.

Verne, Jules. *Le Tour du monde en quatre-vingts jours*. Paris: Flammarion, 1978.

Viatte, Germain. *Geer van Velde*. Paris: Editions "Cahiers d'Art," 1989.

Vigny, Alfred de. *Œuvres complètes*. Ed. François Germain, and André Jarry. Bibliothèque de la Pléiade. Vol. I. Paris: Gallimard, 1986. 2 vols.

Waldberg, Patrick. "Bram van Velde." *Apollo* 398 (April 1958) 130–134.

"Murphy, par Samuel Beckett." Rev. of *Murphy* by Samuel Beckett. *Paru: l'Actualité Littéraire, Intellectuelle et Artistique* 48 (November 1948) 22–23.

"Nicolas de Staël." *Transition Fifty* no. 6 (October 1950) 66–67.

Weingarten, Romain. "Akara." *Transition Forty-Eight* no. 4 (January 1949) 42–59.

Weld, Jacqueline Bograd. *Peggy: The Wayward Guggenheim*. New York: E. P. Dutton, 1998.

Worth, Katharine. *Samuel Beckett's Theatre: Life Journeys*. Oxford: Clarendon Press, 1999.

Wundt, Wilhelm. *Grundzüge der physiologischen Psychologie*. Vol. II. Leipzig: Wilhelm Engelmann, 1902. 4 vols.

Yeats, W. B. *The Poems*. Ed. Richard J. Finneran. *The Collected Works of W. B. Yeats*. 2nd edn. Vol. I. New York: Scribner, 1997. 14 vols.

Zippermann, Charles C. "Literary Landmarks of 1949." *Books Abroad* 24.2 (Spring 1950) 136–141.

ELECTRONIC WORKS CITED

"20th Century." 5 September 2009. web.ukonline.co.uk/m.gratton/Salford%20-%2020th%20Century-Advances%20.htm.

Bibliography of works cited

"About Thomas MacGreevy." 17 August 2009. www.macgreevy.org.

"Buster Keaton Links." Juha Takkinen. 20 January 2010. www.takkinen.se/BusterKeaton/.

"Chaillot, Palais de." 4 June 2010. www.encyclopedia.com/doc/1079-ChaillotPalaisde.html.

"George Wittenborn, Inc. Papers in The Museum of Modern Art Archives." The Museum of Modern Art. 21 November 2008. www.moma.org/learn/resources/archives/EAD/Wittenbornb.

"Kate Harris Interview of Anthony Field." British Library Theatre Archive. 14 March 2007. www.bl.uk/projects/theatrearchive/field.html.

"Robert Carlier (1910–2002)." Les Editions Gallimard. 13 November 2009. www.gallimard.fr/catalog/Html/event/carlier.htm.

Schreibman, Susan. "Introduction to *The Capuchin Annual*." 1999. *The Thomas MacGreevy Archive*. 4 June 2009. www.macgreevy.org.

Van Bork, G. J. *Schrijvers en dicters*. 21 May 2009. www.dbnl.org/auteurs.

744

INDEX OF RECIPIENTS

SUMMARY LISTING OF SAMUEL BECKETT'S WORKS MENTIONED IN VOLUME II

Works are listed below by original title: individual poems or stories are listed separately here, but are listed in the index by collection unless published separately; translations are listed following the title of original here, but in the index are listed by translated title.

Acte sans paroles [I]
All That Fall
"Ascension," see "Poèmes 38–39"

"bon bon il est un pays" (later entitled "Accul," see "Trois poèmes")

"Le Calmant," see *Nouvelles; Nouvelles et Textes pour rien*
"The Capital of the Ruins"
"Cascando" (poem)

"Dante and the Lobster," see *More Pricks Than Kicks*
"Dante . . . Bruno . Vico . . Joyce"
"Denis Devlin"
"Dieppe," see "Poèmes 38–39"

Echo's Bones and other Precipitates ("Enueg I"; "Sanies 1"; "Serena 1")
Eleutheria
En attendant Godot (see also translations as: *Ag fanacht le Godó; Aspettando Godot; Czekając na Godota; Esperando a Godot; Godō wo machinagara; Vi venter på Godot;* *Wachten op Godot; Waiting for Godot; Warten auf Godot*)
"Enueg I" (see *Echo's Bones and other Precipitates*)
"L'Expulsé," see *Nouvelles; Nouvelles et Textes pour rien, Quatre Nouvelles;* translated as "The Expelled" (see *Four Novellas*)

Fin de partie (provisional title *Haam*; see also translations as: *Endgame; Endspiel*)
"From an Abandoned Work"

"The Gloaming" (revised as *Rough for Theatre I*)

"Hommage à Jack B. Yeats"

L'Innommable (see also translations as: *Der Namenlose; The Unnamable*)

"je suis ce cours de sable qui glisse," see "Trois poèmes – Three Poems"
"je voudrais que mon amour meure," see "Trois Poèmes – Three Poems"
"Les joues rouges"

Summary listing

GENERAL INDEX

Names of persons and publications with Profiles in this volume are marked with an asterisk; those with a Profile in the previous volume are marked with an asterisk followed by the volume number (I). The titles of SB's works are given in the summary listing above; individual titles (including translations) are indexed separately, as are poems and stories if they appeared independently; poems or stories that appeared in a collection are indexed by the title of that collection.

480–481, 497–498; Italian, of *En attendant Godot* as *Aspettando Godot* (by Luciano Mondolfo): 489, 503–505; Italian, of *En attendant Godot* as *Aspettando Godot* (by Carlo Fruttero): 608–609, 631–632; Spanish, of *En attendant Godot* as *Esperando a Godot* (by Trino Martínez Trives): 439, 444–445, 447–449, 456–457, 527–530, 535; Spanish, of *En attendant Godot* as *Esperando a Godot* (by Pablo Palant): 440, 493–494, 497–498, 529–530, 544

translator of: the first poem of Apollinaire's *Alcools*, "Zone," 109, 146–147; Duthuit's *Les Fauves* (revision of Manheim translation), 87–88, 157–159, 166, 177, 185–190; Duthuit's "The French Symbolists," 190; Duthuit's "Vuillard and the Poets of Decadence," 266–268, 270–271; Paz's edition, *Anthology of Mexican Poetry*, 177, 181, 184, 192, 195, 197, 200–201, 439, 510, 530, 665–667; Rimbaud's "Le Bateau ivre" ("The Drunken Boat"), 119, 427–428; essays for *Sélection*, 109, 160–163; for *Transition* (proposed, signed, revised, unsigned): 53, 58–59, 66–67, 69, 79, 90–91, 101, 103, 109, 114–118, 120–126, 142, 146, 148–151, 159–163, 177, 202–203, 381, 385–388, 538; UNESCO, World of Art, 223, 225–227; Wahl's "L'écriture est gravure" ("The Word is Graven"), 590

Trinity College Dublin: 396–397, 467–468; Foundation Scholar (1926), Scholars' Dinner, 561–562, 572, 659; Teaching at, 173–174, 467–468

individual poems or stories are indexed by collection unless published independently; translations are indexed by translated title. See Summary Listing preceding General Index, 747–748

Beckett, William Frank* (I), xxvi, 84, 87, 89–90, 92, 174, 435

Beckett and Medcalf, Quantity Surveyors (Dublin), 435–436

Beecham, Sir Thomas, 670–671

Beethoven, Ludwig van, 671; Piano Sonata no. 14 in C# major, 671

Béguin, Albert, 197

Behan, Brendan, 521, 570; *The Quare Fellow*, 521, 569–570

Belis, Andrew (pseud. of SB), see "Recent Irish Poetry"

The Bell, 58

Belmont, Georges (né Georges Pelorson)* (I), 4, 263–265, 278–280, 299–301, 363–364, 661; Editor: *Jours de France, Marie Claire, Paris Match, Volontés*, 301; "Fin de l'élégie" (dedicated to SB), 278–280; *L'Offense* (early draft entitled *Jean ou Les dieux du sang*), 278–280, 299–301; "Mesure de Dieu," 280; "Pavana," 280; "Plans," 278–280; "Vanité de la Grâce," 278–280

Belmont, Joséphine, see Caliot, Joséphine

Belmont, Sophie (m. Genovesi, m. Dinkelspiler), 264–265, 279

General index

Caetani, Princess Marguerite (née
Chapin), 259–260, 262,
310–311, 313, 376–377
Café du Dôme (Paris), 674
Cahiers d'Art, 24–25, 28, 48–49, 51,
87, 105–106, 147, 296, 434
Cahiers des Saisons, see 84: Nouvelle
Revue Littéraire
Caillois, Robert, 363–365
Calder, Bettina, see Jonič, Bettina
Calder, John, 353, 671–672
Calder, John, Ltd. (London
publisher), 590, 671–672;
Pamela Lyon, 672
Caliot, Joséphine (m.
Georges
Belmont), 264–265, 279
"Le Calmant," see Nouvelles; Nouvelles
et Textes pour rien; Quatre
Nouvelles
"The Calmative," see Four Novellas
Campbell, Roy, 36
Camus, Albert, 32–33, 49, 51, 197,
256, 493–494, 676; French
translator and adaptor of
Faulkner's Requiem for a Nun,
676; L'Etranger, 32–33, 493–494
Canadian Broadcast Corporation
(CBC), 608–609, 682
Canisy, Château de Lassay, 19, 21
Capalbo, Carmen, 541, 594, 615
Cape, see Jonathan Cape
"The Capital of the Ruins," 20
Cappella degli Scrovegni (also
Chapelle des Arènes, Arena
Chapel) (Padua), 185–187
Capri, Agnès, 60–61, 76
Le Capricorne (Paris theatre), 61
Capuano, J.-A., 36
Carlier, Robert, 206, 235, 341
Carlisle, Norman and Madelyn, 163;
"The Big Slot-Machine Swindle,"
160–163
Carpentier, Georges, 531–532

Carr, John Dickson, 526; The Seat of
the Scornful, 525–526
Carrefour, 213, 249
Carrickmines Golf Club (Co.
Dublin), 104
Carter, John Grant, 39
"Cascando" (poem), 638
Caspari, Carlheinz*, 391–393; "Zu
Samuel Becketts Theater," 393
Castagne, Helmut, see Fischer
Verlag
Cauvet-Duhamel, Benjamin
Frédéric, 144–147
Céline, Louis-Ferdinand, 493–494;
Voyage au bout de la nuit, 493–494
Censorship, xxi, 36, 357–369,
373–374; Esperando a Godot
(Trives translation, Madrid),
527–529, 534–535; Malone Dies,
615; Molloy, 589, 601; More Pricks
Than Kicks, 419; Wachten op Godot
(Arnhem), 521–524, 526;
Waiting for Godot (Lord
Chamberlain's Office), xxi, 440,
480–481, 484, 602, 645, 663;
Watt, 419, 440
Cercle de la Librairie, 291
Cézanne, Paul, 128, 131, 133,
165–166
Chagall, Marc, 48, 50, 590;
"Illustrations for the Bible," 590
Les Chaînes du destin (No Man of her
Own) (film), 273–275
Champi, see Viéville, Lucien
Chandler, Raymond, 60
Char, Marie-Claude, 313
Char, René, 64, 72, 74, 197, 220,
310–311, 313; L'Abominable
homme des neiges, 216, 218, 220;
Le Poème pulvérisé ("The
Pulverized Poem"), 72, 74
Charensol, Georges, 425
Chase, Stanley, 541, 594

423–424, 428, 439, 441–445,
447–460, 465, 467–468,
480–481, 495–497, 547, 552,
607, 646, 669, 671–672, 682;
banned in Ireland, 589, 601;
English translation, 345–346,
356–358, 381, 385–388,
393–395, 397–398, 407–408,
413, 416, 419–421, 432–433,
439, 444–445, 448–449, 480,
487, 495–496, 498, 502, 508,
512–515, 520, 525, 531–532,
540, 544–545, 547, 550–553,
557, 567–569, 583, 585,
591–592, 601–602, 608–609,
617; German translation,
407–408, 439, 441–445,
448–460, 465, 480–481,
497–498; publication by
Collection Merlin / Olympia
Press, 356, 385, 448, 498, 508,
513, 515, 540, 547, 550, 553,
557, 608–609; publication by
Grove Press, 345, 358, 386, 398,
498, 508, 512–515, 520, 525,
532, 540, 544, 547, 550, 552,
602; publication by John
Calder, Ltd., in *Three Novels*, 590,
672; publication by Suhrkamp
Verlag, 441–443, 449–450, 465,
497–498
Monde Nouveau/Paru, 81, 515
Mondolfo, Luciano, 489, 503–505
Monnier, Adrienne, 566; La Maison
des Amis des Livres, 566
Monteith, Charles*, 603
Montgomery, Niall*, 209, 377,
426–428, 436, 480–481,
560–566, 640, 664–665; "No
Symbols Where None
Intended," 427–428, 480–481,
561–562
Montgomery, Roseanna, 427–428

Moore, George, 612, 621–622, 662,
669; *The Lake*, 622; *The Untilled
Field*, 622
More Pricks Than Kicks, 30, 174–175,
278, 319, 419, 427, 461, 464,
596, 614, 622, 646, 648, 682;
stories in: "Dante and the
Lobster," 319, 427, 646, 648,
681–682; "The Smeraldina's
Billet Doux," 621–622;
"Walking Out," 319; "Yellow,"
319, 427, 614, 621–622,
681–682
Moreau, Gustave, 268, 270–271
Moreland, Manton, 691
Morgenblatt für Freunde der Literatur,
441–443, 447, 449–450
Morris, John*, 656, 675, 688
Morrow, Deirdre, see Sinclair,
Deirdre
Morrow, George, 23
"Mort de A.D.," see "Trois poèmes"
Morteo, Gian Renzo, 467–469;
introduction to "Il Teatro
'nuovo' francese," 468–469; *Il
teatro popolare in Francia*, 468
Motherwell, Robert, 199
"La Mouche," see "Poèmes" 38–39
Munch, Charles, 200–201
Murphy, 14,16, 27–28, 30–32, 36, 49,
53, 55–56, 61, 70, 76, 80, 82, 84,
87, 148, 150, 192, 208, 228,
246–248, 301, 399–400, 427,
441–442, 548, 550–551, 607,
633, 642, 644, 646, 669;
publication by Editions Bordas,
28, 45, 48–50, 55–56, 63–66; 71,
73, 75–76, 191–192, 291, 376,
426; publication by Grove Press,
40, 633, 654, 669, 681–682;
publication by Routledge, 12,
14, 30, 461, 464; Routledge, out
of print, 27, 38–39, 51, 208, 546